ENGLISH COMEDY

ENGLISH COMEDY

BY

ASHLEY H. THORNDIKE

A MARANDELL BOOK

COOPER SQUARE PUBLISHERS, INC.

NEW YORK

1965

Copyright 1929 by the Macmillan Co.

Copyright renewed 1957 by Annette L. Thorndike

Published 1965 by
Cooper Square Publishers, Inc.
59 Fourth Avenue, New York, N.Y. 10003

Library of Congress Catalog Card Number: 65-20100

Printed in the United States of America

PREFACE

When I published a volume, "Tragedy", twenty years ago, I promised myself to write a companion book on English Comedy. Portions of it have been written at various times since then, but its completion has been long delayed, partly because of other matters which have required my attention and partly because of the difficulties of the subject. Not only are there many more comedies than tragedies in English, they are more heterogeneous, and less readily classified or surveyed from any point of view. In one respect, however, my task has been easier, or at least plainer, than it was for the earlier book. When I was writing "Tragedy", the whole history of the English drama was comparatively unexplored and unorganized. Such important and comprehensive works as the fourth and fifth volumes of Creizenach's "Geschichte des neueren Dramas", "The Cambridge History of English Literature", and Sir Edmund Chambers's "Elizabethan Stage" have appeared since then. The Elizabethan drama has been the subject of constant investigation, and in recent years much has been done towards the organization of dramatic history since the Restoration. I have been able consequently to avoid the consideration of minor problems in history or criticism, for it is now possible for anyone with access to a good library to inform himself on the bibliography, texts, and historical data of English comedy. Perhaps there is less need now than twenty years ago for a book on the subject. But I have been attracted now as then by the project of examining all the efforts of one nation during four centuries to provide similar kinds of theatrical amusement and of literary refreshment. Certainly such a survey is

v

not without allurement for anyone who takes either a critical or a historical interest in human affairs.

In addition to my heavy indebtedness to the published works of scholars, I owe much to my own students who have coöperated with me, and also to many of my colleagues, especially to Brander Matthews, Jefferson B. Fletcher, and George C. D. Odell.

ASHLEY H. THORNDIKE.

January 17, 1929.

CONTENTS

PART I

PART II

PART ONE

ENGLISH COMEDY

CHAPTER I

DEFINITIONS

COMEDY may well seem a thing to enjoy and not to define. It belongs to the theater. It lives by the laughter of the audience. But it may become literature by some grace of form which carries that laughter on to one generation after another of readers. The imaginary persons and their talk emerge from the printed page and take on a life that absorbs ours in its merriment or mockery. Then, perhaps, the reflective reader who has yielded to the spell of the illusion may begin to wonder at his own amusement and at the power which evoked it. There is some authority for exalting man as the only animal that laughs. Certainly he is the only animal who tries to define and explain why he laughs. Even comedy must eventually submit itself to philosophy. The Greeks indeed had hardly produced one great comic dramatist before Plato and Aristotle had begun to define and to speculate on the essential significance of those creations of Aristophanes. That speculation and analysis have been carried on ever since by poets and critics as well as by philosophers, so that the writer who today attempts to further this inquiry has plenty of high examples. Those who have written comedy form scarcely as august a company as those who have sought to define it.

For over four centuries the term comedy has been applied to English plays. Though it has covered a great diversity of practice, it has always been used with the intent to indicate a class of plays that could be grouped together because of their common similarities. Though neither practice nor theory has conformed to a fixed definition or to a unified tradition, still they have both recognized certain classes or types of comedy. It is my purpose in this book to look back over the long traffic of the theater and to discuss the emergence of these types and to note their continuation or influence upon the modern stage. This survey will be mainly historical rather than philosophical, but at the start it naturally looks for the guidance of some rough working definition.

If we go to the dictionary or to the average man who reads, we get something like this: Comedy is that form of drama whose chief purpose is to amuse. Such a generalization will not prove very satisfactory either to the philosopher in search of fundamental meanings or to the historian trying to classify the enormous number of plays that at one time or another have received the name comedy. This rough definition stresses rather than solves two main difficulties which confront my inquiry. First, how can we mark off comedies from other plays? Second, what do we mean by amusing, by laughter, by the comic? The answer to either question is likely to involve the other; nevertheless, it will be convenient to take them separately and to begin with the first.

In the early days of the English drama, Sir Philip Sidney declared that there were "no right comedies and no right tragedies but only a mongrel sort of tragi-comedy." This remark might be echoed by a literary student of the present who finds the character and purpose of stage plays too various and too mixed to permit of very precise classification. Sidney's remark, however, shows that he believed there was such a thing as a right comedy, and that it could be sharply distinguished from a right tragedy. Historically this has indeed been a main distinction. Comedy has long been recognized as something quite different from tragedy.

It has been much easier, moreover, to define tragedy than comedy. The great Athenian dramatists created a distinct form of drama known as tragedy, which was defined by Aristotle, revived and imitated in the Renaissance, and has continued as a vital though changing tradition in all modern European literature. From the beginning comedy has been viewed as an opposite to tragedy, and it has tended to usurp the neutral ground between them. As tragedy continued a distinct and limited form, comedy became more heterogeneous and inclusive. In Athens, however, comedy developed a form almost as definite as that of tragedy; and the two, except for the peculiar type of satyric play, were held to comprise all the functions of drama. Aristotle, defining tragedy as concerned with momentous and disastrous actions, with superior and renowned persons, appealing to the emotions of pity and terror, limits the subject matter of comedy to lesser events and persons and its appeal to the sense of the ludicrous.

Whether or not such a division of drama is fundamental is open to doubt. Drama presumably had its origin in mimetic action, first in gesture and dance, and later with speech and dialogue. The efforts of the tribal mimics, in whatever folk rite or religious festival, may conceivably have been directed mainly at one or the other of two purposes, to arouse either the fear or the laughter of the spectators. From dances and rites aiming at the emotions of fear, horror, pity, awe, there might arise tragedy. From the grotesque buffoonery intended to arouse laughter, there might develop comedy. But, even in the more primitive states of society, the crudest mimetic performances might readily excite many other emotions besides unmixed terror or laughter. Among most peoples there is no record of folk drama developing into the two sharply distinguished species.

For England, however, as for all modern nations, it was the example of Athens which counted. By right comedy and right tragedy, Sir Philip Sidney meant those that followed the classical examples of Euripides and Aristophanes or at least of their Latin successors, Seneca and Plautus. But he bemoaned the confusion of the theater with its mongrel tragicomedies. That theater was responding to the taste of its audience, fostered by a long dramatic tradition which desired no sharp separation of the emotions but preferred to take its tragic and comic, its tears and laughter well mixed. The medieval drama in its miracles and moralities had delighted in the mingling of the sublime and the ridiculous and had even found their sharp juxtaposition effective. The English theater for a century after Sidney rarely produced a tragedy without some comic scene, often one that completely justified itself, as, for example, that of the porter in "Macbeth" or of the gravediggers in "Hamlet"; it freely introduced disastrous events and renowned persons into its comedies, as for example, the shipwreck and the Duke in "Twelfth Night"; and it soon recognized tragicomedy as a regular dramatic form. There were then three species, each of which would have seemed very mixed to Aristotle or Sidney.

The distinction of comedy as separated from tragedy is not of great service in modern drama, still it is a distinction that in some degree has continued to be recognized and is not without force today. The test has sometimes been made apart from either the nature of contents or the emotional appeal, solely on the happy or unhappy ending. During the middle ages the terms tragedy and comedy were applied to narratives according as the wheel of fortune turned from good to bad or from bad to good. From the time of Dante's "Divine Comedy," the happy ending has been associated with comedy. A difficulty, however, at once arises as to the meaning of happy. Even when an unhappy ending was thought to require deaths, it was still possible to kill one or two unlikable and unworthy persons without destroying the comic delight of the audience. Tragedies, on the other hand, might reward virtue as well as punish vice. The happy ending indeed became after a time too common to distinguish any dramatic species, except that if the ending was too unhappy the play could not be a comedy.

The practice of the modern drama soon called for

another and quite different distinction. A certain inferior sort of plays were set off from other comedies and assigned the name of farce. Farce is broad or low comedy with exaggeration of character and incidents for ludicrous effect. Or, in Dryden's words, "Farce is that in poetry which grotesque is in a picture, the persons and actions of a farce are all unnatural and the manners false." It may be noted that farce as thus defined conforms strictly to Aristotle's criteria and to the examples of Aristophanes and Plautus. It exactly illustrates our rough generalization, for its chief purpose is to amuse. The feeling seems to be that something more is required of comedy, some truth to life, harmony of organization, or subtlety of appeal. Evidently here is another distinction not easy to make but tending toward a narrower definition. After we have taken out the tragedies and tragicomedies, we must then remove these boisterous and extravagant farces before we can approach to pure comedy.

A comedy cannot be tragic or end too unhappily and it cannot be too continuously and obstreperously comic. To escape the banalities of farce it must have some other interest than mere amusement. It has in fact tried almost every interest. There have been comedies infringing on the appeal to pity which Aristotle restricted to tragedy, and others have entered freely into the boundaries of romance and phantasy. Still others have kept not only to reality but to the commonplaces of every day. Comedy has chosen strange companions. It can yoke itself in service with morality or sentiment, or it can disport with folly and fancy. It suits itself to a caustic censorship of manners or adds savor to the idealisms of lovers. It is a welcome relief and relaxation from anything overserious and taxing; so in drama the tension of the tragic, heroic, didactic, or sentimental is likely to be broken by intervals of appeal to the sense of fun and laughter. The contrasting parts may be sharply separated as are the heroic and comic in Shakespeare's "Henry IV," or they may combine in the very tone and temper of the play as do sentiment and humor in Sir James Barrie's "What Every Woman Knows." The didactic disquisitions do not make a sermon out of Mr. Shaw's comedy "Fanny's First Play." In any given case there may be difficulty in deciding in what species the play should be catalogued, or whether the amount of amusement is sufficient to warrant the term comedy.

One of the most peculiar excursions of the comic muse was into the field of those sentiments closely akin to the emotion of pity. Here, free from tragic grandeur, assured of moral blamelessness, the most tearful stories could be united with sufficient comic relief to afford an agreeable entertainment. Given a most happy ending, even the comic relief might be dispensed with, until the popular "sentimental comedies" of the eighteenth century had nothing left which could be called amusing. The name itself is one of the many modern attempts to coin a term to describe the large tertium quid that might lie between tragedy and comedy. The results have usually been merely neutral words with quite indefinite meaning, such as drame, jeu, spiel, schauspiel, tragicomedy. But the very neutrality of the terms indicates the feeling that the term comedy should be reserved for plays with distinctive qualities, and points to the fact that the plays in the theater have ever been departing from this assumed standard.

Among dramas that have not exhibited these glaring departures from the purpose to amuse, there are still manifold variations and differences. Some gain their power to amuse by satire and ridicule, others by merriment and fun. Some are philosophic and benign, others are scornful and others hilarious. Is there any common ground in the amusement which they afford? Can we extend the word comic to cover such varied appeals? We are brought to our second main difficulty in arriving at a definition of comedy—What do we mean by the comic, by amusement, by laughter?

This is a question for the philosophers, and after long debate they are by no means agreed in answer. Each one has found considerable difficulty in making his explanation of the comic both comprehensive of known facts and harmonious with his own synthesis of the universe. It is needless to recapitulate here the many explanations from Plato and Aristotle through Descartes and Hobbes, Hegel and Spencer, to Bergson and Freud, especially as these have been summarized with admirable wit and judgment by Mr. Max Eastman in his recent volume, "The Sense of Humor." I shall touch on only those theories that have had manifest bearing on the practice of writers or that exhibit a real progress in enlightenment.

One theory which seems tacitly recognized in Aristotle's "Rhetoric" and has been widely held, finds the essence of the comic in incongruity, which produces an emotional shock. Our expectations are suddenly disappointed and we laugh. The clown turns his head and reveals the one cheek painted quite differently from the other. The clown runs full tilt at the barrier, but instead of making the jump, he crawls under the fence. Jeff approaches Mutt expecting the payment of a loan and receives a staggering blow on the head. Dromio returns to his master's house and finds another Dromio holding the door. For the child almost anything new is incongruous and provokes a smile. For the adult, grotesque deformity or an absurd mistake may be required to disappoint expectation with a sufficient shock to raise a laugh. Abnormalities and exaggerations in personal traits and behavior, mistakes and tricks may be wrought together so as to provide an amusing entertainment. "We laugh," says Hazlitt, "at what only disappoints our expectations in trifles." This theory, it may be observed, provides an adequate recipe for farce, but leaves little room for the development of comic characters such as Malvolio, Falstaff and Tartuffe. Though incongruity of some sort is to be found in most jokes, verbal or practical, and though a disappointed expectation is often followed by laughter;

these facts do not carry us far in the analysis of the varieties of humour, and scarcely encourage comedy to proceed without a very generous allowance of farce.

A second theory, almost as widely held as the first, has its beginning in Aristotle's "Poetics," where the essence of the comic is found to lie in the ludicrous and the ludicrous is defined as "some defect or ugliness which is not painful or destructive." This conception of laughter as the outlet for scorn and derision of something inferior has been frequently restated with variations by modern writers. In a famous passage in the "Leviathan" Hobbes declared, "Sudden glory is the passion which maketh those Grimaces called Laughter, and is caused either by some sudden act of their own, that pleaseth them; or by the apprehension of some deformed thing in another, by comparison whereof they suddenly applaud themselves." More recently Bergson has put the case, "In laughter we always find an avowed intention to humiliate, and consequently to correct our neighbor." Although the theory has not gone unchallenged and is now rather generally discredited, it has had a strong influence on the makers of comedy. It was avowedly adopted by Ben Jonson and practised by Molière. It advances comedy far beyond the range of farce and suggests the depiction of manners and character. The follies, affectations, absurdities and even the vices of mankind are held up to ridicule and scorn. The braggart, the coward, the pedant, the pettifogger, the fop, and the hypocrite are revealed as defective and inferior. We glory over Malvolio, and are perhaps purged of that self-love which is his infirmity. We scorn Tartuffe and condemn hypocrisy. The subject matter of comedy may include a wide range of human affairs—the fashion of wearing a hat, an accent in speaking, the pretensions of a religious sect, the pride of a class or a nation; its tone may vary from the gentlest raillery to the bitterest satire. By this theory, however, comedy confines itself to the inferiorities of human society. It may reveal and ridicule these and thus play a large part as critic and censor, but it can have nothing to do with the joy of life.

Under this restrictive definition neither "A Midsummer Night's Dream" nor "As You Like It" could quite qualify as a comedy. We laugh with Touchstone and Rosalind, not at them. It might be possible to feel a superiority over Bottom or even over Titania but not over Puck. It is he who has the sudden glory and cries "Lord, what fools these mortals be!" But neither Puck's laughter nor the tone of the whole play is scornful or satiric. It is not in a corrective exaltation or in a disappointed expectation but rather in his own spirit of mirth that Puck finds the source of laughter.

> And those things do best please me
> That befall preposterously.

Voltaire, himself a master of satire, nevertheless emphatically agreed with what may be called this theory of spontaneous origin. "Laughter arises from a gaiety of disposition, absolutely incompatible with contempt and indignation." The primitive folk dancers by their rude and grotesque mimicry may have expressed their own delight and won a responsive joy from the spectators that had in it little or nothing of fear or ridicule. Comedy has often been amusing because it was joyous and merry. Our feeling towards the butt of the jokes may be not unmingled with sympathy or even envy, as in the case of Falstaff. We laugh in imitation or by contagion rather than in superiority. A play may aim to make us share in a merriment that is relaxing and invigorating. With such a purpose comedy turns to sentiment or romance or fancy and responds to the joy of life rather than to the ridicule of inferiority.

There seems to be no essential likeness in the things that may appear comic. We laugh at pretense, at disappointed expectation, at inferiority, at recognized incongruity. But anything or everything may seem incongruous. Laughter may arise not from any quality or relation of objects but rather in the state of mind which is prepared to find all things "befall preposterously." Emerson finds "the radical joke of life and then of literature" in intellectual perception of the yawning delinquencies of practice from the ideal of right and truth, "His perception of disparity, his eye wandering perpetually from the rule to the crooked, lying, thieving fact, makes the eyes run over with laughter." We may laugh with the philosopher or with Puck, we can certainly laugh in joy as well as in scorn but we can also laugh in sorrow. We often say we scarcely know whether to laugh or to cry. We can laugh when we catch a fish, or when in sudden disappointment we find a minnow where we expected a whale, and we can laugh when the fish won't bite—there isn't much else to do. The longer laughter is discussed the more things are discovered that can be found amusing, and the wider the range of operations that tend towards the comic goal.

Modern theorists have by no means abandoned the effort to discover a unifying explanation for the laughter that arises from so many different objects and under such varying states of mind. It is possible to reduce a multitude of jokes to a very simple formula, but then it is found that accessories seem more essential to merriment than the formula itself. The scientists have sought for a physiological or mechanical explanation, and Freud has sent us to the subconscious for a solution of the comic and of everything else. In general, the trend of recent discussion has been to follow Voltaire's clue and to find the seat of unity not in the external objects but in the state of mind. The psychologists have taught us something in connecting laughter with the play instinct. The child laughs much more than the adult, and the child laughs while at play, while fooling, making believe. The experience seems instinctive and certainly contains no element of scorn or any intellectual perception of wit. Yet, perhaps the gleefulness of Emerson's philosopher as well as that of Puck may be but the growth of this happy playfulness. Laughter of all kinds, from that aroused by tickling to the subtlest forms of irony, may, as Mr. Max Eastman urges, be explainable as the development of an instinct almost universal, but varying widely in individuals. This instinct or, as the older psychologists might have called it, this faculty seems capable of wide application and extensive service. If less vigorous in the adult than in the child, it finds more varied stimuli and relates itself more closely with knowledge and experience. It may possess the intellect as well as the emotions, and it encounters the multitudinous incidents of life, seeking laughter, desiring relaxation, enjoying incongruity and surprise, turning work into play.

The advance of civilization has possibly tended to develop the more kindly sort of laughter. Derision and ridicule may be giving way in actuality to a more genial gaiety. Parents have been learning to laugh with their fellow adults in the same spirit as with their children. Men are coming to find a sympathy and understanding in laughter as well as in tears. The Comic Spirit, like other things, has been evolving. Neither the word comic nor any of the other ancient terms, such as ludicrous, ridiculous, incongruous, satire, fun, merriment, has been found quite sufficient for this enlarging and improving sense of humour. The word, at least, if not the spirit, has undergone an evolution in meaning. Humour is an old word, originally meaning moisture, which has experienced a curious shifting of meanings, until it is now used both to include the widest range of response in smile and laughter and also to denote the most superior of emotions connected with the comic.

Carlyle borrows from Jean Paul Richter this conception: "True humour springs not more from the head than from the heart, it is not contempt, its essence is love, it issues not in laughter, but in smiles which lie far deeper. It is a sort of inverse sublimity, exalting, as it were, into our affection what is below us, while sublimity draws

down into our affections what is above us." Thackeray
in ascribing this quality to Dickens, calls humour "a mixture of love and wit." "What an ornament and safe-
guard is humor!" cries Emerson, "Far better than wit
for a poet and writer. It is a genius itself, and so defends
from the insanities." George Meredith exalts the humorous above the comic: the comic spirit is censorious and
critical, though it may also be sunny and silvery, "but the
humourist, if high, has an embrace of contrasts beyond
the scope of the comic poet."

The thing itself of course existed long before it was
named humour. It is found in Shakespeare's comedies,
and was admirably described by Hegel:

"Inseparable from the comic is an infinite geniality and
confidence, capable of rising superior to its own contradiction, and experiencing therein no taint of bitterness
nor sense of misfortune whatever. It is the happy frame
of mind, a hale condition of soul, which, fully aware of
itself, can suffer the dissolution of its aims."

The sense of humour may be regarded as the consum-
mation of the instinct for laughter. A sufficient sense of
humour will preserve the laughter of the child amid the
"shades of the prison house" or in the adult's "fading
light of common day." The sense of superiority which
accompanies risibility over an unfortunate butt is replaced
by a sort of philosophical amusement at all superiorities
and inferiorities. Comedy may smile at the total incongruity of mankind.

It is, I think, in this enlarging sense of humour that we
must look for our guiding conception of comedy. We
need no longer require a particular quality of ludicrous-
ness as an essential of comic action, and we need not limit
our persons or deeds to an inferior level. Almost any
phase of life or character may be treated, so long as their
humorous aspects are revealed. All drama demands
that the audience yield to the temper of the play, to the
enjoyment of what is not really so, to the mingled pleasure and pain of sharing in the ups and downs of the

persons of the play-world. Comedy mimics the deeds of men so as to appeal largely to our sense of humour.

This does not limit the rest of the drama to tragedy. The religious and the didactic, for instance, are almost as unlikely as the tragic to enter into the spirit of humour. Ecstasy and murder are both outside its pale. A play which aims chiefly, as do some recent examples, at serious discussion and instruction, might have a subordinate comic interest, but would not come under our conception of comedy. The field that remains, however, is large. Comedy may ally itself with whimsy or nonsense as readily as with satire and ridicule. It may indulge in wild exaggeration, in seeing the world topsy-turvy or upside down, or it may linger over the slighter foibles of the mediocre or of the "unco' guid." It may be elfish or Pantagruelian as well as benign. There are few places this side of the grave which humour cannot lighten, few austerities that will not soften under its contrasts. Comedy, says Mark Twain, keeps the heart sweet.

Such a view of comedy frees it from that inferiority implied in Aristotle's definition and accepted by many, both theorists and practitioners, for it is based on a recognition of humour as natural, beneficent and recuperative. The profounder emotional appeal may be reserved to tragedy, but the ministrations of comedy are to be viewed as essential to emotional health and spiritual sweetness. Humour is the salt without which life loses its savour, and comedy is one process of extracting this salt of life from its hiding places and distributing it where it may be available for many. There are, to be sure, many grades and qualities of this humour, but there is as yet no conceivable limit to the degree to which it may be refined, or to either the delicacy or the richness of the flavour that it may add to living.

Comedy finds its purpose aided by the skilful use of words as well as by gesture and mimicry. It avails itself of the arts of the theater and of literature. It delights in song as well as dance, in epigram as well as grimace, in paradox as well as slap-jack, and it can stoop to punning as readily as to buffoonery. Whatever can be used in verse or fiction to amuse and delight can be employed in the drama with the additional advantage of impersonation. It combines the humour of words and voice, of the audible and the visible. Its form and movement, construction and texture, persons and speeches, are all dependent on literary art. Its greatest creative triumphs are won by the pen. The wit of Beatrice, the sparkle of Millamant and the archness of Rosalind exist in the phrase. There is surely beauty both in the stage presentation and in the lines read in the closet of Rosalind and Beatrice as well as of Juliet and Cordelia, or of "As You Like It" and "Twelfth Night" as well as of "Lear" and "Hamlet."

Comedy shares this duality of interest with all drama. It must be acceptable in the theater, and it may have the qualities that make it readable. Even tragedy can with difficulty exist for the reader alone; away from the stage it soon loses all the traits that make for dramatic success. Comedy is still more dependent on the stage for the essentials of its form and the very purpose of its being. Though a play may thrill, instruct or uplift its auditors, it must in the first place entertain them; a comedy may be admirable and have no other purpose than entertainment. It is a form of literature, determined by the requirements of the stage, and its aim is in unison with the main purpose of the modern theater. But it is literature, dependent always on literary skill, creating its illusions and phrases, moulding in some degree the minds and hearts of the people; and there is nothing in its connection with the stage which forbids it from becoming great literature.

The survey that I am undertaking must examine the annals of the English-speaking theater and consider many plays that have long ceased to delight the reader. It must deal with changes in stage practice and in the taste of theatergoers. It should unfold a partial history of a people's entertainment. What, in different periods, has excited laughter? With what in the way of moral or sentiment, have men mixed their amusement? How has the dramatic artist progressed in devising and combining the ingredients of his delightful dish? What kinds of plays have amused the audiences of different periods? Such are the questions that we must encounter while among the varied entertainments of the theater we look for similarities in theme or method that link some together in significant groups, for signs of imitation that mark continuity of effort, or for social changes that cause the decline of one form of comedy and initiate another.

Our inquiry, however, is not concerned with details of scenes, costumes, or the art of acting, but with comedy as a part of literature. To be sure, only a few of the plays which we are to consider still live in the affections of the general reader. Still fewer, it must be added, have survived upon the stage. It is a changing picture, a shifting scene that has supplied the amusement of four centuries. The sense of humour has been tickled by trivialities and temporalities and it has sometimes found its choicer stimuli in poetry or fiction rather than in the drama. But the history of comedy presents an unbroken line of literary endeavour and popular response. There is no sign of its conclusion. The theater of today is crowded with wit and satire, with fancy and frolic, and it appears to be widening its range of humorous appeal. The sense of humour shows no sign of limit or exhaustion. Under its patronage there seem to be no boundaries either to the heights or to the breadths to which comedy may attain.

CHAPTER II

MEDIEVAL AND CLASSICAL INFLUENCES

ENGLISH comedy as a distinct form makes its appearance amid the new and enterprising dramatic activity at the beginning of the sixteenth century. This activity was directed in part by the revival of the classics, but it was based on the long dramatic experience of the middle ages, which had already evolved a certain amount of comic drama and a practice of comic acting. We must first glance at this medieval development and then consider the effect upon it of the influence of classical comedy which reached England with the revival of learning in the sixteenth century.

In the early middle ages nearly all knowledge of the Greek and Roman drama and theater disappeared. Little was known or read of any of the dramatists with the notable exception of Terence. His six comedies were much admired in the scholarly world and even excited certain literary imitations by the nun Hrosvitha. But these apparently were not acted, and only absurd notions survived of the way in which the Roman plays were performed. The very words comedy and tragedy came to be dissociated from the drama and applied to narratives. The medieval drama developed without direct aid from classical theory or practice.

One obscure influence in the direction of comedy, however, must be noted. When the Roman theater finally succumbed to the attacks of the Christians and the barbarians, it had long ceased to present anything worthy the name of comedy. But it still offered boisterous and obscene farces and maintained comic actors. What happened to the Roman mimus—the name for both actor and

18

performance—we do not know. Driven from his theater
and outlawed by the church, he nevertheless continued to
practise his profession and handed down to his children
the art of amusing the crowd. For a few centuries
occasional records of his activity survive, and then he is
completely lost sight of among the minstrels, acrobats,
jugglers and buffoons who survived as entertainers despite
the condemnation of the church. The word mime continued as a term of contempt but without clear connection with any dramatic performance. In the Wyclifite
sermon against miracle plays their apologist is made to
say it is "lesse yvels that thei have thyre recreaceon by
pleyinge of myraclis than bi pleyinge of other japis." We
hear also of "ludi theatrales" in connection with the
Feast of Fools. But we cannot be sure that these ludi
and japis were veritable dramas—and can only surmise
as to their character. In English there exists in a manuscript of the early fourteenth century a fragment of a
version in dialogue of the popular tale "Dame Siriz." It
is entitled "Interludium de Clerico et Puella," and is the
only possible survival from the repertory of the medieval
mimi and histriones. What rude pieces they may have
performed could indeed rarely by any possibility have
been written down and preserved. Their drama must
often have been little more than dancing, horseplay and
clownishness, but they somehow kept alive a tradition of
acting, an appreciation of comic situation and perhaps
some skill in constructing actable plays. Certain comic
passages in the religious plays show a skill in stagecraft
and dramatic technic scarcely to be accounted for except
by such a continuing tradition; but it is not until the fifteenth century, and then mostly in France, that comic
pieces in the vernacular become abundant. This apparently sudden appearance of a comic drama gives
further reason for believing that a submerged vein of
farce by popular entertainers continued throughout the
middle ages.

Another minor contribution to the tradition of play

acting came from the folk games and ceremonies. The Robin Hood plays, especially, exercised some influence on later drama, and the mummers' plays at Christmas and other performances nourished the theatrical instinct. But the main drama of the middle ages arose in the church; and its various forms, of which the miracles and morali-ties were the chief, constitute what we mean by the medieval as distinct from the classical or the modern drama.

This religious drama seemingly had its origin in the church service, in certain texts and ceremonies, first for Easter and then for Christmas. From this there grew a considerable liturgical drama, still in Latin and connected with the service and presenting many events from the old as well as the new testament. Throughout western Europe a gradual secularization brought this drama from the church into the market place, out of Latin into the vernacular, and out of the hands of the clergy into charge of the craft guilds or other lay organizations. By the fourteenth century these miracle plays, usually cycles of short plays illustrating the biblical narrative from creation to ascension or judgment day, became popular spectacles affording to great audiences through their protracted per-formances amusement as well as edification. I must dwell on their element of comedy which delighted the populace and shocked the moralists, but in the main they kept closely to holy writ, their purpose was partly exposition, their form epic or chronicle, and their themes, because of their importance and seriousness, rather on the side of tragedy than of comedy.

Comic or farcical additions, however, are not uncom-mon in the miracle plays. Herod, the tyrant, from an early date was represented as a ridiculous braggart. The minor devils everywhere were employed to excite laughter. There was much fun as they carried off the wicked to hell or even made sallies into the audience after some of the spectators. The life of Mary Magdalene before her conversion gave a manifest opportunity to be no less

amusing than edifying, as in the Digby play. Certain
minor persons, such as the tradesman loosed from hell,
or the spice merchant meeting the Maries on their way to
the sepulchre, or the shepherds watching their flocks, invited a realistic amplification that would delight a popular
audience. In England the play of Noah afforded a
chance for a lively farce on the favorite theme of the
taming of the shrew. When the ark is completed Noah's
wife stoutly refuses to enter and prefers to remain drinking with her gossips even after the rain falls and the
waters gather. A good beating by the husband finally
tames the shrew.

The best and most elaborate of such farcical additions
is the second of the two plays of the shepherds found in
the Towneley collection. We may imagine it as being
played at some time near 1400 at the great fair held by
the canons of Nostel in the fields near Wakefield. One
of the great cycles is being performed with a procession
of wagons, presenting the usual stories from biblical
history. The old testament has been traversed and the
plays of the annunciation and of the salutation of Elizabeth have prepared the way for the nativity. Next comes
the play of the shepherds, the first to greet the new-born
messiah at Bethlehem.

Three shepherds appear and bewail the cold and rain
and cheer themselves with a song. They are very English
and good Christians, who know it is Christmas Eve, and
their racy comments amuse the audience. To them enters
Mak, a suspected thief, and the shepherds are anxious to
know what he is doing abroad at this time of night. With
much audacity Mak at first pretends not to know them
and then professes himself friendly. The shepherds lie
down to sleep and for security compel Mak to lie between
them. As soon as they are asleep, he crawls over them,
steals a sheep, and hastens home where he and his wife
Gib plan a stratagem to hide the booty. He returns and
resumes his place between the sleeping shepherds. When
they awake one tells of his dream that a sheep has been

stolen, and Mak counters with a dream that his wife has given birth to a child. He hastens home, the shepherds go to the flock, discover their loss, and at once suspect that either Mak or Gib is the thief. They run to the house of Mak, who greets them warmly and invites them to drink in celebration of the new-born babe sleeping in the cradle. They find no sheep and their suspicions are allayed and they leave the house; but, remembering they have made no presents to the baby, they return. One insists on having a peek at the child and discovers the nose of the stolen sheep. Thereupon they seize the crestfallen Mak and are tossing him vigorously in a sheet when the angel is heard singing *Gloria in excelsis,* and the shepherds hurry to the Bethlehem stable with their offerings to their Saviour, "the lytyll day-starne."

This "Secunda Pastorum," along with other of the Towneley plays, is the work of a single dramatist of unusual skill and humour. The scheme of the play might serve as a formula or model for much later drama and fiction. The chief actor is a clever rogue who succeeds for a time in his tricks but is finally exposed and punished. In the initial scene there is careful preparation, with incidental characterization, leading to Mak's first success in escaping from his sleeping companions and stealing the sheep. Then there are the prophetic dreams, a device so common in later drama, and the protracted tension for the audience as Mak's trick of concealing the sheep as a baby hesitates in the balance between success and exposure. What a clever bit of dramaturgy is the cradle, the objective of every eye in the audience, while the shepherds stumble over it in their search and Mak pretends that the lively dialogue threatens to waken the sleeper. Then, just before the end, as in tragedy, there is the "final hope" when the shepherds retire and the cradle stands untouched; and finally the discovery and catastrophe. For a long time to come the favorite catastrophe in English comedy was a good beating.

The connection of the play with the larger cycle is not

without skill. The juxtaposition of the blanket-tossing and the angel's announcement of the Messiah is no mere accident but one of those sharp transitions from the ridiculous to the sublime, those conjunctions of the real and the divine, in which medieval art delighted. Even the pretended childbirth of Gib has its contrast to the divine nativity. The very words, "lytyll day-starne" with which one shepherd greets his Saviour, he has used first when offering his gifts to the sheep in the cradle. For sheer dramatic effectiveness for the audience at the Wakefield fair, what could be better than this realistic and homely prelude to the revelation to English shepherds of the birth of the Redeemer? Here, too, in spite of the simple folk story at the basis, are all the essentials and some of the ornaments of comic drama.

In its general characteristics the "Secunda Pastorum" is not unlike farcical incidents in other miracle plays. Like them, it is brief, realistic and racy, and quite medieval in its methods of art and humour. But in dramatic merit it far surpasses all preceding or contemporary efforts. Though much of this excellence is due to the individual initiative of the author, the technic seems too complicated and too skilful to be ascribed solely to his invention. It appears rather as the culmination of a long practice in comic dramatization that has no adequate representation in the surviving miracle plays.

For its equal we have to come down a generation or so later to the most famous of French farces, "Pathelin." In England there is nothing comparable to it until the sixteenth century. Neither in the farcical elements added to bible story, nor in the legends of saints, nor in the few secular stories that found a presentation similar to the miracles, can we trace any consistent development toward comedy. Towneley's "Secunda Pastorum" stands alone, head and shoulders above the rest of the family, and without any direct ancestors or descendants that research has discovered. But within its brief compass it discloses about all the potentialities that existed in medieval farce.

The moralities in the latter middle ages grew up alongside the miracles. They offered a symbolic presentation of life. Instead of the bible story they presented the
conflict of vices and virtues, using personified abstractions
instead of individuals as actors. They were devoted to
a serious purpose and were often extremely didactic in
tone, but they soon found a little comic business helpful
in holding the attention of their audiences. In the sixteenth century they become of much interest in connection
with the rise of comedy, for they present mixtures of
allegory and reality and they desert the general symbolization of life to adventure into the fields of politics, education and religious controversy. They continue even after
the forms of the classical drama are well known, a sort of
degenerate transition type, amalgamating freely with all
species and sometimes combining allegory and farce in a
fashion not unlike that of the "Plutus" of Aristophanes.
But at no time is there anything in the morality that offers
much spur to the comic spirit.

For the development of medieval farce as distinct from
either miracle or morality we are obliged to turn from
England to France of the fifteenth century. In the hands
of various groups of amateur actors, the drama was turning from religious to secular themes and from the purpose
of edification to that of amusement. The Basoche (or
law students), the Enfants sans Soucis in Paris and many
puys and *sociétés joyeuses* in the country acted many
pieces, constituting a secular and even an irreligious
drama. Certain of these conformed to a definite type,
the farce. Gross and realistic, free in their satire,
especially when directed at the women or the clergy, those
plays bear a marked likeness to the fabliaux, the indecent
and vivid tales which had made up so large a part of
medieval popular literature. But in this somewhat limited
field, the farce could exhibit considerable fun and liveliness, and at its best, as in "Pathelin," was an achievement
in dramatic structure and dialogue worthy of rank as
comedy. It must be considered as one of the forms of

drama created by the middle ages without aid from the classics unless through the popular tradition handed down from the mimi.

The Wars of the Roses and other social conditions in England were unfavourable to such a wide outburst of dramatic activity as France witnessed in the fifteenth century. But by the end of that century the conditions of acting were undergoing a revolution. Though the out-of-door performances of the great miracles continue in their established method, and though a long morality is occasionally produced in similar fashion, the tendency is toward shorter performances, fewer actors and a simple stage. At the court there was less simplicity and much pageantry, masking and revelling, but also play-acting. Companies of children, first from the Royal Chapel and later from the choir boys of St. Paul's, become the most frequent performers, though the king has also an adult company. Plays, whether in Latin or English, are performed at the universities and schools, and by amateur organizations, but these are rivalled and after a time surpassed by the professional companies. Since the disappearance of the Roman mimus, we have seen that the professional actor is an unidentified character among the medieval entertainers, but he reappears in England at the court in the Christmas of 1427, when there is a payment for the *jeuues et entreludes* of Jakke Travail et ses compaignons. By the beginning of the next century, such professional companies are far more numerous than in France and are determining the form if not the content of the drama. Protected by the license of some nobleman, they wander from town to town and act at banquets, in school, guild-hall, church, or on the village green, as occasion demands. One company may be composed of five or six men and one or two boys, who take the parts of women. Its costumes and properties are scanty, and it must often reduce or double the characters of a play. The advertisement to "The Nature of the Four Elements" will indicate both the pedantic comprehensiveness in a scholarly author and the new importance of brevity for the professional actor:

A new interlude and a merry of the nature of the Four Elements, declaring many proper points of philosophy natural, and of divers strange lands, and of divers strange effects and causes; which interlude, if the whole matter be played, will contain the space of an hour and a half; but, if ye list, ye may leave out much of the said matter, as the Messenger's part, and some of Nature's part, and some of Experience's part, and yet the matter will depend conveniently, and then it will not be past three-quarters of an hour length. London: John Rastell.

Under such conditions were produced the "interludes." We have already met with the term in *interludium de clerico et puella,* a stray dialogue in a manuscript of the early fourteenth century and again in the performance of Jakke Travail and others at the court of Henry VI. Its origin is unknown, and it was never used with exactness, but it may usually be defined simply as a short play. It might be of any dramatic type from miracle to farce, and it might be performed by any class of actors from choir boys to courtiers, but in the early sixteenth century when the term came into general use, most of these interludes were in part moralities, using allegory and personified abstractions, and most of them had a considerable mixture of farce.

The earliest surviving English play that is neither a miracle nor a morality is the interlude, "Fulgens and Lucres" by Henry Medwall, printed between the years 1513 and 1519 and probably acted at court in 1497. It is in verse and is divided into two parts, "to be played at two times," containing 1432 and 920 lines respectively. Part I seems to have been acted in the interval between banquets, and Part II has a dance and disguising. The serious portion of the play is a disputation based on a popular treatise of the early Renaissance "De Vera Nobilitate" which had been translated into English and printed by Caxton. Lucrece, daughter of a Roman senator, is wooed by Publius Cornelius, noble but unworthy, and Gaius Flaminius, virtuous though of humble birth, and after hearing their long arguments she chooses Gaius. Medwall secures some reality and human interest for the debate, but his dramatic achievement is the comic underplot. Two personages designated as A and B become servants of the chief suitors and rivals for the favor of the handmaid of Lucrece. They engage in a song contest, a wrestling match, a cock-fight, thus supplying a farcical entertainment "to stir folk to mirth and game," while their gross language and vulgar wooing furnish an amusing burlesque on the argumentative love-making of the main plot.

Though Medwall was a humanist, his play gives no hint of familiarity with the classical comedies, and though he may have known the secular dramas already produced in Flanders, he does not imitate them. His clever use of comic underplot to enliven and burlesque the main theme anticipates the practice of Lyly, Shakespeare and many other later dramatists, and suggests the existence of a considerable body of comedies or farces at the court of Henry VII, of which "Lucres" is the only survivor. Medwall's other interlude "Nature" mixes comic realism and the usual allegory of man's temptations.

The morality, indeed, was soon taking long steps in the direction of comedy. If it still kept to the large symbolization of life, as in "Mankynd," it felt the need of amusement supplied by Titivillus the devil who appears as host of a tavern, or it might find amusement and vivacity in depicting youth sowing his wild oats, as in "Hickscorner" and "Youth." Or, it might shift its allegory to educational rather than moral edification, as in the "Four Elements," or to the field of religious controversy, as in the translation of the famous protestant attack on the pope—"Pammachius." These and other of the early Tudor interludes show a widening range of subjects and persons, a tendency from abstract to concrete and an increasing employment of satire, burlesque and farce. The allegorical framework was becoming a loose scheme in which almost anything classical or medieval, tragical or comical might be utilized.

By the time morality and farce were combining, the farce as an integral form had finally made an unmistakable appearance in English in the plays of John Heywood. Employed in youth at court as a singer and later a player on the virginals, epigramist, poet, playwright, the opponent of Cranmer, allied by marriage to More, the favorite of Mary, father of two well-known Jesuits and grandfather of John Donne, his long life was destined to come into contact with many important persons and events of the troubled century. Here we are concerned with his early days at court when he was a leader in the new dramatic activity. His plays fall into two groups, disputations and farces. In the first group are to be included "Witty and Witless," "Gentleness and Nobility" (probably by Heywood), "Love," and "The Weather." These dramatizations of the familiar medieval debate or disputation are tedious enough, though they seem to have afforded amusement in their day and "Love" and "The Weather" are both advertised as new and merry interludes. "The Weather," indeed, approaches the border line of farce, and all might have been described as is "Gentylnes and Nobylyte" in its first edition "compiled in maner of an enterlude with divers toys and gestis addyt thereto to make mery pastyme and disport." The second group comprises three farces, "The Four P's (a newe and very mery enterlude of A palmer, A pardoner, A poticary, A pedlar)," "The Pardoner and the Friar (a mery Play betwene the pardoner and the frere, the curate and neybour Pratte)" and "John, Tib, and Sir John (a mery play betwene Johan Johan the husbande, Tyb his wyfe and Syr John the priest)." These plays all owe something to French farces and they display the characteristic features of the type, resemblances to the fabliau, indecency, satire on the clergy, realistic and coarse fun.

"John, Tib, and Sir John" contains less than 700 lines, which are sufficient for a farcical presentation of the marital triangle. The husband is bewailing his wife's absence and threatening to beat her—when she returns, reduces him to submission and compels him to prepare the table and then go and invite the priest to supper. The priest and Tib sup merrily while John is kept busy mending a leaky pail with wax. The priest tells of some merry miracles which he has performed upon women. John, chafing the wax by the fire, gets nothing to eat and when he protests is beaten, while the wife and priest run off together.

Here at any rate is nothing edifying. No trace of a moral or of an abstraction remains. The sole purpose is to amuse. The play, trifling though its value may be, is indisputably comic. One might indeed speculate why a national drama that could produce the farce of "Mak" by 1400 could produce little else in the way of farce until 1530 and then nothing better than this "mery enterlude" of Heywood's, but in this play and its companions we undoubtedly have the first representatives in English of medieval farce as a form distinct from miracle or morality. Hereafter, as previously, farce is most frequently found in combination with some other and more serious dramatic forms. But few plays written within the next hundred years fail to show some signs of indebtedness to the medieval traditions of farce. And when we speak of medieval farce we mean something very like "John, Tib and Sir John."

By the day of the printing of Heywood's farces, 1533, the medieval drama was about spent, and the revival of the classics was becoming manifest through translations and imitations. It must not be thought, however, that an instantaneous or general adoption of the classical models took place. For a generation more, interludes, quasi-moralities and farces continued to be written that exhibited little or no acquaintance on the part of their authors with the Latin comedies. Even an avowed imitation of the classics was sure to be more medieval than Roman or modern. But the new life in the drama, the new forms and the new themes, and the impetus to new experiment were henceforth derived in large measure from the new knowledge of the classics. The medieval influence survived in comedy as elsewhere, but no one paid it much honor.

The revival of the classical drama began as early as Petrarch, whose "Philologia," written before 1331 and then suppressed, was modelled on Terence. More than a century later a new interest was given to the study of Roman comedy by the discovery in 1427 of twelve hitherto lost plays of Plautus, including the "Menaechmi" and the "Miles Gloriosus." Neo-Latin imitations of Latin tragedy and comedy were now frequent, but written to be read and not acted. It was not until toward the end of the century that a study of the account of Greek and Roman theaters by the architect Vitruvius had encouraged in Italy the presentation of both classical plays and neo-Latin imitations in the classical fashion. By this time Euripides and Aristophanes, as well as Seneca and Plautus, were being studied, edited and translated; and Aristotle and Horace were supplying the basis for a new understanding and criticism of the scope and function of tragedy and comedy.

The main models for Renaissance comedy, however, were furnished by the six plays of Terence, long favorites among medieval readers, and the twenty plays of Plautus, now given new currency everywhere among scholars. These Latin comedies were all translations or adaptations from Greek originals. They offer neither fresh nor extensive reflections of life, nor a novel and enterprising development of dramatic method. They are not the works of great genius, or even the imitations of genius, but rather repetitions of well-worn themes and characters in accord with a conventionalized dramatic practice. They offered to the admiration of the Renaissance a singularly limited range of material for the play of the comic spirit.

The plot is usually a conflict of tricks. A pair of young lovers are engaged in deceiving their elders. The slaves are the go-betweens and the manipulators. Mistakes, misunderstandings, disguises make up the intrigue. Twins are numerous, mistaken identity common, and the recovery of long lost children or parents, a frequent conclusion. But the course of tricks runs no smoother than that of true love. The best planned device usually meets unexpected obstacles, intrigue is met by counter intrigue, and the situation reaches a happy complication when the trickster is tricked. The persons employed in these entanglements conform to rather fixed types. Along with the sputtering old men and love-sick youths are misers, pedants, jealous husbands, braggart soldiers and parasites, whose proclivities are open to easy ridicule. Such types were recognizable in any state of society and gave a certain reality to the picture which otherwise, with its luxurious courtesans and very clever slaves, might have seemed romantically oriental to the Renaissance scholar.

This limited stock of well worn dramatic material had, however, much that was novel and stimulating to the sixteenth century. It presented a new type and scheme of drama, devoted solely to amusement and having a definite structure. Dramatic fable appeared divorced from narrative. A play began in the middle of the story, in the thick of complications which increased until the final dénouement. The lower or middle ranks of society were presented, ridiculed or at least made the sport of laughter. All this seemed justified not by any moral or christian service, but as a contribution to literature that might share in the ancient and imperishable glories of the drama of Greece and Rome.

Further, these Roman comedies, and later, as they became known, those of Aristophanes, supplied what seemed an abundance of new comic situations. The

meager complications and naïve incidents of medieval
farce were enlarged and supplemented. Comedy might
range from the avarice of a miser to the amours of the
gods. Plautus in particular supplied a new fund of plots,
situations, and especially of twists and turns in comic
dialogue. In the reunion of long separated parents and
children were suggestions for sentiment and pathos quite
foreign to farce or morality. The "Andria" and
"Adelphi" of Terence were indeed destined to have
Elizabethan imitators and later to be used as supports for
the moral and sentimental comedy of the eighteenth
century. Fancy and romance as well as realism might
find support in the matter of the classical comedies.
Furthermore, they suggested a still wider extension of the
material of comedy into the great fields of secular story
and of everyday affairs. The plays of Terence also
exhibited a dramatic skill and dexterity unknown since his
day. Incidents, jokes and persons such as anyone might
know, or at least imitate, were woven together with a
deftness of arrangement and a grace of expression that
challenged and baffled the ambition of the modern. These
Roman comedies taught the moderns their dramaturgy
and spurred them to attempt to create literature.

In these larger effects, Latin comedy was destined to
exercise a long and continued sway over the modern
drama. In spite of its limited scope, it supplied a model
better than anything produced in the middle ages. In
spite of its trivial purpose, it called comedy to dramatic
art and poetry. It must have appeared, however, as a
species much less strange than classical tragedy, and its
methods were indeed rather generally and readily
assimilated by Renaissance dramatists. There is not such
a very great difference between a play of Plautus and a
fifteenth century farce, or indeed between a play of
Plautus and a fabliau. Realism, indecency, a plot of
tricks, and much fun, are common to both. The Italians
were producing good vernacular imitations as early as
Ariosto's "I Suppositi" (1509) and the other nations of

Europe shortly followed. In these imitations, both the example of Terence and the desire of the modern audience for excitement soon led to an increase of the complications of the plots.

The classical influence upon sixteenth century drama was exercised not only directly through the Latin comedies but also indirectly through the neo-Latin plays that flourished abundantly. These were the outcome of the humanistic effort to recreate a Latin literature, were known to the scholars of all nations, and for a time seemed to offer a more attractive field for literary talent than did their vernacular rivals. In England during the first half of the century, the schools and universities were very active in dramatic productions and encouraged Latin as well as English comedy. Imitation of the classics was often employed on biblical themes, especially in the Netherlands and Germany about 1530. It was felt that the license and immorality of the classics might be dispensed with or at least balanced by a little morality, and an effort was made to produce a Christian Terence. Stories from the bible were dramatized after the fashion of Seneca or Plautus or Terence, and the story of the prodigal son, in particular, had a great career. All the evils of his prodigal life could be presented with comic effect, and yet the ending preserve the moral. This return to biblical themes and Christian ethics under the guise of Terentian technic soon found itself involved in the great religious controversy and resulted in plays in the vernacular as well as in Latin.

One other variation of the classical influence made itself felt at an early date in the drama. The pagan deities had appeared in Latin comedy and were the constant themes of classical literature. The mythological stories were thrown into dialogue or eclogue, then acted, forming shows that easily combined with pastoral scenes and persons. A remark in Vitruvius in regard to the setting for the satyr play was taken to apply to the pastoral, and later in the century a special pastoral drama with a stage of its own was devised. But before this particular elaboration took place, the ancient gods and goddesses were welcome on the stage or in shows and pageants. Instead of tableaux of abstractions after the fashion of the moralities, the Seven Deadly Sins and other medieval personifications gave place to the rulers of Olympus. In another chapter I shall dwell on the effect of court shows in encouraging classical spectacle and story in the regular drama. Here it will be sufficient to note that classical myths provided the modern drama with both fanciful themes and stage spectacle. The playful or fanciful or burlesque treatment of the ancient stories has continued on to this day one of the chief themes of modern comedy.

Nearly all of the features of the revival of classical comedy exhibited in Italy are to be found in England by the time of Heywood's farces. The "Menæchmi" and "Phormio" were acted by schoolboys at Cardinal Wolsey's in 1527 and 1528. A translation of Terence's "Andria" was printed about 1530. "Thersites" (1537) is based on one of the neo-Latin farces of the French professor Ravisius Textor. But the English humanists who might have written English comedies in the new manner, were soon entangled in the religious clash. From Wolsey's fall to the accession of Elizabeth, most of the plays preserved were more or less controversial in character. It is only with the long peace beginning with Elizabeth's accession that either comedy or tragedy has much chance to develop. However, Udall's "Roister Doister," an imitation of Plautus, was probably acted in 1553, a few years earlier. By that date the medieval and classical influences were fairly joined. But before considering their further amalgamation and adaptation during the ensuing thirty years, I must give one chapter to a different but important source of modern comedy, the host of stories that were coming into print.

CHAPTER III

THE BACKGROUND OF STORY

A MAIN source for Elizabethan comedy is found entirely outside of the drama, whether medieval or classical, in the vast body of narratives which the printing press was making accessible to every reader. The medieval drama translated the bible narrative into performances that could be seen and enjoyed by the illiterate. The Elizabethan drama made the stories of the world vivid and intelligible even to those who could not read. The theater with its new form of entertainment was at first, like the moving pictures in our own day, chiefly a purveyor of old fictions. The new entertainment delighted a public hungry for story.

It is not easy to make exact comparisons between the amounts of story-telling in different periods. The early twentieth century certainly shows an almost appalling increase over the early nineteenth. The millions who go to the movie tonight, the other millions who read the bit of fiction offered in the evening paper, mark a vast expansion over one hundred years ago. The mid-sixteenth century in England offered relatively an even greater increase over the mid-fifteenth. The wealth of story in Greek and Latin, indeed all the wealth stored up in manuscripts classical or medieval had been disclosed, put into circulation, made accessible even for a Stratford lad with only a smattering of education. For the first time, the world's best literature was open to the average man.

This process of collecting, editing, translating and adapting was going on in England throughout the sixteenth century. And meanwhile a new literature, awakened first in Italy and when in the rest of western Europe, was adding its wealth for the printing press to multiply. The great enlargement of the geographical world by the discoveries of Columbus, the vast addition to knowledge wrought by the revival of learning were accompanied by an expansion of commerce, by a quickening of the arts. The sixteenth century not only had for the first time all the stories of the past, it had more tales of its own to tell than had any preceding age, and it was more interested in telling and hearing them. The world of story had added to itself new continents, multiplied its commerce and stimulated all its arts.

History, biography, epic, romance, fiction, adventure, every form of story found its way into the drama. But the service rendered by this great body of literature was not merely that of supplying the plots and persons of plays. It excited the imagination and aroused emulation. The Elizabethan was born into this new world of story, and became possessed of all the privileges and responsibilities of its citizenship. He lived with its persons, shared their adventures and desires, and believed in the wonders they experienced. The streets of London were crowded with Greeks and Trojans, with the deities of Ovid and the knights and ladies of Malory. The life of its own day was reinhabited and reinterpreted in the visions of Ariosto and Plutarch and Homer. Drama was conceived as a new means of adventure in the adjoining realms of illusion and poetry.

One effect of this storyland upon the theater was to unite romance and comedy. These two divisions of literature had never been brought into successful union before this and rarely since. Their tempers are not easily compatible. The strange, remote and ideal are not the most inviting abodes for humor. When a Connecticut Yankee goes to King Arthur's court, romance disappears. But the world of story was all romance for the Elizabethan, all strange, remote, splendid, ideal. The pagan gods, the heroes of myth and legend, the Caesars, Hannibals, and Pompeys, the chivalric knights and ladies, the adventurers to India or America, the wanton ladies and gentlemen of Boccaccio's stories—all presented themselves, not for realistic analysis and portraiture, but as themes for the play of fancy and invention, of poetry and humour. The stories in the books that fired their fancy were heroic, romantic; and the drama, whether tragedy or comedy, naturally took on this romantic coloring. Tragedy was encouraged not to be domestic and moral but to be heroic, grandiose, superhuman. Comedy was invited to mix its jests with adventure, its clowns with lovers, its merriment with heroism. Most of the dramatists soon found that on the stage the unrealities of romance needed the seasoning of wit and mirth. The greatest story-tellers of the age, Cervantes and Shakespeare, discovered absurdities to be ridiculed but they also found beauty and nobility to be exalted.

But there is undoubtedly a certain artificiality in all this romance. The world of the realist ever widens and becomes more clearly lighted. The world of the romancer, ever just beyond these widening boundaries, is necessarily still in the shadows. He is creating brilliant and startling pictures out of what we know to be shadowy. We must share in the deception and often must sacrifice the knowledge of our own day in order to accept the illusions of an earlier period. We must be willing to accept the artificial contrivance which is to convey us to the world of romance.

The Elizabethan knew very well that romance is often in danger of being too conscious, too artificial, too fantastic. Hence the saving grace of a union with comedy; and hence, perhaps, the makers of comedies were willing enough to draw from the most artificial and fantastic creations of storyland. They audaciously matched extravagant story with extravagant farce.

In Greek literature one might find romance everywhere, in the Odyssey, in Herodotus, even in Aristophanes and Menander. But the establishment and amplification of romantic fiction did not come until a late and degenerate age. The Greek romances of the Alexandrian period are the products of a sophisticated culture and an over-conscious art, but they exhibit in remarkable fulness many of the qualities and devices of later romance and they were destined after a long slumber to experience revival and to present themselves with entire freshness and attractiveness to the contemporaries of Shakespeare.

The "Æthiopica of Heliodorus," written in the third or fourth century A.D. is perhaps the most elaborate of these productions and the most influential on Renaissance literature, and the most direct in its effect upon Shakespeare. It may be worth while to attempt a hasty survey of its voluminous expanse.

The heroine is Charicles, chaste, faithful and brave, and also very wily. She is the daughter of the King and Queen of Ethiopia, but miraculously born white; therefore she is exposed, is found and reared by the shepherds, adopted by the priest of Delphi, and becomes a priestess at the shrine. Hither come Calasiris, priest of Isis, who is to serve as her guide, philosopher and friend, and, among other suitors, the hero Theagenes, a Thessalian descendant of Achilles. Then follow love at first sight, elopement, oracles, a long voyage, a ghost, pirates, single-hand combats, mistaken identity, separation, disguises, necromancy, raising of the dead—almost everything which could happen in a romantic tale.

The hero once fails to recognize the disguised heroine and rebuffs her, an incident often remade, as in "Cymbeline." In one of the many minor stories that interrupt the main narrative, a mother is in love with her step-son, and endless complications follow—another oft-used plot. One might, indeed, find on almost every page some plot, incident or motive familiar in nineteenth century fiction. Charicles and Theagenes, though formally married, are vowed to chastity and often separated; so she has countless suitors, and often escapes difficulties by agreeing to marry, and there are many love entanglements.

The story wanders all over the world—as the world was then known—from Ethiopia to Thessaly and back again; and at every port there are fresh adventures and love affairs. All sorts of ups and downs, haps and hazards, coincidences and accidents make up the plot and enliven the artificial, rhetorical, pictorial recital. At first, fortune seems the only guide of the craft; but supernatural powers aid when accidents thwart, and we soon discover that a higher power of fate or destiny is bending fortune to its beneficent purposes. The heroine undergoes a trial of chastity, she is burned at the stake but survives by the aid of a magical stone. Finally, after a great battle, hero and heroine are back in Ethiopia, prisoners waiting to be offered as human sacrifices. But the hero escapes, overpowers a wild bull and horses, defeats the champion athlete, and claims his bride.

Here are most of the incidents of romantic fiction, some of them tragic, but never treated in the tone of tragedy. This mélange of tragicomedy manifestly affords an opportunity for comic relief, and it is completed by the marriage of the lovers, the happy ending for both comedy and romance.

One other late development in Greek literature fascinated the Elizabethans. The pastoral perhaps had a realistic purpose in the songs of Theocritus, but it soon gained an artificial character. The presentation of a golden age, the idyls of love and nature, the conception of a world freed from trouble where love itself was divorced from harshness—all this took its part in Greek romance, and later it proved one of the most fructifying literary traditions of the Renaissance. It seems conventional and insipid today with its nymphs and shepherds, its contests of song and love, its endless conjugations of *amo;* but it answered, at least in fancy, those insistent cravings of modern society for the simple life, a return to nature, freedom from the conventions. It praised the delights of the country—always a romantic appeal so long as one stays in the city—and pictured weather that is rainless and serene. Add to this a simple diet, the joys of love, and the surprises of adventures sure to end happily, and you have the Arcadia that excited countless poets, moralists, novelists, and dramatists.

In the middle ages, as among the Greeks, romance came later than the epic and belonged to a somewhat sophisticated age. But the conditions under which it flourished gave it a far greater vogue and variety, a wider appeal and a more significant representation of life than was achieved by the rhetorical fiction of the Alexandrines. How extensive was its field is now apparent to everyone. The great cycles of stories that gathered around King Arthur, Charlemagne, Alexander and the siege of Troy have been familiarized to modern readers. We know too how great a gain came during the twelfth century through the influx of material from Celtic sources with its fantastic and highly colored tales. As the romances multiplied, they underwent the inevitable processes of sophistication and degeneration. Gradually fewer readers believed the stories or applied them to conduct. Already in the fourteenth century Chaucer wrote a parody holding them up to ridicule, yet in the next century, Malory, though translating from French into English prose some of the late and more adulterated versions of the Arthur story, made one of the most vivid and noble romances in our language.

In the sixteenth century the chivalric romances were still sufficiently alive and compelling to direct the ideals and aspirations of courtiers and warriors and to gain revival and recreation in the great poems of Ariosto and Spenser. They had, however, become familiarized and vulgarized in countless adaptations and chap-books and so-called ballads. They offered a somewhat overused and tarnished material to which the dramatists rarely turned for particular tale or exploit; but they made a great background which supplied everyone who read with conceptions of propriety and conduct. They may be said, indeed, to have established a general formula for romance. It was composed of love, plus adventure, plus marvels, plus courtly or chivalric behaviour. It is not always realized how closely, in the treatment of each of these ingredients, the Elizabethans are bound by medieval precedent. Indeed the medieval formula has never been entirely superseded.

More available material for the use of the dramatist in specific plays was to be found in the great collections of stories representing all phases of medieval fiction—saints' lives, exempla, fabliaux—mixed with products of Renaissance life and classical lore. Chaucer and Boccaccio furnished the most famous fourteenth century examples of such collections, but there were many later gatherings of short stories or novelle. "Painter's Palace of Pleasure," a notable English imitation of the Italian collections, indicates its purpose in its title. Here were a hundred tales—ancient and modern, realistic and romantic, but all designed to create a magically shifting world of illusion, to make the reader's room into a palace, or to give to the bare stage the pomp and circumstance of wonderland.

One other particular source of romance open to the sixteenth century must also be mentioned, the long accumulating tales and ideas of folk lore. Hitherto their preservation had been by the precarious means of oral tradition, now with the multiplication of printed books and the new incentives to authorship, all the material had a new chance of survival. Take Robin Goodfellow, or Puck, to instance a single case. Whence he came no one exactly knows, some say from Bacchus, others say from Ireland; by the twelfth century there are references to him. He seems to be a humble person, belonging not to the court but to the cottage, and chiefly concerned with seeing that the kitchen is clean and that the untidy housemaids are sharply pinched. A great mass of story and superstition collects about him, and by the sixteenth century he is a very composite and accomplished person, sometimes regarded as a companion of fairies, though not a fairy himself—sometimes condemned as a devil and even legislated against as a familiar of witches. By this time he is a figure for invention and romance. Almost every Elizabethan writer of note—Drayton, Jonson, Spenser and many others, make use of him, and Shakespeare made him forever the creature of our fancy, the very type and spirit of romantic comedy.

It would be hopeless to carry much farther our analysis of the romances which were conspicuous in that period when every phase of literature revealed an amalgamation of medieval and classical elements. If anything, classical stories were more romantic than were medieval to the Elizabethans. They were more remote, more foreign, less readily translatable into current experience. Homer and Virgil and Livy were interpreted not with our modern knowledge of ancient art, politics, and philosophy, but on a background of medieval culture and story. Plutarch's Lives were translated into racy, vigorous accounts of the adventures of Elizabethan worthies. Ovid seemed, for a time at least, the noblest Romancer of them all. The amazing tales of his "Metamorphoses" and "Heroides" gave play to the imagination in realms untravelled and misled the youthful Shakespeare as they did many of his contemporaries.

Undoubtedly some of the stories which the Elizabethans reanimated were very imperfect models whether in content or style. I am merely suggesting that this mass of stories, many oft-told, waiting to be told again in the new forms of drama, made it impossible that the experimenting dramatists should see the life of their own day clearly and write of its main issues. Rather they were bound to begin with the stories, and through them come to such revelation of life and character as lay within their vision.

Shakespeare recovered from his youthful infatuation with Ovid and certainly gave attention to the men and women of London as well as to stories. Reality and vigor of characterization became eventually a notable merit in most of his contemporaries. But the interpreta-

tion of human nature grew slowly in power in the general
drama as it did in Shakespeare, and little that is penetrating appeared before the closing years of the century.
Ben Jonson later on was to hold up the classical comedies
as models to lead the Jacobean writers away from fantastic romance to realism and satire, but the models
themselves were not lacking in the exaggerations and
improbabilities of storyland.   The Elizabethans were
attracted by these rather than by Terence's urbanity.
They were not given to delicate analysis of the humor of
the commonplace and familiar.   There was no Trollope
among them.   Even in their most realistic moods they
were searching the life of their day for persons who
should match the supernormal creatures of romance.   A
fat roysterer in the tavern supplied hints for a Falstaff
who should surpass all the braggart soldiers of fiction,
and the absurd persons who thronged Bartholomew Fair
were taken as types that should out-match the caricatures
of Plautus and Aristophanes.   Story-telling continued a
chief function of comedy, which though it gradually
required a share of realism and satire and interest in
current manners, never entirely freed itself from its initial
impulse to romancing.

But the old highways of romance were branching out
into new wonderlands.   There were tales as yet unworn
by literary manipulation.   Outside of fiction the fields of
romance were multiplying.   There was English history,
now being explored and rewritten from Merlin through
Henry VIII.   There was the Ottoman Empire, which for
several centuries had been waging victorious war against
Christianity.   There were voyagers' tales from the East
and from the new America.   Many happenings in the
days of Mary Stuart and the Spanish Armada equalled
the ancient stories in thrills and surprises.   "Truth to
fact" was not then a term synonymous with drab monotony.   Life was not interpreted as a succession of inhibitions.   It was accepted joyfully and wonderingly like a
story.

The men of the sixteenth century were in a fortunate position for romance. They were living in an age of great progress, when knowledge was increasing its domains and reason was leading an irresistible invasion. But the regions open to these conquests had been enormously and suddenly enlarged. The progress of knowledge itself was a picturesque adventure. The world of today, of actuality, of business, was crossed by reports from Florida or Constantinople. The reflections of the most stolid apprentice must have been shot by some visions of unknown but appealing worlds beyond his ken. And these new worlds were picturesque, sensuous, inviting resorts for the imagination. For us today science adds daily to its marvels, but it adds them to the world of fact, and it somehow fails to incite the literary fancy. Experiment and mechanical invention outstrip the romancer and the poet.

But for the Elizabethan his world of fact was environed by a great horizon at every point of which he expected realms of gold. Knowledge had not been divided and catalogued. It nowhere impeded the progress of his imagination. Homer's Greeks, medieval knights, Teutonic fairies, Italian pastoral shepherds and American monstrosities might all be pictured and yet not seem very far from the lives of London shopkeepers. Although there was place in drama as in daily life for the Drakes and Raleighs, the heroic and tragic and superhuman, there was also place for a merry and familiar intercourse with wonderland. In "A Midsummer Night's Dream," Theseus and his amazon Hippolyta from Greek myth, the fairies from confused modern myths, Oberon from romance, and Puck from the household hearth mingle with Anglicized Athenian lovers and a troop of rustic mechanics. Perhaps there has never been a time when you could find romance so close at hand and of so many varieties. It was unfenced by historical accuracy or pedantic knowledge. Its illusions were easily accepted. It had ready entrances and exits from and to reality.

There was a spirited race to see whether fact or fiction, truth or illusion should discover the enchanted islands or provide the most splendid palace of pleasure.

These islands and palaces could be inhabited only by persons of unusual individualities. In our twentieth century we note a tendency in fiction to explain men and women as mere animals, and even divested of the admirable traits which endear to us our dogs and horses. The Elizabethans believed men to be akin to devils and deities. Both their theology and their psychology supported a belief in total depravity and in sublime devotion. The temper of the times and the exploits of their own worthies helped to direct their comedy as well as their tragedy toward an idealization of personality, good or bad, eccentric or typical, trivial or tremendous. Storyland gave a new magnitude and glow to human nature. Characterization became for them a renascence of wonder.

One word more is needed to complete even in meager outline my hints of Elizabethan romance. With all its other advantages, that period was also the time for an extraordinary idealization of woman. Her status had not improved in law or church or perhaps in ordinary life, but in literature the century marked the height of her sovereignty. The reasons for this are many but not easily segregated. The praise of love and women in the Greek romances, the vogue of pastoralism, the chivalric romances with their idealization, neo-Platonism with its worship of the beautiful in woman, the worship of the Virgin Mary in the Catholic church, Petrarchism, the general spread of luxury and prosperity, are a few of the causes that united to compel sonnets, tales, epics and dramas in praise of women. Helen and Andromache, Venus and Minerva, Cressid and Griselda, Cleopatra and Dido, all the fair ladies of the past, whether good or evil, saints or white devils, were exalted anew. If love was the usual motive in fact or in fiction which led to this adoration, it was by no means the sole one. The extraordinary adulation of Elizabeth is one instance of the general sentiment. Woman could excite the admiration of lover or poet or of a whole people.

So it was that the romancer who journeyed to Babylon, Camelot or Arcadia, through whatever adventures or magic, was sure to find among his nymphs and fairies and pirates some woman wiser than Solomon, more beautiful than the stars and more wonderful than all the marvels that vainly sought to block the path between her and her lover. And so the playwright who brought romance to the bare boards of the public theaters and wrote parts for his heroines, to be played by beardless boys dressed in stays and ruffs, sought to convey to his audiences the lovely visions that had enraptured him. Even amid his fun and nonsense he would have beauty. Like his medieval predecessor he mingled clowns and angels.

CHAPTER IV

ELIZABETHAN BEGINNINGS

By the time of Elizabeth's accession to the throne the new drama was well established as a form of entertainment, though whether it was to develop in the hands of amateurs or professionals was not yet certain. It already offered an inviting field for literary talent, though the religious and civil discords of the preceding half-century had choked the beginnings of a poetic revival. Both the scholar and the schoolboy had access to much reading matter which had been hidden from earlier generations. The reading public was expanding, and those beyond its borders could follow a story on the stage. By writing a play, you might hope to win the favour of the queen, the praise of scholars, the applause of the vulgar, or the laurel of undying fame.

But how were you to write your play? What formula was to be followed? In the confused and experimental practice of the time, five fairly definite forms of drama can be discovered which were to lead the way to a distinctive and national comedy:—morality, farce, classical imitation, romantic chronicle, and court show. The first three have already been described and they offered definite enough models for the dramatists of the mid-century. Their formulas, moreover, could be readily suited to a wide variety of comic persons and incidents. Nearly everything that had appeared ludicrous to the ancients of either the classical or medieval world and much that appeared amusing in the experience of the playwright could be put before the audience in the form of either morality, farce or Plautian comedy. Both realism and humanism had their models.

When, however, stories that were not realistic, that told of the wonders of pagan myth or the sentiments of medieval knights or the adventures of sundered lovers, these might be neither tragic nor moral and yet find no place in farce or comedy. A great mass of romantic story pressed for translation into stage show and dialogue. This translation from a narrative to be read into a play that could be acted resulted in something quite unlike either Plautus or a morality, but something that was entertaining and not without fun. This I have called a "romantic chronicle play." If not a very precise dramatic form, it marked the beginning of a notable dramatic advance.

From the pageants, revels and shows at court and elsewhere came definite suggestions for the theatrical presentation of romantic, mythological or fantastic story. There had been a long practice with stage settings, spectacles, properties and costumes, with music and dancing, and there were already beginnings in librettos and dialogues. Choir children well trained in acting were in the early years of Elizabeth's reign the most frequent performers at court and the chief agents in the production of what I have loosely named the "court show." The romantic chronicle and the court show were slow in developing into a drama of literary merit, but they prepared the way for Shakespeare's fancy.

I shall return to these two forms which opened the way for fantastic and romantic comedy but shall first consider the three other forms—morality, farce, and Plautian comedy, whose tendencies were mainly toward realism and satire.

I

The morality at the accession of Elizabeth was still the prevailing form of drama, but morality changing, mixed and disintegrating. The large scheme of drama which should symbolize life through a conflict of the virtues and the vices had given way to allegorical presentations of almost any current question. The allegory was reduced merely to the employment of personified abstractions who could serve as the labelled spokesmen in a dispute or as the authoritative moralists in a sermon. Their eloquence might be directed to pedagogical, theological or casuistical disputation, and the debate might illustrate the struggle of youth with the temptations of the world and the flesh, or the efforts of a schoolboy to learn his letters, or the reign of the antichrist in the person of the Roman pope. Two themes in particular had tended to give incident to the action and individuality to the characters of the moralities, that of the prodigal son and that of the lusty juventus. The youth sowing his wild oats supplied comic incident, the lecturing virtues furnished the moral framework and conclusion. Less helpful to dramatic progress was the absorption of the morality in the bitter Catholic-Protestant controversy, though this gave some opportunities for the beginnings of satirical drama.

The form as well as the content of the morality was uncertain and changing. The short interlude of one thousand lines that had been common in the early years of the century was becoming infrequent. The longer morality might now present a careful division into five acts and scenes in accord with humanist precept. The five act division was, indeed, one of the first requirements of the accepted classical theory to impress itself upon the playwrights. Two plays may be instanced as illustrating some of these varying features. "Nice Wanton," printed in 1560 and based on the "Rebelles," a neo-Latin comedy of the Dutch Macropedius, is one of the liveliest and less allegorical of the later interludes. Ismael and Dalila, the spoiled children of Zantippe, are started on their vicious career, led on by Iniquity, and brought to receive the grievous wages of sin, all in less than six hundred lines. "The Marriage of Wit and Science," printed 1570, takes nearly two thousand lines to proceed through its five acts carefully divided into scenes. Its dramatis personæ are all abstractions although it relates a somewhat adventurous tale. Wit woos Science and after one defeat succeeds with the aid of Instruction, Study, Diligence and Will, in slaying the giant Tediousness and winning the lady. Another difference in form is illustrated by these two plays. Both are in rhymed verse; in "Nice Wanton" the verses are of irregular length though usually with only four accents; in "The Marriage of Wit and Science" there are some pentameters, but mostly Alexandrines and heptameters, sometimes alternating. This last is a common Elizabethan measure.

As Elizabeth's reign progressed, the themes brought into the morality framework became more numerous and the parts taken by most of the personified abstractions more perfunctory. Wealth and Health, Virtuous Life and God's Promise, Strife and Patience, Idleness and Activity, Conscience and Doctrine are couples that hold argument. But Wealth and Health are companions of Hance who "entreth with a Dutche songe"; Virtuous Life and God's Promise sing pious songs in rivalry with Tom Tosspot and Newfangle; Strife and Patience intercede between Tom Tiler and his shrewish wife; Idleness and Action interpret the evangel of St. John; and Conscience and Doctrine comment on the tragedy of Virginia wronged by Appius. Classical, medieval or biblical story, English history, even tragedy might be fitted with an allegorical framework and a concluding lesson.

The possible transformation of the morality play into a type of comedy was apparent, however, less in these modifications and extensions of the allegory than in the admixture of farce. Whatever the story, there was likely to be some farcical incident. The principle of comic relief which we have found recognized even in the miracle plays, was firmly adhered to by both authors and audience.

The connecting link between the farce and the moral allegory was a personage known as the Vice. This term, first used in Heywood's "Play of Love (pr. 1534) and "Play of the Weather" (pr. 1536) has been variously derived. It has seemed to some the survival of a sort of composite of the seven deadly sins, actors conspicuous in the earliest moralities. In fact, the Beverley paternoster play in 1469 had eight pageants, one for each of the seven deadly sins, and one for "Vicious." The Vice later is a sort of generalized sin, as Iniquity in Bale's "Three Laws" or Sin in "All for Money," where he appears with the devil. According to this theory we could trace a theatrical evolution from the devil of the miracle plays, through the Vicious and Composite Evil of the moralities, to the later Vice. This derivation of the term is open to serious objections, but it emphasizes one important attribute of the character. He is usually the main source of evil, the perpetrator of mischief, the manipulator of action in the play.

Another theory finds the term Vice a mere survival of morality nomenclature applied to the clown or fool of the interlude. Certainly the Vice is a buffoon, the source of much laughter, and offering a part for the best comic actor in the company. It is not easy to trace the relationships of the various buffoons—court jesters, domestic fools, performers in such revels as the "Feast of Fools," clowns of the wayfaring actors,—but the Vice might be the descendant of any or all of these. But, as has been noted, he is not merely a mirth provoker, he is also the chief mischief-maker, and he belongs to the moral allegory as well as to the farcical interlude. He is usually the protagonist of the late morality, though he is often put down by the virtuous interlocutors and ends his career in banishment or other punishment.

In these simple pieces one may observe a certain approximation to the method employed in later satirical comedy. Several persons representative of the manners, follies and vices of the day are exposed and reprimanded by other persons who serve as judges or censors. A merry knave keeps the action a-going, interjects some buffoonery, and helps to make his companion knaves ridiculous.

It is a useless task to attempt to trace all the varieties

of the disintegrating morality. Some of the latest, for example "The Conflict of Conscience" (1581), are among the most serious and didactic. The joining of the morality scheme with classical or biblical story in such plays as "Godly Queen Hester" (1561), "Horestes" (1567), "Patient Grissell" (1565-9), "Cambises" (1569), "Damon and Pithias" (1571), "Appius and Virginia" (1575), is mainly significant in the development of tragedy, though it must be noticed that the Vice is usually a prominent figure and the mainspring of the comic scenes. Other Elizabethan moralities offer a general censorship of manners and may be considered as social satires. Such is "A Moral and Pitiful Comedie entitled All for Money, plainly representing the manners of men and fashion of the world nowadays: compiled by T. Lupton, 1578."

The transition from the moral to a satirical comedy of manners is best exemplified in the work of Robert Wilson, a popular actor and playwright, of whom little is known except the three plays to which his name is attached. These were written in the eighties and illustrate various aspects of the changing drama.

The earliest was printed in 1584, "A right excellent and famous Comedy called the Three Ladies of London. Wherein is notablie declared and set forth, how by the means of Lucar, Love and Conscience is so corrupted that the one is married to dissimulation, the other fraught with all abbomination." Though this is called a comedy, the moral allegory is prominent and most of the dramatis personæ are abstractions. Dissimulation, however, is dressed as a farmer, Simplicity as a miller, and a leading part is taken by Gerontus, a Jew, whose virtues are in striking contrast to the dishonesty of an Italian Christian. Simplicity is the fool of the piece and often addresses the audience in set speeches intended to raise a laugh. He is not called the Vice, though he is a link between moral and farce. The play, long popular, is noteworthy for its illustration of manners and for the keenness of its satire.

The sequel to this play, printed in 1590, is "The pleasant and stately Morall of the Three Lords and Three Ladies of London. With the great Joy and Pompe, Solemnized at their Marriages: Comically interlaced with much honest Mirth, for pleasure and recreation, among many Morall Observations, and other important matters of due Regard." It was written after Marlowe and adopts the new blank verse instead of the rhymes of the earlier play; but as its title indicates, it is more of a morality than a comedy. The three lords of London make a brave show against the Spaniards in allegory of the Armada. The part of Simplicity, the clown, however, is given much prominence. As a peddler of ballads and other wares, he is cozened by the rascals, but meantime keeps the audience in honest mirth.

The third of Wilson's plays, "The Cobbler's Prophecy," is a similar medley of comicality and satire, but it is scarcely either a comedy or a moral. Jupiter, Juno and the other classical deities and the Muses appear alongside of such abstractions as Contempt, Folly and Dalliance. Murder is exhibited as well as buffoonery, and the clown's wife runs mad. A fourth play, "The Peddler's Prophecy," has been assigned to Wilson but without evidence. It is a curious and not very intelligible satire.

Vestiges of the morality continue after Wilson, and the satirical presentation of manners is found in "A Merry Knack to Know a Knave," Nash's "Summer's Last Will and Testament" and Lodge and Green's "Looking Glass for London"; but Wilson represents the furthest advance toward satirical comedy made by the morality. His earliest play suggests that the moral framework might be used effectively for a genuine comedy of manners with satiric purpose, but his latest play shows a response to a post-Marlowean demand for spectacle, sounding verse and tragic action. His "Three Lords and Three Ladies" is almost the latest full-fledged and avowed morality to be written for the stage. The time when the allegorical framework could be of service to comic dramatists had passed.

The morality during nearly the whole of the sixteenth century served as a sort of transitional form of drama to which miracle, farce, comedy or tragedy could be attached. Its scheme of allegory afforded an awkward but familiar means of construction, and its personage, the vice, supplied both an important part in the mechanism and a free opportunity for farce or buffoonery. Especially in its shortened form, suited to the so-called interlude, it was easily managed by both actors and writers. But it held little potentiality for the future. The classical comedies offered a superior dramaturgy, and the wealth of available stories about real persons pushed the abstractions off the stage. Allegory was going out of fashion and the rise of the professional actors responded to a popular demand for entertainment rather than instruction. The morality had made only small progress toward a satirical and realistic presentation of manners when it was overwhelmed by the romantic and heroic plays that crowded the theaters after Marlowe. Later we shall look back from the comedies of Jonson to some resemblances in these earlier satires, but he recognized his obligation to classical rather than medieval sources. By 1590 the moral allegory was dead as a dramatic form.

II

Farce, the second form open to Elizabethan writers of comedy, has been defined in terms of the Mak play and of Heywood's "John, Tib, and Sir John." During the first thirty years of Elizabeth's reign we do not find another farce as well made or as amusing as these two pieces unless we turn to classical imitations. Farce, however, continued to exist as an incidental attachment to dramas with a more serious or ambitious purpose. I have spoken of the morality as a transition type to which all kinds of material could be added. Farce was rather a kind of realistic comic incident that could be attached to all sorts of material, moral or tragic, historical or romantic.

In this sense farce includes matter of varied complexity, ranging from mere tomfoolery to a closely knit plot of tricks accompanied by exaggerated characterization. If the vice is bridled and snaffled and kicks his heels about the stage, or if he is carried off on the back of the devil, that is mere buffoonery without much promise of developing into more complex drama. But the rapid growth of the professional actors did give an impulse to the spread and extension of such farcical material, for the professional companies relied very much on clownage. The chief member in each company was the clown. The first actors to become famous were clowns, such as Tarleton, Wilson and Kemp. Whatever might be offered to the public in the way of moral or sentiment, the play could scarcely be put over without the aid of the comic actor. Much was left to improvisation, or to mere jigging, or to impromptu give and take between actor and audience, but there was evidently a demand for as much comic stuff as could be invented. Though much has been lost, yet in the majority of the plays that survive between 1550 and 1590, whether acted at court or in public, by children or adults, the chief part is written for a comedian, variously known as clown, fool, vice or tricky servant.

The curious student of these crude plays may trace some development of comic situation. A sound cudgelling, amusing in itself to Elizabethans, is found to be more amusing if administered by a wife to a husband, or by an undersized opponent to a huge braggart. In the farce of "Tom Tiler and His Wife," for example, there are three beatings arranged in comic climax. The piece deals with the familiar theme of the shrewish wife. Tom's wife, Strife, is drinking with her gossips, Sturdie and Tipple, when Tom appears, and she gives him a good thumping simply to show her mastery and to amaze her friends. Tom Tiler complains to his crony Tom Taylor who suggests a stratagem. Taylor arms himself with a stout cudgel, puts on the husband's coat, and when the wife appears and starts to beat him, he returns blow for blow and beats her black and blue. Tom Tiler then resumes his coat and returns bravely to his wife and lords it for a while, but when he confesses the trick, she falls upon him, gives him double measure, and again humiliates him before her gossips.

The invention of such farcical complication by means of trick and disguise was finding example and incentive from Plautus and Terence. But even if the classical comedies had been completely obliterated with the Roman theater, it is safe to say that the English drama in the sixteenth century would have had its farces and its clowns. The leading comedian was demanding comic speech and business whatever their sources. It was from this vogue of farce and buffoonery that Marlowe in the prologue to "Tamburlaine" promised to free the stage

> From jigging veins of rhyming mother wits,
> And such conceits as clownage keeps in pay.

But soaring tragedy has never been able to drive clownage from the theater.

III

In comparison with the disintegrating morality and the inchoate farce, classical comedy offered a well defined dramatic form that was stirring the admiration and imitation of literary Europe. As we have seen, this comedy had resemblances to medieval farce. It presented deceptions and misunderstandings often brought about by mistaken identity or disguise. It was a play of tricks and farcical entanglements. Anyone who could write an amusing farce ought to be able to invent enough additional complication to build up a five act comedy on the model of Plautus.

The model might be derived directly from the Latin or from a translation or it might be supplied by a contemporary imitation made in Italy or the Netherlands. The author might have seen a play by Plautus reproduced on the stage and he might have buttressed his knowledge of dramatic propriety by a study of Aristotle or Horace or the humanist critics. Sixteenth century attempts to recreate the Roman comic stage provided a background of houses with doors opening on the front stage. Pedantic stage management might strive to particularize the houses and reserve each door for a special purpose, but there was no great difference between this stage-set and those in general use in England. At court a modification of the medieval setting survived, showing practicable structures for the various houses and an open stage in front. As soon as the public theaters were erected, the normal stage had in the rear a door on either side, and a curtained recess under the balcony. Either method could readily represent a street or square, with entrances to houses in the rear.

Though the different ways in which a knowledge of the classical drama was spread through England of the sixteenth century are not easy to trace, yet it may be said that by the accession of Elizabeth any university man who so desired could know a good deal about Latin comedy. He would find it possessed of standards and restrictions that quite marked it off from current plays. In the first place, it was separate from tragedy. It did not deal with affairs of state, with tragic catastrophes, with moral allegory or history, and it had little to do with romance or fantasy. It was devoted to laughter. In the second place, it required organization. Its plot of intrigue, however slight or farcical in content, received a studied elaboration. Trick was to be added to trick, self-deception to self-deception. A simple beginning was to be expanded into a complicated middle and then resolved into a happy ending. The single action thus elaborated was to be substantially continuous. According to the most liberal critics, the actions must be limited to one city and one revolution of the sun. In the third place, fun was to be extracted from the absurdities of human nature as well as from the plot. Certain types of character were passed along, such as the braggart soldier, the pedant, the tricky servant, and the parasite, and these might suggest others. Finally, comedy was a vehicle for poetry and notably for stylistic display. However mean the classical models may appear to modern taste, yet in complication of plot, in characterization and in style they offered an intellectual and artistic interest beyond anything on the English stage.

By 1560, three plays had appeared distinctly imitative of Plautus, "Jack Juggler," "Ralph Roister Doister" and "Gammer Gurton's Needle." Of these the least important though possibly the earliest is "Jack Juggler," "a new enterlude for chyldren to play," licensed in 1562 but apparently written before Elizabeth's accession. The formidable prologue of eighty-four lines announces the author's indebtedness to Plautus and professes freedom from any purpose except to excite laughter.

As now he hath done this matter, not worth an oyster shell
Except percasse it shall fortune to make you laugh well.

The interlude is based on the "Amphitryon," or rather on its opening scene, the quarrel over identity between Sosia and Mercury. Jack Juggler, who takes the place of the tricky god, opens with a speech of seventy lines, and is followed by Jenkin Careaway, the substitute for Sosia, in a speech of over one hundred. Then the action begins and is carried through with some comic force. Jenkin is beaten by Jack, then by his mistress, and then by his master. The laborious long speeches are the framework for a characteristic English farce of multiple beatings. From Plautus the author derived a famous farcical incident, and he translated it into native manners. The household which Jenkin serves is as certainly English as that of Noah in the miracle plays or that of Tom Tiler in the farce.

"Ralph Roister Doister," usually known as the first English comedy, is the first full-fledged imitation of Plautus. Its author, Nicholas Udall, was a prominent scholar, cleric, schoolmaster and courtier, a not unrepresentative figure in English humanism. The play evinces a thorough acquaintance both with the stage-craft of his day and with Latin comedy. The action is simple. A silly braggart makes suit to Widow Custance and, upon being rejected, makes a display of force and gets soundly beaten by the widow and her maids. Merrygreek, who recalls the Latin parasite, is the main contriver of the complications. He and the braggart are the only actors derived from the stock figures of Latin comedy, and Udall did not imitate any single play of Plautus. He did succeed in a remarkable fashion in transferring the spirit and the methods of the Latin dramatist to the early Tudor stage.

Though the play seems childish to a modern reader, it was no small literary achievement in comparison with its contemporary drama. It enlarges the slight action to the dignity of five acts and scene divisions. It observes the unities. It labours over both characterization and style. It displays some real wit and much verbal ingenuity in its set speeches, songs, dialogues and stichomythia. The Plautian model restricted its range of effort, and the rhymed verse in which it was written hampered and stiffened its movement; but the English drama had not hitherto seen such an expenditure of conscious literary invention. A new genre was now open for the more enlightened English men of letters, that of comedy.

"Gammer Gurton's Needle" (1575) was performed at Christ's College, Cambridge, probably about 1560, and written by a Mr. S. who still remains unidentified. The author followed the scheme and methods of Latin comedy as closely as Udall. The play is divided into five acts, the scene is the street before the houses, the time is within twenty-four hours, the action is a series of deceptions manipulated by one trickster, and there is considerable rhetorical display. But the play is nevertheless thoroughly English, showing indebtedness to Latin models only in technic, not in content. The author has taken the material of English farce and expanded it into a comedy of five acts after the Latin manner.

The incidents, manners and speeches are not only native but of a realistic grossness a little vulgar for Christ's College even in 1560. While mending the breeches of her servant Hodge, Gammer Gurton loses her needle. Diccon the Bedlam, or town loafer, seizes upon this misfortune as a possible source of mirth. By his deception, Hodge is led on to unmentionable disaster, Gammer Gurton is induced to believe that Dame Chat has stolen the needle, and the two have a bout of fisticuffs, and Dr. Rat the curate is enticed to attempt an entry into Dame Chat's house and receives a broken head in consequence. All these beatings are accompanied by much abuse and vituperation, and ameliorated by songs, among them the famous

> Back and sides go bare, go bare,
> Both foot and hand go cold;
> But belly, God send thee good ale enough
> Whether it be new or old.

In the end the needle is discovered by Hodge when a blow sends it from its hiding place in his breeches through his skin. The quarrels are ended and all go in to drink.

The realism of manners aids in the lively delineation of character. The rustic servant, the quarrelsome women, and Dr. Rat, the ale-drinking village priest, are vigorously drawn types that reappear in later drama. Still more notable is the trickster. He pulls the strings like the vice of the moralities or the servant of the Latin comedy, but he is a real person, the village beggar, with a surplus of ingenuity and an absence of responsibility, a merry mischief-maker who boldly avows his purpose. When the Baily asks,

Hast thou not made a lie or two, to set these two by the ears?

Diccon replies,

What if I have? five hundred of these have I seen

within seven years.   I am sorry for nothing else but that I see not the sport which was between them when they met, as they themselves report.

This is the very spirit of the new comedy.   Instead of such reproval of vice as the morality insisted upon, the drama could learn from Plautus how to extract mirth even from vice.

Other English comedies after the Roman model during the next thirty years offer little advance on "Ralph Roister Doister" and "Gammer Gurton's Needle."   Two by the versatile George Gascoigne illustrate conflicting tendencies in European imitations.   "The Glass of Government" (1575) follows the methods of the Dutch Terentians, employing both Latin technic upon the theme of the prodigal son and the didacticism of the Dutch school.   In 1566 his "Supposes" was acted by the students of Gray's Inn.   A translation of Ariosto's "I Suppositi," which had been acted nearly sixty years earlier, Gascoigne's play profits from the greater intricacy of plot and the romantic story with which Ariosto had supplemented the Latin model.   In the same year for the same society Gascoigne was also engaged in the translation of Lodovico Dolce's "Giocasta."   He was then a pioneer in bringing Italian versions of both classical tragedy and comedy on the English stage.   But the Italianate manners that clung to romantic drama in the Elizabethan period were due rather to the vogue of Italian story than to any direct influence of Italian drama.

"Misogonus," acted in Cambridge not long before 1577, returns to the prodigal son story like "The Glass of Government" but adds to this a vice Cacurgus and a romantic tale that seems likely to have had an Italian source.   More effective adaptations of Italian comedies are two anonymous plays "The Bugbears" (preserved only in Ms.) based on "La Spiritata" of Grazzini and "Fedele and Fortunio" (S.R. 1584) adapted from "Il Fedele" of Pasqualizo.   The mock conjurer in the first and the braggart captain Crackstone, the pedant and the conjuress in the second are interesting representatives of the stock types.

These comedies imitating the Latin were, so far as we know, performed at schools or universities. We have no evidence that close imitations of Latin comedy had any place on the public stage in the seventies and eighties. Very few plays that were certainly acted by adult professionals have survived from the twenty years before the epoch-making production of "Tamburlaine," so that we can only surmise that in these years efforts were made to adapt Plautus to the general taste. Some predecessors in the public theaters as well as at school and court would seem likely to have prepared the way for the remarkable merits of Lyly's "Mother Bombie" and Shakespeare's "Comedy of Errors" which both appeared at nearly the same time, probably about 1590.

In these plays, this model of Latin comedy was completely adapted to English conditions. Something must be said of them later in connection with the other comedies of their authors, but we may note here that they were both acted before the general public, one by the children of Paul's, and the other by an adult professional company, and that they both show a mastery of the art of plotting as taught by classical comedy, skilfully adapted to the needs of the Elizabethan theater. The imitation in Shakespeare's play is of a particular comedy, the "Menæchmi" of Plautus; in Lyly it is of the general Terentian scheme. Both adaptations, in accordance with the Italian methods and current theatrical demands, show a much greater intricacy of plot than do the Latin models.

Shakespeare, using the well-worn motive of the twins who cannot be told apart, adds twin servants to twin masters, borrows the Sosia-Mercury situation to add to the fun and produces a remarkably effective and amusing farce. Lyly, using the theme of the youthful lovers outwitting their parents by the aid of clever servants, provides four scheming fathers, six children, four tricky and witty pages in addition to various accessory persons, and manages the very complicated plot with unfailing ingenuity. Shakespeare adds to his amusing farce, again following current fashions, a romantic and sentimental story. Lyly slights the romantic possibilities in the passion of the brother and sister and indeed slights the comic possibilities of the plot, after his usual fashion, in order to give full play to the merry pranks and verbal wit of the pages. Neither dramatist found in the Latin model much incentive to the delineation of character or to the study of contemporary manners.

The influence of the Latin comedies was by no means limited to the few close imitators. It was felt throughout the entire field of English drama. Some evidence of it is to be found in almost every comedy after 1580, whether classical, realistic or romantic in story. These evidences appear in the division into five acts, in the confinement of the action to the street before the house, in the use of mistaken identity and disguise, in such stock types as the braggart and the abnormally clever servant; in the recurrence of favourite situations and entanglements, in the whole process of multiplying tricks and mistakes until the final resolution in the last act. Latin comedy supplied not merely a type of drama but the type, from which indeed many circumstances might force the dramatist to depart, but which preserved all that was deemed essential for right comedy. Its influence is manifest in such romantic comedies as "Twelfth Night" and "The Tempest" as well as in Ben Jonson's avowed adaptations, "Every Man in His Humour" and "The Alchemist." Its sway over the theater has perhaps now come to an end but not until it had both directed and limited the genius of Shakespeare and of Molière, and had guided the laughter of centuries of theatergoers.

IV

What I have named "the romantic chronicle" came into existence because of the vast number of narratives that were available for translation into drama but offered no suitability for either the Senecan or Plautian forms. Stories of adventure and romantic love, such collections of fights, travels, escapes and reunions as were found in the "Ætheopica of Heliodorus" or in the chivalric romances, presented material that did not belong in the Latin schemes of tragedy or comedy. The earliest attempts to put some of these stories on the stage resulted in a crude employment of narrative fables. The play began at the beginning of the story not at the crisis, it extended over long periods of time and moved freely from one place to another. It combined a medley of incidents, tragic and comic, realistic or impossible, without any critical feeling for what was fit and what was not fit for stage presentation.

Such medleys of incidents were not wholly out of harmony with the medieval tradition, which was nourished on the representation of any or all the events in holy writ. They were, however, vigorously attacked by both the moralists and the humanists. The moralists who found the new secular drama unedifying had a special grudge against its alliance with romantic narrative. Stephen Gosson in 1579 declared, "I may boldly say it because I have seen it, that The Palace of Pleasure, The Golden Ass, The Æthiopian History, Amadis of France, and The Round Table . . . have been thoroughly raked to furnish the playhouses in London." Sir Philip Sidney, who hastened to defend literature and the drama against Gosson's attack on their immorality, had only scorn for the inartistic translations of narratives that were filling the playhouses.

"You shall have Asia of the one side, and Afric of the other, and so many other under-kingdoms, that the player, when he cometh in, must ever begin with telling where he is, or else the tale will not be conceived. Now ye shall have three ladies walk to gather flowers, and then we must believe the stage to be a garden. By and by we hear news of shipwreck in the same place, and then we are to blame if we accept it not for a rock. Upon the back of that comes out a hideous monster with fire and smoke, and then the miserable beholders are bound to take it for a cave. While in the meantime two armies fly in, represented with four swords and bucklers, and then what hard heart will not receive it for a pitched field?"

Of these many mongrel tragicomedies, these records of lovers and magicians traversing Europe and Asia, very few have been preserved. It is therefore impossible to trace the steps by which thirty years of practice prepared the way for the romantic drama of Greene and Marlowe and Shakespeare. The titles of non-extant plays offer little information except that a large number of the plays acted at court were drawn from classical or Italian sources. A few suggest medieval romance, such as "Knight of the Burning Bush," "Red Knight," "Solitary Knight," "Paris and Vienna." But "Ariodanto and Genevra" (Orlando Furioso), "Timocles at the Siege of Thebes," or even "Ajax and Ulysses" and "The Twelve Labours of Hercules" may have had as little of Seneca or Plautus about them as "The Solitary Knight." The translation of romantic story into dramatic form had begun early in the century in such plays as "Calisto and Meliboea," in the non-extant plays by Ralph Radcliffe— "Griselda," "Meliboeus," and "Titus and Gisippus," and in Grimald's "Troilum ex Chaucero, comoediam"; and we may be sure that this activity went on busily for the thirty years after the mid-century.

There are a half-dozen plays surviving that were acted between 1500 and 1580, that have many traits in common and illustrate the transition from the morality to the "history" or story. They are all written in rhymed verse, all have some features of the morality including the vice, and all tell stories without regard to dramatic precedent. Two, "Cambyses" and "Horestes," may be classed as tragedies because of the predominance of tragic events and the presence of many deaths. Two, "Damon and Pythias" and "Appius and Virginia," were styled "tragical comedies," and thus afford testimony to the widespread feeling of the need for a *tertium quid*. The two other plays, "Sir Clyomon and Sir Clamydes" and "Common Conditions" deal with medieval rather than classical story and unite romance with comedy mainly by means of the vice, who is a prominent figure in both plays. Just as in the later moralities he was the link between morality and farce, so here he is the link between farce and romance. A servant to the knight and lover, or a faithful companion to the lady in distress, he both furnishes the buffoonery and manipulates the adventurous entanglements.

"Clyomon and Clamydes" was first printed in 1599 but probably acted twenty years or more earlier. It is entitled "The Historie of two valiant Knights, Sir Clyomon Knight of the Golden Shield, son to the King of Denmark, and Clamydes the White Knight son to the King of Suavia." King Alexander the Great, "as valiantly set forth as may be, and as many soldiers as can," rules the world of chivalry that is presented. There are three other kings over whose realms the action wanders, as well as the "Isle of the Strange Marshes" and the "Forest of Strange Marvels."

First enter Clamydes discoursing at great length until—

"Lo, where she comes, ah peerless Dame, my Juliana dear."

Juliana bears a white shield which she presents to her faithful knight who is off to slay the flying serpent that feeds on ladies fair. Then enter Clyomon calling for his servant Subtle Shift, whose voice is heard within, confessing that he is ignominiously stuck in a dirty ditch. At last he pulls himself out to "slip onto the stage backwards, as though he had pulled his leg out of the mire, one boot off, and rise up to run in again." He expresses fear that he has lost one leg. Both farce and romance have begun and they continue intertwined. Clamydes has a rival in a magician who imprisons the knight and presents himself to Juliana disguised as her faithful Clamydes. Clyomon has a rival in the King of Norway who carries off Neronis, princess of the Strange Marshes. She escapes disguised in man's apparel, wanders in the forest, is prevented from suicide by Providence (who descends from above), becomes page to her lover, and finally surprises him by a transformation from page to beautiful princess. The vice shifts from one master to the other and occasionally helps along the plot, as when he rescues Clamydes from the magician's powers.

There is considerable stylistic display, both in the stiff speeches of the lovers and in the realistic dialect of the old shepherd who appears with his dog. Only one death occurs, that of the wicked Norway by the hand of the avenging Clyomon; and, though there is much danger, heroism and sentiment, the vice is ever busy to maintain a tone of comedy. He thus proclaims the grand finalé:

> What, is all things finished, and every man eased?
> Is the pageant packed up, and all parties pleased?
> Hath each Lord his Lady, and each Lady her love?

Very similar in content and method and possibly by the same author, is "An Excellent and Pleasant Comedie, termed after the name of the vice, Common Conditions, drawn out of the most famous historie of Galiarbus, Duke of Arabia, and of the good and evil success of him and his two children, Sedmond his son, and Clarisia his daughter, set forth with delectable mirth and pleasant shows." Brother and sister encounter a band of ruffian tinkers, a crew of pirates, and Lord Cordolas who imprisons fair ladies on Morofus Isle. The vice is very resourceful and shifty, and is much occupied in rescuing the lovers from the frying pan and then dropping them into the fire. In addition to the usual functions of clown, servant and trickster, he is for a time captain of the pirates. The course of true love is crossed not only by villainy and misfortune but by the misdirection of love itself. Clarisia is loved by the valiant knight Lamphedon, whose affection she faithfully returns. Sedmond is loved by Sabia, but instead of returning her affection, he while disguised as Nomides falls in love with his own sister, also disguised and already married to Lamphedon. Clarisia, exiled and abandoned, finds solace in a female fool "Lomia the natural." Neither of the texts which we possess brings the story to a conclusion.

The amusement of the reader over the naïveté of these pieces may be succeeded by the reflection that they include much that has delighted the romantic sentiments of many generations in the plays of Greene, Shakespeare and Fletcher, or in the fiction and drama of our own time. Two pairs of lovers are offered for our sympathy. The course of true love for each couple is crossed by separation, misunderstanding, disguise, magic, and perhaps by the temporary unfaithfulness of one. Lovers and ladies pass through adventures, dangers, combats, and rescues to final reunion. Picturesque groups, such as robbers and pirates, bustle upon the stage. A merry servant supplies comic relief to his master's sentimental heroics or cheers his mistress when, disguised as a boy, she makes her way forlorn through the forest. When the excitements and thrills tend to lift the action to the height of tragedy, the antics of the clown or the oddities of some rustic or eccentric restore the balance to comedy. The translation of romantic story into a stage play had been provided, if not with inspiring models, at least with a sort of working formula before Lyly, Peele, Greene and other young men from the university brought their fresh and ingenious wits to the task.

V

For more inspiring directions for spectacle the playwright could turn to the tableaux, pageants, masques, devices and other entertainments that delighted the Tudor courts. I know of no better name than Court Show that can be used as inclusive of all the quasi-dramatic performances of the time. Under Henry VIII, as we have noted, the number and expense of such shows had increased greatly and led to the employment of various groups of actors. After the growth of humanism, either allegorical or chivalrous themes gave place to those of classical mythology. Might and Love, or knight and lady, were superseded by Hercules and Venus. The realm of fancy and of pageantry gained enormously in population, for the newly received immigrants did not altogether crowd out the old inhabitants. Knights and fair ladies, the fairies of Teutonic or Celtic legend, the goblins and spirits of native folk-lore might perform freely together with nymphs, satyrs and other delightful creatures who were the ornaments of revered poesy.

It must not be thought that such shows were confined to the lavish court. They were attempted by country schoolmasters and village mechanics, as we may learn from the shows prepared by Holofernes and the performance of Pyramus and Thisbe by Bottom and his mechanics. Moreover, the frequent progresses of the queen encouraged such exhibitions about the countryside. The poet Churchyard has recorded one near Norwich not unworthy of Bottom himself. The poet had prepared an elaborate show of water nymphs, but rain prevented the performance, and the queen was leaving the city the next day. So Churchyard, determining to pass off his water nymphs as forest fairies, took them to a field, by which the queen v•as to pass on her journey, used some "high and thick bushes" as a screen, and hastily coached seven of the boys to speak seven speeches. "And these boys (you must understand) were dressed like nymphs of the water and were to play by a device and degrees the Phayries, and to dance (as near as could be imagined) like the Phayries. Their attire, and coming so strangely out, I know, made the Queen's Highness smile and laugh withal. And I having this good hope, being apparelled like a water sprite, began to sound a timbrell; and the rest with me, all the twelve Nymphs together (when the seven had repaired in) sounded timbrels likewise. And though I had no great harting, yet as I durst, I led the young foolish Phayries a dance, which boldness of mine had no disgrace, and, as I heard said, was well taken."

The queen saw many strange spectacles on these progresses. Sometimes the tableaux and dances were preceded by an address of welcome, or the device explained by a dialogue. The most splendid entertainment was of course given by Leicester at Kenilworth, and described in Scott's novel. Here one day, as she was going hunting, the queen was met by the poet Gascoigne, "dressed as Sylvanus, god of the woods." He made a long speech running along by her horse, and when she offered to stop, he protested that he could run and talk all day in her majesty's service. It was indeed necessary that he should keep running, for he led the queen to a bush, whence Leicester himself, dressed as "Deep Desire," popped forth and made another speech. Here the professional actors were called from London to aid in the entertainment, in which Arion sang on a dolphin's back, as perhaps Shakespeare remembered when he made Oberon declare:

Since once I sat upon a promontory
And heard a mermaid on a dolphin's back
Uttering such dulcet and harmonious breath
That the rude sea grew civil at her song,
And certain stars shot madly from their spheres
To hear the sea-maid's music.

Two developments in these court shows must be mentioned as marking the early Elizabethan period, the growing use of pastoral material and the increasing part taken by the children actors. There are pastoral personages and devices in the entertainment at Kenilworth in 1575, and the year before we hear of some sort of pastoral at court by Italian players, in which shepherds, wild men, nymphs and Saturn figured. In 1578, the year before the publication of Spenser's "Shepherd's Calendar," there was performed at Wanstead, "The Contention of a Forester and a Shepherd for a May Lady" by Sir Philip Sidney. Here we have for the first time a distinct pastoral setting in an English drama. The old shepherd, the chorus of foresters and shepherds, Therion the hunter, who is rude and sometimes strikes the lady, and his rival Espiles, who is mild and gentle, are types that later become familiar on the stage. The burlesque schoolmaster and the lady dressed like "an honest man's wife of the country" are more unusual in pastoral exhibitions. Henceforth, however, the representation of a pastoral Arcadia is often attempted both by stage decorator and dramatist.

For many years after the queen's accession, the favourite performers of plays at court were the two children's companies, drawn from the choir boys of St. Paul's and the Royal Chapel. Having access to the costumes and properties preserved in the office of the revels and performing for the special pleasure of her majesty, these boys had a far better opportunity than the professional companies to indulge in spectacular stage settings. They apparently had also at an early date demonstrated a superiority over the adults in the presentation of the beings of mythology and fantasy. Gods and goddesses, nymphs and shepherds, could be impersonated by the children in an Arcadian picture that would please the eye and stir the fancy. They became the instruments for the creation of a drama of song, dance and tableau, and of pastoral, romantic or mythological story.

The process of transforming the court show into a five act drama can be traced only in the few texts that have survived of entertainments at court or during the progresses of the queen. The amount of dialogue in these is considerable and they were providing characters, devices and situations for the use of actors and playwrights. Of the plays written for the children by their music masters, two have been mentioned, "Appius and Virginia" and "Damon and Pithias," that partake of the character of the peculiar type of semi-operatic performance that was being developed through these youthful masters of song and dance. But the full development of this species is found in the work of Lyly and Peele, to be considered in the following chapter.

In addition, one anonymous play may be cited as an example of the transformation of the court show into a new type of comedy, "The Rare Triumphs of Love and Fortune" acted at court about 1581.

The play is written in a variety of rhyming measures including doggerel and sonnets. Act One opens with the gods assembling and a Fury stirring debate among them. When Venus and Fortune dispute as to sovereignty, Jupiter summons "The ghosts of them that Love and Fortune slew." To the accompaniment of music and comments from Vulcan, there are exhibited shows of Troilus and Cressida, Alexander, Queen Dido, Pompey and Caesar, and Leander and Hero. The goddesses still disputing, Jupiter orders a final test of their powers on a pair of princely lovers. The next three acts tell of the love of Hermione (a man) and Fidelia, opposed by her brother and aided by an old hermit who is also a banished lord, by the long lost father of the hero, and by a magician who goes mad over the loss of his books. The wiles of a parasite and the buffoonery of the hermit's servant add a little amusement. In the fifth act the gods reappear, a treaty of peace is made between Venus and Fortune, who hasten to bring about a happy dénouement for the distressed human beings in their charge. The Olympian deities serve as a sort of chorus and mock audience, as the directors of the action and contrivers of its happy ending. In the first and fifth acts the court show is used as an introduction and framework for the romantic action which occupies the three middle acts. A five act play results with spectacle, mythology, romance, comedy, and a definite structure.

Although I have tried to indicate five trends toward comedy, it must be remembered that the plays of this period are not easily classified. Some were written for school, some for court and some for professional companies. They are the stray survivals of an experimental period. Their authors were teachers, scholars, courtiers, musicians, actors. As yet comedy has taken no clear direction, and the profession of actor is scarcely recognized. A new development was marked by the advent of university graduates who began to write for the professional companies.

CHAPTER V

LYLY, PEELE AND GREENE

FOR the first three-quarters of the sixteenth century the course of the English drama was tentative, confused and experimental. There was uncertainty whether professional or amateur actors were to be its chief purveyors, whether it was to rely on court or schools or public for its support, whether it was to be imitative of the classics or distinctive and national, whether it was to be merely an entertainment or to contribute a great imaginative literature. Within another dozen years these doubts had all been resolved. In 1576 the Theater was built just outside the London wall by James Burbage of the Earl of Leicester's adult company; in the same year the Children of the Chapel began public performances in a room in the dismantled Blackfriars; and in the following year the second public playhouse, the Curtain, was built and occupied. Henceforth there was no question that the drama was to be in the hands of professional actors, although the children remained for some time dangerous rivals of the adult companies. The success of the public playhouses soon gave assurance that this drama could depend on the public for support, though it might still require the patronage of the court. Within a few years these public theaters were able to attract to the profession of dramatist some of the most gifted of the young men of letters. Peele and Lyly were writing for the children by 1580, and Marlowe and Greene for the men's companies by 1587. These young university men brought poetry to the public stage. By the time that Shakespeare had made his way from Stratford to London, it was clear enough that the new drama was to be popular, national, distinc-

74

tive and poetical. In this chapter we are to consider the development of comedy, and especially romantic comedy, by three of Shakespeare's immediate predecessors.

Lyly, Peele and Greene were all university men who looked to literature as a profession. They were eager to transplant and renew the flora of the luxuriant literature of Italy, both ancient and modern, in the England of Elizabeth. They desired to adorn her court with poesy and story and comedy, and to show the world how gay, and sprightly, and how elegant the English speech could be made. But the profession of letters did not wholly thrive in the court's penurious favour. Disappointed in their hopes for preferment from the queen or some Mæcenas of the court, the three wits were obliged to resort to the booksellers and the theatrical companies. Their artistic ambitions were warped by the necessity of writing a pamphlet that would sell, a poem that would praise a patron, or a play that would please the crowded theater. They were forced to spur their invention to entertain the British public, and in consequence the drama became one of the chief forms of literary endeavour.

There is something touching in the contrast between the brightness of these poets' dreams and the Bohemian squalor in which they were forced to live, between the dazzle of lights and jewels amid which one of their comedies might be performed at Hampton Court, and the dingy lodging to which the author must return after the plaudits. Little of the bread of mirth that they cast upon the waters returned to bless them with happiness. But, amid whatever vicissitudes and disappointments, they kept their lively pens busy devising a memorial of wit and beauty. They flattered the queen, they amused the public, and now and then they wrote a few lines that brought joy to themselves and to many readers since.

I

The grandson of William Lilly, the grammarian, the son of the registrar of Canterbury, John Lyly was a

humanist by inheritance as well as by education and choice.
Born about ten years before Shakespeare, he left Oxford
with bachelor's and master's degrees at the age of twenty-
one. Three years later, in 1578, he published a novel,
"Euphues, the Anatomy of Wit," which went through
four editions in two years, an unprecedented success. The
sequel, "Euphues and His England," met with even
greater popularity in 1580. These novels, comprising
rather diverse matter, satire on the universities, moral
protestations against Italianate affectation and vice, as
well as a love story, were accepted as a compendium and
model of manners. The style in particular was admired
and imitated in conversation and in print. It exhibited
most of the verbal extravagances of the day, classical
allusions, examples from unnatural natural history, a
superabundance of alliteration and word play, but its
firm though artificial balance added a needed element
of structure to prose writing. Everyone read the book,
Euphuism became a fashion at court, Lyly was famous at
twenty-five.

His first play "Campaspe" was probably produced
within a year, and henceforth Lyly is known to us as a
playwright and pamphleteer and as a courtier vainly seeking preferment. He had various ups and downs. For a
time closely attached to the extravagant Earl of Oxford,
he seems to have shared his patron's loss of fortune.
Engaged by the bishops to write in the Mar-Prelate controversy, he was involved in a quarrel with Gabriel
Harvey, had his plays censored, and received no notable
reward. Now we hear of him imprisoned in the Fleet
for debt, again as a member of Parliament and the
servitor of great nobles. After twenty years he wrote
bitterly to the queen:

"Thirteen yeares your Highnes servant: but yet noth-
inge.
"Twenty frendes yt though they saye they will be suer,
I find suer to be slowe.

"A thousand hopes, but all nothinge, a hundred promises, but yet nothinge. Thus castinge up the Inventorye of my frendes, hopes, prommisses, and tyme: The Summa totalis amounteth in all to just nothinge."

The expectations of reward which were so completely disappointed seem to have arisen mainly from Lyly's services as an author of plays. He must, indeed, have turned to this employment with bright hopes. The choir boys of St. Paul's and of the Royal Chapel were giving performances not only at court but in public in their so-called "private" theaters. The spectacular and musical shows which the children had been in the habit of presenting at court could now be practised before a paying audience, but one more select and refined than that which jostled in the pit of the Theater. At Blackfriars, as well as at Hampton Court, ladies seem to have made up a part of the audience. Lyly had written "Euphues and His England" with an eye to pleasing the fair sex and he might hope to devise comedies to their taste. Since women on the stage were impersonated by boys, the number of female parts was restricted to two or three in plays by the adult companies, but in pieces by the children there could be as many women as one chose among the dramatis personæ. There was a chance to create a new kind of comedy that should win reward from the queen and profit from the fashionable public.

We cannot trace Lyly's relations with the children's companies in detail. He failed to win the lucrative office of Master of Revels which he desired. For a short time he was manager of the Blackfriars theater, receiving the lease as a gift from Oxford who supported a company of boys and wrote plays himself. Some taunts by Harvey indicate that he may have been employed in teaching the Paul's boys and that he may have acted with them. He was engaged in writing for the children for a dozen years or more, and eight of his plays have survived, "Campaspe," "Sapho and Phao," "Gallathea," "En-

dymion," "Love's Metamorphosis," "Midas," "Mother
Bombie," and "The Woman in the Moon." All of these
were acted by the Chapel children or the Paul's boys, and
all but one were presented at court.

All of these are in prose except "A Woman in the
Moon," which is in blank verse. All deal with classical
myth or history except "Mother Bombie" which elabo-
rates the Terentian scheme. Several present a pastoral
world and personages. At least three appear to be
allegories glancing at important affairs of court, at the
suit of Alençon, at the rivalry between Mary Stuart and
Elizabeth, and at Philip of Spain and the Armada. In
spite of these and other differences, the comedies resemble
one another closely, and together create a new type of
drama. Its characteristics may be summed up in a sort
of formula.

(1) The story and persons are taken from classical
myth or history, but are treated with free invention. Ovid
often furnishes a hint or two from which Lyly builds up
his plot. This is constructed so as to give opportunity for
stage spectacle, the presentation of gods, goddesses,
shepherds, nymphs, and even mermaids and fairies, and
also in some cases for allegory or references to court and
political affairs.

(2) A love story always forms the basis of the plot.
"Campaspe" shows the simplest complication; Alexander
loves Campaspe but she loves Apelles, the painter. In
"Endymion," the hero is in love with Cynthia, Eumenides
with Semele, Corsites with Tellus and, by way of burlesque, the braggart, Sir Tophas, with the witch Dipsas.
The main entanglement arises because Tellus loves
Endymion. These couplings and crossings afford an artificial rather than ardent treatment of love, but give opportunity for an unusual proportion of women in the cast.

(3) A group of eccentric and humorous personages is
set off against the lovers and the deities. Diogenes and
the philosophers thus form a sort of comic chorus in
"Campaspe." The eccentric persons may be loosely or

closely connected with the myth, and may furnish satire and realistic manners.

(4) A number of pages, acted by the smallest children, appear as attendants on ladies and lovers. They take the place of the clowns or tricky servants that were heretofore usual in stage plays. They afford most of the fun, but this is generally of a refined and verbal character. Puns and repartee take the place of grossness and buffoonery.

(5) The interest lies largely in stylistic display. Set speeches alternate with lively repartee. Euphuism, abundant in the earliest of the plays, diminishes as the fashion wanes, but classical allusions, Latin quotations, puns and quibbles abound. Each play is a contest of wit, an exhibition of verbal fireworks.

(6) Songs are frequent, and occasionally there is a dance. Song, spectacle, artificial dialogue, and the arrangement of characters in groups, give an effect to the performance a little like our comic opera.

If we compare this formula with the usual character-istics of the interludes and comedies of the preceding years, the change is very great. Gone are the septenarius and the doggerel rhyme, gone (except in one play) the vice, the buffoon, the gross jokes, the boisterous farce. All is clever, refined, fanciful. Comedy no longer mimics reality or restores Plautus. It is a pageant, a sublimated court show. It creates a new world in which the deities of Olympus look like the gallants of Elizabeth's court, in which Arcadia is translated to Blackfriars, where the course of true love runs smooth in the end, and where everybody speaks as neatly and prettily as in a book. It is a little childish perhaps, but full of wit and wonder for its audience.

We can today scarcely recover the impressions which the Elizabethans received from Lyly's comedies. The great hall is filled, the queen has entered and taken her place on the dais in the center. A concert of music is playing, the jewels flash in the candle light, the great lords ogle the ladies or glower at their enemies, the queen jests with an ambassador. The concert is over, and the prologue comes forward to announce the piece,

"Most high and happy Princess, we must tell you a tale of the Man in the Moon, which if it seem ridiculous for the method, or superfluous for the matter, or for the means incredible, for three faults we can make but one excuse. It is a tale of the Man in the Moon. . . .

"We present neither Comedy nor Tragedy nor story, nor anything, but that whosoever heareth may say this, Why here is a tale of the Man in the Moon."

Just a wild fancy, the author avows, but that merely leads us to expect some hidden allegory for which we shall have to keep a sharp lookout. The stage is set as a garden, where enter Endymion and his friend Eumenides. Who was Endymion? The learned courtier informs the duchess that he was a shepherd in love with the moon. Yes, that is what he is declaiming on the stage. In love with the Moon, with Cynthia? That must be the queen. Listen, the handsome child who plays Endymion has come down front and is addressing a long speech directly to her majesty:

"Such is my sweet Cynthia, whom time cannot touch, because she is divine, nor will offend because she is delicate. O Cynthia, if thou shouldest always continue at thy fulness, both Gods and men would conspire to ravish thee. But thou to abate the pride of our affections dost detract from thy perfections, thinking it sufficient, if once in a month we enjoy a glimpse of thy majesty." . . .

Of whom is he talking, the moon or the queen? Elizabeth listens without a blush. And who is Endymion? There is the Earl of Leicester, with whom gossip has it she has been in love these thirty years. His face takes a set, self-conscious expression, and the Earl of Oxford, the poet's patron, looks as if he thought he was equal to any part. Does her majesty know who is meant by Endymion?

Now enter Tellus and her confidante. Tellus is in love
with Endymion and swears revenge because he has forsaken her for Cynthia. But who is Tellus? Some
whisper Mary Stuart, some say Lady Sheffield whom
Leicester secretly married against the queen's wishes.
Now enter three little pages and a fat braggart knight,
Sir Tophas. Who can he be? Several corpulent gentlemen about the hall are being nudged by their neighbours.
Here is Tellus again with the old witch Dipsas who is to
cast Endymion into a long sleep—and the act ends.

After the music everyone is curious enough to listen
intently to another long love speech by Endymion.

"I am that Endymion (sweet Cynthia)—whose eyes
never esteemed anything fair but thy face, whose tongue
termed nothing rare but thy virtues, and whose heart
imagined nothing miraculous but thy government. Yea,
that Endymion who, divorcing himself from the amiable-
ness of all Ladies, the bravery of all Courts, the company
of all men, hath chosen in a solitary cell to live, only by
feeding on thy favour, accounting in the world (but
thyself) nothing excellent, nothing immortal; thus
may'st thou see every vein, sinew, muscle, and artery of
my love, in which there is no flattery, nor deceit, error,
nor art."

Now come two of the little pages greeting two girls.
They laugh at their masters sighing in love. "Let them
sigh and let us sing" they cry, and then they egg the two
girls on to quarrel. In a moment they are ready to
scratch, and in another weeping plentifully. There is
laughter at two of the maids of honour who went through
just the same performance not a week ago. The girls
have stopped crying and are being persuaded by the pages
to make giggling love to Sir Tophas who pompously
repulses them. When they go off, Dipsas bewitches Endymion into a deathlike sleep, and a dumb show appears
representing his dreams. Three ladies, one with a knife
and a looking glass, an ancient man—but need we try to

puzzle out these devices? They will be explained before the play is over.

The third act opens upon the entrance of Cynthia accompanied by lords and ladies. How handsome the choir boy is, and how closely his dress matches her majesty's! The ambassador is saying he would not have believed they could find a child beautiful enough to suggest even a shadow of the real Cynthia's beauty, and the queen taps him with her fan in response to the compliment. How stately the boy queens it on the stage! Now the plot thickens. Tellus is put in prison but captivates her jailer, the Earl of Shrewsbury. Semele haughtily refuses the love of Endymion's friend Eumenides, and some think of "Astrophel and Stella," the famous poems that Sir Philip Sidney has addressed to the lady who jilted him in favour of the horrid Lord Rich. The merry pages have put Sir Tophas to sleep in imitation of Endymion, and they wake him with a song:

> "Here snores Tophas
> That amorous ass
> Who loves Dipsas
> With face so sweet
> Nose and chin meet."

It has been revealed to Eumenides at the sacred fountain that Endymion can be awakened only by the kiss of Cynthia. Will Cynthia do it, and what does the queen think of that? And who is Endymion? Now the silly braggart is composing verses to his Dipsas, and the witty pages are having a battle of puns, conundrums, and songs with the stupid watch. Then comes a troop of fairies who dance and sing, gently kiss Endymion, and pinch and bewitch poor Corsites, already badly tricked by Tellus. And who is Tellus? This learned gentleman says she is merely earthly love contrasted to heavenly love represented by Cynthia, but the ladies are inclined to think she is the wicked and beautiful Mary Stuart. Will Cynthia forgive Tellus and will Elizabeth pardon her fair cousin?

The play is coming to an end. Cynthia has graciously kissed the sleeping Endymion, and he awakes an old man with a long beard. He has been sleeping many years! Can this be meant for Leicester? Look, his beard drops off, and he is growing young again. How well acted! The villainy of Tellus is exposed. Semele has been made tongue-tied because she rejected Eumenides. What a crowded stage, not much like those interludes with only four players. Here are fourteen actors on at once, and all splendidly dressed. Tellus confesses and is pardoned and is to be wedded to Corsites. Semele relents and takes Eumenides, Dipsas is reunited to Geron. A tree is transformed into Bagoa and awarded to Sir Tophas, who greets her elegantly, "Bagoa? a bots upon thee!" The play queen arranges all these matches on the stage. Does the real queen approve? Will she restore Leicester to favour and pardon Mary?—or is that what the allegory means? Scholars today are by no means sure and perhaps the audience of 1585 was no surer, but it doubtless applauded the words with which the philosopher Pythagoras closed the performance,

"I had rather in Cynthia's court spend ten years than in Greece one hour."

"Endymion" is perhaps the most pleasing of Lyly's plays, but "Mother Bombie" shows a clever manipulation of the mechanism of Latin comedy, and "Gallathea" and "Love's Metamorphosis" are as elaborate pastorals as had then been presented in European theaters. In "Mother Bombie" the Terentian scheme is amplified so that the plot involves four aged and scheming fathers, their four mischievous pages, three couples of young lovers, one pair of feeble-minded children, a fortune teller, a horse trader, an old nurse, three fiddlers, and Mother Bombie, a "wise woman," who acts as general adviser and counsellor. Tricks and disguises make the comic situations, the pages are full of quips and pranks, and true love is justified in the end. In the pastorals the

Arcadian scene is presided over by Diana or Ceres, and by Cupid who contends with the goddesses for sovereignty. Shepherds or foresters woo the scornful nymphs, girls are disguised as boys and, thus disguised, inspire the tender passion in other girls. Deities, nymphs and foresters all indulge in repartee that is meant to be light and sparkling. Transformations are numerous; a nymph may be changed into a tree, a rock, a rose, or a bird. In one play there are six metamorphoses and four marriages.

The pastoral placidity is also enlivened by strange adventures. In "The Woman in the Moon," Pandora is let loose among the shepherds of Utopia. In "Love's Metamorphosis," Protea escapes from the merchant to whom her poverty-stricken father has sold her, and, transformed into the ghost of Ulysses, rescues her true lover from the lures of a siren, a songstress "half fish, half flesh," who "sing(s) with a Glass in her hand and a Comb." There are no pages and no farcical scenes in this play, but in "Gallathea" there are the comic adventures of three shipwrecked sailors, one of whom becomes a servant first of an alchemist and then of an astronomer.

In these and the other plays we find a deftness in language as well as in plotting, but no indisputable touch of poetry except in the famous and charming song,

> "Cupid and my Compaspe played
> At cards for kisses. Cupid paid."

Lyly's place in our literary history as a considerable innovator was won by cleverness rather than by genius. His writings marked the beginnings of important developments in prose style, in the novel, and in comedy. Though they do not disclose a personality of high distinction, they are the products of a mental ingenuity, quick to seize upon new means of expression, and of an experimenting artistry that made the most of his knack with words. He is partly responsible for the spread of the epidemic of puns, word plays and conceits that infected Elizabethan comedy,

but he is also to be credited with its gain in lightness, ease
and fancy. His dramatic confections were acted in public
as well as at court. They helped to make sentiment and
wit at home in the London theaters. They constitute the
first original English type of comedy, and they provided
a model and method for Shakespeare.

II

George Peele's labours as a dramatist and a poet began
while he was still at Oxford, where he assisted in the presentation of Latin plays by Dr. Gager, and himself translated one of the Iphigenias of Euripides. On leaving the
university he appears to have entered at once upon a
literary career in London, obtaining precarious employment in composing pageants and entertainments for the
Lord Mayor, writing congratulatory verses for patrons,
and plays for the actors. He brought with him to London
a name for conviviality as well as for poetry, and he
became well known as a dissipated man about town. A
volume, "The Merry Conceited Jests of George Peele,"
published a few years after his death, relates some oft
told jokes and pranks for which he could not have been
responsible, but its ascription to him testifies to the character of his general reputation. Like his friends, Marlowe and Greene, he seems to have led a Bohemian
existence shocking to his soberer contemporaries. Even
then, however, there were admirers, like Thomas Nashe,
who wrote of him "for the last, though not the least of
them all, I dare commend him to all that know him, as
the chief supporter of pleasance now living, the Atlas of
Poetry and *primus verborum artifex:* whose first increase,
the Arraignment of Paris, might plead to your opinions,
his pregnant dexteritie of wit, and manifold varietie of
invention wherein (me iudice) he goeth a step beyond all
that write."

"The Arraignment of Paris, a pastoral" (pr. 1584)
was possibly acted as early as any of Lyly's plays. Like
them it was presented at court by children actors and is

effusive in its compliments to the queen. The plot relates the trial by Diana of Paris accused of error in judgment in awarding the prize of beauty to Venus. The decision gives the golden apple to "the Nymph Eliza, a figure of the Queen." The play is written in verse usually rhyming, and its plot, stage devices, classical allusions and songs are the product of independent invention and fancy. Yet in general character and method it resembles the plays of Lyly. Like him, Peele was making use of a court entertainment by children actors for the scenic and poetic representation of his own exuberant delight in classical story.

The stage is thronged by picturesque persons of classical myth, and those who do not appear are alluded to in the dialogue. Ate with the golden apple acts as prologue. Pan, Faunus and Silvanus, accompanied by shepherd, forester and woodman, introduce us to the vale of Ida, where Diana's bower has been richly decorated for the entertainment of the expected goddesses. Flora and Pomona adorn the bower with devices in flowers, and the muses sing in rivalry with "an artificial charm of birds being heard within," and the gods "Hold hands in a hornpipe all gallant in glee." While the rival goddesses prepare for the judgment, nymphs and shepherds are wooing. Paris and Oenone sit under a tree together and when they have recounted the stories of Salmacis, Daphne, Narcissus, Gorgon and others, they sing, "and while Oenone singeth he pypeth":

> "Fair and fair and twice so fair
> As fair as any may be;
> The fairest shepherd on our green,
> A love for any lady."

After a storm of thunder and lightning the goddesses summon Paris and present their shows:

"Juno's Show. Hereupon did rise a Tree of gold laden with Diadems and crowns of gold.

"Pallas's Show. Hereupon did enter 9 Knights in armour, treading a warlike Almaine by droms and fife.

"Venus's Show. Here Helen entreth in her braveur with 4 Cupids attending on her, each having his fan in his hand to fan fresh air in her face."

Helen sings in Italian. The Destinies later on sing in Latin. Everybody is melodious. Colin, the enamoured shepherd refused by Thestilis, sings a lament, and later on the shepherds sing at his funeral. Thestilis, punished by Venus for her disdain, becomes enamoured of a "foul crooked churl," and sings her sorrow, the shepherds echoing her verses. Another nymph refuses Bacchus and Vulcan, but joins with them in a round. Before the assembled gods, Paris delivers his oration of defense in blank verse, but even this, like the other speeches, is lyrical. The musical drama ends in long pæans of praise to the queen,

"For wisdom, princely state, and peerless beauty."

Peele's other comedy, "The Old Wives' Tale" (pr. 1595), is less ambitious but more original. It is a very short play, half the length of "Endymion," and was possibly written some time in the eighties for a special occasion, though the quarto announces it as acted by the Queen's Men, a leading adult company. It is a curious medley of diverse persons and incidents united in a lively spirit of extravaganza. It begins with an induction—a mimic audience intervening between the real audience and the play proper—a device frequently employed by the Elizabethans. Antic, Frolic and Fantastic, names prophetic of the nature of the performance, enter and announce themselves as lost in the woods. A dog barks, a light gleams, a peasant enters with a lantern and conducts the wanderers to his hut where, after a song, they beg Gammer Madge to tell them a tale. Madge begins, but presently the persons of the story appear and act it out with occasional interruptions from Madge and her supposed auditors.

The main action is that which Milton borrowed and immortalized in "Comus," but Peele garnishes it with all sorts of wonders, surprises and absurdities. Sacrapant, who has carried off the beautiful Delia, is a terrible sorcerer who commands the thunder and lightning and two furies, but is finally slain by a genial ghost who goes invisible. The two brothers and the lover of Delia are subject to the sorcerer's enchantments, as is Huanebango, a blustering pedant who makes love in hexameters like those of Gabriel Harvey's:

"Just by thy side shall sit surnamèd great Huanebango: Safe in my arms will I keep thee, threat Mars, or thunder Olympus."

Whereupon Zantippa comments, "Three blue beans in a blue bladder, rattle, bladder, rattle." A mad girl, a sexton, a friar, and harvest men add to the amusing hodgepodge.

An equally incongruous medley is "Edward I," in which history is not raised to the dignity of tragedy in the fashion of Marlowe or Kyd, but treated as a popular and half-comic spectacle. The scene in which the king and his friends play at Robin Hood and his merry men is worthy of note in connection with both earlier and later plays presenting the free greenwood life of the ballads. Peele did not found any school or lead to any development in the drama, but his theatrical inventiveness and his gift of fluent and melodious verse were admired and imitated. His two comedies indicated to contemporary writers how much variety of incident and style might be crowded into an afternoon's entertainment. The same pen could fit the action with an olla podrida of classical allusions or with the sweetest lyrics, with mocking burlesque or spirited adulation.

III

Robert Greene, by repute the most dissipated of the university wits, was certainly the most industrious. His

first novel was registered for printing in the year following Lyly's "Euphues," and for the next twelve years he
kept the booksellers busy with an uninterrupted succession
of publications. He was the forerunner of our present-
day commercial novelists and the most prolific fiction-
writer of his own day. He wrote stories in all the prevailing fashions, Euphuistic, pastoral and Arcadian; and he
usually left room for a Part II in case Part I achieved
sufficient success. He wrote pamphlets which, under pretense of exposing the sharpers of the city, retailed stories
of immorality, and he wrote other pamphlets confessing
his own sins and copiously repenting. Perhaps his most
interesting novels are amplifications of the prodigal son
theme romanticizing his own profligate career. None of
his tales are masterpieces, but they offered to the readers
of his day a gateway to the romance and sensation and
sentiment of story-land. Though he often promises his
readers to forsake love stories for more edifying material,
he is at his best as a sentimentalist.

Greene apparently did not begin writing for the stage
until some years later than Peele and Lyly. In the stories
of two of his prodigals he has described his initiation into
the theater. In "A Groatsworth of Wit" Roberto
("whose life in most part agreeing with mine found self
punishment as I have done") is in despair after his
betrayal by a courtezan and is offered assistance by a
stranger. Roberto inquires how he may be employed.

" 'Why, easily,' quoth he, 'and greatly to your benefit;
for men of my profession get by scholars their whole
living.' 'What is your profession?' said Roberto. 'Truly,
sir,' said he, 'I am a player.' 'A player!' quoth Roberto;
'I took you rather for a gentleman of great living; for if
by outward habit men should be censured, I tell you, you
would be taken for a substantial man.' 'So am I where I
dwell' quoth the player 'reputed able at my proper cost to
build a windmill.' Roberto again asked how he was to
be employed. 'Why, sir, in making plays,' said the other,

'for which you shall be well paid, if you will take the pains.' Roberto, perceiving no remedy, thought it best to respect his present necessity, (and) to try his wit, went with him willingly."

In "Never Too Late," Francesco "Writ a comedy; which so generally pleased all the audience that happy were those actors in short time that could get any of his works, he grew so exquisite in that faculty."

The prosperity of the actors and the demand for writers of plays described in these extracts are evidences of the success of the professional adult actors. In 1583 the best of them had been brought together in a company called the Queen's Men because acting under her majesty's direct patronage, and it was for this company that Greene usually wrote. The earliest play of his which survives is "Alphonsus of Arragon," a servile but absurd imitation of Marlowe's "Tamburlaine," but with a happy ending and some emphasis upon romantic love. "A Looking Glass for London," written in collaboration with Lodge, is a satirical attack on vices of the day under guise of the story of Jonah and Nineveh. "Jonah is cast out of the whale's belly upon the stage." "Orlando Furioso" is a wonderful distortion of Ariosto, with much spectacle and farce, but again with a romantic love story leading to a happy ending. "George a Green, Pinner of Wakefield" uses Robin Hood material and is more successful than the other plays both in its love story and its heroine. Greene was quite likely also the author of the tragedy "Selimus" and possibly a collaborator in "Henry VI," but by far his best and most representative plays are "Friar Bacon and Friar Bungay" and "James IV."

Like his other plays these are medleys of history, spectacle, magic, farce and sentiment, but they alone show definite elements of structure and characterization. In each the course of true love advances to a happy conclusion not merely through adventure and spectacle and shifts of fortune but because of decisive acts of volition. Men

and women make or mar their happiness through their
own choices, and human character is presented as swayed
by ideals of generosity, loyalty, and love.

In "Friar Bungay" romance makes its home in England
though it goes back to the time of Henry III.   Prince
Edward enters "malcontented" and confesses to his companions that he is enamoured with "the bonny damsel
fill'd us drink," Margaret, the keeper's daughter of
Fressingfield. He leaves Lacy, Earl of Lincoln, to woo
the maid for him while he rides off to Oxford where he
is to meet his intended bride, Elinor of Castile.   At
Oxford, Bacon, master of necromancy, performs entertaining marvels and in a prospective glass shows to the
prince Lacy wooing Margaret for himself.   Through
Bacon's magic Friar Bungay, who is about to marry them,
is borne off by a devil to Oxford, and Edward hastens to
Fressingfield to take vengeance on his false friend. Lacy
and Margaret plead their love so successfully that the
prince forgives them but carries Lacy back with him to
Oxford. Here there are fresh marvels, for a necromancer
brought over by the emperor enters into a contest with
Bungay and Bacon.   Bungay conjures up the tree of
Hesperides, the German conjures up Hercules who tears
the branches from the tree, and Bacon conquers by compelling Hercules to carry both the tree and the German
straight back to Hapsburg. Elinor and Edward meet and
are betrothed. Lacy sends a letter of farewell in order
to test Margaret's faith, and she determines to enter a
nunnery. Two of her rejected suitors quarrel and kill
each other. This sad spectacle causes Bacon to break the
prospective glass which had disclosed so much ill, and the
failure of his servant to waken him when his Brazen Head
spoke leads him to give up necromancy. First, however,
he punishes his shiftless servant, Miles, who with Ralph,
the prince's fool, has furnished a good deal of clownage,
and Miles disappears on a devil's back. Lacy arrives in
Fressingfield just in time to save Margaret from the
nunnery, and we have a double wedding at court and

Bacon's prophecy of the matchless flower that shall eventually spring from the royal union.

The magic in this play probably owes something to the success on the stage of Marlowe's "Dr. Faustus," but it is skilfully employed both to afford stage spectacle and to develop the plot. By means of the "prospective glass" the scene is shifted from Oxford to Fressingfield. The contest of the magicians is well integrated with the story of the lovers. The persons of the plot are also endowed with individuality and interest scarcely found in preceding comedies, especially the heroine. There is no great subtlety in the characterization of Margaret. She loves Lacy at first sight, she will have no other, she will have him, and if he won't have her, life is not worth living. This is a simple formula for life or for story, but never before had it been impersonated on the English stage with so much charm and such a touch of reality.

"James IV," though not clearly superior to "Friar Bacon" as a play, is of more interest in illustrating the dramatic possibilities of romantic story, and in its resemblance to Shakespeare's comedies. It begins with an Induction in which Oberon, king of the fairies, enters with Antics who dance about a tomb where a cynic Scot has interred himself. He appears, calls on his two sons, Slipper and Nano, to dance a jig, and then goes with Oberon to the gallery to watch the play. In the act intervals, Oberon and Bohan reappear and witness dances by fairies and others and dumb shows of Semiramis, Cyrus and Alexander, and Sesotris, illustrations of Fortune's pranks. So much of the court show still adheres to the professional stage.

The play, though entitled "The Scottish Historie of James the fourth, slaine at Flodden" has nothing to do with real history. Its story is derived from a novel by Giraldi Cinthio who also made it into a Senecan tragicomedy. The English stage demanded a different treatment, and Greene provided a pseudo-historical framework and a pitched field for a finalé. He also supplied a

villain, Ateukin, who reads Machiavelli, and a number of
farcical scenes. Slipper becomes the servant of the villain,
and Nano page to the queen, and both indulge in the
customary verbal witticisms. King James is married to
Dorothea but is in love with the Countess Ida. He employs the villain Ateukin first to win Ida and then to
murder Dorothea. Ida rejects the king's overtures even
after the death of the queen is reported, and marries the
worthy Eustace. Dorothea is a very Griselda of wifely
devotion. Warned of treachery she flees from court, disguised as a man and accompanied only by her faithful
and humorous dwarf; she is forced to fight and is badly
wounded; she is loved by another woman, the wife of her
rescuer; she remains true to her husband in spite of his
efforts to kill her, and in the end returns to forgive and
save him. It is not only these incidents that remind us of
Sylvia, Viola and Imogen, it is also her modesty, sweetness and loyalty. The dumb-shows, the antics and jokes
of the clowns, the plottings of the villain, and the affairs
of war and state are all incidental, the interest of the
piece is focused on the two women, Ida and Dorothea.
Greene idealizes them most sympathetically, and he wins
for them our belief and approval.

It is in this greater sincerity and reality that Greene
goes beyond the fantasies of Lyly. Their spectacles and
pastoralism and repartee needed something more of
genuine dramatic conflict and serious presentation of
character. These "James IV" supplied and with them a
sort of basic formula for Elizabethan romantic comedy.
Neither Shakespeare, nor later Fletcher, was greatly to
change its outline. Court intrigue, villainy, evil, danger
and even death keep us in some suspense as to the outcome; clowns and nonsense sway us now and then from
heroism and sentiment to farce; lyric outburst and neat
repartee unite with fantastic setting or adventure to persuade us that we are in the world of make-believe; but the
main interest ever depends on our sympathetic attachment
to the idealized heroine. Love cannot be allowed to

become tedious and it is diversified by magic, spectacle, dances and much else, but we are always ready to return to the charming maiden now triumphantly claiming her lover and now wandering lovelorn in some Arcadian seclusion. She makes her choice, and she will be true to it. That is the theme of both plot and poetry. That is the way in which virtue triumphs over harsh reality. In the land of romance sentiment encounters tragedy, farce, heroics, and spectacles, and she is charmingly victorious.

CHAPTER VI

SHAKESPEARE: THE EARLIER COMEDIES

By the time that Shakespeare had established himself in London as an actor, the public playhouses had been open more than a decade, and Marlowe, Lyly, Greene and others had made the profession of dramatist both profitable and literary. Four or five theatrical performances were being given each day, and yet the demand for new plays seemed to be without limit. Naturally the young actor began his career as a dramatist by making plays in the prevailing fashions and following in the footsteps of the brilliant university men who were drawing crowds to the theater. The first documentary record of Shakespeare in London is in the charge of plagiarism in Greene's "Groatsworth of Wit," (1592), which betrays a jealous resentment at the success attained by a mere actor in rivalling Greene and his friends in the creation of poetic drama.

It is not certain whether Shakespeare's earliest efforts were in history and tragedy after the models of Marlowe and Kyd, or in comedy after the models of Lyly and Greene. "Henry VI, Part I" and "Titus Andronicus," are at all events far more imitative and far less suggestive of his mature genius than are his first three comedies, "The Comedy of Errors," "Love's Labour's Lost" and "The Two Gentlemen of Verona." These three plays, however, clearly represent respectively the three types of comedy that we have found prevailing about 1590, those of Plautus, Lyly and Greene.

"The Comedy of Errors" is an adaptation of the "Menæchmi" of Plautus, with an addition from the "Amphitruo." It increases the persons and complications of the original in order to enliven the farce, and it adds

95

a romantic story to heighten the human interest, but in both these variations from his source, Shakespeare is following the practice of Italian and English imitators of the Latin playwrights. His plotting is so ingenious and so superior to that of the other two comedies that many critics have concluded this the latest and maturest of the three. It may well be the latest, though the difference in date is at most slight, but the superiority in plotting must be ascribed largely to the model. Anyone by 1590 could construct a skilful plot on the basis of Plautus, and no one had any certain dramaturgy for romantic comedy. Lyly's "Mother Bombie," of the Roman type, is far better constructed than his allegory "Midas," or his pastoral "Love's Metamorphosis." Where Shakespeare's play surpasses Lyly's and all other imitations of the Roman comedy is not so much in the ingenuity of the plotting as in its adaptability to the stage. Even the romantic story of Ægeon—rather clumsily and stiffly written—meets essential stage requirements. It was necessary that the whole complicated entanglement of the two pairs of twins should be carefully explained to the audience before the action began; and how could it be better explained so as to win their attention than by the shipwrecked father—on trial for his life, destined through the happy outcome of the day's complications to recover life, wife and children? And the farce itself moves with unwavering attention to the dramatic possibilities of comic situation. In comparison with the best plays of the time, "Mother Bombie" included, there is astonishingly little in it that is incidental and adventitious. The action never wanders off into byways and never stops—even for a song. Characterization and witty dialogue never delay the movement. As a result it was funny on Shakespeare's stage and has been just as funny on every stage where it has been acted.

In contrast, "Love's Labour's Lost" seems strangely undramatic and literary. Shakespeare is not here following the well tried model of Roman farce but exercising his own invention in devising a drama along the lines of Lyly's scheme for a court entertainment. Moreover, in the text that we have, the original version seems to have been over-written and the fifth act enlarged out of all proportion to the rest. Presumably writing with a court performance in view, Shakespeare bent his energies to meeting that taste for refined and witty comedy which Lyly had fostered. Though he does not use classical story or allegory, he constructs an artificial and fanciful scheme. The King of Navarre and three gentlemen retire to a little academe whence women are banished. The Princess of France and three ladies arrive and invade the retreat, and after various merry diversions and encounters the four weddings are arranged for a twelvemonth hence. A group of eccentric persons provide the low comedy. Braggart, priest, pedant, clown, constable and page are all familiar types but offer a chance for good-natured satire on some contemporary fashions, and especially at the unnatural and extravagant fads in diction and vocabulary. But the verbal excesses of pedant and braggart are only absurd reflections of the linguistic affectations and displays of the courtiers of Navarre. Indeed, the whole comedy is a very fantasy of that word-play in which Shakespeare, like his age, so greatly delighted.

Such an entertainment does not provide a closely knit plot, nor is it likely to have a universal dramatic appeal. Its witticisms and burlesques pleased its own age, and acted today by school-girls in the freedom of their academe, the play still has power to charm and to amuse, but it has scarcely been heard upon the professional stage since Shakespeare's death. In its composition, however, Shakespeare was acquiring valuable lessons for his further endeavours in comedy. As we have seen he had learned all that Lyly had to teach. He had followed his predecessor in the fanciful scheme, the artificial grouping of characters, the light-hearted treatment of lovers' woes, the burlesque of the more serious action in the absurdities of a group of eccentrics, and especially in the incessant sparkle of repartee and word-play. But in the process he had marked as his own situations and persons that would come again to his call, a clown and his wench, a pompous ass and a mocking page, a witty lady sparring with her lover. Still more, Shakespeare had surpassed his master in copiousness of wit and freedom of fancy, in that delightful power to laugh merrily at one's own arts. It was a saving grace in Lyly that he could mingle high comedy and low so that the low burlesques the high. Shakespeare bettered his instruction. When the pedant presents the preposterous show of the Nine Worthies, he jests at the very dramatic entertainments that Lyly had provided. When pedant and braggart gambol so clumsily with words, they mock the complicated artistry of repartee, echo and sonnet over which Shakespeare himself was straining all his ingenuity. This is more than the exuberance of obstreperous wit and more than a skilful union of sentiment and burlesque, it is of the very essence of humour. The spirit of comedy requires that whenever wit is intellectual, or sentiment refined, or manners courtly, the mimics must be lurking round the corner.

"The Two Gentlemen of Verona," in many particulars of both construction and style, exhibits Lyly's influence, but it is also an experiment in sentimental romance after the fashion of Greene. The main action is drawn directly from "Diana of Montemayor," but the complications were already familiar in stage romance. Valentine and Silvia, Proteus and Julia are the loving couples, and the two gentlemen are fast friends. Silvia's father, the Duke, wishes her to marry a foolish Thurio. Proteus proves false to Julia and betrays his friend to banishment. Julia, disguised as a boy, follows Proteus and becomes his page. Silvia escapes from court to follow Valentine to the forest, where he has become chief of the outlaws. All meet in the forest, the villain repents, Julia is discovered and the proper lovers are united.

This is close to the stock plot of romantic comedy and varies little from the love story in "James IV." Shakespeare added the usual wit contests of the servants; Launce, servant to Proteus, Speed, servant to Valentine, and Lucetta, maid to Julia, occupy a large portion of the earlier acts with their quibbling and with some very bad puns. Launce, however, is far the best clown that had been produced on the English stage, though he and his dog have little to do with the story. Perhaps because this type of romantic play was far less developed dramatically than either the Plautian imitation or the Lylian court entertainment, Shakespeare found it difficult to enliven the action or to enrich the characters. The dénouement is badly hurried and Valentine so far forgets his part as to offer Silvia to the penitent Proteus. Perhaps this fine gesture might be in accord with the code of honour for sworn friends, but it could scarcely be justified on a stage devoted to romantic love.

The spirit and charm of Greene's comedies, however, are by no means lacking. Whatever may be thought of the men, the women have no flaws. Like others on the stage they love at first sight, but each remains utterly single and devoted in her love, and they are the main movers of the action. In Lyly's comedies the manners and talk of ladies are presented, in Greene's an idealized picture; here Shakespeare brings his two love-possessed ladies together, makes them talk and act, shows them always different yet both excellent. But the play is less notable for what it achieves than for what it promises. The two heroines are the first sketches for the great portrait gallery of Shakespeare's women; every situation in which they find themselves was to receive later amplification and enrichment. All that Shakespeare could accomplish in his first attempt was to touch here and there with life the bare formula of dramatic romance.

In order to complete our survey of Shakespeare's apprentice work in comedy, "The Taming of the Shrew" must be added to the three plays already considered, but it cannot be viewed as his independent work. The main plot of Katherine and Petruchio is based on an earlier

and amusing play, "The Taming of a Shrew," and the
subsidiary stories of Bianca's suitors are drawn from
Italian imitations of Plautus, perhaps through the inter-
mediary of English plays. Remnants of these earlier
pieces appear to survive and have led critics to doubt
Shakespeare's authorship of large portions of our text,
but it seems probable that the whole is a theatrical rescen-
sion for which he is responsible. Indeed, the harmonious
conjunction of all the diverse elements into a capital farce
is an achievement beyond any other dramatist then
writing.

What has been accomplished in the various steps of
composition is the blending of medieval and classical farce
into a play of enduring effectiveness. The boisterous
horse-play of taming the shrew derives from a long series
of theatrical versions of the theme going back to Noah's
wife in the miracle plays. The elaborate tricks and disguises of the sub-plot are merely the stock material of
Italian-Roman comedy. Shakespeare is revising and
rewriting, not inventing, but he saves the old situations
from tediousness and triviality by means of the vigour
and humour and general manliness that he writes into the
character of Petruchio. To the induction of the old play
he also gives firmness and vitality. Still more, in spite
of the exaggerations necessary to farce, he does not lose
sight of moral values. The two medieval themes of the
shrew and Patient Griselda continued to find representations on the stage and became the basis of widening
discussion of the relations of husband and wife. Shakespeare's play suggests that for a solution of this vexed
social problem there are at least two requisites, good sense
and good humour.

In these first comedies the young playwright was experimenting in the modes of his contemporaries. In his
next comedy he far surpassed them and created a play
conspicuously original, his first great romantic comedy,
and one of the masterpieces of the world's poetry. There
is no need to dilate on the charm and beauty of "A Mid-

summer Night's Dream." Everyone knows it and loves it, as we do the series of romantic comedies that followed. Everyone knows, too, that it differs from all that had preceded it, even from Shakespeare's own "Love's Labour's Lost" and "Two Gentlemen of Verona," as blossom from stalk, or fairyland from an amusement park.

Yet our study has made plain that the way was prepared for this delightful comedy by years of dramatic experiment and that its rare beauty is no departure from type but rather a fulfillment. It was probably written at nearly the same time as "Romeo and Juliet"; and as that play adopts and transmutes the material and methods of current tragedy, so it consummates the efforts in court show and dramatization of romance to create a national form of comedy. Both plays are the fruition of that creative impulse, aroused by old story and new dramatic opportunity, which had fired the imagination of Elizabethan playwrights, that impulse to romanticize life and to blend both its tragedy and comedy with beauty. We may even recapture, I think, some steps in the process by which that creative impulse, working on Shakespeare's genius, created for his meager theater a veritable poet's dream.

"A Midsummer Night's Dream" was planned for presentation at court in celebration of some special occasion, presumably a wedding. A comedy with spectacle, dances and songs would be expected, and Shakespeare would surely think first of Lyly's methods and his own adaptation of them in "Love's Labour's Lost." The happy idea also occurred to him to throw the play into the form of an entertainment presented at the imaginary court of Theseus and Hippolyta to celebrate their nuptials. The primary interest would naturally lie neither in story nor in characterization but in entertainment of the various kinds that could be provided by a court show. In the finished play there are four rather distinct parts, and these may very probably have occurred to Shakespeare separately as the ingredients proper to his purpose. First there was the framework of the wedding of Theseus and Hippolyta; second, there was the story of the Athenian lovers with their crosses and final reconciliation and marriage. Third, there were the fairies who with their dances and songs should grace the wedding, and, fourth, the dramatic efforts of Bottom and the mechanics, which should afford comic relief and should burlesque the very thing the play was attempting, a court show.

The plan of the play as an entertainment before Theseus and Hippolyta utilizes a common feature of the drama, the induction with a mock audience. The device of a mock audience between the real audience of the theater and the persons of the play had indeed given rise to interesting scenes. In the "Rare Triumph of Love and Fortune," the gods of Olympus supplied the audience before which the love story was enacted. In Greene's "James IV," Oberon, king of the fairies, and a cynic Scot surveyed the fickle course of fortune as presented in the play. In Peele's "Old Wives' Tale," one of the mock audience begins to tell a story which is taken up and impersonated by the actors. Shakespeare himself had elaborated the device in "The Taming of the Shrew" and here he revives it, but without formal separation of the induction from the play proper. There seems to have been a feeling that a prologue or a framework or, best of all, a mock audience helped to bridge the chasm between the actuality of the pit and the illusion of the stage. Theseus and Hippolyta accomplish a more delicate transition; they afford a means of approach to fairyland. A fundamental difficulty in romance is how to get there, how to produce of a sudden the illusion of the impossible. Here the first step is from the London of the court and theater to romantic and legendary Athens; once accustomed to this change, the fancy is ready for the next flight to fairyland. And as in other inductions, so in this, its persons not only furnish a beginning for the play, they supply a framework and unifying scheme for the whole.

The Athenian lovers offer little that is unusual on the stage. The misdirection and crossing of their affections by magic and the use of the forest as the setting for their idyl are in compliance with the accepted conventions of romantic drama. Shakespeare inevitably used in his entertainment the same sort of love story that had been employed by Lyly and Greene and by himself in "The Two Gentlemen of Verona." These Athenian lovers did not need or receive very serious treatment or such dignity of emotion and verse as he had bestowed on the royal couple, Theseus and Hippolyta.

The fairies led by their king and queen, who have quarreled and must be reconciled, have also come to join in the celebration. Along with the monarchs they supply the mythical beings for the stage spectacle. They had often been seen at court, together with satyrs, nymphs, tritons, fauns, devils and witches, and they had appeared on the public stage as well in "Endymion" and "James IV." The occasion of their employment here may have been that Shakespeare's company was permitted to borrow some of the smallest members of one of the children's companies for this court spectacle. Certainly these little actors gave the poet some suggestions. He exaggerates from the first their contrast in size with the adults and reduces his dancers in the moonlight to a tininess never before attributed to them in folk lore. These fairies and imps and even "that shrewd and knavish sprite" Robin Goodfellow, lose all the evil reputation they had gathered in popular tradition and take on instead the irresponsibility and merriment of childhood. Opportunity invited him to make a fairyland out of children; Shakespeare's imagination rose to the challenge.

Others had the opportunity, only he could create that exquisite and merry fairyland which was ushered before Elizabeth's court at the stage direction "Enter a Fairy at one door and Robin Goodfellow at another." The fairy talks of the moon and cowslips, rubies, freckles, pearls, dewdrops, and other delightful things, and Puck retorts with forests, flowers, groves, fountains, starlight and the acorn cups wherein elves hide. In a moment Oberon and Titania are quarreling in the daintiest manner possible, and he has offered the most graceful of compliments to "the imperial votaress," and Puck has been installed as manipulator of mischief alike among fairies and mortals and the little children have sung Titania asleep—"So, good night, with lullaby."

The fourth element of the play, the comic relief, is supplied by Bottom and the mechanics. Theseus and Hippolyta speak sonorous blank verse; the lovers and the fairies frequently use rhymes, the low comedians, except in their play, confine themselves to prose. As in Lyly, so here the low comedy is a foil and a parody of the high comedy. As in "Love's Labour's Lost," so here Shakespeare makes his clowns present a play at court and burlesque what he himself is doing in all seriousness. And happiest stroke of all, the romantic extravagances of all the lovers are absurdly reflected in Titania's infatuation for the transformed weaver, and even fairyland itself is laughed at when her attendants "fan the moonbeams from his sleeping eyes." Then comic reality passes from the forest to the court, and the fun grows uproarious as the mechanics proceed with their play. The author of "Romeo and Juliet" is now composing a "Pyramus and Thisbe" for Bottom. Shakespeare's comic invention is at full tide, and each of his clowns surpasses the other's individual asininity, yet Theseus invites us to reflect that "The best in this kind are but shadows; and the worst are not worse if imagination amend them."

To follow farther the process of the play's creation would be merely to note the dramatic skill and tact with which these four main elements are combined and to praise the sweep of fun and poetry that blends all incongruities into harmony. But the analysis into these four elements has shown perhaps how his imagination was seizing on material and suggestions open to any dramatist of the time, and was following methods and technic that others had applied to comedy. The court show, developed and given an established tradition by Lyly, now becomes transformed into a type of comedy that can only be described as Shakespearian.

If the trend in comedy that we have traced from the court show reached fulfillment in the "Dream," that other development from the dramatic translation of romance came to its Shakespearian transformation in "The Merchant of Venice." The two ancient and improbable stories of the pound of flesh and the caskets were apparently combined in a lost play mentioned by Stephen Gosson in his "School of Abuse" (1579) as "the Jew . . . showne at the Bull . . . representing the greedinesse of worldly chusers, and the bloody mindes of Usurers." In choosing this as the basis for his drama Shakespeare was adopting two procedures already established, first, the combination of two stories in one play, and, second, the use of tragic complications in sharp contrast to the prevailing tone of light comedy. Like Greene and many other earlier writers he was making tragicomedy, but he was careful to emphasize the happy ending. After tragedy is averted, or rather ended, in the punishment of the villain, we return for the last act to the moonlit terrace at Belmont and to the merriments of the reconciled lovers.

There has been general admiration for the technical skill with which Shakespeare ties together the two stories and carries us back and forth from Venice to Belmont without deranging the coherence and rapidity of the action. The stories, however, are of a childish improbability that calls forth all his ripening powers of characterization to make them plausible. There is a perpetual question—would anyone do such an impossible thing?—and Shakespeare's reply—yes, just this sort of person did it. The result is a triumphant humanizing and individualizing that extends to the least important actor in the two stories. Yet, after all, there remains a disparity between the incredible incidents and the veritable persons. Ancient

stories had a way of thus forcing their limits upon the
dramatist. The Elizabethans, hungry for story, gulped
the impossibilities. The modern reader expects events
to develop from character rather than personalities to
grow out of story, and finds it difficult to accept the major
premise of all romantic drama, that the impossible is most
likely to happen. But the play presents Shakespeare's
solution of this difficulty of romance—no matter what the
persons do, he makes them as real and as interesting as
possible.

This difficulty is surmounted but not obliterated in the
character of Shylock. For it, Shakespeare drew many
suggestions from Marlowe's enormously popular "Jew of
Malta." The protagonist Barabas is a usurer and a
villain seeking prodigious revenge upon the Christians
and finally hoisted on his own petard. The medieval
prejudice against the Jews as money lenders and supposed
murderers survived into the Elizabethan period and
found signal exemplification in the execration heaped upon
a Jew, Roderigo Lopez, who was hanged in 1594 for
alleged complicity in a plot against the queen. Indeed,
the case of Lopez may possibly have turned Shakespeare's
attention to the old play as one that might be revised into
a rival of Marlowe's tragedy. Barabas, who was acted
by Edward Alleyn, the creator of Tamburlaine and a
person of majestic presence, begins the play with dignity
and eloquence, but soon degenerates into a Machiavellian
and melodramatic monster. But Shakespeare's creative
process took another course, and he endowed his Shylock not only with the qualities of a detested Jew and of
a stage villain but also with "organs, dimensions, senses,
affections, passions" of a human individual.

Here is a union of the inconceivable usurer of the old
story, the Machiavellian villain of Marlowe's play and
the monstrous Jew of popular hatred, relieved and
enlarged by Shakespeare's humanity. This variability has
led to widely different interpretations, and Shylock has at
different times been acted as a comic butt, a malicious

avenger and racial martyr. If one attends only to his performances, he is clearly a monster like the giants and dragons of story-land; if one attends only to Elizabethan stage practice, he is an avenging villain and the proper butt of the Christians; but as one reads the text, he is a many-sided man, whose revenge is not without justification, whose wrongs weigh against his crimes, and whose contest with his persecutors gains a dignity because he fights single-handed the battle of his race.

The result is not strict consistency of characterization, rather it is richness of personality. Shylock will not stand precise analysis by either Elizabethan or modern psychology, but our continued questioning of his motives and meanings indicates how vital and interesting he still is after three centuries. Shakespeare gave to stories, however improbable, and to situations, however theatrical, the added interest that comes from enriching, enlarging and humanizing their actors. Even Morocco making a silly choice becomes dignified, even Bassanio the foolish becomes agreeable, Jessica stealing jewels from her father is attractive, the clown is individual, Portia disguised as a doctor of laws is magnificent, and Shylock, the deserved butt of laughter of all those delightful people, is pathetic. The old stories were not designed to carry so much meaning, but it is one of the qualities of Shakespearian comedy that it endowed the most improbable romance with humanity.

The date of the writing of the "Merchant" is approximately 1597. The advance shown over Shakespeare's first essays in comedy a half-dozen years before was more than maintained in the three brilliant plays that rounded out the century, "Much Ado About Nothing," "As You Like It," and "Twelfth Night." They complete the series of seven romantic comedies written during the decade from "Love's Labour's Lost" (1590) to "Twelfth Night" (1601). During these years the dramatists in general were, like Shakespeare, mainly occupied with English history and romantic story. They produced many

other romantic comedies, but so far as we know, none of
these except Shakespeare's offered any new developments
in the type.   By 1600, comedy under the leadership of
Jonson was turning to realistic and satiric depiction of
contemporary manners.   The course of romantic comedy
comes to a halt with Shakespeare's three masterpieces.

So far as concerns their main characteristics in plot,
persons and stage effects, these comedies add little to what
was already familiar in the species.   Though each of the
three is very individual and different from the others, yet
they conform closely to the essential elements of the type
as displayed in the "Dream" and the "Merchant."   In
each the main plot concerns two beautiful and noble ladies
and their lovers, and ends with their marriages.   The
focus of interest is always on the idealized heroine.   The
vicissitudes that interfere with the course of true love are
of the usual sort; in two plays they involve villainy and
threaten tragedy, in the third there is the familiar complication of one heroine in love with the other disguised
as a boy.   In all three the low comedy is carried on by
dolts, clowns and clever servants, some of whom make love
and marry as do their betters.   The element of tragedy is
never carried so far as in the "Merchant," and the tone
of refined comedy is maintained by songs, dances, and
especially by witty dialogues.   These include all kinds of
verbal witticisms and are indulged in by the clowns and
servants as well as by the ladies and their lovers.   In only
one play is there spectacle recalling that of Lyly's plays,
or the "Dream," in the pastoral and woodland scenes of
"As You Like It"; but the place of the action is always
foreign and remote, there are picturesque figures such as
sailors, priests and watchmen, and the mood is high
fantastical.   Though in none are there two stories as distinct as those in the "Merchant," the action is diversified
by the two love matches and by the clash of romantic and
comic incident.

Shakespeare is not inventing the entire play as in "A
Midsummer Night's Dream."   He is drawing his material

from widely different sources and is treating it in conformity with the practice of the stage and especially with profit from his own experience in preceding comedies. The persons so far as their dramatic functions go, the situations, the stage devices, offer nothing more novel than a brother who is a villain, a stupid watch, a humorous drunkard, a girl disguised as a page, a lover who hangs his verses on a tree, a duel, and the rest. But his invention is busy improving and enriching all these. One of the outlaws in the forest becomes the melancholy Jacques; the deception of the egoist steward yields the Malvolio scenes so rich in both fun and characterization; the girls in pages' costume become Viola and Rosalind; the witty dialogue expands into the high comedy of Beatrice and Benedick. Shakespeare's transformation, if it can be analyzed at all, may be described as resulting from the dramatic skill and tact with which he blends the familiar ingredients, from the characterization that makes every one from clown to heroine alive and individual, and from the matchless gift of expression that turns everything into wit and poetry.

"Much Ado About Nothing" is reminiscent of "Love's Labour's Lost." Constable Dull is elaborated into Dogberry, and Rosaline and Biron into Beatrice and Benedick. As in the earlier play, the verbal wit and elegance of the court are contrasted with the absurd twistings of language perpetrated by the clowns, but the witty warfare here is of superior brilliancy. The word-play, so universal in Elizabethan drama, reaches its ne plus ultra in both high and low comedy. There had been many scenes exhibiting stupid watchmen and many others displaying clownish misuse of vocabulary and syntax, but Dogberry surpasses all predecessors and his supreme asininity is even further magnified by the feeble echoes of Verges. The lively verbal contests of Beatrice and Benedick are animated by personality as well as by wit. They are both ready for love when the merry deceit of their friends hastens their inclinations and the suffering of Hero unites them in a common sympathy. Love ripens and enlarges their

natures, and it never dilutes into sentimentality nor dulls
their ever-sparkling wit.

This admirable comedy is joined to an old story of a
villain's scheme to break off by slander the marriage of
an innocent girl. It supplies the main plot and several
stirring scenes, but Shakespeare made little effort to give
it probability or consistency, rather he increased its theatrical unreality. Don John is a villain for the comic opera.
He announces at once that "it must not be denied but I
am a plain-dealing villain," and henceforth he is brought
on the stage only for brief intervals just long enough for
him to explain another step in his preposterous deviltry.
Lest the audience may take this too seriously, Don John's
plot is discovered almost immediately after it has begun.
But, lest the audience should feel too assured of the
happy ending, this is delayed by a series of improbabilities.
The stupid Watch, which has caught the villain's accomplices, is not allowed to tell its story, the maid Margaret is dropped temporarily out of sight, and at the altar
the innocent Hero is denounced in outrageous terms by
her lover, his friend and her own father. A counterplot
is promptly devised to pretend that she is dead, and soon
her father and uncle, who know that she is alive, are
denouncing Claudio and Pedro as her murderers, and the
saddened Claudio is reading verses at her tomb and agreeing to marry her unknown cousin. Except when Hero
faints at the altar, there is no sign of sincere feeling in
all this devising. Indeed, the continuous interest of the
play is in Beatrice and Benedick, and the complications
of the main plot intervene only for fleeting scenes and
brief theatrical effects. Tragedy threatens only for a
moment; the prevailing tone is "much ado about nothing."

Our wonder that Shakespeare should have such a
clumsy story is overcome by our admiration for the skill
with which he makes it serve the larger purpose of the
comedy. It is linked to the rest of the play by constant
dramatic tact and by two capital inventions. The villainy
is discovered by the stupid clowns, who thereby get the

opportunity for a further comic exhibition of their own stupidity. The crucial scene of the denunciation of Hero is saved from its melodrama by its revelation of the true characters of Beatrice and Benedick. Villainy and slander are made to subserve the revelation of fun and irony and beauty in human circumstance and character. The whole play is an example of dramatic irony, for there is scarcely a moment when what is said on the stage does not have a different significance to the audience from what it has to the speaker; but it is difficult to suggest in a brief analysis the continual play of irony in contrasted incongruities and subtle surprises of both plot and character. The smart villains are captured by the stupid Watch, the stupid Watch is prevented from telling by the hasty Leonato, and in consequence he is soon hastily accusing his own daughter. The romantic passion of Claudio dies at the intrusion of doubt, while the scoffer Benedick proves the true lover. Don John is the only plain-spoken person in the play, the wittiest are the most sympathetic, but those wittiest are easily tricked into love. And the irony now and again bursts into fun as when Dogberry desires to be writ down an ass or when Benedick in confident and condescending mood deigns to receive the love of the supposedly enraptured Beatrice.

The translation of romantic drama of situation into comedy of character is accomplished in an instant in the amazing scene at the church. The wedding procession enters with whatever pomp and ceremony the theater may afford. Then Claudio spurns the bride, and denunciation after denunciation overwhelm her frightened protestations of innocence. But, as she swoons, Beatrice springs to her support and challenges the world.

"Why, how now cousin! Wherefore sink ye down?"

Benedick takes his place by her side. The wise friar counsels delay and offers a plan that promises relief. Beatrice and Benedick avow their love, but when he vauntingly asks for a test, her sympathy for Hero breaks forth

in the passionate command, "Kill Claudio." They have
been led to love, partly by deceit, but the slander of Hero
has suddenly revealed the truth to themselves and sum-
moned all that is high and generous in their natures to the
union of hearts. The very spirit of the comedy is embodied in the gracious person of its heroine. Lively,
witty, with just a touch of the shrew, her mind is keenly
aware of the incongruities of existence, but too sensible
to be ensnared by plots and sentimentalities, and the
warmest sympathy commands her will.

"As You Like It" is based on Lodge's novel "Rosalynde" written some ten years earlier, and in the main
follows closely the incidents of that tale of romantic
adventure and sentimental pastoralism. Shakespeare's
choice of this novel for dramatization may have been
influenced by the immediate vogue of certain pastoral
plays. Several of Lyly's had been recently revived, and
an imitation, "The Maid's Metamorphosis" (pr. 1600)
presents Arcadian scenes and much love making. A
lady, banished from court, living as a shepherdess and
transformed into a boy, is sought in vain by her lover,
while the court clown makes fun with the boys of the
shepherd and forester. More direct perhaps in their
influence on Shakespeare were the Sherwood scenes in the
"Downfall and Death of Robert Earl of Huntingdon,"
two Robin Hood plays acted in public and at court and
printed in 1600. These undertake to present on the stage
something of the idyllic charm of the free life in the
greenwood and also the charity and kindness which flourish far from the corruption of the court. Shakespeare
may have had them in mind when he added the scenes of
the outlaws in Arden, (which have no counterpart in the
novel), where as we are told in Act I, Scene 1 "they live
like the old Robin Hood of England . . . and fleet the
time carelessly, as they did in the golden world." At all
events, the stage became an enchanted place like the forest
of "Midsummer Night's Dream" or the island of the
"Tempest" and possessing the double charm of the Sher-

wood of Robin's merry men and the Arcadia of the pastoralists.

Much in both the setting and the action of the play must have seemed familiar on the Elizabethan stage. The substitution of the wrestling match for the more knightly encounter of the romance was perhaps a novelty favouring some athletic actor. But the villainous brother, the usurping duke, the heroine disguised as a page who is loved by another lady, the love at first sight, the final conversion of the bad and marriage of all, these are stock incidents and characters. A lover hangs verses on the trees and a shepherd woos a haughty shepherdess as in other pastorals; horns sound and songs are sung and the deer is brought in as in other Robin Hood plays, and the love affairs of the clowns mock the sentimentalities of the courtly lovers as in all comedies.

But Shakespeare is master where the others are novices. Despite a few pastoral affectations, the style is extraordinarily flexible. Blank verse, lyrics, and prose mingle freely, and each serves its purpose with clarity and beauty. A child today may read this fantasy and scarcely stumble over a word or a phrase. And what a population inhabits this delectable forest, where one

Finds tongues in trees, books in the running brooks,
Sermons in stones, and good in everything,

where the fauna and flora include olives, a lion, a deadly serpent, sheep and greenwood trees! Here are gentlemen outlaws, real rustics, pastoral shepherds, sweet singers, lovers and ladies and, as two chief ministers to the queen of wit, Jacques and Touchstone. Jacques belongs to a type that the Elizabethans were fond of discussing, he is of the melancholy humour, and a gentle malcontent. He sees the world as nearly if not quite out of joint, and thanks Heaven that he was not born to set it right. Though he takes no part in the action save to promote the nuptials of Touchstone, his sapient and ironic wit affords a welcome divertisement from the love-making and charity

that prevail in the forest. He is rather sharply chidden
as an immoral idler by both Rosalind and the Duke, but
he takes himself off cheerfully to the religious retreat
where his humour should enliven the minds of the con-
vertites. Touchstone is the prince of clowns and jesters,
having greater resources of wit than any of the others
and a far wider range for the bolts that he shoots from
his vantage ground of irresponsibility. His mirth rustles
like a delightful breeze through the forest, now caressing
the moping Jacques, and now his own Audrey, and leaving
nobody but William disconsolate.

But the spirit of this comedy like that of "Much Ado"
is best expressed in its heroine. Its laughter and irony
and beauty are hers. The familiar disguise becomes a
means for the most charming and playful irony. She
speaks the simple truth and deceives father, Orlando and
Phoebe. She abounds in spirit, initiative and energy, yet
she has a feminine quickness and sensitiveness of emotion.
Whatever there is of mirth or sorrow, she shares, and is
as eager with her raillery as with her tears. She does not
say the wittiest or wisest or most beautiful things in the
play, yet there is no doubt that she deserves all superlatives. She rivals Beatrice in vitality and fascination, and
she is better supported. No queen ever reigned over a
more obedient court. Jacques and Touchstone with their
irony and wit complement her swift joyfulness. The
serene wisdom of the Duke, the songs of the foresters, the
ardors of Orlando, the responsiveness of Celia and the
sweet charity of Arden frame the beauty of "heavenly
Rosalind."

"Twelfth Night," as has often been observed, is re-
capitulatory of the earlier comedies. Shakespeare again
employs the Latin plot of the indistinguishable twins and
the business of the purse which he had used in the
"Comedy of Errors." The heroine disguised as a boy
and loved by another woman, had appeared in "As You
Like It" as well as in Greene's "James IV." A drunken
knight and a silly gull had been exhibited in Falstaff and

Shallow. Even the trick on Malvolio is similar to that practised on Benedick and Beatrice. The friendship between Sebastian and Antonio, love at first sight, a sudden change from one love to another, the shipwreck, and the witty clown, all have their parallels in his earlier plays, and were indeed familiar on the stage. Whatever Shakespeare took from "Gl'Ingannati" or "Apolonius and Silla" or a lost play on the same theme as these, he freely remoulded this material in accord with his own practice in romantic comedy.

Illyria by the sea is a delightful place for a shipwreck. It is just as enchanting as the Forest of Arden and it has more cakes and ale. Instead of shepherds we encounter Sir Toby and Maria. There is not a sober moment while either is on the stage. The wit cannot be better than in "Much Ado" and "As You Like It" but it runs a little faster and conspires more readily for action. It never pauses for a set speech, it is always on tiptoe for sport— a dance, a catch or the famous plot on Malvolio or the duel between Viola and Aguecheek. Malvolio is the sober, efficient, administrative egoist, the essence of everything that is undesirable in the land of romance. And he is more difficult to cure than the villains who sometimes lose themselves there. They can be converted and led safely into matrimony. Modern actors and critics are appreciative of his merits, but there is no one in Illyria who wants to marry him. It is a wonder that the sea air did not drive him really mad, and one has little real hope that the sportful malice which he suffered could rather pluck on his laughter than revenge.

But in the play, wit and laughter when at their height suddenly yield place to sentiment and song. Orsino sighs and Viola sighs and Olivia sighs and Feste sings. Even Sir Toby both sighs and sings. And how charming is the love-making. Viola is less self-reliant than Portia, Beatrice or Rosalind but not less lovable or less humorous. She does not dominate the scene as do they; her wistfulness must be matched to Maria's exuberance if the

ladies are to embody the spirit of the play, but in no other
heroine are girlish fun and tenderness so exquisitely
united. All sorts of contrarieties are blended through the
delicate characterization and the matchless style. Always
subservient to dramatic purpose, never attempting display
or prolonging an opportunity, the words suit themselves
to character, mood or action in faultless harmony. Where
else are drinking scenes so delightful and so innocent?
Verse and prose mingle freely; roistering snatch, plaintive
melody, pun and quibble, each serves the moment's need
of pathos or fun, and all is without a taint of coarseness.
There is not a flaw in the unison of joy and merriment.

"Twelfth Night" is the fairest of all the type, the most
delightful of the romantic comedies—unless you chance
to prefer another. It is the very flower and fragrance
of that gay-hearted spirit which we have been pursuing as
it first gathered force from old story and then danced
lightly over the Elizabethan stage. Shakespeare himself
lost it after "Twelfth Night" and when he regained it
again ten years later in "The Winter's Tale" and "The
Tempest," it had aged and changed a trifle. But no one
can think of the revels of Viola and Feste only as a play
or as a stage in a dramatic development. Even for the
apprentices standing in the dirty pit of the Globe, the
bare stage and the beruffed actors must have been trans-
figured; and over that atmosphere laden with oaths and
tobacco new and lovely dreams must have spread their
dainty illusions. As we read the play today how easily
we arrive at the land of romance. The speeches of
Theseus and Hippolyta transfer us to fairyland; Bassanio and Antonio meet and we are in the Venice of
friendship and love; and here the opening words of
Orsino waft us to the realms of summer:

If music be the food of love, play on!

Music is breathing o'er a bank of violets. We forget
who we are and where we came from. All the hardness
fades out of the world. Within a few minutes we are

experiencing all the pleasure of a morning in June, the happiness of its noon-tide, and the faint melancholy of the moonlight. You feel physically larger and better looking and morally sweeter. Life grows very easy, and the joy of living brisk but not proselyting. All the pleasant easy things you ever did come to your mind, your friends seem to be changing for the better without your assistance, and your own many virtues dance amiably to the music. You feel that it is no trouble to be good and that everything and nearly everybody is beautiful.

There are many countries in the great continent of romance, but the most entrancing is not that of the wonderful, mysterious, supernatural and impossible, nor that of great adventures and perilous escapes. It is a land where the sky is the one Bassanio and Portia knew, where the weather is that of the Forest of Arden, and the nights those by which Jessica and Juliet were wooed and Titania and Oberon danced. It is Shakespeare's realm of romance, bounded on one side by the land of fun, not far removed from the republic of reality, and entirely surrounded by poetry.

There are only three industries in this land, making love, making songs, and making jests. And they make them all to perfection. But it is not permitted to do any of these things too seriously or too long. Some puritans like Malvolio ask for more solemnity and dare to suggest that the last song in "Twelfth Night" is silly, the puns of Feste tedious, and that Viola's love is not up to the twentieth century standard—but such critics have never been shipwrecked on Illyria or faced the lions of Arden. In Shakespeare's romance, one doesn't listen to sermons except in stones, or study lessons save in the running brooks, or even try to look wise. There one would liefer be a Brownist than a politician, and a puritan is likely to have to fight Sir Andrew Aguecheek. There they simply remember the three things to do and let themselves go. Yet they never go wrong. There you can sing all day without growing hoarse, make jokes without being

tedious, and make love all the year round without breaking a heart. Only all these together are better than either
separately. It is well to interrupt the love-making with a
little joking, and the joking with a little music, and per-
chance some cakes and ale, and then back to love again.

People look strangely there, your dearest friends lose
their faults, little weaknesses disappear, all the ladies are
very, very beautiful. Everyone has the most charming
manners, and everyone grows better the longer he stays.
The air has a moral tonic, the sun—it is a very wonderful
sun which always shines—bleaches the freckles out of the
moral complexion; everyone is fair and rosy and bright-
eyed.

A few diseased persons are brought over to be cured—
sick of slow wits or self-love or too much moralizing,
or boiled to death in melancholy—and these prove the
best company in the world—i.e., when you have them safe
in the land of romance. Anywhere else they would be
bores, insufferable, but here the climate brings out their
funny side, the warm breeze from the south sets them
gambolling. They are good at kickshaws. Folly, vanity,
self-esteem make up your masques and pageants. There
is much matter for a May morning, and all are born
under Taurus. When you are tired of the gambols you
can sit out a dance with the most charming company in
the world, with Viola, Beatrice or Rosalind.

Or, if you find you are boring them, you can retire
to the shade and listen to the music of "the spinsters and
the knitters in the sun." There is time for rest and contemplation, the sheep need no watching from the
shepherd—he may lie on his back and play his pipe to his
heart's content. Nobody believes in the strenuous life
there. They have few organizations or societies—only
that ancient and honourable organization of which Dogberry and Verges are the excellent officers, and the society
of the royal foresters of Arden. "There is no clock in
the forest." You may stop work when you will or never
begin, your wages are paid just the same. Everyone—

good or bad, idle or diligent, comes off finely before the play is over. There are no reforms there, or if there are any, they fare hardly, for Sir Toby is chairman of the committee on reform, and all the delegations of prominent citizens in the world and all the doctrinaires would not move him one inch further toward reform than did Malvolio. But in this land it is worth while to bask in the sunshine and simply watch the clouds roll by; that painless operation will fill your soul with poetry and a consciousness of duty well done. For in Illyria the very clouds are lovely fancies, and there it is fancy and not money that buys cakes and ale and wins beautiful brides and in general makes the world go round.

The only fault with this land of romance is that you can't stay there forever. It is no great stretch like the land of the "Faery Queen" or that of Walter Scott's romances, it is only a small patch of forest and field, of terrace and lawn,—a sort of pleasure ground. You can picnic there for a day and then you must back to the land of wind and rain.

> With hey ho, the wind and the rain
> But that's all one, our play is done—
> For the rain, it raineth every day!

But after we are back in the humdrum world, who can forget the music and mirth and maidens of that picnic in romance? We have a long journey yet to go through several thousand comedies, some of which make rather dreary weather. But even the brightest have not the sunshine of Illyria.

CHAPTER VII

SHAKESPEARE: THE LATER COMEDIES

THE plays considered in the last chapter include all of Shakespeare's comedies written before 1600 with the exception of the Falstaff plays. They represent the development of romantic comedy in his hands and the culmination of its general Elizabethan evolution. In order to bring together for discussion the remainder of Shakespeare's comedies, it is necessary to depart somewhat from either a chronological or a logical scheme. They fall into three groups, representing different periods and linking themselves with different forms and fashions of drama.

Plays based on chronicles of English history were very popular on the stage from 1588 to 1603, from the Armada to the death of Elizabeth. In this chapter we may glance at this fashion so far as it turned to comedy, and then consider its culmination in the series of Falstaff plays written between 1597 and 1601, 1 and 2 "Henry IV," "Henry V" and "The Merry Wives of Windsor." These plays were contemporaneous with the last of the romantic comedies, but already there was a marked movement on the stage toward realism under the leadership of Ben Jonson. The full discussion of this movement, lasting from 1598 to 1608, must be postponed until the next chapter, but here we can consider the comedies and quasi-comedies written by Shakespeare during these years and to some degree under the influence of the prevailing fashion for realism and satire, "Measure for Measure," "All's Well That Ends Well," and "Troilus and Cressida." By 1608 the pendulum had turned and was swinging back to romance with new impetus because of the popular success of the plays of Beaumont and Fletcher. A discussion of their plays again must be postponed to a subsequent chapter, but here we must consider Shakespeare's return to romance in "Cymbeline," perhaps following the fashion which the younger writers had set, and then adapting it into the original and final "Winter's Tale" and "Tempest."

I

One of the many extraordinary things about the Elizabethan drama is its presentation of history. In spite of the advance in education there has never been since then an audience so eager for historical information that it could support the Shakespearian histories, English and Roman, that began with "Henry VI" and ended with "Coriolanus." The circumstances, however, that led to this Elizabethan enthusiasm are easy to trace. The popularization of learning after the invention of printing resulted in the compiling of various chronicles of English history and the translation of the classical historians and biographers. To these narratives the early dramatists naturally turned in their search for material. The theme of the fall of princes was highly recommended for tragedy by both medieval and humanistic precept, and the chronicles of English kings furnished abundant and varied incident for use on the stage. The pomp of courts and especially the battle scenes provided spectacle. For the Elizabethan play, a fight of some sort was as indispensable as galloping horses in our moving pictures, and of all fights, a pitched field with contending armies seems to have carried the palm. Then, the increasing national consciousness aroused by the struggle with Spain demanded an expression of patriotism on the stage and maintained the chronicle play in great popularity from the time of the defeat of the Armada until the lessening of national fervor toward the end of Elizabeth's reign.

From the beginning, the historical play followed two methods. It might be moulded to one of the formulas of tragedy, the Senecan, as in "Gorboduc," or the Kydian, as in the "True Tragedy of Richard Duke of York," or the Marlowean, as in "Edward II" or "Richard III." Or it might translate the narrative chronicle with little regard to the requirements of dramatic fable, mixing comic and heroic and retaining the epic or chronicle pattern of the narrative of a reign. Peele's "Edward I" is an example of such a medley of battle, magic, Robin Hood scenes and clownishness. A single reign might be the subject of a sequence of plays, whether epic or tragic in treatment, so that occasionally a play is a sequel relying in some degree on the audience's acquaintance with its predecessor. According to either method, moreover, there was a peculiar stimulus to characterization. The chronicle afforded not only a superabundance of incident but considerable discussion of the characters of the monarchs and statesmen. The dramatist was incited to interpret history in terms of biography and to make his spectacle significant by a study of the conflict of human motives.

Even the tragedies indulged in considerable comic relief. This usually took the form either of episodes displaying the clownishness of the common people, as in the Cade scenes in "1 Henry VI," or of humorous characterization of one of the chief actors, as in the part of Faulconbridge created in the old "Troublesome Reign" and adapted by Shakespeare in his "King John." The conception, indeed, of a popular hero who was not contemptuous of but was hale-fellow-well-met with the common people, won considerable favour from both playwrights and public. The epic method of treatment offered but little more chance for a development into comedy than did the tragic, since in either case wars and battles made up the action, and heroism and patriotism were the themes. Nevertheless, even in the days of the Armada, the chronicle play sometimes took a comic cast. In the old "King Leir" the tragic situations are resolved into a happy ending. In the "Famous Victories of Henry V," the glorious battles of a popular hero are mingled with the comic enterprises of a "lusty juventus." Among the large number of chronicle plays that are lost, such a development toward comedy doubtless received some additions, but, so far as we know, nothing that guided the art of Shakespeare.

After Marlowe, indeed, there was little to guide Shakespeare in the dramatization of the English chronicles. Perhaps his earliest dramatic work was on the "First Part of Henry VI," and he supplemented this with a series of three plays, in Marlowean style, culminating with the tragic downfall of the arch-villain "Richard III" and the triumph of the Tudors. This tetralogy was followed by "Richard II," which opened the way to another series glorifying the hero of Agincourt. An epic rather than tragic plan was natural, and the old play "The Famous Victories" seems responsible for the definite turn to comedy. That rude piece supplied in rough dramatic form an interesting series of incidents—the prince's association with low companions, his share in a highway robbery, his frequenting the Eastcheap tavern, the visit there by the sheriff, the laments of the king over his prodigal son, the stealing of the crown, and the final reconciliation between father and son. In Sir John Oldcastle, Gadshill, Poins and the hostess of the old play there were hints for Falstaff and his associates.

"The First Part of Henry IV" is magnificent in dramatic construction as well as in characterization and style. The serious action is the rebellion of the Percies ending in the defeat at Shrewsbury, and history is altered so that Hotspur becomes the youthful rival of Prince Hal. The comedy is furnished by the intercourse of the prince with Falstaff and other tavern companions. Prince Hal is the pivot of both actions, the cause of much anxiety to the king, but the victor over Hotspur and the rebels, and he is also the mainspring of all the jests in the tavern and the inciter of Falstaff to the height of his wit. His rival in honour, Hotspur, is endowed with a lively humour, and his tavern companion Falstaff takes part in campaign and battle. The serious and comic interests are nicely balanced, and each is enlivened by diversified action and contrasts of character.

The play begins with a scene at court in which Hotspur's success and incipient rebellion are revealed and the king contrasts "this theme of Honour's tongue" with his own son's riot and dishonour. The next scene shows us the prince and Falstaff and discloses the plan of Poins for the highway robbery and the trick on the fat knight. In the third scene we are back at court again listening to the defiances of the rebels and to Hotspur's vaunt, "To pluck bright Honour from the pale-faced moon." So the scenes go on alternating from the heroic to the comic, from court and camp to tavern, until both strains come to a climax in the battle-field of the fifth act. The opening scene with the exchange of defiances and the prince's challenge to Hotspur closes with Falstaff's renunciation of honour. Amid the confusion and clashes of the battle, the prince discovers the bottle of sack in Falstaff's pistol case. In the culminating action the prince kills Hotspur, Falstaff feigns death before the doughty Douglas and later recovers after the fighting is over and—the last word in the union of the heroic and comic—bears in the body of the dead Hotspur as his trophy.

Overflowing as is the wit of Falstaff, it is always linked to the person of Prince Hal, and it is exhibited in dramatic action through the ever memorable scenes on Gadshill, in the tavern and on the field of honour. Brilliant as are the pictures of the historical persons and events, of the King, Glendower, Worcester, Prince John, the Sheriff, Hotspur and Kate, they too belong to the action that frames itself about Prince Hal and Falstaff. The stage has never seen such another union of history and romance and comedy. For anything in literature comparable to it we must wait for the novels of Walter Scott.

Falstaff is more than a part in a brilliant comedy, he is the greatest of comic creations. He lives not merely in stage impersonation but in phrase and word. All that can possibly be said about him has been said, yet every time one reads his lines, one is moved to give some expression to the fresh pleasure one receives. Gross, drunken, a liar, sensualist and coward, he is the summation of butts and braggarts and other stage targets of laughter, yet the mirth that he arouses is never that of ridicule alone. His unfailing wit is his sure defence. His intellectual alertness and his resources of invention can always turn the laugh where they will. And this wit is always without malice and is employed generously at his own expense. This humorous view both of life and of himself, this quickness to observe and to enjoy their incongruities exalts him above all jesters. Instead of the butt of laughter he becomes its master. Humour for him is a philosophy. As he struts before his tiny page, "like a sow that hath overwhelm'd all her litter but one," he meditates on his comprehensiveness as a comic character, "The brain of this foolish-compounded clay, man, is not able to invent anything that intends to laughter more than I invent, or is invented on me. I am not only witty in myself, but the cause that wit is in other men."

Such humour disarms criticism of his immoralities. And they are completely forgotten when he persuades us to join with him whole-heartedly in the great humorous game of make-believe. His vices are scarcely less matters of pretense than his assumed virtues. He lies with the same zest of make-believe that he repents, he feigns cowardice as readily as bravery, and even his reckoning of his consumption of sack is open to suspicion. He knows and he loves the world, the flesh and the devil, but he will not treat them seriously or permit us to do so. All this making fun out of life is for his own relish but also for others' enjoyment. He does not ask us to practise or to forgive his vices but to share his laughter.

It is easiest to forget his sins when, as in Part One, he is constantly ministering to the prince's amusement. In Part Two, there is undoubtedly more difficulty in subduing the moral sense to the spirit of mirth. There

Falstaff is displayed as exercising his genius not as jester
to the prince but for his own profit at the expense of
others. His companions, Pistol and Doll Tearsheet, are
but scurvy substitutes for the prince and Poins. His wit
is less spontaneous, he seems conscious that he has a reputation to sustain. Yet his wit is still unfailing, enormous,
illuminating the absurd satellites that circle in its orbit—
Mistress Quickly, Shallow and Silence. In "The Merry
Wives" he is forced into ridiculous situations and is given
still less chance to excite our sympathy, but his talk is still
witness to his extraordinary gifts. There is nothing like
him in literature unless in Rabelais, and there is nothing
like him in life, for he is the result of a wide experience
with human fact, translated, magnified and revealed
through the imagination of a great humorist.

Part Two of "Henry IV" is inferior to Part One in
construction and dramatic vigour as well as in the characterization of Falstaff. The last years of the reign,
engrossed by the prolonged illness of the king, are not
easily dramatized; the growing responsibilities of the
prince necessitate his separation from the comic action.
The conclusion of the play with the succession of the prince
to the throne and the harsh dismissal of Falstaff is not
quite in the spirit of comedy. But the inferiority is felt
only in comparison to the matchless First Part, for here
as there the union of realistic comedy and historical drama
is consummated with amazing success.

A third play presenting English Harry and Sir John
as rivals of interest was a task that Shakespeare refused.
He preferred to give the hero of Agincourt the center of
the stage and to kill off Falstaff, happily choosing Mistress
Quickly and not the new king as his eulogist. "Henry V"
in consequence relies for its interest on the historical rather
than the comic scenes and focuses that interest upon the
hero. Nevertheless, the battle scenes and orations have
much comic relief, and the play ends, not with the
triumphant return to London, but with the bluff and
humorous wooing of the French princess. As in the two

earlier plays, the method is that of a close interweaving of the serious and the comic interest.

The three plays constitute a type that has few representatives outside of Shakespeare even in his own day, and none since. Polonius might have hesitated whether to call it comical history or historical comedy. It is mainly the supremacy of the humorous characterization in Falstaff that removes the plays from the general category of epic chronicle-histories and places them amongst the greatest of our comedies. It is difficult to conceive the type revived in our theater today, exhibiting a Cromwell or Washington accompanied by "a fellow of infinite jest, of most excellent fancy," or even to imagine heroic history and low comedy combined as they are in "Henry V"—the winter in Valley Forge, the crossing the Delaware and Cornwallis' surrender, the Declaration of Independence and the Farewell Address mingled with roystering soldiers, dancing pickaninnies and Lafayette wooing a Yankee maiden in broken English. Mr. Drinkwater's versions of historical biography, for example, shrink from such comedy and recall rather the repetitive moralities, though he does give General Lee's melancholy meditations a banjo accompaniment. But in moving pictures the presentation of history is felt to need some comic relief, and perhaps we may yet see historical plays in which any moral or partisan propaganda will find a setting in rich characterization and racy comedy.

"The Merry Wives of Windsor" belongs to a different type, that of the comedy of intrigue, presenting domestic manners and eccentric characters. This was a not uncommon form of comedy at the time the play was written, and various companion pieces could be found for it in the work of Marston, Chapman and Jonson, perhaps best of all in the lively comedy on which the three collaborated, "Eastward Ho." The tradition that the play was written in a fortnight upon the command of the Queen to make Falstaff in love, is supported by the general use of prose and by the carelessness in maintaining consistency in characterization. The plot is the usual one of tricks. Falstaff is gulled three times; the first two he is the guller gulled, the third provides also for the elopement of the youthful heroine. Ford, the jealous husband, comes in for some of the gulling, and the Welsh priest, the French doctor, Justice Shallow and the booby wooer add to the amusement. All this makes a delightful and effective play, which has proved more adaptable to the changing theater than have the two earlier and greater comedies of Falstaff.

II

The three plays, "Measure for Measure," "All's Well That Ends Well," and "Troilus and Cressida," do not belong to any definite type but are grouped together because they were probably written within a year or two of one another and because they possess some qualities in common. All exhibit the baser side of sexual passion, all look upon life in a satirical rather than a merry humour, and all are confused in structure, uneven in style, and constrained rather than spontaneous in manner. Two present the complication rather common in Elizabethan drama, but unpleasant to modern taste, in which a wife secretly takes the place of another woman in her husband's embraces.

"Troilus and Cressida" was inserted in the Folio between the tragedies and histories and can scarcely be considered as a comedy. It follows the epic method of a history play diversifying the combats and quarrels of the Trojan war with the scurrility of Thersites and the wiles of Pandarus and the false Cressid. In its present form it was scarcely fitted for presentation on the Elizabethan stage and has rarely been acted since then. "All's Well" is another of Shakespeare's failures. It tells a medieval story of a wife who wins a husband by meeting certain apparently impossible tests. Its sentiment is never made quite delightful, in spite of Helena's charm, and its fun centers on the contemptible Parolles. The play shows two different styles, but we can only guess when it was begun and when it was rewritten. It seems an unfortunate combination of the methods of "The Two Gentlemen of Verona" and of "Measure for Measure."

This last play bears many resemblances to its contemporary drama. Like Marston's satirical tragicomedy "The Malcontent," it uses a disguised duke who spies out the iniquities of his city. Like the underplot of Heywood's "A Woman Killed with Kindness," it presents the casuistical but theatrical problem, shall a sister sacrifice her honour to save her brother's life. Like the current comedies of Middleton and others, it exposes the brothels of a city and has its fun with bawds and panders. Shakespeare would seem to be experimenting in the manner of satirical and realistic comedy of the day, but without becoming absorbed either in the exposure or in the ridicule of vice. The play is redeemed both for the stage and the closet by the character of Isabella. But her virtues and Angelo's self-deception and Claudio's cowardice are themes given an emphasis suitable for tragedy or melodrama rather than for a comedy ending in four marriages and a general amnesty. The clumsy plot almost forbids any interest in the outcome, for the disguised duke manifestly holds all the actors in his power, and both the agonies and the fooleries might be ended at any moment on his command instead of awaiting the needlessly long and explanatory fifth act.

A fourth play may be considered here, "Pericles." It resembles "Measure for Measure" in presenting an idealized heroine against a background of sexual iniquity, in the trial of the heroine's chastity and in the brothel scenes; but the happy reconciliation of the fifth act is more like that of "The Winter's Tale." Shakespeare's hand cannot be discovered in the first two acts, and his share may have been merely rewriting, about 1608, the conclusion of a much earlier play. "Pericles" was very popular in its own day but was often held up to scorn by the more judicious. Ben Jonson speaks of "some mouldy tale like

Pericles," and he was warned by a critic that certain parts
of his own "New Inn" "do displease as deep as Pericles."
It belongs to the class of plays of strange and marvellous
adventures, of which Rowley's "Travels of Three
Brothers" is a contemporary example. The title page of
the 1609 quarto sets forth the plot "With the true Relation of the whole Historie, adventures, and fortunes of
the said Prince; As also, The no lesse strange and worthy
accidents, in the Birth and Life of his Daughter Mariana."
The old-fashioned technic, with Gower as presenter and
chorus, loosely connected situations and dumb shows, is
little like that of the romances, but the story of Mariana
seems a precursor to their tales of marvellous adventure
and happy reunion.

The four plays just considered were written during the
years when Shakespeare was mainly occupied by the great
series of tragedies that began with "Julius Caesar" and
"Hamlet" and ended about 1608 with "Antony and Cleopatra" and "Coriolanus." No one of the four comedies
shows him nearly at his best or marks out any course
that he afterwards was to follow. Though manifestly
taking suggestions from current types and fashions, they
do not reveal any sure inspiration. From such tentative
and uncertain excursions into comedy, it is a relief to come
to three plays that mark the close of his career and a
return to romance.

III

"Cymbeline," "The Winter's Tale," and "The Tempest" were written within the years 1609-11, "Cymbeline"
preceding the other two. They resemble in some ways
the earlier romantic comedies, but "Cymbeline" and "The
Winter's Tale" give a more pronounced development to
the tragic interest. In each, idealized womanhood is submitted to all sorts of tragic trials and misfortunes and the
outcome is kept uncertain until the final dénouement. In
contrast to the tragic entanglements and court intrigue,
each play takes its heroine far from court to share in

simple idyllic scenes. In "Cymbeline," Imogen shares the natural life of her brothers in the cave; in "The Winter's Tale" Perdita is brought up among the shepherds, and the idyl usurps the last two acts. In "The Tempest," where the tragic entanglements have preceded the opening of the play, the idyl of Ferdinand and Isabella develops among the wonders of the enchanted island. In all three plays much effort is spent in multiplying effective situations and in postponing and heightening the happy ending. The whole of "The Tempest" may be said to be an expanded dénouement.

The qualities that differentiate these plays from any others by Shakespeare are in general those that characterize the romantic plays with which Beaumont and Fletcher were winning an early fame in the half dozen years after 1606. I have elsewhere discussed at length the evidence that this new success of these brilliant dramatists led Shakespeare to adopt their materials and methods. In the case of "Cymbeline" he is closest to their type of play and seems to be deriving direct suggestions from their popular "Philaster." Once started again on romance, Shakespeare moulded the new type and technic to his own purpose. The rapidly succeeding and melodramatic situations of the opening acts of "The Winter's Tale" are not unlike those of a Beaumont and Fletcher romance, but the idyllic scenes with the shepherds and the final reconciliation show Shakespeare again at the height of his powers. In "The Tempest," his invention is free and transcendent.

In "Cymbeline" there is no low comedy, in "The Winter's Tale," the happy invention of Autolycus adds another to Shakespeare's great comic characters, and in "The Tempest" drunken boors provide companions and foils for the monster of the island. But in none of the plays do the comic scenes take as large a part as in "Twelfth Night" or "Much Ado," and in none are fun and merriment so unrestrained. The heroines are not witty, they do not represent the spirit of raillery and mirth as do

Beatrice and Rosalind. The tragic adventures which
Imogen and Hermione encounter give them little opportunity for nonsense. They are kept busy exhibiting nobler
qualities. They and the more lightly sketched Perdita
and Miranda are idealizations of all that is noble and
loyal in womanhood, but they are not very individual or
much gifted with humour. Indeed, the contrast between
good and evil, conspiracy and loyalty, baseness and idealized sentiment is too strong for comedy as Shakespeare
has hitherto understood it. Like several of the plays of
Beaumont and Fletcher, these three romances are tragicomedies, a type that was coming to be distinctly
recognized, and, under the initiative given it by Beaumont
and Fletcher, was destined to play a large part in the
subsequent drama. In the contrast between tragic and
idyllic, in the elaboration of the happy ending, and in the
idealization of the heroine, Shakespeare's plays do not
greatly differ from theirs. But in theirs the contrast
of lust and sentiment results mainly in effective stage-
situations, and the idealization of women finds its end in
the poetical decoration. In Shakespeare this form of
tragicomedy becomes the means of expressing a serene
and tolerant view of human existence. The multiplied
stage situations end in reconciliation and reunion. The
idealized women seem to assure us of the victory of spirit
over flesh and circumstance. The dreams of life and its
final sleep are to be viewed with the tranquillity of a
Prospero.

Of the three plays, "Cymbeline" is the least a comedy
and most like the romances of Beaumont and Fletcher.
The plot and characters offer some close resemblances to
those of "Philaster." The pompous king, the wicked
woman, the idealized heroine, the sentimental and jealous
lover, and the boorish claimant to the throne have similar
parts in the two plays. Shakespeare, in imitation of
Beaumont and Fletcher, appears to be straining after
startling situations and a complicated dénouement, but
without much spontaneity. At all events, in spite of tell-

ing situations, the play is tedious on the stage. Only in the idyllic scenes and in the character of Imogen, does Shakespeare show signs of a new conception of romance. Even more than in "Philaster," the simple life is contrasted with court corruption, and the idyl is now placed not among Arcadian shepherds but in the natural and primitive life of the wilderness, perhaps a forecast of the contrast of civilization and primitive society that was to be a theme of "The Tempest."

"The Winter's Tale" is based on a popular romance by Greene, "Pandosto," altered so that the lives of both king and queen are spared and they are finally reunited. The first three acts are tragedy of a theatrical and improbable style, ending with the devouring of Antigonus by a bear and the supposed deaths of Hermione and Perdita. The remaining two acts are really a second play, sixteen years later in time and presenting the idyl and the reunion. In the fourth act we are again in Shakespeare's own land of romance, accompanied by a merry rascal and jogging on the foot-path way to the sheep-shearing festival, where there are flowers and songs and dances and the youthful lovers prove true to each other and Autolycus finds a profitable market. In that happy land reality and fancy are again playmates, and both roguery and sentiment win their games. In the last act we are back at court and ready for the surprising dénouement. Leontes of the furious jealousy has been deeply penitent for sixteen years. Hermione, who during that time has kept herself hidden and unforgiving, is now revealed as a statue coming to life. Improbabilities are forgotten in this effective scene which leads to happy reconciliation.

"The Tempest" is manifestly a spectacular play. The stage interest lies very little in any conflict of persons or events, for the power of Prospero is too mighty to leave opposition any chance of success. The wrongs that he has suffered are related and not enacted, and the plot, which may have been furnished by some Italian novella, survives only in the actions of the bewildered courtiers.

Shakespeare's play is an expansion of the happy dénouement, and in place of tragic action it was necessary to
supply spectacle for the stage interest. Pamphlets
recounting the strange adventures and miraculous escape
of a ship-wreck in the Bermudas suggested some details
and perhaps the general scheme of an enchanted island,
inhabited only by the spirits, their master, a magician, and
his daughter, who has never seen a man. Prospero, Ariel
and Caliban gave novelty and spectacle enough, but
Shakespeare also added pageantry after the style of the
court masques, which had become very elaborate and
fashionable during the early years of the reign of James I.
The betrothal of the lovers in the fourth act is celebrated by a masque in the approved style, the "insubstan-
tial pageant" that excites Prospero's most famous reflection on life. The "strange shapes" that bring in the
banquet and "with mocks and mows" remove it, and the
"divers Spirits in the shape of dogs and hounds" seem to
have been suggested by the new and popular antimasques,
grotesque and antic dances performed by the professional
actors. Just as in "A Midsummer Night's Dream"
Shakespeare turned to the court entertainments performed
by children actors, so here he is drawing from the elaborate and costly masques at the court of James I for the
stage realization of his fantasy.

But even as a stage performance the play was more
than spectacle. If Prospero, Ferdinand and the rest of
the humans have their tragicomedies, so do Ariel and
Caliban. The scene that begins with Caliban's introduction to Trinculo and Stephano and ends with his song of
freedom, though not the most convivial, is certainly the
most amazing of all drunken scenes. The low comedy
parts, like everything else on the island, have been transformed as by a miracle. And the master of sports, the
agent in all the deceptions, is no tricky servant or clever
jester, but a spirit of the air, a singing Ariel, careless of
human worries and, like Caliban, desiring only his freedom. Modern thought has discerned in these creatures

allegories and prophecies that Shakespeare could not have known; but surely he, like everyone since, must have had moments of delight mingled with wonder at these children of his genius.   Yet he seems to have laboured under various artistic impulses, and the style is often curiously involved.   From his own earlier plays he found examples for the shipwreck, the drunken boors, the talkative old man and the youthful lovers; and for some reason he took special pains to set forth all the marvellous happenings in strict adherence to Aristotle's unities of time and place.

Whatever the processes of his creative work, all was harmonized in the final result.   The improbable and supernatural yield to the magic of Shakespeare's invention.   A spirit of the air and a monster half beast and half human seem as veritable as the wise magician who is master alike of nature and of his own soul.   The spectacle, however brilliant, is dimmed by the verse and characterization.   Ariel lives in his songs, not in his stage pranks, and Prospero in his lofty utterance, not in his theatrical magic.   The servant-monster whom Jonson thought an appeal to the vulgar, discloses new significance as with added knowledge each new generation compares civilization and barbarism.   Comedy, spectacle and romance blend in a mood of admiration and delight, inviting us to share Miranda's wonder.

> O brave new world,
> That has such people in't!

IV

In our survey of Shakespeare's comedies we have been reminded occasionally that his environment must be given some credit for offering the opportunities for such a free range of the comic spirit.   His stage permitted almost any story to be acted but required that the spoken word should abundantly supplement its scanty scene.   His audience welcomed improbabilities and was careless of precise exposition or consistency.   His fellow dramatists were poets as well as playwrights, eager to create beauty as well as entertainment, unregardful of rule and delighting in individuality. But these virtues of freedom were accompanied by the corresponding defects. The bare stage demanded as much spectacle and sensationalism as possible. An illiterate audience standing for hours in the pit had to be amused. The busy rivalry of the dramatists produced many new plays hastily written, changing from time to time with passing fashion or fresh success. Shakespeare's genius was bound by these conditions. Yet, in the comedies, there is astonishingly little stooping to the vulgar. There is almost no horse-play. The farcical "Taming of the Shrew" is the only one that can be called boisterous. There is comparatively little indecency, and in many of the plays there is none. So far do they transcend their own theater that they can be acted by school-girls today. Their Elizabethan failing that is most often instanced as undesirable is their word-play. Unquestionably this is open to, objection both as to quantity and quality. It persists even in the latest plays and it furnishes the only lines that one might wish to blot in "The Tempest." But this liking for puns and quibbles is scarcely separable from that intense interest and delight in words which characterizes both Shakespeare's genius and the taste of his time. Without this "dallying with phraseology" the sixteenth century would have had no poetic drama.

In his relations to contemporary dramatists, so far as types of comedy are concerned, Shakespeare has appeared as an adapter and improver rather than as an innovator or inventor. He sometimes followed closely a current model, and then, usually after experimentation, succeeded in transforming it. We have traced especially his developments of romantic comedy, historical comedy and romantic tragicomedy. In other cases, as in "The Comedy of Errors" an example of Plautian imitation, and "Merry Wives," an example of the domestic comedy of intrigue, he was content to give the form but a single trial. But there were numerous other types having many Elizabethan representatives that did not arouse his interest. No play of his can in any strictness be termed a comedy of manners. No play has for its chief purpose satire. He adopted none of the various aims of realistic comedy. There are none which give, as do Middleton's, a vivid reproduction of London life; none based on an analysis of contemporary "humours" or personal characteristics, as are Jonson's; and none that range from individuals to social conditions and problems. Though in every play he is drawing from his observation of real life and depicting manners and men as he knew them, he never seeks primarily a presentation or a criticism of the life of his time. He is neither a realist nor a propagandist. No play definitely offers a thesis or a theory or an analysis or a sermon.

Shakespeare's comedies are stories, drawn from romance or history, laid in past times or foreign places. No effort is spared to make those stories entertaining and amusing on the stage, but little heed is given to dress them in a consistency and probability that will bear a close comparison with actuality. The hundreds of persons so lifelike and human, and the thousands of speeches with their accent of reality, are all framed in events and places that quite remove them from any direct connection with the audience's experience. Occasionally, as in "Merry Wives" and "Measure for Measure," the past time or the foreign scene is a rather thin disguise, but in general each play announces frankly and honestly—this is history or legend or romance, you are not at home, you are in story-land. During Shakespeare's earlier years, such practice was in accord with the common habit of translating stories of all sorts into dramatic form with no desire for verisimilitude. But later, during the period when theory and practice were uniting to require that comedy should employ "deeds and language such as men do use" and should aim "to show an image of the times," his muse flew still farther away from London and reality in such plays as "Troilus,"

"Pericles," and "The Winter's Tale." For him, comedy did not attach itself to a thesis but to an adventure. The main thing was to set the fancy free, and then let reality catch up if it could.

This practice of Shakespeare and the Elizabethans has its difficulties. Storyland has its monotonies as well as real life. What is the story that Shakespeare tells most often? A delightful girl falls in love at first sight with a charming but rather insipid young man. Usually he reciprocates, but, in any case she is bound to have him, and in spite of all difficulties she perseveres until they are married. This tale may be lifelike as well as romantic but it becomes a bit repetitive. Moreover, the adventures and wonders that thrilled the Elizabethans are sometimes beyond the comprehension of sense or humour. In "The Merchant of Venice," "Much Ado," and "The Winter's Tale," one may be excused for wishing that Shakespeare had chosen a different framework on which to weave his tapestries of poetry and character. Why could not means have been found for depicting all these marvellous people except through time-worn plots and wildly improbable inventions? Further, critics have often complained about the distribution of rewards and punishments in this storyland. The moralists do not like the sudden conversions and hasty marriages of the rogues and villains; the sentimentalists do not like to have Falstaff sent to prison or Malvolio kept so long in confinement. I think we must agree that these comedies present life neither just as it is nor just as it ought to be.

On the other hand, it may be urged that history and romance and fantasy gave Shakespeare the fullest opportunity to be lifelike and humorous. He could be as lifelike as he pleased without any constraint that he should always remain so. He could let his humour play where it would without any strict consort with fact or morality. Humour is a wayward fellow who flourishes on improbability. Confined to the land of reality he can do excellent work in the service of ridicule or derision or satire, but

he is a little subdued in these beaten paths. Let him free
in the land just removed from reality and he can roam
where he will. If he finds the court too didactic he goes
to the tavern; if adventures become wearisome he rests
with the yokels; if the stupid fail him he visits the wise.
The love stories in Shakespeare's comedies are monotonous, but the heroines are not, chiefly because humour
comes to their aid. All this is not merely to say that
romance and history afford opportunities for comic relief,
so does a thesis or a criticism; but in Shakespeare's storyland the occupations for humour are without limit. He
makes puns and sings songs, he ridicules and he sympa-
thizes, he is the butt and the jester, he plays pranks and
exercises the intellect, he exposes folly and adorns wisdom. He can see the world just as it is or he can see it
topsy-turvy; he can get back to reality in a moment and
in another he can be far away from it. He can look upon
humans as a Puck or a Falstaff or a Caliban. He invites
us to laugh at ourselves, or at our neighbours, or to laugh
in the sheer joy that we have escaped from reality.

There is a somewhat comparable effect in the tragedies.
They are pitched above the key of ordinary life. They
exalt human aspiration and achievement and defeat. They
reveal life, but in a magnifying mirror. And so Shakespeare's comedies play over a vaster and more significant
range of deed and emotion than any mere analysis of
reality could muster. Falstaff transcends fact as truly as
does Ariel. Beatrice is as much a creation of fancy as is
Titania. We pass from Eastcheap to Fairyland, or from
the archness of Rosalind to the howling of Caliban. It
is a great play world that reflects back to us the sentiment,
fun, nonsense, mirth and irony of our real world, but all
blended and interwoven like the motives of a musical
rhapsody. We recognize this and that familiar strain,
but it never before had such melodic companionship.

CHAPTER VIII

ELIZABETHAN VARIETIES

IN grouping together all of the comedies of Shakespeare I have traversed a period of some twenty-five years, from his arrival in London about 1587 until his retirement to Stratford in 1612 or 1613. This quarter century was a time of brilliant and multifold dramatic activity, including the work of all the major Elizabethan playwrights and affording a bewildering variety of comedies, many of which challenge our admiration for their merit and originality. It is necessary now to turn back and inquire what developments were taking place in comedy during Shakespeare's career that find little or scant representation in his work, but first it may prove convenient to note a few facts and dates in the history of the theater.

I

We have seen that when Shakespeare came to London the drama was well established in the hands of professional actors in permanent playhouses but with considerable rivalry from the quasi-amateur companies of children. These had been an important factor in the creation of refined and fantastic comedy, but this had already ceased to be their exclusive property. The adult companies attracted to their employ a group of dramatists that included Marlowe, Kyd, Greene, Peele, and Shakespeare, and were soon outdistancing their children rivals. Their prosperity, however, was interrupted by the severe plague of 1593 which closed the theaters and broke up the weaker companies. Marlowe died in that year, Greene the year before, and the breaking up of the companies released a large number of plays for publication. In consequence of these facts, we can date many plays as certainly written before 1593, and the cessation of acting during the plague of that year marks a period in the history of the theater. By that year Shakespeare's predecessors had finished their work and the notable development in comedy by Greene, Lyly and Peele was accomplished. By that year too Shakespeare's apprenticeship was over and probably he had written his first comic masterpiece, "A Midsummer Night's Dream."

When the theaters reopened in 1594 there were fewer companies than before and the superiority of the adults over the children was apparently established. By the end of the century, however, the rivalry was renewed. After some years of suppression, the two companies of children began acting again, the Paul's boys in the theater in their schoolhouse, the Children of the Chapel (the Queen's Revels) in the newly-made theater in Blackfriars. At about the same time the two chief adult companies built new playhouses, the Lord Chamberlain's men (the company of Burbage and Shakespeare) erecting the Globe to the south of the Thames, and the Lord Admiral's men retaliating by building the Fortune to the north of the city. In these playhouses where the pit was open to the sky, without seats, and surrounded by galleries provided with seats and a roof, performances were given by daylight. The indoor theaters of the children, which were sometimes termed "private houses," had seats in the pit, were lighted by candles, charged higher prices than the "public playhouses," and apparently attracted a somewhat more exclusive audience. Upon the accession of James I in 1603 both adult and children companies were taken under the direct control of the royal household, and though subject to official censorship and control, profited from an increased patronage of the court.

The revival of the children in the private theaters resulted in some important changes. At first the boys seem to have followed their earlier habit in preferring musical and fantastic pieces, reviving some of Lyly's and presenting others imitative of his work; but they were soon acting plays in no way distinguished from those by their elders, including in their repertory realistic comedy and gruesome tragedy. In fact, these "little eyases" rather specialized in satire as Shakespeare's reference to them in "Hamlet" indicates. They were soon engaging the services of Jonson, Chapman, Marston, Middleton, Beaumont and Fletcher and proving dangerous rivals to the adults. Though this rivalry lasted for barely a decade, it established the popularity of the indoor theaters. In 1608 Burbage took back his lease of the Blackfriars to the children, and henceforth Shakespeare's company occupied this theater, the Globe in summer and the Blackfriars in winter. Other indoor playhouses were opened in Whitefriars, and these became the models for those built after the Restoration.

The stage, whether indoor or outdoor, was a primitive affair compared with its successor of today, but its very defects may be reckoned as of profit as well as of loss to the drama. Its lack of scenery lessened greatly the pictorial effect of a play but encouraged both descriptive poetry and rapid action. The absence of a front curtain explains the necessity for an *exeunt omnes* at the end of each act; and the use of the balcony and rear curtained stage helped to make the succession of scenes rapid and facile. The absence of women actors was in part compensated for by the training of children in the profession. Since an adult company rarely had more than two or three boys, there are usually no more than two or three women among the dramatis personæ. Yet these boys could act well enough to portray Juliet and Cleopatra. The art of acting doubtless developed rapidly along with the theater and the drama. Hamlet's advice to the players alone is sufficient evidence that a careful technic and a sound tradition were established. Speaking from down front, the actor was almost surrounded by spectators whose attention was wrapt in his every word or gesture. Whether the audiences profited from their training to become superior judges of plays and acting, we have no sure means of knowing. The dramatists of that age complained as bitterly of the ignorance and vulgarity of their public as do the dramatists of our own time. It was indeed a mixed and to a large extent an illiterate public, demanding abundant and lively incident and delighting in such spectacle as that stage could afford, but it also seems to have appreciated poetry.

The popularity of the indoor theaters indicates the appearance of an audience more sophisticated and more fashionable than that which still thronged the public playhouses. The drama soon began to be written less for the mob and more for the few, but this change was felt only in the later years of Shakespeare's life. The London that he knew, a city of not over two hundred thousand inhabitants, usually had as many as six theaters open and producing new plays at a rate impossible to our modern methods. Henslowe's players, the only company of which we have records, produced twenty or more new plays annually. Almost every man of literary talent and ambition was drawn into writing for the stage. In this close rivalry and association fashions and types were quickly formed and quickly changed, but there was a constant and rapid growth in every phase of dramatic art.

II

On the basis of the extant plays, it is impossible to analyze surely the growth of distinct types of comedy, or indeed to classify precisely the varied dramatic pieces of the many authors. During the nineties while Shakespeare was writing romantic comedies and histories, these appear to have been the two dominant classes. But domestic, realistic and satirical strains were not absent from comedy, and plots of intrigue, more or less closely following the scheme of Latin comedy, were often used with domestic scenes and persons. "The Two Angry Women of Abingdon (pr. 1599) is a rather crude example of this class of domestic intrigue, to which many later plays may be assigned. By the end of the century a definite reaction set in against romantic and fantastic drama and in the direction of realism and satire and of adherence to classical proprieties. Ben Jonson was undoubtedly leader both in criticism and practice, but the bent toward realism was manifest generally in the majority of comedies from the time of his "Every Man in His Humour," 1598, to that of his "Alchemist" in 1610. By that date the successes of Beaumont and Fletcher had revived romance of a somewhat new and melodramatic order, and henceforth Fletcher's is the outstanding influence on the Jacobean stage.

Jonson and Fletcher require separate treatment as masters of comedy and creators of distinctive types, but before proceeding to the consideration of their plays I wish to examine some of the creations of other dramatists during the busy years from 1594 to 1612. Certain themes repeat themselves; the motives of the shrew who is tamed and of the patient Griselda who wins back an errant spouse reappear in several plays on the marital relations; prodigal sons continue to sow their wild oats; ridicule of braggarts, misers, fops and hypocrites is general and intrudes into the sentimental pieces; general too is the story of romantic love and final happiness, though this may be joined to satire and realism. Tricks, stratagems and deceptions are almost universal, but plays sometimes may be grouped together by the kinds of trick employed. Several use the trick of multiple disguise, requiring rapid changes of costume and face by the chief deceiver. Another group makes use of the device of wandering in the dark, as in "Merry Wives," to produce mistakes and embarrassments. A play depicting London manners may have Italian names and scenes; and another may introduce magic and wonders among English persons and places. Nevertheless, despite these variations, most of the plays can be roughly classified as romantic or realistic, the former belonging to that development from court show and romantic chronicle that we have traced through Lyly and Greene to Shakespeare's masterpieces, the latter still showing signs of morality, farce and Plautian imitation, which from Elizabeth's accession had prepared the way for realism and satire.

In comparison with "The Merchant of Venice" or "Twelfth Night" most of such romantic comedies as have survived are beneath contempt. Few offer any original development or noteworthy variation in type. The majority are medleys displaying the usual contrasts of love, adventure and farce without any dramatic advance. The most popular of those that were printed, if we judge by the number of editions, was "Mucedorus," which is devoid of dramatic ingenuity or literary merit. One, "The Maid's Metamorphosis," a pastoral, follows closely the scheme of Lyly, some of whose plays were revived at the end of the century. Another, "Wily Beguiled," imitates the "Midsummer Night's Dream"; and a later and better play "The Merry Devil of Edmonton" uses the complication of the wanderers at night along with magic and devils and a domestic scene. In general the romantic drama was lawless, delighting in impossibilities of every kind, using myth, legend and spectacle.

Perhaps the most striking example of this romantic confusion is Dekker's "Pleasant Comedy of Old Fortunatus," probably first written about 1594 and enlarged and recast for the court performance in 1598. It is based on the German Volksbuch and shows abundant imitation of Lyly and Marlowe, especially of the latter's "Dr. Faustus." Though called a pleasant comedy and described in the prologue as singing "of Love's sweet war," the story is given a tragic and moral treatment, the vicissitudes of Fortune leading to many deaths and to the triumph of Vice over Virtue. But it comprises all kinds of spectacle and comedy in its rapidly shifting scenes. It begins with an echo dialogue after the pastoral style, followed by a Marlowesque spectacle in which Fortune ascends her throne climbing over the chained and prostrate bodies of four kings, while a shepherd, nymph, monk and others sing the charming song, "Fortune smiles, cry holiday." The peasant Fortunatus, unlike Faustus, prefers wealth to wisdom, and provided by Fortune with a magic purse, starts off on the romance of sudden wealth. At the Court of Babylon he acquires a wishing cap and spends the day in triumph and the night in banqueting. But Fortune, the Destinies, Vice and Virtue pursue him, a dance of satyrs bear off his body, leaving his treasures to his two sons and Shadow, one of the most delightful and witty of clowns. Adventures begin anon, or as the riotous brother says to the solemn one, "Tricks, Ampedo, tricks, devices, and mad hieroglyphics, mirth, mirth, and melody." The intrigues and wonders are, indeed, interrupted by mirth and melody, by merry prose and sonorous verse. The chorus wafts us over the sea; a king's daughter steals the purse from Andelocia sleeping in her lap and is carried off in the air to a wilderness where grow the apples of Sodom. Magic apples cause horns to spring on the heads of the princess and courtiers. The virtuous are praised and the vicious are condemned. Only their Shadow is left to tell how they died. Vice and her train are driven from the stage. "Virtue crowned, Nymphs and Kings attending on her, music sounding," closes the play with a triumph and the song,

> Virtue smiles: cry holiday,
> Dimples on her cheek do dwell.

III

Against such romantic lawlessness there was inevitably a reaction to a more critical and sophisticated view of comedy as a mirror and censor of the times. Apart from the criticism and practice of Jonson this was manifested in several ways: first by comedies of intrigue on the Latin scheme to which were added "humours," i. e., studies of contemporary types of character; second, the exploitation of London scenes and persons, sometimes in

a sentimental but more often in a satirical vein; third,
the presentation of the seamy side of city life and an
emphasis on the problems of sex; and fourth, by the
assumption of a satirical or censorial attitude toward
contemporary follies and vices. All these phases of realism seem to have made their appearance before they were
united in the vigorous efforts of Jonson. Though the
literary terms must be used rather loosely in view of
Elizabethan heterogeneity, it may be said fairly that there
was a marked and sudden shift from romanticism to realism. Jonson himself had been writing miscellaneous plays
not at all realistic and even in the first edition of "Every
Man in His Humour" used Italian names for his persons
and places, but that play was the first of his great series
of realistic and satirical comedies. Chapman's earliest
play, "The Blind Beggar of Alexandria," was at least
quasi-romantic but it was followed by "A Humourous
Day's Mirth," preceding Jonson's play as a realistic
presentation of humours, and by "All Fools" acted about
1599 and exhibiting Terentian complications and London
eccentrics in full accord with Jonson's precepts. Marston's
earliest play, "Antonio and Mellida" Part I, is a romantic
tragicomedy, but two years later in 1601, he was writing
the bitterly satirical "Malcontent." Similarly, certain
romantic elements are found in the earliest of Middleton's
plays, but in the main his comedies from 1600 to 1608
are very realistic pictures of London manners. Moreover, a series of formal poetic satires by Hall, Donne and
Marston gave in the closing years of the century additional zest to the caustic exposure of the humours of
society. "Every Man in His Humour" in 1598 sounded
the tocsin of realistic revolt, and within a year or two
light-hearted, romantic, poetic, fantastic comedy was
mostly a thing of the past. The most notable exception
to this generalization is found in three plays written
between 1604 and 1608 by John Day, a hack writer who
had an original vein of humour. "Law Tricks," "The
Isle of Gulls" and "Humour Out of Breath" display pas-

toral scenes, romantic stories, pages, wit-combats, satire, fantasy and indecency. They are in a way successors to Lyly but they are quite unlike any other plays of their time.

Neither Chapman nor Marston followed up his entry into realistic comedy by any consistent development, both being more interested in tragic themes. Neither is a consistent realist, and they do not hesitate to mingle tragic with comic motives, as for example, in Chapman's "Gentleman Usher" or Marston's "Dutch Courtezan." In general they write comedies of intrigue, the interest depending mainly on the solution of the various tricks, but diverted by some presentation of London manners and of eccentric characters. Both resort freely to indecency as a means of provoking laughter. Chapman is terribly verbose in both the romantic and comic scenes and cannot succeed in uniting them in a coherent movement. About the only distinctive comic purpose that can be assigned to him is the humorous elaboration of character, his most amusing creation being the absurd and long-winded fop who gives his name to the play "Monsieur D'Olive."

Marston appears to have enjoyed a brief popularity and to have been a considerable figure in the drama of the first decade of the seventeenth century, though his plays disclose few attractions to the modern reader. Like Jonson he strove to give the drama a satiric bent, and his plays abound in violent railings at the corruption and hypocrisy of courts and courtiers, expressed in pretentious and uncouth language and often without much bearing upon either tragic or comic purpose. "The Malcontent," published in 1604, with a dedication to Jonson, "amico suo," is perhaps the most successful in uniting satiric purpose to dramatic effectiveness. Altofronto, the dispossessed duke of Genoa, returns disguised to the court of his successor and assumes the rôle of a malcontent. This permits him an outrageous freedom of speech which he vents on all the persons of the corrupt court. In the end

he exposes the sin of the duchess and the machinations
of her minion and secures the retirement of the usurping
duke and his own restoration to power.

"The Malcontent" suggests comparison with two plays
written at about the same date, but probably a little later
than Marston's tragicomedy, Shakespeare's "Measure for
Measure" and Jonson's "Volpone." Like the former
and also like Middleton's "Phœnix," Marston's play uses
the device of a duke who in disguise ferrets out the evils
of his city, and like the latter it presents human vice and
depravity with an intensity scarcely suitable to comedy.
There is indeed little about it to entitle it to consideration
as comedy except that the tragic catastrophe is averted,
the virtuous rewarded and the vicious contemptuously
permitted to go unpunished. Marston's play, like those
of Shakespeare and Jonson, exposes vices rather than
follies and it supplies less comic relief than the other two.
Far inferior to them in the probing of human nature, it
is of some interest as illustrating a tendency of satire,
whether in connection with the drama or elsewhere, to
desert the humorous element of ridicule for wholesale
invective. Its most specific contribution to comedy is its
figure of the railing malcontent, who has an obvious stage
utility that was appreciated in both the Elizabethan and
later theaters.

Much more amusing than any play written by either
Chapman or Marston alone, is the delightful comedy
"Eastward Ho," on which they collaborated with Jonson.
The exact division among the collaborators is not easy to
determine, but the coherence and firmness of the structure,
particularly in the dénouement, seem due to Jonson.
Touchstone, an honest goldsmith of London, has two
daughters, one giddy and extravagant, the other modest
and thrifty, and two apprentices, one idle, the other industrious. The modest daughter and the frugal apprentice
marry and continue models of behaviour throughout the
play. The foolish daughter weds a shifty knight, Sir
Petronel Flash, and they with the aid of the wild appren-

tice indulge in all kinds of extravagance. The knight, at the end of his resources, determines to escape to Virginia, taking with him the wife of an old usurer from whom he has borrowed money. The usurer is tricked into aiding the elopement in the belief that the disguised lady is the spouse of his friend the lawyer. All the precious rascals meet at a riverside tavern for a carouse on the eve of the sailing for Virginia, and then insist on taking boat despite the gathering storm. The boat capsizes and all receive a ducking in the Thames. They succeed in getting ashore at one place or another, the wife manages to return triumphantly to her husband; the knight and apprentice and usurer, after a season in jail, turn penitent and reform.

I quote a little in order to suggest how responsive to both character and situation comic dialogue had become. Gertrude, the foolish daughter, is in jail with her maid, bemoaning her ill fortune but still dreaming of some miraculous intervention. Her singing is interrupted by a visit from her mother.

Enter Mistress Touchstone

O here's my mother! Good luck, I hope. Ha' you brought any money, mother? Pray you, mother, your blessing. Nay, sweet mother, do not weep.

Mist. Touch. God bless you! I would I were in my grave!

Ger. Nay, dear mother, can you steal no more money from my father? Dry your eyes, and comfort me. Alas, it is my knight's fault, and not mine, that I am in a waistcoat, and attired thus simply.

Mist. Touch. Simply? 'Tis better than thou deserv'st. Never whimper for the matter. Thou shouldst have looked before thou hadst leaped. Thou wert afire to be a lady, and now your ladyship and you may both blow at the coal, for aught I know. Self do, self have. "The hasty person never wants woe," they say.

Ger. Nay, then, mother, you should ha' looked to it. A body would think you were the older; I did but my kind, I. He was a knight, and I was fit to be a lady. 'Tis not lack of liking, but lack of living, that severs us. And you talk like yourself and a cittiner in this, i' faith. You show what husband you come on, I wis. You smell the Touchstone—he that will do more for his daughter that he has married a scurvy gold-end man and his prentice, than he will for his tother daughter, that has wedded a knight and his customer. By this light, I think he is not my legitimate father.

Sindefy. O good madam, do not take up your mother so!

Mist. Touch. Nay, nay, let her e'en alone! Let her ladyship grieve me still, with her bitter taunts and terms. I have not dole enough to see her in this miserable case, I, without her velvet gowns, without ribands, without jewels, without French wires, or cheat-bread, or quails, or a little dog, or a gentleman-usher, or anything, indeed, that's fit for a lady——

Sin. (aside). Except her tongue.

Mist. Touch. And I am not able to relieve her, neither, being kept so short by my husband. Well, God knows my heart; I did little think that ever she should have need of her sister Golding.

Ger. Why, mother, I ha' not yet. Alas, good mother, be not intoxicate for me! I am well enough; I would not change husbands with my sister, I. The leg of a lark is better than the body of a kite.

Mist. Touch. I know that, but——

Ger. What, sweet mother, what?

Mist. Touch. It's but ill food when nothing's left but the claw.

Ger. That's true, mother. Ay me!

Mist. Touch. Nay, sweet lady-bird, sigh not. Child, madam, why do you weep thus? Be of good cheer; I shall die, if you cry and mar your complexion thus.

Ger. Alas, mother, what should I do?

Mist. Touch. Go to thy sister's, child; she'll be proud thy ladyship will come under her roof. She'll win thy

father to release thy knight, and redeem thy gowns and
thy coach and thy horses, and set thee up again.

Ger. But will she get him to set my knight up too?

Mist. Touch. That she will, or anything else thou'lt
ask her.

Ger. I will begin to love her if I thought she would
do this.

Mist. Touch. Try her, good chuck, I warrant thee.

Ger. Dost thou think she'll do't?

Sin. Ay, madam, and be glad you will receive it.

Mist. Touch. That's a good maiden; she tells you
true. Come, I'll take order for your debts i' the alehouse.

Ger. Go, Sin., and pray for thy Frank, as I will for
my Pet.

(Exeunt)

Whether in the development of an ingenious intrigue
or in the depiction of London manners or in the inculca-
tion of a sound moral lesson, the play is always lively;
the tale of the idle apprentice has rarely been told with
so much vivacity and spirit. But by the time it was presented, comedies devoted to a realistic depiction of London scenes were becoming common. "Eastward Ho"
(acted probably 1604) seems to have been a sort of
rejoinder to the "Westward Ho" of Webster and Dekker,
and received an immediate reply in "Northward Ho" by
the same authors. These are two of the grossest and least
meritorious comedies of London manners, but they belong
to a class that had already been made popular through
the inventions of Middleton.

IV

Thomas Middleton produced his first play "The Old
Law" probably as early as 1599, and by 1608 had written
at least seven comedies for the children's companies, in
addition to some lost plays and a collaboration with
Dekker on "The Honest Whore." These seven plays,

"Blurt, Master Constable," "The Phœnix," "The Family
of Love," "Your Five Gallants," "A Mad World, My
Masters," "A Trick to Catch the Old One," and "Michaelmas Term," may be said to constitute a definite type of
realistic comedy, and with them may be included other
plays of somewhat later or doubtful date: "The Widow,"
"No Wit No Help Like a Woman's," "The Roaring
Girl," (in collaboration with Dekker) "Anything for a
Quiet Life," and "A Chaste Maid of Cheapside." Still
later Middleton produced notable tragedies, tragicomedies
and comedies, among the latter two highly original and
unusual, "A Fair Quarrel" and "A Game of Chess." It
will be convenient here, however, to limit our attention
to his early contribution to comedy during the first dozen
years or so of the seventeenth century.

His earliest plays follow the current fashion of using
a foreign scene and foreign names for the characters, and
also display some more essential qualities of the romantic
drama. "The Old Law" has a fantastic plot; "Blurt,
Master Constable," a tragicomic story of romantic love,
and "The Phœnix" are both eloquent and moral; but even
in these plays the interest lies largely in the comic presentation of city vices, of sexual and commercial immorality.
In the later plays of this group the action is placed in
London and involves a frank and often licentious but
usually lively and entertaining depiction of the seamy side
of city life. In "The Phœnix" the method is like Jonson's
in the emphasis placed upon satire and exposure. The
son of the duke in disguise discovers the iniquities of his
realm, plotting nobles, Tangle the unscrupulous lawyer,
Falso the judge who takes bribes, his serving men who
commit highway robbery, and one honest and peaceable
citizen, Quieto. But in the plays that follow, Middleton
shows no interest in the presentation of virtue or the
expression of moral indignation, nor does he like Jonson
build his plots upon the humouristic analysis of character.
"Your Five Gallants" and "The Family of Love" expose
evil doers but with an appeal to the baser rather than

more virtuous instincts of the audience. "Michaelmas Term," "A Trick to Catch the Old One," and " A Mad World, My Masters" use the mechanism of ingenious tricks and deceptions, in the course of which the vices go unrebuked, and cleverness is the only virtue that is rewarded.

It is an unsavoury London to which these plays introduce us. The scene shifts from shop to prison, from court of justice to brothel. We meet libertines and prostitutes, tricky lawyers and swindlers, drunkards and usurers, wanton wives and complacent husbands, needy knights and harsh creditors. There are many fools, a few clever scapegraces, and nearly all are rascals. Almost nothing is heard of romantic love or idealizing lovers. If there is a decent girl she appears only as bait for the rogues and reward for the most ingenious. Lust of money and lust of flesh are the dominant motives, but the dramatic struggle is a play of wits, each person striving to outwit the other. Greed and stupidity yield to cleverness, but victors and vanquished are alike unscrupulous in the means that they employ. The gentlemen spendthrifts may in the end win back their fortunes, and the courtezans secure husbands, but they give only faint hints of reformation. Though there are many marriages, none show any indication of having been made in heaven.

"A Trick to Catch the Old One" is perhaps the best of these comedies and is fairly typical of them all. A clever scapegrace, Witgood, who has squandered his fortune, and his cast mistress are the chief manipulators of the plot of deception. They pretend that she is a widow from the country with four hundred pounds a year to whom he is about to be married. His uncle, Lucre, who has seized his lands under a mortgage and has refused to see him, now becomes friendly and loads him and his widow with gifts. His creditors also turn friendly and generous. The pretended widow at once becomes the object of pursuit by several idle gallants, by Lucre's foolish son, and by Hoard, the antagonist of Lucre and his

rival in usury.   Hoard by stratagem and force carries
off the widow to Cold Harbour where he marries her.
Lucre overtakes them there, and on the supposition that
they are not married, promises to surrender the mortgage
to Witgood.   The nephew secures the mortgage and then,
on pretense of a pre-contract with the widow, induces
Hoard to make a settlement with his creditors.   Then
he secretly marries Hoard's daughter.   All these deceptions are explained at a great feast when Hoard celebrates his marriage and discovers that the spendthrift
is his son-in-law and that his own bride is the spendthrift's
cast mistress.

It is impossible in a brief summary to indicate the
innumerable tricks and countertricks by which the plot
proceeds, still less to suggest the dramatic skill and tact
by which the entanglements are made clear and amusing
on the stage.   The plot is similar to that of Roman comedy in that tricks multiply tricks, but in the employment
of a scapegrace as chief trickster and of usurers, lechers,
lawyers and shop-keepers as the chief victims, Middleton
set a model that was long followed.   In other plays he
employs disguise more extensively than in this, but whatever the dramatic devices used, those deceived have their
own greed or lust mainly to blame for their overthrow.
The characterization is sufficient for the intrigue but rarely
goes beyond it.   The persons are authentic enough to
make the plot interesting and plausible without exciting
much interest in themselves.   There is nothing of Jonson's
careful elaboration or Dekker's sympathetic enjoyment
of unusual personalities.   The plays illustrate amply London manners but they do not create individuals.   Both
verse and prose are remarkably easy and natural, suited
to the persons and situations of the action and without
effort for stylistic decoration.   These plays show nothing
of those imaginative flights in poetry and characterization
so typical of the Elizabethan drama in general and
indeed of some of Middleton's later plays, but they established a realistic comedy of London manners, based on

ingenious intrigue and usually expressed in effective and dramatic prose.

Not much can be said in defense of the immorality of these dramas. It is manifest negatively in their lack of sentiment or virtue and positively in their lewdness. Possibly some of his contemporaries are worse than he in grossness of language, but few show less moral scruple in the choice of situation or in the distribution of rewards and punishments. The tendency to turn from the normal and happy to the baser and more sordid aspects of life has often characterized realism in fiction. Among the Elizabethan dramatists this tendency was aided, I think, apart from any moral turpitude or grossness of taste on the part of the author, by the very conception and method of comedy. Their realists were following the conception of Aristotle that comedy was the ridicule of something ugly, and they were following Roman comedy in taking sexual immorality as their main theme. Their method, as exhibited in both Jonson and Middleton, was a concatenation of tricks and counter tricks. But neither tricking nor being tricked is a calling suitable for the virtuous and normal; and their comic scenes were likely to be concerned chiefly with rogues, cheaters, bawds and their victims. So far as it was not merely bestial, human nature in their plays was distinguished by the power of cheating or being cheated. From the narrow limits that this kind of comedy imposed upon him, Middleton did not succeed in escaping by such greatness of artistic design as is shown in "The Alchemist" or by such intensely moral purpose as is shown in "Volpone" or by the breadth of observation and humour of "Bartholomew Fair." But it must not be thought that his coarseness was unaccompanied by genuine wit or that the confinement of a formula prevented his exercise of dramatic invention. His "Chaste Maid in Cheapside," for example, comes closer to "Bartholomew Fair" than any other play in the breadth and raciness of its picture of London manners. In spite of the rather hackneyed plot of deceptions, nothing could be

grosser than its realism or more audacious than its
humour. Whatever its moral value, it is undoubtedly
funny. Perhaps the hearty laughter it arouses is a comic
katharsis sufficient to destroy the contamination of its ugliness. At all events in a type of comedy that discarded
both exciting story and Plautian types of character,
Middleton could be amusing as well as realistic.

V

Although Jonson and Middleton had many imitators,
only two other writers contributed to the rise of realism
during the early years of the seventeenth century plays
of marked distinction and originality. Neither Dekker
nor Heywood was a thoroughgoing realist like Middleton,
and neither appears to have profited much from Jonson's
criticism. They were both actively engaged for many
years in writing for the stage, meeting its various demands
and suiting its changing moods with plays of all sorts and
kinds, and neither hesitated to stoop to the taste of the
most vulgar. Yet both looked into the daily life about
them and saw things which neither Jonson nor Middleton
nor Shakespeare recorded, and in their happier moments
each taught the Comic Muse lessons that she could not
learn from the others.

The earliest work of Dekker of which we have record
was on the highly romantic "Old Fortunatus." For a
number of years, from 1598 on, he was busily employed
for Henslowe's companies, having a hand in as many as
sixteen plays in the course of a single year. From this
miscellaneous and hasty work only a few plays have survived, but these include one of perennial charm, "The
Shoemaker's Holiday," written and acted in 1599, and
presented before the queen on New Year's Day, 1600.
It is based on Delony's "Gentle Craft," a recently published collection of stories about shoemakers, utilizing as
its main plot the rise of Simon Eyre from poverty to the
lord mayoralty of London and as a sub-plot the wooing
of a noble lover who disguises himself as a shoemaker.

It may be classed with other Elizabethan plays glorifying the English craftsman and presumably delighting the apprentices who patronized the theaters. The play marks Dekker's change from romance to realism; but, though it is one of the earliest dealing with the citizens and also one of the vividest in its detail of the daily life of tradesmen, it still keeps the idealism and fantasy of romance. It is indeed a sentimental comedy of London life, the romanticization of the affairs of everyday existence.

There is no dwelling upon vice, and the normal and wholesome are touched by fancy. Even such ordinary occupations as eating, drinking and talking take on a whimsical delightfulness. There is abounding humour as well as sentiment in the characterization and the exuberant prose. How very human and how wholesome are the persons whom we meet!—Margery the wife, Firk, the journeyman, Jane, whose lover has gone to the wars, and above all Simon Eyre himself. Almost any of his speeches will recall the spirit of his madcap mirth. Here is one where Eyre quiets his wife's fears that in the royal presence he won't know how to talk:

Margery. Good my lord, have a care what you speak to his grace.

Eyre. Away, you Islington whitepot! hence, you hopperarse! you barley-pudding, full of maggots! you broiled carbonado! avaunt, avaunt, avoid, Mephistophiles! Shall Sim Eyre learn to speak of you, Lady Madgy? Vanish, Mother Miniver-cap; vanish, go, trip and go; meddle with your partlets and your pishery-pashery, your flewes and your whirligigs; go, rub, out of mine alley! Sim Eyre knows how to speak to a Pope, to Sultan Soliman, to Tamburlaine, an he were here, and shall I melt, shall I droop before my sovereign? No, come my Lady Madgy! Follow me, Hans! About your business, my frolic free-booters! Firk, frisk about, and about, and about, for the honour of mad Simon Eyre, lord mayor of London.

Into the London of tradesmen and apprentices Dekker brought something of that same extravagance of humour and sentiment which Shakespeare carried to Arden or Illyria or fairyland. Nowhere else do we find Elizabethan England so merry or business London so bathed in sunlight.

For the next few years Dekker was still busy with Henslowe, and he also wrote for the Chamberlain's men "Satiromastix," an attack on Jonson, Dekker's contribution to "that terrible Poetmachia lately commenced between Horace the Second and a band of lean-witted poetasters." By 1604 he had gone over to the realists, perhaps mainly under the influence of Middleton and certainly in response to the popular demand for comedies of city life. After the terrible plague of 1603 there seems to have been a great flood of new plays to greet the reign of James; at least a large number may, on what evidence we have, be assigned to the years 1604-5. Among these are two written by Dekker in collaboration with Webster that have little to distinguish them except their coarseness, and two by Dekker with some aid from Middleton himself that displayed marked originality, "The Honest Whore, Parts I and II."

We have seen that at this time sexual immorality in general, and the case of the prostitute in particular, were receiving abundant attention in the London theaters. Marston's "Dutch Courtezan" (1605) had been fiercest in denunciation, but in the comedies the courtezans were usually provided with husbands in the fifth act. No one, however, had tried to present the reformed courtezan after marriage. Dekker, apparently with but little aid from his collaborator, took up that problem. Middleton's assistance seems to have been limited to the scenes introducing the courtezan and to parts of the sub-plot of the humours of the patient man, a sort of male Griselda; the development of the main plot seems Dekker's. Part I begins with Hippolito's grief over the supposed death of his loved Infelice and proceeds to his introduction to

Bellafront, who is entertaining a number of gallants at her house. He returns to denounce her and her trade, unwittingly inspires her love, and brings about her conversion. The long arguments between them are over-rhetorical to our taste, though doubtless effective on the Elizabethan stage. The last act takes us to Bethlem monastery, an asylum for the insane where the patient husband has been confined and where Bellafront, pretending madness, seeks Hippolito. Infelice is restored by her father the Duke to Hippolito, and the reformed Bellafront is married to the unrepentant madcap Matheo who first seduced her. The sensational and melodramatic situations are touched at times by Dekker's poetry and humanity, but the play is far surpassed in both by its sequel.

Seventeen years are supposed to have elapsed. The romantic Hippolito has grown tired of the beautiful and spirited Infelice. Bellafront, true and patient, is living in poverty with the wastrel Matheo who is sunk in dissipation and gambling. Hippolito and Bellafront meet when she is forced to seek his aid for her husband, and now it is he who is mad with love for her and she who refuses temptation. Here are situations challenging to a dramatist, and they found a master hand. Dekker might have made a tragedy in which its heroine, married to one whom she cannot love or even respect, is deeply and truly in love with another and so is driven on to suicide or ruin; or he might have made a comedy exposing and ridiculing human frailty. But Dekker had become sympathetically interested in the persons that he had created and in the truth of the problem that confronted them, and he refused to tamper with their characters in order to heighten the situations. Matheo is always the profligate but his own worst enemy and even at his worst a little likable. Hippolito is always the romanticist, eloquent and imposing, and never quite reliable. Bellafront is not the heroine that either melodrama or modern fiction would draw, but a woman, master of herself, accepting a punishment without questioning its conventional morality, and persevering in what she believes the only road to virtue. Perhaps others could have succeeded as does Dekker in making individuality distinct through the emotional stresses of the plot, and another might even have formed the daring invention of creating Bellafront's old father who has disowned her but now comes to her rescue; but none but Dekker would have created Orlando Friscobaldo. Hazlitt's comment says the last word:

"Old honest Dekker's Signior Orlando Friscobaldo I shall never forget! I became only of late acquainted with this last-mentioned worthy character, but the bargain between us is, I trust, for life. We sometimes regret that we had not sooner met with characters like this, that seem to raise, revive, and give a new zest to our being."

Though it has plenty of flaws, the play is a great stroke of genius. It is one of the happiest illustrations of the way in which genius can turn to its purpose a dubious subject or a worn-out fashion. The triumph is undoubtedly due to the compassion, the tenderness, the humanity of Dekker. But from our point of view the play is not merely a sympathetic and enlightening treatment of persons and motives, it has something that we have not found before in Elizabethan drama, something entirely out of the range of Shakespeare's romances, or Jonson's or Middleton's realism. It is not primarily concerned in telling a story, or in mingling heroics and mirth; it does not depend upon a complication of intrigue or upon the analysis of humours; around a series of dramatic and not impossible situations, he has woven a discussion of social and ethical problems. The very title puts a question before the audience, can the courtezan be converted? The answer is yes, but the conversion is not easy; it means "a slow process involving the horror of past vileness, the anguish of rejected love, and continued hunger, blows and abuse." The play is a little like the sentimental comedy of the eighteenth century or like modern problem and thesis plays, or still more like Heywood's

masterpiece "A Woman Killed with Kindness." But
Dekker offers no thesis and pretends to no solution of
large problems. He leaves Bellafront still with her unre-
formed husband and Infelice with her slightly chastened
Hippolito.

Dekker's solution of the problem is this—he invites
us to view the married courtezan and her trials through
the eyes of the father, Friscobaldo. This whimsical, fantastic, hysterical original is restored to happiness by the
evidence of his daughter's conversion and his view of the
world is both mirthful and tender. "This tough senior,
this impracticable old gentleman, softens into a little
child." But he is not a moralist or a sentimentalist, he
is a humourist. He is a new incarnation of the Comic
Spirit, he sees life with love as well as with amusement,
with truth as well as with fantasy. In this drama of
shops and stews, of Bedlam and Bridewell, comedy rises
to its highest function. To quote again from Hazlitt's
criticism, "It is as if there were some fine art to chisel
thought, and to embody the inmost movements of the
mind in everyday actions and familiar speech."

VI

Though Heywood declared in his preface to "The
English Traveller" in 1633 that the play was "one
reserved amongst two hundred and twenty in which I
have had either an entire hand or at least a main finger,"
only a scant two dozen extant plays can be safely ascribed
to his pen; and neither the approximate dates nor the
general succession of these has been determined with any
certainty. At whatever period of his long career, however, and in whatever variety of play, whether chronicle
history, spectacle based on classical myth, or adaptation
of Plautus, or more original treatment of English manners, he seems to have continued averse to the publication
of his pieces and content in the success of the theater.
He was an actor as well as playwright and knew the
tricks of his stage and the tastes of his audience, but

despite all his vulgarity and clap-trap, he could write simple and affecting dialogue, and he possessed a gentle and genuine human sympathy that won him Charles Lamb's praise as the prose Shakespeare.

In the main his treatment of English manners unites a homely realism to sentiment, adventure and impossible wonders. If his comedies begin in a London tavern or English country house, they are likely to carry us on to Jerusalem or the coast of Portugal, along with our old friends, the peerless heroine and the clown. His personages escape from English middle class surroundings for adventure on the high seas and are capable of very romantic love as well as of a sturdy English protestant patriotism. When realism was flourishing in the theaters Heywood combined it with adventure and sentiment; when romance was flourishing he tinctured it with domesticity and patriotism. An example of this general class is afforded by the early and crude "Four Apprentices of London" that was burlesqued so effectively in Beaumont and Fletcher's "Knight of the Burning Pestle." Another example is "Fortune by Land and Sea," possibly acted about 1609, which takes us from a London gambling house to fights with pirates at sea. The best representative is "The Fair Maid of the West or A Girl Worth Gold" (pr. 1631 as "lately acted"), which begins with a vivid and realistic picture of Plymouth on the eve of the sailing of Essex's expedition to the Azores, and then sends the loyal and redoubtable heroine off to sea, taking her to Morocco, where she rescues her lover after her beauty has overpowered the sultan.

Two of Heywood's domestic plays which are most free from adventure, "The Wise Woman of Hogsden" and "A Woman Killed with Kindness," belong to the decade when Jonson and Middleton were making realism prevalent, while a third, "The English Traveller," is contemporary with the later work of Middleton and Massinger.

"The Wise Woman of Hogsdon" is a clever comedy of intrigue and London manners. As in Middleton, the protagonist is an unprincipled scapegrace who nearly succeeds in duping his father, his betrothed, a London goldsmith and his daughter, and a knight and his daughter. Vice is touched only lightly and the emphasis is less on manner or character than on a skilful development of the intrigues into an elaborate and well constructed dénouement. For the once Heywood was as eager as Jonson to work his intricate complications into a well-rounded plot.

"A Woman Killed with Kindness," certainly acted in 1603, is Heywood's masterpiece. In the main plot, the newly-married Frankford entertains at his house a needy gentleman, Wendoll, who seduces Mrs. Frankford. The husband discovers the guilty pair in bed but when the lover escapes refuses to take vengeance on his wife. She is sent to live in all comfort in a neighbouring manor house, upon the only condition that she shall not seek to see her husband or her children. She repents, pines away, and on her deathbed is visited and forgiven by her husband.

> And with this kiss I wed thee once again;
> Though thou art wounded in thy honoured name,
> And with that grief upon thy death bed liest,
> Honest in heart, upon my soul, thou diest.

There is no mirth in the play, even the clown is tearful; and the sub-plot, which transfers to England an Italian story of a contest of courtly honour—and tells it baldly— offers no sign of comic relief. But the play is far removed from Elizabethan tragedy. It presents middle-class English life—it has no affairs of state, no murders, no soaring style, and it closes with the death of Mrs. Frankford, which is really her victory. It would perhaps have been viewed by the Elizabethans as a comedy, and in any case it lies in that debatable ground between domestic tragedy and sentimental comedy. It is indeed the first play in our language which has the characteristics that made the later sentimental comedy of the eighteenth century, and for that reason one might justify its inclusion here though, like many of the later "comedies" of the class, it has no place under our definition, which requires an appeal to the sense of humour.

It demands our notice for a still better reason because it represents a tendency always latent when realistic drama is in vogue, a tendency to regard contemporary life not in a mood of mirth or ridicule but in one of serious interest. The dramatist may find this interest not easily satisfied by the current modes of either tragedy or comedy; he confronts social and moral problems that demand an honest attempt at an answer. His play presents not so much a story or a plot or a delineation of individuality, but rather discusses a problem or a thesis. Heywood's title, a familiar proverb, is itself a challenge. At a time when adultery was the prevailing theme of the drama, he refused to treat it either as the theme for mocking laughter or for tragic horror. He proposed the question, how shall the husband treat the guilty wife? His answer was an unusual one either in Elizabethan life or drama, but it was the result of a sincere morality and a veracious art. For him the problem was one for the husband's determination. The guilty wife is feebly realized, but the scene of the discovery in which Frankford runs through the gamut of the emotions, is a masterpiece of dramatic truth. The play is not only essentially true, it gives the audience something to think about; its effect is not that of entertainment or satire, but of discussion, a kind of rationalized and intelligent as well as sympathetic understanding of life. The spectator is not appealed to merely for pity for the guilty, as in so many later tragedies, but rather for thoughtful approval of the forgiving husband. The sentimentality not only banishes humour but to our modern taste may seem to cloud both the truth and the moral. But even on the Elizabethan stage and perhaps on any popular stage, sentiment and seriousness both seem needed in order to persuade the general public to revise their moral code. Heywood's

"English Traveller," written much later, has the same earnest appeal for a finer morality, and we shall later examine other Elizabethan plays which in some way approach the modern problem plays, but we shall find none that presents a social thesis with more dramatic persuasiveness than "A Woman Killed with Kindness."

During the quarter century of Shakespeare's writing for the theater, we have found comedy undergoing a rapid and shifting development. For the first half of this period it is prevailingly romantic in material and story-telling in method. But domestic themes and plots of intrigue are not lacking and they continue during the second half of the period when London manners have become the subject of a comedy whose purpose is largely realistic and satirical. Many variations, however, are to be found from this normal development and the plays reflect the moods and fancies of the individual authors rather than conform to any distinct types. It was a time of dramatic experiment, innovation and creation. In the work of Middleton during a decade we note the creation of a definite type of realistic comedy of manners, but in the plays of Chapman, Marston, Dekker and Heywood no such uniformity is discernible. Nowhere do we find as yet any signs of stagnation or conventionality, and few of imitation or conformity. Even outside of the work of Shakespeare and of his chief rivals Jonson and Fletcher we discover abundance of comic invention, many varieties of humour, and more than one masterpiece of dramatic literature. But our view of this hey-day of English comedy is far from complete until we consider the plays of Jonson, who led the movement toward realism, and those of Fletcher, who at the close of the period led a return to romance. To these we proceed in the next two chapters.

CHAPTER IX

BEN JONSON

BEN JONSON was nine years younger than Shakespeare, and when he began writing for the London stage he found the older dramatist well established there. Our first records of Jonson are contemporaneous with "The Merchant of Venice" and "1 Henry IV." In 1597 he was employed by Henslowe as both actor and playwright, and in 1598 he was mentioned by Meres as one of the six poets most excellent in tragedy. In the same year his "Every Man in His Humour" was performed by Shakespeare's company and, according to tradition, was accepted through Shakespeare's effort.

The personal relations between the two poets were to continue friendly and are commemorated in Fuller's "Worthies of England" in the description of those memorable wit combats at the Mermaid tavern between Jonson, the huge galleon "built far higher for learning, solid but slow in his performances," and Shakespeare, that English man-of-war who "took advantage of all winds by the quickness of his wit and invention." In spite of their friendship, a difference in their dramatic theory and practice was manifest from the beginning, for Jonson ridiculed chronicle histories and romantic comedies and proposed a new type of realistic and satirical comedy. "Every Man in His Humour" was the first example of this "comedy of humours," and Jonson's subsequent comedies were in accord with a proclaimed dramatic creed, in promulgating which he could not always resist the temptation to gird at some of Shakespeare's practices that ran counter to his own methods; yet it was Jonson, the critical and arrogant, at the summit of his own career, who penned the noble eulogy which prefaces the "Folio of 1623," the first sweeping and worthy appreciation of Shakespeare's genius.

We have already noted that Jonson began writing plays in accord with current fashions. But he seems early to have formed a program of reform resting on a sharp and general criticism of the plays that had been produced. This criticism is conveyed here and there in his prefaces and introductions and is unmistakable in its main tenets on drama and comedy. Looking over the drama, Jonson found it characterized largely by improbable plots and extravagant expression. Impossible adventures, magic and supernatural powers abounded, and comedy had surrendered to fantasy. If this was true of "The Merchant of Venice," "Endymion," "Friar Bacon and Friar Bungay," and "A Midsummer Night's Dream," it was still truer of "Old Fortunatus" and the popular "Mucedorus." This drama presented a mass of incidents, often brilliantly depicted but mingled together with slight regard to any sense of law or order. There was little unity or simplicity of action. The plots did not observe the laws for dramatic fable, they were merely hasty translations of narratives put together with a minimum of coherence and with no regard to the properties established by classical authority.

The basis of Jonson's protest against this romantic drama was the same as Matthew Arnold's against nineteenth century romanticism, it had not been prepared for by a sound and searching criticism. Further, his ideas as to the nature of such a criticism were also similar to Arnold's; it should rest on a right appreciation of the classics and on a rationalized study of the present. At a time when so few plays had been printed, Jonson may be excused for not perceiving that artistic standards had already been set by Marlowe and Lyly, to say nothing of Shakespeare; but it was also true that in general the Elizabethans, while moved by varied and intense artistic impulses, paid little heed to standards or rules. Jonson

wished the drama to return as far as possible to the purposes and methods of the Greeks and Romans, and he
thought this would be accomplished by obedience to certain laws that criticism had derived from classical practice.
First, were the three unities requiring a single coherent
action, confined at the most to twenty-four hours and to a
single city. Second, there were the laws of decorum
requiring the separation of species and a certain propriety
in characterization. Tragedy and comedy should be kept
distinct, and the mixture of sensational tragedy with
clownish farce was abhorrent. Characterization should
not be capricious and confused but should be based on
some analysis of society resulting in the presentation of
persons who were typical representatives of the different
classes. Any king, for example, should represent kings
in general, a jealous husband should exhibit the typical
traits of jealousy, and neither person should lapse into
mere individual whimsy. Only by adherence to such
principles could flagrant and dangerous departure from
artistic standards be checked.

Jonson singles out the two most popular types of plays
as the most notorious sinners. The Prologue to "Every
Man in His Humour" was not printed in the first edition
and the date of its writing is uncertain; but it represents
opinions similar to those set forth in other of Jonson's
early plays. In this he makes fun of the chronicle histories—perhaps with special reference to Shakespeare's.
He declares that he will not serve the ill customs of
the age:

> To make a child, now swaddled, to proceed
> Man, and then shoot up, in one beard, and weed,
> Past threescore years; or, with three rusty swords
> And help of some few foot-and-half-foot words,
> Fight over York and Lancester's long jars
> And in the tyring-house bring wounds to scars.
> He rather prays, you will be pleased to see
> One such to-day as other plays should be,

Where neither chorus wafts you o'er the seas,
Nor creaking throne comes down, the boys to please,
Nor nimble squib is seen, to make a-feard
The gentlewomen, nor rolled bullet heard
To say, it thunders, nor tempestuous drum
Rumbles, to tell you when the storm doth come.

In the induction to "Every Man Out of His Humour" he laughs at the conventions of romantic comedy, "of a duke to be in love with a countess, and that countess to be in love with the duke's son, and the son to love the lady's waiting maid; some such cross-wooing with a clown to their serving man."

Instead of lawless and fantastic translations from romance and history, Jonson planned a realistic comedy based on a rational and ordered study of life of his own time, contrived with all regard possible on the modern stage to the models of Plautus and Aristophanes. Instead of a haphazard selection of story, scene and persons, he proposed to base his carefully constructed plots on an analysis of society into humours, or dominant characteristics. In so far as these humours represented follies and absurdities, the duty of comedy was to satirize and reform.

These reformative purposes were not entirely novel. Chapman's early plays had delineated humours and exposed follies. There had been a good deal of domestic and realistic comedy, though usually not much above the level of farce; and there had also been much careful imitating of Plautus and Terence, though usually without any very serious study of contemporary manners. The rapid growth and prosperity of the drama naturally made the need of criticism felt, and the growing sophistication of the city audiences must have opened the way for realism and satire. But there is no question that Jonson was the leader in this movement and no doubt that "Every Man in His Humour" surpassed any predecessor in the comedy of humours.

Its prologue promises that it will depict:

> deeds, and language such as men do use:
> And persons, such as Comedy would choose
> When she would show an image of the times
> And sport with human follies not with crimes.

The play proudly fulfills this boast, but it exhibits signs of the conflict that was inherent in Jonson's program. On the one hand is his plan to take a group of persons illustrative of the humours of the time, and from these to build a coherent plot exposing and ridiculing their excesses. On the other hand is the desire to follow the model set by Plautus and Terence both as to its plot of tricks and its types of character. Both the construction of the intrigue and the persons of the play—the jealous husband, the braggart, the confidential servant with his many disguises, the gay young men, the deceived father and the ridiculous gulls—are manifestly suggested by Latin comedy fully as much as by London life. The plot, however, is skilfully dovetailed into London scenes, and the persons are given nct only London manners but a fresh and original development. The play is in fact an admirable example of Jonson's art of character drawing. Each person is distinctly and consistently delineated, yet without the tedious elaboration that he sometimes exhibits, and Bobadill is a triumph. His exploits in lying recall Falstaff's, but his method and manner are entirely different from that chief of all the *milites gloriosi*. Bobadill's is the saturnine temper with a pretense of melancholy and reserve, carefully calculating his chances, watchful of his audience, in his boasting cautiously advancing his parallels until he is ready for the daring assault. His methods help to sustain our interest and bring it to a culmination in the great scene (IV, 5) of his discomfiture. We have no sympathy for Bobadill as we have for Falstaff, and indeed sympathy rarely intrudes on the laughter that the play excites. There is no sentiment, no romance, nothing marvellous or thrilling, only a continuous laugh-

ter at folly. In the revision Jonson deleted one fine passage of blank verse in praise of poetry, and the play is
mainly written in prose, only the ladies and the elders
using verse. Moderation in expression, avoidance of all
excesses, and care in construction united with comic invention, produce a play that was destined for nearly two
centuries to remain a model for the English comedy of
manners.

In the following year, 1599, Jonson's conception of
the comedy of humours was carried on in his "Comical
Satyr of Every Man Out of His Humour." In the induction, Asper, representing Jonson himself, announces a
highly satirical and moral purpose, akin to that of *Vetus
Comoedia*

> Well, I will scourge those apes
> And to these courteous eyes oppose a mirror,
> As large as is the stage whereon we act;
> Where they shall see the time's deformity
> Anatamoised in every nerve and sinew,
> With constant courage and contempt of fear.

A number of affected and absurd persons are thoroughly exposed through the agency of Macilente, who
is also cured of his besetting envy. There may be courage enough in the undertaking, but there is little amusement. The induction and chorus show how carefully considered were Jonson's purpose and art, but the play
exhibits him in one of his most prevailing humours,
indulging in an over-elaboration of uninteresting characters and a too detailed exposure of folly.

In "Cynthia's Revels" (1600) the general scheme is
similar to that of "Every Man Out of His Humour." A
group of ladies and gallants have their follies and affectations exposed through the agency of a censor who
speaks for the author. Further, on the example of Aristophanes, Jonson seems to have ventured on personal
satire, and Dekker promptly took the part of Anaides
to himself. The scene, however, is not in London but in

a forest by a fountain. There Mercury and Cupid are joined by Echo who sings a song and explains that the spring is the fountain of self-love which will infect all those who taste a drop thereof. This is like the setting for one of Lyly's fantastic comedies, some of which were being revived by the Children of the Revels for whom Jonson was now writing. Indeed, the gallants and the ladies, the deities, the songs, and the masque with its devices and dances, all suggest that Jonson was trying to combine Aristophanic satire and Lylian fantasy in a play suitable for the newly revived children actors. But the carefully formed framework is not filled out with mirth or —except the song of Hesperus—with poetry. The moral allegory, however, is fully explained, and the queen rapturously praised. After the masque, the ladies and gentlemen are censured by Crites and go out singing on their way to the Fountain of Knowledge where they are to find cure. In the epilogue Jonson boldly faces the charge that he has drunk too heavily of the other fountain, and boasts of the play,

> By God, 'tis good, and if you like't, you may.

His next play, "The Poetaster," acted 1601, exhibited his arrogance in full length. Jonson is Horace and with his friend Vergil (possibly Chapman) passes judgment on the poetasters Crispinus (Marston) and Demetrius (Dekker). The story of Ovid's love for Julia is introduced very ineffectively, and a swindling and voluble Captain Tucca is constantly on the stage, but the only scene which carries much amusement for the reader of to-day is that in which Marston is made to vomit up a prodigious vocabulary. The play anticipated Dekker's attack on Jonson in the "Satiromastix," and the two were the chief contributions to that War of the Theaters which Rosencrantz describes to Hamlet as taking place between the adult and children companies. Jonson seems to have tried to enlarge his scheme of comedy along Aristophanic lines so as to include satirical allegory, self praise and personal satire, but in "The Apologetical Dialogue," spoken but once on the stage, he refused to carry on further this "poetmachia" and promised to turn from comedy to tragedy.

His return to comedy a few years later was made in collaboration with Chapman and Marston in "Eastward Ho," a play owing much to Jonson's construction and suggestion but discussed elsewhere as representing the best work of his collaborators.

The four comedies that followed, "Volpone" in 1605, "Epicœne" in 1609, "The Alchemist" in 1610, and "Bartholomew Fair" in 1614, rank with "Every Man in His Humour" as Jonson's masterpieces. They are all comedies of humours, but each is an individual development of the type. They all satirize the society of that time and human nature in the large but by different means and with varying intensity. The tone of "Epicœne" is farcical while the satire in "Volpone" exceeds in bitterness the range permissible in comedy. They are all modelled on the classical plays, but in different degrees; the "Alchemist" being a very close though successful adaptation of Latin situations, plot and dramaturgy, while "Bartholomew Fair" is one of the most distinctly English of all our comedies. The plots, firmly constructed, ingenious and highly elaborated, proceed through interesting variations to their common purpose, the ridicule of human folly as illustrated in types of character. There results, in spite of some repetition, an aggregation of clearly delineated persons unrivalled in either numbers or verisimilitude in English comedy except in Shakespeare.

Jonson's method, as has often been repeated, is different from Shakespeare's. He does not start with a story and build up his characterization from the story; he starts with his characters and devises a plot to suit and exhibit them. Though tricks and deceptions make up the mechanism of these plots, the result is something more than comedies of intrigue, and though London and contemporary manners are studied and realistically presented, the result is not merely a comedy of manners. Preëminently these are comedies of character. Jonson is limited in his delineation of human nature by his admiration for the conventional characterization of Latin comedy, and he is limited still more by Elizabethan psychology which saw man governed by some predominant trait or humour, and he did not escape from the fondness of Elizabethan drama for exaggeration and over-emphasis. Individuality appears in his plays chiefly through caricature. He has none of Shakespeare's humour that can perceive wit in a fool, courage of a kind in a braggart, and humanity in a monster. Jonson's comic creations are more like those of Dickens than like those of Thackeray and much more like Smollett's than Jane Austen's. But in the five masterpieces at least, the delineation has both dramatic vigour and literary distinction.

Some further defense of Jonson's verisimilitude will occur to any one who has much acquaintance with the Elizabethans. Though human nature seems much the same in every age, there apparently are periods when its emotions are less restrained, controlled or inhibited than at others. Rarely, it would seem, has there been less of a social consensus as to behavior or less compression of emotions and desires into fixed moulds than in the Elizabethan age. Their fops seem to have been more bizarre than ours, their gluttons more greedy, their braggarts more vociferous. It would be difficult today to find a statesman who would exhibit his good and evil as variously and unreservedly as did Raleigh, or an Englishman in authority who would prove quite as much of the spoiled child as did Essex. One might find evidence that humours ran more wild in Jonson's day than they did even in the London of Chaucer or the London of Dickens. Though the society of the reign of James I was more sophisticated and more corrupt than that of Elizabeth's reign, it was scarcely sufficiently self-centered or self-conscious to afford the basis for a comedy of fashions and modes such as that of Congreve or of Sheridan. Beaux and belles are neither very gay nor fine mannered in Jonson's plays, nor in James's court. But both court and city offered a host of subjects for caricature.

"Volpone" is written in unusually vigorous and flowing verse, and Jonson was justly proud, as he boasted in the prologue, of having written in five weeks a comedy that observed the laws of time, place and persons, and swerved from no needful rule. In the dedication to both the universities where the play had been acted, he excuses the punishment of the vicious in comedy, defending himself by the example of the ancients, and still more because "it is the office of a comic poet to imitate justice, and instruct to life." This is interesting as an adumbration of Rymer's "poetic justice," and as an utterance of the purpose of Jonson's satiric comedy. Other passages in the same dedication give noble expression to the aims to which his art had now arrived, "to reduce not only the ancient forms, but manners of the scene, the easiness, the propriety, the innocence, and last, the doctrine, which is the principal end of poesie, to inform men in the best reason of living." Its proclamation of reform, however, soon becomes characteristically vainglorious and insolently disregardful of his great predecessors and contemporaries. He promises "the maturing of some worthier fruits; wherein, if my muses be true to me, I shall raise the despised head of poetry again, and stripping her out of those rotten and base rags wherewith the times have adulterated her form, restore her to her primitive habit, feature, and majesty, and render her worthy to be embraced and kist of all the great and master-spirits of our world."

The comedy exposes human vices rather than follies. Volpone, a magnifico of Venice, a sensualist and a swindler, feigns that he is dying and receives visits and presents from those who wish to be his heirs. One disinherits his son, another offers his wife to Volpone's lust in hopes of securing his fortune. A corrupt lawyer, a

foolish English knight travelling in Italy and his affected
and literary wife fall into the net. The disguises and
tricks are managed by Volpone's parasite, who announces
himself as the last refinement in that long line of theatrical personages.

> But your fine elegant rascal, that can rise
> And stoop, almost together, like an arrow;
> Shoot through the air as nimbly as a star;
> Turn short as doth a swallow; and be here,
> And there, and here, and yonder, all at once;
> Present to any humour, all occasion;
> And change a visor swifter than a thought!
> This is the creature had the art born with him;
> Toils not to learn it, but doth practise it
> Out of most excellent nature: and such sparks
> Are the true parasites, others but their zanis.

In the end the parasite cheats his master, and both
overreach themselves, are tried and condemned to severe
punishment. Jonson excused himself for the severity of
the catastrophe. "My special aim being to put a snaffle
in their mouths, that cry out, 'We never punish vice in
our interludes'." But "the strict vigour of comic law"
may object to the depravity exhibited rather than to its
punishment. Though the play realizes the Aristotelian
concept of the ridicule of something ugly, the ugliness is
too great for ridicule. Laughter may enter a den of
thieves, but here she is invited into a den of wild beasts.
The grossness of the language keeps pace with the
depravity of the persons and the hideousness of the
situations, but the antics of the greedy beasts seem to
have aroused the hilarity of the Elizabethans, who indeed
could find genial amusement in their madhouses. The
play also "proved very satisfactory to the town" after
the Restoration, and its disappearance from the stage
before the end of the eighteenth century was taken by
some to indicate the growing imbecility of the theatrical
taste. Our stage has never seen such another daring

attempt in satiric comedy to overwhelm vice with both moral indignation and riotous laughter.

The next comedy, "Epicœne," or "The Silent Woman," gives up the Juvenalian ire and returns to something like the manner of the earlier comedies of humours. The scene is London, and the persons exhibit current fashions, including those of foolish knights and ladies collegiate, and they speak in prose. The ingenious plot brings all the fools into the main action with the chief humorist as its focus. Morose, who hates noise above all else, is gulled by his nephew into marriage with a supposedly silent woman, who first proves a noisy tartar, and then—this is the final surprise—proves not a woman at all, but a boy. Of course the clever nephew gets his uncle's fortune. The extravagance of the situations puts the play in the category of farce, but there is wit in the dialogue and an interesting depiction of manners as well as amusement in the unfolding of the absurdities.

In "The Alchemist" Jonson essays another large canvas of tricksters and gulls. Subtle, the alchemist, Dol Common and Face, a housekeeper, have set up their snares in the house of Face's master. Hither come an extraordinary procession of gulls, whose very names are enough to recall the lively scenes—Dapper, a lawyer's clerk; Abel Drugger, a credulous tobacco man; Sir Epicure Mammon, a voluptuary with a Micawber-like gift of eloquent anticipation; Pertinax Surly, a doubting Thomas; Tribulation Wholesome and Ananias, two brethren of Amsterdam who make an effort to serve both God and mammon and also the weaker brethren; Kastrill, a foolish heir; and Dame Pliant, his sister, a widow. One after another, they expose their folly and greed, and add to the fun and entanglement, until the master of the house returns and joins with the clever Face to keep the spoils, including the widow, and to lock the doors on dupers and duped.

If we accept Volpone's iniquity and Morose's horror
of noise as premises, we must admire the closeness of
construction and the vigour of comic invention with which
Jonson proceeds to his dramatic conclusions.   In the
"Alchemist" our admiration is limited by no similar quali-
fications.   The main objects of ridicule, alchemy and
puritanism, require neither the trivality of farce nor the
seriousness of villainy.   They or their counterparts have
always nourished strange humours and are ever in need
of the medicine of comedy.   Our great financiers still
consult clairvoyants and prophets as did Sir Epicure
Mammon, and they do not altogether lack his eloquence;
and every new religious enthusiasm today soon leaves its
followers striving to serve both God and mammon as
did Tribulation and Ananias.   Jonson's comedy displays,
in the manners of the Elizabethans, follies that belong
to the world and to time.

Take for instance the first interview between the simpleton and the two sharpers.   This develops a situation
that has always been a favourite in comedy and is constantly being enacted in real life.   Its particular simpleton, Abel Drugger, gave Garrick one of his greatest parts.

Subtle. What is your name, say you, Abel Drugger?
Drugger. Yes, sir.
Sub. A seller of tobacco?
Drug. Yes, sir.
Sub. Umph!
Free of the grocers?
Drug. Ay, an't please you.
Sub. Well——
Your business, Abel?
Drug. This, an't please your worship;
I am a young beginner, and am building
Of a new shop, an't like your worship, just
At corner of a street:—Here is the plot on't—
And I would know by art, sir, of your worship,

Which way I should make my door, by necromancy,
And where my shelves; and which should be for boxes,
And which for pots. I would be glad to thrive, sir:
And I was wish'd to your worship by a gentleman,
One captain Face, that says you know men's planets,
And their good angels, and their bad.
    Sub. I do,
If I do see them——

Re-enter Face.

    Face. What! my honest Abel?
Thou art well met here.
    Drug. Troth, sir, I was speaking,
Just as your worship came here, of your worship:
I pray you speak for me to master doctor.
    Face. He shall do anything.—Doctor, do you hear!
This is my friend, Abel, an honest fellow;
He lets me have good tobacco, and he does not
Sophisticate it with sack-lees or oil.
    .   .   .   .
A neat, spruce, honest fellow, and no goldsmith.
    Sub. He is a fortunate fellow, that I am sure on.
    Face. Already, sir, have you found it? Lo thee, Abel!
    Sub. And in right way toward riches——
    Face. Sir!
    Sub. This summer
He will be of the clothing of his company,
And next spring call'd to the scarlet; spend what he can.
    Face. What, and so little beard?
    Sub. Sir, you must think,
He may have a receipt to make hair come:
But he'll be wise, preserve his youth, and fine for't;
His fortune looks for him another way.
    Face. 'Slid, doctor, how canst thou know this so soon?
I am amused at that!
    Sub. By a rule, captain,
In metoposcopy, which I do work by;
A certain star in the forehead, which you see not.

Your chestnut or your olive-colour'd face
Does never fail: and your long ear doth promise.
I knew't by certain spots, too, in his teeth,
And on the nail of his mercurial finger.
    Face. Which finger's that?
    Sub. His little finger. Look.
You were born upon a Wednesday?
    Drug. Yes, indeed, sir.
    Sub. The thumb, in chiromancy, we give Venus;
The fore-finger, to Jove; the midst, to Saturn;
The ring, to Sol; the least, to Mercury,
Who was the lord, sir, of his horoscope,
His house of life being Libra; which fore-show'd,
He should be a merchant, and should trade with balance.
    Face. Why, this is strange! Is it not, honest Nab?
    Sub. There is a ship now, coming from Ormus,
That shall yield him such a commodity
Of drugs—This is the west, and this the south?
                            [*Pointing to the plan.*
    Drug. Yes, sir.
    Sub. And those are your two sides?
    Drug. Ay, sir.
    Sub. Make me your door, then, south; your broad
        side, west;
And on the east side of your shop, aloft,
Write Mathlai, Tarmiel, and Baraborat;
Upon the north part, Rael, Velel, Thiel.
They are the names of those mercurial spirits,
That do fright flies from boxes.
    Drug. Yes, sir.
    Sub. And
Beneath your threshold, bury me a load-stone
To draw in gallants that wear spurs: the rest,
They'll seem to follow.
    Face. That's a secret, Nab!
    Sub. And, on your stall, a puppet, with a vice
And a court-fucus to call city-dames:
You shall deal much with minerals.

Drug. Sir, I have
At home, already——
Sub. Ay, I know you have arsenic,
Vitriol, sal-tartar, argaile, alkali,
Cinoper; I know all.—This fellow, captain,
Will come, in time, to be a great distiller,
And give a say—I will not say directly,
But very fair—at the philosopher's stone.
Face. Why, how now, Abel! is this true?
Drug. Good captain,
What must I give?

[*Aside to Face.*

Face. Nay, I'll not counsel thee.
Thou hear'st what wealth (he says, spend what thou
canst),
Thou'rt like to come to.
Drug. I would gi' him a crown.
Face. A crown! and toward such a fortune? heart,
Thou shalt rather gi' him thy shop. No gold about thee?
Drug. Yes, I have a portague, I have kept this half
year.
Face. Out on thee, Nab! 'Slight, there was such an
offer——
Shalt keep't no longer, I'll give't him for thee. Doctor,
Nab prays your worship to drink this, and swears
He will appear more grateful, as your skill
Does raise him in the world.
Drug. I would entreat
Another favour of his worship.
Face. What is't, Nab?
Drug. But to look over, sir, my almanack,
And cross out my ill days, that I may neither
Bargain, nor trust upon them.
Face. That he shall, Nab;
Leave it, it shall be done, 'gainst afternoon.
Sub. And a direction for his shelves.
Face. Now, Nab.
Art thou well pleased, Nab?

Drug. 'Thank, sir, both your worships.
Face. Away.

[*Exit Drugger.*

"The Alchemist" is the culmination of that long imitation of Plautus and Terence which we have traced since its beginnings in "Ralph Roister Doister." It surpasses all rivals in its happy union of English manners with the Roman plot, and it outdistances the Roman models in every element of dramatic vigour and richness. In no other play has Jonson so completely succeeded in accomplishing what he intended to do. There are no tiresome excursuses; the blank verse suits itself readily to the rapid dialogue or to the orations of Sir Epicure; the language is varied, idiomatic and precise; the style finished and animated. The Latin models supply only suggestions for the mechanism; the happy elaboration and the abounding fun are Jonson's.

"Bartholomew Fair" is an extraordinary presentation of Elizabethan London. We are introduced into a noisy and sweaty hurly burly. There are thirty speaking parts and many supernumeraries. In the company of the usual pair of witty censors, we meet a cutpurse, a ballad singer, a tapster, a bawd, a bully. Ursula the pig woman, a silly wife, a foolish widow, a proctor who has written a puppet show, a booby Cokes and his man Waspe, a Puritan zealot, and a pompous judge bent on reform. Most of these persons are either fools or knaves and are very busy exhibiting their characters. Trick rebounds from trick, the biter is bit, the hypocrite exposed, and malodorous epithets fill the air. The action revolves about the stocks which receive several of the company, about Ursula's booth where nearly all, including the Puritan, are regaled, and about the puppet show and its twittering author. Some of the persons are familiar in comedy, but their eccentricities and vulgarities remind the reader of Dickens and Smollett rathe rthan of Plautus and Aristophanes. Nowhere else, perhaps, in literature have so many people been so vividly presented in a three hours' entertainment as here.

In the depiction of manners and character, the play may indeed be held to outrank even "The Alchemist." In many respects, however, its inferiority is palpable. It is unwieldy in structure, its fun is often gross and boisterous, it is overcrowded with persons and incidents. The trouble here, as in other plays by Jonson, is that all the persons are drawn in elaborate detail. If some of the subordinate parts were removed, and others reduced in proportion, the play would doubtless be improved. Certainly, much of Littlewit's puppet play could be spared. But all the persons mentioned and as many more, are drawn not only with painstaking exactness, but also with unflagging animation. A play which unites such masterpieces of comic characterization as Justice Overdo, Cokes and Zeal-of-the-land Busy, together with much uproarious fun, must, surely be accounted an amazing achievement of comic invention.

The amusing induction gives some further hints as to Jonson's theory of comedy. He laughs at the public taste which still delights in such old favourites as Jeronimo and Andronicus, and he scoffs at the recent romantic plays of Shakespeare, "The Winter's Tale" and "The Tempest":

> If there be never a servant-monster in the fair, who can help it, he (Jonson) says, nor a nest of antiques? he is loth to make nature afraid in his plays, like those that beget tales, tempests, and such like drolleries, to mix his head with other men's heels; let the concupiscence of jigs and dances reign as strong as it will amongst you; yet if the puppets please any body, they shall be intreated to come in.

Jonson seems here to refer to the introduction of dances and other elements from the court masques into comedy. By this time he was the chief writer of masques for performance at the court and had helped to give those entertainments an elaborate literary form. Always a precisian, he now seems to have preferred to keep his masques and comedies separate. It is clear that he intended to make "Bartholomew Fair" an example of pure realism. Perhaps for this reason he wrote it, like "Epicœne," wholly in prose, remarkable for its clearness and flexibility, admirably suited to the different speakers and imitative of the manners of the time. Further from classical models than the other comedies, it is nevertheless Aristophanic in the breadth and liveliness of its mirth and in its unhesitating realism. Original in its scheme and subject, daring in its invention, it marks the highest development of the comedy of humours as a national type. The kind of comedy which it presents has continued in prose fiction; but, since the Elizabethan period, our theater has never permitted such robust fun and so unvarnished a presentation of the absurdities of human nature.

In 1616, a year chiefly remarkable for Shakespeare's death, Jonson collected his plays, masques and poems in a Folio edition, and thus asserted again his claim that his dramas be regarded as a part of permanent literature. He was now at the height of his reputation as a dramatist, poet, writer of masques, critic and scholar. At the Apollo room in the Devil tavern he had established a new court of wits, whither the young poets thronged to hail him as oracle. Many of the greatest and worthiest of his time were numbered among his friends. His work in comedy, however, was virtually completed.

"The Devil is an Ass," acted in the same year, betrays a labouring and unhappy invention. Jonson planned to enlarge his collection of gulls by the addition of the devil. Satan sends a minor demon, Pug, to earth to do some mischief, but he proves stupid and unsuccessful. The net result of the humorous conception is to add one more uninteresting dolt to the dramatis personæ. The satire is lively, especially on the exorcism of supposed evil spirits and—taking a more modern tone—on projects and projectors. London was indeed becoming acquainted with some of the adjuncts of commercial prosperity and its attendant luxuries. The chief gull is Fitzdottrel, who aims to become "Duke of Drown'd-land" through participation in a scheme for draining the waste lands of the kingdom, and another project is "serving the whole state with toothpicks." Mrs. Fitzdottrel is portrayed with more sympathy than Jonson usually bestows upon his women, and all the persons are, as usual, carefully differentiated. But the comic entanglements are cumbersome and the movement heavy.

One other comedy, which Jonson did not include in his collected edition, had been published under his name in 1609, "The Case is Altered." It is a Terentian intrigue and was possibly written as early as 1597. It adds nothing to the development of the comedy of humours.

Jonson was now able to withdraw from the stage, and nine years intervened before his next comedy, "The Staple of News" (1625). Though his prologue is as boastful as ever, yet in the induction and the intercalary scenes there are indications that he felt the uncertainty of his powers and was driven back to the stage by want. He went to Aristophanes for a model, composing an allegorical satire based on the "Plutus," from which and from "The Wasps" he borrowed certain passages. The main allegory of Pecunia, Pennyboy, Mortgage and the rest, is tiresome; but there is excellent satire and fun in the scheme of the Canters college and in the picture of a Jacobean innovation which already displayed some characteristics of its successor, the newspaper. But the details of the plan are not fused into a dramatic whole. The play lacks, more than any of his since "Cynthia's Revels," the movement and verisimilitude indispensable in comedy.

The remaining comedies come near to deserving Dryden's harsh criticism, "mere dotages." They reveal him still elaborating large constructions not without comic possibilities, but lacking the power to give these life.

"The New Inn" was incontinently damned at its first presentation and published two years later (1631) with an angry address by Jonson to the reader. The play aims at taking advantage of the current interest in platonism fostered at court by the queen, and both the platonic Lady Frampul and her suitor are treated sympathetically; but the platonic addresses are dull, and so also is the low comedy. The failure of the play called forth Jonson's ode, "Come, leave the loathed stage"; but one's sympathies incline to the audience rather than to the author. Four years later, "The Magnetic Lady," or "Humours Reconciled," attempted a continuation and conclusion of the series of comedies of humours begun thirty-five years before. A marriageable young niece of the magnetic lady is made the "centre attractive, to draw thither a diversity of guests, all persons of different humours, to make up his (the author's) perimeter." This plan is carried out in a half-hearted way, though with the usual attention to details and explanatory intermezzos. But, while the acts conform to the "laws of protasis, epitasis and catastasis," there is no life or wit. "A Tale of a Tub" was acted in the same year. Various references to the queen make it possible that the play was first written about 1597; but the satire on Inigo Jones as In and In Medley must have been incorporated in the 1633 revision. The separation of the early crudities and the later dotages is now impossible. The plot of the trickster-tricked variety shows something of Jonson's old ingenuity, but the persons are all beneath interest.

I shall not comment here on Jonson's masques, which contain many comic scenes, or on his very interesting pastoral, "The Sad Shepherd," left unfinished at his death. This took place on August 6, 1637. He was buried in Westminster Abbey.

Jonson's merits and defects as a comic dramatist have perhaps already been sufficiently indicated. His plays manifestly are the results of wide and painstaking observation. Like a modern realist with his note-books, Jonson must have occupied himself in the systematic collection of phrases, incidents and personal peculiarities to be used in filling out his picture of the follies of the times. Again like a modern dramatist, he was immensely concerned in the construction of a well made play. Nothing is left at loose ends, each scene is complete in itself and fits into the main organization. In these somewhat mechanical excellences at least "The Alchemist" deserves Coleridge's praise for having one of the three most nearly perfect plots in literature. But the chief merit of the comedies is their delineation of character. This is not conditioned by story, as in Shakespeare, but it is limited by the observance of the rules and models of classical comedy and also by Jonson's own purpose to make each person the illustration of a single trait or humour. Due in part to his theory are the long monologues, the extended descriptions of persons, the disgusting coarseness of language, the tendency to exaggerate fact into satire and satire into farce. His aim is to create types rather than individuals, but so much observation of life and care in amplification is crowded into such a type as Bobadill that it assumes individuality. The result is nearly caricature, but the eccentricities of his persons are many and so elaborated that they do not want lifelikeness. Indeed, each person is set forth in such distinctness and abundance of detail that this often distracts from interest in the situation. Jonson will not let go of character or speech or situation until he has wrung it dry. Yet in spite of these obvious limitations his comic characterization remains among the greatest achievements of the English drama because of its clearness and certainty, its richness of humour and its dramatic veracity.

Jonson's plays have many resemblances to other types of comedy; they are comedies of intrigue and of manners, they are like other serious efforts at realism and satire, they are based on a fundamental and systematic analysis of personality. Nevertheless, these comedies of humours make a peculiar species. They give the scantiest place to love and rely less perhaps than any other group of plays in our language on romance and sentiment. They have never stirred a tear or a sigh. Even his moralizing never has a sentimental appeal. He preaches only "the moral obligation to be intelligent." Nor is his picture of society relieved by much refinement of manners or sparkle of wit. High breeding and fine manners are scarcely more conspicuous than delicacy of language and fancy. There is masculine vigour but no feminine charm. This society, he says in effect, is vile but ridiculous; it has however a leaven of intelligence which may be its salvation.

He could depict noble passions and write winsome verse, but he did neither in comedy, which be believed should confine itself to ridicule in the service of intelligence. With these self-imposed restraints, one may wonder that he could create any plays that would please popular audiences or that would be read with pleasure in after generations. But there can be no doubt, I think, of the service of such restricted comedy in literature. As I have written elsewhere, "Comedy, of all forms of literature, has its duties in the street or tavern as well as in Arden or on the sea-coast of Bohemia. Jonson found neither charm nor heroism in the London streets, though they were both unquestionably there. He found neither the truth and passion that lay at the heart of puritanism, nor the joy and fancy that stirred the light-hearted moods of Fletcher, Shirley or Herrick. But he mirrored what he saw of men and manners with an untiring fidelity, heightened and coloured his picture with a hearty and virile humour, and interpreted it by a sound and censorious morality. Imaginative idealism, characteristic of the Elizabethan age and its literature, had another and greater master; but the interest in the depiction and criticism of the actual life of the day—an interest essential to vitality in the literature of any age, and manifest in the golden days of the Armada as well as in degenerate Jacobean times—had its chief exponent in Jonson."

Jonson's influence both as a critic and a practitioner was commanding in his own day and has been felt down to the present. No one then or since has been obliged to accept all of his tenets or methods in order to admire his general service to letters. He endeavored to make the acted drama worthy of a high place in literature and he was also keenly interested in improving the practice of the stage. He not only knew the classical drama better than any of his contemporaries, he tried to adapt intelligently and not slavishly its principles and rules to the peculiarities of the English theater. He wrote his own comedies in the consciousness that they might teach others the desirability of such adaptations, the value of wide observation, careful construction and systematic characterization. These are lessons which he made it impossible for the English drama wholly to forget. But his influence in promoting characterization in comedy has sometimes been over-estimated. English comedy has always had a place for eccentrics, and their continued prominence in our drama, often in disregard of plot or probability, doubtless owes as much to Shakespeare as to Jonson. The Elizabethans by the time that Jonson began to write were intensely interested in human psychology, and he represents only one phase of that interest. In a somewhat different way from Dekker or Heywood or Shakespeare, he supplemented their success in making comedy a study of humanity.

His comedies were imitated as soon as they appeared; witness "Every Woman in Her Humour" (1609, acted by 1600). Beaumont and Fletcher studied in his school, as the "Woman Hater," written by the former, testifies, and Marston, Middleton and Chapman profited from his example. Of later dramatists, Field, Randolph, Cartwright, Nabbes and Brome—to name no others— employed Jonson's methods and wrote plays in his manner. The comedy of humours became, in fact, an established model, which few later writers altogether disregarded. All realistic comedy owned its influence, and reminiscences of its most effective scenes and types of character found their way into every kind of drama. There were other leaders in realistic comedy, Middleton in particular, who may be said to have set an example of a less satirical, less moral, but hardly less Plautian, representation of London manners. But Jonson continued through his lifetime the chief advocate and exemplar of serious realism.

After the Restoration Jonson's reputation for a while increased. Shadwell was his avowed and diligent disciple. Dryden's praise was echoed by Dennis and others, especially by those who were most eager to see neoclassical rules and models prevail in the theaters. His decorum was contrasted to Shakespeare's lawlessness and his "humour" to Fletcher's wit. Both his tragedies and comedies were held in high esteem. The latter found a warm welcome on the stage and maintained themselves there during the long period when Shakespeare's romantic comedies failed to please. "Bartholomew Fair" disappeared (1731) even before "As You Like It" returned to the stage (1740), and neither "Volpone" nor "Epicœne" nor the "Alchemist" outlasted the eighteenth century. The last three were revived by Garrick, who also brought out a revision of "Every Man in His Humour." That play continued on the stage well into the nineteenth century.

Jonson's influence, moreover, has been felt throughout our literature and notably by the novel as well as the drama. His plays have constantly been read and have always encouraged a study of the absurdities of character and the incongruities of manners. Fielding and Smollett felt their incentive, and Dickens, who knew them well and himself acted Bobadill, must have been indebted to no inconsiderable extent to their suggestion. Their laughter still reëchoes through our fiction.

CHAPTER X

BEAUMONT AND FLETCHER

THE career of the two friends and collaborators, Francis Beaumont and John Fletcher, is one of the most astonishing in the entire history of the drama. While still in the twenties they captivated their theater and soon gained a popularity surpassing that of Jonson or Shakespeare, although both these were yet in their prime. The successes of the young poets initiated a return from the prevailing realism of Jonson and Middleton to a dramatic type of romance; but beyond this they instituted changes in theatrical methods and fashions that were destined to dominate the Elizabethan drama until the triumph of puritanism. After the Restoration their reputation remained undiminished and their plays continued to set the taste and fashions of a new age. Two hundred years after their deaths some of their plays were still being acted in the United States as well as England, and one or two were even carried to our mid-western frontier by the pioneer actors who first crossed the Appalachians.

Fletcher's first play was possibly "The Woman's Prize," a farcical sequel to Shakespeare's "Taming of the Shrew," acted in 1604, when its author was twenty-five. Within a year or so came the first effort of Beaumont, then hardly twenty, "The Woman Hater," a comedy manifestly written in discipleship to Ben Jonson. Then shortly followed two very remarkable and novel comedies which seem to have failed of popular success although they won the praise of the judicious. "The Knight of the Burning Pestle," mainly by Beaumont, is a burlesque, drawing its plan from the recently published

"Don Quixote," and making hilarious fun of the plays of adventure that still delighted the apprentices and citizens of the public playhouses. Fletcher's "Faithful Shepherdess" was modelled on Guarini's "Il Pastor Fido" and presented for the first time in English a full-fledged pastoral tragicomedy, designed as a new form of literary drama, and surpassing its model in poetry. Popular success, however, was soon won in a different field and by means of collaboration rather than separate efforts, in a series of tragedies and tragicomedies of which the most famous were "Philaster," "The Maid's Tragedy" and "A King and No King."

Beaumont wrote little or nothing for the stage after 1612. He died in 1616 and was buried in Westminster Abbey amidst the acclaims of all lovers of poetry. Fletcher collaborated with Shakespeare on "Henry VIII" and the "Two Noble Kinsmen" and continued the chief writer for the King's men up to the time of his death in 1625. He collaborated with others, especially Massinger, but he remained by all odds the most popular dramatist of the day and the undisputed leader of the stage. Of the fifty-two plays gathered under the names of Beaumont and Fletcher in the second Folio of 1679, modern criticism has been able to separate with some certainty the writing of Fletcher, but it has not been able to determine exactly the dates or extent of his collaboration with Beaumont, or to indicate his other collaborators with much certainty, except Massinger. In general, after a scenario was determined upon, each author seems to have taken certain portions of the play and to have written these in his own fashion; but there are many cases where the composition seems mixed or revised, and only with Fletcher are style and mannerisms unmistakable. In any case, this determination of authorship cannot go beyond traits of style. It is impossible to say who invented the plots or what suggestions were received from the other by the collaborator who wrote a particular scene. It is clear, however, that while the collaboration of Beaumont and Fletcher lasted they produced plays of high merit and general reputation and of a type and technic that continued to characterize the work of Fletcher and to influence the general course of dramatic practice. In the forty plays probably written after Beaumont's death, Fletcher is certainly the dominating factor. Indeed, the outstanding and distinguishing qualities of all the plays of the Folio are those which characterize the plays by Fletcher alone; most assuredly he is chiefly responsible for their comedy.

Beaumont's humour, however, must not be passed by without another glance at "The Knight of the Burning Pestle," the first and perhaps the best of a long line of dramatic burlesques which includes "The Rehearsal," "Tom Thumb" and "The Critic." The performance is by one of the children's companies, and when one of the boys comes forward to announce the play, he is interrupted by a grocer in the audience who demands a piece which shall glorify and not ridicule the citizens. The grocer climbs to the stage followed by his wife, and they take charge of the proceedings, choosing the name for the play and insisting that their apprentice Ralph take the title rôle. Ralph proves his fitness for a "huffing part" by spouting Hotspur's vaunt on honour and is soon occupied in rescuing maidens, conquering a giant, and in other mock-heroic adventures. At the end his ghost appears and after a prodigious soliloquy dies again, and finally at the behest of the grocer's wife, rises, makes obeisance and exit. Though all this is manifestly suggested by the new "Don Quixote," its adaptation into a burlesque of the favourite plays of the citizens is most ingenious. The action involves the rival loves of the clever Jasper and the doltish Humphrey for the rich and beautiful Luce and also the songs and capers of Jasper's father Merrythought, who is afflicted with chronic mirthfulness. The most amusing parts of the play, however, are the comments of the grocer and his wife which are continually interrupting the progress of the piece. At the end of the first scene they are distrustful of Jasper and Luce.

Citizen. Fie upon 'em, little infidels! what a matter's here now! Well, I'll be hanged for a half-penny, if there be not some abomination knavery in this play. Well, let 'em look to't; Ralph must come, and if there be any tricks a-brewing——
Wife. Let 'em brew and bake too, husband, a' God's name; Ralph will find all out, I warrant you, an they were older than they are.—I pray, my pretty youth, is Ralph ready?
Boy. He will be presently.
Wife. Now, I pray you, make my commendations unto him, and withal carry him this stick of liquorice; tell him his mistress sent it him, and bid him bite a piece; 'twill open his pipes the better, say.

But in the next scene Humphrey, the booby wooer, proves attractive.

Wife. Husband, I prithee, sweet lamb, tell me one thing; but tell me truly.—Stay, youths, I beseech you, till I question my husband.
Cit. What is it, mouse?
Wife. Sirrah, didst thou ever see a prettier child; how it behaves itself, I warrant ye, and speaks and looks, and perts up the head!—I pray you, brother, with your favour, were you never none of Master Moncaster's scholars?
Cit. Chicken, I prithee heartily, contain thyself: the childer are pretty childer; but when Ralph comes, lamb——

They continue impatient until Ralph's entry.

Enter *Ralph,* as a grocer, reading Palmerin of England, with *Tim and George.*

Wife. Oh, husband, husband, now, now! there's
Ralph, there's Ralph.

Cit. Peace, fool! let Ralph alone.—Hark you, Ralph,
do not strain yourself too much at the first.—Peace!—
Begin, Ralph.

Ralph later encounters Jasper and is beaten, to the consternation of the grocer's wife.

Wife. Sure the devil (God bless us!) is in this spring-
ald! Why, George, didst ever see such a fire-drake?
I am afraid my boy's miscarried. If he be, though he
were Master Merrythought's son a thousand times, if
there be any law in England, I'll make some of them
smart for't.

Cit. No, no; I have found out the matter, sweetheart;
Jasper is enchanted; as sure as we are here, he is
enchanted; he could no more have stood in Ralph's hands
than I can stand in my lord mayor's. I'll have a ring to
discover all enchantments, and Ralph shall beat him yet:
be no more vexed, for it shall be so.

Henceforth, whenever Jasper appears, she is terrified.

Wife. Is 'a gone, George?

City. Ay, cony.

Wife. Marry, and let him go, sweetheart. By the
faith o' my body, 'a has put me into such a fright, that I
tremble (as they say) as 'twere an aspen-leaf; look o'
my little finger, George, how it shakes. Now, in truth,
every member of my body is the worse for't.

Cit. Come, hug in mine arms, sweet mouse; he shall
not fright thee any more. Alas, mine own dear heart,
how it quivers!

But when Ralph is victorious over the giant Barbarosso,
otherwise known as the barber, the wife's spirits are
revived.

Wife. To him, Ralph, to him! hold up the giant; set
out thy leg before, Ralph!

Cit.   Falsify a blow, Ralph, falsify a blow! the giant lies open on the left side.

Wife.   Bear't off, bear't off still! there, boy!—Oh, Ralph's almost down, Ralph's almost down!

Ralph.   Susan, inspire me! now have up again.

Wife.   Up, up, up, up, up! so, Ralph! down with him, down with him, Ralph!

Cit.   Fetch him o'er the hip, boy!

[*Ralph* knocks down the barber.

Wife.   There, boy!   Kill, kill, kill, kill, kill, Ralph!

Cit.   No, Ralph; get all out of him first.

The grocer and his wife talk in prose which Fletcher rarely employed in the drama, but I find it hard to believe that he had no share in this most audacious and vivacious dialogue.   Beaumont certainly never did anything else nearly as amusing.

The tragedies and tragicomedies of their collaboration, to which I have elsewhere applied the convenient name "dramatic romances," are distinguished by their sensational plots, contrasting base and exalted love, tragic and idyllic circumstances, and weaving these together by a nexus of surprise and suspense into thrilling theatrical situations.   They display little individualization in the characters, trusting to certain stock types and indulging in extraordinary conversions, but they command an abundance of poetry, always lucid, equal to the requirements of their rapidly changing situations and rising now and then to an exquisite reflection of the current ideals of love and honour.   In comparison with preceding romance on the stage theirs is courtly, artificial and theatrical, but it pleased audiences that were becoming more representative of fashion and sophistication and less of the populace. In technic, in the manipulation of situation, the elaboration of dénouement, the constant employment of surprise, the imitation in blank verse of well-bred speech, these new romances surpassed all that had preceded or followed in sheer immediate theatrical effectiveness.   For the purpose of this book their most significant change in dramatic history lies in the new definition and impetus that they gave to tragicomedy.

In his preface to "The Faithful Shepherdess" Fletcher had borrowed Guarini's definition: "A tragicomedy is not so called in respect of mirth and killing, but in respect it wants deaths, which is enough to make it no tragedy, yet brings some near it, which is enough to make it no comedy, which must be a representation of familiar people, with such kind of trouble as no life be questioned; so that a god is as lawful in this as in a tragedy, and mean people as in a comedy." Though this definition was the outcome of a considerable debate among Italian critics in search for a justification for a *tertium quid* that might take its place between tragedy and comedy as approved by Aristotle, its terms do not differentiate the romances of Beaumont and Fletcher from preceding English practice. Sidney had contemptuously classed early English plays as mongrel tragicomedy, and some of those would have fulfilled Guarini's definition. Most of Shakespeare's romantic comedies would have qualified. Outside of the realistic plays of Jonson and Middleton, there had been few Elizabethan plays that had not either included death or brought some near it. Beaumont and Fletcher, however, were the first to seize upon the full theatrical possibilities that lay in the new species. They made the most of its contrasts of tragic and idyllic, of heroic and comic, of purity and wantonness, and they made the most of the element of averted tragedy, the rescuing of some brought near to death. The dénouement with its happy ending became the main thing. Up to the last act the tribulations and sufferings might be those of tragedy, and the audience held in breathless suspense as to whether the dénouement was to be tragic or happy. Moreover, they attached to this development of tragicomedy their methods and types of characterization and their peculiar devices for stage effectiveness, so that nearly all the

countless tragicomedies which followed derived in some
degree from their example.

The heroic tragicomedies, such as for example, "Philaster" and "A King and No King," come too close to
tragedy and contain too little humour to require our
consideration except to note that Fletcher continued the
type until the end of his career. "The Queen of
Corinth," which he wrote with Massinger, supplies a
typical example of tragedy averted at the last moment.
The fifth act brings the noble queen's evil son to the bar
accused by two ladies of rape. The law requires that
the person guilty of this crime must die unless the woman
wronged will marry him. One woman is willing to marry
the prince, the other demands his death. Which shall
prevail? Or, for another close approach to tragedy, take
"A Wife for a Month," written by Fletcher just before
his death, in which he repeats some of the situations of
"The Maid's Tragedy." The lustful tyrant fails to win
the noble heroine and commands that whoever marries
her shall die at the end of a month. As soon as the
noble hero has wed her, he is secretly commanded to
refrain from living with her as his wife on penalty of
her immediate death if he disobeys or tells anyone of
the secret command. Such sensational melodramas, dealing with the affairs of monarchs and kingdoms and usually
involving conflicts of love and honour include, by Fletcher
alone, "The Loyal Subject," "The Mad Lover," "A Wife
for a Month," and "The Island Princess"; and by
Fletcher with Massinger, or others, "The Queen of Corinth," "The Knight of Malta," "The Laws of Candy,"
and "The Nice Valour"; in the last two Fletcher having
very little share. Such tragicomedies continued after his
death and prepared the way for the "heroic plays" of the
Restoration.

Our interest is rather in those tragicomedies, somewhat less intense in their dangers and horrors, permitting
a larger infusion of mirth, in which the agonies of courtly

love are tempered by a comic rather than by a tragic accompaniment. It is, however, even more difficult to draw an exact line between tragicomedy and comedy than between tragicomedy and tragedy. These distinctions are attempted in the subtitles assigned to the plays in the Folio of 1679 but not always with evident justification, yet it will puzzle anyone to be much more discriminating. With few exceptions, the most important of which are the pastoral and the burlesque already noted, all the plays of Fletcher, written alone or in collaboration, are of much the same pattern. All deal with love and with little else besides love; all employ the most sensational contrasts and situations; all relieve suspense by surprise and throw us into suspense again up to the final dénouement; all are courtly and fashionable in manners and language, and all present a scene, usually designated in a foreign country, which is far removed from reality and created only for the theater. They might be arranged in a sort of scale having the tragedies at one end and the few comedies and farces placed in contemporary England at the other. There would be a gradual descent through the heroic tragicomedies to the tragicomedies with more humour, and next to the romantic comedies, and then to those forsaking romance for wit and manners; and there would be a general lessening of heroics, of intensity of emotion, of height of honour, of state affairs and tragic possibilities; and a general increase in liveliness of movement, in the amount of comic situation, and in the presentation of life in its ordinary walks. Comedy of course is found everywhere, even in the most gruesome tragedy, and it is always about the same in kind, but it is more abundant and hence better worth our observation in the lower half of the scale.

"The Humourous Lieutenant" may serve as an example of middle tragicomedy and the height of our comic diapason. The scene is Greece, and the play presents the conflict between the successors of Alexander the Great, especially the rivalry between the courts of Antigonus and

Seleucus. The warfare is conducted according to the strictest code of honour, but our interest is divided between the prince Demetrius, a paragon of honour, and his mistress, the beautiful and talkative Celia. Moreover, the comic underplot is happily entwined with the main heroic action and is very essential to the play. A favourite theme of tragedy makes its appearance in the rivalry of father and son for the same woman, but tragedy is averted, indeed it is annihilated by a comic incident, and the dramatic conflict is changed to one of those wars between lovers which evoke humour as much as perturbation. A somewhat full analysis may illustrate the nature of Fletcher's theater and the peculiar qualities of his combination of heroic romance and comedy.

The scene opens at court where the ushers are making ready for the presence. Celia appears, eager to see her lover in state, and her sharp tongue causes the guards to give way and let her in. The King enters, ambassadors are received and defiances exchanged. The prince Demetrius discovers Celia and bids her hasten home. The King also has observed her and orders his officers to follow her. Demetrius begs and receives command of the forces to march against the foe. His officers begin preparations, among them a humorous lieutenant who is ill but a brave fighter. This stirring long scene has introduced all the threads of the action and the persons. The second scene of the act shows Demetrius parting from Celia. Honour calls, but love bids him stay. The drums sound a march, and as the sound grows louder it is she who refuses one more last embrace:

> No, the drums beat;
> I dare not slack your honour; not a hand more,
> Only this look; the gods preserve and save ye.

Act II shifts back and forth from the court to the battlefield. At court the King's minions are busy with some incidental comedy in discovering in Celia the slave girl whom the prince has purchased and in preparing to entice her to court. On the battlefield the prince is defeated and some of his officers taken prisoners. He reports the misfortune to the King, but it is followed hard by a still greater blow, the enemy Seleucus returns the prisoners. Thus he has twice beaten Demetrius, once in valour and once in honour. Demetrius rushes off again to war accompanied very reluctantly by the lieutenant who now wishes to get married.

In Act III, Celia is lured to court on the pretext of seeing Demetrius. On the battlefield the lieutenant who has recovered his health proves a sudden coward. His friends persuade the physicians to convince him that he is ill unto death, whereupon his courage returns and he performs prodigies of valour. Seleucus is defeated, surrenders, and sues for peace, whereupon it is the turn of Demetrius to conquer in honour, and after an interchange of fine speeches he restores to the enemy their arms and liberty.

Act IV opens with Celia at court and quite deaf to the King's emissaries. He approaches her himself with jewels, but she pretends not to recognize him, roundly berates him, and refuses the gifts. He is finally forced to disclose his identity and has his love rejected. Demetrius, returning in triumph, learns that Celia has been brought to court and at once denounces his father. The King declares that Celia was false and is dead, and the prince, announcing that he "shall curse all now, hate all, forswear all," shuts himself up in his chamber and forbids anyone to enter on pain of death. The next scene shows a magician conjuring and preparing a love potion for the King's use. It is to be given to Celia in her wine, for whoever drinks it will fall violently in love with Antigonus. Then enters the humorous lieutenant who has been set on to dare the prince in his privacy, but at the door his courage oozes out again. The prince appears with a pistol, and the lieutenant falls dead with fear, just as the woman passes by bearing the potion to Celia. She sets down the bowl to fetch water for the lieutenant, and his friends pour the potion down his throat. The lieutenant recovers, madly in love.

> He talks now of the King, no other language,
> And with the King as he imagines, hourly
> Courts the King, drinks to the King, dies for the King,
> Buys all the Pictures of the King, wears the King's
>   colours.

King Antigonus now visits Celia, believing that she has drunk the potion. He finds her reading a treatise called "The Vanity of Lust" and receives such a vigorous lecture on his sins that he experiences one of those sudden conversions which Fletcher delights in, and first offers marriage, and when that is refused declares himself a humble servant of her virtue. Celia now appears before Demetrius' door and summons him forth. He is astonished to find her alive, but her presence and finery arouse his suspicion and he denounces her at length as false. She bitterly resents his lack of faith, responds with even greater vigour and leaves him with a torrent of reproaches.

> Live a lost man for ever.
> Go ask your Father's conscience what I suffered
> And through what seas of hazards I sayl'd through:
> Mine honour still advanced in spight of tempests,
> Then take your leave of love; and confess freely,
> You were never worthy of this heart that serv'd ye,
> And so farewell, ungrateful.

Although much has happened since Act I, it will be noted that the opening of Act V leaves the lovers farther off than ever from peace and happiness. In the last act, however, events move speedily to the conclusion. The lieutenant recovers from his infatuation. The prince repents and weeps, and Celia forgives but refuses to marry. At this critical moment the noble Seleucus arrives at court and discovers that Celia is his long lost daughter Enanthe, whose marriage with Demetrius unites the kingdoms in peace.

"The Humourous Lieutenant" served as a model for tragicomedy during the remainder of the Elizabethan period and indeed after the Restoration, when Dryden declared that the English "have invented, increased and perfected a more pleasing way of writing for the stage than was ever known to the ancients or moderns of any nation—which is tragicomedy." Somewhere near it on our scale would come "Women Pleased" (by Fletcher alone), "Love's Cure," "The Sea Voyage," "The Custom of the Country," "The Spanish Curate," "Beggars' Bush," "A Very Woman" (all by Fletcher and collaborators), "The Honest Man's Fortune" (Fletcher only in Act V) and "The Fair Maid of the Inn" (very little Fletcher).

Just where on the scale we should draw the line that separates tragicomedy from romantic comedy is difficult to decide, but I should place it a little above such a play as "The Chances." In setting, characterization and plotting its methods are similar to those of tragicomedy, but its tone is lighter, its heroics are less sustained, its tragedy is more readily averted, and its comedy more thoroughly suffused. It is not less extravagant, artificial and surprising, or less romantically removed from probability, but the many jumps from the fire into the frying-pan and back into the fire again rarely fail to arouse amusement as well as surprise.

Two servants open the play by talking of their masters, two Spanish gentlemen, Don John and Don Frederick, now residing here in Bologna for study, but long engaged in an unrewarded pursuit of a certain lady. The masters enter and go out, agreeing to meet within an hour. It is evening, and a number of short scenes succeed, presumably on the streets. Petruchio, Antonio, and their factions enter, vowing vengeance on the Duke who has wronged their family. Don John follows searching for Frederick and, hearing a call from a house that is lighted and opened, enters and has a baby thrust into his arms. Frederick, searching for John, then the Duke, engaged on some perilous adventure, pass on the street; then Don John comes out with the infant, soliloquizes on his predicament, and starts back to his lodging. Frederick enters again and is immediately greeted by a lady who finds she has mistaken him for another, but begs him as a gentleman to succour her. Petruchio and his band pass again on the street, and then the scene discloses Don John at home struggling to persuade his landlady of the truth of his story about the baby. A bottle of wine and the rich jewels with which the infant is laden induce her to take care of the infant who she says closely resembles Don John. On the street again the Duke is rallying his friends. Then at the lodging Frederick appears with the beautiful lady, Constantia, who bids him return to the street and rescue a gentleman whom he may find there hard-pressed by assailants. So ends Act I.

Act II opens with a street affray, and the Duke hard beset. Don John comes to his rescue and saves his life. The Duke conceals his identity but when he finds that Don John has lost his hat gives him his own. Don Frederick overtakes Don John, and the two exchange stories. Don Frederick has promised the lady that no one shall see her, but he agrees to permit the curious and ardent John to peek at the beauty through a crack in the door. At the lodging, they find the servants amazed at the sweet voice singing to a lute. To Frederick's disgust, John presses rather far in his peeking, but the lady seeing his hat bids him enter. Knocking is heard without, and the servant reports Petruchio at the door. The lady dissolves in tears, confesses that she has sinned, and that Petruchio her brother has come to punish her, and begs the support of the two dons. But Don John gets a fresh surprise when he greets Petruchio, who bears a letter of introduction and engages the Don to bear a challenge to the Duke who has wronged his sister.

Act III opens with amusing altercations between the two friends and the landlady, who protests against having the lady as well as the baby in her house. Frederick goes with John to seek the Duke, leaving Constantia, who is now revealed as the lady of their hopeless suit, mourning over the approaching duel between her brother and her lover. The next scene shows Petruchio's friend Antonio wounded and treated by a surgeon but still calling for wine, women and song. In the next the landlady is persuading Constantia to leave her house and the two wild gentlemen, but Constantia will first see the baby. Don John finds the Duke, and the two recognize each other as rescuer and rescued. The Duke appeases Petruchio by declaring that Constantia is his wife contracted before heaven, and that he will marry her as soon as he can find her. The Dons promise to bring him to her and happiness seems at hand. But this is only the end of the third act, and there are many additional complications and much entertainment before the end of the play.

Perhaps even my bald analysis is enough to indicate that the very complications of the tangled plot obey the behests of comedy rather than melodrama. Somewhere near it on the scale may be placed (by Fletcher alone) "Rule a Wife and Have a Wife," "Monsieur Thomas," "The Pilgrim," and "The Wild Goose Chase"; (by Fletcher in collaboration) "The Coxcomb," "The Little French Lawyer," "The Elder Brother," "The Maid in the Mill," "Love's Pilgrimage," "The Captain," "The Nightwalker or Little Thief," and (with little of Fletcher) "The Noble Gentleman." Some of these, as for instance "The Pilgrim" and "The Little French Lawyer," have rather more of tragedy and romance than has "The Chances"; but as we come down the scale romantic adventure, idealized sentiment, and extraordinary events are diminished. Two of the plays, "The Coxcomb" and "The Nightwalker," have their scenes in London, but they are by no means the least supplied with adventure and sentiment. Whatever the scene, it is a place of impossibilities, but the persons converse like ladies and gentlemen of Fletcher's own London. In consequence even his most melodramatic plays have a touch of the comedy of manners, and several of the plays on this list display fully as much of manners as of romance in the development of their intrigue. Perhaps the play in this list which has least claim to the adjective romantic and comes nearest to being a comedy of manners is the once famous "The Wild Goose Chase." Here excitement and adventure give place to tricks and devices carried on in a merry battle of wits between ladies and their lovers.

Mirabel, the wild goose, returns from his travels with his friends Pinac, a lively person, and Belleur, of a stout, blunt humour; and the three gentlemen are at once beset by the wiles of Oriana, desperately in love with Mirabel, and her "airy" friends, Rosalura and Lillia Bianca. Oriana's brother comes disguised as a suitor and awakens Mirabel's jealousy, but a servant discovers the deception. Next Oriana pretends to be dying and Mirabel promises to marry her, but refuses when she confesses the trick. Finally she appears disguised as the sister of a friend who has bequeathed her and his fortune to Mirabel's care, and this time he both makes and keeps his promise of marriage. His two friends have in the meantime been led a merry dance and have been outwitted and won by the airy ladies. The language throughout is blunt and gross, but it seems to have been considered sparkling by Fletcher's contemporaries.

Four comedies in which Fletcher had a share remain that have the scene in London and offer no elements of adventure or romance. "Wit at Several Weapons" is a farcical comedy of manners in which a nephew, who is compelled to earn a living by his wits, cozens the uncle. "Wit Without Money" is a more unusual comedy of manners dealing with the same theme of the gaining by wit of wife and fortune. "The Scornful Lady" is another

battle of wits and tricks between lady and lover. The
fourth play is the amusing farce "The Woman's Prize"
or "The Tamer Tamed" (entirely by Fletcher). These
last two might be grouped with "Monsieur Thomas" and
"The Wild Goose Chase" as the plays most exclusively
and realistically devoted to what is frequently the theme
of Fletcher's comedy, the struggle for mastery between
men and women. In these plays, the content includes
both extravagant farce and verbal repartee; and in the
general artificiality of construction, grossness and liveliness of wit, and unsentimental presentation of sex relations, the way is being prepared for the Restoration comedy of manners. There is something rather modern too
about Fletcher's scornful ladies. They not only win the
lovers they desire and tame them as husbands but they
are outspoken and determined in behalf of the more general interests of their sex. The ladies were evidently
beginning to form no small part of the audience in the
private theaters. It is easy to guess why, when played
before Queen Henrietta Maria, "The Taming of the
Shrew" was only "liked," "The Tamer Tamed" two days
later was "very well liked."

For his many plays Fletcher drew his material from
various sources, chiefly Italian and Spanish fiction, showing a special predilection for the "Novelas Exemplares"
of Cervantes. Though Fletcher's indebtedness to individual Spanish plays is at most very slight, and though it
is doubtful if he could read the language, yet both his
materials and his methods manifestly resemble those of
the cloak and sword drama of Lope de Vega and of the
intricate intrigues of later Spanish plays. But Fletcher's
invention was never closely bound by sources or models
and was ever copious, ready, and, if anything, too self-
reliant. It balked at nothing, it hurdled any improbability, it joined hands with wit in the merriest acrobatics.

In any case he worked over suggestions or stories
to suit the needs of a bustling stage and his particular
formula of sensation and surprise. For example, in "The

Sea Voyage," suggested by "The Tempest," he adds all
sorts of tragicomic complications so that the plot includes
shipwrecks, piracy, cannibalism, a treasure horde, and
two islands, and the opportunities for comedy are supplied by inhabiting one of those islands by a troop of
Amazons led by some shipwrecked ladies, the youngest
of whom, like Miranda, has never seen a man. The
Amazon ladies disarm the gentlemen shipwrecked on the
other island, first decide to parcel them out as lovers,
but then suspecting them of piracy, starve them as slaves.
Elsewhere as here the comic complications offer obvious
opportunities, and Fletcher usually made the most of
them. Petruchio's second wife decides to tame him
(Woman's Prize); an only son returning from his travels
keeps his coarse, rough manners for his sweetheart and
his affected courtesies for his father (Monsieur Thomas);
a brother is brought up at home among the girls while
the sister is trained as a boy in the wars (Love's Cure);
a witless husband offers his friend, who confesses love
for his wife, every opportunity to prove or disprove his
wife's fidelity (Coxcomb); a lady marries a quiet dolt in
order that she may carry on her amours, but the dolt
turns master (Rule a Wife). Such extravagant situations
often gain in their comic force by sharp conjunction with
serious or sentimental action. So, in "The Humourous
Lieutenant," the potion prepared for the lustful king to
overcome the virtuous Celia is drunk by the lieutenant,
who falls in love with the king. Or, in "The Custom of
the Country" a stranger just arrived in a city kills a gentleman and seeks refuge in a house belonging to the mother
of the man he has killed. Out of regard for the law of
hospitality, she releases him, and he escapes, this time into
a house where the comic situation is a little too broad
for a summary. Later he returns to marry the mother,
the son having come to life.

But Fletcher's comic situations are by no means always
novel. He made use of practically everything that the
Elizabethan drama provided. He can present a string of

the usual tricks by which a scapegrace nephew cozens an uncle or a usurer; or he can make his lovers wander in a forest and discourse beautiful sentiments. Disguises, duels, drunken scenes, lovers caught by husbands, and long lost children discovered by their parents are common. The action is always brisk. Persons are just starting on a journey, or just arriving, servants are preparing a meal, bearing a message, or the maid is doing her own wooing as well as that of her mistress, there are many revels and masques. Shops are rare, but the action may leave the court and take us into the country, or linger in the tavern, or cross the seas, and it affords all sorts of bedroom scenes. In "Lover's Progress," a former lover makes his way at midnight into the bedroom of his friend's wife, and the two debate at length on their virtue and the temptation to which it is exposed, until the house is alarmed and they are interrupted; in "Love's Pilgrimage" the heroine disguised as a boy obtains the only room in the inn with two beds, whereupon a young gentleman arrives late and is given the other bed; in "Monsieur Thomas" the graceless lover disguised as a woman gains admission to his mistress's bed, but she forewarned has placed there her blackmoor maid. Fletcher contrives his situations on two principles, first, nothing is what it seems to be; second, whatever is happening, something different will succeed. If a lady seems to be yielding to her lover, he is likely to get his ears boxed. If a coffin is brought on the stage, the corpse will come to life. Comedy is kept lively by surprise and change. Life is usually gay and is always exciting.

I have dwelt on the plots and the situations because they are of the essence of this theatrical comedy. To them characterization is readily sacrificed; indeed Fletcher has little interest in character apart from its service to dramatic situation. The types usual in the early Beaumont and Fletcher romances reappear in the later comedies—the courtly hero, the blunt soldier, the lustful tyrant, the poltroon, the evil woman, and the lovelorn

heroine. The court poltroon more often is reduced to
the rascal who takes beatings with resignation and the
evil woman to the wanton servant maid. The blunt soldier is often a merry fellow who stands by his friend,
lambastes the poltroon, and amuses the ladies. Two
other types are prominent, the scapegrace young hero and
the shrewish, voluble heroine. They are both difficult to
woo and make excellent opponents in the contests of love
and wit. The scapegrace may be something of a woman-
hater and plaindealer, but when it comes to a war of
words, no one can surpass Fletcher's young women.
They are by no means as charming as Shakespeare's
Beatrice, but they are equally competent to take care both
of themselves and their weaker sisters. Celia in the
"Humourous Lieutenant," the scornful lady in the play
of that name, Lamira in "The Little French Lawyer,"
Maria in "The Woman's Prize," are examples.

The frequent revolutions in character which change
serious drama into claptrap have some excuse and value
in comedy, supplying the actors with opportunity and
the spectators with surprise. The cowardly fellow who
unexpectedly turns valiant has several variations in the
humorous lieutenant, the little French lawyer, the scholar
in the "Elder Brother," and Leon in "Rule a Wife."
The apparently virtuous lady who suddenly yields and
the apparent wanton who unexpectedly rebuffs her lover
supply the actor with all sorts of character in a single
part. Clowns of the Shakespearian sort rarely appear,
and humorous or eccentric persons are rather less common than in other drama of the time, but they are sometimes skilfully utilized to help out the comic effect. One
of the best comic complications is that of "The Spanish
Curate" and it depends as much on the characters as on
the situations for its continued laughter. Leandro seeking access to the house of Bartolus, the lawyer, who keeps
his beautiful wife tightly shut in, pretends to be a student
newly arrived in Cordova with a letter from his father
to his old friends the curate Lopez and the sexton Diego.

They are in sad condition, having had but one christening in two weeks and no deaths, but as soon as Leandro offers money they manage to remember his father and mother and agree to get him a place in the lawyer's house. Here he appears as a bashful and bookish student, but soon arouses the interest of the beautiful Amaranta. Given new assurance by their new wealth, the curate and sexton summon their few parishioners and threaten to resign. Lopez declares

Ye have neither faith nor money left to save ye

and Diego refers them to the locked church where

The bell ropes, they are strong enough to hang ye.

The abashed parishioners promise to get more children, to increase the stipends and to die earlier, and the curate relents. He is soon put into a perturbation by several of Leandro's friends who inform him that the supposed American had stolen the money from his master; but this is merely a prelude to a device to draw Bartolus from his house and give Leandro opportunity. The curate fetches the lawyer to the dying bed of the sexton, who it appears has accumulated much wealth and wishes to make the lawyer his executor. The scene of the will making is carried through with much spirit until finally the stratagem becomes apparent to Bartolus, who rushes home only to find the house locked and empty. His wife and Leandro soon appear, but in response to his protests she declares that they have been to church. His hesitation to accept this explanation gives the curate a chance to accuse him of heresy and threaten the inquisition. Bartolus capitulates and invites all to breakfast, where when the dishes are uncovered his guests discover, instead of viands, capiases, citations and warrants. It cannot be said that these situations arise from the characters or display them consistently, but the amusing incidents do gain life and enrichment from the depiction of the absurd persons.

But the best comic union of character and situation is found in the part of Estefania in "Rule a Wife and Have a Wife." Two officers are talking of wars and heiresses when two ladies appear, one with a letter. It is her veiled companion who excites all the romance and cupidity in Michael Perez, who woos and weds her and is completely happy in her great house. Events finally persuade him that she is not the mistress as she had pretended, but the maid, and indeed an accomplished swindler, yet whatever events take place she is always their and his master. By the time he is ready to kill her, she has obtained some money to aid him; he upbraids her, and she replies meekly—

Estefania. I know you have mercy.
Perez. If I had tons of mercy, thou deserv'st none.
What new trick is now afoot, and what new houses
Have you i' th' air? What orchards in apparition?
What canst thou say for thy life?
Estefania. Little or nothing;
I know you'll kill me, and I know 'tis useless
To beg for mercy. Pray, let me draw my book out,
And pray a little.
Perez. Do; a very little,
For I have farther business than thy killing;
I have money yet to borrow. Speak when you are ready.
Estefania. Now, now, sir, now! [Shews a pistol.]
Come on! do you start off from me?
Do you sweat, great captain? have you seen a spirit?
Perez. Do you wear guns?
Estefania. I am a soldier's wife, sir,
And by that privilege I may be arm'd.
Now, what's the news, and let's discourse more friendly,
And talk of our affairs in peace.
Perez. Let me see,
Prithee, let me see thy gun; 'tis a very pretty one.
Estefania. No, no, sir; you shall feel.
Perez. Hold, you villain!

What thine own husband?

Estefania. Let mine own husband, then
Be in's own wits.—There, there's a thousand ducats—

[Shews a purse.]

Who must provide for you?—and yet you'll kill me.

Perez. I will not hurt thee for ten thousand millions.

Estefania. When will you redeem your jewels? I
have pawn'd 'em.

You see for what: we must keep touch.

Perez. I'll kiss thee,
And, get as many more, I'll make thee famous.
Had we the house now!

Estefania. Come along with me;
If that be vanish'd, there be more to hire, sir.

Perez. I see I am an ass when thou art near me.

[v. i.]

No doubt she is a shameful and artful hussy, but she
is so competent and so confident—just the person who
could be the veiled mystery, the generous lady, the humble servant, the meek wife, and yet carry a pistol concealed as a prayer book. No wonder that for two hundred years every actress wished to play Estefania.

Fletcher's style, like his characterization, suits itself
to the plot rather than transcends it, but it is equal to
anything the shifting situations may require. It can be
pathetic or dignified or flippant or rollicking just as
needed. The comic effectiveness of many scenes is
dependent in no small degree on the liveliness and wit
of the verse. He indulges in quibbles and word play
rather less than Lyly or Shakespeare, and his wit is less
premeditated and elaborate than that of Congreve, Sheridan or Oscar Wilde, though at times, as in "The Wild
Goose Chase," the dialogue approaches in matter and
manner that of Restoration comedy. There is rarely a
wit combat merely in words, usually the words supplement trick, device or predicament. Though the humour
of the situation may be shown in few words and unembel-

lished phrases as in the passage just quoted from "Rule
a Wife," yet perhaps the qualities of style that do most
to excite laughter are its readiness and its volubility.
Whatever amusement is created by seeing a poltroon
receive a kick is increased by his profuse explanations of
his enjoyment of the pain and humiliation.   When the
lady has successfully deceived her husband, the moral
sense may be shocked but laughter can scarcely be refused
when his suspicions are overwhelmed by her torrent of
unrighteous indignation.   The tirades of the women,
whether wronged or victorious, are among the most striking comic passages in the plays.   In "The Woman's
Prize" the despairing Petruchio as a last resort to win
his wife, pretends that he is dead, and is brought before
her in a coffin.   She is in black, weeping, and it looks as
if his stratagem had won.   But then she explains her
tears:

> But what's the cause?   Mistake me not; not this man,
> As he is dead, I weep for; Heaven defend it!
> I never was so childish.   But his life,
> His poor, unmanly, wretched, foolish life,
> Is that my full eyes pity; there's my mourning.

Her father asks, "Dost thou not shame?" and she goes on

> I do, and even to water
> To think what this man was,—

and so for many lines more until Petruchio in the coffin
cries for mercy.   It is in such fashion as this that the
flow of words enhances the humour even of the most
absurd situations.

Fletcher does not seem to have had any conscience,
artistic or moral.   His morals, like his poetry, are ready
for any situation but are incapable of sustained and consistent effort.   He depicts the conduct and ideals of gentlemen and ladies but only in accord with the standards
of his own time and even then not often without serious
blemishes and lapses.   Starting with the premise that the

world is mainly concerned in love-making, he gives us examples of all varieties—heroic, ideal, impassioned, tender, sensible, animal, base, and perverted. His lovers may be models of restraint or eager young animals or both in successive scenes. He has less of moral sentiment and delicacy than Beaumont and less of moral vigour and principle than Massinger, but he has been rather too much discredited in comparison with his collaborators. His hand is not in the writing of what seems to me the worst scene from a moral point of view of all the Beaumont and Fletcher folio, Lelia's wooing of her father in "The Captain" (IV, 1). He did write the scenes in the "Custom of the Country" in which Dryden declared there was more indecency than in all the Restoration comedies together, but the scenes have at least the merit of being funny. But there is no defense for Fletcher's licentiousness or for his indifference to moral values. He based his plays on improbable startling situations on which it was impossible to build a sincere and sustained moral interpretation of life. He was not inspired by the muse of comedy to any such tasks as were Ben Jonson and George Meredith, to laugh out of existence the affectations and hypocrisies of mankind, still less to such an accomplishment as Shakespeare's, the creation of a delighted tolerance for the mingling of virtue and folly, nonsense and wisdom. Comedy for Fletcher was neither a means of reforming society nor of idealizing life, it was only an entertainment. You cannot quite say that his drama is artificial, unreal, beyond the facts of life, for it is very true to human nature, convincingly real, truly moral, or immoral,—for a moment, and then the good moment goes, yielding place for some fresh gaiety.

I have been trying to show that, though lacking in the highest values, Fletcher does employ great resources of poetry and invention in the creation of comedy. Measured by the plays of fifty years before, his dramas would seem marvels of creative genius. Compared with his more immediate predecessors, Jonson or even Shakespeare, he discloses new theatrical possibilities for comic effect. Before us on the stage there is revealed a lively world where anything may be expected in truthful or exaggerated or fantastic mimicry of reality. It is gay with an abundance of animal spirits, light-hearted with an absence of moral purpose, and yet animated by a genuine sense of humour. In fact, this sense of humour is perhaps the most genuine thing in that stage world of sentiments, thrills and adventures. The persons are not engaged merely in rushing about the stage, or escaping death or tricking their fellows or displaying virtue and vice; they often have humour and they exercise it. It finds its most direct expression in the blunt old seniors who take life heartily and merrily. They are willing to face danger or love, if necessary, but they prefer a frolic to a fight and they are shy of the responsibilities that love entails. They like to see the young ardent for love and honour, but what they themselves have chiefly acquired by age and experience is this sense of humour. It is neither refined nor profound, it does not delight in subtleties or desire meditation. It asks for movement and action and a bottle of wine. It hates glumness but it is not merely vivacious or boisterous. It mingles freely with honesty and kindness and it is a sound cure for the wounds of pride and melancholy. It is good-natured and friendly rather than penetrating or uplifting, but it is capable of making youth tolerant and age merry.

CHAPTER XI

THE LATER ELIZABETHANS

WE have now considered the main contributions by the Elizabethans to comedy. Later writers felt the domination of the great masters. Shakespeare's influence was potent, and increasingly so after the publication of his plays in the Folio of 1623; imitations of characters, scenes or plays are numerous, though his type of comedy had been in a considerable measure put out of fashion by the successes of Middleton, Jonson and Fletcher. Sincere efforts at realism were likely to follow the methods of Middleton or Jonson or both; lighter mixtures of manners and intrigue, romantic comedy and tragicomedy took the manner of Fletcher.

The theaters no longer demanded an unlimited supply of new plays, they could rely to a larger degree on repertory and produce regularly the favourite plays of the earlier writers. Of the twenty-five plays named among those performed at court from 1621 to 1625, there are thirteen performances of ten plays from the Fletcher list, three by Shakespeare, three by Middleton, two by Jonson, and one by Massinger. Only a few of the plays presented at court are named in the records and many plays acted in public were never given at court, but the figures indicate the continued popularity of Fletcher and, in a lesser degree, of Shakespeare. The rights of the companies in their plays were jealously guarded.

The taste of the theater-goers, however, was undergoing a considerable change. The reigns of James I and Charles I, in the drama as in other matters, carry us away from Elizabethan habits and manners and toward those of the Restoration. From the reëstablishment of the children actors (c 1600), the indoor theaters grew in importance, and the great open-air public playhouses gradually yielded supremacy. The drama depended more and more for its support on that portion of the population connected with the world of court and fashion. Poets sought patrons and scoffed at the populace, and actors sought the applause of the gallants and ladies occupying the benches and boxes of Whitefriars and Blackfriars, rather than of the standing crowds in the pits of the Red Bull and the Fortune. Puritanism was steadily growing in London. The number of theaters and of theater-goers was not increasing and the drama had ceased to be the vox populi, but the drama allied itself to the court. Theatrical taste was becoming more sophisticated, more fashionable and not more moral.

After 1616 the demand for new plays was met mainly by a comparatively small number of writers producing regularly for the leading companies. The King's men, the company of Shakespeare and Fletcher, and later of Massinger and Shirley, maintained its leadership without any close rivalry. The men of a preceding generation who continued writing after Shakespeare's death, Heywood, Dekker, Jonson, Webster, and Middleton, with the exception of the last named, did not add anything novel to the field of comedy. The effect of the changing dramatic fashions may be seen in Dekker's "Match Me in London" (acted c. 1612) and his "Wonder of a Kingdom" (S. R. 1632) and Webster's "The Devil's Law Case," all rather unsuccessful essays in the manner of Fletcherian tragicomedy. Of the new writers, Ford, great and original in tragedy, had no gift for comedy. There are, to be sure, many others, including Randolph, Mayne, Brome, and Davenant, at some of whose work we must glance, but their plays add little to the general view of the course of comedy that may be obtained by an examination of the plays of Massinger, Shirley, and the latest of those of Middleton.

I

The excuse for reserving some of Middleton's plays for special treatment here is that they differ markedly from his earlier work, and partake of the common characteristics of later tragicomedy. We have seen that from 1600 to 1608 he wrote a series of comedies mostly realistic, dealing with city manners. From 1608 to 1616 his work was also realistic, but after 1616 he is found writing romantic tragedies and tragicomedies, sometimes in collaboration with William Rowley.

The earliest of the plays of their collaboration, "A Fair Quarrel" (pr. 1617 and perhaps acted that year), is realistic in content and unique in character. In the main plot, Captain Ager and his friend the Colonel quarrel and the latter applies to the Captain a common epithet which impugns his mother's honour. Ager's suspicions are aroused and he questions his mother, who, at first indignant, soon becomes eager to save his life at all costs and falsely informs him that she was untrue to his father. Ager refuses to fight since his cause is false, until the Colonel annihilates his scruples by calling him coward. As a result of the duel, the Colonel is severely wounded, repents both epithets, and offers his sister and fortune in the way of reparation. Ager's mother confesses her deception, the Colonel recovers, and all are most moral and sentimental. In the sub-plots, Jane rejects the seductions of a physician, and a booby Chough takes lessons in the school of the roarers. The cause of Ager's hesitation is trivial and the arguments fine-spun, but Middleton succeeds in giving reality and appeal to the emotional struggles of mother and son, which won Charles Lamb's warm encomium, "Those noble and liberal casuists could discern in the differences, the quarrels, the animosities of man, a beauty and truth of moral feeling, no less than in the iterately inculcated duties of forgiveness and atonement."

The play would scarcely be considered a comedy to-day,

but in comparison with its Elizabethan fellows it might be viewed as realistic tragicomedy. At least it is a notable effort to extend the dramas of contemporary manners to serious and moral and unconventional issues. It may be compared with Dekker's "Honest Whore" or Heywood's "A Woman Killed with Kindness," for like those plays it propounds a question and proceeds to debate it. But the question—should a man defend his mother's honour without making sure that it is sound?—is not of such import to society as are those raised in the other plays. It is rather one of the extreme casuistries of the code of honour such as are debated by Fletcher's gentlemen.

"The Witch," by Middleton alone, is also something of a theatrical novelty, for it carries all the methods of tragicomedy into the field of the tragedy of revenge and horror. The play has excited interest chiefly because of its employment of witches, as in "Macbeth," and because of the transference of a few passages from Middleton into the text of Shakespeare. The play uses materials of the sort common in the tragedies of Webster, Tourneur and Middleton himself, but in each action the catastrophe is averted and a happy ending substituted. The duchess seeks revenge on the duke for compelling her to drink from her father's skull; Sebastian seeks revenge on Antonio who has married his betrothed Isabella; Antonio seeks revenge on Isabella whom he suspects of adultery. Supernatural and spectacular accompaniments are provided by the witches, aided by "a spirit like a cat." The catastrophe is necessarily complicated. Antonio kills Gasparo and Florida, but they prove to be only wounded. Antonio poisons his sister Francisca, Aberzanes and himself, but his servant has neglected to put poison into the potion. Antonio is reported to have fallen sixty fathoms through a trap door; perhaps if we had the entire text of the play, he also might come to life, but his disappearance is scarcely a calamity since it permits Sebastian and Isabella to unite. The duke is discovered on a couch as dead, but awakens in time to save the duchess. Almachildes, the accomplice of the duchess, who thinks he has enjoyed her, and whom she thinks to be dead, finds that both were mistaken. The duchess is about to be executed for the murder of her husband when he comes to life. All this is accomplished in a series of telling scenes, comic and tragic, surprising and humorous.

"The Spanish Gipsy" is much closer to Fletcher's methods and is a more agreeable play. Middleton, assisted by Rowley, has taken two Spanish stories and combined them into an effective dramatic romance. Like the beggars in "The Beggars' Bush," the gipsies make a picturesque accompaniment, and the suggestion for their use may also have come from Jonson's masque "The Gipsies Metamorphosed." Three gentlemen of Madrid talking on the street at evening see an old couple hurrying home, followed by their beautiful daughter. Two of the men seize the parents while the third, the son of the corregidor, carries off and ravishes the daughter. Roderigo and Clara are discovered in a bedroom in his house; he now repents and they part without either knowing the other's name, but she notes the furniture of the room and carries away a crucifix she finds there. He agrees to declare that he failed in his purpose and to leave the city. Louis, one of Roderigo's companions, is the suitor of Clara, but she refuses him. Roderigo joins a band of pseudo-gipsies, headed by Alvarez, outlawed because he had killed the father of Louis. One of the gipsies, really the long lost daughter of the corregidor, is so beautiful that she attracts various gallants who join the band. The gipsies, who are always singing, come to Madrid and to the court, where they act a play. Clara, who swoons at the sight of one of the gipsies, is carried to the room she recognizes. After she has been married to Roderigo, an entire act is still needed to straighten out happily all the entanglements. Middleton has shown Fletcher a trick or two at his own game.

"More Dissemblers Besides Women" is a slighter piece of the same material. An oratorical cardinal, a profligate nephew, a chaste widow who suddenly becomes enamoured of a general, a lively heroine who loves the general and the profligate and who runs away to join a band of singing gipsies, a plaintive love-lorn heroine disguised as a page, and other persons amorous or comic, and other incidents romantic or farcical are combined by Middleton into a lively comedy exhibiting his usual deftness and even more than his customary amount of double entendre.

These three plays and the powerful tragedies, "The Changeling," and "Women Beware Women," were probably acted within the first half of the third decade of the century. Middleton died in 1627. On "The Changeling," "A Fair Quarrel," and "The Spanish Gipsy," he was aided by William Rowley who has been credited with the romantic and moral tone which they display; but Middleton's change from comedy to tragedy and tragicomedy and from realism to romance seems clearly to have been dictated by the changing theatrical demand. I do not find either in Rowley's unaided plays or in the passages that can be ascribed to his pen in a considerable amount of collaborated work any indication of large dramatic invention or versatility. These qualities are apparent in still another play of Middleton's in this period, "A Game at Chess." Produced in the summer of 1624, it established the first run recorded in an English theater, being acted eight days in succession until closed by the government. It is not wholly intelligible today, but presents the scheme of a Spanish marriage and the miserable fiasco of the journey of Prince Charles and Buckingham to Madrid in an allegory which shows the English triumphant, and it greatly pleased popular feeling of the moment. The White house, with Charles the duke and Buckingham the knight, check the Black king, of whose side the knight represents the Spanish ambassador Gondomar. As a political allegory the play is novel and important, but it scarcely adds anything to our types of comedy. It did not succeed in establishing a type, for it had no followers; but it may furnish a final illustration of the fertility and ingenuity of Middleton's dramatic art and of his cleverness and readiness in responding to theatrical opportunity.

II

Philip Massinger was born in 1584, his father being a gentleman attached to the service of the Earl of Pembroke. He was entered in Pembroke College in 1602 and left Oxford in 1606. We know nothing of him from that date until 1613 or 1614 when he is writing a play for Henslowe. For the next dozen years he was writing in collaboration with Fletcher, having a share in some twenty plays that were gathered in the Beaumont-Fletcher Folios. Before Fletcher's death, three plays appeared in print with Massinger's name attached, "The Virgin Martyr" (with Dekker) in 1622, "The Duke of Milan" in 1623, and "The Bondman" in 1624. It is probable that he produced other plays entirely his own in this period, but the evidence is not conclusive. After Fletcher's death in 1625, he became chief writer for the King's men, and wrote constantly for them until his death in 1640. We have records of the titles of some eighteen plays of his authorship which have not been preserved, and there are seventeen plays extant which he wrote alone or with some other collaborator than Fletcher. Altogether he must have had a hand in nearly sixty plays.

I shall not enter upon a discussion of Massinger's collaboration in the plays that we have already noticed as a part of Fletcher's work. It is large but subordinate, and it contributes very little to comedy or humour. Of tragi-comedies and comedies it includes the following, and possibly a few others where his hand is less evident: "The Laws of Candy" (mostly Massinger's), "The Queen of Corinth," "The Knight of Malta," "The Custom of the Country," "The Spanish Curate," "The Beggars' Bush," "The Sea Voyage," "The Fair Maid of the Inn" (mostly Massinger), "The Honest Man's Fortune," "A Very Woman," "The Little French Lawyer," "The Elder Brother." Massinger's share varies in amount and character, but it is more often concerned in the graver complications than in the comic. For example, his hand is not found in the important comic scenes of "The Spanish Curate," "The Little French Lawyer," or "The Beggars' Bush." In general, his work in collaboration has the same qualities as in his unaided plays.

Massinger is the disciple of Fletcher and often imitates him closely, but both in collaboration and when writing alone he displays some notable differences. Massinger has more moral sense and a more painstaking art than his friend and master. His morality may be superficial but it is usually pointed; he pays some attention to poetic justice, and he is fond of presenting moral wisdom in solemn declamation. His plots are carefully constructed, usually with excellent exposition, and he carries out the scheme of surprises and thrills ingeniously though not as vivaciously as Fletcher. He does not sacrifice characterization to situation as recklessly as does the older dramatist, and he now and then achieves a subtle or a vigorous portrayal of personality. His style has gravity and movement but cannot rise to dramatic crises with anything like Fletcher's power and resource. His verse is readily distinguished from his collaborator's when that is at its best or is most mannered; but Massinger, like most writers of this period, adopts some of Fletcher's tricks, especially the conscious preference for feminine endings. In general, Massinger's style is somewhat colorless, imitative, without much fancy, rhetorical rather than poetic. It is better suited to dialogue or oration than to the dramatic depiction of passion or humour. Both as a poet and as a playmaker he is laborious rather than inspired, sober rather than quick, and without either the great virtues or great vices of his master.

Of the seventeen plays that he wrote apart from

Fletcher, six are tragedies. Two, "The City Madam" and "A New Way to Pay Old Debts," are realistic comedies dealing with contemporary London. The remaining nine are tragicomedies and comedies which might be arranged, as we did Fletcher's, in a scale extending from tragedy to comedy of manners.

These romantic plays present plots drawn from many sources and very similar to those we have already considered. There are wars and insurrections, usually represented on the stage only by duels; there are depositions, banishments, alliances and other court affairs; and there are pirates, Turks and bandits, all serving as a background for the trials of love. Virtue is tempted, jealousy is aroused, a lady solicits a gentleman engaged to another, or a deserted lady wins back her recalcitrant lover. There is likely to be a trial scene, for Massinger liked courts and pleas, in which slander and calumny are exposed and the virtue of the heroine proclaimed. Honour shines brightly in the hero, even though he be disguised as a slave, and attracts the lady. A more subtle variant is the diffidence and modesty with which the heroes are sometimes endowed. There is purity and elevation of sentiment in the heroines also, though we discover it usually through their own declamations. The minor personages, among whom is a sprinkling of doctors, supply a small amount of fun.

Of the tragicomedies "The Maid of Honour" is the best,—serious, eloquent and coming very close to the pitch of tragedy. A little comedy is supplied by the buffoon wooer Sylli, but in the end the noble heroine refuses all suitors, foolish, worthy and unworthy, and becomes the bride of the church. "The Bashful Lover," which skilfully interweaves the stories of Hortensio's modest love for the Princess Matilda and of Maria's recovery of her repentant seducer, "The Emperor of the East," and "The Renegado," are also heroic in tone with only incidental comedy. "The Great Duke of Florence" also belongs in this group but it lacks both the evil motives and the high

passions usual in tragicomedy. The plot, similar to that
of the old play "A Knack to Know a Knave," is placed
in Florence. Cozimo, the duke, intends that his nephew
Giovanni shall marry his ward Fiorinda, duchess of
Urbin, but she loves the Duke's favorite, Sanazarro, and
Giovanni loves Lidia, the daughter of his tutor. Sanazarro, sent by the Duke to bring report of Lidia, falls
in love with her himself and contrives that he and Giovanni conceal her great beauty from the duke lest he
desire her. A foolish servant-maid takes her place in
entertaining Cozimo, but the trick fails, and nephew and
favourite are imprisoned. In the end the Duke pardons
them, the favourite weds the duchess, and the prince, the
Beautiful Lidia. She is a charming heroine despite her
declamatory powers, and the story has unusual refinement. The play is a sort of subdued tragicomedy, grave
in manner but lacking in thrills, yet with only slight
comic passages and without any humour.

"The Bondman" is a heroic play with a large admixture of comedy. It presents the insurrection of the slaves
in Syracuse under Marullo who is in love with the noble
Cleora. After the insurrection is successful Marullo's
restraint and self-control contrast favourably to the absurd
jealousy of the noble lover Leosthenes who had compelled Cleora to go blindfolded during his absence. The
leader of the slaves wins her respect and admiration and
finally her love. The comic sub-plot is very gross but
carries a moral. There is much fine declamation on the
wrongs of slaves, Massinger's eloquence being at his
best. The slaves fight bravely but flee when their masters crack their whips, and the play then proceeds to the
usual sort of dénouement. Marullo turns out to be not
a slave but Pisander, a gentleman of Thebes, seeking
revenge on Leosthenes who has deserted his sister Statilia,
disguised as the slave of Cleora. The proper marriages
follow.

"The Picture" is based on a story that would lend
itself readily to humorous interpretation, but Massinger

makes little of these opportunities. Mathias, a knight of
Bohemia, has a magic picture of his wife which changes
hue according to variation in conduct and sentiment displayed by the absent lady in respect to marital fidelity.
The queen of Hungary, whither Mathias's exploits have
led him, is piqued by his praises of his wife and attempts
to seduce him, and at the same time sends lying courtiers
to tell of his infidelity to his wife and so tempt her. The
picture pales, to the husband's consternation, but the wife's
virtue stands the test, and so does Mathias. The queen
repents, and Mathias gets a sound lecturing from his wife
on account of the jealousy which led him to employ the
magic picture. The protestations of love and fidelity and
the soliloquies on virtue and temptation are all in the
heroic vein, but the discomfiture of the lewd courtiers,
the comments of a blunt old veteran, and the tart recep-
tion by the wife afford a certain realistic and amusing
setting for the high seriousness of the rest of the play.

"The Guardian" gives a more humorous treatment
to a more commonplace plot made up of situations and
motives already familiar, and may clearly be classed as
romantic comedy rather than tragicomedy. Severino, a
nobleman of Naples, banished on account of the supposed murder of his brother-in-law, is the leader of a
band of banditti. His wife, Iolanthe, keeps their daughter, Calista, hid from suitors, but she is in love with a
young libertine Adorio, and is loved by Caldoro, the
bashful ward of the guardian, Durazzo, a lively old
codger. The brother-in-law has not been killed and, disguised as Laval, attracts the love of his sister Iolanthe.
Adorio arranges to elope with Calista but carries off her
maid Mirtilla by mistake, while the guardian and Caldoro
by stratagem carry off Calista. Severino, returning home
in secret to visit his chaste wife, finds her with a banquet
prepared awaiting her lover. He binds her and retires
to consider what form her punishment shall take.
Calipso, her maid, enters to announce Laval, frees her
mistress, and is bound in her place (cf. "Women

Pleased"). She receives a few slashes from the knife of Severino, who again retires. Iolanthe takes a lecture (off stage) from the stranger lover and repents her "loose appetite" and "bad intentions." She resumes her place bound, and to her returning husband declares that the wounds which he inflicted have been cured by miracle and almost convinces him that he has greatly wronged her innocence. Meanwhile, it is now Act IV, the elopers are having their surprises. Calista is greatly disappointed to find that she has been carried off by the bashful lover rather than by the libertine, but is pleased by his courteous manner. Adorio and Mirtilla also discover their mistake and not wholly to her regret. Wandering in the forest, the guardian, Caldoro and Calista come upon Adorio and Mirtilla sleeping with his head in her lap. He has been snoring, rather a realistic detail for such a romantic situation; but it is the situation and not the snoring which makes Calista decide to marry Caldoro. The banditti now rush in and seize both pairs of elopers and later capture the king who has come disguised with Laval into the forest. The king's troops then surround the banditti. All are surprised, pardoned or married.

This piece is cleverly constructed and doubtless afforded an amusing entertainment, offering a nearer approach to Fletcher's extravagance and humour than is elsewhere found in Massinger. Acted in 1633, it represents certain features that had come to be almost indispensable in the late romantic drama. The man supposedly killed who comes to life and the woman who is substituted for another in a critical situation present motives that were indeed employed in every kind of play from tragedy to farce but were especial favourites in devising romantic surprises. So also are two types of character, the libertine and the wife of doubtful virtue. Libertinism may be ridiculed and punished as in "The Picture" or let off easily as in "The Guardian," for the maid Mirtilla to whom Adorio is married, proves of noble birth, but it is always the theme of comedy. The wife, as here and in "The Picture," may be prevented from carrying out her intentions, but in the late drama her intentions at least are usually suspect.

"The Parliament of Love" is a less worthy example of romantic intrigue, built up out of the customary situations and with a very gross sub-plot. Bellisant, a chaste and witty lady, is loved by Montrose. She repulses Clarindore who has wagered three thousand pounds that he will enjoy her, then feigns to yield to him and substitutes in her place his deserted wife Beaupré. Leonora, whose lover Cleremond has been lustful and vows in recompense to do whatever she commands, enjoins him to kill his best friend (cf. "Much Ado"). He provokes a duel with Montrose and kills him. Lamira is solicited by Perigot, who gets tossed in a blanket for his pains. Clorinda is the wife of a physician who doses Novall who attempts to seduce her. In the last act the parliament of love is held. After much declamation, Cleremond produces the body of Montrose, Bellisant explains her innocence of Clarindore's slander, Montrose comes to life and marries Bellisant, Cleremond weds Leonora, and Clarindore is reunited to Beaupré. The minor libertines are punished and repent. The play, like several of Fletcher's, retains some of the trappings and methods of romance while dealing mainly with the intrigues of ladies and their lovers suitable to a comedy of manners.

These examples are enough to indicate both Massinger's general subservience to the Fletcherian type of romantic play and his occasional departures from it. We may surmise that if we had his eighteen lost plays, the titles of many of which suggest romantic treatment, we should find little to change or enlarge our estimate of his contribution to comedy. We turn now to the two realistic plays of London life that look to Middleton and Jonson rather than to Fletcher for a model. In each a serious effort is made to present and to criticize certain social conditions.

"The City Madam" satirizes the extravagance and pride of the wives of wealthy citizens and its final couplet advises them to confess—

> In their habits, manners, and their highest port,
> A distance 'twixt the city and the court.

The plot, however, focuses upon the character of Luke Frugal. He has been a spendthrift and wasted his fortune, and at the beginning of the play holds a menial position in his brother's household, subject to the insolences of Lady Frugal and her daughters. Sir John Frugal pretends to retire to a monastery and leaves his family and fortune in charge of Luke, whose meekness and piety have won the good opinion of Lord Lacy but have not concealed his hypocrisy from the audience. Sir John and the two suitors, who have been disdainfully treated by his daughters, are recommended to Luke's care, disguised as Indians from Virginia. On coming into the possession of power and fortune Luke shows himself a monster, ruins the debtors whom his brother helped, punishes severely those whom he himself set on to riotous living, and even plans to transport his sister-in-law and her daughters to Virginia as sacrifices to the devil. The lively pictures of the city madams, the idle apprentices and the prostitutes remind us of Middleton, but the studied characterization of Luke gives the comedy a weighty and moral significance that is Massinger's own. The play is an important addition to Elizabethan comedy, but its characteristics are paralleled and its merits surpassed in its more famous companion piece.

"A New Way to Pay Old Debts" is, like "The City Madam," a comedy of London manners satirizing the new wealthy class that threatens the privileges of the gentry and nobility. Its plot is in part borrowed from Middleton's "A Trick to Catch the Old One"; the spendthrift Wellborn, by means of a feigned marriage, secures funds to settle with his creditors whom he gathers in a procession headed by a drum. The spendthrift, however, is not married, the wealthy widow who aids him being reserved for the noble Lovell, and the heiress for her attractive young stepson. These persons are much pleasanter and more virtuous than those in Middleton, and the minor incidents of the story are set forth more easily and vivaciously than is common in Massinger. But in the main, the plot grows out of Massinger's sustained and dramatic revelation of the leading character, Sir Giles Overreach. He is not an ordinary usurer but a merchant prince.

> But this Sir Giles feeds high, keeps many servants,
> Who must at his command do any outrage;
> Rich in his habit, vast in his expenses,
> Yet he to admiration still increases
> In wealth and lordships.
>
>   He frights men out of their estates
> And breaks through all the law-nets, made to curb
>   ill men,
> As they were cobwebs. No man dares reprove
>   him:
> Such a spirit to dare, and power to do, were never
> Lodged so unluckily.   [II.2.

His ruthless march to wealth, however, is controlled by another purpose than greed. He plans to marry his only daughter to a nobleman and thus triumph over the aristocracy.

> And, therefore, I'll not have a chambermaid
> That ties her shoes, or any meaner office
> But such whose fathers were right worshipfull.
> 'Tis a rich man's pride; there having ever been
> More than a feud, a strange antipathy
> Between us and true gentry.   [II.1.

In carrying out his purpose, this London parvenu proceeds with blind self-confidence and basest malignity. Like Barabas, Shylock and Volpone, he is a monster,

defeated in the end by his own greed and arrogance, and,
like other Elizabethan villains, he is frank in his avowal
of iniquity and atheism. Success has made him half-mad,
and he rushes on to his purpose in reckless fury. The
action is like that of a tragedy in which a Barabas or a
Richard III piles crime on crime to hasten his own
destruction. Overreach treats both his accomplices and
his foes with ferocious contempt. He will suffer no
impediments or delays, nor take any counsel of policy or
prudence. In the most powerful scene of the play (III,
2) he bids his daughter disregard her maiden purity in
order to make sure of his lordship, and then exultingly
imagines himself forcing the lord to cure her wounded
honour by marrying her. He consents to a secret marriage and is easily gulled into signing a direction to
"marry her to this gentleman," who proves to be All-
worth and not the desired Lord Lovell. When the trick
is exposed he falls into a frenzy and tries to kill his
daughter. It is perhaps a logical outcome of his passion,
and not merely an Elizabethan extravagance, that he ends
in raving madness.

The character of Sir Giles has been criticized from
different points of view. Massinger imposes his own
morality in an external fashion, and it is out of character
for Sir Giles even in madness to ascribe his own defeat
to the "undone widow" and "wrong'd orphans." This
is not dramatic confession but Massinger's own denunciation of the speaker's sins. Further, Massinger seems to
view the parvenu's desire to wed his daughter to nobility
as the basest infamy. It would be possible to regard this
as a harmless ambition which might help rather than
humiliate the gentry, but Massinger makes it the motive
for Overreach's greatest malignities, including his unnatural treatment of his daughter. This is a little like attacking a political creed by proving that a conservative, or a
radical, is a scoundrel. But, despite its lapses in dramatic
veracity and its peculiarly narrow social view, the characterization of Overreach has a sustained forcefulness and

a general truth to type that render it not only a most effective part for the actor but one of the great imaginative achievements of our realistic comedy.

Like "Volpone," the play goes beyond the usual limits of comedy, and it borrows a villain from tragedy, but its Marlowean superman is a trader and his villainies belong to the modern commercial world. Massinger comes nearer than had either Jonson or Middleton, to arriving at a formula that could henceforth be repeated in modern realistic comedy. Let your play deal with some social evil, in this case the threat of the rich commercial class to usurp the place of the gentry, and in the main give it a comic treatment, as here in the hangers-on of the rich man, the servants of the lady, and the tradesmen with their changing attitudes. Let the chief figure of the play be a representative of the social evil, and on him or her focus both the dramatic development, the social satire and the moral preachment. Character then dictates the action, but that action may be melodramatic or even tragic in the intensity of its emotions, against a setting of comic satire.

There is not much laughter in Massinger's plays and very little to edify the sense of humour. He is at his best when maintaining serious characterization and patent moral teaching whether in romantic or realistic plays. But this service to comedy was exercised over many years. Though his plays were rather strangely neglected during the Restoration period, the best of them were later revived. "The Maid of Honour," "The Bashful Lover" and "The Bondman" were on the stage in the last quarter of the eighteenth century, and "The City Madam," as "Riches," held the stage until 1822. After its revival in 1748, "A New Way to Pay Old Debts" attracted Kemble, Cooke, Kean, Junius Booth and later Edwin Booth and Davenport. It may be said to have kept the stage throughout the nineteenth century, and to have outlasted all other Elizabethan plays except those of Shakespeare.

III

James Shirley was born in 1596, studied for a time at Oxford and took both the bachelor's and master's degree at Cambridge. He entered the church and in 1621 became head-master of St. Albans Grammar School, a position which he resigned in 1624 because of his conversion to Catholicism. In February of the next year his first play, "Love Tricks," was licensed and henceforth Shirley was occupied as a dramatist in London until 1636, when he went to Dublin and for four years wrote for the theater there. Upon the breaking out of the Civil War Shirley entered the royal service under his patron, the Earl of Newcastle. For a time during the Protectorate he seems to have kept a school and he continued at this occupation after the Restoration. Though some of his plays were revived, he does not appear to have had any personal connection with the new theaters. He died in 1666 in consequence of exposure during the great fire.

Shirley does not contribute to English comedy any such powerful and original plays as "A Fair Quarrel" and "A New Way to Pay Old Debts." Rather he sums up and includes all that was best in comedy during the reign of Charles I and continues the traditions and practices of the great writers of the earlier period. His own relations with the court were close, and the plot of one of the comedies, "The Gamester," was suggested by the king himself; and his plays represent a theater that was becoming more and more devoted to one class of society. The London merchants and their wives and their apprentices, so common in the drama of the early years of James I, scarcely appear in Shirley's comedies. When they deal with contemporary manners, it is with the courtiers at a ball or the upper middle classes at the races or with knights and their ladies seeking the gaieties of fashionable life. Their romance too is of the courtly fashion of Fletcher, where plots and misfortunes and insurrection fail to dim the cardinal virtues of loyalty to king, a high sense of personal honour, and gallant devotion to your mistress.

When Shirley began to write for the stage, all of Shakespeare's plays and most of Jonson's and Middleton's were in print. During the Protectorate he aided in bringing together the still unpublished plays of Beaumont and Fletcher in the Folio of 1647. A reader and a student, Shirley had a better opportunity than any earlier writer to profit from the great treasure-house of poetry that the English drama had already collected. No earlier dramatist presents so many reminiscences of Shakespeare in phrase, characterization and incident, and he often imitates Jonson, particularly in the drawing of some "humorous" person. But his plays in their main characteristics naturally adapt themselves to the models of Fletcher and Massinger, whose work dominated the theaters of his day. Massinger was his main rival during the decade that he wrote for the Queen's men, and in the last years he succeeded Fletcher and Massinger as the chief writer for the King's men at the Blackfriars. He carried on their tradition but he brought it perceptibly nearer to the Restoration. Indeed, he must be remembered as one of those dramatists who lived through the interval of the Protectorate, and who saw his plays acted in the theaters both of Charles I and of Charles II. He is almost as close to the heroic play, the tragicomedy and the comedy of manners of the Restoration as to the romances and comedies of Fletcher.

Shirley wrote at least thirty plays in addition to a few on which he collaborated. With the possible exception of "St. Patrick for Ireland," they might all be arranged in a scale similar to that which we have suggested for Fletcher and Massinger, varying from tragedy through tragicomedy, romantic comedy, to comedy of manners. Love is the main theme in all, and all are primarily plays of intrigue rather than character. We meet the now familiar personages and situations, the slandered lady,

the gentleman killed but coming to life at the nick of
time, the love-lorn girl disguised as a page, the lady
whose virtue is triumphant though sorely tested, the gentlemen rivals in love and honour, the intriguing favourite
of the king, but all these are tricked out with new
surprises. If we compare these romantic plays with
Fletcher's, they are distinguished by a greater probability
and nicety in the management of intrigue. Their plots
are not so sensational or striking as his, though they are
varied, surprising and lively; and impossibilities are not
admitted without an explanation, or changes of character
without an excuse. If we compare Shirley's romance with
Massinger's, it is distinguished by ease of manipulation
and charm of style. Shirley has a lightness of verse, a
grace of phrase, a flight of fancy, that suit themselves
readily to sentiment and strained situations.

Of the tragicomedies "The Young Admiral," though
based on Lope de Vega's "Don Lope de Cardona," follows an established formula also represented in "The
Doubtful Heir," "The Imposture," and "The Court
Secret." Two kingdoms are involved in war as well as
rivalry in love. The succession to the throne, duty
to country, loyalty to king or mistress are all at stake,
but happy marriages result, including the union of two
royalties. The comic scenes in each of these plays are
negligible. "The Gentleman of Venice" provides a
romantic treatment of the imaginary cuckold theme combined with the story of the love of a man of humble rank
for a great lady. As is now usual in tragicomedy, two
distinct stories are tied loosely together. "The Coronation," which was included in the Beaumont-Fletcher Folio
but seems mainly, if not entirely, by Shirley, is in less
heroic vein, an example of tamed romance and with little
humorous accompaniment.

Less heroic too is "The Royal Master," like "The
Coronation" and like Massinger's "Great Duke of Flor-
ence," which it resembles in plot as well as in tone. The
King of Naples, a widower, entertains the Duke of Flor-

ence as suitor to his sister Theodosia. Montalto, the
king's favourite, is himself in love with the princess and
plans to break off the match by introducing the duke to
Domitilla, a beautiful young girl living in the country.
Montalto proceeds on his machinations by carrying tales
between the princess and the duke and by slandering her,
but he is defeated through his old enemy Riviero, disguised in the duke's service. The king has planned to
marry Domitilla to Montalto, but when he broaches the
subject to her she misunderstands and thinks he himself
is her lover. Montalto is sent to prison, and the duke
won back to the princess. It remains for the king to
cure the charming Domitilla of her infatuation. He does
this by pretending to the rôle of the lustful monarch and
arouses her virtuous indignation, which is upheld by the
brave Octavio, Riviero's son, to whom the king gives her
in marriage.

This is an admirable example of the tamed and purified
tragicomedy, in which the plots and clashes and jealousies
are brought down to some degree of ordinary humanity
and probability. The ducal suitor, the villain favourite,
the banished noble, the lustful monarch, the royal lady,
the love-lorn heroine, all play their usual parts but with a
difference; and the elaborate intrigue is very deftly
handled. The princess, wild with jealousy because the
duke appears to have forsaken her, draws a dagger on
her girl rival; then Domitilla, kneeling, begs her

To tell the King how willing I die for him." [VI.1.

Thus with one dramatic gesture, the princess's jealousy
is banished and Domitilla's secret disclosed. Or again
in the closing scene the king's rather theatrical proposal
to make Domitilla his mistress leads not only to the
cure of her infatuation but to her love for the hitherto
neglected Octavio. Charming too is her acceptance of
her new defender with its reference to the promise she
had made to marry whomever the king proposed—when
she hoped he would propose himself.

My lord, you now deserve I should
Be yours, whom, with the hazard of the King's
Anger and your own life, you have defended.
There is a spring of honour here, and to it
I' the presence of the King, his court, and Heaven,
I dare now give my heart, nor is't without
My duty to a promise.

There is something here of the tenderness and grace
of a Shakespearian heroine, but there is little of Shakespeare's humour in the comic scenes.   These deal with
Domitilla's secretary, Bombo, who is much addicted to
books though he can neither read nor write.   He enters
with a book in hand like the soliloquizers in the old
revenge plays, and otherwise is mildly amusing.

Slightly less intense in their passions, more diversified
in plot, and somewhat more comic in intention are the
romantic comedies: "The Brothers," "The Grateful
Servant," "The Arcadia," based on Sidney's romance but
with little stage pastoralism, "The Humourous Courtier,"
"The Bird in a Cage" (a romantic extravaganza), "The
Opportunity" (based on a play by Tirso de Molina),
"The Sisters," and the early medley "Love Tricks."   Of
these perhaps the most representative is "The Grateful
Servant."   Leonora, princess of Milan, once betrothed
to the Duke of Savoy, runs away as a page in order to
escape marriage to her uncle.   She is accompanied by
Valentio, a friar, and they are taken prisoners by banditti.   Valentio escapes and the princess is rescued by
the noble Foscari who takes her into his service as a
page and despatches her to his mistress Cleona to
announce his return despite his reported death.   The
princess-page finds Cleona courted by the Duke of Savoy.
When she reports this to Foscari, he circulates again the
report of his death, magnanimously hands Cleona over to
the duke, and prepares to enter a monastery.   The priest
whom he consults is Valentio whom the page recognizes,
and the two succeed in preventing Foscari's design.   The

duke marries Leonora and Foscari, Cleona. The extensive sub-plot deals with one of Shirley's favourite themes, the reformation of a libertine. The duke's brother, the rake Lodwick, commands his follower Piero to commit adultery with his wife in order that he may have grounds for divorce. Grimundo, his former guardian, undertakes his cure and offers to lead him to a lady of surprising attractiveness. The libertine is brought to a beautiful garden, where he is welcomed by a masque of nymphs and satyrs, and by a fascinating but uncanny lady. She finally admits that she is a devil, and Lodwick escapes to his home where he finds Piero with his wife. At first Piero says that he has succeeded, and then confesses the truth that the lady is innocent. One other encounter with the she-devil (Grimundo's wife disguised) is necessary to ensure the libertine's reform.

There is scarcely a situation here which can not be paralleled in many earlier plays or indeed in other dramas by Shirley. Even the lady appearing as a she-devil occurs in his "Lady of Pleasure." But each situation is developed into an effective scene and neatly linked to the next. The dialogue is clever, the movement quick. There are no dull spots; and romance, sentiment, profligacy and morality all play their parts without straying beyond the control of comedy.

It is in the romantic rather than the realistic plays that Shirley's talent shows to the best advantage—at least to my taste; but the realistic comedies have an interest for our inquiry beyond their intrinsic merits because of their historical position. The romantic plays belong to a species which was to receive no further development of importance, the comedies of manners proceeded in certain directions beyond Jonson and Fletcher and toward the masterpieces of Congreve and Sheridan. Nine of Shirley's comedies have the scene in contemporary London, which may be sufficient excuse for classing them as realistic: "The Wedding," "Changes," "The Gamester," "The Example," "The Ball," "The Witty Fair One,"

"Hyde Park," "The Lady of Pleasure," and "The Constant Maid." But no sharp line of difference is to be found between their plots and situations and those of the romantic plays. Six of the nine have the theme of the converted libertine which we have just seen figuring in "The Grateful Servant." Six have the yet more tragi-comic situation of the dead coming to life. They are all comedies of intrigue rather than of character or manners, mixing tricks and rivalries, slanders and defenses of virtue; presenting in fact what had become the stock material of the Elizabethan drama.

A distinction may be drawn, however, among these nine plays of London between those which develop their plots without any noticeable attention to actual London conditions, and those which accompany their intrigues with definite pictures of local manners. In the first group are "The Wedding," "Changes," "The Example" and "The Constant Maid." "The Wedding" presents a story of slandered innocence similar to that of "Much Ado." Marwood, the slanderer, is supposed to be killed in a duel by Beauford the lover. The coffin supposed to contain Marwood's body, when opened, reveals Gratiana, the slandered lady, whose innocence is established by the confession of her servant who has substituted her own daughter Lucibel. Marwood comes to life in time to marry Lucibel, who has appeared in male disguise. In the comic underplot rival suitors, one a fat glutton, the other a lean miser, and a mock duel, help to add to the fun. "The Changes" and "The Constant Maid" also have very complicated plots of love crossings, and "The Example" has a conflict on a "point of honour" between husband and rejected suitor. The two minor actions are comic, one presenting a lively maiden who disposes of her foolish or dissolute suitors, and the other dealing with the Jonsonian humours of Sir Solitary Plot and his assistants. The main action has the seriousness and extravagance of tragicomedy. Lord Fitzavarice attempts to seduce Lady Peregrine by offering to pay all of her

husband's debts.   In admiration of her constancy he presents her with the mortgage and jewels, just at the
moment that the husband arrives home from the wars.
A challenge follows, but the husband is arrested for debt
and naturally assumes that this is at the instigation of
his lordship.   Fitzavarice pays the debt, overwhelms Sir
Walter with kindness and convinces him of his wife's
innocence.   Fitzavarice next raises the point of honour.
His payment of the debts will lead some to suppose
that he has bought Sir Walter's complaisance in his
wife's dishonour or at least his consent to abandon
the duel.   Honour demands that the duel be fought;
both draw blood, honour is satisfied; Fitzavarice
is married to Jacinta of the sub-plot, and the play
ends.

Of the plays of the second group, "The Witty Fair
One" makes the least of London manners.   The two
heroines are kept busy in the usual fashion, Violetta in
marrying the gentleman of her choice instead of the booby
designed for her by her father, Penelope in out-tricking a
very foul-mouthed libertine and bringing him to repentance and marriage.   Brains, the clever servant in charge
of Violetta, is the best of Shirley's "humourists" and is a
happy burlesque on the theatrical type that he represents.
His dogged confidence in his own prowess leads to amusing discomfiture.   The London gaming rooms and the
habits of the gamblers form the setting for the complicated plot of "The Gamester."   The reformation of a
libertine, the coming to life of a gentleman killed in a
duel, appear again, but with new permutations and surprises.   "The Ball" has only a slight plot, the scornful
lady ridiculing her suitors but caught by one of them, and
the two ladies who are merry rivals for a lord; but these
actions are enveloped in the brisk repartee and the amusing figures of society's latest diversion—the ball.   The
records of the master of revels show that the play as first
performed caused considerable scandal because of its

mimicking of certain court notabilities. It carried realistic comedy into the highest circles of society.

In "Hyde Park" three stories are combined. Carol, a "scornful lady," repulses all her suitors, but when Fairfield begs of her one boon—that she will never seek to see him again—she begins to waver, and after a series of tricks and countertricks she yields and marries him. Her cousin, Mrs. Bonavent, whose husband is thought to be dead, is married to Lacy, whereupon her husband returns and claims her. Julietta, sister of Fairfield, is affianced to the jealous Trier, who introduces the libertine Lord Bonvile to her in order to test her virtue. She cures the libertine but breaks with her jealous lover. All three stories are carried along together in successive meetings in the drawing rooms or in Hyde Park at the races. The flow of conversation is easy, the manners up to date, and the details added to the old plots well adapted for theatrical effectiveness. In Act I, for example, the two suitors, Rider and Venture, boast of the presents they have received from their mistress Carol, and then discover that each has received the gift that the other gave the lady. In Act II, at his wedding Lacy compels the stranger Bonavent to dance before the ladies; and later in the Park, Bonavent at the point of his sword compels Lacy in turn to caper to the music of a bagpipe. Venture, the foolish gallant, is thrown from the horse he is riding in the race and enters covered with mud. The scenes in the Park are enlivened not only by the racing and betting but also by songs from the foolish Venture and from a nightingale and a cuckoo. Something is always happening and the play of words between the ladies and their lovers, if not especially witty, never lacks animation. The characters too are distinct. Lord Bonavent is a good-natured sportsman as well as the conventional libertine. The sprightly Carol recalls other scornful ladies but foreshadows Millamant. She recounts the pleasures of the single life, and asks her cousin, the widow

And will you lose all this, for
"I, Cicely, take thee, John, to be my husband"?
Keep him still to be your servant:
Imitate me; a hundred suitors cannot
Be half the trouble of one husband.   I
Dispose my frowns and favours like a princess;
Deject, advance, undo, create again;
It keeps the subjects in obedience,
And teaches 'em to look at me with distance.   [I.ii.

Here is a formula manifestly capable of much variation and of adaptability to any stage.   The fashionable diversion of the moment may be made to afford a novel background for ladies of varying temperaments and their suitors, foolish, profligate or worthy.   Still closer to the Restoration comedy of manners is "The Lady of Pleasure."   Sir Thomas Bornwell, in despair over the extravagance and frivolity of his wife, determines to outrival her. Though she goes so far as to keep an assignation with a lover blindfolded, when her lover boasts that he has lain with a she-devil and when her husband declares that he has lost his fortune, she professes repentance and congratulates herself on losing the lover and retaining her husband and his fortune, which proves to be unimpaired. In contrast to the frivolous Aretina, is the widow Celestina aged sixteen.   She maintains her good sense and virtue amid the gaieties of fashionable life, aids Sir Thomas in his plot and cures her suitor Lord A. of his libertinism.   The detailed depiction of fashionable manners and affectations and the flippant conversations half conceal and half reveal the lewdness of contemporary society.   The plot suggests resemblances to the "School for Scandal"; and though there is less wit and more preaching than in Congreve, the method and manner are not unlike his.

In spite of many improprieties in language and situation Shirley has often been praised for his morality. Perhaps he deserves this in comparison with Fletcher and

Middleton, or with his immediate contemporaries or Restoration successors. He usually keeps away from bawds and prostitutes, makes his profligates repent, rewards the virtuous, and does not prolong his ribaldry. But he does not bend his humour to satire or censorship, and he is not above suiting it to lewdness. His comedy finds love in two spheres, the one romantic, passionate, the abode of heroisms and idealisms, where humour is necessary to give relief or moderation; the other realistic, fashionable, where humour prefers to regard the ladies and suitors as playing a game rather than imperiling their souls. He is far below Middleton or Jonson or Fletcher in his powers of comic invention, but he sees the inconsistencies and affectations of mortals and the incongruities and absurdities of their actions and can persuade us to see and to smile with him. If not very witty, he is rarely stupid, usually brisk without being boisterous, amiable rather than satiric. His humour is personified in his sprightly ladies; they desire pleasure, employ what wit they possess, and put a little vivacity into the game of existence without losing a saving quantity of good sense.

IV

I shall not pause long over the minor comic writers of the reign of Charles I. They produced singularly little that offers any variations of importance from the average work of Middleton, Massinger and Shirley, and nothing comparable to the best work of these masters. They did, however, produce a great many plays representative of all the dramatic types then in fashion. Tragicomedy was perhaps the favourite form. Ford's plays in this class are unworthy of his great genius, being often either imitative or mawkish. Those by May, Davenport, Mayne, Randolph, Glapthorne and others add little that is new in the way of either humour or romance. D'Avenant and Carlell are the chief writers next to Shirley in developing the Fletcherian model somewhat closer to the heroic play of the Restoration. Of romantic comedies,

Suckling's "Goblins" has originality and sprightliness. In the field of realistic comedy of London life, the followers of Jonson are numerous but uninspired. Jasper Mayne's "City Match" has the merit of farcical liveliness which kept it on the stage until the end of the next century.

We shall gain a sufficient view of comedy at the close of the period if we look at the fifteen plays of the most prolific of the sons of Ben. Richard Brome, once the servant of Jonson, was later accepted as a literary disciple and praised by his master for his achievement.

> By observation of those Comic Laws
> Which I your Master first did teach the Age.

In his own prefaces and prologues Brome shows himself a little self-conscious and uneasy. Though he likes to display his Latin, he disclaims any merit as poet or scholar. He does not share in the fashion for plays

> In scene magnificent and language high

and professes his interest in "low and home-bred subjects." Nevertheless, as we shall see, he was as successful in tragicomedies with foreign and historical stories as in plays on contemporary London. Though he is often spoken of merely as an imitator of Jonson, yet as a matter of fact he borrowed freely from Shakespeare, Fletcher and Middleton. From Ben he learned his elaborate construction of plots and his detailed drawing of eccentric personages; but in general his plays, even more than Shirley's, echo everything that was famous in the drama. Lacking Shirley's poetry and delicacy, always gross in language, often licentious in their appeal, his comedies are at once representative of the average of their own time and very close in most of their traits to those that were to follow after the Restoration.

Brome, however, was by no means a mere imitator. He does not rehash old material without striking changes. Like others, he seeks constantly for surprise, and this demands some ingenuity. His plays are always clearly introduced, but a first act of excellent exposition is followed by a bewildering array of tricks, discoveries, transformations and reconciliations, often working out to a conclusion that could scarcely be guessed from the persons or circumstances at first disclosed. All the stock tricks of classical comedy are employed, and disguise in particular is used more frequently and improbably than by any preceding dramatist. All the devices of romantic story are also utilized, especially madness. Some one is always exhibiting real or pretended madness and being practised upon by real or pretended physicians. Brome's effort is to give the old intrigues or situations a new complication, and in consequence his romance and realism are both conventional and theatrical. But we can't tell what will happen. The scapegraces, rascals and prostitutes are not what they seem or else they get converted. Like Fletcher and Shirley, he is willing to deny truth or poetry or satire for the sake of theatrical surprise.

His fifteen plays range themselves in a scale such as I have applied to Fletcher and others, except that most of Brome's plays are realistic presentations of London life. Only three have foreign scenes, but romantic elements are not lacking in some of the London pieces.

At one end of the scale are the tragicomedies. One of these, "The Queen's Exchange," is placed in Anglo-Saxon times and has some of the trappings of the early historical plays. It exhibits two courts, four clowns, six ghosts who dance, a hermit, a king's fool, a villain, a genius, a prison, madness, and many passages reminiscent of Shakespeare. But all the historical paraphernalia merely provides a background for love complications of the usual sort which end happily when Bertha, queen of the West Saxons, marries Anthynus, worthy son of Segebert, and Osrick, King of Northumbria, weds Mildred, Segebert's daughter. "The Queen and Concubine" is equally serious and laudatory of virtue. The queen, slandered and exiled, proves patient and forgiving and adds to the virtues of Saint Griselda those of a school teacher seeking to instruct her poor subjects,

And by practice give them literature. [IV. 1.

Needless to say, her saintliness triumphs in the end over the mad pride of the concubine and brings the lustful king to repentance. "The Love-sick Court" is much more in the Fletcherian manner and borrows directly from "The Two Noble Kinsmen." Next to these three plays on our scale, may be placed "The Novella," which has less heroic trappings and tragic dangers than they but has the scene in Venice and a tragicomic plot. Victoria takes the rôle of a courtezan, "the novella," advertised to be sold to the highest bidder, as a means to win back her true lover Fabritio.

At the other end of the scale from these tragicomedies are a number of realistic plays of London manners. Little is to be found here which was not already familiar on the stage. We meet again light wives in search of gallants, spendthrift nephews seeking to recuperate their fortunes, young lovers outwitting miserly or choleric parents, needy knights consorting with projectors, country bumpkins gulled by city wits, jealous husbands nagged by clever wives, prostitutes disgraced, cowards kicked, and bullies out-bullied. The manners of court and fashion are imitated, but Brome is more at home among the vulgarities of the city. No one had written so many plays of this sort since Middleton; but unlike Middleton, Brome usually provides for the final repentance of the rogues and the triumph of the virtuous. These transformations in persons and events require that the London scene should be filled by plots and improbabilities worthy of an Arabian night.

"A Mad Couple Well Match'd" is as shameless in language and incident as one of Middleton's plays, but ends in conversions. "The Court Beggar" is more Jonsonian, stupider, and fully as gross. "The English Moor" presents as its chief novelty an English girl disguised as a moor. "The Weeding of Covent Garden" gives a boisterous exhibition of the roysterers and prostitutes of Covent Garden which is also invaded by several respectable but eccentric citizens. "The New Academy" has a school of fashion, many intrigues, a widower who is always weeping or reciting his verses, a merchant who has married his maid and caught a tartar, an uxurious citizen who won't be jealous, a doting mother, her foolish son, and a boastful libertine. " 'Sparagus Garden," like several others of the plays, makes its action center on a place of assignation. As usual, the young lovers encounter the opposition of their families; but this Juliet by pretending to be with child manages to bring about marriage with her Romeo and reconciliation between their parents. "The City Wit" has the old plot of a disguised person discovering and exposing the follies and vices of the city, but this Haroun al Raschid is a young citizen on the verge of bankruptcy who, instead of one disguise, gallivants about in many. He recovers his fortune and shames his opponents and his wife. He is aided by his apprentice Jeremy who, unknown to his master, goes about disguised as a woman, so there is a double discovery at the end. In spite of ingenious plotting such as this and some skill in the depiction of eccentric character, these London comedies are mostly noisy and tedious.

By far the most interesting of the London plays are the few which introduce fanciful or romantic elements. These may be given a place midway in our scale between the tragicomedies and the realistic London pieces, and they are the most original of Brome's plays.

In "The Damoiselle" the persons are of the familiar types, an old usurer, a decayed knight, a humorous justice, two gallants and so on. But the story unfolded is as miraculous and virtue is as triumphant as in one of the tearful comedies of a century later. The exposition gives no hint of these developments. The opening act introduces us to a Shylock-like usurer who has disowned his worthless son and clings to his only daughter, but presently the son appears and carries off the daughter. In the second scene of the act we meet Justice Bumpsey, whose daughter has just married Valentine, son of Dryground, who has just mortgaged his last land to the miser. Bumpsey accepts the challenge to divide his fortune with his son-in-law, and then to equal him either in squandering or saving. These humorous beginnings work into a plot in which a supposed courtezan offered to the highest bidder surprises everyone by proving to be a man in disguise. Our sympathies are excited by the ruined gentleman Brookeall and a beggar child Phillis. The angel who rescues them is the old knight Dryground who repents the wrong he did to Brookeall's sister fourteen years earlier. He discovers the woman he wronged, their long-lost daughter Phillis, and Brookeall's son; and after many tears and upbraidings he rights all wrongs and brings about the desirable marriages and reformations. Similarly in "The Northern Lass" complicated intrigues and London humours are crossed by pathos and loyal love. The love-lorn heroine, the northern lass, is supposed to excite our pity by her devotion and simplicity and in the end she wins the man she loves. Songs and dances further diversify the entertainment.

More original is the scheme of "The Antipodes." Perigrine is brain-sick because of too much reading of Mandeville's and other books of travel. A physician under the patronage of a phantastic Lord Letoy undertakes his cure by persuading him that he is in the Antipodes. A play is staged for this purpose and considerable merriment goes on both among the actors and the audience. Though little is made of the manifest possibilities which the scheme offers for either satire or fancy, still this is far from being the ordinary comedy of intrigue. In spite of early appearances to the contrary, Letoy proves benevolent as well as phantastic and cures all ailments that interfere with happiness.

Still more romantic is "A Jovial Crew or the Merry Beggars," a play suggested by Fletcher's "Beggars'

Bush," but ingenious and original.   Springlove, the
steward of a great estate, has settled his accounts early
because it is "well-nigh May" and the spring fever possesses him to wander with the beggars and gipsies.   A
nightingale sings and he is off.   The two young daughters
of the great estate also feel the desire for adventure and
persuade their lovers to run away with them and join the
beggars.   Their later experiences are not so romantic as
they expected, and the rest of the play is largely taken
up with the hardships and mishaps that result from their
masquerading.   But we have much jollity and humour
and many songs.   As an opera the play kept on the stage
through the eighteenth century.

   Brome's plays bring us even closer than those of most
of his contemporaries to the Restoration.   Their grossness and noisiness, their loose women and tricky spendthrifts, their humours and intrigues remind us of the
comedies that were to come in the reign of Charles II.
Nevertheless he is still unmistakably of the Elizabethan
tradition.   He imitates Jonson and Fletcher and Shakespeare.   He is not poetical but he tries to be.   Though
very vulgar he does not dare to be immoral.   He delights
in human nature, the joy in reporting one's observations
on the human species.   Though he is imitative and theatrical rather than inventive and imaginative, still he does
present a broad and varied view of his Englishmen.   The
spirit of the great Elizabethans was by no means dead
in a theater than could produce "The Antipodes" and
"The Merry Beggars."

CHAPTER XII

CONCLUSION TO ELIZABETHAN COMEDY

In a review of Elizabethan comedy, two dramatic species that have been referred to only incidentally, the pastoral and the court masque, may need a further word. Each for a time mingled its waters freely with the main stream of English comedy, though in the end each found a separate and well defined channel of its own.

Pastoralism, as we have noted, was a considerable element in Renaissance literature. It attempted to express man's perennial craving for the simple life in terms of the golden age, following the models of Vergil and Theocritus. It made its way into various forms of literature, into lyrical, descriptive and satirical poetry, into the novel and the drama. Its entrance into the drama was by several doors. Accompanying mythological persons and stories, it early found a place in spectacles and shows, shepherds and nymphs appearing on the stage with the deities of Olympus. Again, it took the stage in the form of dramatized eclogues. Spenser's "Shepherd's Calendar," which embodied nearly all the themes and modes of pastoral poetry, was published in 1579, and one year earlier came the first English pastoral play, Sidney's "Lady of May." Again it took the stage through the dramatization of pastoral novels, so Lodge's "Rosalynde" supplied story and shepherds for "As You Like It," and Sidney's "Arcadia" furnished the themes for several later dramas. Finally, the pastoral was equipped with a special stage of its own. Following the division of Vitruvius of the classical stage into three kinds of scenes for tragedy, comedy and satyr, the last of which was "decorated with trees, caverns, mountains, and other rustic objects delineated in landscape style," Italian humanists felt that the pastoral could be made to fit these specifications of a special setting and of a species distinct from both comedy and tragedy. Guarini's "Pastor Fido" was an elaborate and laborious literary effort to meet this critical demand for a pastoral tragicomedy, and it was imitated most skilfully by Fletcher in his "Faithful Shepherdess."

Pastoralism was thus enabled to aid comedy from time to time in different ways, supplying spectacle and picturesqueness, song and music, romance and fantasy, sentiment and idealization. The effect of the artificial exaggeration of the amatory emotions such as is found in "The Faithful Shepherdess" can be traced throughout the tragedies and tragicomedies of Beaumont and Fletcher, and indeed on into the heroic plays of a later generation. A good deal of the idealization of love in the earlier drama owes something to the imitation of pastoral idyls; certainly the refinement and delicacy as well as the artificiality of Lyly's comedies are in harmony with their use of pastoral themes and persons. Pastoralism served an injunction on the farce and buffoonery that were always threatening to possess the stage. After the clown, the shepherd was not unwelcome; upon the exits of the low comedians, enter the love-lorn nymph or the pleading swain. Shakespeare indeed carried his clowns to the Forest of Arden and to the sheep-shearing in Bohemia, and in those secure retreats real and pretended rustics dwelt together. In general, however, the drama did not have much success in depicting a genuine countryside or the humours of country folk. The pastoral tradition encouraged fancifulness rather than observation and linked itself more readily to romantic story than to comic reality.

After "The Faithful Shepherdess" the pastoral was recognized as a distinct form of drama, admired by the cultivated though too delicate for the vulgar stage. Under the patronage of Queen Henrietta Maria it had a revival. Inigo Jones devised scenes for "The Faithful Shepherdess" at court (1633-4) and the queen and her ladies acted in the French pastoral "Florimène" (1635). Of the new pieces composed, Randolph's "Amyntas" used the Italian scheme in a more humorous fashion than had his predecessors, but Fletcher's masterpiece had only one really worthy successor, the unfinished "Sad Shepherd" by Ben Jonson. Drawing on folk-lore, mingling real and fanciful creatures, aiming at the creation of a distinctively English pastoral, Jonson planned what might have been a literary triumph and a dramatic innovation. But it seems unlikely that Jonson's interesting experiment, if completed, could have availed much to maintain the pastoral as a distinct form of drama.

It may be noted, however, that comedy in later, as in Elizabethan times, has often profited from some form or other of pastoralism. It is ever in danger of becoming too citified, too sophisticated, too ingenious, and it needs the refreshment of country air. Though it may do without sheep and shepherds, song contests and echo dialogues, it needs to return from time to time to the simpler virtues and the quiet life. The drama requires some quiet moments in order to give play for its crises and thrills and movement; and comedy may view the placidities as well as the absurdities of mankind.

Masques are common in the early plays and add the gaiety of dance and the colour of dress to the spectacle of comedy. Pastoral sentiment, the machinery and costumes of the court masque, a romantic love story, and burlesque by the low comedians—this would serve as a sort of recipe for romantic comedy. As the masque developed in the hands of Inigo Jones and Ben Jonson into a very expensive spectacle with music, songs, scenery, and libretto, it passed beyond the reach of the regular theaters. It seems to have stirred the creative fancy of both Fletcher in "The Triumph of Time" and Shakespeare in "The Tempest," as I have tried to show elsewhere. And in particular, the antimasques, grotesque and extravagant dances in costume by professional actors, were repeated or imitated in "The Triumph of Time," "The Two Noble Kinsmen," "A Winter's Tale," and "The Tempest." After Shakespeare's death, masques continued to appear frequently in the regular drama, but they could have been only faint reflections of the court performances, which increased in musical and scenic complexity. Their glories ended with the revolution but not before they had furnished the form for Milton's "Comus" and helped Shakespeare to create the enchantments of "The Tempest."

Both pastoral and masque continued as recognized species of drama long after the Restoration, but they gave place to a new form, the opera. Henceforth the musical and the spoken drama are constant rivals, though comedy of course never entirely surrenders song, dance and spectacle. The masque was practically absorbed by the opera shortly after the Restoration. The pastoral tradition has never been lost entirely and has reappeared from time to time, sometimes in the spoken but more usually in the musical drama.

Another relationship between species was the use of comic scenes in tragedy. This practice was virtually universal during the Elizabethan period and occasioned the nurse in "Romeo and Juliet," the porter in "Macbeth," the grave diggers in "Hamlet" and the fool in "Lear." Little contribution to comedy as a form of drama was made by such employment of comic relief, but some extension of comic material was provided. The purpose of such scenes was contrast and heightening as well as relief, so the low comedians found themselves performing in strange juxtapositions of tears and laughter, horror and merriment. To modern taste some of the most grotesque combinations arise in the presentation of madness, which may be frankly comic as in Middleton's "Changeling" where two gallants with designs on the keeper's wife become inmates of an asylum, or which may be at the same time tragic and comic, as in "The Duchess of Malfi" and "Lear." Shakespeare is often suggesting that tears and laughter are close kinsmen, but nowhere does he dramatize this intimacy so powerfully as in the babbling of the fool to Lear.

A far less daring combination is the use of the populace or of menials to afford relief to the tragedies of monarchs, as the citizens in "Julius Caesar" or the insurrectionists in "Philaster." These contrasts have a certain propriety, and Jonson in "Sejanus" was careful to keep his comic portion closely interwoven in the main plot. But after Shakespeare there are few highly imaginative unions of the tragic and the comic. No one else can create comic grave diggers, to say nothing of the Prince of Denmark. Incidental comic scenes become banal, though they are still numerous in tragedy. In heavy tragicomedy the two principal actions were often supplemented by a little buffoonery, but it is usually lifeless.

The clown had, as we have seen, a long career, and though the clown, or fool, as a recognized figure is rarely found after Shakespeare, yet a certain amount of horseplay and buffoonery occurs in comedies of all sorts to the very end of the period. Wit, humour, and romance, as well as tragedy, accepted the relief of a little boisterous fun. In this as in other instances the Elizabethans took the ingredients of their dramatic fare well-mixed. Whatever their other emotions, they enjoyed hearty laughter, and they did not tolerate any form of drama without some clowning. But of course low comedy was not restricted to mere uproariousness; it gave the chance for creating eccentric and whimsical persons and for introducing them into laughable predicaments. It offered a place for the grave diggers, for Dogberry and Autolycus, for the motley denizens of "Bartholomew Fair," for the grocer and his wife in "The Knight of the Burning Pestle," for Lopez and Diego in "The Spanish Curate" and for a host of other most comic revelations of human nature.

Elizabethan comedy is low and high, refined and boisterous, witty and farcical, fantastic and realistic. In tracing the formation of types, it has been necessary to remind ourselves that opposite characteristics are often united in the same play and that few pure examples of any type are to be found. Nevertheless, it has not proved difficult to trace the main changes and developments under the convenient though over-used classification of romantic and realistic. Though often confused and indistinct yet the broad line of this distinction persists. Romantic comedies are marked by adventures, improbabilities, foreign scenes, fantasy, poetry, and by the idealization of love and other sentiments and of personality. Realistic comedies are distinguished by reflection of current life and manners, especially of London, by domestic incidents, by unidealized sentiments and personalities, by a slighting of love or a stress on its baser aspects, by a tendency to criticism and satire. Toward the end, the two classes were both somewhat conventionalized; romantic comedy usually keeping to persons of rank, foreign scenes, and verse—realistic comedy to London, to persons of the middle or lower classes, and to prose.

Romantic comedy, I have followed from its early origins in storyland and spectacle, through the various contributions of Lyly, Peele and Greene in mingling fancy, sentiment and fun, to Shakespeare's apotheosis of the type in "As You Like It" and "Twelfth Night." After that the old materials remain and are given a new and brilliant life, though coarsened and theatricalized, by Fletcher and his followers. If these plays lack Shakespeare's woodland fancy wild they still take a cheerful view of life and of virtue; as, for example, in Shirley's "Grateful Servant," or more light-heartedly in Brome's "Jovial Crew." Buoyant spirits, lofty sentiment, idealized love, and generous human kindness sweeten verse and action. Their purpose is to take us away from actuality on a delightful or at least an entertaining excursion into romance.

The march of realism we have followed from the moralities and Plautus to some of its chief exponents,

Jonson, Middleton and Massinger. But here the development is not so consistent as in romance, and the crossings of purposes and methods are more confusing. I wish to attempt a further analysis of these varying forms, one which is not inapplicable to the romantic plays but which I shall apply chiefly to the realistic comedies. I shall take some of the terms that have since then come into general use and inquire how far they will aid in analyzing the dramatic realism of the Elizabethans. How far can the plays that we have been considering be classified as comedies of intrigue, of manners, of character, of satire, of social problems?

When we look for intrigue, it is everywhere. Nearly every comedy, romantic or realistic, is based on tricks, and the discovery of the deception makes the dénouement. This is true of "Twelfth Night" and "The Merchant of Venice" as well as of "The Alchemist" and "A New Way to Pay Old Debts." These tricks are by no means confined to love-making, they may lead to death or disaster as in the cases of Shylock and Overreach, or may be only a playful gesture like Portia's game with the ring, or a theatrical coup like Estefania's prayerbook for a pistol case. But though tricks are omnipresent, some plays rely almost exclusively for their interest on their plots or intrigues; or at least this plot interest overshadows any concern in character, wit or moral. These are the comedies of intrigue.

One or two peculiar groups may be noticed where the relationship is wholly that of a special plot. "Look About You," "The Blind Beggar of Bethnal Green" and "The Blind Beggar of Alexandria" are alike in using multiple disguise, one person tricking everyone by quick changes of costume. Another group is defined, though less sharply, by the use of the errors of persons wandering about in the dark. Another group, later in our period, copies the lively hide and seek of Spanish comedies of mistakes. The majority of English plays, however, model their tricks more or less on those of Plautus and Terence, often very closely, as in the case of "The Comedy of Errors," Lyly's "Mother Bombie," or Jonson's "Case is Altered." Very few plays confine the intrigue solely to the pursuit of illicit love, as was so common in Restoration comedy and in modern French farce; and very few employ such extravagant and improbable tricks that they result in mere farce. A great many plays, however, depict manners or character so slightly or so incidentally or so ineffectively that they have little interest beyond the contraptions of their plots. This is true of several by Chapman and a number by Middleton, Fletcher, Massinger and Shirley. Heywood's "Wise Woman of Hogsdon" is an elaborate example. Of Fletcher's comedies, "The Woman's Prize" and "Monsieur Thomas" are perhaps the most farcical; and "The Chances" and "A Wild Goose Chase" are examples of intrigue with some mixture of manners and wit. Of Jonson's plays, "Epicœne," and of Shakespeare's, "Merry Wives of Windsor" come the nearest to being comedies of intrigue. The six plays last named represent well enough the Elizabethan species and they were all received as admirable examples of comedy after the Restoration.

Our second main class is the comedy of manners, by which I shall mean plays whose chief interest lies in the exhibition of the habits, manners and customs of the society of the time. Manners is a word which may mean almost anything from fashion to character, but I take it as having less reference to the individual and more to society, less to moral decisions than to habits and modes. Romantic comedy has little direct interest in contemporary life, and during the vogue of romance little attention was paid London society. After the realistic movement about 1600, comedies of manners became numerous. They are rarely presented with a photographic impartiality, they are usually given with a sentimental, satirical, farcical or moral bias, but this bias should not be excessive if the play is to be a true comedy of manners.

Certain plays are devoted frankly to the exploitation

of some phase of London life, perhaps a trade, or a sect, or a custom. Of trade plays we hear of "A Shoemaker is a Gentleman" and "Six Clothiers," and Dekker's "Shoemaker's Holiday" is the masterpiece of this class. Middleton's "Family of Love" is a satirical exposure of a religious sect; his and Dekker's "Roaring Girl" tell of a notorious personage. A larger group is concerned especially with the seamy side of city life, with prostitutes, swindlers and other rogues, and their manners may be presented in humorous travesty or in realistic accuracy without any satire. Such are "Northward Ho" and "Westward Ho" and several of Middleton's. Other plays deal more at large with the manners of the London citizens, as in "Eastward Ho," which traces the careers of the idle and the industrious, or "A Match at Midnight" or Fletcher's "Wit at Several Weapons" or Massinger's "City Madam."

Domestic conflicts in family life are the themes of others. The old prodigal son story survives in "The London Prodigal," but in general the Elizabethans were less interested than are we in the differences between parents and children. Griselda and the shrew still furnish the patterns for a discussion of marital relations; but the sport of taming the shrew is supplanted by that of the scornful lady who refuses all suitors, and the old theme of the lusty juventus by that of the libertine converted or the husband tamed. In the later part of our period, comedy becomes more concerned with the affairs of women and fashion. Shirley's "Hyde Park" and "The Ball" and Fletcher's "Wild Goose Chase" are examples of a growing tendency to depict high life and smart society.

One other group includes plays by Jonson and his imitators which seek a carefully wrought analysis of contemporary manners and typical characters. Such plays may transcend the limits I have placed on "manners" and become genuine comedies of character. But often when they fail really to create human beings, they do succeed in presenting an analysis of manners, as for example,

"Every Man Out of His Humour," "The Staple of News," or Brome's "Antipodes." "Every Man Out of His Humour" is indeed primarily a comedy of manners, and the interest in the characters is incidental to the study of current habits and follies. I am reserving, however, from this group those plays in which the characterization, or the moral satire or the social implications give a value and interest beyond that of mere manners; but perhaps I should note here that the presentation of contemporary manners usually requires the adornment of wit. Cleverness is not only an ornament but often, rather than morality or desert or fortune, becomes the arbiter of events. In the citizen plays the clever scapegrace fools the shopkeepers, and in the comedies of fashion the witty lady disarms and puts to rout all suitors, or the contest for mastery between the sexes becomes a battle of wits.

The third class includes those plays in which the interest goes beyond intrigue and manners to character. Though the delight in characterization is manifest in almost every Elizabethan comedy, very few develop their plots from the persons. Ben Jonson is almost the only dramatist who consciously endeavours to construct comedies of character in that sense. In his "Alchemist," "Bartholomew Fair," "Volpone" and to a less degree "Every Man in His Humour," the complications may be said to spring naturally from the characters of the persons involved. In spite of some extravagances in plot, the same may be said of Massinger's two realistic comedies, or of Middleton's "Fair Quarrel." But such is never the case in Shakespeare, who begins with story and develops character interest out of the persons of the story; and in most realistic comedy even when imitative of Jonson, the humours are merely additions to a plot of tricks. Under my definition, the personalities depicted are not necessarily the mainsprings of the plot, but they are presented with so much vividness or emphasis that they overshadow all else.

Under such a classification it is often difficult to draw

the line. "Eastward Ho," for example, has a plot of tricks and it is a remarkable picture of London manners, but it also presents well defined characters who excite an interest in themselves apart from plot or manners. In a different way the character interest in Fletcher's "Rule a Wife" certainly surpasses that of the plot. Often the depiction of eccentric or whimsical persons supplies the chief comic force of the piece, as in Chapman's "Monsieur D'Olive," Fletcher's "Humorous Lieutenant" and "Spanish Curate," or Brome's "Antipodes." Again, a number of Elizabethan plays fairly run loose on characterization and crowd the stage with comic personages who are responsible for all the fun. Without counting Falstaff and his crew, it would be difficult to match elsewhere in the drama such freedom and vigour and abundance of comic personalities as we have in "A Chaste Maid in Cheapside" or "The Spanish Curate" or "The Knight of the Burning Pestle" or "Bartholomew Fair."

My fourth class, comedies of satire, is somewhat aside from the preceding divisions, for manifestly satire does not distinguish itself from intrigue, manners or character. It presents a special purpose on the part of the author which might be compared with other purposes, sentimental, burlesque or idealizing. But I wish merely to call attention to the large part which satire played in Elizabethan realistic comedy. Marston, Massinger and Jonson are the most serious, but Chapman, Middleton and others are vigorous. The objects of satire are usually certain types of persons, gulls, cheats, roaring boys, cast captains, prostitutes, usurers, puritans, parvenus, hypocrites; but often the censure extends to sexual immorality in general or to the demerits of large classes such as merchants or courtiers. For a brief time during the war of the theaters, personal satire and caricature are indulged, and we even hear of a suppressed play which represented James I intoxicated. Other plays, such as Middleton's "Phœnix," or any of Jonson's, assumed a serious censorship of the age, presented a lengthy and detailed indictment of the times. Occasionally the purpose of amusement is lost sight of in the fierce indignation which denounces rather than ridicules. Comedy is no longer light-hearted, it must show the course of evil and punish its rascals, as does tragedy, and expose folly as allied to vice. Jonson's "Volpone" is the most striking example, but with it may be grouped Marston's "Malcontent" and Massinger's "New Way to Pay Old Debts."

Our fifth class introduces another special division not coördinate with the others and comprises plays engaging in the discussion of social and moral problems, not altogether unlike problem and thesis plays of today. The audience is asked not only to be amused and thrilled but also to consider a question and to share in a debate. The Elizabethan dramatists did not go very far toward turning their stage into a forum but they well understood the dramatic value in a question. Should a sister sacrifice her honour to save a brother's life?—is the sensational and casuistical problem proposed in "Measure for Measure" and in the sub-plot of "A Woman Killed with Kindness." Should a son defend by a duel his mother's honour, if the slander is true?—is the theme of "A Fair Quarrel." Usually the question proposed concerns the relations of the sexes and involves a realistic study of social conditions; but whether sincere, verbal, casuistical, or sensational, the question is kept to the fore and is of interest to society at large. The issue is not merely as to the conduct of John or Mary, the persons of the play, but rather as to the attitude that society should take on the question. In comedies of character the solution is derived from the individual personalities; in satirical comedies the assumption is that the audience knows what is right and the author is denouncing what is wrong; in problem plays the question is proposed and argued before the audience as a tribunal. Of course the three classes are not mutually exclusive, but "A New Way to Pay Old Debts," "A Fair Quarrel," "The Honest Whore,"

"The English Traveller" and "A Woman Killed with Kindness" are the Elizabethan comedies which go farthest towards a discussion of serious social problems. Of these "A Woman Killed with Kindness" is most revolutionary both in its social thesis and in its departure from current types. It gives warning of the enormous field open to domestic drama inspired by a reformatory or questioning purpose.

My analysis may suggest the range of experimentation in Elizabethan comedy and the extent to which it anticipated later developments. But all its efforts did not arrive at any consensus of opinion or any critical agreement as to the limits or the form of the species. A division into five acts was about the only rule obeyed, and a very foolish rule. Neither Shakespeare's invention nor Jonson's criticism resulted in any such model of comic method as Molière was to leave the French theater. Shirley's comedies at the close of the period come as near as anyone's to summing up what was acceptable to his own day, but even these do not present a distinct and definable type of drama. After nearly a century of free experimentation comedy was still marked by variety and contradiction, richness and confusion, brilliancy and ineptitude.

This bewildering diversity makes it difficult to assess the merits of the Elizabethan drama. Many a critic or reader on turning back to his first love is confronted by some glaring defect which had been scarcely perceptible in the enthusiasm of his earlier admiration. The dramatic construction, even at its best, is not in accord with modern methods. The wit even in Shakespeare sometimes seems trifling. The invention is a little unregulated. But, whatever its faults and weaknesses, this drama does meet the great test, it does give a highly imaginative interpretation of human nature. In comedy as in tragedy, in the minor authors as well as in Shakespeare, its great merits lie in its poetry and in characterization.

By poetry I do not mean merely those flights of fancy that enliven even the most humdrum passages, nor merely the gracious phrase or the unexpected image that are likely to delight us anywhere. These are but the indications of a spirit that animates prose as well as verse and the dialogues of the clown as well as the lyrics of the lovers. In comedy it seeks beauty in grace, in surprise, in mirth, in an exuberant vitality. It manifests itself in a joy in words, in a quest for images, or in audacious invention. It accompanies pensive thought or quick laughter or moral indignation. Nothing arouses its enthusiasm more than the excitement of human nature. The great adventure of expressing human nature in English words was responsible for much bad verse and defective prose, but it gave all discourse an ambition and daring such as it has rarely possessed in the drama. Standards of style, rules of propriety, the common usages of society offered no fetters to a bold initiative always in search of a wider vocabulary, new comparisons, and melodious phrase. Elizabethan comedy might be of any or all varieties; it always afforded an opportunity for poetry.

In the spirit of imaginative surprise the poets undertook the dramatization of men and women. They were not very critical or analytical. They accepted life as a thing of wonder and the humours of human beings as amazing and stimulating. "What a piece of work is man!" "What a paragon is Elizabeth!" "How despicable is a coward!" Of modern analysis, modern psychology, modern belittling of personal volition, they knew nothing. They tried to depict the stupidities and gaieties of our species truthfully but wonderingly. They marvelled at ugliness as well as at beauty. Jonson's method is more critical and deliberate than Dekker's, but in comparison with moderns, Jonson and Dekker differ only in degree, not in kind. Jonson intended that Sir Epicure Mammon and Bobadill should arouse exclamations of wonder and admiration no less than Friscobaldo or Falstaff. Wit and humour and the invention of comic situation display themselves mainly in the dramatic portraiture. When they wish to make us laugh, these Elizabethans create a man. They are constantly engaged in proving how amazing, how charming, how contemptible, how irresistibly funny is human nature.

In Shakespeare often, and now and then in a lesser man such as Dekker, the imagination reveals how slight is the division between tears and laughter, pity and amusement, and the tenderest tolerance gleams in Comedy's smile. But most of the comic writers are at least open-minded and curious and rarely doctrinaire or intolerant in the probing of human motive. Joy in life, wonder at mankind and zeal for poetry are still abundant in Fletcher and Shirley, and discernible even in Brome and D'Avenant. Comedy continues to be, up to the closing of the theaters, a poetic tribute to the humorous delight furnished by men and women. The nineteenth century novel offers a somewhat similar though more prosaic tribute, but nowhere else in the drama except in this Shakespearian period is there such evoking from human nature "of infinite jest, of most excellent fancy."

PART TWO

CHAPTER XIII

THE RESTORATION, 1660-1680

THE Puritan revolution caused an interruption of the drama. The theaters were closed in 1642; and, although there were occasional performances, especially in the last years of the Commonwealth, they were not reopened until the Restoration of Charles II in 1660. There has been no other break in the English drama so prolonged and so complete since the first playhouse was built in 1576, or, indeed, since the first performance of miracle plays on Corpus Christi day. We begin in this chapter with new theaters, new drama and a new age.

There is danger, however, in overemphasizing the change. Old playhouses, old actors and old plays were employed at the beginning of the new epoch, and no complete revolution occurred in the practice of the stage or in the habits of the people. In every respect the new was a continuation of the old. The drama of the period from 1660 to 1700 rests on the Elizabethan tradition and is the direct descendant of that from 1600 to 1642.

At first the actors made use of the old theaters, the Red Bull, the Cockpit, and Salisbury Court, but soon new buildings were provided and everyone was commenting on the novelty of women actors and movable scenes. In spite of these decorations, the new stage still bore many resemblances to the Elizabethan. It was divided into two areas, front and rear. The apron, or the part in front of the proscenium arch and curtain, extended far into the auditorium and was entered by doors on either side of the arch. Scenery was confined to the rear stage which, though deeper and larger, was still employed in much the same way as in Elizabethan times.

Changes of place were often indicated by closing or opening scenes, just as by closing or opening the curtains of the old theater. If persons are supposed to be in a bedroom, the scenes close and they enter through the doors on the front stage and are on the street or elsewhere. Occasionally, in fact, scenes close while the actors remain in sight of the audience and are transferred from one place to another merely by a shift of the background. Scenery was for a long time used sparingly in the regular drama, but the new public theaters were enabled to present spectacles and operas with a magnificence comparable to that which had formerly been reserved for the court masques. Scenes and machines as well as music and dances became formidable rivals of the actor even in the regular playhouses. It was some time before the opera had a building to itself, and a still longer time before the stage was gradually transformed by the cutting down of the apron into a picture frame with a front curtain. On the whole, however, the physical theater of the Restoration was nearer to ours than to Shakespeare's and offers fewer difficulties than his to our understanding.

The theaters and companies, like those in the earlier Stuart period, were under royal license and censorship. Where six playhouses had been usual in Elizabethan London, two were found sufficient after the Restoration, and for a time the two companies were united. D'Avenant and Killigrew, the first managers, were veterans from the pre-revolution days and they gathered old actors to form the basis of the new companies. At first boys continued to play the parts of women, and Kynaston's grace and beauty were long remembered, but soon actresses thronged the stage. Instead of the two or three women customary in an Elizabethan comedy, there were now five or six or more. While it is impossible to make sure comparisons with the earlier period, we at least know much more about the acting than ever before. Many theatergoers have left their comments and appreciations of various actors, and we can form fairly definite notions of the stage effects. On the whole the acting seems to have been of marked excellence. A comparatively small group of persons were thoroughly trained after the most arduous methods of stock companies, acting in from fifty to one hundred plays in a single season. Betterton, Nokes, Mrs. Barry, and Mrs. Bracegirdle have left famous reputations in theatrical history. One effect of the small number of actors in comparison with the large number of plays was to increase the influence of the actors on the dramatists. A play had to be written for the one company or the other and it was inevitably suited to particular performers. Nokes was partly responsible for the blundering bumpkins and Nell Gwyn for the madcap girls of Restoration comedy.

The number of Londoners who went to the theater appears to have been relatively much smaller than in Shakespeare's time. The sober middle-class, already estranged in the time of Charles I, now stayed away. Two playhouses proved more than enough for a growing city of three or four hundred thousand inhabitants, and there was very little play-acting in England outside of London. Though a play was now continued on successive nights, there were few runs of more than five or six performances, and the bill was constantly changing. New operas and spectacles were necessary to keep up the attendance, while the success of a regular play might depend mainly on an accompanying dance or song. The audience was dominated by the King and courtiers, and many went to the theater, as did Pepys, partly to get a look at the court ladies. Charles II was fond of the theater, attended regularly, and exercised a personal influence on the drama much greater than that of any preceding or succeeding monarch. In spite of the presence of royalty and fashion, the theater was far from being a place of decorum. During the reign of Charles, in particular, it was a place of assignation and riot. Fights were frequent in the pit and not unknown on the stage. The picture of the stage in Shadwell's "A True Widow" recalls the hurly burly of Hogarth's print "Strolling Actresses in a Barn," and it did not go beyond reality. The wits and courtiers of Charles do not appear to have been any more attentive or well-behaved than the apprentices who thronged the pit to hear Marlowe and Shakespeare. Perhaps the later audience was more homogeneous, though even as early as 1666 Pepys complains that the number of mechanics and low people has increased. It was not until after the revolution of 1688 that the theaters began to be somewhat less given over to disturbance and immorality and more representative of the general public.

When the companies were reëstablished they naturally began with the old plays that were in repertory in 1642. Shakespeare's romantic fancy did not please, and "The Taming of the Shrew," in altered form, "1 Henry IV" and "The Merry Wives of Windsor" were his only comedies that were popular on the stage until well into the next century. Ben Jonson's chief comedies were constantly acted, much admired, and frequently imitated. Nearly all those of Fletcher and Shirley and some of Massinger's were revived, and a considerable number of Fletcher's long held the stage. A few other plays, such as Brome's "Jovial Crew" and "Antipodes," made up the Elizabethan representation on which all new dramatic composition was inevitably based; and in addition to those that continued unchanged on the stage, many others were altered and acted under new titles and still others were freely robbed for incidents or persons. Some of the dramatists, like D'Avenant and Killigrew, had written for the old theater, and newcomers, such as Dryden and Shadwell, avowed their efforts to follow the old models. Restoration comedy began where Elizabethan had left off. Tragicomedy, praised by Dryden, continued for a time, but romance was confined to the heroic plays or to the heroic portions of the tragicomedies. Comedy was prevailingly realistic, following the models of Jonson's humours or of the comedy of fashionable manners as exemplified in Fletcher and Shirley. It is only a short step from Fletcher's "Wild Goose Chase" and Shirley's "Lady of Pleasure" to the comedies of the reign of Charles II.

New influences, however, were felt from abroad. Spanish drama, already influential before the Puritan revolution, was much drawn upon for plots of complicated intrigue. Sir Samuel Tuke's "The Adventures of Five Hours" (1663), based on a Spanish play suggested by the King himself, had a great popular success and helped to fix the taste for such ingenious contrivances of suspense and surprise. Then there was the great example of the French theater. Many of the courtiers had lived in France, and intercourse between Paris and London was easy. The English drama felt at once the influence of both French theory and practice. In theory the English dramatists were led to a consideration of the three unities, a closer connection of scenes, some study of the classics, and a restriction of comedy to definite species. Acquaintance with French drama and criticism tended to make the English writers conscious and curious of dramatic methods. Dryden's prefaces and essays are the best but by no means the only discussions of the laws of comedy, the merits of the English masters, the advantages of rules and decorum. In practice the playwrights borrowed very freely from the French and especially from Molière, sometimes lifting a scene or two, often translating and adapting a whole play. Usually they made many changes, increasing the number of persons and the amount of action, and altering the general effect. They seem to have missed the higher qualities of his humour and humanity and to have kept mainly incident and situation. Restoration comedy is far from being an imitation for either better or worse of French comedy; but its general characteristics were in some measure determined by French precept and practice. It is no longer like the Elizabethan, a story-telling drama; it is still a comedy of incidents, tricks and mistakes, but coloured by an observation of society. Romantic elements are lessened, the old clowns and buffoons are discarded, certain methods of stage intrigue are standardized. The Latin and French comic writers, as well as the Spanish drama and the plays of Beaumont and Fletcher, all encouraged a comedy largely concerned with intrigue, but Molière as well as the English poets, manifestly offered something besides a mere complication of situations. The tendencies that we have already traced in Jonson, Middleton and Fletcher towards a comedy of manners were strengthened and developed by French example.

The new comedy became indeed not merely a follower of English or French models but very distinctly the reflection of the manners of the new age. The drama must always respond to its audience, and perhaps no drama ever did this more completely than that of the Restoration. This audience, as I have noted, was not representative of the whole public, but of a dissolute King and his followers just returned from long hardships to a debauch of pleasure and prodigality. Comedy represents a leisure class devoted to wine, woman, and song, and also to "scowering," duelling and adultery. Society, like the King, was selfish and sensual, and it delighted in its depravity. Its audiences desired a comedy that is restricted in subject to adultery and seduction and that is not merely plain spoken but foul-mouthed. There is a striking contrast when we turn from the plays of Wycherley or Congreve to those of Molière with their complete freedom from indecency. But the court of Louis XIV, though corrupt, was decorous and the court of Charles II was nothing if not indecorous. The riots and indecencies of the young bloods of his circle might, I suppose, be duplicated in the annals of the courts of Elizabeth or Victoria, but at no other time have they received general applause, royal favour and a recital in literature. The way in which the taste of this class affected the theater may be illustrated by the single instance of "The Parson's Wedding." This play by Tom Killigrew was produced probably just before 1642; if so, it carries the prize as the most indecent and obscene play up to that date, but when it was revived after the Restoration, to give it an added attractiveness it was played entirely by women. The words bawdy, smutty, and lewd, often in use in the literature of the time, may fittingly be applied to many scenes and to not a few plays as bad as "The Parson's Wedding." But apart from immorality, the demand for indecency injured comedy by greatly narrowing its range. Its laughter is confined mainly to certain sexual matters; it cannot rise above the gaieties of flirtation and it can sink to almost any depth of obscenity. Instead of the great field of story open to Elizabethan fancy, or the observation of the whole of society open to a resourceful comedy of manners, humour, after the Restoration, is directed to a most limited range of human behaviour. Its everlasting subject is cuckoldry and its ever-recurring situation is that of the wife and lover interrupted by the husband; and the efforts of dramatic art are exhausted in discovering new ways for the lover to escape or the husband to be deceived. Inevitably comedy so restricted tends to become farcial and repetitious.

But the society of the reign of Charles II in spite of its baseness was concerned about standards and manners, and it imposed these on its drama. It was convinced that there was a genteel way of doing everything, entering a room or writing a prologue, managing a seduction or fighting a duel. Fashions were not as changeable or as eccentric as in Tudor days, the "mode" approached the fixity of a code. This was far different from our social code, for it did not take much account of cleanliness or of the prevention of disease, but it was scarcely less fixed in its inhibitions and standards. Rochester and Buckingham won the admiration of all by their presence and address and by their way of entering a ball-room. The aspiration of men and women of fashion was not for virtue or valour but for style. And they cared for style in talking and writing. They criticized the solecisms and archaicisms of the earlier writers and sought to establish an accepted usage in language. The King was an arbiter of taste in diction. The most dissolute courtiers, Sedley, Rochester and Buckingham, prided themselves on their skill as writers, and they were not wholly undeserving of Dryden's extravagant comparison of them with the Elizabethans:

> Our ladies and our men now speak more wit
> In conversation, than those poets writ.

Wit, indeed, was the final word in style and manners. The courtiers lay awake nights trying to form happy epigrams and repartees that they could use the next day. They were fond of comedy partly because its lively dialogue gave an exhibition of the game of wit at which they were all practising. And the drama could scarcely fail to be witty under the patronage of the king who "never said a foolish thing nor did a wise one." It was not only on the stage but in society that every action was capped by a pungent comment, an indelicacy by an innuendo, and a follow by a witticism. Among all the bedroom interruptions in the drama, is there any scene more cleverly handled than the actual incident when by Buckingham's design the King unexpectedly entered the apartment of his mistress, Lady Castlemain, and discovered her with young Jack Churchill? The future Duke of Marlborough saved himself half-clothed by jumping through the window but did not escape recognition by the King, who called after him, "I forgive you, for you do it for your bread." What is perhaps the most characteristic witticism of the age was not made by a person in a play but by Sedley's daughter, who became the mistress of the Duke of York, afterwards James II. The lady is reputed to have had a squint and to have been more lauded for her sharp tongue than for her comely features. She remarked that she was at a loss to explain the ardour of the royal passion. "It cannot be my beauty, for he must see I have none; and it cannot be my wit, for he has not enough to know that I have any."

Such a society as this helped to create a comedy of manners reflecting its modes and conditions. There is scarcely a play that could have been written at any other period, the effort is always to write for the age and not for all time. Even a play mainly occupied with complicated intrigues will also mirror the ways of fashion; and fashion is the theme of farce or burlesque, satire or wit. This comedy of manners highly embellished by wit takes its most characteristic and admirable form in the so-called artificial drama, best represented by Congreve. This particular species is generally held to have found its first representation in Etherege; and in its beginnings it pictured a very real state of manners, for Etherege's man of mode was supposed to be drawn from Rochester. But this comedy of fine manners, indecency and wit, continued into the next generation when it had ceased to represent the society of its own time. By the end of the century the mode is no longer that of the Rochesters and Sedleys, and the comedy of Congreve, Farquhar and Vanbrugh is in some degree the perfection of a literary and dramatic tradition rather than the mirror of its age.

I have divided my treatment of Restoration comedy into two chapters, the first extending roughly to about 1680, and the second ending with the century but running over into the reign of Queen Anne in order to include Vanbrugh and Farquhar. Most of the masterpieces of artificial comedy come in the second period, as does also the beginning of the reaction to morality and sentimentality. The first period includes only Etherege and Wycherley among the finished practitioners of the "genteel" species, but it contains a large number of comedies mostly reproducing the manners of the time, seasoned with some spice of wit. In spite of the small opportunity afforded by only two theaters, there was a remarkable output of new plays, and in spite of the restriction that limited the scope of comedy, they display considerable variety. Nearly every one who made any pretence to wit appears to have written at least one play, and there were then, as always, many who desired novelty rather than superiority.

I shall not be able to glance at the many varieties of expression which the comic muse found upon the stage in the under-plots of tragedy, in farces, burlesques, operas, pantomimes and spectacles. Certain accompaniments which came to be regarded as essential to comedy must, however, at least be noticed. Every play was introduced by a prologue, interrupted by songs, and concluded by an epilogue, and each of these accompaniments was thought to offer an opportunity for both wit and indecency. The success of a piece might be assured by the banter of the prologue, or its chief novelty or audacity might be reserved for the epilogue. Dryden, who put his genius whole-heartedly at work on these ephemera, describes the importance of the new fashion in the prologue to "The Rival Ladies":

> In former days
> Good Prologues were as scarce as now good plays.
> For the reforming poets of our age
> In this first charge spend their poetic rage.
> Expect no more when once the prologue's done;
> The wit is ended ere the play's begun.

Of the songs, there is little to be said except that they are always present. Even after comedy had been reduced to prose and realism, it could pause to listen to the lyrical sighs of Strephon and Chloe. There were songs of good life as well as love songs, and on the whole Bacchus is more successfully praised than Cupid. The songs indeed partake of the usual tone of the plays but they at least introduced the welcome relief of melody.

Nor shall I attempt to notice all the comedies, or even all of those pieces that have some historical importance because they helped to initiate or direct new develop-

ments. The unacted and unactable plays by the Duchess
of Newcastle, various efforts by the Duke of Newcastle
and other persons of quality, John Wilson's two Jonsonian comedies, Sir Robert Howard's "Committee" and
Sedley's "Mulberry Garden" have an interest mostly as
ineffectual experiments. The "Committee" (c. 1662),
written in praise of the cavaliers and satirizing the Puritans, had a long life on the stage owing mainly to the
popularity of the low comedy part of Teague, the Irish
servant. An adaptation, "The Honest Thieves,"
replaced it in repertory in 1797. "The Mulberry Garden" (1668) is one of the early instances of the comedy
of manners and wit, but is inferior to Etherege's early
attempts in the same school. Sedley's "Bellamira"
(1687), based on the "Eunuchus," is a better and wittier
play, but Wycherley had preceded him in extracting about
all the fun and indecency possible from the theme. Of
the miscellaneous productions, by far the most amusing
and most famous was "The Rehearsal" (1671), composed by Buckingham and others, burlesquing the heroic
plays and many practices of the stage, and focusing its
ridicule on Dryden. Its only predecessor in the field of
dramatic burlesque was "The Knight of the Burning
Pestle," but it had many followers, of which Sheridan's
"Critic" is the chief. My purpose, however, is merely
to examine the main experiments and developments in
the comedies of the period, and these are sufficiently
exemplified in the four leading writers, Dryden, Shadwell,
Etherege and Wycherley.

I

Dryden's connection with the stage extended for nearly
forty years, from his first play in 1663 to the epilogue
for Fletcher's "Pilgrim," revised for his benefit in the
year of his death. He tried his hand at almost every
kind of play then in vogue, tragedies, heroic plays, operas,
tragicomedies and comedies; he wrote drama in rhyme,

prose and blank verse; he imitated and emulated both
Shakespeare and Molière; he was a dramatic critic keenly
interested in theory as well as practice; and he contrived
to please Charles II and his court. In comedy Dryden
is not at his best, but he is very representative, exhibiting
both the defects and the merits of contemporary practice,
and illustrating both its range and its ambition.

He began naturally where the Elizabethans had left
off, and he constantly restudied the creations of Fletcher,
Jonson and Shakespeare, but he was soon also under the
tutelage of the French stage, with its insistence on
decorum and structure, and of the comic invention of
Molière. His comedies fall into about the same sort of
classification that we have applied to all since Fletcher's.
The theme is always the intrigues of lovers, but these
may be of a heroic character involving dangers and
affairs of state, turning the piece to tragicomedy; or they
may avoid the heroic and mix with the "humours" of
ordinary life in pure comedy. What romance exists is
of the exalted sort called for by "honour" and best exemplified in the emperors and princesses of the heroic plays;
this is usually reserved for the serious section of a tragicomedy; but the more realistic and comic portion rarely
descends to buffoonery and beatings, it rather maintains
a lively action of intrigue variegated by eccentricity and
wit. What gradually removes Dryden's persons both
from a stilted romance and from humoristic realism is
his growing sense of an established society, a code of
manners and a criterion of style. He feels that the puns
and the fisticuffs of the Elizabethans are out of date and
that there are new standards both of honour and of gaiety.
He himself attributed the excellence of his style not more
to the observance of rules or the study of the past masters
than to a familiarity with the conversation of the King
and his circle. To that conversation he perhaps owed
this—the recognition of standards of usage, of methods
of wit, of style in expression based upon a social consensus. Though his continued fondness for quasi-roman-

tic tragicomedy hindered him from going further than
to point the way toward a comedy of manners and style,
he hailed with enthusiasm its attainment in Etherege and
Congreve.

His first comedy, "The Wild Gallant" (1663), is placed
in London. A scapegrace wins an heiress, to the accompaniment of the humours of Justic Trice, who shakes dice
with himself, and of Bibber, a tailor who admires wit.
The borrowed Spanish plot is complicated and absurd
and the language very gross. "The Rival Ladies or
Secret Love" in the next year is a tragicomedy, also
drawn from a Spanish source. Love is always debating
with honour, which is a powerful motive even with robbers. Some of what Professor Saintsbury calls the
"scenes of amatory battledore and shuttlecock" are in
rhymed verse (IV. i) and quite after the heroic fashion.
There is no obscenity. "A very innocent and most pretty
witty play," thought Pepys. The two plays are commonplace examples of their types.

Three years later, in 1667, Dryden produced three
plays which illustrate varied experimentation. With
D'Avenant he attempted to improve Shakespeare's "Tempest" by the addition of spectacle and ingenuity. Miranda
and Caliban are each provided with a sister, and the
enchanted island is further blessed by a youth who never
saw a woman. It is rather shocking to know that Dryden
was pleased with these inventions; he "never writ anything with more delight." In the second piece he turned
with happier fortune to Molière, reworking the Duke of
Newcastle's translation of "L'Etourdi" into the original
and successful "Sir Martin Mar-all." This is a triumph
of what Dryden called humour as distinguished from wit,
i.e., of comedy arising from a humorous or eccentric personality. Sir Martin is a blunderer who puts his foot
into it and spoils all just as the intrigue of his clever
servant is at the point of success. His absurdities
furnished Nokes his most famous part. The lady whom
he misses elects to wed the clever servant. Wit will do

almost anything in Restoration comedy, but it did not often win a lady for a valet.

The third play of the year, "Secret Love, or the Maiden Queen," is a tragicomedy which reveals Dryden almost at his best. The heroic portion represents the noble and beautiful queen struggling against her passion for the favorite Philocles, who is in love with another, the sister of the high-born Lysimantes, who in turn is in love with the queen. The comic portion tells of the wild gallant Celadon, who makes love to all the ladies but is captured by the frisky Florimel, in spite of the scorn that both pretend for love and marriage. The construction is regular, and Dryden's style is brilliantly masterful both in the heroics and the gaieties. Nell Gwyn captivated the audience as Florimel, especially in the scene when, dressed as a boy, she wins the two admiring girls away from Celadon. The King cannot have been more pleased than was Pepys. He declares "so great performance of a comical part was never, I believe, in the world before as Nell do this, both as a mad girl, then most and best of all when she comes in like a young gallant, and both the motions and carriage of a spark the most that I ever saw any man have. It makes me, I confess, admire her."

This is the first worthy presentation of a main comic theme of Restoration drama—flirtation. It differs from Elizabethan love-making, not so much because of its greater licentiousness as because of its recognition of a code and a manner. True love has little to do with the case, the young man always wants the young woman on first sight, and she is equally determined in her desire for him, and in the end they are usually safely and happily married. But that is not the comedy. They are young ladies and gallants of a leisure class playing a game of hide and seek. The code says that marriage is a dull bondage and love a dangerous disease and that either is intolerable without wit. The first duty is to flirt. Any result may be excused if the game is only well played.

Dryden returned to the same theme the next year, but the result was called "very profane" by Evelyn and "very smutty" by Pepys. "An Evening's Love, or the Mock Astrologer," derived from Calderon by way of Thomas Corneille's "Le feint Astrologue," rather overplays the flirtation. There is no romantic or heroic plot, but the entire action is devoted to the busy intrigues of four gallants and three ladies. Wildblood and Jacintha, acted by Hart and Elinor Gwyn, are the successors of Celadon and Florimel, lively scorners of love and adepts at flirtation, who are finally caught in the net of matrimony. "The Assignation or Love in a Nunnery" (1672), is another brilliantly written comedy that seems to have had but slight success on the stage. The duke and his son both make love to Lucretia, a novice in the nunnery. Two other gentlemen are carrying on love affairs, which are constantly interfered with by their servant, who is of the pattern of Sir Martin Mar-all. The intrigues are artificial and their setting in a nunnery offended even Restoration taste.

In the next year came Dryden's comic masterpiece, the tragicomedy "Marriage à la Mode." The serious plot presents two long-lost children, Leonidas and Palmyra, who succeed to the Sicilian throne after a good deal of very honorable and exalted love-making. Two ladies of the court carry on the flirtations; Doralice, the neglected wife of Rhodophil, with his friend Palamede, and Melantha, a lady who affects French phrases and manners, with Rhodophil, though she is betrothed to Palamede. The intrigues are amusing but of the usual theatrical kind, the flirting couple being always interrupted in the nick of time; but what is most unusual is the brilliant life-likeness of both the manners and the persons. Doralice is admirably drawn, a lady of much sense as well as self-assurance; but the great part for the theater is that of the charming, impertinent Melantha. Colley Cibber, forty years later, still waxed enthu-

siastic over his recollection of Mrs. Mountfort's impersonation.

"Melantha is as finished an impertinent as ever flut-
tered in a drawing-room; and seems to contain the most
complete system of female foppery that could possibly
be crowded into the tortured form of a fine lady. Her
language, dress, motion, manners, soul and body are in
a continual hurry to be something more than is necessary
or commendable. And, though I doubt it will be a vain
labour to offer you a just likeness of Mrs. Mountfort's
action, yet the fantastic expression is still so strong in my
memory that I cannot help saying something, though fan-
tastically, about it. The first ridiculous airs that break
from her are upon a gallant, never seen before, who
delivers her a letter from her father, recommending him
to her good graces as an honourable lover. Here, now,
one would think she might naturally show a little of the
sex's decent reserve, though never so slightly covered.
No, sir, not a tittle of it: Modesty is a poor-souled
country gentlewoman; she is too much a court lady to be
under so vulgar a confusion. She reads the letter, therefore, with a careless drooping lip, and an erected brow,
humming it hastily over, as if she were impatient to outgo
her father's commands, by making a complete conquest
of him at once; and that the letter might not embarrass
the attack, crack! she crumbles it at once into her palm,
and pours down upon him her whole artillery of airs,
eyes, and motion; down goes her dainty diving body to
the ground, as if she were sinking under the conscious
load of her own attractions; then launches into a flood
of fine language and compliment, still playing her chest
forward in fifty falls and risings, like a swan upon waving
water; and, to complete her impertinence, she is so
rapidly fond of her own wit that she will not give her
lover leave to praise it. Silent assenting bows, and vain
endeavours to speak are all the share of the conversation
he is admitted to, which, at last, he is removed from by

her engagement to half a score of visits, which she swims from him to make, with a promise to return in a twinkling."

The two ladies finally give up their flirtations and determine to be happy with their husbands. Palamede cannot win Melantha's attention long enough to make serious love until he drowns her chatter with singing, and then she accepts him in this fashion: "Hold, hold; I am vanquished with your *gaité d'esprit*. I am yours and will be yours, *sans nulle reserve, ni condition.* And let me die, if I do not think myself the happiest nymph in Sicily—My dear French dear, stay but a *minute,* till I raccammode myself with the princess, and then I am yours, *jusqu'a la mort. Allons donc.—*"

Here is a precursor of Millamant and a bit of genteel comedy worthy of Congreve. Dryden has succeeded in his desire to offer "neither so little of humour as Fletcher shows, nor so little of love and wit as Jonson," and he has contributed to what he calls "our refining the courtship, the raillery, and conversation of plays."

His remaining pieces did little to advance this type of comedy, though they illustrate certain contemporary tendencies. "Mr. Limberham," which was intended as a satire on keeping mistresses, has a certain cleverness in plotting that is insufficient to relieve its disgusting indecency. "Amphitryon" is a reworking of Plautus and Molière, and is admirable enough in both its verse and its stage bustle and fun; but it exhibits Dryden's genius occupied, as so often, on a task that is scarcely worth its pains. "The Spanish Friar" (1680) is one of Dryden's better plays, vigorous in style and humour, and it had a long career on the stage, but in form and method it marks a reversion to Elizabethan tragicomedy rather than a progress in the comedy of manners. It is much more like Fletcher than like Congreve. In the serious part the unlawful queen and the lawful heir proclaim their love in fervent eloquence; the comic part is copied from

Fletcher's "Spanish Curate," with a notable transformation of the curate into a grotesque friar. The play, which is blatantly Protestant, was forbidden during the reign of James II and came into favour again after the glorious Revolution, though the lines of the usurping queen are said to have caused Queen Mary some perturbation when she first heard them at the theater. Though one of the best of Restoration tragicomedies, it marks the waning of that species.

None of Dryden's comedies deserves a rich immortality. None reveals him at his best, though none is lacking in passages of lively wit and of comic delineation of manners. They are among the best of their time, they are making the way for Congreve and Farquhar, but they do not escape the faults that beset all their contemporaries. Love is treated either as the set theme for the perfervid declamation of the tragicomedies, or as the opportunity for trick and indecent jest. A generous and humorous insight into life is wasted on situations too impossible for anything except opera or farce, and finds its expression only occasionally in the absurdities of an eccentric, or in the gay flirtations of impertinent coxcombs and coquettes. His critical writings abound in sensible and informing remarks on comedy, and he always planned and wrote with a certain effort to make the most out of what his theater would accept, but his wit and invention found their best opportunity in poetic satire rather than in the comic drama.

II

Thomas Shadwell was unfortunate in attracting the enmity of a much superior wit, and so his memory is preserved chiefly in Dryden's satire as a dull poetaster "who never deviates into sense." He was in fact a writer of considerable force and invention, who, in spite of drinking and opium taking, habits also recorded in Dryden's attacks, worked most industriously, completing some eighteen plays. Two of these, the revision of

Shakespeare's "Timon" and "The Libertine," are tragedies, two are operas, one a pastoral, and the remaining
thirteen are comedies, extending from the year 1668, the
date of production of "The Sullen Lovers," to 1693, the
year after his death, which saw "The Volunteers or The
Stock Jobbers." These plays were of importance in the
history of comedy and present today a vivid and interesting picture of the time; and they display, if little poetry,
the sense and wit that Dryden denied him and also the
sturdy partisanship which made him poet laureate when
the Whigs triumphed.

In the preface to his first play he proclaims his discipleship to Ben Jonson, "Whom I think all Dramatick Poets
ought to imitate, though none are like to come near; he
being the only Person, that appears to me to have made
perfect Representations of Human Life." Again and
again in subsequent prefaces he repeats his allegiance to
the principles of his master. Like Jonson he will create
a comedy of "humours," types of character based on the
observation of real life and holding up to ridicule the
affectations and vices of society. Wit will be incidental;
"humour," *i.e.*, realistic characterization, the main basis
of his design. The satire of folly is always his avowed
purpose. Jonson's method, as we have observed, led to
caricature rather than individualization, and Jonson's
own genius was readily betrayed into an over-elaboration
of detail and a tedious insistence on the gross or uninteresting foibles of his own day. Shadwell's plays always
partake of the faults of his master's theory and practice,
without ever equalling the great examples of Jonson's
realistic satire. Nevertheless he does succeed in presenting a record of the manners of his time, something
like that which our cartoonists are supplying of our
own day.

"The Sullen Lovers," though based on Molière's "Les
Fâcheux," is very like Jonson in its main scheme. The
two lovers are the censors before whom are paraded a
long string of fools. As in some of Jonson's plays, per-

sonal satire seems intended, and Sir Positive was at once identified with Sir Robert Howard, and Ninny with his brother Edward. But the satire is also general, directed against prevailing habits and it is sustained dramatically both in the individual persons and the general construction.

In "The Humourists" the two "sullen" lovers are replaced by Raymond, a gentleman of wit and honour, and Theodosia, "a Witty, Airy young Lady of a great Fortune." Henceforth in each play Shadwell presents at least one pair of lovers who appeal for our sympathy and approval and whose courtship and union, despite the interference of parents and fools, make up the principal action of the play. In some cases the heroine is lively and witty, in others she is marked by sensibility and, disguised as a page, attaches herself to her lover; the hero is usually a man of wit, but he too may be subject to moral sentiments. "The Humourists" repeats some of the personages of the preceding play and helps to establish a group of stock characters who are henceforth always recurring in Shadwell's plays. He does indeed vary and add to his collection, but in any subsequent play we may encounter persons like these humorists: Crazy, "in Love with most Women, and thinks most Women in Love with him"; Drybob, a pompous and "a fantastick Coxcomb, who makes it his business to speak fine Things and Wit, as he thinks"; Brisk, "a Brisk, Airy, Fantastick, Singing, Dancing Coxcomb;" Lady Loveyouth, "a vain, amorous Lady, mad for a Husband"; and Mrs. Errant, "a running Bawd."

The presence of one or two novel humours is not sufficient relief from the rather dreary round of bullies, coxcombs, henpecked husbands and flighty wives; nor could Shadwell devise an action that would not rely for its interest largely on drinking scenes, roistering, beating, duelling, and other devices to secure noise and bustle. He protests often against the farces of his day, which delight the audience, "when one fool tumbles over another or throws a custard in his face"; but his own comedy very frequently resorts to similar slap-stick methods.

No dramatist, I suppose, resorts oftener to that prime scene of all farce where the lovers are just embracing when the husband enters. He has certainly succeeded in devising many variations for the escape of the lovers; in one instance the scene opens and discovers them on the bed, the husband enters, but they succeed in persuading him of their innocence; in another instance three different couples are driven to hiding in the closets and woodholes of a single bedroom; but perhaps it is unedifying to specify further his exploits in this kind of device. Further illustration of the way in which Shadwell's serious and critical intentions succumbed to the general practice of the stage may be found in his next two plays, "The Miser" and "Epsom Wells."

The preface to "The Miser" begins: "The Foundation of this Play I took from one of Molière's call'd L'Avare; but that having too few Persons, and too little Action for an English Theatre, I added to both so much, that I may call more than half of this Play my own; and I think I may say without Vanity, that Molière's Part of it has not suffer'd in my Hands; nor did I ever Know a French Comedy made use of by the worst of our Poets, that was not better'd by 'em." This passage indicates Shadwell's blindness to the real opportunities lying in the comedy of character, and his contentment with the bustle and laughter afforded by the most commonplace figures of the English stage. His main additions to the dramatis personæ consists of Rant and Hazard, two gamesters and bullies; Squeeze, a usurer, and his booby son; Timothy, who becomes the wooer of Theodora (Elise); and two women of the town, Lettice and Mrs. Joyce. The scenes in which these persons are occupied are such as will be found in almost any Restoration comedy, drinking, gaming, "scowering," wooing by the booby, marrying the cast mistress to the booby, and so on. In addition Shadwell provides a complicated series of tricks and counter tricks to render the dénouement a little more theatrical and impossible than even the reconciliation of the long separated father and children in Molière. The Harpagon of Molière may be unmotivated and exaggerated, but he stands out a very clear and amusing piece of dramatic characterization. Translated into Shadwell's Miser, he becomes scarcely more than one of a crowd of over-busy stage buffoons.

In "Epsom Wells" (1672), a play that held the stage for fifty years, the chief humour is that of Clodpate, a country justice, "an immoderate Hater of London and a Lover of the Country" who is paired with Mrs. Jilt "that pretends to be in Love with most Men, and thinks most Men in Love with her." The other persons are three "men of wit and pleasure," two bullies, two citizen cuckolds, two young ladies of wit, beauty and fortune, and three married women eager to cuckold their husbands. There are four instances of the wife and lover being interrupted by the husband, several duels, innumerable beatings, and rather more wit and gaiety than is usual in Shadwell. When Caroline, one of the nice young ladies, expresses to the other, Lucia, aged seventeen, a fear that their lovers are too wild, Lucia replies, "An they be naturally wilder than I, or you either, for all your simpering, I'll be condemn'd to Fools and ill company for ever." These two madcaps take their share in the contest of wits and tricks by which their gentlemen are vanquished.

The four comedies that followed are not without a certain inventiveness both in persons and situations. In "The Virtuoso" (1676) he boasts that four of his humours are entirely new; and two at least are out of the ordinary, Sir Nicholas Gimcrack, the virtuoso and amateur naturalist, and Snarl, "a great admirer of the last age and a declaimer against this." Of his next play "A True Widow" (1679) he again boasts in his dedication to Sedley that three of the humours are wholly new and that the scene in which Lady Busy tries to persuade Isabella to become the mistress of Bellamour will live when the stuff of his contemporary scribblers has been razed out of the memory of men. But the main interest today in the comedy lies in the play within the play which gives a realistic presentation of the riotous Restoration theater. In "The Woman Captain" (1679), again his invention is less manifest in the prodigals, bullies, and misers of the dramatis personæ than in the novel trick of the miser's wife. In the uniform of a captain and accompanied by a sergeant, she compels her husband and several coxcombs to enlist and puts them through a rigorous drill. Her part must have been very effective on the stage. In "The Lancashire Witches and Tegue O' Divelly, the Irish Priest" (1681), Shadwell attempted still greater novelties, combining political satire with the spectacular doings of the witches. His Whiggism led him, however, to satirize a clergyman of the Church of England, popishly inclined, as well as an Irish priest; and in consequence the censor cut large portions of the play. His witches are even more prankish than his ordinary mortals.

Shadwell was ever diligently seeking new material for theatrical effect and he won his greatest success toward the end of his career with "The Squire of Alsatia" (1688). This procured the author one hundred and thirty pounds on the third night, the largest sum ever received at a benefit performance, "and the house was never so full since it was built, and vast numbers went away that could not be admitted." The sharpers, rascals, decoys and bullies who took refuge in the privileged precincts of Whitefriars are known to us in Scott's "Fortunes of Nigel" and had been depicted in various dramas before Shadwell, but his picture yields to none in comprehensiveness and realism. The play has twenty speaking parts besides officers, fiddlers, watchmen, rabble, etc.; it uses many cant words and phrases; and calls for an unprecedented amount of noise. This presentation of vice and crime is curiously combined with a story from the "Adelphi," and very like those of later sentimental comedies. Belfond senior, who has been bred with great rigour and severity by his rigid and morose father, becomes "abominably vicious" and the easy victim of the sharpers. Belfond junior, bred "with all the tenderness and familiarity and bounty and liberty that can be" by his uncle, "a man of great humanity and gentleness and compassion towards mankind" is a noble youth "possessed with all gentleman-like qualities." He has, however, some piccadilloes to his debit, having seduced "a young beautiful girl of a mild and tender disposition," and having neglected his mistress, "a furious, malicious, and revengeful woman." Before he can marry the lovely Isabella he has to settle his debts with these other ladies. This is accomplished through his uncle's aid in a most compassionate and humane fashion. He nobly lies to save Lucia's reputation, and his uncle gives her fifteen hundred pounds, whereupon she offers a thousand thanks, and promises she will hereafter "outlive the strictest nun." The cast mistress is also quieted by means of an annuity and the promise that her child shall be provided for like a gentlewoman. The hero is thus enabled to offer marriage in these terms: "A long farewell to all the vanity and lewdness of youth. I offer myself at your feet as a sacrifice without a blemish now." "Rise," exclaims the lady, "I beseech you, rise."

The real triumph of virtue occurs, however, when the severe and rigid father acknowledges that the kind and lenient guardian had chosen the better way; and the play ends with the moral advice to the father, "by gentleness and bounty make your sons your friends."

The remaining comedies, written after the Revolution and during Shadwell's poet-laureateship, do not differ greatly from those already considered. They offer some evidences of the growing fashion for sentiment and moral-ity, but they retain the usual intrigue, farce, boisterous-ness and indecency. "Bury Fair" (1689) takes us out of London to a fair in a country town; "The Amorous Bigot" (1690) continues the adventures of Tegue O'Div-elly to the accompaniment of a Spanish plot. "The

Scowrers" (1690) amplifies what had been a favourite
theme of most of Shadwell's plays, *i.e.*, the amusing practice of young bloods to enter houses and taverns, drive
out the inmates, dance and roar, break the windows, and
beat the watch; but in this case the chief of the "scowrers"
has a tender heart and yields to virtue and love. Very
virtuous also are the hero and heroine of the last play,
"The Volunteers or The Stock Jobbers," produced in the
year after the author's death. The play is not quite filled
out, and Shadwell may have intended a fuller satire on
the stock jobbers; but the old major-general is well drawn
and the volunteers in the service of their country sufficiently extolled, and room is found for the usual collection of coxcombs, sharpers, affected girls, and wayward
wives.

In comparison with his contemporaries, Dryden, Etherege and Wycherley, Shadwell's lack of gaiety may occasionally seem to justify Dryden's epithet of dull. But his
dulness is due to over-elaboration of detail or repetition
of tiresome humours and noisy scenes rather than to any
real want of wit. His plays can flash, though not so brilliantly as the best of his rivals. They are somewhat more
given to humours than those of the others, somewhat
more serious in satire than any with the exception of "The
Plain Dealer," perhaps no more indecent, but more vulgar
and less spirited. They do not succeed in developing plot
out of character, though they attempt it; they rather attach
some eccentric and satiric characters to an intrigue, often
ingenious but too much supported by noise and farce. He
did not contribute much that was new or important to
the development of comedy; he did very little that others
did not do fully as well; he represents in our dramatic
history rather the petering out of the Jonsonian tradition
than the creation of any new tendencies; but his diligent
efforts to enlarge the scope of comic characterization
make his comedies, despite their repetitions and trivialities, a very full dramatic record of the time.

III

The initiation of that particular type of the comedy of manners which reaches its height in Congreve has been universally attributed to Sir George Etherege. "The dawn," said Hazlitt, "was in Etherege, as its latest close was in Sheridan." His three plays possess therefore a certain historical as well as inherent interest, and the last, "The Man of Mode," has long served as an archetype of the Restoration comedy both for the admirers and the detractors of that species. Of Etherege's life little is known; he apparently lived in France long enough to gain an intimate knowledge of things Parisian; he was a gay man about town, the companion of Rochester and Sedley, married a fortune, was knighted and at fifty left England for a diplomatic career at Ratisbon. French literature and manners perhaps helped to form his style and dramatic method, but his plays are manifestly a reflection of the manners and the wit of the London circle of which he was thought one of the ornaments.

His first play, "The Comical Revenge or Love in a Tub" (1664) has little to distinguish it from other plays of that date. The serious plot in which love and honour appear in their loftiest mien is written in rhymed couplets, then a novelty; and the realistic scenes are in prose which is at least vastly superior to the verse. The confusion of heroics, humours and intrigues gives little hint of a new dramatic development, unless in the occasional wit and gaiety of Sir Frederick Frollick and his impudent French valet, borrowed from Molière.

"The Comical Revenge" appears to have excited so much interest that the second play "She Wou'd if She Cou'd" (1668) was greeted with extraordinary excitement, Pepys finding the theater crowded and "1000 people put back that could not have room in the pit." The piece did not at first meet the public expectations, but it soon won general admiration, Shadwell declaring it "the best comedy that has been written since the restoration of the stage." It shows indeed a marked improvement over the earlier play. Sentiment and heroics have disappeared, and though both intrigue and humours are commonplace, they are brightened by wit, with enough hints of characterization to give verisimilitude to the clever dialogue. Courtal, the self-contained and cynical gentleman, directs the tricks and the wit, frees himself from the seductions of the middle-aged Lady Cockwood and captures for himself and his friend Freeman the two young heiresses, "sly girl and madcap." This seems to have been the epitome of life and the triumph of wit as understood by Restoration comedy.

"The Man of Mode or Sir Fopling Flutter" was not produced until eight years later, after Dryden's "Marriage à la Mode" and all four of Wycherley's comedies. It is, however, nearer to Congreve and Sheridan than any of those plays, and unquestionably a fine example of the pure comedy of manners. It is free from sentimentality or heroics and from practical jokes or impossible tricks, while its humours are confined to the affected Sir Fopling Flutter, the first of a long line of stage fops airing French styles on the English stage. Five gentlemen encounter six gentlewomen in various drawing-rooms or on the Mall, and both action and conversation move nimbly and naturally without any excess unless it be of wit. The chief personage is the arrogant, clear-headed and cold-hearted Dorimant, thought at the time to have been patterned after Rochester. His manners are admirable when he wishes them to be; his wit equal to any occasion and master over his emotions or even his vanity. He coldly insults and discards one mistress, the ardent and hysterical Mrs. Loveit, as coolly dismisses her successor, the timid but amorous Belinda, and carries off the heiress, overcoming by his politeness and self-control the alarms of her mother and her own sharp-tongued defense.

A few lines may be enough to recall the exquisite finish and the dramatic point of the dialogue. The stage has filled for the closing scene. The two cast mistresses have intruded on the company but have failed in their purpose to injure Dorimant. The mother of the heiress graciously accepts him.

Lady Woodvil. Mr. Dorimant, every one has spoke so much in your behalf that I can no longer doubt but I was in the wrong.

Then Mrs. Loveit speaking to Belinda, the other cast mistress, fires her parting shot.

Mrs. Loveit. There's nothing but falsehood and impertinence in this world, all men are villains or fools; take example from my misfortunes, Belinda; if thou wouldst be happy, give thyself wholly up to goodness.

Harriet, the heiress, now hastens to take a shot at her retreating rival.

Harriet (to *Loveit*). Mr. Dorimant has been your God Almighty long enough; 'tis time to think of another.
Loveit. Jeered by her! I will lock myself up in my house and never see the world again.
Harriet. A nunnery is the more fashionable place for such a retreat, and has been the fatal consequence of many a belle passion.
Loveit. Hold, heart! till I get home; should I answer, 'twould make her triumph greater.

> [*Is going out.*

Dorimant does not speak to the furious lady, or even escort her to the door, but in two words he completes her humiliation by passing her over to the odious fop.

Dorimant. Your hand, Sir Fopling—
Sir Fopling. Shall I wait after you, madam?
Loveit. Legion of fools, as many devils take thee!

> [*Exit.*

But the lovers do not now rush into each other's arms. That is not the fashion. Lady Woodvil invites Dorimant

to visit them in the country, and the last words of the
lovers before the final dance are as follows:

Harriet. To a great rambling lone house that looks as
if it were not inhabited, the family's so small; there you'll
find my mother, an old lame aunt, and myself, sir, perched
up on chairs at a distance in a large parlour, sitting moping like three or four melancholy birds in a spacious
volery. Does not this stagger your resolution?
Dorimant. Not at all, madam. The first time I saw
you, you left me with the pangs of love upon me, and
this day my soul has quite given up her liberty.
Harriet. This is more dismal than the country,
Emilia; pity me who am going to that sad place.
Methinks I hear the hateful noise of rooks already—
Knaw, knaw, knaw. There's music in the worst cry in
London. *My dill and cucumbers to pickle.*

Everyone has admired the wit that distinguishes all the
persons of the play, but there has been difference of opinion as to how far it presents a natural or an artificial
view of society. Etherege has been denied skill in characterization; and Dryden's criticism, extravagant if applicable at all, has been sometimes echoed in regard to his
masterpiece—"being too witty himself, he could draw
nothing but wits in a comedy of his; even his fools were
infected with the disease of the author. They overflowed
with smart repartee, and were only distinguished from
the intended wits by being called coxcombs though they
deserved not so scandalous a name." Etherege anticipates such criticism when he makes Emilia say of Sir
Fopling, "However you despise him, gentlemen, I'll lay
my life he passes for a wit with many." But really his
pseudo wit and affected asininity are made apparent,
although without exaggeration or horseplay. And the
gentlemen and ladies are sufficiently individualized in spite
of the fact that they all exhibit skill in dialogue and repartee. They do not attempt to lay bare their souls, but
they never speak out of character, and we have some

satisfaction in knowing that such superior gentlemen as Dorimant and Bellair find ladies who match them in wit. Superior wit is, of course, always artificial in comparison with the dulness of ordinary conversation, but the dialogue in "The Man of Mode" presents a real society and real persons. "I allow it to be nature," cried Steele in "The Spectator," "but it is nature in its utmost corruption and degeneracy." Well, Etherege's view of human nature is assuredly not that of the sentimentalists or idealists, but he holds up for admiration neither corruption nor degeneracy but good manners and good dialogue. He sees the comedy of life, not through sentiment or fancy, nor with either malice or kindness, nor with any emotional prepense whatever, but with a cynicism and wit that both spring from the intellect. This is something new in our dramatic art, and it is not, I think, without a refreshing moral stimulus.

IV

Within the eight years that separated Etherege's second and third play were produced the four comedies that made up the entire dramatic work of William Wycherley. His first, "Love in a Wood, or St. James's Park," in 1671, introduced the handsome young author to the favour of the king's mistress, the Duchess of Cleveland. "The Gentleman Dancing Master" (1672), "The Country Wife" (1675), and "The Plain Dealer" (1676) established a great reputation in the theater and gained the encomiums of Dryden and all the wits. After that he wrote no more for the stage though his plays maintained their popularity; he married a countess, was imprisoned for debt, supported by a pension, patronized Pope and was patronized by him, and lived on until 1715.

Wycherley's plays belong to the same general species as Etherege's. They give a realistic depiction of the manners of the age and enliven and emphasize these manners by their wit; but they differ in many particulars from "She Would if She Could" and "The Man of

Mode." In the first place, Wycherley covers a wider range of manners, he takes us to the city as well as to the court and includes a larger observation of London life. Again, he has greater dramatic invention than Etherege or any of his predecessors. Though he borrows freely, and especially from Molière, he contrives his situations skilfully and plays every one of them for its full dramatic value. His danger lies in carrying the game too far and running off into farcical extravagance. Again, he is more indecent than any of his contemporaries, more frankly animal in his flirtations and seductions. Again, he is more like Shadwell than Etherege in his satirical bent. He is not content merely to indicate affectation, hypocrisy and greed, he holds them up to scorn and condemnation. Moreover, alongside of his rakes and harlots, bawds and pimps, he usually presents one instance of unselfish and devoted love. He offers us something for admiration as well as condemnation. And finally, as his contemporaries recognized, Wycherley has a marvellous vigour, a boldness of execution that distinguish him alone among Restoration dramatists.

All those qualities are exemplified to a sufficient degree in "Love in a Wood" to raise it far above the average of contemporary comedy. Though borrowed in part from Molière's "L'École des Maris" and "L'École des Femmes," the construction is masterly, the intrigues are ingenious but not out of keeping with the characters, and every speech fits into place. The behaviour of the dramatis personæ is for the most part worse than that of animals, but there are some superior enough to interpret it with the gloss of wit; and there still survive examples of moral as well as intellectual virtue. The pure affection of Christina and Valentine, however, seems almost incredible amid the affectations and lechery of the coxcombs of the town and the usurers and bawds of the city.

"The Gentleman Dancing Master" is surer in tone, without these contrasts of morality and immorality, but it is less serious in purpose and more extravagant in its

situations. Foppish imitations of French and Spanish
manners are brought into ridicule, and a forward miss
of fourteen shields her lover under the pretense that he
is her dancing master. This is excellent farce or farcical
exaggeration of manners, but not much more.

In "The Country Wife" the comedy of manners is
supported by brilliant farce, but it is a triumph of the
theater. The basis of its plot is from Terence's
"Eunuchus" which supplies the suggestion for the part of
Horner, and Wycherley again draws on Molière for the
jealous husband who tries to keep his young and ignorant
wife from general society. A city knight and his dissolute ladies, and one worthy woman, who finally escapes
marriage to a coxcomb and secures a gentleman who is
at least witty and resourceful, supply the rest of the action.
It is mostly indecent but always amusing. It might be
disputed whether or not the abundant innuendos temper
the immorality of the piece, but there can be no doubt
that they increase its theatrical effectiveness. The entanglements of the situations gain immensely from the rapid
play of dramatic irony and double entendres. Wycherley's wit is perhaps as intellectual as Etherege's or Congreve's and it is certainly more dramatic than either, better interwoven into both situation and character, surer to
win the laughter of the audience. The famous China
scene is unquestionably the acme of this audacious combination of indecency, dramatic cleverness and sheer wit,
but the dénouement in the last half of the last scene is
only a trifle less overwhelming. The play held the stage
for nearly a century before it was cut and adapted and
its "esprit du diable" diminished. A more moral and less
outspoken age may still envy the art that created and the
laughter that greeted this masterpiece of the Restoration.

In "The Plain Dealer" Wycherley shifts from farce
to satire. Again turning to Molière he found a suggestion in "Le Misanthrope" and imitated the "Critique de
l'École des Femmes" in the criticism he introduced on
the indecency of "The Country Wife." But Wycherley's

Manly offers little resemblance to Molière's Alceste. He is surly, brutal, exposing the ugly relations of life. As he avows in the Prologue:

> But the coarse Dauber of the coming scenes,
> To follow Life and Nature only means,
> Displays you as you are, makes his fine Woman
> A mercenary Jilt, and true to no Man:
> His Men of Wit, and Pleasure of the Age,
> Are as dull Rogues as ever cumber'd stage:
> He draws a Friend only to Custom just,
> And makes him naturally break his Trust.

Manly, a brave sea captain, comes back to London to find that the lady, Olivia, whom he loved and to whom he gave his fortune, has married his trusted friend. She is not true even to her new husband but entertains the fops of the town and is eager to make an assignation with Fidelia, who disguised as a boy has followed Manly to sea and now plays the part of Shakespeare's Viola between him and his former mistress. The main action leads to Manly's revenge on Olivia and his marriage to the devoted Fidelia. The sub-plot deals with the wooing by Manly's lieutenant Freeman of the petulant, litigious Widow Blackacre. But both actions are to the accompaniment of constant denunciation and exposure of human frailties and vices. The widow and her son, bred to the law, lead us to amusing satire on the lawyers; but the contempt of Manly is too severe to be amusing; in the main action satire runs to mere denunciation.

Society is depicted as vile and loathsome, and so it was. Many critics seem to feel that the only impression a modern reader can receive is that of disgust, and this is certainly produced by the repulsive nature of the revenge Manly takes on his Olivia. In defense it can only be said that this substitution motive had been very common in preceding English drama, and that it was the kind of brutal joke of which the Rochesters and Lady Castlemains were quite capable. Of the presentation of manners, I think we may justly admire the powerful writing, the skilful adaptation to dramatic need. Wit, to be sure, is no longer merely a fine dress for cuckoldry, adultery and seduction, it exposes and derides and shames pretense and falseness. I had occasion to use the word cynical in speaking of Etherege, but the adjective is more often applied to Wycherley. I am not quite sure of its precise appropriateness. There is scorn and contempt, but there is also earnestness in this plain dealing, a moral indignation. The play is by no means heartless; alongside of the odious Olivia he chooses to draw the devoted and loyal and pathetic Fidelia. And when he turns on his own plain dealing it is with a touch of genuine humour rather than cynicism. Freeman, who is denounced by Manly as a time-server, manages to pursue a temperate and witty course and in the end retorts on the converted misanthrope "I think most of our Quarrels to the World are just such as we have to a handsome Woman; only because we cannot enjoy her as we would do."

If we look at the play as a product of its age, we must view it as astonishingly moral. We can understand Dryden's praise, "the author of the Plain Dealer, whom I am proud to call my friend, has obliged all honest and virtuous men by one of the most bold, most general, and most useful satires which has ever been presented on the English theater."

If the comedy of manners could readily quicken its gaiety into farce without becoming vulgar or noisy, it could also take on the dignity of satire and moral purpose. Wycherley's example, however, was not followed. The moral reaction led to sentiment and propaganda for various reforms; but no one else appeared capable of addressing bold and general satire from the stage. The great satires of that age turned naturally to the themes of politics and religion, which could scarcely be treated with any freedom in a censored Stuart theater. "The Plain Dealer," alone of the plays, presented the manners of the age with an art comparable to that of "Hudibras" or "Absalom and Achitophel." For its peers in English satirical comedy we should need to turn back to the masterpieces of Ben Jonson, or forward to the very different modes of Shaw and Galsworthy. They are keener perhaps in questioning the validity of the props on which society seems to rest, but I do not know that we have ever had a bolder and more general satire on the vices which fashionable society appears to foster than in Wycherley's "Plain Dealer."

We have surveyed now the first twenty years after the Restoration. In the later plays of Dryden and Shadwell we have proceeded somewhat beyond the proper limits of that period, and in the next chapter we shall be obliged to go back into the seventies to find the early pieces of those authors who flourished in the theater from Wycherley to Congreve. By the end of the reign of Charles II, however, Fletcherian tragicomedy, though still followed by Dryden, was a waning type, the Jonsonian comedy of humours in spite of Shadwell's devotion had failed to take a real growth, but the comic stage, if still occupied largely by farce and intrigue, had to its credit a novel and brilliant species in the comedy of manners of Etherege and Wycherley.

CHAPTER XIV

MANNERS AND WIT, 1680-1700

BEFORE the end of the reign of Charles II, comedy had assumed a new and distinctive character and was establishing traditions of its own. Many of the plays that we have examined in the last chapter were kept in repertory and acted every year and so supplied modes and standards for the future. Dependence on the Elizabethans was gradually lessening, although the chief comedies of Jonson and Fletcher were still to be seen on the stage. The superiority of the English drama to the French was freely boasted by the very authors who filched from Molière. Comedy was recognized as the fashionable form of literature, approved and patronized by king and court, practised by the greatest wits, and attempted by every ambitious young writer. There was indeed a justifiable pride in the drama that within twenty years after its re-establishment had produced the best comedies of Dryden, Shadwell, Etherege and Wycherley.

Those writers, however, represent the best rather than the average fare of the theaters, and their excellences should not blind us to the fact that comedy continued very much limited in subjects and methods. All of the plays rely heavily on intrigue, to which the humoristic characterization is only incidental. Some reflection of current manners and as much wit as the old situations and persons could command, complete the recipe. The first essential is a trick, an intrigue, a deception. There is no Restoration comedy which does not contain a trick, usually it will have a whole bag full. But these tricks which make up the plot are much alike, a trick by means of which the gallant may marry an heiress, a trick by which the rake

may fool the husband. These stratagems meet with difficulties and counterplots, and they breed new plots, and
their success or failure makes up the fable. You go to
the theater to see some one deceived, to laugh at the out-
tricked miser or fop or parent or husband. Along with
this pleasure in trickery, however, goes amusement in the
absurdities of certain persons, the country booby, the
amorous old lady, the city fop, the Puritan clergyman, the
avaricious alderman. These are likely to be bamboozled
but they are supposed to be funny even though unduped.
Act one presents the gentlemen or ladies or both, and discloses their plots to obtain one another. Acts two, three,
and four elaborate these plots and counterplots, deceptions and mistakes, varying the confusion by the antics of
the eccentrics. Act five reveals certain tricksters successful and others defeated. But there is no success without a trick.

This fundamental scheme for comedy might, as I have
said, be enlivened by manners and wit as well as by
"humours," it might also be relieved by sentiment. At
first this was usually put into blank verse or rhyming
couplets and confined to the more serious or heroic parts
of tragicomedy. There the noble and virtuous, however
beset by stratagem, could resort freely to the most exalted
sentiments and extravagant idealizations. Such sentimentality when exercised by renowned persons in foreign
scenes might be discounted as far removed from fact; but
its need was soon felt even in prose pieces dealing solely
with the affairs of seventeenth century London. We have
seen it finding a place even in the satires of Shadwell and
Wycherley; in fact, after 1680 it was both frequent and
increasing in comedy. This moral relief usually appears
in one of three ways: first, in a pair of decent and virtuous lovers who contrast with the rakehells and madcaps
and who indulge in sentiments rather than in raillery;
second, in a devoted girl who goes disguised as a page and
finally wins her lover through her loyalty and tenderness;
third, in a fifth act repentance or conversion in which the

triumph of virtue over vice receives some emotional exploitation. All three methods increase in frequency as the century advances to its close and were doubtless approved by that growing protest against immorality which found its most striking expression in Jeremy Collier's attack on the stage. There is not a little sentimentality in Aphra Behn and D'Urfey as well as in Shadwell, and later in the early work of Cibber. We encounter fleeting appeals to pathos and compassion, praises of natural feeling and virtue, and occasionally even a glimpse of a social problem, as in Shadwell's "Squire of Alsatia," but we shall find no comedy of the seventeenth century in which the treatment is mainly sentimental. The wonder is that at a time when Southerne and Otway were writing their tragedies, so little appeal was made in comedy to pity or tenderness.

But a strong feeling existed that neither the poetical rhapsodies of the heroes nor the prose sentimentalities of the virtuous had any place in pure comedy. The creaky mechanism of the intrigue could be adorned only with manners and wit. Comedy was supposed to be forbidden by its ancient laws to concern itself strenuously with either vice or virtue, but it was encouraged to paint the difference between good and bad manners. Though neither the wicked nor the pure in heart had any place in strict comedy, it had a welcome for all the refinements as well as the impurities of fashion. Both the affectations and the graces of high life, its foppery and its conversation, its coquetry and its banter, were the proper themes of a form of drama which attained its highest art in the discrimination between the counterfeits and imitations of false wit and the intellectual quickness and polished phrase that denoted true wit. Etherege and Wycherley continued to be the models for such comedy of manners and wit; but between Wycherley's first play in 1671 and Congreve's appearance twenty-one years later, no new writer of distinction made his debut on the comic stage.

In the meantime satire had no more successful exponents than wit. Wycherley's "Plain Dealer" found no
worthy successor. A new bent for satire was, however,
indicated in a group of political plays, first by the Tories
exulting in the downfall of Shaftesbury and later by the
Whigs celebrating the glorious revolution of 1688. These
gave the opportunity for personal satire and political
invective, but they developed nothing noteworthy or novel.
The average play kept pretty close to the norm. The
author used what wit he possessed and employed both
indecency and sentimentality rather indiscriminately, but
he relied mainly on the old bundle of tricks and the
familiar types of persons. The inevitable tendency was
to multiply the tricks and exaggerate the persons to the
verge of farce.

Crowne's "Sir Courtly Nice" (1685), a very popular
play which held the stage for over a century, may be cited
as a rather rare example of success through the exaggeration of character. Excepting Shadwell's, no other play
owes its success so largely to caricature. The eccentrics
are mostly Crowne's additions to a Spanish plot, and
include Testimony, a fanatic, Hothead, a zealot against
fanatics, Aunt, an amorous veteran, and the chief eccentric, the fop, Sir Courtly, to whom Bellguard will marry
his sister. Sir Courtly is balanced by the drunken and
boorish Surly; and these persons together with Crack, who
as the crazy nabob makes another eccentric, are constantly
airing their peculiarities in amusing conjunctions and
antitheses. Testimony and Hothead are always meeting
and fighting; Surly interrupts Sir Courtly at his toilet,
which is being accompanied by music, or breaks in on his
wooing when it has reached its most exquisite stage. The
two clever girls are chiefly occupied in setting the humours
at play. Leonora encourages her foppish suitor to air
his affectations, but when he pauses to admire himself
in a mirror, she steals away and Aunt promptly steps into
her place and receives the compliments and avowals that
follow. As a play this is a poor thing, but it is made up

of amusing scenes in which all the fun possible and not a little wit are extracted out of the eccentrics.

The tricks in this case are childish but the dramatists were acquiring considerable skill in manipulation. They ransacked the Spanish drama, used Molière's plays over and over; and as soon as one of Fletcher's plays went out of fashion on the stage, they seized upon it like so many crows, picking it over for situations and devices. It is useless to enumerate many examples of the comedies of intrigue for they are so much alike that in synopsis one can scarcely be distinguished from another. In truth, nothing can be more tedious than a succession of average Restoration plays with their recurring fops, jilts and cuckolds, their disguises, eavesdroppings and missent letters, their endless tricks and mistakes. Under such repetition, vice itself loses half its charm by losing all its novelty.

Most prolific among these later writers are Ravenscroft, D'Urfey, and Mrs. Behn. Ravenscroft is remembered chiefly as the reviser of "Titus Andronicus" and as the author of "London Cuckolds," a very lively and indecent play which kept the stage up to Garrick's time; but his skill lay mainly in farce and he was one of the first to introduce the Italian sort with scaramouch and harlequin. D'Urfey is perhaps as representative as any one of the general practice of the years from 1680 to 1700, and his twenty comedies must employ every trick that is known to Restoration drama. He can be sentimental as in "Love for Money," or indecent as in his "Don Quixote," which brought him the honour of sharing with Congreve the attacks of Collier and the prosecution of the Middlesex grand jury; but his chief distinction is in his indefatigable complication of his plots. The best examples of the comedy of intrigue, however, are to be found among the plays of Aphra Behn, who was fully as skilful as the others in managing her plots and who also succeeds in giving her plays a somewhat distinctive character and personality. Her dramatic career almost exactly coin-

cides with the twenty year interval between the first plays
of Wycherley and Congreve.

I

The first woman to write regularly for the stage, Mrs.
Aphra Behn, had some twenty plays produced, for the
most part successfully. She was born Aphra Amis, in
1640, spent her girlhood in Surinam, the home of the
royal slave Oroonoko, who was to become the hero of
her most famous novel. She returned to London not long
after the Restoration, married Mr. Behn, who shortly
died, served as a political agent in Holland, fell into want
and distress, and then turned to her pen as a means of
livelihood. Her entire writings lend support to the
stories told during her lifetime and later of her loose
living; but, whatever the facts about her amours, she was
unquestionably a hard working writer kept very busy earn-
ing a living by her pen. She courageously challenged the
male dramatists in the competition for money and fame,
and she fairly held her own with them in what were then
deemed the chief essentials in the art of comedy, bustling
intrigue, indecency and wit.

Her plays do not display much invention. She borrowed freely from French and Spanish romances and
from Middleton, Molière and other dramatists, but she
was very clever in manipulating her bundle of tricks.
Though they are not lacking in manners, wit or humour,
her plays are mainly comedies of intrigue, marking the
tendency toward farce rather than that toward the artificial comedy of manners. They have, however, an individuality of their own and preserve in our literature an
impression of a spirited personality.

Like Dryden, she had a fondness for tragicomedy and
romances. Her early plays mark a descent down the
Fletcherian scale from the thrilling and passionate to the
realistic and domestic. Her first play "The Forced Marriage" (1670) is a tragicomedy in blank verse, reminiscent of the Beaumont-Fletcher romances. The king, the

prince, the favourite, the princess and the favourite's daughter play their usual parts in the tangles of love and jealousy, and there is little comedy. "The Amorous Prince" (1671) is also in blank verse but with fewer thrills and more laughter. Cloris, debauched by the prince, serves him disguised as a page and eventually marries him. This tender and romantic episode is accompanied by other incidents more characteristic of the contemporary stage—the husband who urges a friend to attempt the seduction of his wife, two sisters who by changing clothes greatly confuse their lovers, and ladies of quality who appear disguised as courtezans and thus add to the mistakes. The next play, "The Dutch Lover," based on a Spanish romance, treats of the favourite tragicomic theme, the love of a (supposed) brother and sister, but it is mostly in prose and many of the complications are unromantic. "The Town Fop or Sir Timothy Tawdrey" (1676) carries us still farther away from romance toward realistic comedy. It is taken from an Elizabethan play, Wilkins's "Miseries of Enforced Marriage," and like other of Mrs. Behn's plays offers an unhappy marriage as an excuse for adultery. The girl disguised as a boy, to whom another girl makes love, reminds us of the old romantic tradition, and there is some sentiment. But the brothel scenes, the fop knight, the serenades and the bedroom discoveries are all customary material of current comedy. "The Debauchee or the Credulous Cuckold" (1777), ascribed to Mrs. Behn by Langbaine, is an adaptation of Brome's "The Mad Couple Well Match't."

All the methods of stage intrigue practised in these first plays reappear in "The Rover or the Banished Cavaliers," Part I (1677). This proved Mrs. Behn's most popular play and held the stage for nearly a century. It is taken from Tom Killigrew's "Thomaso," an unacted comedy that cannot boast of much originality for its devices, the most unsavoury being borrowed from Middleton's "Blurt, Master Constable." The scene is Naples, but the chief

actors are Englishmen who seem to practise the manners
of Restoration London, slightly romanticized, and the
Spanish ladies who by their devices help to complicate
the action after the fashion approved in their national
drama. Willmore, the rover, a bold libertine, suggests
Dryden's Celadon and Wildblood. A famous Neapolitan
courtezan, played by Nell Gwyn, has posted her picture
offering herself for 1000 crowns a month. Willmore
tears down the picture, forces his way into her apartment,
and declares his love and poverty. She becomes enamoured and pursues him until the end of the play. Meanwhile he is busy pursuing, either by mistake or intention,
each and all of the other ladies of the play, until he is
finally captured by the madcap Hellena. Of his companions, the most interesting is Blunt, a country gentleman, rough in manners and unlucky in love. The married
woman whom he pursues tricks him sadly, and he returns
to his lodging clad only in shirt and drawers and covered
with filth. Here he is shortly visited by one of the ladies
of quality who has made her way into the wrong chamber.
Songs, masquerades, disguises and duels enliven the love
chases. There is no less stage bustle than in one of
Shadwell's pieces, but the action is less grotesque and
noisy, and to quicker music. It is all diverting and
improper.

"Sir Patient Fancy" (1778) is closer than any of the
preceding plays to what by that date was the norm of
comedy. It is borrowed from Molière's "Le Malade
Imaginaire," enlarged with incidents from other of his
comedies and furbished with London manners and
humours. Sir Patrick, the hypochondriac, is cuckolded by
Wittmore. Four times the husband discovers his wife
with her lover, though once another gallant has, unknown
to her, taken Wittmore's place. In the end she obtains
money from her husband sufficient to render her independent, and he decides to quit the rôle of hypochondriac
husband and turn gallant and spark. Lady Knowell is a
precieuse ridicule and Sir Credulous Easy is a country

bumpkin, affording a fine part for Nokes. Two peculiarities in the intrigue may be noticed; one which happily does not occur again, the employment of a child, Fanny, of seven years, who overhears, conceals, or discloses all the amorous plots, and the second, which frequently recurs, the use of a half-darkened stage. The mistakes necessary to the complicated plot can scarcely be managed by masks and disguises, so Mrs. Behn and other dramatists frequently use the device of persons groping, embracing, fighting and mistaking one another in the dark. The stage, though supposed to be dark, can of course be seen readily by the audience. The play aroused what its author styles "the most unjust and silly aspersion woman could invent to cast on woman, and which only my being a woman has procured me, that it was baudy." She defends herself most wittily, but this was the first though not the last of her plays to furnish justification for Pope's couplet:

> The stage how loosely does Astrea tread
> Who fairly puts all characters to bed.

Mrs. Behn's other plays repeat with variations the materials and methods that I have noticed, but they are never lacking in some novelty and considerable vivacity. Two, "The Young King" and "The Widow Ranter" are outside the strict range of comedy, the former being a stilted tragicomedy written many years before it was acted, and the latter combining comic scenes and persons with the tragic history of Bacon's rebellion in Virginia. "The Feign'd Curtezans or A Night's Intrigue" (1679) and "The Younger Brother or The Amorous Jilt," acted after the author's death, are sufficiently described by their titles. The Second Part of "The Rover" (1680) carries on the amorous adventures of Willmore after the death of the wife whom he had won in Part I. He makes love to all the ladies in Madrid, escapes marriage and concludes with the favours of the beautiful courtezan La Nuche. The entanglements of the plot become farcical when they include the pursuit of two Jewish heiresses, one a dwarf and the other a giant who can be saluted only by the aid of a ladder.

Next in order are the two political plays that varied the customary intrigues by Tory exultations over the downfall of Shaftesbury and the Whigs. "The Roundheads" (1681-2) is a revamping of Tatham's "Rump," a rude and popular burlesque of the parliamentary leaders after Cromwell's death. To this Mrs. Behn adds the intrigues of two cavalier lovers with two leading Puritan ladies. Much is made of Lady Lambert's pride and pretension, but her lover Loveless proves noble and constant and comes to her rescue after her husband's downfall. "The City Heiress" satirizes Shaftesbury who is represented as Sir Timothy Treatall, who keeps open house for Whigs and traitors and is gulled into believing he is to be king of Poland; but the plot is taken from Middleton's "A Mad World, My Masters" with the addition of two characters from Massinger's "Guardian." Sir Timothy is gulled of his money by his witty nephew and married to the nephew's cast mistress. Wilding, the nephew, marries a beautiful and devoted heiress, but not before he has had a long bedroom scene with a widow, Lady Galliard, who yields only after a protracted debate. Even in such a medley of political lampooning and immoral melodrama, we find, as so often in Mrs. Behn, some genuine sentiment and passion.

"The False Count" (1682) and "The Lucky Chance" (1686) are also farcical in the extravagance and improbability of their incidents. The first is taken from Molière, the second from Shirley's "Lady of Pleasure." This play required another sprightly defense on the charge of indecency. In addition to Shirley's device of the lady who secretly meets her lover who is persuaded that he has been with a she-devil, Astrea adds that of the avaricious husband who, on the chance of winning five hundred pounds, plays the parts of pander and cuckold. From such recurrent ribaldry it is a pleasant change to a farce of a different sort, "The Emperor of the Moon," acted in 1688, shortly before the death of the author. It is elaborated from "Arlequin Empereur dans la Lune" by Biancoletti, the head of the Italian actors in Paris, and employs songs, choruses, instrumental music, spectacles and the acrobatic antics of scaramouch and harlequin. Italian actors and the commedia del arte were not unknown in England, but the great success of this extravaganza or pantomime farce seems to have helped in popularizing such entertainments for many years to come.

Mrs. Behn contributed to the continued sway of incident and intrigue in English comedy. Though her plays pleased by their licentiousness and sprightliness, they are more likely to run to farce than to cynicism and they are rarely without traces of sentiment. Though she does not sermonize, or moralize, or satirize anyone except the Whigs, she has a code of her own, that of the tender passion. Neither her ladies nor her courtezans are free from its tyranny; the wives offer excuses and arguments when they are untrue to their husbands, but those who are untrue to their lovers are condemned as hopeless jilts. Astrea may have trod the stage loosely, but she was not heartless. If she had lived in a time when sensibility and sentiment ruled the theater she might have preferred pity to wit as a means of pleasing her public. But perhaps we may prefer her plays as they are, and such as possibly no woman will ever compose again. She wrote for a stage where compassion had no place, where she presented life gaily and wittily and somewhat too coarsely, where she stirred merriment for the escapades and frailties that follow in love's wake and yet asked a little tenderness for its victims.

II

The first of Congreve's four comedies, "The Old Bachelor," was produced when he was twenty-two, and the last, "The Way of the World" a few days after his thirtieth birthday. The first was a great success, the second, "The Double Dealer," though less favourably received on the stage, elicited Dryden's magnificent commendation:

> Heav'n that but once was prodigal before,
> To Shakespeare gave as much; she could not give
>   him more.
> Maintain your post: that's all the fame you need;
> For 'tis impossible you should proceed.
> Already I am worn with cares and age
> And just abandoning th' ungrateful stage:
> Unprofitably kept at heav'n's expense,
> I live a rent-charge on his providence.
> But you, whom every muse and grace adorn,
> Whom I foresee to better fortune born,
> Be kind to my remains; and oh, defend,
> Against your judgment, your departed friend!
> Let not th' insulting foe my fame pursue;
> But shade those laurels which descend to you:
> And take for tribute what these lines express:
> You merit more; nor could my love do less.

The third comedy, "Love for Love," was a complete triumph in its own day and remained a favourite on the stage up to the nineteenth century. The last, "The Way of the World," though indifferently received in the theater, was at once acclaimed by critics as the masterpiece of its species, an opinion often repeated, as in Swinburne's superlatives—"the unequalled and unapproached masterpiece of English comedy. The one play in our language which may fairly claim a place beside, or but just beneath, the mightiest work of Molière." Congreve lived for nearly thirty years, the holder of moderately lucrative offices, loved by Mrs. Bracegirdle and the Duchess of Marlborough, the recognized chief of English letters, admired by Steele, Swift and Pope; but he wrote nothing more of consequence.

"The Old Bachelor" is assuredly an amazing play for a youth just out of college and, though it is inferior to the others, it shows Congreve's formula for comedy almost full-formed. In substance it differs very little from a play by Etherege and departs in no particular from the tradition already established for the comedy of manners. Two gentlemen of wit marry two heiresses, one of whom is capricious and affected; a cast mistress is passed off on a wittol; a citizen's wife is seduced by one of the wits, and a surly bachelor, hater of women and gallantry, is saved by his friends from marrying the forsaken mistress. The themes, as usual, are cuckoldry, flirtation, asininity, and the language is gross. These familiar plots and persons are, however, treated with a finesse peculiar to the author. The intrigues are not multiplied, in fact the tricks are very few, and there is no bustle, noise or beating, except for the kicks bestowed upon the braggart soldier. Little attempt is made to tie together the various plots and counterplots into an elaborate construction. On the other hand, great care is spent in making the most out of a given situation. Take, for example, the discovery of the wife and her lover by the husband. Bellmour goes to Fondlewife's house disguised as a Puritan preacher, with a volume of Scarron's novels in place of a prayer-book. He succeeds in persuading the wife; and the scenes drawing disclose "Laetitia and Bellmour, his cloak, hat, etc., lying loose about the chamber." When the husband unexpectedly returns and Bellmour escapes into another room, he does not leave his hat or cloak behind him— that device was too old—he takes everything with him except the prayer-book, and the husband's suspicions are aroused only when he discovers this to be a novel "The Innocent Adultery." This is of course a mere detail; the husband's suspicions are finally lulled, and Bellmour escapes and later utilizes his clerical disguise in performing a mock marriage—another trick essential to the plot.

This deftness in handling the situation is paralleled by a refinement in characterization. Vainlove is not merely the usual gallant in love with all, but has the peculiarity of delighting in the ardours of the chase more than in the satisfactions of success.   Belinda, who was played by Mrs. Mountfort, is an affected coquette but not to a ridiculous or excessive degree.   There are at least faint indications of the effort that Congreve was to make in his later comedies to maintain consistency and individuality of characterization in spite of a general distribution of wit.

In "The Old Bachelor," however, the merit lies less in the characterization than in the wit.   Congreve's style, if not yet at its best, is flexible, pointed and easy, already capable of a dialogue superior to that of Dryden or Etherege or Wycherley.   And the wit is ever sparkling. The opening conversation starts the scintillations, and they continue until the very end.

Bell.   Vainlove, and abroad so early!   Good-morrow; I thought a contemplative lover could no more have parted with his bed in a morning than he could have slept in't.

Vain.   Bellmour, good-morrow.   Why, truth on't is, these early sallies are not usual to me; but business, as you see, sir—*(showing letters).*   And business must be followed, or be lost.

Bell.   Business!   And so must time, my friend, be close pursued, or lost.   Business is the rub of life, perverts our aim, casts off the bias, and leaves us wide and short of the intended mark.

Vain.   Pleasure, I guess you mean.

Bell.   Ay; what else has meaning?

Vain.   Oh, the wise will tell you——

Bell.   More than they believe—or understand.

Vain.   How, how, Ned!   A wise man say more than he understands?

Bell.   Ay, ay!   Wisdom's nothing but a pretending to know and believe more than we really do.   You read of but one wise man, and all that he knew was, that he knew nothing.   Come, come, leave business to idlers, and wisdom to fools; they have need of 'em.   Wit be my faculty, and pleasure my occupation; and let Father Time shake his glass. Let low and earthly souls grovel till they have worked themselves six foot deep into a grave. Business is not my element—I roll in a higher orb, and dwell——

Vain. In castles i' th' air of thy own building. That's thy element, Ned. Well, as high a flier as you are, I have a lure may make you stoop. *(Flings a letter.)*

"The Old Bachelor" is more "artificial" than any of the plays of Etherege or Wycherley, partly because of its excess of wit, partly because of the greater refinement in character and intrigue, and partly because it is twenty years later. It follows an established dramatic tradition, it does not attempt to picture life. It accepts the matter and the methods of the comedy of manners that had grown up in the society of Charles II. There is no sign of any fresh observation of life by the youthful author, nothing that he could not have found in an earlier comedy, scarcely a thrust of wit that did not merely improve on some lessons learned in the old fencing school. The problem of dramatic art for Congreve is to clothe the old intrigues and indecencies in new artifices of manners and wit. Sympathy and emotion are out of place and satire is merely incidental, since for him comedy deals with manners and not with morals, and since, with his accredited material, wit must be cynical. In the three comedies that follow there is scarcely more depth or freshness in the view of human nature than in the first, but there is far more skill and invention in remodelling the familiar type, more ingenuity, more comic force, and a mastery of style and wit.

"The Double Dealer" abounds in comic life. The fops, male and female, are irresistible, and they reveal themselves in every action and every word. Congreve has attained variety and individuality in the manners of his persons and bridled his wit to the task of revealing rather than commenting on their absurdities. Here is the roster of fools: Lord Froth, a solemn coxcomb; Lady Froth, a great coquette and pretender to poetry and learning; Brisk, a pert coxcomb and also a poet; Lady Plyant, insolent to her husband and easy to any pretender; Sir Paul Plyant, an uxurious, foolish old knight. One might spend a lifetime searching the frivolities of society or the creations of comedy and not find five greater sillies than those, and each one is silly in his or her own special fashion. They blunder into wit or innuendo in different ways; their tongues babble to different rhythms; and their minds display five different kinds of vacuity. It is difficult to imagine where an exercise of free-will might lead five such futile volitions, but under the conventions of the stage their careers are predestined. Lady Froth must succumb to Brisk, and Lady Plyant to any gentleman who offers himself, and Lord Froth and Sir Paul must remain static in complacent cuckoldom. The way in which Congreve manages all this without resorting to mere farce is a marvel. How inimitably absurd is the flirtation of the simpering poets— Lady Froth's vapid cachinnation echoes even from the printed page! And what *vis comica* in that amazing scene in which Lady Plyant accuses the bewildered Mellefont of seeking, under cover of a marriage with her stepdaughter, to lead her astray and then answers her own scruples against being led astray before the astounded gallant can discover what she is talking about.

Lady Plyant. Nay, nay, rise up; come, you shall see my good-nature. I know love is powerful, and nobody can help his passion. 'Tis not your fault; nor, I swear, it is not mine. How can I help it, if I have charms? And how can you help it, if you are made a captive? I swear it is pity it should be a fault. But my honour,— well, but your honour, too—but the sin!—well, but the necessity—O Lord, here's somebody coming, I dare not stay. Well, you must consider of your crime; and strive as much as can be against it,—strive, be sure. But don't

be melancholic; don't despair. But never think that I'll
grant you anything. O Lord, no. But be sure you lay
aside all thoughts of the marriage, for though I know
you don't love Cynthia, only as a blind for your passion
to me, yet it will make me jealous. O Lord, what did I
say? Jealous! no, no, I can't be jealous, for I must not
love you; therefore don't hope,—but don't despair
neither. Oh, they're coming, I must fly. [II, v.

In his epistle dedicatory Congreve answers two criticisms made against the play. He first defends his use
of soliloquy on the ground that the convention is permissible provided the soliloquizer is unconscious of any
one listening. But his use of soliloquy is not only
excessive in this play, he indulges in the overheard
soliloquy as a device for plot until it becomes almost as
obvious an artifice as the mistaken letter or the darkened
room. The second criticism was to the character of
Maskwell, the double dealer; and the debate on this
charge has continued, some finding this villain and his
fellow conspirator, Lady Touchwood, out of place in
comedy, others finding them admirable. Unquestionably
their characters account for their plots, and their plots
help to give unity and vigour to the action. Moreover,
their characters are presented with consistency and force.
But I do not think that there is any addition to the
humour of the play by this borrowing from tragedy the
stock figures of the Machiavellian villain and the passionate and revengeful lady. Furthermore, the presence
of so much villainy makes it necessary to set up Mellefont and Cynthia as models of virtue; and that is a bit
out of keeping with the merry immoralities of Ladies
Froth and Plyant. Their affairs might belong to that
Utopia of cuckoldry that Charles Lamb defended, but
the revengeful amours of Maskwell and Lady Touchwood
belong to melodrama.

"Love for Love" provides variety of incident and persons without intruding on the field of tragedy. The list

of dramatis personæ is longer than before. The men are the hero Valentine, his father who is trying to disinherit him, his friend who is free-spoken, Tattle, a beau who tells tales while pretending to secrecy, Ben, the younger brother, a sea-dog, Foresight, a peevish addict of astrology, and Jeremy, a most witty servant. The women are Angelica the heiress beloved by Valentine, Prue, a country girl, and the two flighty sisters, Mrs. Foresight and Mrs. Frail. Valentine pretends madness in order to postpone his signing away of his estate and to win the sympathy of the clever and competent Angelica, and this stage trick is given a new effect because Valentine mad is almost as witty as Valentine sober and is more poetical. This main action is supported by several minor intrigues, Ben's and Tattle's wooings. Angelica's pretense of marrying the father, Scandal's deception of the astrologer in order to court his wife, and the tricking of Tattle and Frail into marrying each other.

The persons are more natural, less "artificial" than in the other comedies. No one is a villain, and no one except Tattle is a fool. Sailor Ben is a great addition from the outside world, and his sea metaphors seem to slip from Congreve's pen as readily as do polished epigrams. The simplicities of little Miss Prue and the superstitions of the astrologer give an opportunity for broad and popular comic effects. The bodkin dialogue is perhaps the best of the comic scenes, but the Frail sisters are not as mirth-provoking as the others of that family in "The Double Dealer." The fun is a little commonplace, the appeal of the wit a little obvious and the art of the whole play less refined than in the masterpiece that followed. But it is only by comparison with Congreve at his best that "Love for Love" seems inferior or uncharacteristic. Raillery, satire and cynicism are always at play, though in the end both Valentine and Angelica confess to having hearts. The concluding speeches may be quoted as an example of Congreve's style in sober mien and of his moralizing, not very fervent or profound but not too cynical.

Scan. Well, madam, you have done exemplary justice in punishing an inhuman father and rewarding a faithful lover. But there is a third good work which I, in particular, must thank you for: I was an infidel to your sex, and you have converted me. For now I am convinced that all women are not like fortune, blind in bestowing favours, either on those who do not merit or who do not want 'em.

Ang. 'Tis an unreasonable accusation that you lay upon our sex: you tax us with injustice, only to cover your own want of merit. You would all have the reward of love, but few have the constancy to stay till it becomes your due. Men are generally hypocrites and infidels: they pretend to worship, but have neither zeal nor faith. How few, like Valentine, would persevere even to martyrdom, and sacrifice their interest to their constancy! In admiring me, you misplace the novelty.

> The miracle to-day is, that we find
> A lover true; not that a woman's kind.

In "The Way of the World," except for the indecency, the process of refinement is complete. There is little appeal to the vulgar. Action is reduced to a minimum. No ladies are seduced, no bedrooms disclosed, no duels fought, no beatings administered, and the only broadly comic scene is the wooing of Lady Wishfort by the bogus Sir Rowland. This impersonation by the disguised Waitwell is the only trick presented on the stage, for the plots of Fainall and Mrs. Marwood and the counter-attacks of Mirabell are scarcely parts of the action; they are merely recited parts of the conversation. The misdeeds of Mrs. Fainall and Mrs. Marwood are likewise merely narrated. The play indeed has little dramatic construction; the plot might be printed on the play-bill and it would be clearer to the audience than it is when acted,

and fully as exciting. It might be put briefly as follows:
Mirabell, a witty gentleman, wins the hand and fortune
of the coquette Millamant in spite of the stratagems of
his cast mistress and her new lover and in spite of the
failure of Mirabell's scheme to lure into a mock marriage
with his servant old Lady Wishfort, who controls part of
Millamant's fortune.   Congreve could neglect but he
could not escape this jejune complication.

Striking and obvious character-parts are as lacking as
is intrigue. Fainall and Mrs. Marwood play the parts of
villain and revengeful mistress, but not with the melodramatic emphasis given to similar parts in "The Double
Dealer." He does not soliloquize at length and she does
not storm and rage. They are kept within the tone of
comedy and they are clever enough to join in the game
of wit. The triumph of humour lies, as Congreve
explains in his dedication, in the creation of persons not
naturally fools but making fools of themselves by affectation. Witwould is certainly one of the great comic inventions, a coxcomb perpetually prattling in the hope that he
may somehow deviate into repartee, and he has a perfect
foil in the affectedly surly Petulant. Of Lady Wishfort
opinions differ, one critic finding her "almost too offensive
for comedy," another pitying this "miserable tragedy of
a love-sick old woman." Both critics seem a little finical.
Such moralizing might occur to one when reading the
play but would hardly come to one's mind in seeing it
acted. After all, if comedy is to take a look at human
affectations, why shy at an affected old woman (she is
only fifty-five) making a fool of herself in love. Sir
Wilfull is the only natural unaffected person in the piece,
and, though he is not as interesting as Sailor Ben in
"Love for Love," his boorishness and drunkenness supply
a needed low comic relief from the niceties of wit, and
of course he is another capital foil for Witwould.

The hero and the heroine represent the last possible
refinements of their parts. They embody all that the
wits and coquettes who preceded them on the stage have

to offer, except that they play no practical jokes and indulge in no stage deceptions on each other. Wit, irony, sarcasm, sobered by experience and judgment, make Mirabell the most self-possessed of all fine gentlemen, and therefore splendid game for the most witty and fearless of Dianas. The play undertakes to depict their courtship, unmarked by one sacrifice, one rescue, one embrace, or, on the part of the lady, by one moment of real hesitation or by the disclosure of one palpitation of the heart. If we accept the convention that love is a game of wit, they are the perfect lovers.

Following the plan of "The Old Bachelor," Congreve keeps his ladies off the stage throughout the first act, which is devoted solely to the conversation of the real wits and the would-be wits. It is all expository of the plot and the persons and is most brilliantly written. The longest speech is Mirabell's *confessio amantis* which has fully as much truth as well as more wit than most such confessions.

Fainall. For a passionate lover methinks you are a man somewhat too discerning in the failings of your mistress.

Mirabell. And for a discerning man somewhat too passionate a lover, for I like her with all her faults; nay, like her for her faults. Her follies are so natural, or so artful, that they become her, and those affectations which in another woman would be odious serve but to make her more agreeable. I'll tell thee, Fainall, she once used me with that insolence that in revenge I took her to pieces, sifted her, and separated her failings: I studied 'em and got 'em by rote. The catalogue was so large that I was not without hopes, one day or other, to hate her heartily. To which end I so used myself to think of 'em, that at length, contrary to my design and expectation, they gave me every hour less and less disturbance, till in a few days it became habitual to me to remember 'em without being displeased. They are now grown as familiar to me as my own frailties, and in all probability in a little time longer I shall like 'em as well.

With Act II the ladies appear, but it is half over before Millamant is at length discovered. "Here she comes," cries Mirabell, " 'i faith, full sail, with her fan spread and streamers out and a shoal of fools for tenders." Hazlitt's superlatives are not too great for this scene; there is nothing like it anywhere. No one can refrain from quoting: "Oh, ay, letters—I had letters—I am persecuted with letters. Nobody knows how to write letters; and yet one has 'em, one does not know why. They serve one to pin up one's hair." To Millamant lovers are much like letters. "Beauty the lover's gift; Lord, what is a lover, that it can give? Why, one makes lovers as fast as one pleases, and they live as long as one pleases, and they die as soon as one pleases; and then, if one pleases, one makes more." In vain Mirabell tries his epigrams upon her; she is gone as she came. "Gone! Think of you? To think of a whirlwind, though 't were in a whirlwind, were a case of more steady contemplation, a very tranquillity of mind and mansion."

In the third act we come to Lady Wishfort's house, and the plot thickens—what there is of it—at least there is a constant coming and going of persons. Millamant sets her wit to teasing Marwood, ending with the song:

If there's delight in love, 'tis when I see
That heart which others bleed for, bleed for me.

In Act IV she subdues the drunken Sir Wilfull, and she and Mirabell again match wits as they draw up their articles of marriage; and she finally owns she has a mind if not a heart to him.

Mrs. Fainall. Fie, fie, have him, have him, and tell him so in plain terms: for I am sure you have a mind to him.

Millamant. Are you? I think I have; and the horrid man looks as if he thought so too. Well, you ridiculous thing you, I'll have you. I won't be kissed, nor I won't be thanked.—Here, kiss my hand though, so hold your tongue now, don't say a word.

Mirabell is silenced and so is Congreve. Millamant has exhausted him and he gives her scarce a word during the rest of the play. Lady Wishfort takes up her courtship with the pseudo Sir Rowland. "You have an excess of gallantry, Sir Rowland, and press things to a conclusion with a most prevailing vehemence. But a day or two for decency of marriage——" The humour broadens and grows hilarious; and when the deception is discovered, then the fifth act is occupied largely by Mirabell's explanations. Neither he nor his author cared to trust Millamant with the management of the fifth act, which she could, if she wished, have done as efficiently as Angelica or even Portia or Rosalind. She does lend a hand to help her lover, but she appears indifferent to prosy explanations and exposures of what every one knew before, and just a trifle impatient for Mirabell to take her.

If we judge the play from the point of view of Restoration comedy, Congreve's success is overwhelming. As the presentation of manners of a particular social group, as the refinement of raillery, flirtation and affectation, as a model of style and wit, it is close to perfection. Its obvious faults, except that of feeble structure, are chargeable not to it alone but to all its contemporaries, indelicacy of language, restriction to the superficialities of human nature, and a hardness and cynicism in tone. Since its own day, it has been the subject of both extravagant praise and blame but usually in the course of a debate on the question of its immorality. Charles Lamb has gallantly defended it on the ground that it takes us to an artificial, imaginary world where everyday morals do not exist, but nineteenth century moralists have usually been very stern in their condemnations. Perhaps the most telling indictment is to be found in Leslie Stephen's charge of "a perpetual gush of cynical sentiment." This might be defended as a part of the conventions of Restoration comedy, as a sort of pose, a pretense that must be kept up as an accompaniment of the display of affectation and folly; but no doubt an excess of cynicism is almost as wearying as an excess of sentimentality and almost as immoral. Worse than either alone is a mixture of both, and Congreve at least deserves some credit for refusing to sugar-coat his pill. But Stephen becomes absurd when on the ground of the asphyxiating atmosphere of the plays he denies them any right of comparison with Molière's. Congreve is doubtless inferior to the master of comedy, especially in the range and depth of his humour, but in style and wit and in the treatment of such comic situations as come within his range he may surely challenge comparison even with Molière.

Why should every comedy within its three hours' duration be required to exploit our moral sentiments and either bemoan the depravity or extol the goodness of mankind? Such was not Congreve's view of comedy or Charles Lamb's idea of an evening's enjoyment at the theater. Our age seems more likely than its predecessor to relish Mirabell's wit even when it sneers and to enjoy with Millamant, and for that matter with Witwould, their attitude of make-believe, of playing a game with zest. Half-cynical, wholly amused, a little heartless, Millamant's pleasure in the frivolities of existence comes near to justifying Lamb's defense of this play-world where the "privation of moral light" is a necessity for imaginative mirth. Her merriment has the insouciance of Puck's and the airiness of Ariel's. Happy in her own quickness of wit she exults less at the inferiority of others than at her own celerity which outdistances all competitors. Has she a heart, is she unselfish, and would she meet the realities of life as cheerfully and fearlessly as she frisks with its follies? There is nothing in the play to negative these questions, but they are not positively answered in the course of this three hours' entertainment. It would take another play to tell us whether Alceste would have found her more worthy than Célimène, or whether Mirabell has won a wife who will help him to be a better man. We may suppose that Congreve didn't know or that he didn't care to say what were the qualities of her heart and will; but the Comic Spirit was surely in a playful rather than a saturnine mood when she guided his pen to create Millamant's wit and laughter.

III

The comedies of Sir John Vanbrugh do not carry farther that process of refinement which we have observed in Congreve. Though his two best plays long held the stage and deserve high rank among comedies of manners, they add little or nothing that is new in the development of that species. Vanbrugh has both wit and style, but he is inferior to Congreve in these particulars and is at his best rather in making the most of such comic effects as were afforded by the now familiar situations and types of character.

After a residence in France including an imprisonment in the Bastille and after some experience as a soldier, Captain Vanbrugh found himself in London "with a heart above his income" and with an ambition to write plays. This was excited to action by Colley Cibber's first play, "Love's Last Shift." The piece offered a certain novelty in its plot which turns on the reclamation of a dissolute husband by a devoted wife, one of the many instances of the growing sentimental and moral interest in comedy, and it also presented an amusing character, Sir Novelty Fashion, another in the long list of affected fops. The problem proposed by Cibber seemed to Vanbrugh to present a different answer, and he promptly wrote a sequel, "The Relapse, or Virtue in Danger," which carries on the affairs of the persons of "Love's Last Shift," showing the reclaimed husband again unfaithful and the devoted wife severely tempted. The fop reappears as the newly created Lord Foppington and is cheated out of the country heiress by his younger brother. The play is in some

degree an answer from the realistic school to an early
effort of moral sentimentality as shown in Cibber's play,
but Vanbrugh, like authors of the sentimental school,
debates a problem and depicts the triumph of virtue in
the faithful wife Amanda, who after long debates in
blank verse finally converts Worthy's "wild flame of
love" into pure adoration for her merits.

More interesting and much more diverting are the
scenes in prose that tell of Foppington and his brother
and of the brisk wooing of the young widow Berinthia
by the relapsed Loveless. Lord Foppington, like Congreve's Witwould, is "a man whom nature has made no
fool" but "who is very industrious to pass for an ass,"
and his mincing conversation is almost the last word in
foppism.

Lord Fop. Why, that's the fatigue I speak of,
madam. For 'tis impossible to be quiet, without thinking: now thinking is to me the greatest fatigue in the
world.

Aman. Does not your lordship love reading then?

Lord Fop. Oh, passionately, madam.—But I never
think of what I read.

Ber. Why, can your lordship read without thinking?

Lord Fop. O Lard!—can your ladyship pray without devotion, madam?

Aman. Well, I must own I think books the best entertainment in the world.

Lord Fop. I am so much of your ladyship's mind,
madam, that I have a private gallery, where I walk
sometimes; it is furnished with nothing but books and
looking-glasses. Madam, I have gilded 'em, and ranged
'em so prettily, before Gad, it is the most entertaining
thing in the world to walk and look upon 'em.

Aman. Nay, I love a neat library too; but 'tis, I think,
the inside of a book should recommend it most to us.

Lord Fop. That, I must confess, I am nat altogether
so fand of. Far to mind the inside of a book is to enter-

tain one's self with the forced product of another man's brain. Naw I think a man of quality and breeding may be much better diverted with the natural sprauts of his own. [II, i.

Less carefully drawn, but amusing on the stage are Miss Hoyden and her father Sir Tunbelly who, when visitors approach his country house, locks up his daughter and arms his servants.

Vanbrugh followed up the success of "The Relapse" (1696) by producing two plays within a few months, "Æsop," a translation from the French of Boursault, and "The Provoked Wife." The first is a string of episodes in which Æsop acts as adviser and arbiter and announces his decisions in rhyming fables. The piece was so enriched by Vanbrugh's wit and invention that it secured a long popularity on the stage. "The Provoked Wife" is his masterpiece. The chief faults of "The Relapse," its uncertain shifts from grossness to sentimentality and its failure to connect the two stories, are here avoided, and the play is excellently constructed along the approved lines of the comedy of manners. Sir John Brute is the brutal husband; his wife, seeking consolation in a lover, his niece wooed for lawful wedlock, and Lady Fanciful, an affected impertinent, are the ladies; Constant and Heartfree, the lovers; and the valet and maid, as in French comedy, are kept very active.

The dramatic management is skilful in avoiding the extremes of high and low comedy. The conversations are always sprightly though never protracted into a tiresome succession of epigrams without incident; the stage action is always dramatic and humorous without ever resorting to mere noise and bustle. Two instances may be given to illustrate the nature of Vanbrugh's achievement. Sir John Brute figures in drinking and scouring scenes similar to those in other plays, but the character of this bully and coward is maintained by a variety of devices that kept it long upon the stage and made it a

great favourite with Garrick. The most amusing scene
in the brute's career is when after arrest he is brought
into court disguised as a parson. Objections were raised
to this defamation of the clergy, so Vanbrugh rewrote
the scene, disguising him as a woman and presenting the
edifying picture of a drunken virago in court. At least,
he enlarged the comic effectiveness. A second instance
of dramatic resourcefulness is found in the device of
repetition. Lady Brute and Belinda, masked and poorly
dressed, seek an adventure in Spring Garden, where they
encounter the drunken Sir John and, in order to escape
him, are compelled to disclose themselves to their lovers.
Belinda and Heartfree walk away, and Constant is left
alone with Lady Brute. He makes advances rapidly and
urges her toward a close arbour nearby, but the jealous
Lady Fanciful and her maid have hid there and bolt out
upon them just as he is forcing her to enter. So far the
scene follows a common pattern. But in the next act
when Lady Fanciful's maid relates the incident of the
arbour to her lover, the valet Rasor, they re-enact the
scene, mimicking Lady Brute and Constant,—"as she
speaks, Rasor still acts the man, and she the woman."
On the score of immorality this scene deserves a black
mark, but there can be no doubt that the repetition
greatly enhances its comedy.

"The Provoked Wife" is much more than merely a
play of intrigue, it is a genuine comedy of manners
worthy of a place with those of Etherege and Congreve.
It is artificial inasmuch as it adorns by wit and ingenuity
manners and incidents long familiar to the stage, without
much effort to compare these with the actual life of its
time. Vanbrugh does draw to some extent on nature and
still more on his dramatic inventiveness to supply spirit
and vivacity, but I do not know what Mr. Palmer means
when he declares that "Vanbrugh killed the comedy of
sex for the English theater." He cannot have forgotten
Berinthia's faint cries as Loveless carries her off and the
mimicking of Mademoiselle and the raillery of Lady

Brute and Belinda. Flirtation may be less a conflict of wits than in Congreve, but sex still supplies abundant comedy in Vanbrugh.

"The Relapse" and "The Provoked Wife," both produced just before the publication of Jeremy Collier's "Short View of the Immorality and Profaneness of the English Stage" in 1798, naturally became shining marks for the attacks of that non-jurying clergyman. Vanbrugh defended himself in one of the many pamphlets that followed in the wake of that famous assault, but it cannot be said that he did much to improve the morality of his subsequent plays. Collier's attack was only one symptom of the growing protest against the looseness of the theater and it naturally did not produce an immediate revolution. But the Restoration type of comedy was losing the support of a changing society and was in need of a closer contact with fact as well as with morality. Vanbrugh was unable to supply either, for by this time he was taking an active interest in his profession of architect; and the best energies of his later years were given to building the stupendous palace of Blenheim and to quarreling with the vindictive old duchess. For several years, however, he continued to prepare translations and adaptations, though he produced no other original play. In 1700, on the occasion of the benefit for Dryden, he remade Fletcher's "Pilgrim," mainly by reducing the blank verse into prose. The prologue and epilogue were written by Dryden, and Anne Oldfield won her first success in the rôle of Alinda. "The Country House," a slight but amusing farce from Dancourt's "Maison de campagne" and "Squire Trelooby" from Molière's "Monsieur de Pourceaugnac" were unimportant. "The False Friend" (1702), from Le Sage's "Traître puni," with some borrowings from its Spanish original, was a failure at first but long kept a place in repertory, as did "The Mistake" (1705), which follows closely "Le Dépit Amoureux" of Molière. These are both comedies of intrigue rather than of manners; they lose nothing in

briskness in their English dress.   More popular than
either of these and more indebted to Vanbrugh's wit and
comic force is "The Confederacy" (1705), from Dancourt, "Les Bourgeoises à la Mode."   Two city wives
imitate the gaities and gambling of the ladies of quality
to the consternation of their stingy husbands, and each
extorts money from the husband of the other by encouraging his advances.   This amatory quadrangle is developed into a well constructed play that exhibits some
recognition of the social phenomenon that was taking
place, the rise of the middle classes.

At his death Vanbrugh left unfinished a comedy, "A
Journey to London," which might have ranked with "The
Relapse" and "The Provoked Wife."   Colley Cibber
revamped it with much added sentimentality into "The
Provoked Husband," which proved a lasting favourite.
Sentimentality, now in fashion, thus had its revenge on
Vanbrugh for the desentimentalized sequel that he had
written thirty years earlier to Cibber's first play.   "A
Journey to London" bade fair to take a pronounced
satirical tone, for according to Cibber, Arabella, the gaming wife, was to be turned out of doors by her husband.
In its unfinished form it shows a more realistic and varied
presentation of manners than its predecessors.   Act one,
describing the arrival of the Headpieces in London, is
like a chapter in Smollett or a print by Hogarth in its
realism and humour; and the picture of high life is no
less animated.   The device of repetition is again used
very effectively.   Husband and wife have a violent quarrel that is much like other such quarrels, but it gains new
effect in Lady Arabella's narration of it to her friend
Clarinda.   The passage may serve as a closing example
of Vanbrugh's humour and style.   Clarinda girlishly
envies married people who can give themselves the same
turn in conversation.   "Oh, the prettiest thing in the
world!" exclaims Arabella.   Thereupon Clarinda ventures to wonder if two people do not exhaust topics of
conversation.   Not in the least, replies the lady; we

have a few things that we can always talk about, and she proceeds to give an instance:

Lady Arabella. Oh, there's no life like it! This very day now, for example, my lord and I, after a pretty *tête-à-tête* dinner, sat down by the fireside, in an idle, indolent, picktooth way for a while, as if we had not thought of one another's being in the room. At last (stretching himself and yawning twice), my dear, says he, you came home very late last night. 'Twas but two in the morning, says I. I was in bed (yawning) by eleven, says he. So you are every night, says I. Well, says he, I am amazed how you can sit up so late. How can you be amazed, says I, at a thing that happens so often? Upon which we entered into conversation. And though this is a point has entertained us above fifty times already, we always find so many pretty new things to say upon't, that I believe in my soul it will last as long as we live.

Clarinda. But in such sort of family dialogues (though extremely well for passing of time) don't there now and then enter some little witty sort of bitterness?

Lady Arabella. O yes; which don't do amiss at all; a little something that's sharp moderates the extreme sweetness of matrimonial society, which would else perhaps be cloying. Though to tell you the truth, Clarinda, I think we squeezed a little too much lemon into it this bout; for it grew so sour at last, that I think I almost told him he was a fool; and he talked something oddly of turning me out of doors.   [II, i.

IV

The year of the publication of Collier's "Short View" was marked also by the appearance of the first play by George Farquhar, a youth of twenty who, during the few years that intervened before his early death, added new lustre to the school of Etherege and Congreve. It has been noticed that these plays of immorality and wit were sometimes written by boys barely out of college. Indeed,

the libertines who were taken as models for the stage
heroes had often begun their careers at a still earlier age.
A few weeks after his eighteenth birthday, Rochester was
imprisoned in the Tower for attempting to abduct an
heiress by force and he was then already notorious for
his debaucheries and drunkenness.   Lord Mohun, when
tried for the murder of the actor Mountford, could plead
that he was only seventeen years of age.   Both Farquhar's life and his comedies display the venturesomeness
if not the viciousness of youth.   He was born in Ireland,
left college after a year or so of attendance, became an
actor, accidentally stabbed a fellow actor on the stage,
followed his friend Wilks to London, writ a comedy, discovered Anne Oldfield, then aged sixteen, reading "The
Scornful Lady" behind the bar of the Mitre tavern, introduced her to the stage, adopted her as his mistress, won a
great success with his "Constant Couple," obtained a commission in the army, married a lady who deceived him
into believing that she was an heiress, fell into great
poverty, continued to write plays, sold his commission to
pay his debts on the promise of the Duke of Ormonde to
give him a captaincy, and upon the failure of the duke
to keep the promise died before he was thirty, leaving to
the care of Wilks "two helpless girls."   He described
himself as "habitually melancholy," but within eight years
he wrote one farce and seven light-hearted comedies.

His first play, "Love and a Bottle," is very much like
one of Mrs. Behn's.   The hero Roebuck, "an Irish gentleman of a wild and roving temper, newly come to London," is of the pattern of her popular Rover.   Lovewell
in contrast is a sober and devoted lover, like Vanbrugh's
Constant and Worthy.   Vanbrugh makes one of his rovers admit, "To be capable of loving one, doubtless is
better than to possess a thousand," and this theme is
somewhat developed in Farquhar's contrasted gallants.
But in the main the play is a collection of oft-used
intrigues.   The dark room, the garden, the duels, the girl
disguised as a page, the cast mistress who is married to

the booby, all reappear in a lively series of tricks and mistakes.

In the next play, "The Constant Couple, or A Trip to the Jubilee" (1699), Farquhar goes over to the school of Congreve and Vanbrugh, although his hero is still of the rover type. This comedy and its sequel, "Sir Harry Wildair" (1701), called for by Wilks's success in the title rôle, are defiant answers to Collier's animadversions and consciously flaunt their immorality. Sir Harry affects gaiety and freedom in his behaviour and even refuses to risk losing the pleasures of his £8,000 a year by fighting a duel. He desires to possess a thousand rather than to be capable of loving one, but is married at the end of the first play; and though in the sequel his wife is reported dead in order to give him freedom for his carefree lovemaking, she reappears before the end of the play and takes him in hand. Colonel Standard, the constant lover, fares very badly in comparison with his friend, for he is married to the jilt Lady Lurewell, who continues her wiles and extravagances in the second play. The smart dialogue, the flippant tone and the comments on the fashions of the day link these plays to the artificial comedy of manners, but they still carry a good deal of intrigue. Indeed, what Hazlitt wrote of Vanbrugh is fully as applicable to Farquhar, "his best jokes are practical devices, not epigrammatic conceits." "The Constant Couple" consists of a series of deceptions planned by Lady Lurewell, the jilt, and Vizard, a hypocritical villain. The jilt tricks all her lovers and finally traps and exposes Vizard and Smuggler, his uncle, disguised as a woman, in her own chamber. Vizard's main device is to tell Sir Harry that Angelica is a prostitute, while he tells Angelica that Sir Harry comes as an honourable suitor. The mistakes that result delighted the theater of 1700, but to us today they rather seem to justify Collier's criticism.

The next play, "The Inconstant" (1702), is a rewriting of Fletcher's "Wild Goose Chase," changing the blank verse to prose, reducing and simplifying the sub-plot, preserving Mirabel's part for Wilks, and supplying a new fifth act. This addition, said to be based on fact, sends Mirabel in pursuit of "a woman of contrivance," who is about to have him robbed and murdered when Oriana, disguised as his page, brings relief. This is a rather melodramatic and moral finish for "Fletcher's great original," as the epilogue styles it. That play had maintained its looseness and wit until the very end, and in this and other respects had been imitated by Restoration comedies of manners. But Farquhar was perhaps a little more worried by Collier than he cared to admit. His scheme seems to have been to be as naughty as you please but to bring in some moral sentiment just before the final curtain.

A similar avoidance is attempted in "The Twin Rivals" (1702), where four acts of cynicism and grossness are capped by the administration of poetic justice in the conclusion. In an ironical preface the author professes that he is profiting by Collier's advice but blames the ill success of the piece to its lack of "a beau, cully, cuckold, or coquette" and to its punishment of the "rake." The play has amusing scenes and persons, especially the midwife and the Irish servant, but these are placed in an improbable and complicated fable, the stratagems of a villainous and deformed younger brother to obtain an estate. This vivacious and bustling presentation of villainy and virtue is not convincing enough to give any significance to the author's assertion that he is now turning comedy to the exposure of vice as well as folly. "The Stage Coach," a farce in three acts, is merely an adaptation of a French piece.

In his last two plays, however, Farquhar came to his own. "The Recruiting Officer" (1706) brings new matter to enliven the comedy of manners, and combines successfully the oil and vinegar of sentiment and cynicism. It was succeeded in the next year by "The Beaux Stratagem," an even finer example of fresh invention, a delightful manner and a mastery of dramatic manipulation. But the promise that these plays offered for a notable and original development in English comedy was cut short by the death of the author during the triumphant initial run of "The Beaux Stratagem."

"The Recruiting Officer" draws upon Farquhar's own experience and takes us to Shrewsbury, where we are introduced to methods of recruiting, fully as amusing as those of Falstaff, and also to the courtships of two gentlemen with the local heiresses. A free and lively time is enjoyed by all. The two tricks that make up the plot, the disguise of Sergeant Kite as a fortune-teller, and the disguise of Silvia as a boy, are nicely varied from their usual employment so that they fit into the probabilities of their merry environment. Sergeant Kite as a conjurer prophesies the fortunes of the country bumpkins so as to induce them to take the queen's shilling with great expectations. Thomas, the smith, is persuaded that he is to be captain of the forges and he goes out to look for his fate in the hands of a tall slender gentleman with a cane; Pluck, a butcher, is promised that he shall become surgeon general and departs to look for a gentleman with the tip of his handkerchief hanging out of his right pocket. Melinda, the coquette, receives a warning from the devil and goes home to seize upon her last chance when her lover calls for tea at ten the next morning. Sylvia in disguise is no whining page but a madcap youth, and as a woman she is both warm-hearted and sensible. Though there is doubtless a good deal in the play to offend our taste, particularly in the double entendres of the scenes with Rose, the cynicism and immorality are confessedly largely affectations. Captain Plume, the hero who was supposed to represent the author, is neither rake nor rover nor cynic. "No, faith, I'm not that rake that the world imagines; I have got an air of freedom, which people mistake for lewdness in me, as they mistake formality in others for religion. The world is all a cheat, only I take mine, which is undesigned, to be more excusable than theirs, which is hypocritical. I hurt nobody but myself, and they abuse all mankind." Throughout the play the thin veneer of smartness is ever cracking to let natural instinct or romantic sentiment show through. The wit too is never studied but has that same "air of freedom" which wins our liking for Captain Plume and the redoubtable Sergeant Kite.

In "The Beaux Stratagem" we again forsake the city for the invigorating air and fresh acquaintances of a country town, this time Lichfield. Two cavaliers of broken fortunes are seeking adventures and heiresses, one as master, the other as servant. They are to change their parts from town to town, but in Lichfield Aimwell is master and Archer servant. They put up at the inn, where they are suspected of being highwaymen and where they encounter a talkative host, his charming and clever daughter Cherry, an Irish chaplain to the French officers paroled in the town, and finally the real highwaymen. In Lichfield live Lady Bountiful, a nice old lady fond of curing her neighbours of all distempers, her daughter the heiress Dorinda, her doltish son Squire Sullen, and his discontented wife. Here are some old stage friends in a new setting and some new persons, the bountiful lady, the highwaymen, the French officers and their chaplain, and Scrub, the competent man of all work: "of a Monday I drive the coach, of a Tuesday I drive the plough, on Wednesday I follow the hounds, a Thursday I dun the tenants, on Friday I go to market, on Saturday I draw warrants, and a Sunday I draw beer."

If we must have tricks in comedy, what could be fuller of comic possibilities than the main stratagem of the gallants' incognito which has also the special advantage of introducing the irresistible rover, always played by Wilks, in the disguise of a footman. One comic device leads on to another and we are hurried from incident to incident, never very improbable and always unexpectedly amusing. The complications come to a crisis in the bedroom scene, and what an innovation is there, for the wife and her lover are interrupted—not by the husband but by burglars! How vivid and how comic is the manipulation, Archer's confident protestations, Mrs. Sullen's struggles between her scruples and her inclinations, her apparent yielding. Then suddenly her cries, "Thieves, thieves, murder!" that bring first the distracted Scrub and then the real thieves. With Mrs. Sullen sentiment is really in the ascendant, as it is with Dorinda, who will have her lover, rich or poor, or with Aimwell, who at the point of success confesses his deception, "she has gained my soul, and made it honest like her own." As for Archer, he has high spirits which are often as acceptable as moral sentiments. "The devil's in the fellow," says the captivated Mrs. Sullen, "he fights, loves, and banters, all in a breath." The play has indeed an excess of high spirits in which all share. Wit and repartee shun satire and cynicism and ally themselves to good nature. All are gay and debonair, clever and witty, even the highwaymen and Scrub. No wonder they give Squire Sullen a headache, their Lichfield was no place for the spleen or the sullens.

I have tried to suggest the delight that these plays still afford to one who comes to them after reading the comedies of the preceding forty years. They maintain some of the conventions of Restoration comedy, but with what freshness of invention and spirit! They have little of the superior air of Congreve and Addison and nothing of the satire of Wycherley and Swift, and they are scarcely equalled by Steele or Fielding in their more care-free moods. Nothing so genuinely light-hearted had been seen on the stage since Fletcher, and I do not know that we have had any such contagious gaiety since. They disclose the way in which comedy might have advanced to a wider but not less entertaining view of manners and to a recovery of natural mirth without the loss of wit and raillery.

So the curtain falls on Restoration comedy. Farquhar's two plays are really after-pieces acted beyond the time the period should properly close. The actors come forward once more for the final plaudits, the men in their huge periwigs, their laces and ribbons, with their swords and their snuff-boxes, the ladies in their soaring head-dresses, their spreading hoops, their laces and ribbons, with their patches and fans. What bows and what cour-tesies! What manners! How many out of the hundreds of plays since the Restoration may we summon for the final curtain call as perfect specimens of the comedy of manners? Only half of Dryden's "Marriage à la Mode," for the rest is too romantic, and is not the "Plain Dealer" too serious and satiric, and is "The Old Bachelor" quite proficient? Etherege's "Man of Mode," Wycherley's "Country Wife," Congreve's "Double Dealer," "Love for Love," and "Way of the World," Vanbrugh's "Relapse" and "Provoked Wife," Farquhar's "Recruit-ing Officer" and "Beaux Stratagem,"—these nine take the final call. It was a strange age for which we must now turn off the lights. It had its share of war, rebellion, religion, science and misery as well as of pleasure, luxury and glory. It produced Milton's "Paradise Lost" and Bunyan's "Pilgrim's Progress," the constitution under which England is still governed, Sir Isaac Newton and the law of gravitation, and nine comedies of manners that no succeeding age has been able to equal.

CHAPTER XV

THE RETURN OF SENTIMENT, 1700-1730

THOUGH the great masters of the comedy of manners had ceased to write, their influence continued long after the death of Farquhar. Their plays were acted year after year and were constantly imitated. At the beginning of the eighteenth century the regular repertory of the theaters retained a few of Jonson's and Fletcher's comedies, and Shakespeare's "I Henry IV" and "Taming of the Shrew" but was made up in large part of Restoration plays. Out of a hundred or more nights devoted to comedy at one of the playhouses, scarcely a third would be free for new plays. Moreover, as time went on and new plays appeared to take their places in repertory, the majority were largely modelled on Congreve or Vanbrugh. Even at the mid-century a large number of the comedies acted in any season were either selected from the masters of the school of manners or from later plays written in imitation of them. But by the beginning of the century a tendency toward sentiment was already manifest, and this as well as a somewhat general improvement in decency continued to spread. The old comedy of manners and wit soon had a new rival in the drama of sensibility.

I

The real leader in the effort for morality on the stage and one of the creators of sentimental comedy was Richard Steele. The desire for a less immoral theater was indeed widespread and many writers preceded Steele in adding sentimental elements to their plays; but no other dramatist was so consistent and untiring in his devotion to

342

morality and to a virtuous view of love and marriage. All his plays are true to these principles, and the last, "The Conscious Lovers," is sentimental comedy par excellence.

When Captain Steele produced his first comedy "The Funeral" in 1701, he was a young man under thirty. He held a commission in the Coldstream Guards, was a friend of the wits, including Congreve and Vanbrugh, and had fought a duel; but he had also repented his irregular habits, astonished his old companions by publishing "The Christian Hero," a little book on applied religion, and had become an admirer of Collier and a partisan for morality on the stage. His play was consequently very different from the first plays of Congreve, Vanbrugh, Farquhar or Cibber in that it was almost free from indecency or innuendo. No earlier comedy dealing with contemporary London had been so blameless against the charge of lewdness. The atmosphere is entirely changed. Virtue is recognized and acclaimed. Not only are we asked to sympathize with the virtuous, they pay us back with moral counsel. The tendency is so apparent that Hazlitt noted, "it is almost a misnomer to call them comedies; they are rather homilies in dialogues." Lord Hardy the virtuous thus remonstrates with his livelier friend, Campley: "Ay, Tom, but methinks your head runs too much on the wedding night only, to make your happiness lasting; mine is fixed on the married state. I expect my felicity from Lady Sharlot, in her friendship, her constancy, her piety, her household cares, her maternal tenderness." Campley himself proves no less serious a lover and promptly cures his lady of coquetry. Even the songs proclaim their new attitude toward love and marriage and praise sweet reason and loyal love,

Chloe my reason moves and awe.

One happy effect of this new moral purpose is to turn the conversations and incidents from the old conventional themes to new subjects. The undertaker and his man exposing in their talk the tricks of the trade, the lawyer and his clerk, the soldiers, the widow and her lady visitors, the widow again at a toilet "talking with Tattleaid, her mouth full of pins," all these provide dialogue that is diverting and fresh. The rather far-fetched stratagems by which the vicious are exposed and the virtuous rewarded are thus ornamented by a sufficiently lively ridicule of undertakers, lawyers, and scandal-mongers as well as by the decorous courtship of the lovers. There is considerable humour and not too much rapture even in this part of the play. Lady Sharlot thus meets the blameless Hardy—"Now is the tender moment now approaching. [*Aside.*] There he is. [*They approach and salute each other trembling.*] Your lordship will please to sit. [*After a very long pause, stolen glances, and irresolute gesture.*] Your lordship, I think, has travelled those parts of Italy where the armies are." (II, iii.) The raptures are confined to the stage directions, the trembling lovers can't get away from Italy, war and travel. It is not until the last act that their sensibility finds full utterance, then it soars into blank verse as in a tragicomedy.

Steele's next play, "The Lying Lover" (1703) is more explicit in its avowal of a moral purpose. In the preface he declares "I thought, therefore, it would be an honest ambition to attempt a comedy which might be no improper entertainment in a Christian commonwealth," and in his dedication he adds "The design of it is to banish out of conversation all entertainment which does not proceed from simplicity of mind, good nature, friendship, and honour." He afterwards described in his "Apology" how the play was written in emulation of Collier's principles and "was damned for its piety." It is based on "Le Menteur" of Corneille and the first four acts give a very amusing picture of Bookwit, the engaging and inventive liar, and of the rivalry his gay advances cause between the two girls Penelope and Victoria. So far, except that there is no indecency and that Steele now and then intrudes a homily of his own, the play is of the general pattern of Restoration comedies, for Bookwit is brother to the Rover and Sir Harry Wildair and other men of mode, and Penelope is another of the many coquettes. But with the fifth act Steele departs entirely from Corneille and presents the moral lesson that preceding comedy usually lacked. Bookwit who thinks he has killed Lovemore in a duel repents and reforms. Penelope who thinks she has lost Lovemore discovers that she truly loved him, and all ends in tears, blank verse and marital felicity.

> Let all with this just maxim guide their youth,
> There is no gallantry in love but truth.

Sir A. W. Ward declared this play "the first instance of Sentimental Comedy proper." "Instead of contenting himself with making vice and folly ridiculous, the author applies himself to provoking a response from the emotion of pity." The play certainly goes beyond any preceding comedy both in its opposition to current stage morality and in its appeal to compassion. Once started in these directions both Steele and other dramatists, as we shall see, were destined to make this process of sentimentalization cover all five acts and not merely the last as here. But perhaps the essentials of sentimental comedy are sufficiently plain in this act—decency in language, praise of virtuous love and marriage, attack on a social abuse, here duelling, and an emotional appeal to compassion.

> While generous pity of a painted woe
> Makes us ourselves both more approve and know.
> > *Epilogue.*

"The Tender Husband" (1705), which owes a suggestion to Cibber's "Careless Husband" of the preceding year, is less successful as a moral document because its sentiment is involved in stage intrigue. The main tricks on which the plot rests are of the approved fashion; a husband tests his wife's fidelity by employing his mistress disguised as a man to make love to her; and a younger brother employs devices and disguises to marry the heiress, her booby suitor being left with the cast mistress. Steele is ardent enough in his sentiment and virtue, but he is happier in the innocent mirth that he devises for the lovers. Bridget Tipkin, the heiress, has sensibility, has read deeply in the romances and despises her name and longs for a Philocles or Oroondates as a lover. The crafty Clerimont, his arm in a sling, thus begins his wooing:

Cler. We enjoy here, madam, all the pretty landscapes of the country without the pains of going thither.

Niece. Art and nature are in a rivalry, or rather a confederacy, to adorn this beauteous park with all the agreeable variety of water, shade, walks, and air. What can be more charming than these flowery lawns?

Cler. Or these gloomy shades—

Niece. Or those embroidered valleys—

Cler. Or that transparent stream—

Niece. Or these bowing branches on the banks of it, that seem to admire their own beauty in the crystal mirror?

Cler. I am surprised, madam, at the delicacy of your phrase. Can such expressions come from Lombard Street?

Niece. Alas, sir! What can be expected from an innocent virgin that has been immured almost one-and-twenty years from the conversation of mankind, under the care of an Urganda of an aunt? [II, i.

He is soon proposing himself as a Musidorus to her Pamela and she begs him for an account of the battle of Blenheim where he was wounded, "Were there not a great many flights of vultures before the battle began?" Then he begs to know her name, and she is thrown into confusion. She informs him that she has discarded Bridget for Parthenissa, and he offers to change Tipkin to Clerimont. Bridget, though delighted, feels that he is progressing much more rapidly than is becoming to a hero in a romance; and the approach of her Urganda interrupts his fervours.

Niece. That had been a golden age, indeed! But see, my aunt has left her grave companion and is coming toward us—I command you to leave me.

Cler. Thus Oroondates, when Statira dismissed him her presence, threw himself at her feet, and implored permission but to live.

[*Offering to kneel.*]

Niece. And thus Statira raised him from the earth, permitting him to live and love.

[*Exit Cler.*]

Steele is really at his best in passages of this sort, entertaining without being either indecent or moralizing.

Much happened to Steele in the seventeen years that elapsed between "The Tender Husband" and his fourth and last comedy. He was married twice, the second time to "Dear Prue" of his charming letters. He had carried on his task of reforming manners in "The Tatler" and "The Spectator" and in those familiar essays had found a better medium for his humour and sentiment than comedy could afford. There he had also continued his attack on the immorality of the old comedies as well as his protests against duelling and other abuses of the age. He had been at the top of fortune and in bankruptcy. He had been prominent in politics, knighted, and made patentee of Drury Lane and written and printed a thousand pamphlets, including that dedication to his wife which ends: "I will end this without so much as mentioning your little flock, or your own amiable figure at the head of it. That I think them preferable to all other children, I know is the effect of passion and instinct. That I believe you to be the best of wives, I know proceeds from experience and reason." He had his follies and mistakes, including too much drinking and gaming as well as too much writing, but he was still the same lovable and ardent

partisan of virtue as when he penned "The Funeral."
On November 7, 1722, "The Conscious Lovers," long in
preparation and long eagerly expected, was produced
with Mrs. Oldfield, Mrs. Younger, Booth, Wilks, and
Cibber in the principal parts, and won an enormous
success.

This is sentimental comedy full-fledged and unadul-
terated and as different as possible from any Restoration
play. In the preface Steele avows the general moral purpose and the specific attack on duelling. "The chief
design of this was to be an innocent performance . . .
nor do I make any difficulty to acknowledge that the
whole was writ for the sake of the scene of the fourth act,
wherein Mr. Bevil evades the quarrel with his friend."
For guidance in this new venture Steele turned back to
what had been the primary source of the comedies that
he found immoral, to the Latin dramatists, and took the
suggestion for the plot of this triumph for virtue from
Terence's "Andria." Young Bevil, obedient to his father,
prepares to wed the heiress Lucinda, daughter of Mr.
Sealand, but he is really playing a virtuous trick on his
father because he knows Lucinda won't marry him and
he is in love with the mysterious stranger Indiana. His
friend Myrtle plots and disguises in order to marry
Lucinda, but certain appearances excite his jealousy and
he challenges Bevil, who with difficulty preserves his virtue and refuses to fight. Lucinda is also wooed by a
pompous coxcomb of an ancient family, Cimberton, who
coolly appraises her points as he would those of a filly.
In the end Indiana is discovered to be Sealand's daughter
by his first wife, the mystery is solved, the long-lost child
is restored and all ends in tears, happiness and marriage.

Virtue abounds, not a coarse or profane word is
spoken. No one is vicious, not even the pedantic Cimberton or the shallow Mrs. Sealand. Even the servants
are faithful and decorous, and Tom and Phillis make
love just as sentimentally and more prettily than their
superiors. The dialogue which describes how they fell

in love was rewritten by Steele from a description in "The Guardian":

Tom. Ah! too well I remember when, and how, and on what occasion I was first surprised. It was on the 1st of April, 1715, I came into Mr. Sealand's service; I was then a hobbledehoy, and you a pretty little tight girl, a favourite handmaid of the housekeeper. At that time we neither of us knew what was in us. I remember I was ordered to get out of the window, one pair of stairs, to rub the sashes clean; the person employed on the inner side was your charming self, whom I had never seen before.

Phil. I think I remember the silly accident. What made ye, you oaf, ready to fall down into the street?

Tom. You know not, I warrant you—you could not guess what surprised me. You took no delight when you immediately grew wanton in your conquest, and put your lips close, and breathed upon the glass, and when my lips approached, a dirty cloth you rubbed against my face, and hid your beauteous form! When I again drew near, you spit, and rubbed, and smiled at my undoing.

Phil. What silly thoughts you men have!

Tom. We were Pyramus and Thisbe—but ten times harder was my fate. Pyramus could peep only through a wall; I saw her, saw my Thisbe in all her beauty, but as much kept from her as if a hundred walls between— for there was more: there was her will against me. Would she but yet relent! O Phillis! Phillis! shorten my torment, and declare you pity me.

Phil. I believe it's very sufferable; the pain is not so exquisite but that you may bear it a little longer. [III, i.

The virtue of the chief lovers is indeed so great and so transparent that they engage our hearts as soon as they appear. "Be patient, then," says Bevil, "and hear the story of my heart." Here is no rover, no Wildfire, here no flirtation and banter, nothing of the cavalier, but here is the pattern for all the sentimentalists and romanticists to come. "I shall appear, Humphrey, more romantic in my answer than in all the rest of my story; for though I dote on her to death, and have no little reason to believe she has the same thoughts for me, yet in all my acquaintance and utmost privacies with her, I never once directly told her that I loved." His virtue never leaves him, it breathes through his soliloquies as through his conversations. The interview with Indiana, on the day that he is supposed to wed Lucinda, is a model of propriety such as we now try to indicate by the epithet "Victorian." "There is nothing unusual," argues Bevil, "in the expense the unknown benefactor is showering on her. He does not waste his money on anything else."

Bev. You may depend upon it, if you know any such man, he does not love dogs inordinately.
Ind. No, that he does not.
Bev. Nor cards, nor dice.
Ind. No.
Bev. Nor bottle companions.
Ind. No.
Bev. Nor loose women.
Ind. No, I'm sure he does not.   [II, ii.

No blank verse is needed for such a paragon, his virtues shine even in ordinary prose, but there are tears and embraces at the finish. Both lovers disdain any interest in their ladies' fortunes—and thus the last prop of Restoration comedy yields to sentimentality.

Bev. Jr. I hear your mention, sir, of fortune, with pleasure only as it may prove the means to reconcile the best of fathers to my love. Let him be provident, but let me be happy.—My ever-destined, my acknowledged wife.
Ind. Wife! Oh, my ever loved! My lord! my master!   [V, iii.

But the persons are not only in possession of the most virtuous sentiments, they distribute them freely to all. The homilies that Hazlitt mentioned abound. It would be difficult to enumerate all the moral lessons that are gently inculcated. Never strike a servant; treat a servant like a humble friend; don't sell your vote for beer; treat a musician like a gentleman; don't fight duels, etc., etc. Wit devotes itself to making sermons, and every adventure or repartee points a moral. Yet one must grant that Steele made a brave effort to turn all this morality and sentiment into situation and conversation and plot, and even retained a pleasing undertone of something faintly resembling comedy. It is to be regretted that he could not have stopped half-way, and having rid his plays of indecency and immorality, found scope for his natural bent for humour. "The Funeral" is not a great or brilliant play, but it is a delightful and promising comedy. "The Conscious Lovers" is scarcely a comedy at all. But neither Steele nor subsequent dramatists nor the general public could stop half-way, and this play was to have many successors which reveal virtue in act one and ask for it our incessant sympathy during the excitements of an improbable story, which present problems and attack evils of society with moral earnestness, which excite us to morality by both preaching and weeping, and which have little room left for fun or wit.

In connection with Steele's plays mention must be made of Addison's "Drummer," acted first in 1716 and revived and republished with a preface by Steele in 1722. Lady Truman, a widow of fourteen months, is pursued by a free-thinking fop who is frightened by another suitor Fantome, the ghostly drummer, who in turn is frightened by the husband, who was not killed in battle after all. Marital love is praised as heartily as in Steele, but virtue has the aid of satire and fun in making a pleasant entertainment. The play was long popular and seems to have gained a European renown even earlier than "The Conscious Lovers."

II

While Steele was acting as the evangelist of sentiment and morality upon the stage, Colley Cibber was giving to those same causes the less ardent but scarcely less effective service of an astute playwright who understood his audience and his actors. During the first third of the century he was the leading figure of the theater, one of the best comedians, an excellent manager, an unrivalled critic of acting, and the most successful dramatist. The record of these achievements has been preserved in his entertaining "Apology" published when he was nearly seventy. Five years later, in 1745, he again appeared as actor and author, playing Pandulph in his own version of Shakespeare's "King John." He died in 1757 at the age of eighty-six. He had obtained employment as an actor before he was twenty, married when he was twenty-two, and in order to help support his family, taken to writing plays before he was twenty-five. "It may be observable too," he writes in the "Apology," "that my muse and my spouse were equally prolific; that the one was seldom the mother of a child, but in the same year the other made me the father of a play. I think we had a dozen of each sort between us, of both which kinds some died in their infancy, and near an equal number of each were alive when I quitted the theater." He was in fact the father by creation or adoption of some twenty-five theatrical pieces including tragedies, ballad operas, pastorals, and one masque. A dozen of these were comedies.

We have already noted that his first play "Love's Last Shift" (1696), which impelled Vanbrugh to write "The Relapse" as a sequel, had a sentimental fifth act. Amanda, who has been deserted for ten years by her rakish husband and is not recognized by him, wins him back as a lover. When she makes herself known he decides to return to her. "Oh! why have I so long been blind to the perfections of thy mind and person? Not knowing thee a wife, I found thee charming beyond the wishes of luxuriant love. Is it then a name, a word, shall rob thee of thy worth?" The piece may not offer a larger or sincerer appeal to sentiment than others of the later years of the seventeenth century but it is theatrically more effective, for it combines the attractiveness of a licentious action and a sentimental conclusion. Not much can be said for the morality of the first four acts or for the trick by which the wife wins back the husband, but the moral is fervently proclaimed at the end: "The greatest happiness we can hope on earth,

> And sure the nearest to the joys above,
> Is the chaste rapture of a virtuous love."

The epilogue, however, adds this flippant comment:

> He's lewd for above four acts, gentlemen,
> For faith he knew, when once he'd chang'd his fortune,
> And reform'd his vice, 'twas time—to drop the curtain.

His next comedy "Woman's Wit, or the Lady in Fashion" (1697), was a failure, but it is interesting as illustrating how closely Cibber fitted his plays to his actors. In the preface he explains that he wrote the first two acts during a temporary secession to the Lincoln's Inn Fields, where Mrs. Barry and Mrs. Bracegirdle were playing; the last three acts were designed for the less experienced actors of the Theatre Royal, but with a low comedy part added for Doggett. It afterwards served as basis for a farce "The School-Boy." In 1700 came his alteration of "Richard III," which was to hold the stage until 1821.

"Love Makes the Man or the Fop's Fortune" (1700), is a skilful combination of two plays by Fletcher. The first two acts are taken from the first three acts of "The Elder Brother" and the last three acts from the last four of "The Custom of the Country." The material retained is that of Fletcherian romance showing the course of true love beset by adventures, dangers, and surprises, rather after the fashion of tragicomedy than of the comedy of intrigue. Cibber, however, has retained the striking and surprising situations and yet tamed them to the Restoration manner, partly by changing Fletcher's verse to prose and partly by balancing the romantic elder brother by a pert coxcomb of a younger brother, played by Cibber himself. He has also omitted the ribaldry of the "Custom of the Country," which was too strong even for Dryden, and added some sentimental rhetoric. Fletcher converts his amorous and wicked lady very suddenly but he does not make her mealy-mouthed. When she decides to resign the hero to his true love, she merely says:

> It is in vain
> To strive with destiny; here my dotage ends.—

Cibber's lady:—"Release the lady—go. And now farewell my follies and my mistaken love; for I confess the fair example of your mutual faith, your tenderness, humility and tears have quite subdu'd my soul; at once have conquer'd and reform'd me: O! you have given me such an image of the contentful peace, th' unshaken quiet"— etc. with many more Oh's and pardons and thanks.

Two years later, 1702, came another quasi-romantic comedy, "She Would and She Would Not, or the Kind Imposter," based on Learned's "Counterfeits" (1678), in turn drawn from a Spanish original. Hypolita a madcap, though really in love with Don Philip, repulses him, whereupon he posts off to Madrid to marry the unknown Rosara, whereupon Hypolita dresses as a man and posts after him determined first to win his mistress and then to marry him. She manages to carry out both purposes with the assistance of the rascal servant Trappanti, but not without many difficulties partly caused by Rosara's testy old father and by her lover Octavio. Cibber has again subdued romantic material to the requirements of his theater. As the prologue boasts, he has observed the unities, confined the wit to the plot, completed the exposition in the first act, and developed a lively and closely integrated action. The play long remained a favourite and was occasionally revived throughout the nineteenth century.

His next play, "The Careless Husband," 1704, was

original and in several ways an innovation. The scene is Windsor, the action takes place within a single day, there are only seven persons in the cast, three men and four women. Their parts are the usual ones in the comedy of manners: Lord Morelove, in love with the coquette; Lord Foppington, a coxcomb planning to win the coquette; Sir Charles Easy, unfaithful to his wife with both her woman Mrs. Edging and with Lady Graveairs; Lady Betty Modish, the coquette; Lady Easy, the wronged wife; Lady Graveairs, the mistress; Mrs. Edging, the presuming servant. The action as usual is largely flirtation but it results in the favour of virtue. Lady Easy by her tenderness and good sense wins back her husband to a repentant fidelity; Lady Betty is brought to repent of her coquetry and to reward her patient and loyal lover with marriage.

Cibber had admitted the truth of Congreve's stricture on his first play that it "had only in it a great many things that were like wit, that were in reality not wit"; but there is no great improvement here. The conversation is pleasant and well-bred rather than sparkling. The flirtation of Lady Betty and Lord Foppington brought together Mrs. Oldfield and Cibber, whose mutual efforts were destined to delight the theater for thirty years to come. The play does not bring to the comedy of manners fresh wit and dramatic invention as do the plays of Vanbrugh, or new material and spirit as do those of Farquhar; its departure from the conventions of the species are to be found in its sentimental additions. These comprise, besides the virtuous ending, the well drawn figure of Lady Easy. Though a patient Griselda in her long suffering, she is good-humoured rather than tearful, and she holds our sympathy from the beginning without ever forcing an appeal to our pity. However, one famous scene is of a tenderness hitherto unknown in domestic comedy. She discovers Mrs. Edging and her husband together, sleeping in armchairs, and fearing her husband may catch cold without his periwig, places her steinkirk over his unprotected head. When he awakes and discovers this evidence of her kindness he at once repents and reforms. The reformations of the last act are accompanied by a large amount of moral lecturing. The theses established inculcate proper sentiments toward love and marriage, though I am afraid they emphasize especially the desirability of sweetness and submission on the part of women. At all events, there is more sensibility here than in any preceding comedy unless it be Steele's "Lying Lover," acted the previous year; and like that play, "The Careless Husband" marks a definite response to Collier's demand for morality and an advance toward the establishment of a new species, sentimental comedy.

The most novel thing about the play, however, seems to me its freedom from tricks. The only trick employed is the "design" by which, because of Morelove's attentions to Lady Graveairs, Sir Charles Easy pretends to Lady Betty to believe that she has ruthlessly thrown over her lover, so the coquette is piqued into repentance. This design is given the usual paraphernalia of a stage trick, the preliminary conspiracy and the final revelation, but it is scarcely a trick at all and the same results might have been accomplished without any plotting. The negligibility of this element of deception helps to bring the play very close to a modern drama in both materials and methods. The opening act discloses a situation which presents certain social problems. The remaining acts are devoted to conversation which discusses those problems as exemplified in the persons of the piece and develops theses which are proclaimed both in incidental aphorisms and in prolonged lectures. If we allow for the differences in both manners and sentiments, Cibber is pretty close to a nineteenth century thesis play.

Of the next four comedies only one offers any sentimentality or any resemblance to a thesis play. The other three are adaptations and belong to the school of manners and rely a good deal on intrigue. "The Comical

Lovers or Marriage à la Mode" (1707) combines the comic portions of Dryden's "Secret Love" and "Marriage à la Mode" and was often played under the latter title. This double dose of flirtation and affectation brought together two rival "impertinents," Mrs. Bracegirdle as Melantha and Mrs. Oldfield as Florimel, and presumably helped to determine the famous contest of this season which resulted in Mrs. Oldfield's victory and Mrs. Bracegirdle's retirement. "The Double Gallant or The Sick Lady's Cure" (1707) takes its title and part of its plot from Thomas Corneille's "Le Galant Double" and makes up the rest of its complicated intrigue from three plays that had recently failed, "Love at a Venture" by Mrs. Centlivre, "The Reformed Wife" and "The Ladies' Visiting Day" by Burnaby. The result is again a superabundance of intrigue, flirtation and affectation with scarce a trace of sentiment. One scene, considerably improved on Burnaby, is worthy of Wycherley or Vanbrugh. Lady Sadlife is expecting a letter from Atall, the rover of the play, and when this letter is intercepted by her husband, Sir Solomon, she is overcome with fear. Sir Solomon waxes ferocious as he reads the epistle; but the gallant has addressed it to Mrs. Wishwell, my Lady Sadlife's woman, so Sir Solomon begins to think he has been unjust to his weeping wife and she quickly recovers her countenance.

Sir Sol. Come! come! dry thy tears, it shall be so no more—but, hark ye! I have made a discovery here—your Wishwell I'm afraid is a slut—she has an intrigue.
Lady Sad. An intrigue! heavens, in our family!
[III, iii.

Wishwell now appears and, smoking the situation, claims the letter as from her intended husband and asks Lady Sadlife to write a reply. So, with suggestions from her husband and her servant, the lady pens a note making an assignation with her own lover. But the other scenes fall considerably below this in wit and ingenuity. The

rifling of four plays only succeeded in assembling about
the usual sort of humours and intrigues; and these Cibber
has freshened a little to show the manners current in the
reign of great Anna.   The play had a long popularity,
but "The Rival Fools," a somewhat similar revision of
Fletcher's "Wit as Several Weapons" proved a failure.

In "The Lady's Last Stake, or The Wife's Resentment" (1707) Cibber again returned to sentiment and a
thesis.   In the dedication he declares "A play without a
just moral is a poor and trivial undertaking," and the
prologue explains that the piece is intended as a pendant
to "The Careless Husband," presenting a jealous and
angry wife who is finally persuaded to try tenderness and
good humour, and also attacking the fashionable vice of
gaming.   There are only seven persons, apart from servants, to carry on the double plot.   Lord and Lady Wronglove are the erring husband and the jealous wife.   Lord
George Brilliant, played by Cibber, is the profligate really
in love with the vivacious Mrs. Conquest, played by Mrs.
Oldfield, but seeking an amour with Lady Gentle by
involving her in gaming debts.   Sir Friendly Moral is
the lecturer on virtue who reconciles the married couple
and supports Mrs. Conquest in her devices to win the
profligate.   Miss Notable is an amorous tell-tale who
plays tricks on every one and does all she can to thwart
the moral stratagems.   The play has, indeed, an abundance of tricks.   Mrs. Conquest, disguised as her twin
brother, challenges Lord George, pretends to be wounded
while rescuing him, and then wins his submission and
repandance. Lord George, through a confederate, cheats
Lady Gentle of £2000 at the card table and she, though
of "impregnable virtue," risks a cast, the money against
her permission for him to hope.   She loses, but the money
is provided, and when he attempts to force her, Mrs.
Conquest's twin brother appears.   The jealous wife dis-
dains the gentleness of Lady Easy, follows her husband
in a coach, makes herself generally disagreeable, and is
at the point of separating from him when she is brought

back to sweetness and submission through the intervention of Sir Friendly Moral.

It will be observed that the theses are addressed mainly to the ladies, enjoining them to be tender towards their husbands and not to gamble; but the play, like "The Careless Husband," preaches sincerity rather than affectation in courtship, and loyalty after marriage. It may also be observed that these conversions and repentances afford an actor a fine chance. Mrs. Oldfield could flirt recklessly for four acts and then show herself in a new rôle, melting and repentant; the rake and the tender husband were played by the same actor; the jealous shrew and the clinging vine were in the same part. Naturally there was a tendency to exaggerate these opposite aspects, and the sentimental displays soon surpassed in artificiality anything that wit or immorality could devise. When compared with the usual discourse of one of the persons, the style of his sentimental flight becomes incredible.

Lord Wronglove is reproached by Sir Friendly Moral with the fact that he sleeps in a separate bed from his wife, and he explains the origin of this domestic problem in the following very natural as well as humorous discourse.

Lord Wrong. I could never sleep with her—For tho' she loves late hours, yet when she has seen me gape for bed, like a waiter at the Groom-porter's in a morning, she wou'd still reserve to herself the tedious decorum of being first solicited for her company; so that she usually contriv'd to let me be three-quarter asleep, before she wou'd do me the honour to disturb me. Then, before this, I was seldom less than two nights in four, but in the very middle of my first comfortable nap, I was awakened with the alarm of tingle, tingle, for a quarter of an hour together, that you'd swear she wanted a doctor or a midwife; and by-and-bye down comes Mademoiselle with a single under-petticoat in one hand, and rubbing her eyes with t'other; and then, after about half an hour's weighty arguments on both sides, poor Mademoiselle is guilty of not having pull'd the sheet smooth at her feet, by which unpardonable neglect, her ladyship's little toe had lain at least two hours on the rack of a wrinkle, that had almost put her into a fever—— This when I civilly complain'd of, she said she must either be easy in the bed, or go out of it—— I told her, that was exactly my case; so I very fairly stepp'd into the next room, where I have ever since slept most profoundly, without so much as once dreaming of her.   [IV, i.

But when he yields to a sentimental reconciliation his style suddenly soars.

Lord Wrong. Now I should blush ever to have deserv'd these just reproachful tears; but when I think they spring from the dissolving rock of secret love, I triumph in the thought; and in this wild irruption of its joy, my parching heart cou'd drink the cordial dew.

Lady Wrong. What means this soft effusion in my breast? An aching tenderness ne'er felt before!

Lord Wrong. I cannot bear that melting eloquence of eyes. Yet nearer, closer to my heart, and live forever there—Thus blending our dissolving souls in dumb unutterable softness.   [V, i.

There is much more, but perhaps this is enough to indicate that sentimentality was acquiring a fixed style of speech that forbade individuality of character, humour, or naturalness.

By this time Anne had been on the throne for five years and the Augustan age of English literature was well under way. The signs of a changing era are already apparent in Cibber's comedies—a chastening of conversation and manners, the increased prominence of women's fashions, the growing self-consciousness of society in place of Restoration carelessness, and the appearance of sentiment and morality rather than wit as arbiters of taste. The next decade was to see further progress in all these

changes, and a marked increase of sentimentality in literature. Rowe's "Jane Shore" was to join his "Fair Penitent" in stressing the appeal of tragedy to pity. "The
Tatler" and "The Spectator" were to lead in the work of
softening manners and cajoling the fair sex into propriety,
and Shaftesbury's "Characteristics," asserting the power
of natural virtue or "the moral sense," was to afford a
philosophical basis for the sentimentalists everywhere in
Europe. But it was also the era of Swift, Defoe and
Mandeville, and the cause of sentimentality advanced
very slowly on the stage. Only two comedies show
marked traces of it during the fifteen years from "The
Lady's Last Stake" to Steele's "Conscious Lovers"—
Addison's "Drummer" (1716), and Cibber's "Non-
Juror" (1717).

"The Non-Juror" is audaciously partisan. Molière's
Tartuffe is made over into Doctor Wolf, a Jesuit priest
posing as an English non-juror and seeking to debauch
the principles and the wife of Sir John Woodvil. Against
such hypocritical villainy, virtue naturally takes a strong
stand; and the play at once resolves itself into a contest
in intrigue between the two sides. The virtuous are:—
Lady Woodvil, her daughter Maria a coquette, who soon
shows she has both a heart and a head, young Woodvil,
Mr. Heartly, suitor to Maria and an indefatigable moralist, and Charles, assistant to Dr. Wolf but soon converted. The appeal to sensibility is made chiefly in the
penitent Charles who is a forlorn admirer of Maria and
is finally restored to his long-lost father; but virtue is
ever exalted and vice denounced. The excellent articulation of the scenes, the few characters, the pronounced
alignment of our sympathies, and the admirable part for
Mrs. Oldfield, are Cibber's contributions, and these along
with Molière's hypocrite make a play that was not
unworthy of the huge success assured to it by its political
appeal.

The Tories did not dare to attack "The Non-Juror"
but they took their revenge on Cibber's Whigism by mak-

ing a faction against other of his plays, and possibly their opposition may account for the failure of "The Refusal" (1721), an amusing comedy of manners, owing hints to Molière's "Les Femmes Savantes." It was not until 1728 that he had another theatrical success, and then in the most "sentimental" of his comedies, "The Provoked Husband."

Though this retains the persons and the exposition of Vanbrugh's unfinished play, both its outcome and its entire spirit are changed from the original. The low comedy provided in abundance by the London adventures of the Wrongheads is retained, contrary to the usual practice in Cibber's more genteel efforts, but it is kept down in quantity and softened in quality. In the main action the usual elements of intrigue and flirtation are eliminated. The amusing and witty quarrel between Lord Townly and his pleasure loving wife, as Vanbrugh wrote it, now takes from the start a serious tone and soon becomes an elaborate debate between virtue and vice that ends, after much eloquence, in tears and tenderness. Virtue is further represented by Lady Grace, a pattern of female domesticity, who is justly admired by Mr. Manly, the benevolent moralist, who devotes some of his virtue to setting to right the Wrongheads as well as the Townlys. It must be added that the sentimental style is not so farfetched as in the "Lady's Last Stake" and that enough of the comic force of Vanbrugh's situations is retained to relieve the heaviness of the moral eloquence. And the play has no long-lost child or parent.

The play gained a great success and continued in repertory for nearly a century. It goes somewhat further than any preceding comedy, except Steele's "Conscious Lovers," in exalting virtue and sentiment and the blessedness of home. Domestic problems are proposed and debated at great length, and if the solutions proposed are against the independence and extravagance of women, they show a genuine and not merely rhetorical regard for love, marriage and family.   The moral against gaming and extravagance is made all the plainer in that no one is seeking to tamper with Lady Townly's virtue, and the usual theatrical motive of sex jealousy does not appear.   Virtue is represented by persons who excite our sympathy from the start and who never deviate from the commands of a lofty and delicate morality.   Perhaps Cibber, like Steele, is here too anxious to personify the virtues, but his Manly and Lady Grace have a temperance even in their sensibility.

Cibber's plays illustrate and in fact largely represent the course of comedy in the first thirty years of the century.   In comparison with those of the preceding period they are notably clean in language and decent in morals. They are not original in invention, in fact many of them made over the work of others, of Molière, Fletcher, and Dryden, or of contemporaries such as Burnaby.   The majority are not sentimental, "The Careless Husband" and "The Lady's Last Stake" being the only plays markedly so before "The Provoked Husband."   Fletcherian romance and Spanish intrigue appear as well as comedies of manners in the style of Congreve and Vanbrugh. In fact, Cibber is in the main a deviser of plays of intrigue, exhibiting the manners of his day and enlivened by wit.   Where he departs from this Congrevian formula is not only in greater decency of language and in a tempering of manners to suit the changing age, but also in further steps of refinement,—reduction or removal of low comedy, simplification of plot, and the added interest of social problems.   Occasionally his plays become very modern in their exemplification of the dramatic effectiveness of a debate over a thesis.   That these theses should ally themselves with sentimentality was perhaps unfortunate for comedy but was inevitable in that age.   The change from "The Provoked Husband" as Vanbrugh conceived it to the play as Cibber finished it, indicates the victory for sentiment.

III

It will be remembered that the first seven years of the century brought a number of notable additions to the repertory of the theaters, including Farquhar's brilliant comedies of manners and the essays of Cibber and Steele in sentimentalism. For the next twenty years or so, not only were there few sentimental plays but few comedies of any kind of sufficient merit to secure a place in the regular offerings of the companies. There was no well contested struggle between the cohorts of sentiment and of wit. The triumphs of sensibility were won by two or three plays; the followers of wit succeeded only in farce and intrigue. Certain hangers-on of the theater, Christopher Bullock, Charles Johnson, and Taverner, showed some skill in making over old plays; and Charles Shadwell wrote one very popular play with "humours" that might have delighted his father, "The Fair Quaker of Deal or The Humours of the Army" (1710). "Three Hours After Marriage," a gross and stupid farce written by Gay, Pope and Arbuthnot, was damned, but possibly rather because of its personal satire than because of its coarseness. Gay's somewhat novel "What d'ye Call It" (1715) succeeded but it is too uncertain and farcical to count for much. Theatrical taste was probably turning towards decorum and virtue, but it does not seem to have been very hospitable to new comedies. The new theater in Lincoln's Inn Fields under the management of John Rich prospered by producing pantomimes in which he (Lun) played the part of harlequin. At Drury Lane, too, there were pantomimic and operatic performances, and the offering of the regular company was drawn largely from repertory, and the public taste for high comedy was sufficiently supplied by Restoration and Elizabethan favourites. Farces, both as afterpieces and as full evening entertainments, helped to meet the demand for laughter and still further reduced the opportunity for new plays. Only two or three new comedies were acted each season, and usually no one of these would establish itself as a lasting success. The twenty-three years from 1707 to 1730 produced fewer comedies of real merit or continued popularity than had the first seven years of the century.

The only author who in these later years wrote several plays to rival in success "The Non-Juror," "The Provoked Husband" and "The Conscious Lovers" was Mrs. Centlivre. Her plays may be taken as representing the continuation of the Restoration methods, with even fewer traces of sentimentalism than attach themselves to the contemporary plays of intrigue by Bullock, Johnson and Taverner.

Mrs. Centlivre's first play, a tragedy, was acted in 1700 when she was about twenty-three years of age. She is supposed to have had various amatory adventures before that date, including one escapade when, dressed as a boy, she lived for a time at Cambridge under the protection of Anthony Hammond. She may have been married to an officer Carroll, the name which she uses in some of her earlier publications. Evidently she took to writing for the theater and acting in provincial companies in order to earn her living. About 1706 she married Mr. Joseph Centlivre, cook to Queen Anne and George I. She continued to write after her marriage, producing some eighteen comedies or farces before her death in 1723. Her work in many respects resembles that of Mrs. Behn; she is nearly as immoral, even less sentimental, and even more skilful in theatrical contrivance. Few of her plays are wholly original, but all owe something to her ingenuity, and two proved their excellence by their long survivals.

Her first comedy, "The Beau's Duel" (1702), is after the usual patttern, abounding in intrigue, fluent but without much wit or style. The second, "The Stolen Heiress," is adapted from a Spanish source; and the third, "Love's Contrivance or Le Medecin Malgre Lui" from Molière. The next, "The Gamester" (1705), had a great success.

Based on Regnard's "Le Joueur," it combined lively intrigue with an exposure of the evils of gambling and with some moralizing and sentimental touches not found in the original. "Love at a Venture," drawn from T. Corneille's "Le Galant Double," apparently was acted only in the provinces but furnished Cibber with most of the plot for his popular "Double Gallant." "The Bassett Table" is another exposure of the evils of gambling, and contains a good many amusing passages, especially those describing the young girl who is of a scientific turn. When her lover comes a-wooing, she is discovered "with books upon a table, a microscope, putting a fish upon it, several animals lying by." She entertains her lover with views in the microscope of *Lumbricus Laetus* and other wonders, but empties the tub of her precious fishes and hides him under it when they are surprised by the entry of her father. Lady Reveller, who keeps the bassett table, is cured of her gaming and coquetry and marries her sober and deserving lover. The conversion, however, is not produced after the sentimental fashion but by means of a trick. In connivance with her lover, his friend makes love to her, gets her into a room with him and locks the door; she resists him and her cries bring the waiting hero to her succour. "The Platonick Lady" was the author's seventh comedy of intrigue before 1707.

In 1709 came "The Busy Body," Mrs. Centlivre's greatest success. The many stratagems by which two gallants plan to marry two heiresses are frustrated by the mistakes of the well-intentioned but blundering Marplot. He is an improvement on Dryden's Marall because his self-sufficiency and prying lead him to mistakes in action as well as in speech. He is not merely an amusing character, he is a constant participator in the plot, upsetting the best-laid plans of the lovers. Mrs. Centlivre seems to have learned from her study of Molière and other French dramatists how to keep farcical situations a little above the range of mere farce by skilfully repeating and varying the performances of a central character.

Marplot never stops meddling, and, as Hazlitt says, he "whiffles about the stage with considerable volubility." In addition to his misdeeds there are other amusing contrivances, counterplots, and deliverances, but the action is simple and well integrated, to a degree unusual in English comedy.

Several comedies intervened before the production of her second great success "The Wonder: A Woman Keeps a Secret" (1714). The plot in its main outline is a familiar one and presumably from a Spanish source. Violante conceals Isabella in her own room and keeps the secret although Don Felix, her lover, becomes furiously jealous, believing that she is hiding a man. Isabella is the sister of Felix and in love with her rescuer Colonel Briton, a stranger in Lisbon. The complications are of a quasi-romantic kind, resting on improbable situations and coincidences as well as on stratagems, and they involve a most ingenious use of the postponed or potential discovery.

In this device our attention is fixed on a door—or some other object—which conceals something or somebody whose discovery will cause a great commotion. We are always expecting that the door will be opened, the deception discovered, and the fat thrown on the fire; but when our anticipations are raised to the bursting point, the door is only half opened and the discovery is avoided. But the door is still there and the disclosure is only postponed, and we again begin to rise on tiptoe. The theatrical effectiveness of the device appears to rest on the theory that anticipation is usually more delightful than realization.

Once in the play the chambermaid is hid in the clothes press, and as various persons come and go we are in continued suspense lest she be discovered at the wrong moment. But the most remarkable instance is in Act IV. Violante, on Isabella's persuasion, secretly receives Colonel Briton and by their conversation becomes convinced that he is truly in love with Isabella and makes appointments for their clandestine marriage. Before the colonel has a chance to find where he is or who is speaking or whether or not it is all a fairy tale, the chambermaid enters and whispers to Violante that her lover Felix is crossing the garden. Violante tells the colonel that her father is coming and thrusts him into her bed-chamber. Behind its closed door, he now becomes the potential or threatening discovery. Felix is humble and repentant for past jealousy; Violante cold at first and then forgiving. Enter the chambermaid again to announce that now Violante's father is really coming up the back stairs and in a temper. Felix starts to hide in the bed-chamber and gets the door partly opened before the women stop him —and the audience is deprived of the expected disclosure. Felix is provided with a riding-hood and passed off on the father as the maid's old mother, but this takes time and many inventions, and meanwhile the half-opened door is still threatening. Violante quiets her father, who has found the back door opened and has locked it, cutting off Felix's escape; and promising to enter a nunnery as he wishes, she leaves the stage with him. The coast is now clear, and the maid calls the colonel out and directs him how to escape by the roof, and the audience is again deprived of the expected discovery and encounter. But now re-enter at one door Felix, and at another door Violante. She does not see him and runs at once to the door of the chamber where she supposes the colonel still is, calling, "Sir, sir, you may appear." Felix, wild with jealousy, draws his sword, and pushes by her into the chamber. Violante is in despair, but her maid returns with the news that the colonel has escaped. Violante now takes a high tone with the bewildered Felix, assuring him that she has played a trick on him to expose his jealousy, and the curtain falls on a humbled and repentant lover.

In the next act, however, when Felix and the colonel are introduced in the house of their friend Frederick, the colonel innocently recounts his strange adventures leading to his concealment in the bedroom, in such a way that Felix's jealousy is excited anew and the complications begin again. The play. is, indeed, a masterpiece of intrigue. There is unity in spite of the rapidly shifting action, for attention is focused on the room where Isabella is hiding, on the secret which Violante is keeping, and on the confusion of Don Felix—and the three are really one. Though little effort is made at characterization, the changes in temper of Violante and Felix make excellent acting parts. Mrs. Oldfield was triumphant in one, and Garrick was so fond of the other that he chose it for his last appearance on the stage.

Several farces and one tragedy intervened before another notable success, "A Bold Stroke for a Wife," (1718). The play is original and is developed from a situation which, while extravagant in the English rather than simple in the French manner, gives ample chance for caricature and intrigue. Mrs. Lovely, with a fortune of thirty thousand pounds, is the ward of four guardians, the consent of all of whom must be obtained before she can be married. The four are an old beau, a silly virtuoso, a 'change broker, and a Quaker hosier, and afford opportunity for ridicule of their different eccentricities. Colonel Fainwell, the lover, is hard put to it in many disguises before he tricks all the guardians into consent and carries off the heiress.

Finally, in 1622, came "The Artifice," a failure on the stage but one of the most amusing of her plays and decidedly in the Restoration manner. Here is a full-fledged comedy with all sorts of stratagems, discoveries, interruptions, escapes, with plenty of fun while it is going, and no moral lectures; but the play seems to have failed even with Mrs. Oldfield playing the naughty Mrs. Watchit. Perhaps it was too spicy for the theater which the next month gave a great triumph to "The Conscious Lovers."

Mrs. Centlivre was the last able and loyal maintainer of the Restoration tradition. She lacked style but she had enough characterization, fluency, and observation of manners to give vivacity to her ingeniously contrived plots. One must own a lively admiration for this wife of the royal cook who could devise so skilfully and write so fluently. No woman in the two centuries since her time has contributed as much as she to the English comic stage, and no one, man or woman, has surpassed her in the comedy of intrigue.

IV

The year 1728, which witnessed the success of Cibber's "Provoked Husband," saw the still greater success of Gay's "Beggar's Opera," and the rather timorous début amid these triumphs of the first comedy of a great humorist, Henry Fielding. "The Beggar's Opera" initiated an immense vogue for comic or ballad operas, and Fielding's humour was to affect the theatrical taste through his farces and burlesques rather than through his comedies. The year of 1728 may be remembered not only as marking a victory for sentimental comedy but also as introducing these new recruits to the irregular drama which was destined to drive comedy proper out of the theaters. Henceforth for nearly forty years there are no comedies of sentiment comparable to those of Steele, no comedies of manners comparable to those of Vanbrugh or Farquhar, no comedies of intrigue comparable to those of Mrs. Centlivre, and no writer as skilful in any one of the three as was Cibber. Ballad operas, farces, burlesques and pantomimes engage the talents of the new writers, and the attempts to produce genuine comedies meet with little public approval except in a few sporadic instances. In the next chapter I shall consider these somewhat illegitimate forms of comic drama that flourished during the middle third of the century, but here I wish to examine a brief activity in comedy that manifested itself from 1728 to the licensing act in 1737, synchronizing with Fielding's dramatic career. Most of the few comedies that appeared, including some of Fielding's, paid their respects to virtue and contained sentimental passages. John Kelly's "Married Philoso-

pher" (1732), was a translation of one of the earliest of
French sentimental plays, "Le Philosophe marié," by
Destouches. Theophilus Cibber's "Lover" (1731), made
much of a hypocritical villain, guardian, seducer and rob-
ber. Boadens, Miller, and Popple mixed sentimentality
and immorality, but without achieving anything successful
on the stage or influential upon the types of comedy. No
doubt the theaters demanded morality and sentiment to
a larger degree than before, but they were influenced by
the great success of Lillo's tragedies and by the general
course of the times rather than by any new initiative in
comedy. That lack of initiative and the state of the
theaters may be made sufficiently apparent by a brief
review of Fielding's career and without further consideration of his immediate contemporaries.

Fielding's first play, "Love in Several Masques," produced before he was twenty-one, is a commonplace affair,
professedly modelled after Congreve and Wycherley but
really subdued to the Cibberian manner. The country
squire has some individuality, but the fop, the jealous
lover, the blunt honest suitor, the coquette who is converted, and the amorous old lady who is repulsive, are
trite enough. Two years later, in January, 1730, his
"Temple Beau" was produced with fair success by the
second rate company in Goodman's Fields. Wilding, the
beau, is of the type of Mrs. Behn's rover, and makes
love to everyone, but in the end aids his friends Veromil
and Valentine in their serious love affairs. This scheme
manifestly has merits for a comedy of intrigue and it
was later used by Hoadly in his "Suspicious Husband"
with much greater effectiveness than Fielding achieved.
Fielding's characterization and wit run off into boisterous
fun, as in the scenes where Lady Pedant, the coquette,
and her sister Lady Gravely, the prude, seek the favours
of Wilding. If those passages were too indelicate for
the taste of the day, they were interspersed with scenes
of the most approved style of sentimentality, including
an imitation of the famous duel scene in "The Conscious

Lovers." The play has little unity in tone or definiteness in plan or purpose.

Within a few months of the appearance of "The Temple Beau," Fielding's burlesques "The Author's Farce" and "Tom Thumb" were crowding the little theater in the Haymarket. Of these and other burlesques and operas which he wrote, something will be said later. Their great success doubtless encouraged him to bring out at the Haymarket later in the season another full-fledged comedy, "Rape upon Rape, or the Justice Caught in his own Trap," later renamed "The Coffee-House Politician." There is almost no sentimentality but a good deal of comic force in this comedy, in which the humour has some of the flavour of the later novels. Two characters, the dishonest justice and the coffee-house politician, are elaborated with a richness of detail and a vigour of satire scarcely found on the stage since Shadwell's imitations of Ben Jonson. But the humour and satire are confused by a superabundance of intrigue. The two young ladies while adventuring get their gallants exchanged, and the two gentlemen are arrested for rape and carried to jail. Then follow tricks to deceive the dishonest and lustful Justice Squeezum, his amorous wife and the chatterbox politician. A constable, a jailor, and others supply the low comedy, but most of the humour is broad rather than high. Such extravagances of plot and exuberances of fun, though suitable to farce and burlesque, were no longer welcomed in a five-act comedy.

The next season Fielding was busy re-writing and enlarging "Tom Thumb" and in adding new pieces for the Haymarket until that playhouse was closed by the government. The following season, 1731-1732, he went over to Drury Lane, bringing out four short pieces and one full-fledged comedy within a few months. The comedy, "The Modern Husband," met with opposition but in revised form was acted fifteen times, though never again revived. It is Fielding's most ambitious attempt in the drama, a manifestly sincere but futile effort to revive satirical comedy. There are eight persons representing three households in high life, Mr. and Mrs. Modern, who present the problem; Mr. and Mrs. Bellamant, who are the sentimental pair, and their daughter Emilia and their son, Captain Bellamant; Lord Richly, his nephew Gaywit and his ward, the coquette, Lady Charlotte. The problem is the husband who makes financial profit out of his wife's unfaithfulness. The cold-blooded bargaining of Mr. and Mrs. Modern could scarcely be made plausible on the stage, still less could it be made amusing. The presentation of manners which delighted Lady Mary Wortley Montagu by its verisimilitude when she read the manuscript, aroused quite properly the hisses of the audience at Drury Lane.

During the next two seasons Fielding brought out two translations that long held a place on the stage. "The Miser," an excellent adaptation of Molière's "L'Avare," and "The Intriguing Chambermaid," a two-act farce from Regnard. These circumstances illustrate the lack of welcome for new comedies. "The Miser" was the only new comedy performed in London in 1732-3, and none was given at Drury Lane in 1733-4. The following season Fielding's "The Universal Gallant" was vigorously damned. The chief scene in the play suggests again Fielding's fondness for farcical extravagance and his failure to mark any line between what was funny on the stage and in a novel. The jealous husband has forged a letter from his wife making an assignation with a worthless fop. They meet in a darkened room, the husband on the couch impersonating his wife. All this was common farce, but what is intended to be funny is that the fop does not respond to the supposed lady's solicitations and is doing his best to escape when they are interrupted and discovered. Something of this sort might do in "Joseph Andrews" but how could it be acted with plausibility? But the play is dull as well as dirty and deserved the damning which grieved and surprised its author.

For two seasons at the Haymarket Fielding won success with "Pasquin" and other pieces of a satirical nature until the licensing of 1737 closed the theater, and he turned to the study of law. Several years later he had a chance to prepare a comedy for Garrick. At first Fielding proposed an old piece re-written. The manuscript was later lost, recovered long after Fielding's death, retouched by Garrick and Sheridan and produced by the latter with prologue and epilogue by the former, November 30, 1778, as "The Fathers, or the Good-Natured Man." Based like Shadwell's "Squire of Alsatia" on Terence's "Adelphi," setting forth the opposite plans for training youth, it is more serious than any of Fielding's other pieces, but it has little vitality. Instead of this, Fielding gave Garrick "The Wedding Day." It is by no means without wit but it is carelessly built on the popular formula of lewdness for four acts and virtue in the last. At the beginning Millamour is receiving two bawds who bring letters from two mistresses. Clarinda is to marry old Stedfast that very day, but she feigns illness and Millamour attends her as a physician. All this is amusing according to the Restoration manner, but then miracles begin to happen. Clarinda is discovered to be the long-lost daughter of the man she was to marry. Millamour repents, restores the infatuated Charlotte to her true lover, denounces the bawd, and marries Clarinda. Here are both sentiment and humour but badly mixed. By this time Fielding's "Joseph Andrews" was carrying the ensign of humour and ridicule against the triumphant sentimentality of Richardson's "Pamela," and one wishes he had followed the advice of Macklin in the prologue,

You'd better stuck to honest Abraham Adams, by half:
He, in spite of critics, can make your readers laugh.

As Arthur Murphy, his biographer, remarked, if Fielding "had resolved to shape the business and characters of his last comedy into the form of a novel, there is not one scene in the piece which, in his hands, would not have been very susceptible of ornament; but as they are arranged at present in dramatic order, there are few of them from which the taste and good sense of an audience ought not, with propriety, to revolt."

Murphy relates a story of this last performance, illustrating Fielding's contempt for his public. Garrick had begged him to omit a particular passage likely to give offense. "No, damn 'em," replied Fielding, "if the scene is not a good one, let them find that out." But when the passage was spoken, Garrick, "alarmed and uneasy at the hisses he had met with, retired into the greenroom, where the author was indulging his genius and solacing himself with a bottle of champagne. He had by this time drank pretty plentifully; and cocking his eye at the actor while streams of tobacco trickled down from the corner of his mouth, 'What's the matter Garrick?' says he, 'what are they hissing now?' 'Why the scene I begged you to retrench; I knew it would not do, and they have so frightened me that I shall not be able to collect myself again the whole night.' 'Oh! damn 'em,' replies the author, 'they have found it out, have they?'"

Professor Cross, Fielding's latest biographer, refuses to believe the story, but it seems characteristic of Fielding the dramatist and, except for the tobacco, not very unbecoming. A playwright is compelled to go to school to his audience, but there is no sign that Fielding ever learned anything from this master. It was not in his temperament, as it was in Cibber's, to adjust lewdness and sentiment in such proportions as to excite and edify a capricious public; and it was not within his skill to confine his humour to what could be represented effectively by an actor. The wit and humour which made the rollicking burlesque of "Tom Thumb" and enlivened farces and operas for the comic genius of Kitty Clive were never trained to the regular measures of high comedy. Though part of his failure must be attributed to the conditions of a theater that eagerly demanded farce and burlesque but gave no encouragement to any attempt to write comedy after the fashion of the old masters; yet the wonder persists that so great a humorist could write such paltry comedies. His genius indeed matured slowly, but it would never have found in the drama the opportunity which the novel supplied to instruct mankind in both humour and morality. His comedies fail in both particulars, they added nothing fresh in the way of humour and their immorality offended an audience that had been pleased by sentiment. So far as his plays may be regarded as a revolt against sentimentality they were impotent. The future course of comedy is foreshadowed not more by the success of "The Conscious Lovers" and "The Provoked Husband" than by the failure of so brilliant a wit as Fielding to produce anything comparable to the still popular plays of Congreve and Vanbrugh.

CHAPTER XVI

PANTOMIME, OPERA AND FARCE, 1730-1760

THE dearth of comedy during the middle third of the eighteenth century has not received sufficient emphasis by historians of the stage and drama. They have usually jumped from Cibber and Fielding to Goldsmith and Murphy and Sheridan but have assumed that there was something in between. As a matter of fact there were almost no new comedies. Though the two leading theaters continued to bring out one or two new tragedies each year, and though both presented many new operas, farces and pantomimes, season after season often went by without a single comedy. During the period from 1735-36 to 1759-60, only two appeared that kept any lasting hold on the stage, Hoadly's "Suspicious Husband" and Moore's "Foundling," both in the forties. In the fifties no new comedies were acted. Only in the early sixties are there again a few notable first performances.

The activity that we have noticed in Fielding's day was partly due to the second-rate companies in Goodman's Fields and the Haymarket, but the licensing act ended this. In the season of 1735-6 Professor Nicoll records three new comedies, one each at Drury Lane, Lincoln's Inn Fields, and the Haymarket. In 1736-7 there is only one, Hewitt's "Tutor for the Beaux" acted three nights at Lincoln's Inn Fields; in 1737-8 only one, the Rev. James Miller's "Art and Nature" acted once at Drury Lane; for the next three seasons there are none. In 1741-2 Garrick's advent at Goodman's Fields resulted in his "Lying Valet," and Dance's version of "Pamela," and the next season Fielding's "Wedding Day" was damned at Drury Lane. Professor Nicoll records two comedies

377

in '43-'44, three in '44-'45, none in '45-'46, Hoadly's successful "Suspicious Husband" at Covent Garden in '46-'47 and Moore's "Foundling" at Drury Lane, '47-'48. From this time on, no new five-act comedies are produced at either of the two main theaters, Drury Lane and Covent Garden, until the season of '60-'61, when Arthur Murphy's "Way to Keep Him," which appeared in three acts the year before, was enlarged to five acts, and Colman's "Jealous Wife," partly drawn from "Tom Jones," made a great hit. Murphy and other writers were now producing plays in two or three acts which are difficult to classify as farces or comedies, but I think none that could rightly be called a comedy had appeared before 1760. After that date, though comedies are still rare, there are at least one or two a year. Colman's management of Covent Garden in 1767 and the rival performances of Goldsmith's "Good-Natured Man" and Kelly's "False Delicacy" inaugurate a new age of comedy, that of Goldsmith, Sheridan and Cumberland.

I

This period, so unproductive in comedy, and for that matter in tragedy of merit, was a time of improvement in the theaters and of excellent acting. Garrick made his famous début in "Richard III" at Goodman's Fields in 1741 and was soon delighting the town in all the principal parts in both comedy and tragedy. In 1747 he and Lacy became joint managers of Drury Lane, and in spite of theatrical wars, riots and rebellions, maintained an unrivalled company of actors until his retirement in 1776 and the sale of his share to Sheridan. Garrick's impersonation of many of the famous rôles in comedy led to the revival or renewed popularity of old plays and helped to crowd the season with stock plays to the exclusion of new productions. The most important additions to the old repertory came through the revival of Shakespeare's long unacted comedies. "Merry Wives" and "Measure for Measure" were put on at Loncoln's Inn Fields in 1721-2 and later at Drury Lane. "As You Like It," "Twelfth Night" and "The Merchant of Venice" were all revived at Drury Lane in 1740-41, and "The Winter's Tale," "All's Well," "Much Ado" and the "Comedy of Errors" before 1750. Garrick aided greatly in maintaining the new popularity of these comedies, though he was guilty of some regrettable adaptations. Shakespeare henceforth held his place as the chief contributor to a repertory that also included the best comedies of Wycherley, Congreve, Farquhar, Steele, Cibber and Mrs. Centlivre. There has never been a time since Garrick's day when so many representative English comedies could be seen in a single season. The public constantly had plenty of first rate comedy, and in consequence may not have desired novelty except in farce or opera.

It may be worth while to stop a moment to look at the list of the plays in stock from 1730-1760, for it includes every type of comedy that we have been considering. In a given season thirty or forty comedies were usually acted at Drury Lane and nearly as many at Covent Garden. The stock lists of the two theaters were not very different, but some of the plays in stock were brought out at infrequent intervals, so that the entire number must have approached one hundred. The main change from 1730 to 1760 consists in the addition of Shakespeare's comedies. There were also many adaptations. "The Tempest" appeared as Shakespeare wrote it and also as it was rewritten by Dryden and Davenant, and again as a re-made opera. "A Midsummer Night's Dream" supplied matter for two operas; "The Winter's Tale" appeared in two operatic versions, "The Sheep-Shearing" and "Florizel and Perdita"; even "The Two Gentlemen of Verona" was revived, with alterations and additions; and "Catherine and Petruchio," the farce from "Taming of the Shrew," had great popularity.

The theater-going public for the first time in a century had an opportunity to enjoy the humour and the poetry of Shakespeare's land of romance. Rosalind, Viola,

Beatrice, Portia again became queens of stageland. Touchstone, Sir Toby, Dogberry, Malvolio again mingled their mirth and absurdity with the fantasies of the lovers and the melody of the verse. Here was a new theatrical life for a kind of comedy quite different from that of the Restoration, a comedy full of romance and sentiment, though not sentimentality, and bound to influence the taste of each new generation of theater-goers, actors and writers.

Of the other Elizabethans, a few of Jonson's comedies were still acted, as they had been since the Restoration. "Bartholomew Fair" was no longer given, and "Volpone" only infrequently. "The Alchemist" and "The Silent Woman" held their places; and in 1751 Garrick appeared as Kitely in his own adaptation of "Every Man in His Humour," which henceforth continued in stock. Of other realistic Elizabethan comedies there were two notable revivals, Massinger's "New Way to Pay Old Debts," in 1748, and "Eastward Ho" (in place of the "London Cuckolds"), 1751-2. Brome's, "Jovial Crew" and Mayne's "City Match" still held the stage.

The plays of Beaumont and Fletcher continued in repertory but in diminishing numbers and subject to alterations. Of the tragicomedies "The Humorous Lieutenant" still appeared occasionally and "Women Pleased" was revived. Of the romantic comedies "Rule a Wife" maintained its popularity, as did "The Chances" in Garrick's revision of Buckingham's revision, "The Beggar's Bush" remade into "The Royal Merchant," "The Pilgrim" in Vanbrugh's adaptation, and Cibber's "Love Makes a Man" ("The Elder Brother" and "The Custom of the County"). Of the comedies of manners, "Wit Without Money" still kept the stage, "The Scornful Lady" was seen but rarely, and "The Woman's Prize" was reduced to a farce known by its second title, "The Tamer Tamed." "The Wild Goose Chase" had a revival but was chiefly known through Farquhar's adaptation, "The Inconstant." Not much of Fletcher's verse

was heard in the theater, but his lively situations and
surprises were reworked into many plays besides the
adaptations noted.

Of the Restoration dramatists revivals were growing
rather infrequent. Howard's "Committee," Shadwell's
"Squire of Alsatia," Betterton's "Amorous Widow,"
Crowne's "Sir Courtly Nice," Mrs. Behn's "Rover" and
"Emperor of the Moon" were still to be seen, as was the
disreputable "London Cuckolds," which was continued at
Covent Garden even after Garrick had dropped it from
Drury Lane. Of Dryden, "The Spanish Friar" was the
only regular representative, though "Amphitryon" was
acted occasionally and "Marriage à la Mode" survived in
Cibber's "Comical Lovers," and later in a popular farce.
"The Rehearsal" was constantly acted.

Of the masters of the comedy of manners, Etherege's
"Man of Mode" was occasionally revived, Wycherley's
"Plain Dealer" and "Country Wife" rarely until Garrick's
adaptation, "The Country Girl," was substituted for the
latter. Congreve's four comedies kept the stage without
much apparent abatement in popularity. All of Vanbrugh's continued in stock : "The False Friend," "The
Confederacy," "Æsop," and "The Mistake," as well as
"The Relapse" and "The Provoked Wife." Of Farquhar, "The Constant Couple," "The Recruiting Officer,"
"The Inconstant," and "The Twin Rivals" were often
acted, and "The Beaux Stratagem" continued perhaps the
favourite comedy of the period. Whatever the growth of
sentimentality and niceness, little sign appeared of any
decrease in favour for the masterpieces of the school of
manners.

The sentimental comedies, however, seem to have
increased their hold on the public, perhaps at the expense
of the Restoration authors. Steele's "Funeral," "Tender
Husband" and "Conscious Lovers" are frequent on the
lists, and his "Lying Lover" was remade into Foote's
"Liar." Addison's "Drummer" also kept a place in
stock, and Cibber's "Love's Last Shift," "Careless Hus-

band," "Lady's Last Stake," "Non-Juror" and "Provoked Husband" were all favourites.

The non-sentimental comedies of the early eighteenth century, however, were equally popular. Cibber's "She Would and She Would Not," "Love Makes a Man," "The Double Gallant" appear frequently, and "The Comical Lovers" less often. Mrs. Centlivre's "Busy Body," "Bold Stroke for a Wife," "Gamester" and "The Wonder" were all regularly acted. Fielding's "Miser," the younger Shadwell's "Fair Quaker of Deal," Johnson's "Country Lasses," Baker's "Tunbridge Walks," and Norris's "Royal Merchant" ("Beggar's Bush") are about the only other comedies that kept a place in repertory.

With the revival of Shakespeare's comedies, the London theater now gave adequate representation to two great and intermingling national traditions in comedy, that of the Elizabethan era, and that of the Restoration. Their intermingling was of course much greater than our list indicates, for Fletcher's influence was unmistakable on many plays in addition to those which were confessedly adaptations, Jonson's theory as well as his practice was before the mind of every dramatist, and Middleton, Shirley, Massinger and others of the Elizabethans supplied many an unacknowledged hint for scene or plot. But the Restoration drama, carried to excellence in the comedies of manners, had also become a distinct tradition, the integrity of which became the more evident when the masterpieces of Congreve and Vanbrugh were brought into theatrical rivalry with those of Shakespeare. Several other dramatic traditions also find representation in our repertory. Roman comedy, long forgotten or misunderstood, then revived to be the model for all nations in the Renaissance, and continuing directly or indirectly to guide the dramatic practice of each succeeding generation, is represented in translations such as Dryden's "Amphitryon," in borrowings such as Shadwell's "Alsatia" and Steele's "Conscious Lovers" as well as in the adaptations by Shakespeare, Jonson and Molière. Italian influence appears in some of the personages and tricks of the commedia dell' arte, and Spanish drama supplies several comedies of intrigue with their plots. Most important, however, of foreign influences is that of France. Among direct translations are Vanbrugh's "Æsop" and "Confederacy" and Fielding's "Miser"; among less direct adaptations Wycherley's "Country Wife" and Cibber's "Non-Juror." On the comedies since the Restoration the influence of Molière is stronger than that of Shakespeare or Jonson and possibly than even that of Fletcher.

It is the purpose of this book to trace the results of such contending influences, to note how a tradition is transformed and combined and reanimated into something new, and to note the differences that distinguish the successful types of English comedy; but it may be observed that in spite of marked peculiarities, there is a close family likeness in these ninety or a hundred plays which represent the survival of the fittest. They are alike even in their mechanical form; they all have five acts. Nearly all have a marriage in the last act, and the majority have two or three. In most of them courtship occupies a considerable part of the other acts, and in many cases the ardent love-making of a pair of young lovers is contrasted with the more amusing affairs of their servants or with the illicit love of other couples or with the ludicrous wooing of some absurd person, such as Malvolio, Lady Wishfort, or the miser. Even the ridiculous persons who are exhibited for our laughter can be catalogued mostly under a few types: miser, braggart, drunkard, jealous husband, fop, coquette, coward, hypocrite. In practically all, the plot rests at least in part on tricks or deceptions, the action often proceeding from the initiation of the deception in act one to its disclosure in act five. Plays as different in their effects as "Twelfth Night," "The Alchemist," "The Country Wife," "Love for Love," "The Beaux Stratagem," and "She Would and She Would Not" conform to this general form.

Even the means used for deception do not make a long

catalogue. How many conversations are overheard, how many letters missent! Disguise is very common and is often the mainspring of the plot, while the girl in boy's clothing trips through nearly half the plays. The same stratagems are plotted again and again and are thwarted in the same ways. The most popular protagonist is the trickster tricked, though he may combine this part with the miser robbed, the hypocrite exposed, the profligate reformed, or the rake married. Discovery scenes in bedrooms are by no means confined to Restoration plays, and an unexpected interruption or a discovery of some sort seems almost essential to comic success. The tension is maintained not only by the action on the stage but by the uncertainty when the door will open and who will enter. One discovery may be enough for a play, as when Lady Easy finds her husband and the chambermaid napping in adjacent chairs, or there may be a succession of interruptions, as in "The Merry Wives" or "The Double Dealer." The differences between any two plays are usually in degree rather than in kind. Wit abounds in "The Way of the World" but is attempted in all. Low comedy and farce are excluded from very few even of the most sentimental; a modicum of boisterous buffoonery is almost as essential as witty dialogue. Songs and dances are not more common than drinking, beating, and duelling.

"The Humorous Lieutenant," "The Spanish Friar," "The Winter's Tale," and one or two others introduce heroic and tragic themes, and some other plays, as "Volpone" and "The Plain Dealer," carry their satire into an exposure of villainy and wickedness, yet none of these plays depart in any very marked degree from the normal traits which I have noted. The two parts of "Henry IV" in their absence of love-making and weddings and in their inclusion of historical material, are the most striking variants; among post-Restoration plays only "Æsop" and the farce "What D'ye Call It" show any marked abnormality. "The Conscious Lovers," perhaps the most origi-

nal of the additions to the repertory, borrows its scheme
from Terence's "Andria"; and Cibber, a most accomplished playwright, utilizes Fletcher, Dryden and
Molière.   All the interesting experiments and variations
in the English theater during two hundred years have not
produced a result very far removed from the product
of the French or the Spanish theaters during the same
period.   And modern comedy, however varied, still bears
a recognizable likeness to the plays of Plautus and
Terence.

Comedy was still from 1730 to 1760 a well defined
form of drama, though it attracted but few practitioners.
I shall not attempt to discuss at large the causes why the
many plays regularly acted and representing various traditions still powerful should fail to encourage new dramatic
experiment.   In some measure these causes are doubtless
to be found in general social and literary conditions.   The
theater, though it was gradually extending its appeal to
the middle classes, had not regained the popularity that
it had in Elizabeth's reign.   It was superseded during the
eighteenth century by pamphlet, periodical and novel as
popular forms of literature.   Sentimentalism was to find
its great proponents not in the plays of Steele and Cibber
but in the novels of Richardson.   Prose fiction and not
the drama was to provide the opportunity for Fielding's
genius.   The beginnings of Gothicism and romanticism
were to get expression in poem and tale rather than in
play, and many of the new tendencies toward sentimentalism, medievalism, humanitarianism were scarcely pro-
vocative of comedy.   Apart, however, from these general
conditions, the state of the London theaters did not
encourage new plays.   The Licensing Act of 1737 cut off
the minor theaters that were beginning to appear and
confined the drama to the two patented houses.   Both of
these supplied the public not only with stock plays but
with pantomimic and operatic entertainments.   There was
a constant demand for new music, new shows, and new
short and lively farces and burlesques, so that what

dramatic and comic talent was available was likely to be
employed on these pieces rather than on full-fledged
comedies. The cessation of any development in comedy
proper gives us an opportunity to look back at the
progress of these quasi-dramatic forms in so far as they
have any relation to comedy. I shall group them roughly
under three heads—pantomimes, operas, and farces; and
while I cannot pretend even to indicate the extent and
characteristics of any one of these, I may hope to show
their influence on comedy.

II

Perhaps a word should first be said in regard to the
two plays that in the course of these thirty years secured
places on the roster of stock comedies. "The Suspicious
Husband" is a very clever contrivance, utilizing and
improving on the plot of Fielding's "Temple Beau."
Ranger, who loves all the ladies, eventually aids his two
friends in their serious love affairs. On a drunken prank,
he ascends a ladder that has been used by the elopers and
enters the bed-chambers of the ladies, fluttering the dove-
cotes. He escapes, leaving his hat behind, and this
arouses the suspicions of the husband against his entirely
devoted and innocent wife. In the end these suspicions
are removed by the good-natured Ranger. Not since
Cibber, had a comedy so skilfully combined the attractions
of lewdness and sentiment. "The Foundling" (1748),
by Edward Moore, the author of the powerful domestic
tragedy, "The Gamester," professes a more serious intention. As the prologue announces:

> He forms a model of a virtuous sort
> And gives you more of moral than of sport;
> He rather aims to draw the melting sigh
> Or steal the pitying tear from beauty's eye.

The main situation, similar to that of Marina in "Pericles," then recently revived, or of Johnson's tragedy,
"Caelia," gives opportunity enough to harrow the feel-

ings of the audience.   The heroine passes from evil
hands into the doubtful protection of the profligate Belmont, but the process by which he becomes converted and
marries her is marked by comic complications and intrigue,
with very little appeal to sensibility.   So far as sentimental comedy is concerned neither of these two plays
adds anything new.

In France, however, this species was flourishing during
this very period when it was quiescent in England.   Destouches, who resided in England for some time, was a
friend of Addison, and married an English lady, produced in 1727 "Le Philosophe Marié," celebrating a virtuous and submissive wife.   "La Chaussée," with his
"La Fausse Antipathie," in 1733, is generally considered
the founder of *la comédie larmoyante*.   "La Mére
Confidente" (1735), and "Les Fausses Confidences"
(1737) of Marivaux treat sentimental love with delicacy and charm.   Voltaire, quick to take advantage of
the new fashion, wrote "L'Enfant Prodigue" in 1736
and "Nanine" in 1742, based on Richardson's "Pamela"
and commended by Rousseau as a sort of document for
social democracy.   The new sentimental comedy was
making its way both in the French theater and in French
criticism.   Moreover, by the mid-century Lillo's "George
Barnwell" had been translated into French and was being
hailed by Diderot and by Lessing in Germany as inaugu-
rating a new epoch for virtue and sentiment in drama.
It is rather curious that at this time in England the drama
of sensibility should have so few followers and should
provoke so little discussion.   We turn to the forms that
did interest the English public, pantomime, opera, and
farce.

III

Of the three, the first has the least connection with
comedy, but it was an enormously successful kind of
entertainment in the eighteenth century.   Pantomime in
the more general sense of the word had long played a
part in acting and is to be found in the Elizabethan

drama—in the dumb shows, in the special antics of the clowns, and in the antimasques, grotesque and acrobatic dances which formed a part of the court masques. After the Restoration, pantomimic action seems to have been introduced into the operas, but it took a new turn from the presence of companies of Italian actors in Paris and London, and the introduction of certain personages of the *commedia dell' arte,* scaramouch, harlequin, columbine, etc., into plays and spectacles. I have already noticed one of these pieces by Mrs. Behn, "The Emperor of the Moon," (1687), which long held its place in the London theaters. Such a combination of drama, songs, spectacles, and the pantomime of harlequin and scaramouch, made up what was sometimes termed a "pantomimic farce." The kind of performance, however, that through the eighteenth century was known as Pantomime seems to have been invented by a dancing master, John Weaver, who brought out at the Drury Lane in 1702 "The Tavern Bilkers," which he calls "the first entertainment that appeared on the English stage, where the Representation and story was carried on by Dancing Action and Motion only." In 1717 he brought out another at Drury Lane, "The Loves of Mars and Venus"; and in the same year John Rich (Lun) produced two at Lincoln's Inn Fields, "The Jealous Doctors" and "Harlequin Executed." In these, as in similar shows to which the French gave the name vaudevilles, a story was told by means of spectacle, music, dancing, transformations and pantomime, though not without some aid from speech and dialogue. Lun's creations came to take a fairly definite form. A story, usually based on classical myth or fable, was presented by means of scenery, ballets and music, and this was interspersed by the adventures of Harlequin and Columbine in pantomime, often grotesque or acrobatic, and with tricks and transformations accomplished by Harlequin's wand.

Rich succeeded his father as manager of the new theatre in Lincoln's Inn Fields in 1714, and there and later at Covent Garden he presented pantomimes annually

from 1717 until his death in 1760. These were usually
money makers, with prices of admission doubled, and
they naturally occasioned rival shows at Drury Lane.
Lun always played harlequin and was generally recognized as unrivalled. He is credited with surpassing the
Paris performers because, while they spoke,

> When Lun appeared, with matchless art and whim
> He gave the power of speech to every limb;
> Tho' mask'd and mute, convey'd his quick intent
> And told in frolic gesture what he meant.

This is from so competent a judge as Garrick, and
leads one to conjecture that Lun's talents may have had
an influence in encouraging the more natural and lively
style of acting which Garrick introduced. It will be
remembered that he criticized a French actor mimicking
a drunkard because "he was not drunk in the legs."
What effect the pantomimes had on comedy, except to
crowd regular plays out of the theaters, is difficult to
say. They usurped not only the theaters but a large
number of stories which they vulgarized, and their composition attracted the services of some men of letters,
among them Lewis Theobald and T. Cibber. Subjects
of many sorts which might readily enough have been
chosen for comedy—Perseus and Andromeda, The Rape
of Proserpine, The Harlot's Progress, The South Sea
Director, The Loves of Mars and Venus—were used for
these spectacles.

The success of these shows naturally aroused satire
and ridicule among the wits. Rich's removal to the new
theater in Covent Garden produced a picture by Hogarth
and a print with this legend:

> Shakespeare, Rowe, Jonson, now are quite undone;
> These are thy triumphs, thy exploits, O Lun!

A number of farces satirized or burlesqued the exploits
of Harlequin, notably, Fielding's "Author's Farce"
(1730), in which Monsieur Pantomime is one of those

favoured in the court of Nonsense, and "Tumble-Down Dick," dedicated to Mr. John Lun, vulgarly called Esquire. Pantomimes, however, continued to thrive, and later on pantomimic acting was to play a large part in the vogue of melodrama.

IV

The term opera has been applied to almost every variety of entertainment with songs, and it is not always easy to draw the line between a drama with incidental songs and an opera with dialogue. The word is first used in England during the Commonwealth period; and immediately after the Restoration, operas began to be frequent at the playhouses. These were dramas in blank verse or rhyme, interspersed with songs and dances and furnished with elaborate scenes and machines. This new musical drama virtually absorbed two Elizabethan forms, the masque and the pastoral. Sporadic examples of these long continued to be written and performed, Colley Cibber producing "Venus and Adonis," a masque, and "Love in a Riddle," a pastoral, but such pieces on the stage were indistinguishable from operas. In the late years of the seventeenth century English opera acquires literary excellence in Dryden's "Albion and Albanius"; and owing to the genius of Henry Purcell becomes of some importance in the history of music, but it has little concern for comedy. We occasionally hear of a "comical opera" as in Settle's "The World in the Moon" (1697), which mixed comic incident and dialogue with its scenic effects; but in the main this opera was heroic or tragic in theme and rarely sought for any comic effect.

It found a formidable rival shortly after 1700 in the introduction of Italian singers and of operas after the Italian manner. Efforts were made to have recitative in English, but the Italian language prevailed, and after 1710 the great theater in the Haymarket was turned over to Italian grand opera. It was supported by Handel's music, and not injured by the competition of occasional

English operas such as Addison's "Rosamond." The
satirists of the time, however, have a great deal to say
about the extravagance and lack of patriotism shown by
people of fashion in preferring the foreign species, and
there were many demands for a return to English speech
and song.   In response to this demand John Gay produced "The Beggar's Opera," a comedy in prose interspersed with songs written to familiar English airs.   He
had already tried his hand at dramatic novelties, "What
d'ye-Call-It" in 1715, which he called a tragi-comi-pas-
toral farce, and which had the additional elements of song
and burlesque, and, in collaboration with Pope and
Arbuthnot, the farce "Three Hours After Marriage" in
1717.   Swift's proposal of "a Newgate pastoral" suggested the scheme of the play, and possibly the songs
composed for Scottish airs in Allan Ramsay's "Gentle
Shepherd" gave the hint for the employment of familiar
tunes.   The result was something quite new, for which
ballad opera is the most descriptive of the various names
applied.

The piece is too well known for description, but it
may be noted that if the songs were omitted it would
still be very clever and satirical comedy.   The opening
act with the disturbance in the Peachum family because
Polly has married is written with a gay irony unsurpassed
by Mr. Bernard Shaw in his wittiest onslaughts on love
and matrimony.   Her father, the receiver of stolen goods,
cries: "Do you think your mother and I should have lived
comfortably so long together if ever we had been married, baggage?"   Her fond mama puts it: "Love him!
worse and worse, I thought the girl had been better bred;"
and again, "If she had only an intrigue with the fellow,
why the very best families have excused and huddled up a
frailty of that sort. 'Tis marriage, husband, that makes
it a blemish."   But the songs, of course, are essential.
The satire might have grown heavy and the irony tedious
without them.   No wonder that the audience was a trifle
dubious through the first act.   Gay's Tory friends found

little of the attacks on the government which they desired, and the crowd could scarcely see the bent of the persiflage. But just as the burlesque is getting extravagant and the Peachums are deciding to have her lover impeached and hanged, the pretty and girlish Polly sings:

> Oh ponder well! be not severe;
> So save a wretched wife!
> For on the rope, that hangs my dear,
> Depends poor Polly's life.

This plaintive appeal, we are told, decided the success of the piece; the act ends in a salvo of songs that inaugurated one of the greatest of theatrical triumphs.

No one of the elements which make the success of the opera is in itself of transcendent merit, neither the songs, nor the novel scheme, nor the realism of manners, nor the wit and irony. But they are all combined with a fitness and finality perhaps never equalled in later efforts in comic opera. The songs, which are witty as well as tuneful, are a relief from the realism, and the very familiarity of their airs helps to lull into contentment any uneasiness that may be felt over the novelty and the satire. The basest wretches sing pleasantly and are quite like virtuous mortals in their domestic discussions and disputes. Captain Macheath conducts his amours and meets his destiny with the gallantry and breeding of a man of quality, so that we are betrayed into crying with the mob for his reprieve. The satire on our social conditions is never so disturbing that it does not quickly vanish into mirth or song. The irony is tinged by sentiment and the actuality by nonsense.

So delightful and extravagant a fantasy has inevitably aroused the tempers of the moralists and the pedants. Sir John Fielding, who succeeded his brother as police magistrate, requested Garrick to suppress "The Beggar's Opera" because of the encouragement it gave to thieves and highwaymen, and this charge was frequently repeated in the eighteenth century though scoffed at by Dr. Johnson, who had a way of applying good sense even to moral principles.

One wonders what he would think of a present-day moralist who, writing after the recent revival of the opera, finds its moral virtue in Macheath's inspiring request that Peachum and Lockit be brought to the gallows. "In this little passage Gay points the whole moral of the piece. It is not, as so many people have thought, a glorification of the lives of thieves and highwaymen, but an exposure of the vile system which allowed such men as Lockit and Peachum to exist, to make criminals for their benefit, and to betray them to justice after they have served their turn, for the reward." How reassuring this is; it puts the play up a peg and enables us to regard even our own laughter at it with moral approval. Other students have discovered that Gay was attempting an elaborate satire on the corrupt Whig government; but if this is true, he either did not try very hard or else did not succeed. In one purpose he did succeed, in delighting mankind with his nonsense and song. If we must have a moral, let us stick to that which after the usual fashion he set forth in a closing couplet, the refrain of the final chorus,

> Then think of this maxim, and put off your sorrow;
> The wretch of to-day may be happy to-morrow.

The classic account of the opera's success is given in Pope's note to "The Dunciad":

"The vast success of it was unprecedented and almost incredible. . . . It was acted in London sixty-three days uninterrupted and renewed the next season with equal applause. It spread into all the great towns of England, was played in many places to the thirtieth and fortieth time, at Bath and Bristol fifty, etc. It made its progress into Wales, Scotland, and Ireland, where it was performed twenty-four days together; it was lastly acted in Minorca. The fame of it was not confined to the author only, the ladies carried about with them the favourite songs of it in fans, and houses were furnished with it in screens. The person who acted Polly, till then obscure, became all at once the favourite of the Town. Her pictures were engraved and sold in great numbers, her life written, books of letters and verses to her published, and pamphlets made even of her sayings and jests.

Furthermore, it drove out of England for that season the Italian opera, which had carried all before it for ten years: that idol of the nobility and people which the great critic, Mr. Dennis, by the labours and outcries of a whole life could not overthrow, was demolished by a single stroke of this gentleman's pen. This happened in the year 1728."

It was acted wherever the English language was spoken and was translated into French and produced in Paris. It held the stage constantly through the eighteenth century, was frequently revived in the nineteenth, and again revived in the twentieth for a run of nearly four years, 1919-1923, at the Lyric Theater, Hammersmith. Gone are Gay and his Duchess of Queensbury, gone are Newgate and the highwaymen of romance and the Tories who hated Walpole, and gone the stage with spectators on the sides and candles overhead; but Macheath still wishes one dear charmer away and Polly still sings,

> No power on earth can e'er divide
> The knot that sacred love hath tied.
> When parents draw against our mind,
> The true-love's knot they faster bind.

The sequel, "Polly," feared because of its political appeal, was suppressed by special command of the King and was not acted until fifty years later. Gay's pastoral opera, "Acis and Galatea," was produced in 1731 with Handel's music, and his burlesque opera, "Achilles," in 1733, the year after his death. None of these is comparable in merit with their great predecessor or influential in the further course of comic opera.

As soon as "The Beggar's Opera" had achieved its success, the stage was crowded with imitations. Everyone was busy patching up old pieces to suit the new fashion. Thomas Walker, who played Macheath, turned an old play on the adventures of Jack Shepherd into "The Quaker's Opera," Henry Carey revamped his farce "The Contrivances" with songs; Charles Johnson wrote "The Village Opera," and Cibber "Damon and Phillida." For the next ten years everything that could be was made into a ballad opera, but then the fashion waned. These pieces include all varieties, sentimental, pastoral, and realistic, but the majority are short farces or burlesques. Some of them, especially those of Fielding, we shall examine as farces; none are of much consequence as operas. A different kind of comedy and of opera is to be found in Dalton's adaptation of "Comus" for the stage. Fitted out with some songs by Dalton and with music by Dr. Arne, this scored a success in 1738, was performed for the benefit of Milton's granddaughter in 1750, and held the stage until superseded by Colman's abridgement in 1772. It was, however, over thirty years after Gay before another author appeared with a real knack for uniting story, comedy and songs. Bickerstaffe's "Love in a Village" and "The Maid of the Mill," based on "Pamela," with both old and original airs, inaugurated a new popularity for comic opera early in the sixties.

Gay can scarcely be said to have created a distinct form such as "opera buffa" or "opéra bouffe" or even "opéra comique," although the latter combined songs and dialogue as did Gay's, but he did set an English tradition for the lyric stage that has bloomed from time to time, most recently in the operas of Gilbert and Sullivan. But "The Beggar's Opera" was also the first successful union of comedy and song, and this success constantly repeated in the theater served as a stimulus to innu-

merable attempts at musical shows in which mirth and
melody should mingle. Ballad farce was a name given
to the earlier and briefer of such efforts; but burlettas,
burlesques, extravaganzas, masques, pastorals, operas, or
whatever they were called, from this time on are com-
petitive with the spoken drama. Gay stopped Italian
opera only for a season but he added another kind of
entertainment that was ever after to attract spectators
away from pure comedy. Henceforth the historian of
comedy must frequently listen to musical shows to make
sure that they are not more humorous or more entertaining than the pieces which still carry on the traditions
of Shakespeare and Congreve.

V

Farce is a term even more difficult to define precisely
than pantomime or opera. Indeed, the word has already
been used in this book with several different applications.
Farce in the medieval drama denoted a short play on a
secular theme, usually realistic and gross. In Elizabethan
literature the word was little used, but we are accustomed
to distinguish farces from comedies, as plays more
improbable in plot, more extravagant in character, more
boisterous in humour. For example, we speak of "The
Taming of the Shrew" as a farce, or consider "The
Merry Wives of Windsor" closer to farce than is "Much
Ado." This sort of distinction was made much of by
critics of the Restoration, who were forever drawing the
line between true comedy and her unworthy sister. Nevertheless some of the dramatists preferred the jade, and
we have noted as a sort of counterpoise to the "refinement" of the comedy of manners, the popularity of the
farcical pieces of Ravenscroft and D'Urfey. Farce
toward the end of the century had shown two tendencies,
one the vulgarization of the usual material of comedy by
increasing the tricks and buffoonery, the second the
employment of harlequin, scaramouch and other Italianate antics to increase the bustle.

From the beginning of the eighteenth century there is an increased demand for short farces, to serve as after-pieces. In Elizabethan days jigs and dances had been so employed, and in Restoration times shows, spectacles and dances of various sorts were used to fill out an evening's entertainment. Later, when no comic relief was offered in the declamatory tragedies and very little mixture of low in the high comedies, a dramatic supplement of farce seems to have proved acceptable. The term became generally applied to any short piece of one or two acts with comic intentions. Among the earliest of these are Vanbrugh's "Country House," Farquhar's "Stage Coach" and Cibber's "The School Boy," the first two taken from the French, the third utilizing persons and incidents common in English drama. For a time pantomimes and, later, ballad operas were more favoured for afterpieces, but by the mid-century they were both outranked by farces.

In the main these farces require little attention from us, for they offer little that is new. They are either translations from the French, or re-makings of the comic or vulgar portions of old English plays, or the mere repetitions of incidents and characters long familiar. While they were in demand as afterpieces in the regular theaters, these short and snappy pieces were also useful in efforts to make the little theater in the Haymarket a summer house for light comedy. Fielding in 1730 and again in 1736-7 crowded the house with his burlesques, and later Foote rebuilt the theater as a home for his farces. After the licensing act of 1737, which stopped Fielding, the drama was confined to the two patented theaters except for such a special dispensation as Foote obtained or for some such pretense of a concert, with a play given gratis, as that under which Garrick made his début at Goodman's Fields. Farce in combination with music and songs, or with spectacle, or entering the field of burlesque and satire of current events, plays or persons, might thus afford the basis for a very amusing entertainment and might provide novel themes and audacious fun. Such a

short piece might be extended to two or three acts and
it might be realistic or satirical or even sentimental rather
than merely boisterous and extravagant. Such a play
might claim to be comedy rather than farce, an evening's
entertainment rather than merely an afterpiece. Or, the
two-act piece, if successful, might be padded out into a
regular five-act play. Such were some of the changes
that were actually taking place during the years from
1730 to 1760 when comedy of the regular sort was
gaining so few recruits at the patented theaters. The
changes took place mainly under the auspices of Fielding
and Foote, and we must look at their contributions with
some care, giving a glance or two at several of their contemporaries.

Fielding's first short piece was contributed in March,
1730, to the Haymarket, then under the management of
Samuel Johnson of Cheshire, whose "Hurlothrumbo"
had been having a great success, "The Author's Farce
with a Puppet Show called the Pleasures of the Town."
Its main action tells the plight of Luckless the author,
dunned by his landlady, in love with her daughter, and
finding no help from the theatrical managers or the
booksellers, but finally facing the public with his so-called
Puppet Show. This is a burlesque with songs, in which
Don Tragedio, Sir Farcical Comick, Dr. Orator, Signior
Opera, Monsieur Pantomime, and Mrs. Novel appear as
the pleasures of the town, and descend to the lower world
to contend before the Goddess of Nonsense, who awards
the palm to Opera. In the end the author and the landlady's daughter are discovered to be children of kings
and they sail off together to claim a throne in the Kingdom of Bantam, where they promise to find employment
for the persons of the puppet show. Cibber, Wilks,
Curll the bookseller, Orator Henley the preacher, and
others are objects of good-natured banter in this medley
of farce, burlesque and opera.

"Tom Thumb" made its first appearance in 1730 as a
two-act afterpiece for "The Author's Farce." Two

additional scenes and a prologue and an epilogue were soon added, and the next year the piece was enlarged to three acts, supplied with a preface and notes of a mock-scholarly character, and published under the title "The Tragedy of Tragedies, or The Life and Death of Tom Thumb the Great." It is a parody on the favourite trage-dies of the time, with especial attention to Thomson's "Sophonisba." Like the burlesque part of "The Author's Farce" it owes something to the still popular "Rehearsal" and perhaps surpasses its model in fun. To our taste the tragedies imitated are so ridiculous in themselves that Fielding's travesty is the comic equivalent of painting the lily, but it is not difficult to understand the success of his hilarious nonsense. It reached a culmination in the origi-nal piece when the ghost of Tom Thumb was slain by Grizzle, his rival for the hand of Huncamunca. Swift said that he had never laughed but twice in his life, once at this scene. For some unknown reason Fielding omitted this in the enlarged play, but it was occasionally still retained on the stage.

In the same year as the enlarged "Tom Thumb," appeared a farce in three acts, without songs, "The Let-ter Writers, or A New Way to Keep a Wife at Home," which was a complete failure. It presents Mrs. Wisdom and Mrs. Softly, who are plotting to cuckold their foolish husbands by means of Rakel. It is without a touch of sentimentality and it would have pleased a Restoration audience, but it failed utterly even at the Haymarket. Fielding's next effort, "The Welsh Opera," indulged in some political satire on Walpole, was rewritten as "The Grub Street Opera" and was suppressed by the govern-ment. Then followed in 1732, at Drury Lane, "The Lottery," a farce in the form of ballad opera, which suc-ceeded at once and had a long popularity. The various abuses connected with the state lotteries are exposed in the story of Chloe, a girl from the country who comes up to London with a lottery ticket and the expectation of winning £10,000. The fun comes in because her confidence deceives certain sharpers into thinking she already possesses a fortune. At first in two scenes, the piece was soon enlarged to include the actual representation of the drawing in the Guildhall. Miss Raftor (Kitty Clive) was the singing heroine who helped to give this amusing trifle a great success.

This same year Fielding provided two pieces for a summer opening of Drury Lane. "The Old Debauchees" (1732) in three acts is sometimes called a comedy, possibly because it had no songs, but it is a gross and boisterous farce. Much attention had been attracted to the case of Father Girard of Toulon, brought to trial in 1731 for practising sorcery to seduce a girl to whom he was confessor, and a ballad opera on the subject, "The Wanton Jesuit," had already been performed at the Haymarket. Fielding pays little attention to the case of Father Girard but paints his Jesuit in the blackest colours. His attempt to seduce the girl is balked by her lover, who substitutes himself for her, receives the priest in her chamber, and exposes his villainy. The Jesuit as a seducer was already a familiar stage figure, and Fielding offered nothing new. Since "The Old Debauchees" had but three acts, Fielding provided an afterpiece, "The Covent Garden Tragedy," a ballad opera in form, burlesquing Ambrose Philips's "Distrest Mother," a tragedy still in stock. The scene is placed in a brothel where the "distressed mother," Punchbowl the bawd, does her offices with beaux, bullies and their mistresses. Taken with "The Old Debauchees," the evening's entertainment surpassed in indecency anything since Charles II. The afterpiece was damned, but "The Old Debauchees," after considerable revision, was accepted, and Fielding promptly fitted it with a new companion piece, "The Mock Doctor, or The Dumb Lady Cured." This is a translation of Molière's "Le médecin malgré lui," shortened, coarsened and supplied with some new scenes and nine songs. It is characteristic of Fielding's fooling that the doctor prescribes a brandy punch for the dumb lady; the additions were for Kitty Clive, who played the mock doctor's wife. The piece long continued among the most popular of farces on the stage. "Deborah," the next year was a failure and was not printed.

"The Intriguing Chambermaid" (1734), another very successful adaptation from the French with some enlargement and songs for Kitty Clive, was followed by the ballad opera "Don Quixote in England," which scarcely had a chance on the stage. In the next year "An Old Man Taught Wisdom, or The Virgin Unmasked" scored a success and took a place in repertory.

In 1736 Fielding was managing the Haymarket and produced his "Pasquin, A Dramatick Satire on the Times: Being the Rehearsal of Two Plays, viz. A comedy call'd The Election; and a Tragedy call'd The Life and Death of Common Sense." This is about the same sort of entertainment as was provided by "The Author's Farce" and "Tom Thumb," with this addition that the burlesque comedy furnished an amusing satire of a country election.

In the same season Fielding produced a very funny burlesque on Lun's pantomimes which has already been mentioned, the nature of which is somewhat fully expounded in the title, "Tumble-Down Dick, or Phaeton in the Suds. A Dramatick Entertainment of Walking, in Serious and Foolish Characters. Interlarded with Burlesque, Grotesque, Comick Interludes, call'd Harlequin a Pickpocket. . . . Being ('tis hop'd) the last Entertainment that will ever be exhibited on any Stage." In the following season Fielding, who had now allied himself to the opponents of the government, went more boldly into political satire with "The Historical Register for the Year 1736." As usual, he has many digs at Colley Cibber, including as a parody on one of the laureate's odes, an ode to the new year, which begins:

This is a day, in days of yore
Our fathers never saw before
This is a day, 'tis one to ten
Our sons will never see again
    Then sing the day,
    And sing the song,
    And thus be merry,
    All day long.

But this merry fooling was finished. The government became alarmed by the satire and by others which it produced, and passed the licensing act requiring the censorship of plays and limiting performances to the two patented theaters. Cibber now had the chance for a retort and in his "Apology" he described Fielding as "a broken wit" and again, "This Drawcansir in Wit, that spared neither Friend nor Foe! who to make his Poetical Fame immortal, like another Erostratus, set Fire to his Stage by writing up to an Act of Parliament to demolish it."

Two other pieces complete the list of Fielding's actual productions. "Eurydice" was produced at Drury Lane February 19, 1737, as an afterpiece to "Cato," but there was constant rioting that night over the presence of footmen in the boxes and so much yelling and noise that the farce had no chance to be heard. "Eurydice Hiss'd," a comic explanation of the incident, was added to "The Historical Register." The hasty but clever skit deserved a more tender fate. It is another mock mythological piece with the scene again in the lower world, where Plutus is henpecked by Proserpine, and Eurydice, a fashionable lady, is not at all inclined to return with Orpheus to earth and married life. "Miss Lucy in Town," a sequel to "The Virgin Unmasked," was prepared for Drury Lane in 1742. This is a commonplace treatment of the "country wife" theme.

Few of these pieces were without songs. "The Grub Street Opera" and "Don Quixote," because of their length and their many songs, perhaps deserve the title of opera. Of the others the most distinctive are the burlesques. There is scarcely anything funnier than good burlesque when the theater laughs at itself, and all its arts are employed in mocking and mimicking its own performances. In this kind of fun Fielding was free and at home and a delightful though somewhat uproarious host. Of the remaining pieces two were translations from the French, and some of the others reworkings of old material. But these farces added some new or unusual themes, such as a country election, a state lottery, and the mocking of classical myth. This is considerably more theatrical novelty than is to be found in his regular comedies. Fielding did not set any standard or method for light comedy, but he did show certain opportunities, some Aristophanic possibilities which might be developed to beat Menander. In spite of their lack of finish, it was his short pieces and not his comedies that preserved his influence in the theater.

Somewhat similar to Fielding's burlesques were the ballad farces of Henry Carey. "The Contrivances," acted first in 1715, was revised after the success of "The Beggar's Opera" to fit the prevailing mode, and in this form long held the stage. "The Tragedy of Chrononhotonthologos," a diverting absurdity that owes much to "Tom Thumb," "The Honest Yorkshire Man," a ballad opera, and "The Dragon of Wantley," a burlesque, are among the other productions that followed in the thirties, the last obtaining a great success at Covent Garden in the same year, 1737, that Fielding's "Eurydice" was hooted from the stage at Drury Lane. But the same year witnessed at Drury Lane the triumph of an afterpiece of a very different sort, Robert Dodsley's "The King and the Miller of Mansfield." Dodsley was one of several persons of humble birth in the eighteenth century whose poetical talents won the attention and patronage of persons of fashion. While in service as a footman he began to write verses and was soon able to publish a volume,

"A Muse in Livery," that could boast three duchesses and one duke among its subscribers. He then composed the dramatic satire, "A Toy Shop," and set up a bookshop. He later became a famous bookseller, one of the publishers of Johnson's Dictionary, editor of Dodsley's Old Plays, and author of a tragedy, of "a new species of pantomime," of a volume dedicated "To Morrow," and of much else; but something of the ingenuity and adaptability that were to be displayed so variously are discernible in his second dramatic attempt, "The King and the Miller." The story is that of the King who loses his way in Sherwood forest, where he is entertained by John Cockle, the miller, and where he interferes in a love affair. Peggy has been seduced by the wicked Lord Lurewell and now bitterly repents her faithlessness to her wrongly accused lover Richard. The King commands Lurewell to marry Peggy; she refuses him; the King then commands him to settle £300 a year upon her, but she asks that this be given to Richard:

As to myself, I only sought to clear the innocence of him I loved and wronged, then hide me from the world, and die forgiven.

Dick. This act of generous virtue cancels all past failings; come to my arms, and be as dear as ever.

The democratic and revolutionary sentiments of this little play might have been considered as more dangerous than those of Fielding's "Historical Register," but its tearful virtue shielded it from prosecution. So far as I know, it is the earliest sentimental afterpiece. A sequel, "Sir John Cockle at Court," is less sentimental but most moral.

Garrick also began writing for the stage with a moral farce, "Lethe, or Esop in the Shades." It owes the main scheme to Vanbrugh's play and the scene in the underworld to Fielding. The various visitants from London— fop, lord, drunkard, lady of fashion, miser, etc.—are submitted to the moralist's examination and their vices are exposed. A counter burlesque might have represented Charon ferrying back a few of the Restoration wits to experience the edification of a moralized theater. Henry Fielding must have heard the piece and have let a pious ejaculation escape him at its concluding maxim:

'Tis vice alone disturbs the human breast;
Care dies with quiet—be virtuous, and be blest.

Garrick's other pieces are less comprehensive in their moral pronouncements. They are usually brisk without being very boisterous and present persons and situations long familiar on the stage. They are condensed comedies speeded up for the requirements of an afterpiece. "The Lying Valet" presents the lady disguised as a gallant visiting and aiding her lover who is much involved by the deceptions of his tricky servant. "Miss in Her Teens" exhibits two foppish lovers drawn into a mock duel by the heroine while her true lover in hiding enjoys the spectacle. Perhaps the best was his last, acted in 1775, "Bon Ton, or High Life Above Stairs," quite in the manner of the older comedies of manners and intrigue, though with a moral ending. The secondary title refers to one of the best farces of our period, "High Life Below Stairs" (1759), by James Townley. The servants are known by the titles of their masters, and their affectation and insolence are constantly ludicrous.

Samuel Foote, after squandering a fortune and after a doubtful success as a regular actor, determined to exploit his skill in mimicry and to open the Haymarket in 1747 with an entertainment of music and farce. He circumvented the legal prohibitions by issuing invitations to "a dish of chocolate" instead of tickets to a theatrical performance. Concerts, farces and burlesques were mingled with his mimicry of actors and other persons. These entertainments were interrupted because Foote received a second fortune and went to Paris to spend it. Two years later he was back in London acting again at the regular theaters and producing various farces. The first of these, "Taste" (1752), was a two-act account of the tricks played by the fabricators of objets d'art. In the summer of 1760 he opened the Haymarket with "The Minor," written a few months earlier and now enlarged to three acts. It had a great success and has often been praised as the best of his plays. It is a gross caricature of Whitfield and the Methodists. The next season he and Arthur Murphy took Drury Lane for a summer and produced several new short pieces by Murphy. In 1766, while visiting at a nobleman's country place, Foote was persuaded to mount a spirited horse and was thrown, breaking his leg. In recompense, the Duke of York, who was one of the practical jokers, obtained for Foote a patent to erect a new theater in the Haymarket with the privilege of giving plays there yearly from May 14 to September 14. The new theater was opened in 1767, and proved most profitable. The next year his farce, "The Devil Upon Two Sticks," brought Foote nearly £4,000, of which he lost £1,700 to card sharpers at Bath on his way to Dublin, where the play again recouped his fortune.

Foote usually published his pieces as comedies and insisted that they deserved the name because of their faithful depiction of manners. Not much, however, can be said for their wit or their manners, but they do take a freer and wider range in their ridicule and satire than had been customary in regular plays. The pretended connoisseurs of "Taste," the Methodists of "The Minor," the parvenus from India in "The Nabob," the silly fop of "The Englishman Returned from Paris" are examples of satire which comedy might properly have made its own. But Foote's stories as well as his persons were often drawn from actual life, and have no significance except as gossip. "The Maid of Bath," for example, presented as Miss Linnet, the Miss Linley with whom Sheridan afterwards eloped; and "The Trip to Calais," printed after its acting was prohibited, ridiculed the extravagant mourning of the Duchess of Kingston (Lady Crocodile). Some of the pieces are made over as "The

Liar," from Steele's "Lying Lover," and none show very much originality in plan or persons. The famous "Devil Upon Two Sticks" is fairly representative. The eloping lovers in Spain free a devil who takes them to London, where he exhibits a most ludicrous burlesque war between the doctors and the apothecaries. Occasionally he gives us a touch of sentimentality. In "The Minor," Mrs. Cole (played by Foote) is a bawd and a Methodist much addicted to Whitfield's sermons. She procures a young girl, Lucy, and brings her to Sir George Wealthy, the young profligate, who is won over by her virtue, and thus proves his own worth to his father, Sir William, and the value of kindness to his harsh Uncle Richard, who discovers in Lucy his runaway daughter. But in general Foote is often gross and never moral for long.

Foote was now firmly established under royal favour and he continued on his course of caricaturing private persons, thus gaining the extravagant title of the English Aristophanes. Usually he talked freely about his plans, thus advertising his intentions and giving the persons to be caricatured a chance to join in the advertising. Dr. Johnson, however, brought matters to a halt by sending word that in case he was impersonated he would go from the boxes on the stage and chastise Foote before the audience. Finally he caught an ever worse tartar in the notorious Duchess of Kingston. She managed to have the play prohibited; lawsuits ensued; serious charges were brought against Foote; and, though his innocence was established, his health was broken by the ordeal. In 1777 he sold his patent to Colman, started for the south of France, and died at Dover.

Foote was an amusing scallawag and he could win over even his enemies to laughter. "The first time I was in company with Foote," says Dr. Johnson, "was at Fitzherbert's. Having no good opinion of the fellow I was resolved not to be pleased, and it is very difficult to please a man against his will. I went on eating my dinner pretty sullenly, affecting not to mind him. But the dog was so very comical that I was obliged to lay down my knife and fork, throw myself back in my chair and fairly laugh it out. No, sir; he was irresistible." If he could make the good doctor forget both his hostility and his dinner, imagine what he could do with a theater full of admirers who had paid money for a chance to laugh. But the buffoonery cannot live in the printed page, and the famous wit has grown stale, only rarely renewing its flavour with age, as in this passage from "The Maid of Bath." The conversation has turned on the new freedom of women, particularly of married women. Whereupon the aged rake Sir Christopher Cripple exclaims "What vast improvements are daily made in our morals! What an unfortunate dog am I, to come into the world at least half a century too soon! what would I give to be born twenty years hence! there will be damned fine doings then! hey, Tom." (I. i.) This was in 1771.

Like Fielding, Foote represents an audacious attempt to revive pungency and hilarity in the comic drama, but he succeeds only in short pieces, too hasty and too extravagant to have much value apart from his own impersonations. They left behind them a tradition that was confined mainly to farce. He succeeded where Fielding failed in establishing a playhouse that broke the monopoly and the monotony of the private theaters, but he achieved very little for the future of English comedy.

In this period farce was no more successful than ballad opera in acquiring a definite technic, and it did not produce any individual piece of outstanding merit. There are no farces as skilful in workmanship as Molière's "Le médicin malgré lui," and there are none whose fun is still irresistible today. But farce did enlarge its material and its scope, allying itself readily with burlesque and realistic satire and forming a combination with song and show that was of lasting theatrical import. All this remained rather rough and raw, without the nicety of entanglement or the dramatic ingenuity or the daring fun which were becoming characteristic of the French models. The vogue for farce, however, helped to create a kind of short play designed for an afterpiece or half an evening's entertainment, which might or might not be farcical in nature. Those afterpieces which extended to two or even three acts were often mere revampings and condensations of old comic stuff, but they might risk a venture in new fields. They permitted some experiment in the field of comedy and an easy alliance with song and dance. They gave freedom from the rigidity into which the five-act drama was falling, and at a time when the old form was in disuse they supplied a light-hearted and easy-going substitute.

CHAPTER XVII

THE REVIVAL OF COMEDY, 1760-1800

THE revival of comedy which began in 1760 continued until near the close of the century. Each year several new comedies were produced, Drury Lane and Covent Garden rarely letting a season go by without rival offerings, and the Haymarket continuing after Foote's death with a summer season in which light comedy was usually conspicuous. Toward the end of the century minor theaters began to appear, limited by law to pantomimes, burlettas, or other kinds of "illegitimate" drama. Provincial theaters were becoming of more importance, notably that at Bath, which for several years kept Mrs. Siddons from the metropolis, and those in the United States which after the Revolution began to produce new American plays as well as the London successes. But with few exceptions all new comedies of any consequence were first acted at one of the three London theaters which through their patents held a monopoly over the legitimate drama. In the nineties both Drury Lane and Covent Garden were rebuilt and greatly enlarged.

Of the new pieces many were kept in repertory and displaced some of the older favourites. Shakespeare, however, continued to be popular at all the theaters, and there were frequent revivals of other Elizabethans. The elder Colman during his management of Covent Garden was especially active in such revivals from Fletcher and Massinger, but without much success except for "Philaster," which kept the stage pretty well through this period. The dependence of the London theaters upon Paris continued. Any theatrical novelty was quickly

410

brought across the channel, and English playwrights were ever borrowing from the French. Molière and Destouches continued to be filched from; more recent dramatists such as Diderot and Voltaire were translated; French sentimental comedy was imitated; and the great successes of Beaumarchais were at once reproduced in London, "Le Barbier de Seville" in 1777 and "Le Mariage de Figaro" as "Follies of a Day," in 1784. The new German drama also found a hearing in England, "Minna von Barnhelm" ("Disbanded Officer"), in 1786, a version of "Werther" in 1785 (at Bath), and "Emilia Galotti" in 1794. The theatrical world was widening and communication between its different capitals becoming more rapid. The closing years of the century witnessed a world-conqueror in the German dramatist Kotzebue, whose plays were soon receiving the plaudits of every playhouse in Europe and America. The triumph of this theatrical Napoleon inaugurated a cosmopolitanism that has since continued. Whatever is new or successful in one city is likely to be tried soon on all stages.

Comedy after 1760 was still faced by the formidable rivals of the preceding period, pantomime, farce and opera. Though farce tended to mix with pantomime or to become musicalized, yet it probably never before and never since has occupied so distinctive and so important a place in our theater. All the varieties noted in the last chapter continued to flourish. Practically every serious play had its farcical afterpiece. Foote's notable and peculiar entertainments continued until 1776. Burlesques of all sorts were popular, culminating in the best of them all, Sheridan's "Critic." Afterpieces, extended to two acts, were provided with first pieces of slightly greater length, or triple bills were offered to fill out a long and varied evening's entertainment. Many old plays were reduced to the shortened forms of one-act farce or three-act comedy. Outside of the regular plays of five acts, this period discloses a considerable body of

comic drama, including not only the products of such
mechanics of farce as O'Keeffe and Dibdin, but also
many pieces of two or three acts by the most skilful writers of comedy, Garrick, Colman, Murphy, and others.
But by the end of the century neither farce nor light
comedy could easily stand alone without the assistance
of music, pantomime and spectacle.

Comic opera won new popularity in the productions
of Bickerstaffe, Sheridan, and others, and musical shows
became even more in fashion than after the success of
"The Beggar's Opera." In few of these pieces is there
any considerable attempt at lyric or comic excellence, the
desire is rather for novelty and spectacle. All sorts of
specious innovations are tried. "The Beggar's Opera"
was revived in 1777 with a new conclusion, which sent
Macheath to breaking rock, and was again produced with
immense success in 1781, when the women's parts were
taken by men actors, and vice versa. "Tom Jones" was
drawn upon for a sentimental opera in 1769. In 1785
"Omai," a piece celebrating the adventures of Captain
Cook, made a great hit, and in 1791 there was a ballet
pantomime based on Ossian. It is difficult to enumerate
all the names employed for musical shows and combinations of music, farce, and pantomime. Comic operas,
operettas, operatic farces, musical trifles, burlettas, are
only a few. The term burletta gained a legal definition
as a piece with music, and the minor theaters soon
began to evade the licensing act by producing legitimate
plays with some slight musical accompaniment. But
burlettas and all kinds of musical and spectacular shows
were also the delight of huge audiences at Covent
Garden and Drury Lane and tended to crowd the regular drama from their stages. The most successful pieces
of this sort were the extraordinary jumbles of farce,
tragedy, and opera devised by Colman the younger,
but consideration of these may be postponed until we
come to the melodrama of the next century for which
they prepared the way.

The rebuilt theaters were so large that they proved unsuitable to the spoken drama, and especially to new plays. The minor theaters, which by the end of the century were becoming of some importance, could produce regular drama only by an evasion of the law, and the two patented theaters were rendered by their size unsuited to anything except opera and pantomime. The legitimate drama was almost swamped by burletta, and even the triumphant Kotzebue was decked out with songs upon the English stage. These conditions, however, became of full effect upon the drama only in the nineteenth century. In our period comedy maintained a valorous though a losing battle against the encroachments of musical shows. Especially during the first two decades the "legitimate" proudly held its own. The period is notable not only for the great names of Goldsmith and Sheridan, but for a large number of new comedies of merit and interest. Not since the death of Farquhar and not again until the close of the nineteenth century was there a period of such activity in English comedy.

The conflict between the traditionalists and the sentimentalists became more open and definite than before. After the outbreak over Jeremy Collier's attack had subsided, English criticism had had little to say about the new species of drama that Steele, Cibber and Lillo were establishing. Meanwhile, new possibilities for sentimentality in literature had been opened, first by Richardson and then by Rousseau, and the French theater had developed a definite type of comedy dealing with the delicacies and refinements of sentiment. Some efforts were made, as in Whitehead's "School for Lovers" (1762) to establish this form in England, but the English sentimentalists scarcely succeeded in creating a well defined species. They usually mingled comic persons and scenes with improbable plots, tearful reconciliations, moral preachments, and examples of benevolence and sensibility. Mrs. Sheridan, Mrs. Griffith, Hugh Kelly and, most notably and consistently, Richard Cumberland, established such plays in popular favour in the sixties and seventies. Meantime, opposition to French refinement and to the general sentimentalization of comedy was considerable. The success of Kelly's "False Delicacy" (January 23, 1768) and the condemnation of the bailiff scenes in Goldsmith's "Good-Natured Man" (January 29, 1768) won a temporary victory for the sentimentalists which brought as a rejoinder Foote's ridicule in "Piety in Pattens" and the success of "She Stoops to Conquer" in 1773. But neither this triumph for the fundamentalists nor the still greater success of Sheridan's "Rivals" and "School for Scandal" had any considerable or lasting effect upon the vogue of sentimentalism. Tearful and moralizing comedies continued to thrive on the stage until the end of the century, when all theaters succumbed to the sentimental clap-trap of Kotzebue.

The critical debate which may be traced in journals, prologues, dedications, and in the plays themselves, is not very illuminating. One party is never tired of affirming that the chief aim of comedy is to amuse and entertain; the other party is as tireless in declaring that the drama should teach and edify. This debate, however, indicates a fairly well marked division—albeit with many compromises—that may be made between the plays of the period that carry on in some measure the tradition of Congreve, Vanbrugh and Farquhar, and those that follow Steele, Cibber and the French sentimentalists; between the comedy of manners, wit and satire, and the comedy of sentiment, thrills and benevolence. Morality is no longer in question. No plays exhibit the indecencies of the Restoration era, all are decorous enough. The rake and the rover are no longer heroes, and they usually are treated as villains or as repentant prodigals. A light-hearted or comic treatment of marital infidelity never survives through the last act. Those who are trying to be naughty give up the effort before the final curtain. No couples are discovered in bed, wit never becomes gross. Few followers of the old school get along without a certain amount of sentimentality, such as even Sheridan displays in the "Rivals," and most of the praisers of benevolence and sensibility relieve their palpitations with some laughable and ridiculous personages. The audiences evidently found that thrills and laughs went well enough together, and most dramatists were willing to try both to entertain and to edify. The student of dramatic types needs to proceed cautiously in attempting to classify this very miscellaneous comedy into two main divisions. Nevertheless, the distinction is both apparent and significant. The exponents of the old comedy, including Goldsmith and Sheridan, were really marking the end and not the revival of the old tradition, and the sentimentalists of various sorts, though they produced no masterpieces comparable to "The Rivals" and "The School for Scandal," were pointing to the future.

In the succeeding chapter I shall try to trace the course of sentimental comedy from Whitehead and Mrs. Sheridan to Kotzebue and to note its importance both as a social record of its times and as a basis for the social drama of the nineteenth century. In the present chapter I wish to deal with defenders and revivers of the old tradition.

I

The farces and the afterpieces and the "petite comedies" were in the main on the side of the old tradition. Only rarely did they take on a sentimental tone, and even more rarely were they free from comic characters and ridiculous situations. They naturally inclined to the extravagance and rapidity of farce but they not only preserved much of the method and material of the old comedy, they also widened the range of its satire and ridicule. We have noted the extent to which Foote's entertainments added to the list of comic personages and kept the ridicule of manners quite up to date. A number of his pieces held a place in repertory after his death —"The Minor" (1760), "The Liar" (1762), from

Steele), "The Mayor of Garratt" (1762), "The Patron" (1764).

The fashion which Foote promoted of offering short plays of two or three acts also gave an opportunity for maintaining the purpose and methods of a true comedy of manners. As a matter of fact, there never was any real reason for dividing a play into five acts, and the difficulty was considerable of building up such an elaborate structure for a drama that should be constantly witty, satirical or laughable. English writers rarely learned the comic value of the repetition, with variations, of a situation, such as is often exemplified in Molière; and bowing to the demand of their audience for variety and incident, they found five acts of amusing entanglement rather a task. The sentimentalists had the advantage of being able to resort to a story with mystery, thrills and a final reconciliation, but the upholders of old comedy clung to the traditional plot of deception and exposure. And then, prolongation is the essence of sentiment, but brevity is the soul of wit. For a plot of tricks, illuminated by wit, two or three acts were well adapted. In addition to Garrick and Foote, some of whose pieces have already been mentioned, Colman the elder and Murphy were notable contributors to this abbreviated form.

Colman's "Polly Honeycombe" (Dec. 5, 1760) was published as "a dramatic novel in one act." Polly is a great patron of the circulating libraries and elopes with Scribble, who poses as an author. Her parents, an absurd old couple, still very fond lovers, design her for Ledger. The elopers are brought back, and Scribble is discovered to be an imposter and the nephew of Polly's nurse. The ridicule of the sentimental novel-reader, which Sheridan later repeated in "The Rivals," is capped by old Honeycombe's concluding remark—"a man might as well turn his daughter loose in Covent Garden, as trust the cultivation of her mind to a Circulating Library." In "The Deuce is in Him" (Nov. 4, 1763) Colman again attacks sentimentality. Colonel Tamper is possessed by the deuce, *i.e.*, by an excess of sentimental egoism which demands that Emily should love him for himself alone. He returns to her from the campaign at Havana with one leg and one eye missing. His appearance is a little too much for her "pure and disinterested passion," but Prattle, an amusing and gossiping physician, gives away the colonel's trick for testing the purity of her affection. Emily proceeds to play a trick on the colonel, and both receive considerable sensible advice before they are reconciled.

Murphy's "Citizen" (July 2, 1761), which kept the stage for sixty years or more, is a very lively afterpiece in two acts, in tone and incident very much like the old comedies. Sir Jasper Wilding, a hunting squire, has come to London to marry his daughter Maria to the son of an old city miser, Philpot. Young Philpot, though he works in the city in business hours, sets up as a man of fashion in the West End, drives a coach and keeps a mistress, Corinna. Maria is a gay madcap, teases her lover Beaufort and fools young Philpot, first by appearing to him as a simpleton and then as a literary young lady quoting poetry. In Act II old Philpot solicits Corinna, offering her twenty guineas ("There are some light guineas among them. I always put off my light guineas in this way"). His son interrupts them; old Philpot hides under the table; young Wilding (Maria's brother) enters, quarrels with young Philpot; old Philpot's watch strikes ten under the table; general confusion. In the last scene Beaufort, disguised as a lawyer, tricks the old squire into signing papers for his marriage with Maria, who by this time has refused old Philpot as well as his son.

In his "Three Weeks After Marriage" Murphy continued his ridicule of the parvenu citizen seeking to become a person of fashion. The play was damned on its first appearance as an afterpiece, "What We Must All Come To," but when revived, March 30, 1776, became a great success. Drugget is the citizen who has retired to the country "almost four miles from London," and is delighting himself with strange freaks in horticulture. His oldest daughter has been married three weeks to Sir Charles Racket, and the parents, delighted in this alliance with fashion, are thinking of giving their second daughter, Nancy, to the beau Lovelace instead of to the worthy Woodley. Sir Charles and Lady Racket come in from a rout where they have been playing cards; she thinks he should have played a diamond, and he insists that his club was right, and they fall into a great quarrel. Sir Charles sends for his horses, calls his wife names, and creates general consternation and misunderstanding. The Rackets are reconciled but soon return to the old dispute over the club and the diamond. The Druggets, disillusioned by this exhibition of high life, decide to marry Nancy and Woodley, even if the new son-in-law doesn't approve their taste in gardening.

It will be noted that these pieces create new persons and situations, some of which were borrowed in later plays, as well as give new point and life to some of the oft used complications of the old comedy, such as the man hidden under the table, and the marital quarrel. Indeed, as one looks back over the history of the drama, it is these short plays which seem to have offered the most promising lead for a reviving and continuation of the comic tradition. Discarding the elaborate five-act structure and keeping close to the manners of the day, the dramatists might have found ample scope in the social changes of the period for both laughter and instruction. But the ambitious dramatist, though he might write afterpieces for the theater, kept in view as his goal a five-act comedy that should rival Congreve and Wycherley.

The masterpieces of these dramatists were not acted as often as a generation before. Wycherley indeed was now endured only in adaptations, but even these adaptations preserved something of the old spirit. Garrick's "Country Girl" (October 25, 1766), an alteration of

Wycherley's "Country Wife," loses much of the vigour as well as the indecency of the original, but it was very popular and not at all sentimental. Sheridan's "Trip to Scarborough" (February 24, 1777), an adaptation of Vanbrugh's "Relapse," cannot escape the charge of sentimentalizing but it preserves a good deal of the old play. Sometimes, indeed, the old favourites suffered the humiliation of being reduced to one-act farces or three-act afterpieces, but even so, they preserved something of the comic tradition. There was much in the repertory of the theaters to stimulate the ambition to produce a new and great example of the comedy of manners.

Colman's "Jealous Wife" (February 12, 1761) succeeded as far as the approval of the theater was concerned. It was immensely popular and held the stage well into the next century. It is indeed a notable effort to keep to the canons of high comedy, tuned down to the taste of the times, but without any yielding to sentimentalism. Mrs. Oakly's jealousy is always absurd, and no one, not even the lovers, is troubled by extreme delicacy. Harriot flees from home to escape marriage to Sir Harry Beagle, is followed to London by her irascible father and by the "horsey" Sir Harry. At her aunt's, Lady Freelove's, she is insulted by Lord Trinket, her foppish suitor, escapes to the house of Oakly, and is suspected by Mrs. Oakly of being her husband's mistress. His son Charles, who is in love with her, and his brother, Major Oakly, secure her escape from Lord Trinket, who has had her father and Sir Harry seized by a press gang headed by Captain O'Cutter, a pugnacious and vociferous Irishman. O'Cutter mixes two letters of Trinket's, a challenge to Charles and a plotting one to Lady Freelove, and thus exposes the tricks of the conspirators. Sir Harry swaps his right to Harriot with Trinket for a horse. Mrs. Oakly is ridiculed; her husband makes a stand, and she declares herself cured. Charles marries Harriot. Here is a play with sufficient entanglements for five acts, with considerable social satire, and with something of a moral lesson directed to jealous wives who have tantrums and to henpecked husbands who submit. It is never first-rate comedy for a minute, but it is a painstaking effort to write satirical and entertaining drama.

Colman and Garrick as dramatists and as managers of the two theaters had been on the side of the old rather than the new comedy, but they combined to write a play, "The Clandestine Marriage," which may serve as the most striking example of a compromise between the comic and the sentimental tendencies. We are introduced into a family where much that is amusing occurs and where the comic aspects of human nature are constantly exhibited. The *nouveau riche* Sterling and his sister, the formidable Mrs. Heidelberg, are entertaining Sir John Melvil, the proposed suitor for Miss Sterling, and his father, the gay old beau, Lord Ogleby. Sterling pesters my lord with his attentions, showing him his possessions and his ruins.

Sterling. Ay, ruins, my lord, and they are reckoned very fine ones, too. You would think them ready to tumble on your head. It has just cost me a hundred and fifty pounds to put my ruins in thorough repair. This way, if your lordship pleases.

Lord O. (Going, stops.) What steeple is that we see yonder? The parish church, I suppose.

Sterling. Ha, ha, ha! that's admirable. It is no church at all, my lord! it is a spire that I have built against a tree, a field or two off, to terminate the prospect. One must always have a church, or an obelisk, or something, to terminate the prospect, you know. That's a rule in taste, my lord.

Lord Ogleby, one of the old school of stage fops, is even more amusing than Mr. Sterling and also has amusing servants. But underlying all these comicalities we are soon aware of a suspense that holds the heart. Fanny, the youngest daughter, has made a clandestine marriage to one of her father's clerks, Lovewell. Sir John Melvil, designed for the elder daughter, falls in love with Fanny, as does the old beau, Lord Ogleby. The dénouement is accomplished with theatrical éclat by the old situation of the discovery of a man in a lady's chamber. Here the discovery is participated in by the entire household, jealous sister, outraged aunt, father, lovers, and servant, but it ends with a pæan for sensibility and benevolence.

[*Fanny is pulled out of her chamber.*]
Fanny. I am, at this moment, the most unhappy—most distressed—the tumult is too much for my heart—and I want the power to reveal a secret, which, to conceal, has been the misfortune and misery of my—
[*Faints away.*]

[*Lovewell rushes out of the chamber.*]
Lovewell. My Fanny in danger! I can contain no longer. Prudence were now a crime; all other cares were lost in this. Speak, speak to me, my dearest Fanny! let me but hear thy voice; open your eyes, and bless me with the smallest sign of life.

As he continues eloquently to avow the marriage, Betty, the maid, remarks, "I could cry my eyes out to hear his magnanimity." But it is only in the chance aside like this that the authors' tongues go into their cheeks. The play was a great success, partly because the audience wept with Betty over the affecting magnanimity of the dénouement and partly because Lord Ogleby and Mr. Sterling are capital comic parts. No play of our period utilizes so skilfully what was theatrically effective in both the comic and the sentimental traditions. But what real merit it possesses belongs to its ridiculous persons and situations.

A mixture of the old and new styles of comedy to a somewhat different effect is to be found in two popular pieces by Charles Macklin, the actor. His farce "Love à la Mode" (1759) is an amusing sketch of the humours of a Scottish, an Irish and a Jesuit wooer, but has a sentimental ending in which a true lover, indifferent to for-

tune, wins the lady. His "Man of the World" was first
acted in abbreviated form at Dublin in the year after
"Love à la Mode," but the prohibition of the censor prevented its performance in London until 1781. In the
main it is a humorous and satirical depiction of Scots
speech and manners and a very satirical attack on time-
serving and place-hunting politicians. The satire, however, is joined to a sentimental story obviously borrowed
from Voltaire's refinement of "Pamela" in his "Nanine."
As in Voltaire's comedy, the hero is an entirely admirable
young man who, unlike Richardson's Mr. B., has every
regard for the heroine's honour. She is a dependent,
not a menial, in his family, and suspicions are aroused
against her because of her relations with a gentleman,
who turns out to be her father, an old soldier who has
seen better days. This story is told sympathetically, but
the main interest of the piece is in its satire on the Scotch
and the place seekers, combined in the person of Sir Pertinax Macsycophant, who is portrayed with Jonsonian
elaboration and vigour.

A more loyal follower of the old tradition than either
Colman or Garrick is to be found in Arthur Murphy.
No dramatist of this period yielded less to the entice-
ments of the popular sentimentalism. His first play, a
farcical afterpiece, "The Apprentice," appeared in 1756,
his last comedy, "Know Your Own Mind" in 1777, but
most of his pieces were produced in the sixties. The
majority were short, two or three acts, of which we have
already noticed the two most successful, "The Citizen"
and "Three Weeks After Marriage." Of his five-act
comedies, "The Way to Keep Him" and "Know Your
Own Mind" also held the stage into the next century.
None of his plays show much invention. He drew largely
from the French, from Destouches, Voltaire, and especially from Molière, his "School for Guardians" (1707)
borrowing its persons and incidents from three or four
of Molière's plays. But if not greatly gifted with originality, Murphy had a sense of stage requirements, dra-

matic tact and ingenuity, and skill in dialogue. "I don't know," said Dr. Johnson, "that Arthur can be classed with the very first dramatic writers; yet at present I doubt much whether we have anything superior to Arthur."

"Know Your Own Mind," drawn in part from "L'Irrésolu" of Destouches, is an excellent comedy, a skilful re-working of the old material of the comedy of manners. The harsh father, the indulgent father, the man of wit, the hypocrite, the true lover, and the irresolute lover, are the men of the dramatis personæ; and the madcap, the sly puss, the poor relation, and the amorous widow are the ladies. These are stock types, but there is fresh shading in the characterization, as there is ingenuity in the situations that expose to ridicule the defects and follies of the persons, and as there are life and wit in the dialogue. The villain who seeks to ruin the poor relation is both a hypocrite and a sentimentalist who declares "There is, however, something voluptuous in meaning well." The usual love entanglements are conducted with both decency and spirit, but the tone is antisentimental. Lady Bell is a capital heroine, and a fine part for Mrs. Abington. Her gaiety, coquetry and teasing recall the best madcaps of the old comedy.

"The Way to Keep Him" was even more successful on the stage and has the merit of greater originality. It was first written in three acts as a companion piece to the romantic "Desert Island," but the next season enlarged into five acts (Jan. 10, 1761). The moral conveyed in the title is that a wife should not mope but should exercise her charms to hold a husband, but the action of the play also suggests that husbands would better stay at home. Lovemore, of a roving disposition, is neglecting his wife and making love both to Lady Constant and the widow Bellmour, representing himself to the latter as Lord Etherege. Sir Bashful Constant is engaged in concealing his admiration for his wife, scolding her in public and sending her presents in secret by his friend

Lovemore. Sir Brilliant Fashion, another friend, is making love to all three ladies. Here is a setting for a Restoration comedy on the principle that marriage is a means for adultery; but that view is held up to ridicule in the affectation of Sir Bashful, and the contrary principle that you should love your own wife and no others is set forth in lively scenes. The sprightly widow Bellmour (another fine part for Mrs. Abington) repulses Lovemore when she discovers his imposture and aids his moping wife to wake up and put her best foot forward. Lady Constant repulses both Lovemore and Sir Brilliant and secures the homage of her husband. The morals of the old comedy are reversed, but the methods are the same. The value of constancy is discovered through intrigue and celebrated by wit. The drama appeals to good sense through ridicule, never to sentiment through pathos. The ladies admit some slight faults on their side, but it is perhaps indicative of the growing power of women in the theater that at the end of the play the three ladies are quite triumphant and award forgiveness to their repentant husbands and lovers.

II

Oliver Goldsmith's first play, like those of Murphy, was written avowedly in protest against the vogue of genteel comedy and in accord with the traditions of "the last age," but "The Good-Natured Man" (Jan. 29, 1768) has a good deal of sentimentality and is far from exemplifying the methods or tone of Wycherley and Congreve. There is excellent satiric characterization in Sir Thomas Lofty, who pretends to aid Honeywood by his political and social influence, and in Croaker, who is always borrowing trouble; and the bailiff scenes were considered so "low" that they led to the condemnation of the play on its first presentation; but the main plot celebrates the loveliness of virtue. Young Honeywood, a believer in universal benevolence, carries his amiability and generosity so far that he is imposed upon by every one and is saved from disaster only by the tender care and timely interference of Miss Richland, whom he marries. Humanity, charity and tenderness are exalted as highly as in "The Vicar of Wakefield" or in any comedy by Kelly or Cumberland. The sub-plot is more amusing, though its main situation is rather like that of "The Conscious Lovers." Croaker has sent his son, Leontine, to France, to bring his sister, long resident there; the young man returns with Olivia with whom he has fallen in love and whom he passes off as his sister. The young people, fearing that their deception is to be discovered, plan to start off for Scotland separately. Their plots get mixed and lead to comic entanglements and ludicrous scenes at the inn. As in "The Clandestine Marriage," comic persons and scenes alternate with those of extreme sensibility, and the contrasting elements are not fused in any single decisive dramatic purpose.

"The Good-Natured Man" is by no means a comedy of the first rank, but it has certain qualities unusual and promising. First, there is Goldsmith's gift of style, so agreeable and so unforced. Cumberland, his opponent, paid him a generous but deserved compliment when he wrote "It is to be lamented that Goldsmith did not begin at an earlier period to turn his talents to dramatic compositions; and much more to be lamented, that after he had begun, his life was so soon cut off."—"There is something in his prose that to the ear is uncommonly sweet and harmonious; it is clear, simple, and easy to be understood; we never want to read his period twice over, except for the pleasure it bestows; obscurity never calls us back to a repetition of it." Since Steele, simplicity and charm had scarcely been found in comic diction.

Along with gracefulness of phrase, goes a real sense of humour. Always unaffected, sometimes a little boyish, it is ever on the lookout for opportunities. It gives point and satire to the comic characterization of Lofty and Croaker, adds sprightliness to the scenes at the inn, and slyly intrudes an attack on the sentimentalists into the talk of the bailiff.

"I love to see a gentleman with a tender heart. I don't know, but I think I have a tender heart myself. If all that I have lost by my heart was put together, it would make a—but no matter for that. . . . Humanity, Sir, is a jewel. It's better than gold. I love humanity. People may say that we, in our way, have no humanity; but I'll shew you my humanity this moment. There's my follower here, little Flanigan, with a wife and four children, a guinea or two would be more to him than twice as much to another. Now, as I can't shew him any humanity myself, I must beg leave you'll do it for me. . . . Sir, you're a gentleman. I see you know what to do with your money." [III, i.

This humour reminds us now of Steele and now of Farquhar and it gives promise of that distinctive quality which was to make Goldsmith's next comedy a classic of the stage and the finest expression of his own personality.

"She Stoops to Conquer" was acted at Covent Garden on March 15, 1773, under favourable circumstances. The play had been accepted by Colman only with some reluctance and after vigorous urging from Dr. Johnson. On the day of the performance, as Cumberland relates, Goldsmith's friends assembled for dinner at the Shakespeare Tavern with the redoubtable doctor at the head of the table "in inimitable glee," and thence proceeded to the theater where they took prearranged posts and carried the play to success by their applause. It is difficult, however, to believe that preconcerted signals were required to establish the points for laughter or that it was necessary for the solemn Cumberland to explain to Drummond of the sonorous and contagious laugh when to cut loose with its music. Where, indeed, in this delightful comedy should one refuse to laugh?

It is admirable in construction and incident apart from its charms of style and humour. How simply and pleasantly the opening scene introduces us to an old-fashioned house in the country and its occupants—Mr. Hardcastle, with his fondness for silly old stories and a silly old wife; Mrs. Hardcastle with her absurd hopes of what a year or two of Latin may do for her son Tony; Tony himself bawling and prancing over the stage; Miss Hardcastle and her friend Miss Neville so natural and unaffected in their maidenly views of fortunes, marriages and the expected suitors. Miss Hardcastle soliloquizes:

Miss H. Lud! this news of papa's puts me all in a flutter. Young, handsome: these he put last; but I put them foremost. Sensible, good-natured; I like all that. But then reserved and sheepish; that's much against him. Yet can't he be cured of his timidity, by being taught to be proud of his wife? Yes; and can't I—But I vow I am disposing of the husband, before I have secured the lover.

How naturally the second scene in the alehouse introduces Tony and the two lovers and the practical joke which directs them to his father's house as an inn. Here is excellent exposition, everybody introduced, the main action started, our expectation aroused for amusing complications, and yet no hint given of their development. The mistake of the house for an inn may be improbable enough, but it is well prepared for and carried along. And as a stage trick it has the great virtue of novelty.

How novel too are the succeeding incidents and how cleverly they are developed and interwoven! Tony's pranks, so rudely designed, bring about such unforeseen results. Laughter shifts from one person to another like the box of Miss Neville's jewels, which is ever being won and lost. The most preposterous situation is always saved from buffoonery and heightened to merriment, as when Mrs. Hardcastle at the end of her long ride finds herself kneeling to her own husband in her own back yard, or in the final scene when Marlow's mistaking of Miss Hardcastle for a servant reaches its culmination in his ardent proposal of marriage, her arch raillery, and their fathers' perplexity.

The play follows the old comic formula of a series of deceptions, but the tricks are new and so is the trickster. Never before had the manipulator of the strings in the entanglement been a boisterous oaf playing crude practical jokes which nevertheless triumph over circumstance and superior intelligence. One is reminded of Puck playing with the mortals and laughing at their folly, but Goldsmith, no more than Shakespeare, emphasizes the irony or the morality of wisdom falling at the beck of folly. No one, I hope, desires to have Tony reformed or even held up as an example of anything. The play has that happy sufficiency of humour which can maintain its vivacity without stressing its own merits.

This humorous view of life separates the play from the two opposing schools of its own day. It is certainly unsentimental without any parade of refined sensibilities even in its heroines, and it is pure comedy throughout, eschewing tears and reforms. But it is also free from the sarcastic or satirical attitudes of Congreve or Wycherley, and it offers no view of high society or modish wit. It can scarcely be called "high" comedy either in the sense that it is concerned with the refinements of humour and manners as opposed to "low" and obvious excitements of laughter, or in the sense that its plot is determined by its characters. The main action and many of the incidents are essentially farcical, and Tony Lumpkin is a triumph of "low" comedy, yet both the naturalness and consistency of the persons and the freedom from boisterous buffoonery are far above the requirements of farce. Laughter is free and unrestrained yet does not forbid a tenderness or liking for the very objects of our amusement. The ancient edicts of comedy are disobeyed as completely as in "As You Like It" and "Twelfth Night." The purpose of the laughter is not satire or ridicule, its objects are not contemptuous or ugly. On the other hand, nothing is idealized or moralized. There is no glamour of romance as in Shakespeare, and no one is wept over or converted as in Cumberland.

It is indeed not easy to reduce Goldsmith's comic muse to a definition. She bears no likeness to Cumberland's as Goldsmith described her:

"Like a tragedy queen he has dizened her out."

And she is no child of woodland fancy wild. She has neither the superiority nor brilliancy of Congreve's. Perhaps she is nearest in mood to the deity who guided Farquhar's pen to the creation of Cherry and Scrub. She has a special fondness for practical jokes but she is not merely a romp. She usually likes those at whom she laughs, and they are nearly everybody. She prefers to win our homage in a homespun gown, but whatever she wears has the grace of style. She stoops to conquer but with a glee not less inimitable and even more winsome than Dr. Johnson's at the Shakespeare tavern.

Though the success of "She Stoops to Conquer" in March was matched by that of Kelly's sentimental "School for Wives" in December of the same year, it perhaps helped to get a hearing for two unsentimental comedies, "The Man of Business" (Jan. 29, 1774) by Colman, who was just retiring from the management of Covent Garden, and "The Choleric Man" (Dec. 19, 1774) by no other than the chief of the sentimentalists, Cumberland. Goldsmith, who died in March, 1774, did not live to welcome as a temporary convert to the ranks of pure comedy the man whom he had just described in "Retaliation" as,

"The Terence of English, the mender of hearts,"

or to witness the début on January 17, 1775, of a new master of wit in "The Rivals."

III

Richard Brinsley Sheridan was born to the theater, his father an actor and his mother a dramatist, and he was schooled in its ways and traditions. The drama

offered him the readiest means for the attainment of fame
and for the expression of his extraordinarily brilliant
mind.   Moreover, his temper as well as his education
gave him certain advantages that have been helpful to
many dramatists, including Shakespeare and Molière.
He was willing to make use of any matter which had
been successfully employed on the stage and was liked
by the actors, and he was eager to please his audience
and not at all unintelligent in finding out what it desired.
His immediate and enormous success was due in part to
a cleverness in bettering his examples and in meeting the
popular taste as well as to his great dramatic and literary
powers.

His first play, "The Rivals," was produced when he
was barely twenty-two, on January 17, 1775, at Covent
Garden.   On November 21 of the same year appeared
his opera "The Duenna," acted seventy-five times that
season, and long a great favourite.   The next year he
became owner and manager of Drury Lane and produced
there on Feb. 24, 1777, "A Trip to Scarborough," a
revision of Vanbrugh's "Relapse," and on May 8, the
"School for Scandal."   Two years later came the burlesque, "The Critic," on October 30, 1779, which virtually ended his dramatic career.   He was to win great
laurels in Parliament as an orator, so that Byron could
say that he had made the best comedy, the best opera,
and the best speech of his time, but his long management
of Drury Lane was disastrous and his adaptation of
Kotzebue's "Pizarro" in 1799, though very popular,
added nothing to his fame.   Portions of an unfinished
opera were found in his manuscripts at his death.   His
dramas were produced within four years, when he was
in the twenties, and include an opera, a farce, an adaptation, a burlesque, and two comedies.

Of these pieces only the two comedies require our consideration here.   "The Duenna" surpassed all contemporary operas in popularity and for a time bid fair to outdo
even "The Beggar's Opera," but the libretto shows

scarcely a stroke of Sheridan's real genius.   It is an excellent comedy of Spanish intrigue, better than the others of its time but not much better.   The "Trip to Scarborough" is a clever reworking of the "Relapse," preserving all that the theater would stand of the original but changing the Loveless-Berinthia story to meet moral and sentimental requirements.   "The Critic" is better than "Tom Thumb" and better than "The Rehearsal," which it displaced after a century of life in the theater, and it is as irresistibly funny now as the day when it was first acted.   The attack on Cumberland as Sir Fretful Plagiary is one of the most effective personal caricatures in the drama, and the nonsense and the persiflage are inimitable.   But his contribution to comedy is to be found in "The Rivals" and "The School for Scandal."

"The Rivals" failed on its first performance owing to the ineptitude of one actor, but with some abbreviation and with a new Sir Lucius it soon established itself in the position that it has ever since maintained, as one of the most diverting comedies on the stage.   Though the emotional refinements of Faulkland and Julia are quite in the style of the sentimental drama and equally dull, the remainder of the play is wholly in the comic vein, with the spirit of Farquhar and the wit of Congreve.   The main situation is farcical or at least theatrical—a young spark making love under an assumed name to the very girl designed for him by his irascible father—and the accompanying incidents and persons might seem drawn from the repertory of the theater; but their creator knew Bath and had eloped with a reigning beauty and fought two duels, and he had the wit to give the old situations both verisimilitude and vivacity and to inspirit the characters and their juxtapositions with a new comic force. The art of heightening by contrast the comic aspects of character has rarely been exhibited more amusingly than in the conversations of Mrs. Malaprop and Bob Acres with the others, or more exquisitely than in the dialogues between Captain Absolute and his father Sir Anthony.

Bob Acres and Mrs. Malaprop are doubtless caricatures but they are the work of genius. The coward reluctantly engaged in a duel is one of the oft-repeated situations of the stage, but nowhere worked out so effectively as here. Every bit of the elaboration counts,—his boorish gaiety that irks the somber Faulkland, his dressing, his learning to dance, his confidences with his servant, the challenge, and all the complications of the duel. At every moment his follies shine in contrast to the absurdities of others, especially to the ebullient pugnacity of Sir Lucius. Like Bob Acres, Mrs. Malaprop has a great stage part and is always presented in dramatic contrast with other persons, but she would be magnificent even alone and in monologue. How easy it is to invent malapropisms, once you have been shown how, and yet of all the specimens produced are there any which equal the masterpieces of the originator—"He is the very pine-apple of politeness," "a nice derangement of epitaphs," "Was it you that reflected on my parts of speech?"

"The School for Scandal" was produced near the close of Sheridan's first season as manager of Drury Lane, on May 8, 1777. It had long been expected and Sheridan had laboured over it with unusual pains and diligence, writing and rewriting up to the very moment of presentation. Its success was triumphant. We are told that passers on the streets near Drury Lane that evening were astounded by the tremendous noise in the theater. The screen had fallen in the fourth act, and the applause reverberated. Sheridan had attained a great ambition, to write a full-fledged five-act comedy equalling or surpassing the best of Farquhar, Vanbrugh, and Congreve, yet not too cynical, too immoral or too satirical for his own generation. That triumph has been maintained in the century and a half since then, the play still delights any lover of the theater, and by general acclaim would probably be held the best comedy of manners in our language and the best play of any kind since Shakespeare.

The general character of the play is dictated by the

stage tradition. The persons are not unusual—a choleric old husband and a sprightly young wife, two brothers, one a hypocrite who passes as a model of virtue, the other a spendthrift with a warm heart, a long-absent rich uncle who returns from abroad to test his nephews, an intriguing widow and a sweet young heiress. The main outlines of the plot are as familiar as these types of character. The old husband and the extravagant young wife quarrel. The hypocrite Joseph plots with the widow so that he may win the heiress and she win the spendthrift Charles. Joseph has an affair with the young wife, and the play must come to a climax in the scene in which they are discovered by the husband; but, to suit the morals of 1777, the affair must not go too far and the hypocrite must be foiled and the lady must repent. The uncle in disguise will test the character of the nephews, baffle the villain's plot, and help secure the heiress for the warm-hearted Charles. This much of the play is merely the standardized formula of the old comedy of manners adapted to the sentimental decorum of the reign of George III.

Sheridan's development of this framework is a marvellous work of art. He gives his persons sufficient vitality so that the complications of the action seem to spring from their dispositions. He adds minor characters, Snake the accomplice, Moses the Jew, and Mrs. Candour, a stroke of genius. He carries on the action through a series of notable and elaborate scenes, the quarrels of the Teazles, the scandal club, the auction of the family portraits, the screen scene, each in itself meeting every requirement of dramatic effectiveness. He clothes everything in a prose style that is a delight in itself and is decorated with the most brilliant wit. Each part is nicely fitted with every other part, and the whole structure is a model of design.

One of the happiest strokes of invention in this design is the enveloping the main action in the atmosphere of scandal. Instead of the forthright adultery and knavery of

Restoration times, we are introduced to a society which is most interested in talking about these subjects. This gives the play its satire and at the same time preserves some of the piquancy and wit without the grossness of the older comedies. And the scandal club rather puts us in the mood of make-believe. We are seeing persons and facts through a nimbus of comic misrepresentation. Mrs. Candour seems to say, This is real life—to be sure —but it is also high comedy.

The affair between Lady Teazle and Joseph does not proceed through scenes of love-making and flirtation, but through her quarrel with Sir Peter and the gossip of the scandal-mongers. Lady Teazle appears as a sharer in their frivolity and wit, but there are many suggestions that she and Joseph are only making believe—playing the parts. The other main course of the action, the prodigality and repentance of Charles, has a different setting, not of scandal, but of wine and song followed by the theatrical coup of the auction. In defending the extravagance of Charles, Sheridan was perhaps writing an *apologia pro vita sua,* but his praise of the generous heart never takes a seriousness that makes us lose the vein of comedy. The saving grace of refusing to part with the picture of his uncle and his lavish generosity with money not his own, are contrived for the applause of an excited audience rather than for thoughtful approbation.

These two actions concerned with the two brothers unite in the screen scene of the fourth act, the masterpiece of artificial comedy. What a metamorphosis of the bedroom discoveries of the Restoration drama! What a clever utilization of the ancient devices of the overheard conversation and the postponed discovery! With what contrast and irony one person is set off against another, and how surely every speech adds to the dramatic play and yet sparkles with wit! In the fifth act we return to the scandal club; and from its poison, the inno-

cent and virtuous—not too innocent or too virtuous—
purge themselves by repentance and reform—but not
beyond the requirements of good sense and good nature.

The play teaches no lesson and points no distinctive
moral unless it be Sir Peter's that true wit is nearly allied
to good nature. Sheridan had no desire to use the drama
as a means of direct instruction. In "The Critic" he disclaims any purpose in comedy except entertainment. He
had his own beliefs on social and political matters but
he did not preach them in his plays. In this respect
he was unlike his sentimental confrères who sought to
inspire benevolence and also to inculcate specific lessons,
and he was unlike most of the dramatists of his century,
who were inclining more and more to place emphasis on
particular moral or social instruction, and he was unlike
his contemporary Beaumarchais, who could smuggle revolutionary sentiments into the merriest theatrical divertisement. This lack of moral purpose has, I think,
resulted in some lowering of Sheridan's reputation
through the nineteenth century, and now with a turn in
taste critics arise who accuse him of spoiling "The School
for Scandal" by making it too moral. But the play, like
the others of Sheridan's, is a picture of life from which
you may draw your lessons as you choose.

Is this picture of life anything more than comic? is it
real or true or important? It certainly does not reflect
a mind seriously concerned over the problems of society
as do the plays of Ibsen and Mr. Bernard Shaw. Nor
does it reflect the manners and social views of a period
with any such clearness as do the comedies of Etherege
and Wycherley. We are not quite sure whether the
manners of Sheridan's comedies belong to his own or
to an earlier age, whether they are drawn from life or
from preceding drama. We can scarcely assert that they
present a profound or searching study of the universali-
ties of human behaviour. They were the work of a young
man, gallant, witty, a great dramatist and a great

humorist. His powers as a dramatist are displayed in design, in dialogue, in a most effective representation of comic characters. His powers as a humorist are to be found in a wit that is unequalled in readiness and abundance, in the high spirits which will find a laugh anywhere, and in a view of mankind which discovers plenty that is amusing without probing too deeply. If his representation of life seems sometimes artificial or theatrical, it is well to remember that it is unique. Is there any other picture of English society so vivid and so entertaining as "The School for Scandal"?

Sheridan had no rivals and few followers. It is absurd to say that his successes revived the comedy of manners and killed the sentimental species. It would be nearer the truth to say that he killed the old form. No one could emulate him, and his plays virtually end the great tradition that began with Dryden and Etherege but had been sadly lapsing after Farquhar, until this later bloom in Murphy, Goldsmith and Sheridan. There were of course plays of this type after Sheridan but none of importance. Farces and light comedies still preferred the comic to the tearful; lively intrigues, low comic scenes, and even attempts at wit were to be found in sentimental pieces, but only rarely an attempt was made to write high comedy that was both amusing and witty.

In fact, only one had any considerable popularity or merit, "The Belle's Stratagem" (Feb. 22, 1780) by Mrs. Hannah Cowley. She had begun writing for the stage four years earlier with a sentimental comedy, "The Runaway," and she produced in all nearly a score of tragedies, farces and comedies. A number of her plays are comedies of intrigue borrowing their inspiration and sometimes their plots from those of Mrs. Behn and Mrs. Centlivre. The most popular, "A Bold Stroke for a Husband," has the scene in Spain, where a deserted wife dons men's clothes and makes love successfully to her husband's mistress, while another donna pretends to be a vixen and repulses all suitors until she captures the desired one. Here, as in other pieces, a rather hackneyed plot is carried off with a good deal of dash. In "The Belle's Stratagem," the young lady who is scorned as shy and lifeless by her prospective husband, just returned from abroad, puts on a mask and boldness and wins his high-and-mightiness; while in the second plot a subdued country wife tastes some of the excitements and dangers of fashionable London. Thus ends the comedy of manners. It is a long time before anyone can devise new entertainment out of witty beaux and madcap belles.

When the revival of comedy began, about 1760, England was on top of the world. A reasonable freedom of the press and of assembly had been secured at home, and the Empire had been extended over India and America under the rule of a limited but not exclusive aristocracy. London had become the seat of luxury and culture, the abode of a society more cultivated and more urbane than it had ever known before. This settled and self-satisfied society, this triumphant and happy aristocracy, this metropolis of the world, would seem to supply the conditions under which a comedy of manners might flourish. But this mood of national magnificence was of brief duration. By the time Sheridan began to write for the stage, England was already involved in an irremediable quarrel with her American colonies, and before long the French Revolution was shaking the foundations of social order. The last quarter of the century was to know wars and agitations and suppression and intolerance and all things hateful to the comic muse. In such times men may be cynical or hysterical, they can scarcely be humorous. The comedies of Goldsmith and Sheridan represent a period of peace and prosperity, of national exultation, the age of Chatham, Burke and Johnson out for a holiday. If "The School for Scandal" does not preserve with exactness and thoroughness the manners of that age, it does reveal something of its spirit. We are invited to join in the merriment of gentlemen, gay, superior, a little arrogant, but not without some sense of social responsibility. They are not in a mood for tears or sermons and they mean to laugh at all the world beneath them, but they know that at times it may be brave or it may be kind to laugh.

CHAPTER XVIII

SENTIMENTALITY TRIUMPHANT, 1760-1800

WITH the increase of new comedies that began about 1760, there was every reason to expect a large appeal to sensibility. Sentimental comedy had long been established on the stage where the plays of Steele and Cibber continued to be favourites. The revivals of Shakespeare's romantic plays, and particularly the popularity of his "Cymbeline" and of Fletcher's "Philaster" gave further examples of the presentation of distressed and perplexed virtue. The new French *comédie larmoyante* was already known in London and continued to appear in translations, adaptations and imitations. Sentimentalism indeed was sweeping like a summer shower over the literature of western Europe, promising to revive it and as yet bearing no portent of the revolutionary tempest. Richardson and Rousseau were proclaiming the fascination and the value of the tender heart. The old conventions and established practices of European society seemed almost ready to dissolve and change before this emotional appeal. In England the middle class was growing, leisure was becoming more widespread, especially among women, and Methodism was quickening the religious emotions among the masses. Humane and liberalizing reforms were being agitated. The morality of the Puritans was being revived, but accompanied by an un-Calvinistic faith in the possibility of human betterment here and now. How far the manners and morals of English society were really changing it is difficult to say, but at least the audiences of the theaters seem to have disliked cynicism and cold calculation on the stage and eagerly endorsed the praises of virtue, benevolence, and the tender heart.

439

On February 10, 1762, appeared a very remarkable and original comedy, "The School for Lovers" by the poet-laureate William Whitehead. It is based on Fontenelle's "Le Testament," a closet drama with the scene in ancient Greece, but it tells a story of English lovers of its own day with freshness and delicacy. It offers no repentant prodigals, no converted rakes, no long-lost children, no lecturing moralists to excite the sympathies of the audience, but asks their interest solely in the perplexities of natural if over-sensitive lovers. Cælia is the ward of Sir John Dorilant, and to him by her father's will goes her estate unless she marries him when she comes of age. He is in love with her but too high-minded to force her inclinations and is fearful of mistaking her gratitude for affection. She is a charming girl, in love with her guardian, but desiring love in return and momentarily touched by the tender solicitations of a philanderer. This is the main action, two estimable lovers, perplexed through the over refinement of their sentiments. It would be less difficult to bring the two together for the happy dénouement, as Araminta, Sir John's sister, remarks, "had my brother a little less honour and she a little less sensibility."

A comic element is supplied by Cælia's mother, who has designs on Sir John herself, an intrigue by Modely, engaged to be married to Araminta but plotting to carry off Cælia and her fortune. Modely, however, is not a villain or a libertine but merely a conceited philanderer who is speedily brought to his senses; and Araminta is a spirited and intelligent woman who does not despair of all things when the man whom she loves disappoints her but at once sets to work to punish and instruct him. The deception and manipulation of the plot really detract very little from the interest in the love perplexities of Cælia and Sir John. Professor Bernbaum, the first critic to give the play its due meed of praise, rightly declares, "To introduce such characters, to write the dialogue between them with a purity and grace corresponding to their fastidiousness, was an achievement for which Whitehead deserves more credit than he has received." It is rather surprising that Whitehead succeeded in his own theater; the play was performed fifteen times in its first season, and was later revived. It might be difficult to persuade a theatrical manager that any audience to-day is possessed of such genuine refinement of feeling as that of the Drury Lane of 1762. Certainly the success of the "School for Lovers" indicates a great change of manners in the eighty years since Wycherley's "Plain Dealer."

Too much credit must not be given to Whitehead for originality in the analysis of the debates of the sentiments. He may have been imitating the best manner of Marivaux. Since "Pamela," many novelists and dramatists had been engaged in praise and vivisection of sensibility. The conflict between sentiments both generous and refined had been dramatically illustrated in the dialogues between Bevil and Indiana in Steele's "Conscious Lovers," indeed similar conflicts of love with honour or loyalty or propriety had been common in the heroic plays and in the tragicomedies of Massinger and Shirley. The scruples that were once thought to honour the princes and princesses of romantic poetry are here made the natural attitudes of ordinary English gentlemen and ladies. Perhaps the play may be said to mark the date when such emotional scrupulosity became common and popular. With the rise of the middle classes, all the peculiar possessions of knights and gentlemen were claimed by all—including that of sentimental sensitiveness. Few novels or plays in English since Whitehead's day have failed to exploit it; and up to the recent post-war anarchy it was accepted in our popular literature as a sure mark and evidence of virtue.

Whitehead's example, however, had few direct followers. The closest imitation of his play seems to have been of its title, which was borrowed for a score of comedies, "School for Rakes," "School for Scandal," "School for Guardians," etc. Few dramatists failed to

give some exhibition of emotional refinement; fewer dared
to present it without sensational accompaniments; the
majority sought excess rather than delicacy of sentiment. As a matter of fact, this balancing of sensitiveness is a precarious business in the drama: "I love you,
but though you protest you love me I fear it is only pity."
"Nay, I love you, but you are moved by duty". . . etc.
This kind of supersensitive debate soon wearies and
offers even less visible than auditory satisfaction to
the audience. Even Whitehead's elegance seems a trifle
stilted. The English audience was supposed to require
more excitement and slapstick, and to be affronted by
French simplicity and delicacy. The dramatic problem
was how to mix this virtuous and instructive fastidiousness with something else—comic personages, a sensational and pathetic story, an evil-doer reformed with due
emphasis on her career "in gaudio," or with the music
and song of opera. All of these and other accompaniments were tried in the decade which followed "The
School for Lovers" by Mrs. Sheridan, Mrs. Griffith,
Kelly, Bickerstaffe, Cumberland, and later on by many
more.

Mrs. Sheridan's "Discovery" (Feb. 3, 1763) acted the
year after "The School for Lovers" with even greater
success, was often revived, and has had the distinction of
being rewritten recently by Mr. Aldous Huxley. It relies
on comic scenes for a large part of its interest and on a
sensational brand of sentimentalism. The amusement is
supplied by the newly-married Flutters who are constantly
quarrelling and by a formal old beau, Sir Anthony Bran-
ville, played by Garrick. The sensationalism appears in
the relations of Lord Medway, a roué in financial difficulties, and his noble son Colonel Medway. The father
sees his only escape from financial ruin through the marriage of his son to a wealthy widow, Mrs. Knightly, but
the son is devoted to the poor relation of the widow,
Miss Richly. The plot reaches its highest tension in
a rivalry of renunciation. "I deserve the ruin I have

brought upon myself," says My Lord, "and am content to sink under it." "Not while I have power to help it," replies the Colonel.

Lord M. I cannot ask it, son.
Col. M. I'll give up all, even my love, to save you.

Miss Richly supports the Colonel in his sacrifice of her to save his father, but happily the sacrifice is not necessary. Mrs. Knightly proves to be no other than the long-lost daughter of Lord Medway himself, and her munificence permits all the nice young people to get married. Such sentimental generosity as the Colonel shows is so silly that it is almost immoral, but it is the kind of gesture well suited to the new theatrical taste.

Two years later sentimentalism triumphed in the opera "The Maid of the Mill" (Jan. 31, 1765) by Isaac Bickerstaffe. It owes a little to Fletcher's play of the same name but is mainly a revamping of "Pamela," transforming Richardson's Mr. B. into Lord Aimworth, a model of worth and sensibility. In this the opera resembles Voltaire's dramatization of the novel, "Nanine," but it does not follow that excellent comedy in plot, and still less in style and tone. The debates between Lord Aimworth and Patty (Pamela) are in the most exalted tone, each vying with the other in nobility and sentiment, but just as they reach a tearful crisis they burst into an insipid song. What merit the play has is devastated by the songs which are below the usual low level of Georgian opera. Here is the one which ends their perturbations:

Duet

Lord A.   My life, my joy, my blessing,
   In thee such grace possessing
     All must my choice approve.

Patty.   To you my all is owing
   O! take a heart o'er flowing
     With gratitude and love.

Lord A. Thus enfolding,
             Thus beholding,

Both.   One to my soul so dear;
             Can there be pleasures greater?
             Can there be bliss completer?
             'Tis too much to bear.

Bickerstaffe was a clever purveyor to the theater, writing plays of all kinds as well as operas, most of which won striking success. Without conscience or principle, artistic or otherwise, he knew the theater and the easiest way to please the taste of the moment. Heretofore the drama had been regarded as a part of literature; but its production was about to pass largely into the hands of men who possessed little literary talent or sincerity but much skill in creating popular theatrical confections. Of these Bickerstaffe was one of the earliest and most successful. He had already written several pieces, including the pleasant and slightly sentimental opera "Love in a Village," but he seems to have taken special pride in the lofty tone of his version of "Pamela." He even had the audacity to write "This sort of comedy (appealing to the heart and understanding), if pleasantry be not entirely excluded, is certainly the most commendable of all; and the author begs leave to observe that the 'Maid of the Mill,' a piece written by himself, however trifling in other circumstances, was the first sentimental drama that had appeared on the English stage for near forty years." He is apparently dating back to Cibber's "Provoked Husband" and overlooking Lillo, Moore, Whitehead, to say nothing of Dodsley's sentimental opera, "The King and the Miller of Mansfield" (1737). But while Bickerstaffe's boast is preposterous, it may be granted that he was the first to succeed with sentimental comic opera. "The Maid of the Mill" had many followers and it doubtless did much to maintain the popularity of sentimentalism in the theater.

A much better sample of Bickerstaffe's talents and an

even more popular opera appeared three years later, "Lionel and Clarissa" (Feb. 25, 1768). The comic portion in which an irascible father is fooled into providing for the elopement of his own daughter is amusing, the songs have life and the sentimental portion is neither absurd nor jejune. Lionel, tutor to Clarissa, is under great obligations to her father and, though torn between honour and love, finally tells her that he cannot marry her. Sir John Flowerdale, the father, overhears this renunciation, and after chiding the two lovers for not confiding in him, gives them his blessing. Here is the way the opera begins:—

Scene I. A chamber in Colonel Oldboy's house: Colonel Oldboy is discovered at breakfast, reading a newspaper; at a little distance from the tea table sits Jenkins; and on the opposite side Diana, who appears playing upon a harpsicord. A girl attending.

Trio
Ah! how delightful the morning
How sweet are the prospects it yields;
Summer luxuriant adorning
The gardens, the groves, and the fields.

Perhaps we may dispense with the second stanza in order to find room for a little of the Colonel's pleasantry. He has had a serious quarrel with his wife and explains:

Col. A little affair of jealousy. You must know my game-keeper's daughter has had a child, and the plaguey baggage takes it into her head to lay it to me. Upon my soul, it is a fine fat chubby infant as ever I set my eyes on: I have sent it to nurse; and, between you and me, I believe I shall leave it a fortune.
Jenkins. Ah, Colonel, will you never give over?
Col. You know my lady has a pretty vein of poetry; she writ me an heroic epistle upon it, where she calls me her dear, false Damon; so I let her cry a little, promised

to do so no more, and now we are as good friends as ever.

This, it will be noted, is quite in the vein of the old comedy, and so is much of the action and the dialogue of the piece, in artful contrast to the sentimental heroics. But the character of Lionel is well conceived though his idiom is not that of our twentieth century youth. He is parting from Clarissa:

Lionel. Oh! my Clarissa, my heart is broke; I am hateful to myself for loving you: yet, before I leave you forever, I will once more touch that lovely hand—indulge my fondness with a last look—pray for your health and prosperity.

Clarissa. Can you forsake me? Have I then given my affections to a man who rejects and disregards them? Let me throw myself at my father's feet; he is generous and compassionate;—he knows your worth—

Lionel. Mention it not; were you stript of fortune, reduced to the meanest station, and I monarch of the globe, I should glory in raising you to universal empire; but as it is,—farewell! farewell!   [III, ii.

The next entrant into the sentimental field after Bickerstaffe was Mrs. Elizabeth Griffith with "The Double Mistake" (Jan. 9, 1766). The basis for harrowing our feelings is unfortunately farcical. By absurd mistakes a gentleman is twice discovered in the heroine's chamber, and she suffers greatly from the suspicions occasioned. A much better play is the author's "School for Rakes" (Feb. 4, 1769), an adaptation of Beaumarchais' "Eugènie" (1767). The play comes closer perhaps than any since Whitehead's to the French model. The later comedies by Mrs. Griffith, "A Wife in the Right" and "The Times," are more commonplace and add nothing new to the sentimental genus.

Two years after "The Double Mistake," Hugh Kelly scored a success with "False Delicacy" (Jan. 23, 1768).

Because this play came into rivalry with Goldsmith's "Good-Natured Man," it has often served as a butt for the attacks of the critics, but it is really far from being stupid or ridiculous. It is an interesting and novel attempt not merely to intermingle but to unite the humorous and the sentimental views and to reconcile sense and sensibility. The two plots both lead to sentimental agonizing. Lady Betty has refused Lord Winworth from false delicacy, and he requests her to convey a proposal of marriage to Miss Marchmont. This perturbs Lady Betty, who really loves Lord Winworth herself, and it perturbs Miss Marchmont because she does not love Lord Winworth but fears she ought not to disregard the wishes of Lady Betty, to whom she is under the greatest obligations. In the sub-plot Sir Harry Newburgh is persuading Miss Rivers to elope against her father's wishes, but father and daughter outdo each other in perturbation and magnanimity. These sentimental complications are exposed to ridicule through Cecil and Mrs. Hurley, a vivacious widow, who exclaims, "The devil take this delicacy! I don't know anything it does besides making people miserable," and then adds, "and yet somehow, foolish as it is, one can't help liking it." Lord Winworth and Lady Betty are finally brought from their false to their true sentiments, not through their own understanding, but by the artifice of these humorous censors, who, however, are not above joining in the finalé of tears, generosity, and platitudes. It is impossible to tell whether the audience was better pleased by the ridicule of false delicacy or by its pathos. Doubtless Mrs. Hurley and Cecil made the play go on the stage, but they would not have been amusing except in contrast to the sentimentalists. And the dubieties of two sensitive souls in love with each other are realized with humour as well as with delicacy. To the success of the play is attributed the rapidly increasing vogue of sentimental pieces.

Kelly's next play, "A Word to the Wise" (March 3, 1770), is even more ambiguous in its mixture of comic and sentimental interest. Its materials are those that were by this time familiar in the dramas of sensibility, a girl leaving home for her lover who then proves unwilling to marry her, another girl in love with her father's secretary and disdainful of the wealthy prig who has been chosen for her, a duel which is prevented by the tearful entreaties of one of the ladies concerned, a long-lost son who is rescued from dependency to wealth, a converted libertine, and so on. But amid the mental sufferings of parents and daughters, considerable fun is had at excessive sensibility. The spirited Miss Montagu comments on "A very florid winding up of a period, very proper for an elevated thought in a sentimental comedy." Sir George Hastings, a pompous gentleman of the finest principle, plays a mock-heroic part in acceding to Miss Dormer's request to take upon himself the blame of breaking their engagement. This is perfectly proper for a hero of sentimental comedy, but his embarrassment is comic, not pathetic. Finally, the dénouement, as in "False Delicacy," is brought about in a very unsentimental way. Miss Willoughby, escaping from Capt. Dormer, places herself in the protection of Miss Montagu, to whom the Captain is coming to pay his addresses. Miss Willoughby hides in the closet. Miss Montagu leads the Captain on to express his devotion to her and his freedom from any attachment to Miss Willoughby, whereupon the latter comes from the closet, pulls him by the sleeve, and the two girls make great fun of him. For the girl, just saved from seduction and in an agony of mind, to play tricks in this fashion on her lover is adding a good deal of spice to sentiment. The worthy Sir George also has comic difficulties in proposing to Miss Montagu. The play was prevented from a hearing by Kelly's political opponents, the friends of Wilkes, but was acted in the provinces where presumably no great objection was made to the medley of humour and sentiment.

Kelly possessed both and he mingled them more adroitly in his "School for Wives" (Dec. 11, 1773), a

play that long held the stage.   Captain Savage and Miss
Walsingham are in love, she ingratiates herself with his
father the General, who proposes to her, but in such a
way that she thinks he is proposing for his son and he
thinks he is being accepted for himself.   Mrs. Tempest,
who is kept by the General, and rules the roast, finally
compels him to relinquish Miss Walsingham to his son.
Belville is the roving husband who decoys the stage-mad
Miss Leeson on the pretext that he is a theatrical manager, but she escapes from his lures and he is challenged
by her brother whom he disarms.   He also makes love
to Miss Walsingham, but she makes fun of him; later
he receives a letter in her name making an assignation
at the masquerade, where he discovers his masked partner
to be his own wife.   Of considerable importance in manipulating these complications are Torrington, an unusual
lawyer for the stage, "a downright Parson Adams in
good-nature and simplicity," and Lady Rachel Mildew,
a dramatist who is ever taking notes for her next sentimental comedy and always a good deal disappointed when
her friends are not sufficiently distressed to make good
copy.   In spite of this back fire at his own methods, and
in spite of the laughable scenes, Kelly's main purpose
is effectively carried through—to praise serenity and
patience in wives and to deplore the unfaithfulness of
husbands.   Mrs. Belville is not only admirable in character but very eloquent in her condemnation of libertinism
and duelling (IV. 2).   And he closed the play with a
very neat defence of his aim in comedy.

Belville.   I sha'n't, therefore part with one of you 'till
we have had a hearty laugh at our adventures.
Miss Walsingham.   They have been very whimsical,
indeed; yet, if represented on the stage, I hope they would
be found not only entertaining, but instructive.
Lady Rachel.   Instructive! Why, the modern critics
say that the only business of Comedy is to make people
laugh.

Belville. That is degrading the dignity of letters exceedingly, as well as lessening the utility of the stage. A good comedy is a capital effort of genius and should, therefore, be directed to the noblest purposes.

Miss Walsingham. Very true; and unless we learn something while we chuckle, the carpenter who nails a pantomime together will be entitled to more applause than the best comic poet in the Kingdom.

The next débutant in the sentimental world was Richard Cumberland with "The Brothers" (Dec. 2, 1769). He had already written a tragedy and had an opera performed, and in the course of his dramatic career, which extended through the century, he produced over forty pieces of various kinds. But he was destined to be known chiefly for his sentimental comedies, of which the first won a considerable success. The scene is in Cornwall. There has been a shipwreck, but all are saved, including a strange lady, Violetta, rescued at sea, and Belfield, Jr., the hero, and Captain Ironsides, a rough old tar. They have come ashore near the residence of Belfield, Sr., an avowed villain, who has slandered his younger brother to Sophia Dove, whom he now woos for himself. Really he has been secretly married to Violetta; and Lucy Waters, who has aided him in his villainy, now goes back on him and confesses to Sophia. The strange lady Violetta introduces some further complications, but in the end Belfield, Sr., confesses and repents, and Belfield, Jr., marries Sophia. Sir Benjamin Dove, a henpecked husband, Lady Dove, an amorous termagant, and Captain Ironsides make some stir and fun, while the other persons indulge in morality and pathos.

This hasty summary may be enough to indicate the essentials of Cumberland's formula which reappear in his later pieces. There is a complicated plot, comedy and villainy as well as sentimentality, and a very happy ending involving the entire conversion of the villain and the complete vindication of virtue and benevolence. The

various items in the plot are not exactly novelties; the
rescued but unknown lady had been a commonplace since
"The Conscious Lovers"; and the two brothers, one very
wicked and the other very nice, had been familiar in a
great many plays since "As You Like It" and "King
Lear."   But Cumberland surpassed his contemporaries
in the skill with which he manipulated the stock dramatic
situations into new excitements.   Instead of giving his
lovers time to brood and debate over their emotional
refinements, he rushes them on to new thrills and hurries
them through dangers and rescues to a final haven of
blessedness.

His next comedy, "The West Indian" (Jan. 19, 1771),
performed twenty-eight times the first season, and long
continued in repertory, added a new element in his formula.   He has told us in his Memoirs how he determined
that universal benevolence should be illustrated by exalting those types of character which had hitherto had few
or no defenders.

I fancied there was an opening for some originality,
and an opportunity for showing at least my good will to
mankind, if I introduced the characters of persons who
had been usually exhibited on the stage as the butts for
ridicule and abuse, and endeavoured to present them in
such lights as might tend to reconcile the world to them,
and them to the world.   I thereupon looked into society
for the purpose of discovering such as were the victims
of its national, professional, or religious prejudices, in
short, for those suffering characters which stood in need
of an advocate; and out of these I meditated to select
and form heroes for my future dramas, of which I would
study to make such favourable and reconciliatory delinea-
tions as might incline the spectators to look upon them
with pity and receive them into their good opinion and
esteem.

So, as he says, he "took the characters of an Irishman
and a West Indian for the heroes of his plot.   The stage

and the London public had not been accustomed to view these types as heroic or noble, but Cumberland's experiment proved entirely pleasing. O'Flaherty, the Irishman, is brave, generous, contemptuous of meanness, and patriotic. Belcour, the West Indian, is a child of nature, with the passions intensified by a tropical climate but without any of the selfishness and insincerity of corrupt society, and with instinctive goodness of heart, beaming at every gesture. In spite of his virtues, however, he is a good deal livelier than most sentimental heroes. The plot includes about everything possible. The long-lost son appears in Belcour, who is united to his father, the benevolent merchant Stockwell. The innocent girl, betrayed by a bawd but rescued, is Louisa Dudley, finally wed to Belcour. The prevented duel is between Belcour and her brother Charles. The change of fortunes by which a large property is transferred from the bad to the good restores their inheritance to the Dudleys. It will be observed that the emotional agonies in these sentimental plays are caused by money as well as love. Final happiness is secured only by the possession of both. The villain here, who for a time holds the money and oppresses the poor and worthy, is Lady Rusport, a puritan with a "heart of flint."

In "The Fashionable Lover" (Jan. 20, 1772) Cumberland's propaganda is directed at the national and theatrical prejudice against the Scotch. Colin Macleod, the steward, possesses every virtue; his thrift is unselfish and he helps to rescue the heroine. The author proudly avows his purpose in the closing words of the play. "I'd rather weed out one such unmanly prejudice [as that against the Scots] from the hearts of my countrymen than add another Indies to their empire." Sentiment thus takes a national, non-imperialistic, humanitarian swing. But the plot is very hackneyed and a little involved. The heroine, a poor dependent in the family of a rich merchant, is pursued by the libertine and spendthrift lord who is to marry the daughter of the merchant. Mortimer, cynical externally but benevolent at heart, Macleod the Scotch steward, and Tyrrel, the poor but worthy lover, aid the heroine. Her long-lost father comes home from India in the nick of time and regains his fortune, stolen by the villain merchant in whose family his daughter had suffered humiliation. The heroine marries the worthy lover. The rake reforms.

Owing possibly to the successes of Goldsmith and Sheridan, Cumberland turned aside from sentimental comedy for a time, devoted himself to tragedy and musical plays and even produced one non-sentimental piece, "The Choleric Man" (1774), but he soon returned to his formula and in the eighties and nineties employed it in more than a dozen comedies. Some of these were very popular and some failed, but Cumberland's dialogue and characterization are almost always skilful, and indeed his handling of complicated plots is usually ingenious if we admit the conventions of his theater. The balanced rhetoric in which the eighteenth century clothed its sentiment as well as its wit makes both a little ridiculous to our taste, and his pieties are not ours, but no small amount of brains and good intention went into the making of these plays. Cumberland cannot of course be credited with inventing a formula, but he may be said to have established it and by his skilful employment assured its general adoption. The use of an elaborate plot full of improbabilities and coincidences, daring escapes, rescues, and discoveries, had been justified in Shakespeare, and indeed his comedies would supply parallels to many of Cumberland's situations. But the use of these romantic entanglements for the presentation of contemporary manners and sentiments inevitably seems incongruous and artificial. Sentimentality could scarcely stand alone as Whitehead attempted, or maintain its virtue mingled with irony, as Kelly seems to have designed; it needed action to support it on the stage. A thrilling and romantic plot was perhaps just as likely to be original or interesting as the contrivance of tricks and deceptions employed in the comedy of manners. But the question was naturally raised, are such thrillers with their torturing of sensibilities, with their insistent morality, still to the viewed as comedies? They had happy endings and a considerable proportion of undeniably comic persons and situations. This comic relief often saved the day in the theater and served to offer sufficient excuse for the title, comedy, but in Cumberland the comic is always subordinate to the sentimental. An exciting story which reaches its high points in the emotional doubt and suffering of its heroes and heroines, relieved by comic scenes, and culminating in the complete triumph and reward of virtue—this combination, very familiar since Cumberland's day in novel and melodrama, may come as near tragedy as comedy, and not very close to the traditional forms of either. If we apply our general test—does it intentionally appeal to a sense of humour—that question must be differently answered according to the qualities of individual plays. If the pangs of sensibility are too much expanded, if the plot is too improbable, the situations too theatrical, if the moral aphorisms are too thick or if the faith in universal benevolence is too much exploited, humour is crowded out of doors. But it is possible to deny the thrills long enough to give humour a chance; sense and sensibility may dwell together even in Cumberland's formula. I may note one instance among his later plays where he keeps within the bounds of comedy and two others where his fondness for preaching and for plot make any humorous intent impossible.

"First Love" (May 12, 1795) has much the same basis of plot complication as "The Brothers," written twenty-five years earlier. Sabina Rosny is the foreign lady secretly married to Lord Sensitive but deserted by him, brought to England by Frederick Mowbray, whom she has nursed through an illness. Mowbray's first love, Lady Ruby, is now a widow, and his father, who opposed his marriage to her, now desires it, but Frederick feels himself bound to Sabina. Lord Sensitive courts Lady

Ruby but has pangs of conscience over Sabina. Frederick and Sensitive are the sentimental protagonists, each beset by scruples and perturbations. The Wrangles, a quarrelsome pair of newlyweds, David Mowbray, a downright naval officer, and Mowbray, Sr., who gradually learns not to run other people's affairs, furnish some amusement without any over-refinement of emotions. But the balance of sense and humour as against sensibility is supplied by Lady Ruby, who does not require either tricks or scruples in order to manage everybody with cleverness and expedition. She shames Sensitive into repentance, secures Frederick for herself, and is constantly good-humoured and entertaining in her conversation. Her character, admirably drawn, keeps the play from running off into melodrama and holds the interest to the life-likeness of the characterization rather than on the improbabilities of plot. The sentimentality is extreme enough in spots, but it never gets clean away from reality and a sense of humour. One humorous person, given full play among a crowd of sensitives, would, one suspects, always make a comedy.

Without any such humorous alleviation are the two best known plays of Cumberland next to "The West Indian," "The Jew" (May 8, 1794) and "The Wheel of Fortune" (February 28, 1795). The first of these was written to rescue the Jew from the undeserved contempt of Englishmen; and the hero, frankly reminiscent of Shylock, practises penury only that he may give, proves a universal benefactor, and out-Christians all the Englishmen. His forgiveness and gratitude, indeed, become so superlative that one feels an unworthy preference for Shylock, whetting the knife. One remark in the play may be quoted. Daughter and mother are having a heart-to-heart talk, cheering each other in recounting their tribulations. The mother sums up the situation, " 'Tis a distressful interim." That is the word; the play, which includes the usual clandestine marriage and prevented duel, is composed of "distressful interims," until finally the Jew dispenses fortune and happiness on the worthy. Even more than "The West Indian" and "The Fashionable Lover" this is a play with a purpose, an effort to change public sentiment. Its tone is sentimental and its plot artificial, but it is no more a comedy than are the social plays of Ibsen and Brieux.

"The Wheel of Fortune" (February 28, 1795) is still farther removed from comedy; indeed it proved far more moving to the emotions than any of the tragedies of the day. In his Memoirs Cumberland gives credit to the exquisite acting of Kemble in the leading rôle and to himself for hitting on so moving a plot. What a plot it is! Act I, Scene I, "The cottage of Penruddock seated in a group of trees, with a forest scene of wood and heath." Enter Weazel, a lawyer, in search of Penruddock, the hermit, to inform him that his cousin has died and left him a huge fortune. Nay, nay; the hermit scorns the money. Aye, aye; but do you remember Arabella Woodville? The hermit starts; twenty years have not effaced the memory of that name. This fortune puts her in your power and also that wretched Woodville, her husband. "Money can give you something, for it gives revenge." Scene II: Another part of the forest. Enter Woodville, followed by his servant. He has ruined himself, his wife, and his son, long a prisoner in France and just returning home. He has brought pistols to propose to the hated Penruddock the duel which he had avoided twenty years before. But look! another has also found this lonely spot, Syndenham, the philanthropic and humane. He goes with Woodville to Penruddock's cottage. The two foes meet; pistols are drawn. But stay! here is a parcel from Arabella directed to the hermit. He seizes it and retires to the cottage. Syndenham draws Woodville away—"Come Woodville, we have thrown that cynic cur a bone; so let him gnaw it."

Manifestly such a beginning presages much serious business. All the interims are distressing. Henry Woodville, the son, has several encounters with Penruddock, who discloses the villainy of his father who had won Arabella by deception and slander. Then Henry goes to his father and mother. The father is weeping. "Sir, be a man! . . . Penruddock charges you with acts, long past, indeed, but of the blackest treachery. How stands the truth?" . . . *Woodville.* "I'll give no answer." . . . *Mrs. Woodville.* "Take it from me.—'Tis true." Now Henry must return to Penruddock, his proud head bowed low, pleading not for justice but only for mercy. The cynic is unyielding—but list! "A word before we part:—you bear a strong resemblance to your mother— will you be troubled with a message to her?" When Kemble's voice trembled over these words, sobs were heard all over the house. The highest point of tension was reached. The cynic was turned philanthropist. " 'Tis done!" he cries, "the last bad passion in my breast is now expelled, and it no longer rankles with revenge." Everything moves on to noble music, to marriage, for-giveness and fortune, and to Penruddock's final aphorism, "the true use of riches is to share them with the worthy; and the sole remedy for injuries to forgive them."

In this breaking from any attachment with comedy, Cumberland not only opened up a new field for senti-mentalism but also invented a new species of drama, a serious moral or social lesson attached to a thrilling plot and a happy ending. However hackneyed his plots or sentimentalized his instruction, he is manifestly pointing the way for the serious drama of the next century. His immediate followers accepted both his leads, sometimes they kept sentimental conflicts tuned to the lighter music of comedy, but more often they joined them to social propaganda, to sensational situations, and to an earnest effort to prove that the good are always happy.

Of those who took the less serious purpose, perhaps the most skilful was the General Burgoyne whose sur-render at Saratoga was the turning point of the American Revolution. Before taking this command he produced a sentimental opera, "The Maid of the Oaks" (November

5, 1774), and after he had returned to England another, "The Lord of the Manor" (1780), still harping on natural innocence and virtue, and a comedy, "The Heiress" (January 14, 1786). The General had a sense of humour and a deftness of style, neither of which was displayed in his boastful proclamations to the Americans, but both of which temper the sentimentality of a very successful comedy. Horace Walpole thought that this "delicious comedy" would charm the stage after Burgoyne's battles and speeches were forgotten. Alas for prophecy, every American schoolboy knows of his battles, while no English schoolboy studies either his speeches or his play. Its plot has been traced to Mrs. Charlotte Lennox's novel, "Henrietta," and her play, "The Sisters," and to Diderot's "Le Père de Famille," but it is also very close to that of Cumberland's "Fashionable Lover" and indeed of other sentimental comedies. Lord Gayville is intended for the rich merchant's daughter, Miss Alscrip, but pursues a Miss Alton, who becomes a dependent in the Alscrip household. She turns out to be the sister of Clifford, a dependent on Sir Clement, uncle of Gayville and Lady Emily, with whom Clifford falls in love. In the end an honest lawyer discovers that the Alscrips have stolen the Cliffords' fortune, so the poor girl becomes the heroine and marries the reformed libertine, "her persecutor and her convert"; and the poor brother, after turning his fortune over to his sister, marries the rich Lady Emily. There is, of course, an abortive duel between Gayville and Clifford. These turmoils of the heart are fortunately accompanied by much amusing ridicule of the parvenu Alscrips and of the brother and sister Blandish, social hangers-on and flatterers who bet on the wrong heiress, and by much exchange of wit between Emily and Sir Clifford. Lady Emily, as her uncle says, presents sensibility and vivacity uncommonly blended and is a high-spirited girl who manages everybody and prevents any conversation from becoming tiresome. As the advocate of the warm heart, she carries on a duel with her uncle, the devotee of self-interest. After her Clifford's exhibition of matchless magnanimity at the close of the last act, she cries triumphantly to her uncle, "Now, sir, where's the suspicion? Where is now the ruling principle that governs mankind? Through what perspective, by what trial, will you find self-interest here? What, not one pithy word to mock credulity?" But Sir Clement rises to magnanimous heights himself, bestows a fortune and happiness, and rejoins, "If you think me a convert, you are mistaken: I have ever believed self to be the predominant principle of the human mind: my heart, at this instant confirms the doctrine. . . . To reward the deserving, and make those we love happy is self interest in the extreme." Here is a dramatic union of comedy and sensibility, displaying no considerable departure from Cumberland's formula, but escaping gracefully from mere repetition and commonplace.

From Thomas Holcroft, who beginning as a stable boy advanced to an extremely active career as man of letters, radical, and revolutionary, a development of the drama toward social propaganda might naturally have been expected. But Holcroft's political opinions find no specific expression in his plays. Those opinions were indeed so much out of favor that some of his pieces appeared anonymously, as even the name of the radical would have insured their damnation. In the "School for Arrogance" (February 4, 1791), sponsored at first by another dramatist, he has much to say about the equality of man versus rank and title, but in the main the plays keep to the safe and well-trodden course of denouncing gambling, libertinism, duelling, and of exalting the warm heart and the good intention. Holcroft's variation from Cumberland consists chiefly in the heightening of the story interest by the addition of tragic elements. Sentimentality is jazzed up. The old situations recur with greater emphasis on their tragic or sensational aspects, and the characters are extravagantly good or bad, sentimental or eccentric. The dialogue goes with a breathless rapidity. There is a wild rush to the conclusion, the prodigal returning on the run, the villain being trampled upon and kicked downstairs, and the sentiments spouting like geysers.

"The Road to Ruin," the best and most popular of his plays, and successfully revived as late as 1873, illustrates what advantages there may be in Holcroft's method. Young Dornton, son of a rich banker, is the prodigal spendthrift and gambler but has a tropical heart. His losses bring the banking house to the verge of ruin, when in repentance and haste he proposes to forsake his loved Sophia and to marry her mother, the detested widow Warren, so that her fortune may save his father from ruin. The widow's fortune, however, is due to a lost will, which has got into the hands of the villain Silky, instead of the honest Sulky. Silky plots to destroy the will and to marry the widow to Goldfinch, and to disinherit Sophia and the illegitimate son Milford. So far the plot is serious enough, but Goldfinch is the best of the many "horsey" stage eccentrics. Holcroft's youthful experience at the race track enabled him to fill out the type with amazing vivacity. But even without Goldfinch the play has a good deal of novelty and life. The first act, for example, is a fresh and admirable introduction to the prodigal son story. Harry has lost £10,000 at Newmarket, and the news has preceded him home. His father is enraged, vows not to receive him, but will hear no ill word about him from anyone else. Harry arrives with his friend Milford. The doors are closed. His father threatens from a window with a blunderbuss, "Knock again, you scoundrel, and you shall have the full contents, loaded to the muzzle, rascal!" Harry bets Milford a hundred that the door will open in less than fifteen seconds. It opens. His father refuses to see him and dismisses the servant who let him in. Harry lets the servant in again. Sulky, partner in the banking house, discourses on the impending ruin, the lost will, and other matters. Father enters—still in a rage. Harry bows to the storm, but now the warm heart of his begins to beat.

Dornton. I'll no longer act the doating father, fascinated by your arts.

Harry. I never had any art, sir, except the one you taught me.

Dornton. I taught you! What? Scoundrel? What?

Harry. That of loving you, sir.

Dornton. Loving me!

Harry. Most sincerely.

Dornton struggles against his warm heart for a moment but recovers and declares that he will never speak to his son again. Harry begs him to say good night.

Harry. Reproach me with my follies, strike out my name; I deserve it all, and more; but say, "Good night, Harry!"

Dornton. I won't! I won't! I won't!

Harry. Poverty is a trifle; we can whistle it off; but enmity—

Dornton. I will not.

Harry. Sleep in enmity? And who can say how soundly? Come! good night.

Dornton. I won't! I won't! (*Runs off.*)

Harry. Say you so? Why then, my noble-hearted dad, I am indeed a scoundrel.

(*Re-enter Mr. Dornton.*)

Dornton. Good night!

Harry. Good night.

Such dramatic rapidity leaves little opportunity to translate the conflicts of the emotions into prolonged debates. The temperature of the heart rises quickly until it boils over into action, generous or sacrificing, forgiving or repentant. The plots will take us not through distressful interims, but along roads to ruin, where the warm heart must contend against cold and calculating iniquity. Ruin is usually expressed in commercial terms.

The name of the goddess of the revolving wheel is now applied only to pounds, shillings, and pence. The comic relief is rarely as large as in Goldfinch; Holcroft's "comedies" are really plays of villainy, impending ruin, and final salvation.

In "Duplicity" (October 13, 1781), his first play, Osborn plays the part of villain, bringing Sir Harry Portland to ruin through gambling, but in the end he restores the property and proves a benefactor. In "Seduction," Sir Frederick Fashion, a libertine, plots to keep an assignation with Lady Morden and to elope with the heiress Emily in the same evening, but his tricks are completely upset by the counter tricks of Lady Morden's brother who is disguised as a servant. The sentimental interest is supplied by Lord Morden, cured of infidelity by the stratagem of his wife who pretends to be giddy. In this piece the complexity of plot arises through the multiplication of deceptions, but the result is a reversal of that of the old comedy, for here the virtuous win all the tricks. In "The Deserted Daughter," on the other hand, the heightening of the story is in the direction of tragedy.

The innocent daughter, long separated from her father, befriended by his honest Scotch steward, and lured to a house of ill fame—is taken from Cumberland's "Fashionable Lover"; and the impetuous Cheveril, who rescues and marries the girl, is of the type of the West Indian. Mordant is the errant husband, and Lady Ann the usual patient Griselda. But in addition, Holcroft has made Mordant desert his daughter by his first marriage, and presents him at the beginning of the play broken in fortune and conscience, despairing and frantic. He is the victim of his own misdeeds and of those of a villainous agent who has become possessed of his property and also of that held in trust. Not knowing his own daughter, Mordant plans to aid a friend to secure her and visits her in the house of ill fame. Of the many other complications that are added to this ghastly situation, we may merely note that the lovely daughter not only follows the old fashion of appearing disguised as a boy but also a new mode—she has studied the human countenance, has read Lavater, and is adept at interpreting character from physiognomy. Of course, in the end the virtuous win; the errant husband reforms; the villain and his confederate are exposed; and the lovers, young and true, embrace.

In these plays of Holcroft we come even closer than in Cumberland to the plots of the novels of Dickens and of nineteenth century melodrama and twentieth century movies. A villain has stolen a fortune and is willing to add seduction, abduction, or adultery to his crimes. He will get thoroughly exposed and damned before the play ends. In the meantime the innocent and pure and beautiful are brought to the verge of ruin. And those who have wandered from the paths of virtue have plenty of suffering and discipline to guide them to the stool of repentance. Eccentric persons and comic scenes furnish relief for our sympathetic suffering and lead us to trust in the final happiness which is sure to come.

Rather more successful with the public than Holcroft and not less varied in her themes and methods was Mrs. Elizabeth Inchbald, the chief of a considerable band of women sentimentalists that included Mrs. Sheridan, Mrs. Griffith, Mrs. Cowley and Miss Lee, and the last of the long series of women dramatists who had purveyed to the eighteenth century theater. She wrote between 1784 and 1805 some thirty pieces for the stage, including adaptations from the French and German and a number of farces and "petite comedies." These shorter pieces are usually brisk and unsentimental. "Appearance is Against Them," for example, has a bedroom scene. Lord Lighthead, a rover, is visited by Miss Audley, who hides in his bedchamber when his uncle Walmsley is announced. Walmsley in turn seeks refuge there when Lady Loveall enters. Miss Audley hides in the bed when Walmsley enters, and he jumps under the counterpane when Lady Loveall searches the chamber. She thereupon discovers the two in bed together. Explanations are difficult. "The Midnight Hour" is an excellent comedy of the customary brand of Spanish intrigue, and "Animal Magnetism" is a piece in three acts ridiculing a new fad. But Mrs. Inchbald's longer plays are all extremely sentimental, with plots almost as elaborate and thrilling as Holcroft's, though with somewhat more emphasis on social propaganda.

She may indeed be regarded as the most thorough-going exponent and apologist of sentimental comedy. The comments prefixed to the plays in her collection, "The British Theatre" (1806-9), are often significant both of her own attitudes and the new public taste. Of Cibber's "She Would and She Would Not," still popular, she remarks "This comedy has neither wit nor sentiment, but it has instead swearing, lying, and imposture." Of "The Beaux Stratagem" she observes, "It is an honour to the morality of the present age that this most entertaining comedy is but seldom performed. . . . The well drawn characters, happy incidents, and excellent dialogue . . . are but poor atonement for that unrestrained contempt of principle which pervades every scene." Sentimental comedy, she affirms, is not only right in morality but also right in art. "Scrupulous purity of character and refinement in sensation are the delightful origin of all those passions, those powerful impulses of the mind, on which works of the imagination are chiefly founded."

It might be supposed that a person holding such opinions would find a sense of humour as undesirable as an evil conscience. Mrs. Inchbald seems to have compromised on a distinction similar to the famous romanticist separation of fancy and imagination. Fun and merriment might be given rein in such trivial and fanciful pieces as farces and petite comedies, but should have only a slight and secondary place in the works of the imagination extolling, as the sentimental plays assuredly did, "scrupulous purity of characters and refinement in sensations."

"Such Things Are" (1787) has its scene in Sumatra

but presents as its model of perfection Haswell, who was intended as a portrait of Howard, the great English reformer of prisons. The story is a curious combination of romance and humour. Twineall, just arrived from England, plans to make his way by flattering the members of the English colony, but is misdirected so that instead of flattering he rubs their sore spots when he talks to Sir Luke Tremor of battles, to Lady Tremor of family, and to Lord Flint of sedition. He gets at once into hot water and then into prison, and is likely to lose his head. The romantic and sentimental portion of the play introduces the Sultan, really a usurper and a Christian, who has filled the prisons with his enemies. Haswell ministers to the prisoners, and obtains pardon for some. One of them, Zedas, steals his purse, but on discovering his true nobility, penitently returns the purse, an incident that aroused great applause at the first performance. The Sultan's long-lost Christian wife, Arabella, is discovered in prison and restored to him amid the usual flood of forgiveness, which releases the poor flatterer Twineall.

Three of the comedies which followed were taken from the French and illustrate the methods of French sentiment. "The Child of Nature," from Madame de Genlis (November 28, 1788), a very successful play in four acts, tells of the love of a girl and her guardian opposed by scruples similar to those in Whitehead's "School for Lovers." "The Married Man" (July 15, 1789) is a version of "Le Philosophe Marié," by Destouches, already presented in "The Married Philosopher" of 1732. "Next Door Neighbours" (July 9, 1791) was from "L'Indigent" of Mercier and "Le Dissipateur" of Destouches. Her next play, "Every One Has His Fault" (January 29, 1793), follows a scheme similar to that of "Such Things Are"; two stories, one humorous, the other serious and sentimental, are tied together by a model hero who is also the chief manipulator of the happy ending. Harmony, who has the habit of telling everyone that others praise them, is the reconciling angel.

He brings into harmony Placid, the hen-pecked, and Mrs.
Placid, Sir Robert Ramble and his divorced wife, and
Solus, a bachelor, and Miss Spinster. This is the humorous plot; in the serious story Harmony has an arduous
time. Lord Morland has never forgiven his daughter
for her marriage to Irwin, but has secretly adopted her
son. Irwin, in poverty and despair, denied by his old
friends, assaults and robs Lord Morland and is arrested,
charged with the crime. The pleadings of the child are
necessary in addition to the wisdom of Harmony before
Lord Morland relents. Here, perhaps for the first but
certainly not for the last time, the child appears as a
dramatic agent of forgiveness and reconciliation. At a
time when "King John" with Arthur and "Bonduca" with
Hengo were often acted, it seems rather strange that the
child had not often been employed in new plays as a
means of exciting pathos, especially as nearly every
comedy dealt with differences, separations and reconciliations between parents and children. But during the eighteenth century the young child had not been the center of
interest that he was henceforth to become both in literature and life.

The next comedy, "Wives as They Were and Maids as
They Are" (March 4, 1797) presents a perennial theme
for moralizers, the virtues of the past and the giddiness
of the present generation. Miss Dorillon, representative
of what was then the giddy younger generation, runs her
course of extravagance which lands her in prison for debt,
from which she is rescued by her father, returned from
India after a long absence; and, after due repentance,
she is married to the sentimental lover Sir George Evelyn.
Lady Priory, the obedient wife of her rigorous lord, is
the example of the rectitude of the elders. She is carried
off by Bronzely, a rover, to his house, where he informs
her that she is in his power. Her response is rather a
novel one and may be commended to all similarly distressed females, "Lady Priory sits down and takes out
her knitting." This foils the villain, who takes her home,

where she does not neglect the opportunity of reading her husband a sound lecture.

Although comic interims and aspects relieve these plays, their main appeal is not to a sense of humour. Imprisonment, robbers, poverty, sentences of death, all kinds of serious impediments interfere with the path of virtue and block the way to the union of peace and righteousness. But the final word in theatrical sentimentalism was attained by Mrs. Inchbald's adaptation of Kotzebue's "Lovers' Vows" (October 11, 1798). The all-conquering German had made his invasion of England on March 24th of the same year with "The Stranger," acted twenty-six times at Drury Lane in the brief remainder of the season. Covent Garden at once responded, presenting "Lovers' Vows" during the first month of the next season, and, while it was being acted forty-two times, also producing three other adaptations. At the close of the season Drury Lane joined in with Sheridan's "Pizarro" ("Die Spanier in Peru"), which brought everybody, even George III, to the theater. By the next season most of these pieces were being acted in New York as well as in London. "The Stranger," presenting the errant wife who is forgiven, is perhaps a more daring stroke of sentimentality than "Lovers' Vows," but the latter was venturesome enough to excite considerable debate as to its propriety among the young people of Jane Austen's "Mansfield Park." It is a good example of Kotzebue's methods. He intensifies all that was theatrical and improbable in the English sentimental pieces and gains his appeal not from truth of characters or feelings but from the excitement of theatrical situation and the showiness of the sentiments expressed.

Ill and penniless, Agatha is thrust out of the inn by the landlord and sits on a stone by the roadside. Then she rises, comes down stage, kneels and prays God that she may once again see her son, her only joy; and, continuing, she asks heaven's blessing on that son's father, her seducer. In a moment, enter Frederick, dressed as a

German soldier; impulsively he starts to aid the suffering woman.—Mother!—Son! After five years he is home on a furlough in order that he may secure his birth certificate. His mother sees that the secret can be kept from him no longer, and she painfully unfolds the tale: he is the natural son of the Baron Wildenhaim, whose castle towers over the neighbouring village. The two find from humble cottagers the refuge which the inn denies and then learn that the baron's wife has recently died and that he has just returned to the castle for the first time in twenty years. Agatha faints. Frederick leaves the cottage to beg aid and money for his mother. At the castle are the baron, the daughter Amelia, a French count, who is suitor for her hand but whose frivolity pleases neither father nor daughter, a comic butler, and the young pastor, a model man, with whom Amelia is in love. Frederick, in despair, begs money of the baron and threatens his life, and gets carried off to prison (a situation close to that in Mrs. Inchbald's "Every One Has His Fault"). The count's avowal of his infidelities stirs the baron's conscience to recall his own betrayal of Agatha, and softens his heart toward Amelia, who avows her love for the pastor and begs pardon for the prisoner. Frederick faces his father and reveals the truth. The baron is proud to find a brave and generous son and readily promises recompense; but no, he will accept no favours unless the baron performs the long deferred act of justice and marries his mother. Pastor Anhalt also urges this, and the humbled baron at last puts his conscience to peace. Forgiveness, embraces and a final tableau. "Frederick throws himself on his knees by his mother; she clasps him in her arms. Amelia is placed by the side of her father, attentively viewing Agatha; Anhalt stands on the side of Frederick, with his hands gratefully raised to heaven."

Sentimental comedy had begun in Steele and Cibber as a protest against cynicism and indecency on the stage, and against gaming, libertinism, duelling and other vices in society. It had praised the home and the family, sentimental love and marital fidelity, and had discovered in the everyday life of its own times some of the finer virtues and sentiments that had heretofore been reserved on the stage for the heroes and heroines of tragedy and romance. Beyond this accomplishment it had not greatly advanced in the course of the century. It had failed to create a species on the French model devoted to the refinements and delicacies of sensitive souls in our modern environment. It had failed to expand its material into a searching or critical study of its own times or to enlarge its efforts in behalf of a variety of social reforms. As a species it developed little beyond Steele's "Conscious Lovers," and by the end of the century had become addicted to a hackneyed plot, an excessive appeal to a few emotions, the repetition of the same sentiments. Its arguments and conventional emotional appeal were handed down to the melodrama of the nineteenth century and to the moving pictures of today.

The popularity of this type of drama was no doubt due in part to the rise of a commercial middle class in England. The stress placed on money and fortune is noticeable. But this drama can scarcely be denominated bourgeois. Its heroes are mostly of high rank, success in trade is rarely praised, the virtues exalted are not those supposed to characterize the bourgeoisie, thrift, sexual fidelity and honesty. Rather our admiration is elicited for the warm-hearted, careless of money or prudence, pursuing love and ideals with the fervour of adolescence. The vogue of sentiment on the stage seems to have been one of the early manifestations of that wave of humanitarianism which swept over the rationalism and restraint of the eighteenth century. It owed as much perhaps to the existence of peace and prosperity as to the philosophy of Shaftesbury or the imagination of Rousseau, and it owed still more to the growing influence of women in our society and literature. That amiable human desire to find free play in our dreams and our reading for those dénouements and reconciliations which are so difficult to bring to pass in actuality was exalted into a sort of gospel or cult of benevolence. The wave receded with the Napoleonic wars but it was renewed in Victorian peace; and after the inevitable materialistic reaction following the great war, it will presumably renew itself again. Why should not all be virtuous and happy?—that is the popular burden of a humanitarian and liberal movement. Why, indeed? scoffs the realist who has a sense of humour. But sentimental comedy replies, Look, we are. See, here on the stage are virtue and happiness united as we desire.

This kind of drama may, as we have seen, exist without any intent to rouse the sense of humour and without any of the traditional attributes of comedy except the happy ending, a sop to popular sentiment and a symbol of dramatic mediocrity. A comedy that possessed imagination and ambition might have encouraged and enlightened and directed to useful activity the sentiments of its audience. The novel later seized with enthusiasm on the opportunities which the drama had neglected, and great poets were soon exalting the principles and emotions which comedy had merely vulgarized. The revival of comedy failed to make the theater the continuing home of genius or even of respectable literary talent. Such great humorists as Burns, Scott, Lamb and Byron were to find little impulse toward writing comedies. The English drama of sensibility in the eighteenth century had engaged no minds of the first class, and it left comedy a forceless and futile instrument, destined to lie long unused in the literary workshop.

Yet there is something rather engaging—mediocre and tedious though they be—in these efforts to make the stage instruct and edify a growing democracy. The sentimentalists at least display the good intentions that they prize so highly—Steele's ardour for simplicity and sincerity, Whitehead's attempt to write a modern idyl, Cumberland's devotion to those abused by the majority, West

Indian, Irishman, or Jew, Holcroft's belief in the ultimate goodness of a society that persecuted him, Mrs. Inchbald's faith that art flourishes only on "scrupulous purity of character and refinement of sensation." Their faith was greater than their works, their morals more admirable than their art. Their plays have not continued lasting monuments in our literature, and even what power they had of edification is lost. We do not believe as they did in the value of sudden repentances and conversions. But at least these comedies remain a testimony to that enthusiasm for goodness, to that trust in the warm heart which stirred the eighteenth century. No one wishes these sentiments to vanish from any part of human intercourse, least of all from the theater.

CHAPTER XIX

THE ILLEGITIMATE, MELODRAMA, ROMANCE AND CLAPTRAP, 1880-1840

I

In the last years of the eighteenth century, English literature was being stirred by new ideas and a new spirit which were to inspire the great writers of the next generation. This age of Wordsworth, Coleridge, Scott, Byron and Shelley is usually described as a part of the Romantic Movement manifest everywhere in western Europe and everywhere stimulating imaginative expression. This movement of ideas and of artistic impulses is only faintly recorded in the English drama, and the greatness of our poetry and fiction from 1800 to 1830 has no parallel in the theater. The great romanticists wrote tragedies, but the best of these, "Cain," "The Cenci" and "Prometheus Unbound," were suited for reading in the closet rather than for representation on the stage. Almost no comedies of any literary merit or even of any literary pretensions were produced during the first half of the new century. Romanticism, which received poetical expression in the early plays of Goethe and Schiller, and later in those of Victor Hugo, found no worthy dramatic utterance in the London playhouses.

The term romanticism is vaguely and varyingly used to include diverse implses and purposes. These I have elsewhere summarized under six captions, a new sympathy for humble life, a delight in external nature, a fondness for the past, especially for the middle ages, a zeal for change and reform, an appeal to wonder and awe, and an intense interest in individual personality. Most of these tendencies may be observed in the drama.

472

The plays of Steele and Lillo had been the precursors of a European drama of sensibility which took regard of the humble man and of the emotional variabilities of the individual. Medieval castles and stories, specters, mysteries and wonders were common enough on the stage before the turn of the century. Appeals for democracy, relief for the poor, reform of social abuses were by no means unknown. But nothing great or original in drama resulted. The theater attracted no geniuses. Its sentimentalism and humanitarianism and medievalism remained superficial and commonplace. A part of the responsibility for this separation between literature and the theater may be charged to the nature of the literature itself. Poetry tended to concern itself with individual experience, with spiritual debate and longing, and it did not acquire that basis of a rich and varied contact with both life and books which was so essential to Elizabethan dramatic literature. Much of the best romantic literature is undramatic in content and form; except for Scott's novels and Byron's "Don Juan" there is a lack of wide and vigorous human interest. Humour was indeed praised most highly as the almost supreme attribute of personality, but it was not viewed as something that could be conveyed to the multitude from the stage. It is difficult to imagine a romanticist school of comedy.

The theaters, however, must be charged with some of the causes for the gradual decline of the literary drama. The patent theaters, which still held the monopoly on the legitimate drama, were rebuilt after the destruction of both in the season 1808-9 and enlarged to such huge dimensions that they were unsuited to the spoken drama and only fit for music and shows. The smaller theaters were restricted by law to the illegitimate drama, pantomime, operas and burlettas. The first third of the century may be described theatrically as a war between the patented and the minor theaters. Drury Lane and Covent Garden were kept going only with difficulty. New plays, especially those relying on diction and style, had little chance of being understood in their great auditoriums. The familiar plays of the repertory and especially the tragedies of Shakespeare succeeded because of the dominant personality of such a great actor as Kean. Covent Garden was literally saved from bankruptcy in 1829-30 by the attractiveness of a new Juliet, Miss Fanny Kemble. But more and more these theaters were forced to resort to all kinds of spectacles and pantomimes, real waterfalls, troops of horses, even elephants. The death of Kean in 1832 removed their main support in the "legitimate." By this time the minor theaters were acting almost anything they wished, and the legal monopoly of the patent theaters was finally destroyed in 1843.

The struggle for a free stage was also a war between the legitimate and illegitimate drama. The inroads of farce, pantomime and opera had already in the eighteenth century nearly crowded new comedies off the stage. The revival of comedy in the sixties and seventies, as we have seen, finally resulted in the disintegration rather than in the reëstablishment of the species. So far as comedy was concerned, the "legitimate" was almost extinct by 1800. The vogue of sentimentalism had led to plays exciting, thrilling, moralizing, but employing comic scenes only as a relief for the thrills and the sermons. The nondescript term, "play" or "drama" was beginning to be used in England, as in Germany and France, to describe performances that clearly departed from the traditions of both tragedy and comedy. Kotzebue's popularity completes the success of such emotional drama. At the end of the century, plays of mystery and horror, such as Lewis's "Castle Spectre," gave a vogue to romantic and medieval pieces also known as "dramas," and certainly bearing no resemblance to the old comedy. Meanwhile, the "illegitimate" was displaying a renewed vigour in rivalry with the disorganized cohorts of legitimate comedy. Almost every dramatic performance was embellished by song and spectacle. The ingenuity of George Colman the younger created a fresh and most illegitimate mixture of species which combined tragedy, farce, and opera, and anything else that came handy. When Cumberland wrote his "Memoirs" in 1807 he could boast of his own devotion to the legitimate with the proud loneliness of a sole survivor of a lost cause.

In 1802 the "illegitimate" received a new and powerful ally. Holcroft took advantage of the brief peace to go to Paris and to bring back to London the libretto of the latest Paris novelty, the melodrama, "The Tale of Mystery," which was at once produced with enormous success. Henceforth the English and American stages were crowded by specimens of this new kind of show, which was destined to prove the most popular dramatic type of the century. As a form, however, melodrama is difficult to define precisely. In 1802 it was a combination of spectacle, pantomime, drama and musical show. Scenery and machines were elaborate, and the spoken dialogue was minimized. Its place was taken in part by pantomime, and both pantomime and speech were accompanied by descriptive music—harsh for the villain, soft and sweet for the lovers. All of these characteristics are to be found in earlier drama, but the French combination of them was felt to be new and set the model. At first, the tales of romance and mystery proved well adapted to this form, and in the course of time nearly all of Scott's novels were melodramatized. But with a change of taste, the melodrama proved also well suited to stories of modern life. Instead of castles, instruments of torture and bridges over chasms, spectators were thrilled by the railroad train hastening across the stage to crush the hero bound to the track; instead of the baron's daughter kidnapped by the bandit chief, the poor girl from the mills defying the advances of her employer's son. Gradually, the peculiar characteristics became less distinguishing, and the term melodrama was applied to almost any sort of sensational play. The accompanying music by the orchestra, however, was long considered essential, though this was soon adopted by all kinds of plays. So late as twenty years ago, a popular melodrama would carry forty or more cues for music. For a full century, sentiment spoken on the stage had the support of soft music from the orchestra.

The melodrama, like other species of the "illegitimate," was a sign of the popularization of the drama. It appealed to persons who had only a restricted vocabulary and a slight acquaintance with literature, and it prolonged its career in the United States for audiences of foreign birth who spoke little English. Its advent was also synchronous with the use of gas in lighting the theater, a tremendous aid to shows intended mainly for the eye rather than the ear. Since the melodrama abounded in dangers, deaths and other excitements, it supplied a popular successor to tragedy rather than to comedy. It soon found, however, the usefulness of comic relief and moulded itself into a combination of excitement, sentiment and comic eccentricity, not very different from one of Cumberland's thrillers. The great tradition of comedy seemed indeed to be dwindling down to the comic relief supplied to melodrama, spectacle, pantomime, musical shows and operas. This afforded opportunity for little except broad and extravagant and conventional farce.

II

The theatrical conditions which I have been describing manifestly did not encourage a young wit emulating Congreve to offer a comedy that was a refinement of the literary tradition, or a young moralist like Steele to initiate in the theater an appeal for a reform of social manners. The playhouses no longer offered an opportunity for literary ambition or merit, but they required workmen, acquainted with the mechanics of the stage and the taste of the audience, who could turn out shows that would succeed. The playwright must be a master, not of dramatic art but of the new theatrical technic which involved stage carpentry, song-making and lighting effects; and he must be as familiar with the interests of the moment and as careless of literary distinctions as those other purveyors to democracy, the journalists. After Waterloo the public demanded a free press as well as a free stage, and an increased quantity of both news and amusement.

This public of tired business men and their wives and daughters liked sensation and it liked also fine sentiments, fun, good humour and lively movement, and its needs soon gave employment to a score of facile playmakers. The nature of theatrical entertainment for fifty years or so may perhaps be most readily suggested through a glance at the work of two or three of the busiest of these writers.

John O'Keeffe was born in 1747, began as an actor at an early age, and soon became a prolific writer of farces and comic operas. At fifty he became totally blind but still continued composing for the stage. It is related that when the opening performance of one of his pieces was to take place, he would go to the stage door and listen tremblingly at the keyhole for the first noise of approval or condemnation. His new efforts soon failed to please, but he lived on until eighty-five, maintaining some of his geniality amid misfortune and poverty. When nearly eighty he published his "Recollections," in which he lists sixty-eight pieces of his authorship. Several of these—"The Agreeable Surprise," "The Young Quaker," "Fontainebleau" and "The Castle of Andalusia"—had a long popularity, as did his best essay in the "legitimate," the comedy "Wild Oats" (1791). Here the usual accompaniments of sentimental drama are amusingly blended with farcical whimsy and drollery. The leading person is Rover, a high-spirited strolling actor, who spouts quotations from old plays to fit or misfit every occasion and person, and who turns out to be the long-lost son of Sir George Thunder by a supposedly sham but really true marriage to the forsaken Amelia, and who wins the love of the wealthy quaker, Lady Amaranth. The numerous dramatic tags are a somewhat literary addition to O'Keeffe's usual offering of bustle, slapstick, gag and song, but the piece evokes a rather engaging picture of the amusements of our ancestors. The sentiment is so naïve, the fun so hearty, the delight of the author in his creation so contagious that even the printed pages summon up visions of the bustling stage and the delighted audience. The aged dramatist took some umbrage when told that Scott had used the phrase "From Shakespeare to O'Keeffe," and remarked, "Ah! the top and the bottom of the ladder; he might have shoved me a few sticks higher." The top of the dramatic ladder remains where it was, but we have certainly extended it several rungs downward since O'Keeffe's day.

More prosperous and more versatile than O'Keeffe was Frederic Reynolds, who began his dramatic career in 1785 with a version of Goethe's "Werther," made a success with his comedy, "The Dramatist," in 1789, and proceeded to occupy the next fifty years by the composition of over one hundred pieces of all sorts and kinds. One of these creations, "The Caravan" (D. L. December 5, 1803), introduced a live dog that leaped from a rock into real water and saved a child from drowning. For a number of years, 1814-1822, he was employed at Covent Garden as "thinker" for the management. His chief service in this office seems to have been the operatizing of Shakespeare's comedies, beginning with "A Midsummer Night's Dream," which was followed by "The Comedy of Errors" and "The Merry Wives" and nearly all of the rest under the direction of Reynolds or others. This operatizing consisted of the addition of many songs, mostly from other plays of Shakespeare, and of elaborate scenery and spectacle. In "A Midsummer Night's Dream" the procession for the final tableau introduced "The Cretans, the Amazons, the Centaurs, the Minataur, Ariadne in the Labyrinth, the Mysterious Peplum, or Veil of Minerva, the Ship Argo, and the Gold Fleece." Act II of the "Comedy of Errors" ends with a hunting scene, "a rustic bridge across a river surrounded by mountains, whose tops are covered with the snow." This snow was introduced most happily so that a quartette and chorus could sing "When Icicles Hang by the Wall" from "Love's Labour's Lost." Who cares how a song is introduced provided that it is a good song? Reynolds's last contribution to the stage was the Christmas pantomime in 1840, the year before his death.

An even more versatile deviser of shows was Thomas Dibdin. He was the illegitimate son of the elder Charles Dibdin, actor and composer of songs, operas and entertainments, and was the brother of Charles Dibdin the younger, who managed Sadler's Wells theater when it was famous for its nautical shows, having an enormous tank full of real water under the stage and another tank overhead for waterfalls. Thomas wrote more songs and plays than his father, though perhaps not as complete an artist, for the elder Dibdin was the sole performer in his celebrated entertainments—"he sang and accompanied himself on an instrument, which was a concert in itself; he was in fact his own band." This virtuoso deserted first his wife and then his mistress with three young children, who were befriended by Garrick. At the age of four Tom played Cupid to the Venus of Mrs. Siddons, and at eight he was a choir boy in St. Paul's. When he was eighteen he ran away from the upholsterer to whom he was apprenticed and found employment under an assumed name as actor, scene painter and composer of songs and burlettas. He wrote many pieces for Sadler's Wells, where his lifelong friend, Grimaldi, was varying the water pageants with his clowning, and where Dibdin became stage manager and prompter. In 1798, when he was twentyseven, he adopted Cumberland's suggestion and hastily devised a piece with songs to celebrate Nelson's victory at the Nile. This was performed at Covent Garden and followed by an incessant stream of operas, pantomimes, melodramas and other forms of the "illegitimate." Almost the only piece making pretensions to comedy was "Liberal Opinions," in three acts, afterwards enlarged to five acts as "The School of Prejudice"; but his operas, including a version of "The Lady of the Lake," were very profitable. Dibdin made great sums of money which he lost in theatrical speculations and managements. In the new Drury Lane he was employed at an annual salary of £520 as writer of pantomimes, but in 1816 he took charge of the Surrey (old Royal Circus) where he tried melodramas and lost a fortune. But whether prompter, actor, manager or speculator, he seems constantly to have been composing theatrical pieces, nearly two hundred he tells us in his "Reminiscences," of which only ten failed and sixteen were notably successful. He also wrote two thousand songs, doubling his father's record. He died in 1841 in his seventieth year.

A younger but not less industrious writer than these was William Thomas Moncrieff (1794-1857) who composed about two hundred pieces of various orders. He became connected with the theater in his teens and at different times was manager of a number of minor playhouses, the Regency, Astley's, the Coburg, the Adelphi and Vauxhall Gardens. His offspring were mostly illegitimate and of a variety that may be indicated by a few titles: "The Dandy Family," an equestrian drama; "Lear of Private Life," in which Junius Brutus Booth played the hero; "The Cataract of the Ganges" with a real waterfall; "Zoroaster," a melodrama; "Tom and Jerry" (1821), a dramatization of Pierce Egan's "Life in London," which had an enormous popularity; "The Bashful Man," a comedy for Charles Mathews; "The Somnambulist or The Phantom of the Village," and "Sam Weller and the Pickwickians." In his later years, like O'Keeffe, he became totally blind.

III

But of all these playwrights, these purveyors of the illegitimate and debasers of the dramatic tradition, the chief in talent, versatility, resource and audacity was unquestionably George Colman the younger (1762-1831). The son of an actress whom Colman the elder married at the cost of a fortune and a seat in Parliament, he was bred in the theater, and after a cursory education at Westminster, Oxford and Aberdeen, he was producing musical farces by the time he was twenty and in 1787 won a great success with his opera "Inkle and Yarico." For the next twenty years he was far and away the most popular and successful of all writers for the stage, and a number of his plays that were hailed as masterpieces in their own day managed to keep hold on the stage almost to the present time. His most daring innovation was the construction of what the chronicler Genest always refers to as "jumbles" of tragedy, farce and opera. Such pieces, "The Siege of Calais," "The Mountaineers," "The Iron Chest," though they have plenty of comic relief, were played by Kemble and Kean, and may be considered illegitimate tragedies rather than comedies. They anticipated and prepared the way for melodrama and led the way in debasement of tragedy into sensationalism and claptrap. But except in a few five-act comedies, Colman shows little reverence for dramatic traditions. Each piece is a gallimaufry of gambols, designed, however, with the greatest talent for winning applause whether by pun or pathos, low or high comedy, song, sentiment or spectacle. His own life was as varied and inconsistent and unprincipled as one of his theatrical triumphs. Though he received what were then the highest payments on record for dramatic work, £1200 for "John Bull," he wasted a fortune in ostentation and was always dodging his creditors. Though extravagant in expenditure and a high liver, he was mean and litigious in his business management and always involved in law suits.

Most audacious in his burlesquing of other writers and in his mingling of the serious and impertinent, he was extremely sensitive to criticism and ever quarrelling with the newspapers. The author of very indecent poems, he became, when appointed censor of plays, most meticulous in his deletion of profanity and other improprieties. He would not permit the use of "O Lord" or even the word "Heaven" and objected to a lover addressing a mistress as "angel." When reading one of his compositions, it is difficult not to imagine him as writing with his tongue in his cheek, enjoying his broad comedy and burlesque, and laughing at the heroic and sentimental tirades with which he caught the house; but it is perhaps charitable to suppose that there was a screw loose somewhere in his mental makeup which prevented any unity of purpose in his work and merely concentrated his brilliant talents to the perpetration of one claptrap after another. Nevertheless, though he borrowed freely from the French and elsewhere, his work never loses its peculiar individuality; and he goes his own way both before and after the success of Kotzebue and melodrama.

I do not wish to consider here his more extravagant and miscellaneous pieces, but only those that conform to the general requirements of comedy. Though younger than Cumberland or Holcroft or Mrs. Inchbald, he began writing at a time when their plays were most successful, and all his comedies have a strong infusion of sentimentality. They also abound in low comedy and amusingly eccentric persons, and they repeat about every comic device ever employed on the stage from Shakespeare to O'Keeffe; yet in spite of their conventionalities they have more freshness and fun than any other comedies of that period and are not undeserving of the applause that they sought. Colman demands our attention less for his extraordinary contributions to the illegitimate than for his part in carrying on into the new century what was left of the literary tradition.

"Inkle and Yarico," based on Steele's tale in No. 11 of

the "Spectator," is, like the operas of Gay and Bickerstaffe, merely a comedy interspersed with songs. Inkle, a
calculating young man of business, on his way to the
Barbadoes to marry the governor's daughter, is lost in
an American forest, where he is befriended by Yarico, a
noble savage girl. He escapes with her to Barbadoes,
where he at first offers to sell her as a slave, but finally
repents and marries Yarico. The comic relief is supplied, after a long-used formula often adopted by Colman, by the servants of the chief actors, by Trudge, the
Englishman, and Wowski, the attendant of Yarico.
Scene I displays Inkle and Trudge lost in the forest and
indulging in a brisk and punning dialogue. Scene II,
though enlivened by songs and attacks by the natives, is
largely scenic.—The ship which is waiting off shore sails
away, leaving Inkle and Trudge stranded in thick American forest inhabited, as it soon appears, by lions, leopards
and negro cannibals. Scene III discloses them in the
cave, in an inner recess of which they discover the sleeping Yarico, "beautiful as an angel," and Wowski, "a nice
little plump bit in the corner." They awake and show
an ability to speak English; Trudge and Wowski retire,
and we have this delineation of love at first sight:

Inkle. How wild and beautiful! sure there is magic
in her shape, and she has rivetted me to the place. But
where shall I look for safety? let me fly and avoid my
death.

Yarico. Oh! no—don't depart.—But I will try to preserve you; and if you are killed, Yarico must die too!
Yet 'tis I alone can save you. Your death is certain
without my assistance; and indeed, indeed, you shall not
want it.

Inkle. My kind Yarico! What means, then, must be
used for my safety?

Yarico. My cave must conceal you: none enter it,
since my father was slain in battle. I will bring you
food by day, then lead you to our unfrequented groves

by moonlight, to listen to the nightingale. If you should sleep, I'll watch you, and awake you when there's danger.

Inkle. Generous maid! Then, to you will I owe my life; and whilst it lasts, nothing shall part us.

The duet which follows is sentimental, but the wooing of Wowski and Trudge both in dialogue and songs is much less stilted.

Acts II and III are in the Barbadoes. Trudge refuses to sell Wowski. But it is only at the conclusion when convinced of the error of his utilitarian principles that Inkle becomes truly noble.

Inkle. Ill founded precept too long has steeled my breast—but still 'tis vulnerable—this trial was too much —Nature, 'gainst habit combating within me, has penetrated to my heart; a heart, I own, long callous to the feelings of sensibility; but now it bleeds—and bleeds for my poor Yarico. Oh, let me clasp her to it, while 'tis glowing, and mingle tears of love and penitence. (Embracing her.)

Wowski leads the assembled party in a flood of happy tears, and then they join in a merry and resounding chorus.

This absurd medley was long popular and apparently because of the exquisite sensibility which found an angel in this negro child of nature. Twenty years after it was first acted Mrs. Inchbald praised the play for its teaching of moral duty:

"This opera was written when the author was very young; and, should he live to be very old, he will have reason to be proud of it to his latest day—for it is one of those plays which is independent of time, of place, or of circumstance, for its value. It was popular before the subject of the abolition of the slave trade was popular. It has the peculiar honour of preceding that great question. It was the bright forerunner of alleviation to the hardships of slavery."

"Ways and Means, or A Trip to Dover," acted at the Haymarket in the year following, is an amusing and lively comedy largely farcical in character. Colman avowed that his only objects in "Ways and Means" were "laughs and whims," but for several years the pieces which he prepared for the Haymarket added to those desirabilities, history and tragedy, music and spectacle. It was not until 1797 that he returned to legitimate comedy with "The Heir at Law." The themes and persons are mostly old stage acquaintances. The comic portion of the play presents the absurdities of the parvenus who have become Lord and Lady Duberly and the Honorable Dick Dowlas. The sentimental portion is supplied by the separation of Dick from Cicely whom he had loved in poverty and by the distress of Caroline betrothed to Henry Moreland, the rightful heir, who is supposed to have perished in a shipwreck. He escapes from the shipwreck, returns to London, Caroline and the barony, and brings about a generally happy dénouement.

The original element in the play is the character of Dr. Pangloss, who is employed by Lord Duberly to tutor Dick, has his pay doubled by Dick to neglect his duties, and doubled again by Lady Duberly that he may teach her son French and dancing. The doctor's flattering subserviency is broken by his frequent quotations from the classical and English poets, to which he always appends the author's name and an apologetic cough. This makes the stage part; you know a quotation is coming and listen for it. The art of characterization consists simply in finding the appropriate tags, but this is accomplished with the greatest dexterity. Here is the close of the interview in which he informs Dick of the new fortune, title and tutorship:

Dick D. Come, now, tutor, go you, and call the waiter.

Dr. Pan. Go and call! Sir, Sir!—I'd have you to understand, Mr. Dowlas—

Dick D. Aye, let us understand one another, doctor. My father, I take it, comes down handsomely to you, for your management of me?

Dr. Pan. My Lord has been liberal.

Dick D. But, 'tis I must manage you, doctor, acknowledge this, and between ourselves, I'll find means to double your pay.—

Dr. Pan. Double my——

Dick D. Do you hesitate—why, man, you have set up for a modern tutor, without knowing your trade.

Dr. Pan. Double my pay!—say no more—Done,— *"actum est."* Terence. Hem! Waiter!—Gad, I've reached the right reading at last——
"I've often wish'd that I had clear,
"For life, *six* hundred pounds a year,"—Swift.—Hem!—Waiter!

Dick D. That's right, tell him to pop my cloaths and linen into the carriage, they are in that bundle?

[Enter *Waiter.*

Dr. Pan. Here, put all the Honourable Mr. Dowlas's cloaths and linen into his father's, Lord Duberly's, chariot.

Waiter. All,—where are they, sir?

Dr. Pan. All wrapt up in the Honourable Mr. Dowlas's pocket-handkerchief.

Dick D. See them safe in, doctor, and I'll be with you presently.

Dr. Pan. I go, most worthy pupil. Six hundred pounds a year! However deficient in the classics, his knowledge of arithmetick is admirable!—I've often wish'd that I had clear, for life——

Dick D. Nay, nay, don't be so slow?

Dr. Pan. Swift.—Hem! I'm gone.   [II, ii.

When one sees how skilfully Colman can build up such a part, one cannot help lamenting that he did not some-

where show us the best he could do.   The play was acted
clear through the century and perhaps is still performed—if so, let us hope the epilogue is not omitted.
Each character asks for the audience's favour in high
sentimental style.

Henry.   While filial duty animates each youth
While virtuous passions warm the heart of truth
With qualities like these to Britons dear,
Henry may surely hope for favour here.
Caroline.   And may Caroline applause secure,
Who to all these adds feelings for the poor.

And finally Dr. Pangloss:

Does anybody want a tutor here,
My terms are but—three hundred pounds a year.
On their own merits modest men are dumb—
Plaudite et Valete—Terence—Hum!—
Then on my merits I shall lay no stress,
I'm L. L. D. and—and—A Double S.

In his next plays Colman combined music and drama,
anticipating in the "Feudal Times" in 1799 nearly all the
features of the melodrama which three years later was
to be hailed as something new from France, but in 1801
he returned to comedy with "The Poor Gentleman,"
followed in 1803 by "John Bull" and "Who Wants a
Guinea" in 1805.   All three use the established formula
—an improbable story of suffering and distress, in which
virtue aided by benevolence triumphs, the strong sentimental appeal being relieved by comic scenes and eccentric
persons.

In "The Poor Gentleman," a half-pay officer, his
beautiful daughter, and his faithful corporal are the virtuous sufferers.   The chief benefactor is Sir Robert
Bramble, supported by a well-drawn servant, Humphrey
Dobbins, and a nephew Frederick, a child of nature fresh
from Russia, who saves Emily from abduction, escapes a

threatened duel, and is rewarded with heroine and fortune. Ollapod, the apothecary, possessing military ambitions and an amazing jargon, is the chief humorist, and there are various other oddities. The comedy is rather more slapdashy and the sentiment more soapy than usual.

In "Who Wants a Guinea" a village has been destroyed by fire, but a bevy of philanthropists are on hand to relieve distress. Even the grouchy village miser has a boy of seven who practises benevolence upon a wanderer in a touching way. The other patrons of virtue are Torrent, an impetuous practitioner of universal benevolence; Heartly, his eloquent friend; Barford, misanthrope on the surface but with a heart like that of Vesuvius; Oldskirt, a modest and benevolent architect; and Solomon Gundy, the prize eccentric, rat catcher and gentleman's dresser, who talks a Malapropian jargon in both English and French. All these philanthropists are interested in behalf of Fanny, the young female in distress, who has been engaged as housekeeper for Torrent in the manor house. But Fanny by mistake gets into the wrong house which is the temporary refuge of an Irishman, Sir Larry, hiding from his creditors and looking for a little gaiety. The servants of course are comics. To this house come all the philanthropists seeking the lost Fanny, but Sir Larry withstands them all, refusing to give her up. He orders the impetuous Torrent deposited in the hen house and prepares to fight a duel with Fanny's lover Henry; but when Barford declares that she is his daughter, then Sir Larry relents and turns virtuous amid the applause of the house:

"This is the case, sir, you see. Does an Irishman love a pretty woman? sure, sir, he does; but when he's bullied by a wicked advertizing alderman, on one side of him; and a man in trowsers on the other, damn the bit of answer will he give.—I—give me your hand, sir—there's no standing a father's asking for his child. Sir, I'm a

gentleman, a little wild, perhaps.   But upon my honour
and conscience, she's safe; and dam'me if an Irish gentleman will ever do a dirty action!"   [V, iii.

One other passage must be quoted as a tribute to Colman's invention.   Barford is relating how his wife was
seduced by Torrent's brother.   He had overtaken their
carriage and "the bosom traitor threw out his sword
unsheath'd and exclaim'd he was ready, on the instant,
to give me satisfaction."   Then comes the most extraordinary of happenings.   "The hilt of his sword stuck deep
in the soil of the road, while the blade pointed upwards
to that heaven which had witnessed his villainy.   In leap-
ing out, he fell upon it; it pierced his body, and he expired
at my feet."

But the best of his comedies in the estimation of his
own day, and the favourite of several generations of play-
goers was "John Bull."   The improbable story is as follows: Peregrine, heir of the Rochdales, ran away to sea
when a boy and was befriended by Job Thornberry, a
warm-blooded and hot-headed brazier of Penzance, who
gave him ten guineas.   Just thirty years later Peregrine
escapes from a vessel about to be wrecked on the Cornwall coast, near Penzance.   At this moment, Thornberry's daughter Mary, seduced by Frank Rochdale,
leaves home in despair, and her father's business is
brought to bankruptcy through his misplaced trustful-
ness.   Frank is in love with Mary but intends to obey
his father and marry Lady Caroline, his parvenu father,
Sir Simon, paying her father £40,000 for the honour of
the alliance.   Tom Shuffleton, a smart and fashionable
friend of Frank's, manages, however, to steal a marriage
with the gay and petulant Lady Caroline.   Peregrine has
saved from the ship only a trunk containing £10,000, the
profits on the original ten guineas; however, he not only
relieves Job but brings about the marriage of Mary and
Frank.   In the end his ship is saved and he recovers all
his wealth accumulated abroad as well as the Rochdale

properties, but he promises to continue a general benefactor.

The plot involves about all the elements familiar in
sentimental drama, but Colman shuffles and plays his
cards with unfailing skill. He keeps the action away
from tragedy, and there is no deep-dyed villain. Sir
Simon is absurd, Frank kindly, and Tom Shuffleton not
without wit and spirit, so even the evil-doers contribute
to comedy, while the eccentric and humorous Dennis Brulgruddery and Job Thornberry furnish its main interest.
Every action is a direct appeal to a sense of humour or to
a sentimental sympathy, and sometimes the two are combined. But every action is accompanied by speeches
which adroitly direct our emotions and instruct us whether
it is time to laugh or weep or cheer. Nearly every line
is a claptrap, but the story of virtue in distress, relieved
by benevolence and miracle, had never been told with
more skilful effectiveness for the popular theater.

The dramatic manipulation indeed established a sort
of standard and set a model for the next half-century.
We have had occasion to analyze a number of well constructed comedies of different periods and different types,
"Twelfth Night," "The Alchemist," "The Country
Wife," "The School for Scandal"; and in all these we
have found plots and counterplots essential in the comic
mechanism. In "John Bull" there is only one trace left
of the old plot of tricks, Shuffleton's story to Frank that
Peregrine is Mary's lover, and this is negligible. The
first act brings before us the accessory comic persons, the
lady in distress and the benefactor, and discloses the story
of distress and promises relief. The second act shows
the relieving of distress on its way, but this is crossed
and retarded by various not improbable interferences.
Mary is not content to let Peregrine work out her salvation but sends a letter to Frank. Shuffleton, sent by Frank
to Mary, tries to deceive her, and later finds that Frank's
fiancée is a lady whom he has been courting. Job can't
wait for Peregrine and goes with Mary to the manor

house to demand justice of Sir Simon. This is the great theatrical scene for which the fifth act is reserved. Job seats himself in a chair in the middle of the room and refuses to budge until justice is done by the magistrate. Exposition in the first act, a rapid but clearly marked progress of events and disclosure of the story until, in Act V, the grand scene precedes the happy ending for all. This is a dramatic scheme not unlike that already used by Kotzebue and later refined and varied by Scribe, but Colman fits it out with comic "eccentrics", dear to the English heart, and carries it through with a dash of his own that is indescribable.

Perhaps, however, one glance at the opening of the play will help to recall Colman's wiles. The place is the inn of the Red Cow on the heath. Enter Dennis Brulgruddery the landlord and Dan the servant. We learn that the night has been "blustratious," that the inn has no guests, that the beer is sour, and that Dennis is a character, drunken, vociferous, genial and honest. A stranger is sighted in the offing. Great excitement and preparation for his welcome. Enter Peregrine, escaped from the shipwreck, bearing his little trunk. What is it stuffed with? "That which keeps the miser awake—money!" The stranger finds he is close to Penzance and must leave at once to seek Job Thornberry. He asks for brandy, but Dennis informs him this has been drunk by Mrs. B., and reluctantly brings forward the sour beer. Just as Peregrine is about to drink, "A shriek is heard at a distance." "Ha! the voice of a female in distress! Then 'tis a man's business to fly to her protection." He reënters, supporting Mary. Dennis's sympathies and his wife's suspicions are aroused. They retire, leaving the heroine alone to tell her story to her benefactor.

Colman was at the height of his power and he never did anything afterward nearly as good as "John Bull." Indeed, it is hard to see how anything better could be done with that story and with the only purpose, theatrical effectiveness. That no better comedy should be written by anyone for many years is merely an indication that an honest presentation of life was unwelcome in our theaters and that no one else could excel Colman in yoking humour and dramatic skill to the service of claptrap.

IV

Second only to Colman in popularity and profits was Thomas Morton (1764-1838). He made many contributions to the "illegitimate" and perhaps his greatest success was the melodrama "The Slave," but the longest-lived of his pieces were his comedies; of these, "The Way to Get Married" (1796), "A Cure for the Heartache" (1797), "Speed the Plough" (1800) and "The School of Reform (1805), provided famous parts and held the stage to a time within the memory of present theater-goers. His formula differs little from Colman's except that he relies rather more on the sensational and melodramatic situations and less on comic characters than did the author of "John Bull." The distressed heroine has a strenuous time of it; she goes to prison in one play, is rescued from a burning castle in another. Villains and rascals abound and are painted very black. But Morton also provides plenty of comic relief and numerous eccentrics and some incidental reflections of the changing times. In one play one of the eccentrics is a speculator on the stock market who talks much of bulls and bears; in another an inventor of all kinds of contraptions. "Town and Country" (1807) opens: "Scene I—a romantic country—large cotton manufactory. Canal, with wheels in motion occupying the foreground—a gentleman's house in the distance.—In the background a mountain.—Porters are carrying bales of cotton." This is rather early for the cotton factory on the stage or in literature, and it is treated with respect and admiration and as not incongruous to romance. The most famous of Morton's comic creations is a character in "Speed the Plough," who does not appear in person but only in the gag, "What will Mrs. Grundy say?" The most amusing of the comedies is "The Cure for a Heartache" because of the parts of the two Rapids, old and young, played first by Munden and Lewis. They are tailors who have acquired wealth and Young Rapid is eager to make the money fly. He is always on the jump, and his favourite gag, "Push on, Keep moving," became a byword, as did one other of his phrases, "Approbation from Sir Hubert Stanley is praise indeed."

For nearly a quarter of a century after these successes of Colman and Morton, few comedies found their way into repertory or deserved to. Colman and Morton in their later years apparently found melodrama more profitable than comedy, and no one appeared with comic invention comparable to theirs. The theaters were supplied by constant borrowings from the French and a few from the Germans, by melodramatizations of novels, Cooper's as well as Scott's, and by many farces, pantomimes, melodramas, operas and spectacles, none of which offered anything new or permanent as an addition to the comic drama. In light opera nothing of marked originality appeared, and little is now remembered except the song, "Home, Sweet Home," from John Howard Payne's "Clari." Of the numerous farcical pieces Poole's "Paul Pry" (1825) and "Twixt Cup and Lip" were about the only additions to the comic repertory.

One product of the illegitimate drama, however, offered a novel and delightful exhibition of the comic spirit, the extravaganzas of J. R. Planché. He had a burlesque produced at Drury Lane in 1818 when he was twenty-two, and, during the next five years wrote librettos for harlequinades, melodramas and operas, and designed the historical costumes and scenes for Charles Kemble's revival of "King John" (1823). Before his death in 1880, Planché had won distinction as an antiquary and an authority on heraldry and as the author of a great variety of successful dramatic pieces. His extravaganzas, the best of which were collected in 1875 in a testimonial edition of five volumes, were performed during a long period, the first in 1825, the last in 1871.

The earliest to show their distinctive character was "The Olympic Revels, or Prometheus and Pandora, a mythological, allegorical burletta" written for Madame Vestris at the Olympic theater and performed in January, 1831, based on the tale of "The Sun Poker" by Colman the younger. Unlike most preceding burlesques, this displayed neatness and sprightliness of wit in its libretto and propriety in the classical costumes. Later pieces added appropriateness in scenery as well as in dress, and restraint instead of buffoonery in acting. Each year the town was delighted by one of these combinations of tastefulness and nonsense, of beauty and absurdity. I shall hazard one or two brief quotations in the vain hope of suggesting the lightness and whimsicality of the total effect of one of these pieces. In "The Paphian Bower, or Venus and Adonis," Christmas, 1832, Venus is away from home, and Cupid and the Three Graces receive a call from the Nine Muses.

> [There is a *ra ta ta tat* without, and Exit a *Love*.
> *Cupid.* Run to the door!
> Some Post from Greece or Rome.
> [The *Love* returns.
> The Nine Miss Muses. Will you be at home?
> *Cupid.* Always to them.
> *Hymen.* Oh, show 'em up, of course.
> *First Grace.* Have they all come upon their flying
> horse?
> *Love.* No, please your Grace, whene'er they visit
> us,
> They come in Clouds' blue-bodied omnibus.
> The man behind politely pulls the line,
> And says in accents soft, "Descend ye nine."
> [Exit *Love*.
> *First Grace.* The omnibus for ladies of their rank!

Second Grace.   They run from Mount Parnassus to
   the Bank.
Cupid.   Run to the Bank! no, no, you silly wench,
From Mount Parnassus they run to the *Bench.*

In "The Deep, Deep Sea, or Perseus and Andromeda"
(1833) the monster is the sea serpent, who seems to have
derived some of his dialect and manners from the American actor, James Hackett, who had already played some
of his Yankee parts on the London stage.   The serpent
thus introduces himself:

[Music—*Serpent* appears above.
Ser.   I say!   You eternal nigger!
Your boiler must have burst, I calculate,
To stir the sea up at this mortal rate—
You've made me figure in tarnation attitudes;
I've lost my way, I swear, in these strange latitudes!
[*Descends.*
Amphitrite.   You give yourself strange latitude of
   speech,
And for your longitude—Gods! what a reach
It makes!   I ne'er beheld a snake so lanky!
Neptune.   Sir, by your accent you should be a
   Yankee.
Ser. (*advancing*).   Guess I am, stranger.   A United
   Stater!
Half man, half horse, and half an alligator.
Nep.   I ought to be no stranger, sir, to you;
My name is Neptune.
Ser.   Mister!   How d'ye do?
I've heard of you before.
Nep.   And now *your* name
And purpose,—whither bound, and whence you came?
Ser.   Neptune, I shan't say no when you say yes;
My tale's a mortal long one, though, I guess,
So long you'll hardly stop while I unfold it;
But you may hear, although you can't behold it.
All bones but yours will rattle when I say,

I am the sea serpent from America.
Mayhap you've heard that I've been round the world;
I guess I'm round it now, mister, twice curled.
D'ye call that nothing? Don't think me a dreamer.
Listen—you'll find I'm nothing but a screamer!
Of all the monsters through the deep that splash,
I'm "number one" all to immortal smash.

Planché departed from classical myths in "High, Low, Jack, and the Game" (1833), in which the actors represent the playing cards, and three years later turned to fairyland, adapting "Riquet à la Houppe" and preserving the qualities which he attributed to the French "feérie folie"—"sparkling with wit, pregnant with refined satire, exquisite whim, and delightful persiflage." The following year he made a second incursion into fairyland with "Puss in Boots." Among his later entertainments are other adaptations from the French, including some of the operettas of Offenbach, but to the end he far surpassed any English rivals in originality and taste. His pieces prepared the way for the operas of Gilbert and Sullivan, and have been forgotten mainly because they have been surpassed in their own excellences of music, verse, spectacle, wit, and nonsense by their more delightful successors. But they preserve some of their charm even for the reader, an interest, it may be noted, quite unlike the wit and satire of Congreve or the emotional excitement of Cumberland. Their mirth tickles the intellect as well as the fancy, but creates neither hard feelings nor self-satisfaction. Nothing else so blithesome is to be found between Shakespeare and Gilbert.

V

At the other end of the theatrical scale from farce and burlesque were a few pieces of literary merit whose success seemed for the moment to promise a revival of poetic and romantic comedy.

Literary romanticism, as we have seen, made itself felt

in tragedy and in the main neglected comedy, but exceptions must be made in the case of two minor poets, John Tobin and Sheridan Knowles. Tobin's life in some respects resembled that of Keats. Articled to a solicitor, he devoted all his spare time to writing plays, mostly in verse, and had thirteen successively refused by the managers. The fourteenth, "The Honey Moon," was accepted by Drury Lane, to the author's great joy, but the signs of consumption had become manifest; and at the advice of physicians Tobin set sail on a voyage to the West Indies. He died the first day out, December 8, 1804, before his play could be put on the stage. It was performed the next month with marked success. It is written in blank verse tastefully imitative of the Elizabethans and is a sort of romanticization of Shakespeare's "Taming of the Shrew." It contains one claptrap which is sometimes still remembered:

The man that lays his hand upon a woman,
Save in the way of kindness, is a wretch
Whom 'twere gross flattery to name a coward.   II, i.

After the success of "The Honey Moon," the managers brought out others of Tobin's pieces—"The Curfew" (1807), a romantic drama of the time of William the Conqueror that equalled "The Honey Moon" in favour; "The School for Authors" (1808), a light prose comedy in three acts, which borrows from Foote's "Patron" and gave Munden a good part in Diaper; and "The Faro Table, or the Guardians" (1820), a comparative failure. Other plays of his were published in 1826.

James Sheridan Knowles, like many other English dramatists, was born in Ireland. His youth was employed in various ways, in the army, in studying medicine, in teaching school, in acting Hamlet and other parts, and in writing poems and plays. He became a friend of Lamb, Coleridge and Hazlitt, and an ardent disciple of romanticist principles in poetry. His tragedies, "Caius

Gracchus," "Virginius" and "William Tell," won theatrical success and some literary fame. Hazlitt praised him in "The Spirit of the Age" as the first tragic writer of the time. His earliest comedy, "The Beggar's Daughter of Bethnal Green," was damned at Drury Lane in 1828, and Knowles at once set to work on "The Hunchback," which after much delay was produced at Covent Garden, April 5, 1832, with Fanny Kemble as Julia and the author as Master Walter. It was an immense success. Julia, who in pride has slighted the worthy Clifford and promised to marry the Earl of Rochdale, is disciplined by her guardian, the hunchback, and is not released from her pledge to the hated Rochdale until the last moment. The hunchback then reveals himself to the tortured Julia as her father and the rightful earl. The plot is absurd and confused, the humour childish, and the soliloquies numerous and ornate; but many felt that the drama was being reformed because of the tolerable blank verse, imitative of Shakespeare, and full of long similes and metaphors.

Slighter as a play but more truly a comedy was "The Love Chase" (1837). It is composed of elements often employed in the old comedies. Constance is the flirt or tease or madcap of the old comedy, and her wooing is a contest of stratagems and counter stratagems. Lydia, who is in love with the seducer whose proposals she rejects, is a typical heroine of sentimental comedy. The Widow Green is the inevitable stage widow. Some of the situations are amusing but highly artificial. These old materials are dressed up in a blank verse which is at its best in descriptive passages. All is pleasant enough but not especially romantic, poetic, humorous or dramatic.

These plays did not bring about a literary revival but they held the stage long after their initial successes and doubtless encouraged other efforts in the poetic drama. Knowles deserves credit at least for showing that the theaters would welcome something besides farce and claptrap.

VI

In this, as in earlier chapters, I have not attempted to observe closely the chronological bounds of the period discussed. I have included some plays by Colman and Morton that were acted before the beginning of the century because they served in a way as models throughout the period, and I wish to include here the plays of Douglas Jerrold, although some of them were written later than our terminus, 1840, three years before the freedom of the theaters.

Douglas Jerrold's "Black-eyed Susan" was produced in 1829 and broke all theatrical records. Jerrold was then twenty-six and a much experienced man. After a childhood in the theater at Sheerness, of which his father was manager, he served as midshipman in the navy for nearly two years, then lived with his family in poverty in London, working for a printer and at the same time studying and writing busily. At fifteen he wrote his first play, which was later acted, and he was writing pieces for the newspapers as well as all sorts of plays for the Coburg Theater, when Elliston produced his "Black-eyed Susan" at the Surrey with T. P. Cooke as William. It was acted over four hundred times at various theaters during its first six months, ran for nearly a year at the Surrey, and continued for a number of years to be acted everywhere. Jerrold went on writing for the stage until a few years before his death in 1857, but after a time he became mainly occupied in non-dramatic work, as contributor to the press, editor of various journals, and one of the mainstays of "Punch," established in 1841. The early experiences of Jerrold and of his friend Charles Dickens were much alike and gave them both a generous sympathy for the poor and downtrodden and an acquaintance with the thrills and humours of everyday life. It is obvious, I think, that the plays of Cumberland, Colman, and the rest, fed the mind of the great novelist and helped to direct his art. Jerrold's early plays may also

have had their effect on Dickens; at all events, he was
giving the drama a flavour of Dickens even before Dickens
had written a novel.

"Black-eyed Susan" differs from most preceding melodrama in substituting a domestic story for the usual
romantic plot and in supplementing this by sprightly dialogue and humorous scenes.   Sentiment and thrills are of
course not neglected.   Susan's William is condemned to
death for striking a superior officer.   The final prayer has
been said and William is embracing the Union Jack—
when Captain Crosstree rushes in, crying "Hold! hold!"
It has been discovered that William's discharge had been
secured before his offence was committed, but was concealed by the villain.   He is free!   The seamen give
three cheers, William leaps from the platform, Susan is
handed on by Crosstree, etc.

Though Jerrold wrote plays on Nell Gwyn, the
Flying Dutchman, Thomas à Becket, Beau Nash and
other historical or legendary themes, the most characteristic of his pieces, whether melodramas or comedies,
are domestic and usually drawn in part from Jerrold's
own experiences; they are at least original without borrowing from the French.   The comedies are of varying
length, from one to five acts, and have a rather large
range of subjects and persons.   They keep the old stories
of distressed females rescued and of fortunes lost and
won, but they put much less stress on story than do his
melodramas.   They produce a certain enlargement,
though no elevation, of the comic field, by new subjects,
new jokes and new "humours."   Though no one of them
is as good as are several of Colman's, half a dozen surpass in vivacity and fun anything since "John Bull."   The
dialogue is bustling and the action is hustling.   Some one
is always entering or exiting; no one sits for long; tears
and laughter both come in bursts; soliloquies are strings
of ejaculations.   Sometimes, as in "The Catspaw," a
farcical piece of many disguises, this rapidity would be
almost unintelligible if there was anything to understand.

But whatever its faults as a whole, each comedy has some amusing bits of repartee or of action, of whimsical satire or humorous caricature.

"The Wedding Gown" (1834), in two acts, shows the heroine in poverty employed in sewing the wedding gown of another, but in the second act she wears it to her own wedding. "The School-fellows" (1835), in two acts, depicts a schoolmaster serving as philosopher and friend to some of his old pupils, who have fallen into difficulties through run-away marriages, long-lost parents and similar mishaps. "The Prisoner of War" (1842) presents English prisoners at Verdun in 1803, including Pall Mall, a typical Englishman abroad, who scorns everything foreign and boasts of everything English—"Talk of *consommé de grenouilles,* did you ever taste our *habeas corpus?*" "Doves in a Cage" reveals its lovers in Fleet prison. "Retired from Business" (1851), in three acts, depicts life in the suburban Garden of Eden known as Pumpkinfield, where the inhabitants are retired business men and the lines of caste are drawn very strictly between retail and wholesale. On the outskirts live Gunn and Tackle, retired officers of the army and the navy respectively, and Tackle has a wonderful garden which he surveys with a fieldglass searching for sprouts. This is a cheerfully new environment for the usual old plot, and it is perhaps an indication of the changing times that the poetic young lover is an engineer. But the union jack is not forgotten, it is used in the grand finale for the ingenue to hide under. "Isn't she under her own flag, and wasn't that made to cover innocence and beauty!"

The most popular of the comedies was "Time Works Wonders" (1845). Act one introduces Professor Truffles and Felix Goldthumb waiting for their bacon and eggs at a country inn.

Felix. But I was about to ask, were you ever in Arabia—odoriferous Arabia?

Truff. I've travelled much; but not—I—I think in Arabia.

Felix. This perfume, stealing from the kitchen.

Truff. Though 'tis a dish I never heard of, it promises well. It really——

Felix (looking towards window). Eh! what's this? A postchaise and—yes—one of our Oxford men. Petticoats, too! Professor Truffles, you have seen the world. Is that really a postboy, or Cupid?

Truff. (rising from table, and approaching window). Worse, sir,—worse—Hymen. Yes; if I know anything of horseflesh, those chestnuts are bound for the church. (Returns to table.)

Felix. Poor beasts! 'Twould almost appear they knew as much; for they seem resolved not to budge another foot. Oh, Professor! See you that lovely girl?

Truff. Sir, I am now nine-and-forty; and 'tis at least twenty years since I saw any girl answering that description.

Felix. What eyes—what lips. What—why, it's the baker's daughter!

Truff. That any man can think of such trifles before his dinner!

Felix. It seems but a few weeks since she was a wild thing, running about in a pinafore, and eating bread-and-butter.

Truff. Yes; and you'll think the innocent creatures will go on eating it for years to come, when somebody whispers "bride-cake,"—and down drops the bread-and-butter.

Felix (aside). Eh, Clarence Norman, the proud baronet's nephew! *He* the swain! *He* marry! I hope he means fairly now. I trust it *is* the church. Beautiful creature! Yet, looking at her with a doubt, a fear, her beauty falls like a shadow on me.

Truff. Where, sir, where is this Araby you spoke of?

Felix (aside: Stay, is she the bride? Is it she or her

companion?) Now, Professor, your judgment on these girls.

Florentine and Clarence, accompanied by Bessy (Mme. Vestris), have run away to be married and are soon followed by Miss Tucker, the girls' schoolmistress and an old flame of Professor Truffles. The girls are carried back to school and the act ends in disappointment for all the males. Five years are supposed to elapse before Act II, and circumstances are then changed so that four acts more of dialogue are required to get the couples of Act I happily married and reconciled to their parents.

One more quotation may further illustrate the quality of Jerrold's dialogue and humour. "Bubbles of the Day," in five acts (1842), opens with the servants discussing their master, Lord Skindeep, who is a parliamentary orator, and it soon appears that Corks, the butler, is in the habit of lampooning his master in the papers under the pseudonym "Brutus the Elder."

Corks. They've flayed him alive, though. Oh! ha! ha!!—given him such a scourging. (Takes newspapers from his pocket.)

Kimbo. Is it very cruel? Pray read it.

Corks. No—no; here's the papers—there's the speech. (Gives a newspaper to each.) Read for yourselves. And yet, here is a little bit of abuse in the leader, that does one's heart good.

Guinea. Abuse of his lordship? Oh! read—read!

Corks. A staring likeness of him. Listen. (Reads.) "As for the member for Muffborough, he is one of those wise philanthropists who, in time of famine, would vote for nothing but a supply of toothpicks."

Kimbo. The very man.

Corks (reads). "He ventures on a state benevolence as a timid spinster ventures on sea-bathing. He stands shivering on the brink of good intentions; dabbles, splashes a little; and, making noise enough to bring all the world about him, never has the heart to plunge right in."

Guinea. Beautiful bitters!

Corks (reads). "In a word, Lord Skindeep may be called the Punch of Parliament!"

All. Ha! ha! ha! The Punch of Parliament!—the Punch of—

> [Enter *Lord Skindeep,* down the stage. *Guinea* and *Corks* drop papers and run off.

Skindeep. The Punch of Parliament! Now, although I know every member of the house, who can those menials mean? Kimbo, is my library turned to a debating-room? Ha! the morning papers! (Aside: I stand in the midst of 'em like a conjuror in a circle of snakes.) (*Kimbo* picks up the papers and presents them.) Go. I can see by the scoundrel's look of satisfaction, somebody has abused me.

> [Exit *Kimbo.*

Jerrold's plays bring us into a new theatrical era, marked among other changes by the passing of the repertory theaters. During the period traversed in this chapter the importance of the patent theaters and their repertory of old comedies had been decreasing in comparison with the minor theaters and their miscellaneous offerings, but the old comedies had still been acted and had exercised their influence on a new public and on new writers. Nearly all of Shakespeare's comedies, Jonson's "Every Man in His Humour," Fletcher's "Rule a Wife" and Massinger's "A New Way to Pay Old Debts" held their places; Congreve's "Love for Love," Vanbrugh's "Confederacy" and Farquhar's "Beaux Stratagem," "Inconstant," and "Recruiting Officer" were still acted, though more infrequently. The old favourites by Cibber and Mrs. Centlivre maintained their popularity; and Hoadly's "Suspicious Husband," Colman's "Jealous Wife" and "Clandestine Marriage," Garrick's "Country Girl," Murphy's "All in the Wrong," and Mrs. Cowley's

"Belle's Stratagem" were among the plays of the Georgian era which were still known to all theater-goers. "The Rivals," "The School for Scandal" and "She Stoops to Conquer" continued popular, and so did certain of the plays of Cumberland, Mrs. Inchbald, and Holcroft; so did Kotzebue's "Stranger" and "Lovers' Vows." Of musical pieces, "The Beggar's Opera," "The Duenna," "Lionel and Clarissa" were frequently repeated. To this repertory were added the plays mentioned in this chapter, notably those by Colman the younger and Morton and the two verse comedies by Sheridan Knowles.

If the great inheritance of comedy had been little increased during the first forty years of the nineteenth century, at least some experiments had been started which were to be continued in the second half of the century. Tobin and Sheridan Knowles had many successors in the effort to revive poetic and romantic comedy. Douglas Jerrold gave a new lead in domestic drama. Planché demonstrated the great possibilities of humour that lay in burlesque and extravaganza. But in the main, comedy was still in alliance with melodrama, and Colman the younger was the king of the theater in 1843, just as he was in 1800.

CHAPTER XX

THE VICTORIAN ERA, 1840-1890

I

THE reign of Victoria witnessed vast changes in the ways of living and thinking that could not fail to affect the theater and the drama. When she came to the throne the drama was still ostensibly in the hands of the two patent theaters, patronized by the government, and maintaining a repertory of the best English plays of the past. For two periods at least under the management of Macready, Covent Garden in 1837-9 and Drury Lane in 1841-43 were restored to their old distinction. But within a few years after the repeal of the patent privilege in 1843, their preëminence was lost among a dozen playhouses. Henceforth the democratization of the theater went on apace. The protest of the middle classes against the immorality of the drama had begun to wane, and the London public patronized the theater as it had not done since Shakespeare's time. The audiences were swollen not only by the great increase in urban population but by the ease and cheapness of transportation by the railways which were soon sending thousands to the capital on pleasure as well as business. In a lesser degree each provincial city repeated the experience of London.

Theaters sprang up in peculiar localities and acquired special services. The playhouse at Sadler's Wells once devoted to aquatic shows became the home of Phelps's notable revivals of Shakespeare, and in our own day the Old Vic has experienced a similar metamorphosis. The managers soon discovered not one but many publics of many tastes and appreciations, for which different playhouses specialized their offerings. In the mid-century

506

the Princess, under the direction of Charles Kean, occupied a leadership later taken by the Lyceum under Irving. The Olympic, under Madame Vestris, was famous for Planché's extravaganzas, as later the Savoy was famous for the operas of Gilbert and Sullivan. British melodrama for a time had its special home at the Adelphi, and high comedy and stage reform at the Prince of Wales.

This diversification of theatrical services and the competition in expensive productions led eventually to the disappearance of stock companies playing repertory. Each manager aimed to produce a new piece which should run for the whole or the better part of a season; and if he undertook the revival of an old play, it was in hopes of a similar run. This change after a time extended itself to the provincial theaters, and then second companies were organized to take on tour the London successes. Instead of stock companies at Manchester and Leeds playing repertory and occasionally supporting a star on a visit from London, each provincial town came to rely on visits from the touring companies, carrying their own scenery and costumes.

This revolution in the business of the theater was well under way by the sixties and nearly accomplished by 1880. The physical theater also changed. The reign of Victoria began by gaslight and ended with electricity. The first box set, that is a room with three practicable walls, is usually said to have appeared on an English stage in "London Assurance" in 1841. At the beginning of the reign, the apron still extended far in front of the proscenium, and the scenery was composed of wings and flats well to the rear, and the methods of shifting the stage sets differed but little from those of the time of Cibber. By the end of the reign the apron had disappeared, the proscenium arch framed a picture, flooded with light, and created by means of every artifice of painter and costumer. Whether symbolic or realistic or fantastic, the drama was a series of pictures, designed with an art and executed with a brilliance that the theater had never known before. Between the beginning and the end of this transformation,—from the use of closing and opening wings to present changing scenes and machines, down to the creation of a picture stage with a few elaborate sets,—was a period when constant and increasing attention was paid to the improvement of the mechanism and the pictures of the stage, to the increase of its appeal to the eye.

Each manager could experiment on setting and costume as a particular production might demand, and he could suit the accommodations and offerings of his theater to a special public. By the second half of the century, stage management became recognized as an art. A company must be specially organized for each new piece and trained to make the most of all its possibilities. The acting text was interlarded with the most minute directions as to business, furniture, properties, scene shifting, lighting and music. A play needed not merely good acting but acting especially instructed and disciplined to the piece, and aided by every device of costume, setting and lighting.

All these changes in production and management were taking place everywhere in Europe and America. Until toward the end of the century, Paris in fact maintained a primacy in all the details of stage effectiveness. But in France as elsewhere on the Continent, certain theaters were subsidized by the government and sought to preserve the tradition without much regard to the populace. Nowhere else were the effects of democracy and industrialism as rapid and sweeping as in England, and nowhere else was the theater surrendered so completely to free competition. A close second was the United States, at first far inferior in wealth, but after the Civil War rapidly developing in the northern cities a theater rivalling that of London. Throughout the century a constant interchange of actors and plays proceeded. Even before Victoria's accession Hackett's Yankee parts were adding, as we have seen, to the gaiety of London audiences. Dion Boucicault, the most popular and prolific dramatist of the period, lived much of the time in the United States and catered to the favour of both nations. By the end of the century New York was almost ready to surpass both Paris and London in its theaters. But during most of the reign of Victoria England led all nations in manufacture, railways, commerce and wealth, and was spending a large share of her resulting economic surplus upon the theater. The drama, to be sure, shared with other amusements—with games, horse-racing, gambling and drinking, though not as yet with automobiles and the cinema—but perhaps never before, not even in Periclean Athens, had the theater obtained a larger share of the national wealth or of popular interest.

The drama changed with the theater. At the beginning of the reign few of the new theatrical pieces had any value as literature, and few men of literary talent were writing for the stage. The long union between the stage and literature seemed to be dissolved, and the successes of Bulwer Lytton and Douglas Jerrold were among the few signs of a reunion. Comedy, even more than tragedy, was scorned by play-makers and poets alike. At the close of the reign, Henry Jones, Pinero, Grundy, and Oscar Wilde had written brilliant plays, and the stage was set for Shaw, Barrie, Synge, and Galsworthy. But this impressive renaissance of the drama came only in the last decade of the nineteenth century and links itself to the twentieth. The fifty years from 1840 to 1890 were singularly lacking in dramas of high merit or in promising experiments. Not in comedy proper but rather in the operas of Gilbert and Sullivan in the seventies and eighties do we find the chief Victorian tribute to the Comic Muse.

These fifty years, though they supply very few comedies of importance, are of considerable interest to the student of the history either of the stage or of comedy, and are the subject of this chapter. Plays there were in great numbers, but no one has attempted to record their titles and lists of actors, as Genest did those before 1830. Many of the plays were never printed; most of them were borrowed from the French, few contributed anything novel to the art of comedy. In a half-century when theater-going was constantly on the increase, the theater welcomed no writer of high literary rank, no comedies that are still acted to-day; and such innovations as it produced in the dramatic art have been mostly forgotten in the livelier activities which succeeded them.

The profession of the dramatist had fallen to a low ebb in the early decades of the century, as we have noted in the last chapter. The interest of audiences and managers seems to have focused on almost anything rather than words and ideas. The making of plays was given over to the mechanics of the theater and to translators from the French. The vogue of melodrama continued, of plays telling sensational stories by the aid of elaborate scenery and machines. Comedy as well as tragedy gave place to it, or to something very close to it, ambiguously named a drama, or play (drame, schauspiel), also with strong situations and some comic relief. No man thought of reading one of these pieces, few were printed except for use in the theater, full of technical stage directions.

The conditions for the dramatic writer were much worse than in the days when Colman, Jr., received £1,200 for "John Bull" finished at top speed while the waiting manager gathered up the scattered sheets as they came hot from his pen. The manager would pay well the actors or scene makers or artists who designed the costumes, but instead of paying an author he merely hired a hack to translate a French piece or to melodramatize a novel. Douglas Jerrold received only sixty pounds for "Black-eyed Susan," which made thousands for the manager. Tom Taylor, who was one of the most popular dramatists of the mid-century, had only from £100 to £200 for a play. Like Kotzebue, the French were turning out what William Archer has named "exportable" plays, so well contrived in respect to situations and structure that they could be acted anywhere. No international copyright existed, and British and American managers stole freely. Moreover, the novel was beginning to offer an exceedingly profitable field for literary talent. The new reading public was absorbing enormous quantities of fiction before it had acquired much taste in the drama; in fact, novels were determining the dramatic taste of the Victorian public. The publisher could afford to pay huge sums with a certainty of a sale at a guinea and a half a novel; and periodicals were offering an immense field for profits on fiction outside of book publication. Meanwhile the theaters were risky speculations, as yet uncertain of the public taste and support. Thackeray, Dickens, Reade and others who loved the theater wrote novels, not plays. Young writers tried their hands at journalism or novel writing, not at comedies. After a time Boucicault demanded and received royalties instead of fixed sums for his plays. But it was not until after the repertory companies were ended and the custom established of long runs and secondary companies for successful pieces, that royalties began to be enormous. The author then shared the speculation with the manager and might get great rewards. By this time the public was used to the theater, increasingly discriminating as well as generous in its patronage, and the dramatic art began to advance.

II

Although it is aside from our story, something must be said of the French theater which during most of the nineteenth century dominated English comedy. At the end of the eighteenth century the state of comedy in France was not very different from that in England. The sentimental school had created a new type that offered possibilities of development in at least two directions, one, in the consideration of social problems and reforms; two, in the telling of an exciting story with comic relief and a happy ending. These two possibilities, apparent in the plays of Cumberland, Holcroft and Colman, Jr., had resulted in nothing of further importance in England during the first third of the century. In France they encountered the same difficulties as in England, a restricted theater, the invasion of Kotzebue, literary romanticism, and the vogue of melodrama and the illegitimate; and they encountered the still greater difficulties of an unsettled society, uprooted by the revolution, tyrannized over by Napoleon, and after Waterloo long unsettled and disturbed. Nevertheless, at the accession of Victoria, the drama was far more interesting and important in France than in England. Inspired in part by the visit of English actors in 1827, Victor Hugo in "Hernani" and Alexandre Dumas in "Henri III" had inaugurated a romantic revolt, and Eugene Scribe was turning out scores of light comedies that were to set a new standard in dramatic construction.

During the rest of the century, Paris continued the theatrical center of the world. It had better theaters, more novelties, better melodramas, better vaudevilles, better operettas, better plays, better criticism. After Scribe's reorganization of the Dramatic Authors Society, the theater offered large rewards to writers, and the drama continued one of the best worn pathways to literary glory. The dramatists made fortunes and were admitted to the Academy, and their plays were evaluated by a keen and versatile criticism. Of the course of drame and comédie in the fields of social discussion, only a word can be said here. French drame and comédie during the century confined themselves largely to sexual relations and chiefly to the theme of adultery. The earlier sentimental drama had spent its tears on the virtuous wife or the maiden betrayed by deception. Kotzebue had caused floods of tears to be shed for the errant wife. Dumas fils in "La Dame aux Camélias" opened the flood-gates for the courtezan; but in the main French dramatists discuss sexual relations with reference to their bearings on society. Whether in the journalistic patter of Sardou or in the thesis plays of Dumas or in the thoughtful arguments of Augier, marriage, the family, and particularly the position of woman in modern society, became the subjects of a frank and searching discussion.

The English drama has nothing of this, until much later. The one point of superiority that English dramatists claim over the French is their morality. Even Thackeray and Gilbert stress, as if it were the supreme test, the suitability of a play for the ears of a young girl. It would be difficult to find among the English plays of 1840-1890 a single expression that would bring a blush to the chastest cheek or a sentiment unbecoming to the most circumspect curate. This mid-Victorian propriety restrained comedy from any frankness in the discussion of sexual relations. There are no English plays to compare with Dumas's "Demi-Monde" (1855), Augier's "Le Mariage d'Olympe" (1855) and "Le Fils de Giboyer" (1862) or "Frou-frou" (1869) by Meilhac and Halévy. The bridge from sentimental comedy of 1800 to the social drama of Ibsen, Zola, Brieux, Shaw and Galsworthy was not made in England but in France.

A considerable number of French plays could not be presented in England or the United States without drastic alterations. "Camille" was forbidden in England and produced in America in a version which made Camille a coquette engaged to Armand. Even the masterpieces of Augier were too French in their problems and persons for London or New York. But an abundance of plays remained, unprotected by copyright, open to the world. An English play of this mid-century is pretty certain to borrow its plot from a novel or another play; if from a play, it is sure to be French. Scribe and his collaborators and followers had excelled in invention and construction, in the devising of innumerable theatrical situations and in writing these in skilful plots. The process from surprise to suspense, or to another surprise, the escape from dilemma, the glossing of improbability, give dramatic construction a deftness that it had never possessed before. The English dramatists not only borrowed situations and plots, they made their own concoctions under the French standard of "the well-made play." Dramatic construction, the telling of a story by using all the resources of the nineteenth century stage, became an object of worship by everyone connected with the theater, until the inevitable reaction resulted which found the old god an idol of theatricality and preached a new return to nature.

The skilful unfolding of a story, such as we find in the best plays of Dumas fils or Augier and Sardou, is perhaps of more importance in drama or melodrama than in comedy. I wish, however, to note two particular effects on comedy. First, it tended to change the species, making comedy merely the telling of a story with a happy ending, and of that we shall find a-plenty in England. Second, it created a special form of comedy, wholly dependent on deft manipulation of plot and situation. Nothing quite like this had been known before. The clever audacities of plays of Spanish intrigue, or of Fletcher and Mrs. Centlivre, seem timid beside the ingenuities of Scribe and Sardou.

Plays of this kind have the fascination of a puzzle, of a game of chess, of a detective story, or a murder mystery. The fun doesn't come necessarily in the situations themselves, still less in the persons or in their conversations; it arises from the mental pleasure in following the dramatist in his intricate dodgings. He has constructed a labyrinth, and at each turn gives us a hint instead of a key. He is the hare dropping a few papers for a scent, and we are the hounds that follow. In comedy, of course, the game is not to supply rescues and other excitements by the aid of stage machinery; the game is to employ an ordinary company of actors—leading character, walking lady, comedy, first juvenile and the rest—in composing the puzzle, and to keep the interest of the audience in its solution constantly rising and constantly baffled until the very end.

A good example of this game of hide-and-seek is to be found in Scribe's "Bataille des Dames," translated by both Reade and Robertson; but the model par excellence is Sardou's "Les Pattes de Mouche" translated as "A Scrap of Paper." After the persons of the play have been introduced, we learn that a letter which had been placed in a porcelain ornament three years earlier is still there. The woman who wrote it, now married to a jealous husband, and her lover who failed to receive it now discover its hiding place and manœuver for its possession. The lover secures it, carries it to his lodgings, and hides it among some papers. Meanwhile its author has secured the aid of a friend, an unattached lady, who is glad to match her wits against those of the thief. The two ladies invade his apartment, where of course the husband follows the wife, who escapes. But the other, now the leading lady, finds the letter, burns it in part, surrenders it back to the thief, now her lover, who uses it as a spill to light a candle, and tosses it out of the window, where it falls at the feet of the husband returning from shooting. It is picked up, however, by his companion, an entomologist (leading comedy), who makes of it a little cornucopia, which he wraps about a beetle and leaves by his gun. There it is found by his pupil, the first juvenile, who writes another love letter on its back, which gets misdelivered to the wrong woman, the entomologist's wife, is read by her husband, read on the other side by the other husband, and captured at last by the leading lady and her lover, who have lost their hearts to each other while vainly searching for the piece of paper. What deception, what tricks, what coincidences, what inventions, and with what skill and wit they are fitted into a three hours' entertainment!

The English drama has nothing of the kind equal to this. But English dramatists were nearly all admirers of this type of construction, and evidence of its influence may be found in most of them, in Boucicault and Robertson, and later in Jones and Oscar Wilde.

III

In the early years of Victoria's reign two comedies were acted with great success that were representative in various ways of the drama of the next thirty or forty years. In 1840 came "Money," by Bulwer Lytton, already an accomplished and famous novelist; in 1841, "London Assurance," by Dion Boucicault, an unknown youth who as actor and playwright was to prove one of the mainstays of the Victorian theater.

Before "Money" Lytton had already produced the tragedy "Richelieu" and the drama "The Lady of Lyons." The latter is written in prose with occasional bursts into blank verse, and its quasi-romantic story is placed in Lyons forty years before. It is a successor of the sensational sentimental pieces of Cumberland and Kotzebue. "Money" is much the same sort of theatrical contraption. It has strong situations, surprises, heroics, and an abundance of claptrap, but also comic persons and a somewhat humorous interplay of the worldly and the true-hearted, of cynicism and sentiment. Evelyn and Clara, dependents in a worldly and hypocritical family, are in love with each other, but she refuses to marry him for fear that their poverty will injure his prospects. An Indian multi-millionaire passes over the other kinsman and leaves his fortune to Evelyn, who still misinterprets Clara's refusal as signifying a lack of love. He spends his money lavishly and showily and then, in order to test his newly acquired friends, he pretends to gamble away what remains of his fortune. All this lends itself to strong situations, such as that at the gambling club, to emotional acting and to much declaiming. In the end Clara proves true and saves Evelyn from despair at humanity's baseness. The closing speeches may indicate the way in which humour is used to supplement the insufferable heroics and to turn the melodrama into comedy.

Evelyn. Ah, Clara, you—you have succeeded where wealth had failed! You have reconciled me to the world

and to mankind. My friends—we must confess it—
amidst the humours and the follies, the vanities, deceits,
and vices that play their parts in the great Comedy of
Life—it is our own fault if we do not find such natures,
though rare and few, as redeem the rest, brightening the
shadows that are flung from the form and body of the
TIME with glimpses of the everlasting holiness of truth
and love.

Graves. But for the truth and the love, when found,
to make us tolerably happy, we should not be without——

Lady Frank. Good health;

Graves. Good spirits;

Clara. A good heart;

Smooth. An innocent rubber.

Geor. Congenial tempers;

Blount. A pwoper degwee of pwudence;

Stout. Enlightened opinions;

Gloss. Constitutional principles;

Sir John. Knowledge of the world;

Eve. And—plenty of Money!

Lytton made no further attempts to hold his position
in the theater, although he wrote a comedy "Not So Bad
as We Seem" (1851) for Dickens's amateur company
and, much later, a rhymed comedy, "Walpole." The
meagre rewards of the stage could not tempt an author
who in 1853 received £20,000 for ten years' copyright on
a cheap reprint of his novels. Lytton's ripening humour
is shown in such novels as "The Caxtons" and "The
Coming Race," but not upon the stage. We shall later
in this chapter glance at other men of letters who made
sporadic essays at comedy, but no other succeeded as did
Lytton in popular favour. "Money," "Richelieu," and
"The Lady of Lyons" remained prime favourites until
the close of the century.

Dion Boucicault was another of those gifted young
Irishmen, like Steele, Farquhar and Sheridan, who could

write a comedy by the time he was twenty. "London Assurance" is a comedy of manners of the old fashion, the plot resting on a string of deceptions and counterdeceptions so improbable as to be almost farcical; the dramatis personæ all well developed types, excellent stage parts, and each having numerous good lines to speak. Sir Harcourt Courtly—old beau—goes to Oak Hall, the country house of Max Harkaway—horsey squire—to marry Grace Harkaway under the terms of a will devised to fit this play. He is preceded there by his son Charles and his companion Dazzle, a cheeky adventurer. Charles has hitherto passed himself off to his father as a milksop, aided in the deception by Cool—sagacious valet—but he is really a gay youth and promptly makes love to Grace, now passing himself off to her and his father—too old to see and too vain to wear spectacles—as an Augustus Hamilton. In Act III the group at Oak Hall is enlivened by the arrival of Lady Gay Spanker—dashing and horsey—and her timid spouse. Young Courtly finds it advisable to get killed as Hamilton and to return in his own person and rightful name. Lady Gay conspires to entrap Old Courtly into an elopement and then to turn the coach over to Grace and young Charles. Grace considers herself insulted by Charles's cavalier stratagems. Meddle—tricky pettifogger—eavesdrops, and Spanker shows some spirit. Lady Gay involves Sir Harcourt and her husband in a duel and then discovers to her surprise and pleasure that she is concerned for her husband's safety. Old Harcourt, doubly fooled, resigns Grace to Charles. Dazzle, who has been constantly busy with one trick or another, confesses that he has no means of support except his assurance.

This play is exaggerated and farcical but not much more so than Sheridan's "Rivals," and in cleverness of dialogue, distinctness of characterization, and sense of theatrical effectiveness, it came nearer than any play produced for thirty years before or after it, to measuring up to the standards of the comedy of manners. It launched Boucicault on a long career.

He followed "London Assurance" by several other comedies, including a notable success, "Old Heads and Young Hearts" (1844). A simple-hearted clergyman, Jesse Rural, supplies the great acting part and about him revolve the stratagems of the giddy lovers, enlivened by much epigrammatic dialogue and smart satire of modern manners. The next four years Boucicault spent in France, where he acquired an intimate knowledge of the language and the theater. In 1852 he made his first appearance in London as an actor, and the following year married Miss Agnes Robertson and went to the United States, where they were enormously successful. "Such," we are told, "was the enthusiasm created by Miss Robertson amongst the ladies of Boston, that her promenades through the streets were beset with crowds . . . and the corridors of the Tremont House, where she resided, were blocked up with fair admirers who fairly invaded her apartments." Boucicault returned to London from time to time to superintend performances or to dissipate a fortune in theatrical managements. For over twenty years he was constantly before the public as actor, manager and dramatist. After a retirement to America in 1876 and a separation from his wife, he again resumed his theatrical career which continued almost to his death in 1890.

Boucicault invented few plots but followed the prevailing practice of taking his material from novels or French plays. No more skilful adapter ever worked. He knew just the touches necessary to transform "Le Gamin de Paris" into "The Dublin Boy," or "Les Pauvres de Paris" into "The Poor of New York," and then into "The Poor of Liverpool," and finally into "The Streets of London," or to make of Feuillet's febrile comedy, "La Tentation," a great New York and London success in "Led Astray." He adapted a French piece, and then discovered that it was a dramatization of

Dickens's "Cricket on the Hearth." He revised Colman's "John Bull" and remade "Rip van Winkle" and produced "Faust and Marguerite," "The Trial of Effie Deans," and "Mimi" ("La Vie de Bohème"), and in the year of his death was working on "The Luck of Roaring Camp." In fact, he dramatized anything and everything, women's rights and prohibition in "Apollo in New York," the negro problem in "The Octoroon," which made a tremendous success even after "Uncle Tom," the relief of Lucknow in "Jessie Brown," the Civil War in "Belle Lamar." He was a very skilful craftsman, readily adapting French models to English taste and to his own powers in Irish parts, and his pieces are usually excellent in theatrical construction, as it was then understood. They are worth studying simply as a revelation of the theatrical taste of the mid-century.

Boucicault did a good deal to change the theatrical conditions under which he worked. He had an influential part in establishing royalties as the form of payment for dramatists, in securing a dramatic copyright law in America, and in beginning the practice of touring companies repeating the metropolitan successes. He made little use, however, of his notable dramatic and literary gifts for the improvement or freshening of comedy.

His most original plays, though they are partly borrowed, and those that offer the most novel additions to comedy, are the three Irish dramas, "The Colleen Bawn" (1860), "Arrah-na-Pogue" (1865), and "The Shaughraun" (1870). These are all melodramas having complicated scenic effects, accompanying music, deep-dyed villainy, and sublime and sacrificing virtue; but they are most artful in construction and genuinely imaginative in their creation of Irish life. In each Boucicault made a part for himself—a careless disreputable, lovable, loyal, and resourceful Irishman. In the two later plays, which have more comedy than "The Colleen Bawn," the plot is substantially the same—a patriot exile returns to Ireland, meets the beautiful girl whom he loves, but is threatened with capture and death through a miscreant villain police spy. Working for his rescue or pardon are the British officers (the plays were for English audiences), the lovely girls, the peasantry of the countryside, and the resourceful paddy. The similar plots, however, are developed by different devices and mechanisms and illustrated by a wealth of whim, fancy and wit, mostly in brogue.

The hero of "Arrah-na-Pogue" is Shaun the post, who has got himself put in prison in place of his chief Beamish. His sweetheart, Arrah Meelish, separated from him on their wedding day, is on the cliff above the prison. Shaun soliloquizes. A stone falls through the chimney. It carries a letter from Arrah. Her voice is heard singing. Shaun climbs on a table to get at the window in an effort to see her. He tries the bars; the stone splits; splash! it has fallen in the waves below. The soliloquizing, which has been interrupted fifteen times by stage directions, comes to an end as Shaun resolves to climb the cliff to Arrah:

The wall is ould and full of cracks—the ivy grows agin' it. It is death, maybe, but I'll die sthrivin' to rache my girl, an' chate the gallows that's waiting for me. She's on the road to hiven, annyway; and if I fall may the kind angels that lift up my sowl stop for one minnit as they pass the place where she is waiting for me till I see her once ag'in. (*Exit through broken windows. Music, mostly tremolo, throughout the following changes.*)

Scene changes.

Sink table and close the trap. Draw in side sets, L. and R. Discover the frame set flat, and the set wall, with Shaun half way up the steps. Shaun climbs up, stops, ivy falls on him as his hold slips, and the foliage falls over him, covering him as it hangs. The flat ceases to descend. Soldier shows himself, looks down and up. Arrah sings, as before.

Sergeant (looks out of window in flat). It's all-right. (*Other Soldiers shown at windows, R.*) It's only that girl above there—she has displaced some of the masonry. (*All go off, R.*)

Soldier (with musket, shoulders it). All's well.

(*Voices less and less loud, repeat*) : All's well! (*Off R.*)

Wall descends. Shaun climbs up as wall descends, and by the ledge reaches second flat of wall. Climbs up as it descends, and upon the set platform of room, when the Soldier (coming on and going off R.) has his back to him. Shaun goes up to the cannon, climbs on it and out of gap. Soldier comes on, looks off front, down the wall, while Shaun climbs through gap. Soldier exits, R. Shaun to exit, R. All is worked down. Gas up.

Arrah, singing on top of the cliff, is being attacked by the villain Feeny.

Arrah struggles with him. He is just overpowering her when Shaun's hands appear; then his head; then Shaun seizes Feeny's ancles, the stone and Feeny fall into trap-hole. Pause. Music all through struggle, dies away, Shaun climbs up exhausted and falls full length on stage beside Arrah. Drum-beat heard, below stage level. Arrah and Shaun embrace, start, go over L. I. E., where Shaun hides behind ruins, Arrah before him.

Feeny has fallen over the cliff into the lake below. The rescuers, with Shaun's pardon, rush on, but suppose that it is he that has been drowned.

Shaun (comes forward). Spake out, ye thafe, and tell me am I dead?

Amid the general rejoicings he receives his pardon.

Arrah. D'ye hear that, Shaun?

Shaun. I do, dear, but it's a mistake; it isn't a pardon I've got. Instead of death, I'm to be transported for life—and it's yersilf that's to see the sintince rightly carried out, my darlint!

I have quoted at length in order to indicate the skill with which Boucicault employed all the resources of his theater and actors to construct his melodramatic scenes and yet kept drollery and fancy ever ready to relieve the excitement. Such stage machinery and setting as were necessary to picture Shaun's escape and climb up the ivied cliff permitted a visualization of stories that the earlier theaters could not have used, and, as we have seen, reduced the spoken words to a secondary place in dramatic narrative. But Boucicault's humour never failed when words were needed.

Only rarely, however, does humour dominate the setting and the action. The best example is in "The Shaughraun," where Conn, the character lead, pretends to be dead and has the pleasure of attending his own wake. The scene is in his mother's (Mrs. O'Kelly's) cabin; Conn is lying on a shutter supported by a table, stool, and keg. Eatables and drinkables are in abundance. Male and female choruses sing "The Oolaghaun," and the music continues softly as the Keeners begin their rhapsodies.

Biddy. None was like him—none could compare, and —Good luck to ye, gi' me a dhrop of something to put the sperret in one, for the fire's getting low.

  (Sullivan hands her his jug of punch.)

Mrs. O'K. Oh, oh! it's mighty consolin' to hear this, Mrs. Malone, you are not ating?

Nancy. No, ma'am, I'm drinkin'. I dhrink now and agin by way of variety. Biddy is not up to herself.

Reilly. Oh! wait till she'll rise on the top of a noggin.

Biddy (after drinking places the jug beside her, L., and rises on low stool). He was brave! he was brave! he was open-handed! he had the heart of a lion, and the legs of a fox.

Conn (takes the jug, empties it quietly, and, unobserved by all, replaces it on the stool).

Biddy. His voice was softer than the cuckoo of an

evening, and sweeter than the blackbird afther a summer shower. Ye colleens, ye will nivir hear the voice of Conn again. (*Sits and blows her nose.*)

Conn (aside). It's a mighty pleasant thing to die like this, once in a way, and hear all the good things said about ye afther you're dead and gone, when they can do you no good.

Biddy. His name will be the pride of the O'Kellys for evermore.

Conn (aside). I was a big blackguard when I was alive.

Biddy. Noble and beautiful!

Conn (aside). Ah! go on out o' that!

Biddy (taking up her jug). Oh, he was sweet and sthrong—Who the devil's been at my jug of punch! (*Goes up to crowd.*)

Mrs. O'K. (sobbing and rising). Nobody is dhrinkin' —yez all despise the occasion—if yez lave behind ye liquor enough to swim a fly—oh, hoo! There's a hole in your mug, Mr. Donovan, I'd be glad to see it in the bottle—oh, hoo!

(*Knock without, R. D.*) (*The door is opened.*)

Sullivan. What's that?

Enter Molineux. They all rise.

Mol. I don't come to disturb this—a—melancholy— a—entertainment—I mean a—this festive solemnity—

Mrs. O'K. (wiping own chair for him with her apron). Heaven bless you for coming to admire the last of him. Here he is—ain't he beautiful? (*Leads him up.*)

Mol. (aside). The vagabond is winking at me. I've a great mind to kick the keg from under him and send him reeling on the floor.

(*Sullivan offers him snuff, R.*)

Mrs. O'K. How often have I put him to bed as a child, and sung him to sleep! Now he will be put to bed with a shovel, and oh! the song was nivir sung that will awaken him.

Conn and Shaun are not merely effective parts, they are imaginative creations, embodying in their personalities many of the virtues and much of the wit of their race. It is a pity that they are kept so busy helping to work out the creaking plots; we could have stood with less virtue if they would have given us more wit. Boucicault's theatrical cleverness is now antiquated, and no one of his many ingenious constructions is now performed. His plays have never been collected and scarcely ever read. But anyone who will peruse the stage copies will find abundant evidence of gifts of dialogue and characterization which found but slight employment in those mid-century melodramas.

Only second to Boucicault as an adapter of French plays was Tom Taylor. He gave, however, only a part of his time and talents to the stage. He was a fellow of Trinity, Cambridge, and a successful coach, a professor of English literature for two years, a member of the bar, an official in the civil service, then a journalist and the author of various books of biography, long connected with "Punch" and its editor from 1874 to his death in 1880, yet he found time among all those occupations to write over seventy plays in the course of thirty-five years. He began with several burlesques in 1844, and won a number of great successes—"Still Waters Run Deep" (1855), "Our American Cousin" (New York, 1858), which gave Sothern the basis for his "Lord Dundreary," "The Overland Route" (1860), and "The Ticket of Leave Man" (1863). He did not have Boucicault's gifts of phrase and epigram, but he was a skilful theatrical artificer who knew how to please a public that demanded thwarted villainy and happy virtue in every play above the level of farce or burlesque.

"Still Waters Run Deep" is a fair example of his domestic comedy, and purported to be original. John Mildmay, an undemonstrative soul, finds himself a secondary figure in his household which is governed by his mother-in-law. She is infatuated by a swindling pro-

moter, Captain Hawksley, who seeks to win her money
and her daughter's love. But Mildmay, though still, is
deep, and he wins back his wife, recovers his mother-in-
law's letters, saves the family fortune, and exposes
Hawksley as a felon. This sensational stuff permits some
comic interplay of persons and rapidity of dialogue. The
following conversation indicates the kind of wit that the
editor of "Punch" dealt out to the theater. Mildmay is
on a ladder painting the trellis:

Potter (in turning round, sees Mildmay on ladder, C.).
Egad! there's Mildmay upon the ladder.

Mrs. Sternhold (L. C.). Mr. Mildmay? Well, sir,
I suppose you don't see us?

Mildmay (C., on ladder). Yes, I see you *(looking
down quietly)*.

Mrs. S. And do you see Captain Hawksley?

Mild. Oh, yes. I don't stand on ceremony with him.
I'm sure the captain will allow me to finish my job.
(Continues his painting.)

Hawksley (R. C., sneering). Oh! I never disturb an
artist at his work. Fresco, I think.

Mild. No—"flatting"—that's the technical term.

Hawks. Indeed! A punster might be provoked into
saying it was proper work for a flat. *(All laugh.)*

Mild. Flat? Oh! I see. Very good—very good
indeed. Would *you* like to try your hand?

Hawks. No, thank you; I've no talent for the fine
arts. Charming colour; isn't it, ladies? One would say
Mildmay had a natural eye for green.

Mild. You're very kind. Yes—I think it's rather a
success—and when the creepers come to be trained
over it——

Hawks. Why, you don't suppose any creepers will be
weak-minded enough to grow there?

Mild. Why not? Parasites thrive uncommonly well
in this house, you know, captain.

Hawks. Parasites!

Mild. That's the technical name for what you call creepers.

Charles Reade, who occasionally collaborated with Taylor, affords an interesting illustration of the difficulties which beset a man of literary gifts who desired to write plays. He graduated A.B. at Magdalen College, Oxford, in 1843 and was elected fellow. Though he held college offices and retained his fellowship and his pleasant suite of rooms until his death, he spent most of his time for a number of years after graduation in London, playing the fiddle, collecting old violins, and going night after night to the theater. His great ambition was to write a play, but his first piece to see the stage was "The Ladies' Battle," which he translated from Scribe and Legouvé's "Bataille des Dames" (1851). He felt no compunction about this theft, as he afterwards confessed, until later on the Americans began to steal his own plays. The next year, in addition to several other pieces, he produced in collaboration with Tom Taylor the very successful comedy, "Masks and Faces."

This is a sentimental comedy of a new kind with a courtezan as heroine, and acted in the same year as "La Dame aux Camélias" of Dumas fils. But Peg Woffington has a very different rôle from Camille. She falls greatly in love, but she restores her infatuated lover to his wife and acts as ministering angel to a family sunk in poverty and distress. The best comic scene—which has been traced to various sources—is that in which Peg puts her own face in place of that which Triplet has slashed from his portrait and listens to censures of the art critics upon the supposed painting.

In the same year that this brilliant little comedy was acted Reade formed the acquaintance of an actress, Miss Seymour, who had captivated his heart years before when she played Aspasia, and with whom he remained on terms of intimate friendship until her death. Under her encouragement he turned his comedy into a novel, "Peg Woffington." Henceforth he was occupied in collecting materials, classifying and arranging notes taken from a very wide research, and writing volume after volume, novel after novel. From these came his large financial rewards and his literary reputation. But his heart was always in the theater. He continued to write plays, to dramatize his tales, and to engage in all sorts of theatrical speculations. He put five new dramas on the stage in 1855, none of them with much success, but in 1865 triumphed with his dramatic version of "It is Never Too Late to Mend." As late as 1879 he produced "Drink," a dramatization of Zola's "L'Assommoir," in 1882 "Love and Money," and in 1883, the year before his death, "Single Heart and Double Face." Most of his plays are sensational dramas or melodramas; among his comedies are "Two Loves and a Life" (with Tom Taylor) and "Dora," a pastoral that had considerable success in the United States, and is perhaps about all that could be made out of Tennyson's poem.

If circumstances had favoured, it is difficult to see why Reade might not have been as distinguished a dramatist as novelist. In Paris he might have poured forth his reforming philanthropy in thesis plays, as did Dumas, or, like Zola, he might have employed his documentary collections to make plays as well as novels. He might have produced dramas more significant if not more sensational than those which he did compose. His dramatic or melodramatic power is apparent enough in most of his novels, and he delighted in exposing abuses and urging reforms. One may doubt, however, if any age or theater could have held his genius to comedy. He loved sensation and controversy and, although "Masks and Faces" showed that he could work with charm in parvo, he was at his best on an enormous canvas such as "The Cloister and the Hearth."

IV

The Victorian theater was not prepared in Reade's time for a searching discussion of social problems, but it was ready for amusement provided without machines or claptrap or staginess. The pieces of Douglas Jerrold had pointed the way toward a pleasing but entertaining domesticity, and the time was ripe for more realism and less melodrama on the stage. The leader in these mild innovations and in some measure the forerunner of greater changes to come was Tom Robertson.

Robertson was bred in the theater, acted for some years, and was making a precarious livelihood as a journalist and translator when he induced the actor E. A. Sothern to produce his comedy, "David Garrick," which he had based on a French play, "Sullivan." The piece was a great success in 1864, when Robertson was thirty-five, and for the seven remaining years of his brief life he wrote constantly for the theater, composing, along with pieces of various kinds, ten comedies.

"David Garrick" was followed by "Society," the first of his plays to be given at the Prince of Wales's Theater then leased by Miss Marie Wilton, afterwards Mrs. Bancroft. This had a run of one hundred and fifty nights, beginning on November 11, 1865; and the next year "Ours," presented first in Liverpool and then at the Prince of Wales, gained a huge success, soon repeated in the United States. "Caste" the next year (1867) was another triumph and won praise both for Robertson and the company at the Prince of Wales as sharers in a revival of the drama. His later comedies are similar in character but show no distinct advance. In 1868 came "Play"; in 1869, "Home," adapted from Augier's "L'Aventurière," "School," "A Breach of Promise," and "Progress," from Sardou's "Les Ganaches"; and in 1870, "M.P." and "Birth."

The brief titles suggest rather extensive surveys for the comic muse, and they do introduce us to many different scenes, to London's literary Bohemia, to a girls' boarding school, to a German resort, to a soldier's hut in the Crimea, but they do not disclose any ambitious desire to discover the many aspects of the comédie humaine.

Although Robertson was well acquainted with contemporary French drama and adapted one of Augier's plays, he makes little effort to analyze social conditions and problems. His comedies are all domestic and sentimental, presenting the course of true love as it triumphs over mistakes or poverty or the scoffs of a fashionable and worldly and Thackerayan society. They avoid in the main the sensational and melodramatic and keep sentimentality from running to excess. This quiet realism gave point to the jibe which fastened the name of "cup and saucer" school on Robertson and his followers. The dramatic themes are a little insipid but they provided a change from the melodramatic standards of their day; the style is epigrammatic and brisk, and the characters are modern and pleasantly contrasted. The type of comedy can be fully illustrated in its three earliest specimens.

"Society" is a sketchy and poorly organized series of scenes which depict literary Bohemia, a fashionable soiree and a country election. A number of eccentric and amusing persons help to fill out these pictures and to enliven the story of Sidney Daryl, poor but noble, who wins Maud Hetherington, lovely but lifeless, in spite of the wealthy and vulgar John Chodd, Jr., abetted by the cynical and worldly Lady Ptarmigant. The long-lost child so often employed in sentimental story is played for a new dramatic effect. Lord Ptarmigant has a sleeping part, dozing ostentatiously on every occasion until the last scene, when the discovery that he has a granddaughter brings him suddenly to life and action. This is a fair example of Robertson's translation of homely humour into stage character; and in the hands of that fine actor, Mr. John Hare, the sleeping gentleman became the hit of the play.

In "Ours" the contrasts in setting, characters and dialogue are more artfully managed than in "Society." The set for Act I is the park of a country seat in England with the autumn leaves falling from the trees. The set for the third and last act is a soldier's hut in the Crimea, very rude, "roof covered with snow and icicles," "wind and snow as the door opens." The suitors of the beautiful Blanche are Angus, a young and penniless officer, and the Russian prince Perovsky, old, rich but worthy, who becomes a prisoner in the last act. The drawling and listless Chalcot, teased by the madcap Mary Netley (Miss Marie Wilton) in the park, becomes the gallant crippled soldier who aids Mary in cooking the mutton and pudding in the camp. The absurdly jealous Lady Shendryn, who refuses to say good-bye to her husband, begs forgiveness as he comes back wounded from battle. The play opens with the announcement of the birth of twins to Sergeant Jones of "Ours," the regiment of Sir Alexander Shendryn's quartered near his house. Soon the family and guests are amusing themselves, raising a subscription for the twins, playing at bowls, dodging the rain, flirting and quarreling under the trees of the park; but, in the second act, war is declared with Russia and partings are made while the regimental band plays "The Girl I Left Behind Me," and finally "God Save the Queen." In the last act the ladies have joined the gentlemen at the battle front, and the love matches are made to the accompaniment of bugles and cannon.

Variety and contrast in the conversations are aided by a device that Robertson often employs—two couples, each supposedly unaware of the other, carry on two contrasted dialogues which reach the audience with a sort of antiphonal effect. During the rain the lovers, Blanche and Angus, are standing on the seat under the tree on the right of the stage, while the estranged husband and wife sit back to back on the stump to the left. Angus takes off his coat and tenderly wraps it about Blanche; the baronet is quite indifferent to Lady Shendryn. The cynical and sentimental antiphony proceeds:

Lady S. If you walked to the Hall, you could send me an umbrella.

Sir A. I'd rather you got wet. Just now you wished me to stay for fear of highwaymen.

Lady S. I might catch cold.

Sir A. I should be sorry for the cold that caught you.

Lady S. It might be my death.

Sir A. Lady Shendryn, the rain fertilizes the earth, nourishes the crops, and makes the fish lively; but still it does not bring with it every blessing. You have no right to hold out agreeable expectations which you know you do not intend to realize.

> *These conversations to be taken up as if they were continuous.*

Angus. What was that song you sang at the Sylvester's?

Blanche. Oh!

Angus. I wish you'd hum it to me now.

Blanche. Without music?

Angus. It won't be without music.

Blanche. You know the story; it is supposed to be sung by a very young man who is in love with a very haughty beauty, but dare not tell her of his love.

Angus. Of course he was poor.

Blanche. N—o.

Angus. What else could keep him silent?

Blanche. Want of—courage.

Angus. How does it go?

Blanche (sings. Air, "Le Chanson de Fortunio," in Offenbach's "Maître Fortunio").

> If my glances have betrayed me,
>   Ask me no more,
> For I dare not tell thee, lady,
>   Whom I adore.
> She is young, and tall, and slender,
>   Eyes of deep blue,
> She is sweet, and fair, and tender,
>   Like unto you.
> Unless my lady will me,
>   I'll not reveal,
> Though the treasured secret kill me,
>   The love I feel.

Lady S. Advertising our poverty to the whole country; a filthy, old rumbling thing, not fit for a washerwoman to ride in. I won't go out in it again!

Sir A. Then stay at home.

Lady S. Why not order a new carriage?.

Sir A. Can't afford it.

Angus. The air has haunted me ever since I heard you sing it. I've written some words to it myself.

Blanche. Oh, give them to me, I'll sing them.

Angus. Will you?

    Gives her verses, which he takes from pocketbook in coat pocket.

Lady S. Oh! I feel so faint, I think it must be time for lunch.

Sir A. I'm sure it is *(looking at watch)*. And I'm awfully hungry. Confound it!

Blanche (reading verses which Angus has given her). They're very charming. *(Sighs.)*

Angus. You're faint. They'll lunch without us.

Blanche. Never mind.

Angus. You're not hungry?

Blanche. No; are you?

Angus. Not in the least.

Blanche. Cousin, do you know I rather like to see you getting wet. May I keep these?

Angus. If you wish it.

Lady S. Where does all your money go to then? And what is that Mr. Kelsey, the lawyer, always coming down for?

Sir A. You'd better not ask. You'd better not know.

Blanche. But tell me, cousin, have you ever been in love?

Angus. Yes.

Blanche. How many times?

Angus. Once.

Blanche. Only once?

Angus. Only once.

Lady S. I know where the money goes to.

Sir A. Do you? I wish I did. Where?

Lady S. I know.

Sir A. Where?

Lady S. I know.

Blanche. I shouldn't like a husband who was too good, he'd become monotonous.

Angus. No husband would be too good for you; at least, I think not!

*   *   *   *   *   *   *

Lady S. I suppose that when that woman——

Sir A. Lady Shendryn!

Lady S. That Mrs.——

Sir A. Silence! *(Distant thunder and lightning.)*

Lady S. (rising and clinging to Sir Alexander). Alexander!

Sir A. Dou't touch me!

Angus (nearing her). Blanche!

Blanche. Angus!

"Caste" has all the merits of the two earlier plays and a more definite structure and moral. The Hon. George D'Alroy makes love to the ballet dancer Esther Eccles, "Act One—Courtship"; their happy marriage is interrupted by the arrival of his mother, the Marquise, and by the orders which send him off to India with his regiment, "Act Two—Matrimony"; and the mourning of Esther with her baby is brought to a happy conclusion by the return of her supposedly dead husband, "Act Three—Widowhood." The madcap Polly Eccles (Marie Wilton) is wooed and won by Sam Gerridge, gas fitter and plumber, and their lower-class love-making supplements and relieves the main story. George's friend, Captain Hawtree, and the Marquise sufficiently illustrate the upper classes. Further diversion and moral are supplied by old Eccles, an idle drunkard and rascal who becomes a radical agitator indulging in much talk of the rights of the working class. On the first run of the piece it was objected that the very effective acting of this part was a little out of the picture. The part itself is indeed given a magnitude quite disproportionate to its real service—an offence of exaggeration much rarer in Robertson than in many English dramatists. Two box sets, one of "the little house in Stangate," the other of "lodgings in Mayfair" are sufficient to carry the story and to suggest the differences of caste.

"Caste" was hailed enthusiastically by the critics as well as by the public. On the morning after its first production an eminent critic wrote:

"Society" and "Ours" prepared the way for a complete reformation of the modern drama, and until the curtain fell on Saturday night it remained a question whether Mr. Robertson would be able to hold the great reputation which those pieces conferred upon him. The production of "Caste" has thrown aside all doubt. The reformation is complete, and Mr. Robertson stands preëminent as the dramatist of this generation. The scene-painter, the carpenter, and the *costumier* no longer usurp the place of the author and actor. With the aid of only two simple scenes—a boudoir in Mayfair and a humble lodging in Lambeth—Mr. Robertson has succeeded in concentrating an accumulation of incident and satire more interesting and more poignant than might be found in all the sensational dramas of the last half century. The whole secret of his success is—truth!

The perspective of sixty years makes this realism seem a little shadowy and renders old-fashioned most of the novelties of the play of 1867. We find its sentiment and fun rather obvious, its soliloquies and asides artificial, and its story and moral commonplace. But in many ways it is closer to our theater of today than any comedy that we have examined. We find ourselves no longer looking at actors across the vast distances of Drury Lane where every stroke of humour or passion must be exaggerated on the stage if it is to reach the galleries. We are seated in the orchestra of a little theater, no apron separates us from the proscenium arch, which frames a picture of rooms and persons very like those which we know in real life. Much that was customary in the theater of Colman, Jr., has been discarded, the low comedy is less eccentric, the emotional crises less exciting, the pathos less prolonged, the claptrap less vociferous. It is all less theatrical, more natural, or at least more subdued. The remarkable coincidences, the cleverly disguised surprises, the artifices of Sardou are mostly lacking. No chance is offered for an emotional actress. The story develops simply and every person on the stage helps to tell it.

The pleasant concoction is not strong drink, it is served in cup and saucer. But how much of our comedy since Robertson has afforded a stimulation very like that of his mild tea. The slight story so easily followed, the satire and sentiment pleasantly varied and spiced by moments of hilarity, the timely reflection of social conflicts or fads, —these reappear in the new plays of each succeeding season. Sentiments, manners and social contrasts change a little from year to year but they seem to unite in the same blend. The humour of this style of comedy may indeed be more ample and original than Robertson's but it will not go too far, it will remain domestic rather than imaginative. The purpose of comedy becomes somewhat confined and regulated. It does not aspire to the unrestricted fields of entertainment or instruction, it seeks merely to provide a pleasant and a quiet evening. The limit of its aspiration is geniality.

Robertson's reforms were in large part matters of the theater. His successful comedies were mostly produced at the Prince of Wales, a small theater where stalls were placed in the pit and the management catered to a select audience. This theater, under the Bancrofts, was to continue a progressive career after Robertson's death, but it was his initiative that promoted one of the most far-reaching of theatrical changes—the sending on tour of a well trained second company to play the season's successes in the provinces. This practice, already begun in the United States, marks the beginning of the end of the stock companies. Robertson himself was a careful director, and he made the most of his tiny stage, rehearsed thoroughly, wrote nearly as long stage directions as Bernard Shaw, and planned every exit and entrance and every grouping of persons as a part of the picture. Years later, Sir W. S. Gilbert bore this testimony: "I look upon stage management, as now understood, as having been absolutely invented by him." He made good use of his intimate acquaintance with the theater and with French comedy. No earlier writer had employed so intelligently the resources of stage, costume and acting to mirror and reënforce some of the phases of sentiment and humour in modern life.

After Sheridan Knowles the poetic drama had few successes during the mid-century. None of Browning's plays are comedies, and what comic characterization is to be found in "Pippa Passes," or a "Soul's Tragedy," or "Colombe's Birthday," has little fitness for the stage. A more persistent exponent of verse in drama was John Westland Marston. His "Patrician's Daughter" (1842), an effort to treat contemporary differences of caste with elevation and passion, was followed by a number of dramas and tragedies, written with more literary skill and emotional sincerity than the stage was commanding from any other writer. His comedies are of less consequence. Only one is in verse, "Donna Diana" (1863), and that is based on Moreto's "El Desden con El Desden." "Borough Politics" (1846) is a commonplace sketch of love crossed by family pretensions. "A Hard Struggle" (1858) relates how Reuben relinquished Lilian to Fergus and found some hope in the devotion of Amy, aged thirteen. It succeeded, drew tears from Dickens, and is perhaps as good as Reade's "Dora." "The Wife's Portrait" (1862), with another girl of thirteen, and "Pure Gold" (1863), are domestic dramas that permit of much sentiment but nothing humorous.

A less literary but more popular contributor to domes-

tic comedy was Henry Byron, friend and benefactor of
Robertson, actor, journalist, and author of many farces,
burlesques and extravaganzas. Of his domestic comedies,
"Cyril's Success" won general favour, but "Our Boys"
made the great hit, breaking all records by a continuous
London run from January 16, 1875, to April 18, 1879.
Two sons, two fond fathers, one an aristocrat, the other
a rich plebeian, two girls, an old maid aunt, and a comic
but tender-hearted slavey. Each boy selects the wrong
girl; they are disowned by their fathers; they live in poverty in a garret, where they are discovered by the girls
and the fathers; and after a few amusing complications
the curtain drops on forgiveness and reconciliation. This
is about as good a recipe as can be given for a four years'
run; it might be improved by a baby in the last act, as in
Robertson's "Caste." "Abie's Irish Rose," which has
now broken the New York record for a long run, varies
this recipe only slightly, making the fathers represent different races and creeds, confining itself to one couple,
but providing twins in the last act. My formula does not
carry a sure guarantee of success, but apparently no
comedy is likely to have a long metropolitan run that
strays very far from the simple story of domestic differences and reconciliation.

A word or two must be said also of three mechanicians
of farce and translators from the French who were among
the chief purveyors to the public's demand for laughter.
Of these, J. Madison Morton, son of the dramatist
Thomas Morton, was perhaps the most prolific producer
of light comedies and French adaptations. Benjamin
Webster, famous character actor and manager of the
Haymarket from 1837 to 1853, was the author of over
one hundred pieces and the bestower of a prize of five
hundred pounds for the best comedy, which was awarded
to the once celebrated Mrs. Gore for a play that excited
more derision than praise. Webster's successor at the
Haymarket, John Baldwin Buckstone, was another comic
actor and author who batted out his century—mostly of

farces. Morton, Webster and Buckstone combined to live over two hundred and forty years and to write some four hundred plays that afforded great enjoyment to thousands of audiences in England and the United States. These many thousand nights entertainments aroused sighs by their sentiment and sobs by their pathos, but they kept the playhouses forever ringing with laughter. It is rather cheering to realize how readily and how continuously the Victorians laughed. I dare say these pieces might still be amusing on the stage; but in print, those that survive do not disclose a wide perspective of fun.

In fact, in commenting on the authors who took part in that democratization of the drama which was proceeding during Victoria's reign, I have not had occasion to notice much originality or richness of humour. In an age of great humourists, comedy remained commonplace and thin. Even the most amusing of farces, "Box and Cox," remade from two French pieces by the younger Morton, no longer convulses us as it did Queen Victoria. Neither those writers who tried to give comedy poetic or literary values, nor the craftsman like Boucicault, nor Robertson and his followers were notably lavish with their mirth. But a great revival of humour on the English stage was taking place during the very years when the feeble fun of "Our Boys" was delighting London, and its creator, W. S. Gilbert, deserves a chapter to himself.

CHAPTER XXI

SIR WILLIAM SCHWENK GILBERT

THE reviver of humour on the English stage and its greatest comic dramatist during the nineteenth century won his rights to those titles not by his comedies but by his operas. Though he wrote many plays, some of which had long runs and later revivals, he created nothing of great originality and made no marked departure from contemporary practice in the way of comedy proper. Nor did his comedies directly prepare for the operas or reveal the characteristics of their humour. That new and original humour, what Gilbert was himself fond of calling topsy-turvydom, had its forerunners in his "Bab Ballads," from which it borrowed hints for plots, persons, incidents, and versification.

At first thought it may seem a little absurd to consider the words apart from the music which must be credited with much of the charm and some of the humour of the operas; but Gilbert's librettos to which Sullivan fitted his music are as delightful on the stage today as forty or fifty years ago, and their incomparable nonsense may still be enjoyed by a tone-deaf reader. With unique powers as versifier and humorist, Gilbert was also most accomplished in the arts of the theater, and the librettos are both dramatic and literary masterpieces. Though they owe little to comedies of the past and though they are not exactly comedies themselves, still they helped to revive comedy in England. Their topsy-turvydom proved a stimulating discovery and gave direction to the wits of Oscar Wilde, Bernard Shaw, Sir James Barrie and many others. After their example, wit and humour could scarcely refuse to frolic.

William Schwenk Gilbert was born in 1836, graduated B.A. at the University of London, and after four "uncomfortable years" in the civil service, was called to the bar and spent four years more in nearly briefless practice as a barrister. By the time that he was twenty-one he had written a laughing song for the stage, and in 1861 he became a member of the staff of "Fun," engaged to contribute a column of copy and a half-page drawing every week. During the sixties he was busy as a journalist, writing articles of all sorts as well as stories and verse for various periodicals. In 1869 was published the first collection of "Bab Ballads, Much Sound and Little Sense," with illustrations by the author. These verses, drawn from the columns of "Fun," and added to in later editions, are enough to establish Gilbert's fame as a humorous versifier. He had a precursor in the nonsense verses of Edward Lear, and the most famous of all discoveries in topsy-turvy land had been accomplished by the publication of "Alice in Wonderland" four years before the first collection of his Bab Ballads. But there could be no doubt of their originality or of their author's amazing ingenuity as a versifier. They were recognized almost at once as classics. Everyone "chortled over" "The Bishop of Rum-ti-foo," "Gentle Alice Brown" and the cannibalistic "Yarn of the Nancy Bell."

> Oh, I am a cook, and a captain bold,
>   And the mate of the Nancy Brig,
> And a bo'sun tight, and midshipmite,
>   And the crew of the captain's gig.

Among Gilbert's associates on "Fun" were Tom Robertson and H. J. Byron. Robertson persuaded him to write for the stage, and his first piece, "Dulcamara" (1866), followed the manner of Byron, then the chief composer of theatrical burlesques. Other successful burlesques followed, and between 1869 and 1872 Gilbert wrote many sketches for the German Reed entertainments given at the Gallery of Illustration in Regent Street, the

music for these operettas being composed by Frederick
Clay. A musical play by Gilbert and Clay later furnished
suggestions for "Ruddigore," and Gilbert's blank verse
burlesque, "The Princess," performed at the Olympic in
1870, was later worked over into the opera "Princess
Ida." Within the next few years Gilbert tried his hand
at many of the current types of drama, but his principal
non-musical pieces may be grouped in two classes, (1)
blank verse fairy plays and (2) prose comedies and
dramas.

The four blank verse plays are "The Palace of
Truth" (1870), "Pygmalion and Galatea" (1871), "The
Wicked World" (1873), and "Broken Hearts" (1875).
The first three were acted at the Haymarket, and all four
had Mr. and Mrs. Kendal as actors. All deal with fairy
or magical transformations and are ambitious efforts to
create a type of poetical and fantastic drama.

"The Palace of Truth" treats of the disclosures of
character and the crossings of love brought about by the
magical palace where everyone unknowingly speaks the
truth. The dramatic treatment is clumsy and without
climax. "Pygmalion and Galatea" had a great success
with Mrs. Kendal as Galatea and has often been revived,
notably by Mary Anderson in 1884 and 1888. The story
of the statue which comes to life and then falls in love
with her creator is given a considerable amount of stage
effectiveness but not much real dramatic interest. "The
Wicked World," later remade into the opera "Fallen
Fairies," depicts the evil transformations wrought in the
fairy world in the clouds by the introduction of human
love. In this as in the other two plays romantic love and
its attendant passions evoke abundant sentimentality, but
in "Broken Hearts" it is excessive to the degree of mawk-
ishness. Four broken-hearted maidens withdraw to an
island, pledged to love no living thing, and fix their affections on a time-dial, a fountain and other inanimate
objects. The man arrives, possessed of a scarf that
makes him invisible, and woos the maidens, speaking as

from the sundial and the fountain. Two sisters fall in love with him, and after a struggle in generosity, the younger fades away. Gilbert told Miss Anderson that there was more of him in "Broken Hearts" than anywhere else, but fortunately this strained pathos did not appeal to the public.

The blank verse of these plays has felicitous passages and in general a workmanlike quality, but it is very stiff, surprisingly so in comparison with the ease and deftness of his rhyming measures. The characterization and moralizing are also stiff, even in "Pygmalion," both being made to type or pattern without any freedom of invention. The dramatic structure, with a partial exception for Pygmalion, has many clumsy devices. The overheard conversation, for example, is too much employed. Before the close of each dialogue, some one is pretty sure to steal on behind and overhear the closing and significant words, which of course leads to the next deception or entanglement. Even Gilbert's ironies are a little stagy. The plays mark another failure to revive the poetic drama and they add very little to the development of comedy, although "Pygmalion and Galatea" is possibly as good as any poetical comedy for a long time. They suggest nothing of that rich and mobile humour which was to be revealed in the operas.

The prose plays have more variety and humour. Four of these are sentimental and melodramatic pieces, with less machinery than Boucicault's and more villainy than Robertson's. No less sentimental, however, than the verse plays are "Sweethearts" (1874), a sketch in two acts showing the lovers parted at the end of act one and reunited after a lapse of thirty years, and "Dan'l Druce" (1876), a melodramatic and humourless romance. Much more comic dialogue and social satire are to be found in "Randall's Thumb" (1871) and "Charity" (1874). The latter is a problem play defending the woman who has expiated her mistake by a life of sacrifice and charity, but the problem is badly argued, for the persons who accuse the lady are proved to be unmitigated hypocrites and criminals. In "Randall's Thumb" the satire is lighter, but the comedy is invaded by a designing villain whose nefarious schemes trouble the frivolities and deceptions of the guests at a seaside hotel.

"Tom Cobb" (1875) and "Engaged" (1877) were both announced as "farcical comedies" and are happily free from excessive sentimentality or villainy. In the first Tom Cobb pretends he is dead and thus gives his rival a chance to capture his sweetheart, the daughter of an Irish adventurer; but the supposed pauper, also named Tom Cobb, who really dies, turns out to be rich and a relative of the other, hence many complications. In "Engaged" the entanglement is still more complicated, and the preposterous plot is carried through with a pretense of logicality as later in the operas. A young man who proposes marriage to every girl he meets; a house, part of the garden of which is in Scotland, so that a Scotch marriage by mutual declaration is legal; a will in which a sum of money is left to one young man only so long as the other man doesn't marry—these are some of the premises which result in a great deal of funny dialogue before four couples are finally paired off. The spirit of extravagance and burlesque runs through the dialogue as well as the plot and brings us closer than in any other play to the prose of the operas.

Even after the great success of "Pinafore" and the consequent incentive to produce a new opera every year, Gilbert turned back from time to time to the spoken drama. He found the task of fun-making often irksome, and to the last had a desire to preach and sentimentalize on the stage. "Gretchen" (1879), a serious play based on "Faust," and "Rosencrantz and Guildenstern" (1891), a travesty, are in blank verse. "Foggarty's Fairy" (1881) is a fantastic fairy play, and "The Fairy's Dilemma" (1904), with music, was called a "domestic pantomime." "Brantinghame Hall" (1888) is a sentimental melodrama in prose. Perhaps the best of these later pieces are two one-act sketches, "Comedy and Tragedy" (1884), a brilliant scene, in which the actress delights the company by her improvisations while her husband is fighting a duel with her traducer in the garden outside, and "The Hooligan" (1911), a powerful sketch of the criminal awaiting his execution, acted in the year that Gilbert lost his life trying to save a guest from drowning.

If Gilbert had died before "Pinafore" was produced, he would not deserve much attention in a history of English comedy. Still, he would require some notice as one of the most ambitious and successful of the dramatists of his era and some special credit for originality in two directions, romantic poetic comedy, and topsy-turvy farce. "Pygmalion" and "Engaged" would be cited as two pieces superior in their respective fields and offering promise for future achievement. His later plays, however, make it doubtful whether he would have ever advanced much farther than these in the non-musical drama. He yielded too readily to those banes of the nineteenth century theater—sentimentality and melodrama; and these were fortunately scarcely permissible in light opera. His puckish humour and fancy had a far better opportunity and discipline in the somewhat narrow limits of a libretto than they could find in the loose articulation of farce.

His experience in writing plays gave him a thorough acquaintance with the stage and with dramatic technic. Advancing years sharpened his wit and gave a wider play for his fun and disciplined his intelligence. What these needed for an accompaniment was not blank verse or sermons, but music as graceful and delightful as his best fairy fancy. At about the right period in his career and at a most happy moment for the English stage, Gilbert former a partnership with a brilliant young composer, Arthur Sullivan.

The collaboration of Gilbert and Sullivan began with "Thespis, or The Gods Grown Old," an "entirely original, grotesque opera in two acts," produced at the Gaiety

Theater, December 23, 1871. Though a failure, its verse and nonsense often show Gilbert almost at the top of his form. A company of actors appear on the summit of Mt. Olympus on a picnic. The Olympian deities, somewhat decrepit and out of date, agree to descend to earth, leaving the running of the universe in the hands of the Thespians. After two acts of unhappy consequences the gods resume their places. Gilbert and Sullivan renewed their partnership three years later in "Trial by Jury," "a dramatic cantata," produced at the Royalty, March 23, 1875, as an afterpiece to Offenbach's "La Périchole." The chorus, composed of jurymen and bridesmaids, takes a dramatic and musical importance greater than in any of the earlier pieces; but the cantata, unlike the later operas, contains no spoken dialogue. The theme, a satire on courts and lawyers, is one to which Gilbert frequently returned. Under the management of Mr. D'Oyly Carte, the author and composer were next induced to prepare an opera that would provide a full evening's entertainment; and "The Sorcerer" was acted at the Opéra Comique, November 17, 1877.

In comparison with the later operas, "The Sorcerer" is still a little experimental. The plot, to carry the increased length of the entertainment, is cumbersome and hackneyed. The sudden shifts and exchanges of the lovers which usually form a main element in Gilbert's topsy-turvydom, are here accomplished by the use of a potion that causes the sleeper to fall violently in love with the first person seen on awakening. Since a charm for this purpose was administered by Puck to the Athenian lovers, it must have been employed in thousands of stage extravaganzas, in Gilbert's "Gentleman in Black" among others. But, though the ancient plot creaks, and though his verse and fun are a trifle thin and strained compared with the products of his fully matured art, yet all the constituents and the main pattern of the later operas are present. The chorus, here an undistinguished one of villagers, the ensemble scenes, the love

songs, the comic songs, the patter song, the duets, the
soprano part, the tenor part, the prose dialogues which
connect the musical numbers—all the ingredients which
make up the recipe are here determined upon in proper
proportions and arrangement.

The male and female choruses and the male and female
soloists, including elderly as well as youthful amorists,
have their love affairs twisted and turned through the
instrumentality of the leading comic actor, here as always,
a characteristically Gilbertian "humour," John Welling-
ton Wells (of J. W. Wells and Co., Family Sorcerers).
Mr. George Grossmith took this part with some hesitation and upon going over it with Gilbert he said, "For
the part of a magician, surely you require a fine man
with a large voice?" "That," replied Gilbert, "is exactly
what we don't want." He was to write many patter
songs for Grossmith, who played the comedy lead successively as First Lord of the Admiralty, as Major General,
as a fleshly poet, and as Lord Chancellor. By this time
Gilbert knew exactly what he wanted and what he didn't
want. "The Sorcerer" helped him to find the actors and
singers for whom he must make appropriate parts and
find the general pattern into which he must work the parts.
His invention was now quite ready for the stupendous
task of filling these requirements with originality and
variety.

After a run of six months, "The Sorcerer" was succeeded at the Opéra Comique on May 28, 1878, by
"H. M. S. Pinafore," which ran for two years. The
authors went to the United States to superintend a performance there and produced "The Pirates of Penzance"
in New York December 31, 1879. It was given in London
three months later, April 3, 1880, with about the same
cast as "Pinafore" and was followed on April 23, 1881,
by "Patience." The Savoy Theater, built especially for
the operas and the first public building in England to
be lighted entirely by electricity, saw the première of
"Iolanthe" on November 25, 1882, followed in 1884 by

"Princess Ida," in 1885 by "The Mikado," in 1887 by "Ruddigore," in 1888 by "The Yeomen of the Guard," in 1889 by "The Gondoliers," in 1893 by "Utopia Limited," and in 1896 by "The Grand Duke." Gilbert also wrote "The Mountebanks" with music by Alfred Cellier, produced in 1892, "His Excellency" with music by Osmond Carr, in 1894, and in 1909, two years before his death, "Fallen Fairies," based on "The Wicked World," with music by Edward German. All of the Gilbert and Sullivan operas were produced in the United States, and the chief of them have been frequently revived down to the present time. They have been translated into foreign languages, but Gilbert is untranslatable. In spite, however, of the British character of the themes and allusions, the operas have been even more popular in the United States than in England, and time has not yet impaired their charms.

Gilbert was responsible for nearly everything that made an opera effective except the music. He planned every detail on a miniature stage with three-inch blocks for the male performers, and two and a half inch blocks for the females. He was his own stage director and rehearsed the company most rigorously. He drew designs for costumes and he had a hand in much else besides the verse and the wit. These are of almost unfailing excellence. Even in "The Grand Duke," which failed, and in the librettos written for other composers than Sullivan, Gilbert's extraordinary technical skill in versification remains unimpaired, and his fun is as obstreperous and nearly as spontaneous as ever. The dozen operas written within twenty years after "The Sorcerer" reveal an amazing fertility of wit and invention.

Among so many operas certain differences are perceptible in aims and methods. Gilbert's own preference was for "The Yeomen of the Guard," and some capable critics agree that there both he and Sullivan reached their highest achievement, but no one who is valuing the operas mainly on the basis of their humour can approve of this

judgment. Gilbert, like many humorists, was a sentimentalist and moralist at heart and tired of the rôle of
fun-maker. In a letter to Sullivan (Feb. 20, 1889) he
speaks of "The Yeomen" as "a stage in the direction of
serious opera," and continues, "Personally I prefer a
consistent subject. Such a subject as The Yeomen is far
more congenial to my taste than the burlesquerie of
Iolanthe or The Mikado." In "The Yeomen," indeed,
topsy-turvydom disappears, and we have a time-worn
romantic plot, while the humour is mixed with the usual
sort of pathos in the jester Jack Point, who, like Gilbert
himself, finds jesting an onerous business. It is a stage
toward serious or sentimental opera, and its libretto
inspired very charming music, but its humour is comparatively commonplace and uncharacteristic. Of the others,
"Princess Ida," with the dialogue in blank verse and the
subject drawn from Tennyson, is one of the less inventive
and less sparkling. But of the rest, "Pinafore," "Pirates
of Penzance," "Patience," "Iolanthe," "The Mikado,"
"Ruddigore," "The Gondoliers," each will choose his
favourite as he will. In all of these Gilbert's humour is
at its prettiest.

This humour is a great creation for the stage and a
lasting influence in comedy; but it is not altogether new
and original. Gilbert made his operas in considerable
part from the whimsicalities of the Bab Ballads, and
these, as we have seen, came after Edward Lear and
Lewis Carroll. The fun of viewing things turned upside
down or inside out had indeed had a great exponent in
the drama in Aristophanes and has been cropping out ever
since in comedy, as in the pranks of Puck or in Falstaff's
oration on honour. From the time of "The Beggar's
Opera" this topsy-turvy nonsense had characterized the
whole course of burlesque, extravaganza and light opera.
The majority of English musical shows and burlesques
were doubtless very poor when Gilbert began to write,
and they have been ever since and still are. But Gilbert
did not furnish the only exception to the rule of medioc-

rity and vulgarity, nor did he succeed in leavening the huge lump of inferiority. He learned a good deal from his predecessors. The musical drama had attracted a number of wits since the time of Gay's success, and English burlesque had gained a freshness and delicacy of humour in the delightful extravagances of Planché. He prepared the way for Gilbert, who also learned something from the French fairy drama, praised by Planché, it will be remembered, for just the qualities that we find in the Savoy operas, "sparkling with wit, pregnant with refined satire, exquisite whim, and delightful persiflage." Moreover, there can be no question of a general indebtedness of Gilbert and Sullivan to Offenbach, who had virtually created opéra bouffe anew and to Halévy and Meilhac, who composed his librettos. Their operas were at the very height of their world success when Gilbert was beginning as a writer for the stage. Indeed, it is worth noticing that in 1866, the year when Gilbert produced his first extravaganza—quite inferior to Planché's best—Planché at the age of seventy was adapting "Orphée aux Enfers" for the Haymarket.

The writer of the article on opera in the Encyclopedia Britannica says of French opéra bouffe, "Sullivan assimilated its adroit orchestration as Gilbert purified its literary wit, and the result became a peculiarly English possession." The conclusion of this generalization is undoubtedly true, and it is also true that the wit of the Savoy operas is much purer than the wit in Offenbach's; but it is scarcely sufficient to regard Gilbert's invention as purely literary or as merely a work of purification. It would perhaps be a more adequate generalization to say that Gilbert after learning all he could about extravaganza and opera from Planché and Offenbach and about staging a play from Tom Robertson, proceeded to make over the jests and suggestions of the Bab Ballads and others of his fresh discovery, amplifying and elaborating them into operatic form.

He was of course immensely fortunate in finding Sullivan for a composer, for without Sullivan's genius and compatibility, all his efforts must have been abortive. He is writing operas and not plays, and all his comedy is carefully designed for music and dance, and relies on picturesque setting and costume and all the operatic accompaniments. His whim and banter are barely conceivable without a song or a frolic. But the libretto of each opera is a work of laborious though exquisite art. The framework provides the fundamental absurdity, and the jokes and sallies decorate it. To make the House of Lords a singing and dancing chorus is a joke. To balance this male chorus by a chorus of fairies with whom the peers fall in love is to devise the source for the ever gushing mirth of "Iolanthe." Gilbert's artistry is as unflagging as his humour. They work together to frame the plot, develop the situations, inspire the music, fill in every joint and crevice of the dramatic structure. Puns and allusions and phrases embellish every part. Gilbert constructs veritable palaces of nonsense, delicate and airy, but well-built and completely furnished.

The picturesque scenes and costumes create an unreal and delectable setting—on a warship, in fairyland, in Japan, among the pirates, or in a South-sea Utopia. The opposing choruses of sailors and the female relatives of the First Lord of the Admiralty, or of the peers and the fairies, or of the pirates and policemen and the major-general's daughters, or of the æsthetic maidens and the heavy dragoons, or of the professional bridesmaids and the wicked ancestors from the portraits—these announce the method and mode of hilarity. Then, a preposterous plot is unfolded, and adhered to with pretended exactitude. The hero, son of the Lord Chancellor and a fairy, is presented as half-fairy and half-mortal (from the waist downwards)—or the hero is heir to the wicked baronets who must sin and die, and to escape this curse he seeks disguise as a humble villager. The absurd love entanglements and crossings usually burlesque the sentimentalities both of actual life and of the lyric and spoken drama.

And a partaker in the various contretemps is the most preposterous personage of all—a commander of the Queen's navee, or a lord chancellor, or Pooh Bah—Lord High Everything Else.

Under the bewildering auspices are introduced a host of persons and a multitude of topics for song or conversation. Each person and each topic presents an unexpected side, an absurd aspect. All are objects of laughter. Some excite more and some less, but none are spared. Sympathy and sentiment, an interpretation of character, a genuine concern in the realities of life are not suffered to exist for longer than a moment. Humanity is not usually an attribute of Gilbert's humour. And yet an astonishing range of English life is touched upon by his persiflage and drollery. No professions or persons are sacrosanct. Ridicule hits lawyers, judges, jurymen, the clergy, the nobility, the army, the navy, the police, and even royalty itself. Place-seeking politicians, stock jobbers, company promoters, æsthetes, young girls of all sorts, ingenuous, rapturous, love-sick, and collegiate, middle-aged and heavyweight amorists, aristocrats and republicans, all get a touch of satire. And the wit plays about such themes as official incompetency, British insularity, upperclass pride, democratic aspiration, jingoism, æstheticism, smugness, and what not? Though many of the references are to local and contemporary follies and affectations, most of them remain pat enough today —even the account of the ways in which the Duke and Duchess of Plaza-Toro earn their living.

Duchess. And vow my complexion
    Derives its perfection
    From somebody's soap—which it doesn't—
Duke (*significantly*). It certainly doesn't.

The English comic stage had never before held up to ridicule so many habits and personages generally accepted or even highly prized by the British public. Laughter mocked at everyone from sentinel to major-general, from queen to schoolgirl.

Yet it seems to me a mistake to view Gilbert simply as a satirist. Only once, in "Patience," does ridicule of contemporary manners become the main theme of the opera; often it is confined to some particulars, such as the duchess lending her face to a soap advertisement. Usually the fun is too extravagant to hurt. The Victorian age is presented to us and is laughed at, but it is not condemned and is scarcely censured. No effort is made to excite us to revolution or reform; not much pabulum is offered to the enthusiast or the dreamer. Little time is allowed for any one to sigh or to think about the shortcomings of society. The satire may run into burlesque or parody, but not into denunciation or a jeremiad. Lightness of touch is never lost. Therein lies the difference between Gilbert's fun and that of some more recent magistrates of topsy-turvydom. Paradox and whimsy and incongruity are not prolonged to enforce a lesson or to preach a crusade. Gilbert was a middle-class Victorian tory of many crotchets and prejudices. He endured without great dissatisfaction most of the things that he laughed at. He had humour enough to see something funny in many things, but he also had humour enough to know that almost anything is funny when looked at upside down. He did not hold things upside down as an argument that they were useless. His banter and irony were intended to reach the average intelligence, but not to alarm or disrupt it.

The humour has certain definite limitations. It is never improper. It never brings a blush to the chastest cheek. Gilbert wrote constantly with his female relatives in view as auditors. They did not need to wear masks or carry fans. Only a very Victorian Mrs. Grundy could detect the slightest indelicacies. The masculine sense of humour in matters of sex gets no gratification here. Subjects which had stirred the wit of Aristophanes, Rabelais, Wycherley, Swift and Sterne find no mention. No guffaws and no smirks are permitted. When we consider the temptations offered to a representative of the male sex with a vocabulary and a dexterity in words such as Gilbert possessed, the decency and delicacy of the language of the operas is no inconsiderable achievement.

This delicacy is secured without running off into sentimentality. The humour rarely disturbs our emotions. Except in "The Yeomen of the Guard," the operas make only fleeting appeals to our sympathies, and they show only a passing acquaintance with the more general sentiments and passions of mankind. None of Gilbert's humorists work their way into our affections as do Falstaff or Sam Weller. Pooh Bah is perhaps the nearest to a fully developed personality, but no one loves him. Even the young lovers are not allowed to coo or to lament too long, they are likely to be dismissed with something like a box on the ear. Home, heaven and mother are kept off the stage. The lack of tenderness makes the humour seem a little inhuman at times. The young lovers and their companions are mostly gay, amusing, delightful, but we can't put ourselves in their places. Only on such themes as the passing of youth or love, the momentariness of life and joy, is the verse suffered to sound a plaintive but transient note.

In spite of the coöperation of music and costumes and scene to excite the eye and ear, the absence of emotional appeal leaves the humour with a distinctly intellectual cast. Though disdaining philosophy or reform, the librettos very craftily bring the intelligence into play. The humour, to be sure, depends almost entirely on the old appurtenances of surprise and incongruity. This is seen in the choruses, the settings, the plots, the characters, in what we may style the main incongruities. It appears too in the preternatural gravity of the actors in performing their absurdities and speaking their impertinences, and in the rather careful logicality and precision with which the plots are argued and explained. But it appears also in jingles and proper names, and in phrases and rhymes and in places where only a well trained intelligence can discover its exquisite impropriety. It is an enormous tribute to the wit of our much abused public that it can take delight in something as novel and mentally exciting as the librettos of "Iolanthe" and "The Mikado."

It is hopeless to attempt to describe humour so variable and extravagant as this, and it is too ubiquitous to need illustration. But let us look for a moment at a few instances of the minor incongruities that surprise us in a single act. The queen of the fairies, a full-sized, even massive, person, is debating on her love for Iolanthe, while the other fairies listen sympathetically—"Who taught me to curl myself inside a buttercup?" exclaims the queen, and answers, "Iolanthe! Who taught me to swing upon a cobweb? Iolanthe. Who taught me to dive into a dewdrop—to nestle in a nutshell—to gambol up a gossamer? Iolanthe!" Whereupon one of the listening fairies comments, "She certainly did surprising things!" Strephon, Iolanthe's son by a mortal, soon enters, dancing and playing on a flageolet. He complains of his unhappy construction as a fairy to the waist, but mortal from the waist down. "My brain is a fairy brain, but from the waist downwards I'm a gibbering idiot. My upper half is immortal, but my lower half grows older every day, and some day or other must die of old age. What's to become of my upper half when I've buried my lower half I really don't know!" The fairies exclaim in pity, but the queen has a remedy. "I see your difficulty, but with a fairy brain you should seek an intellectual sphere of action. Let me see. I have a borough or two at my disposal. Would you like to go into Parliament?" Strephon's love-making is interrupted by the entrance of the Procession of Peers marching and singing. They are funny enough without words, but recall the words of their chorus:

Loudly let the trumpet bray—
  Tantantara!
Gaily bang the sounding brasses—
  Tzing!
As upon its lordly way
  This unique procession passes!
    Tantantara! tzing! boom!
Bow, ye lower, middle classes!
Bow, ye tradesmen! bow, ye masses!
Blow the trumpets, bang the brasses!
    Tantantara! tzing! boom!
We are peers of highest station,
Paragons of legislation,
Pillars of the British nation!
    Tantantara! tzing! boom!

Somewhat later Lord Tolloller delivers himself of this
pathetic appeal:

  Spurn not the nobly born
    With love affected,
  Nor treat with virtuous scorn
    The well-connected.
  High rank involves no shame;
  We boast an equal claim
  With him of humble name
    To be respected.

But I do not mean to quote all the famous things in the
act, such as the Chancellor's song—

  When I went to the Bar as a very young man,
    (Said I to myself, said I),

or the merry fooling over the youthful-looking mother,

I wouldn't say a word that could be construed as injurious
But to find a mother younger than her son is very curious;
And that's the kind of mother that is usually spurious.
    Taradiddle! taradiddle! tol-lol-lay!

I will note only two other minor embellishments. After
the queen has decided that in Parliament Strephon shall
turn things topsy-turvy, she ends her prophecy with this
inconceivable disaster:

> Peers shall teem in Christendom
> And a duke's exalted station
> Be attainable by Com-
> Petitive examination!

And here is a bit of the final ensemble:

Fairies. Your lordly style
   We'll quickly quench
  With base *canaille.*

Peers.   (That word is French.)

Fairies. Distinction ebbs
   Before a herd
  Of vulgar *plebs.*

Peers.   (A Latin word.)

Fairies. 'Twould fill with joy
   And madness stark
  The οἱ πολλοί.

Peers.   (A Greek remark.)

Such humour has the exhilaration of a game. Take
all possible pleasure from the music and the spectacle,
and you still lack the mental whirl and excitement of the
libretto. Listening to it is like watching a skilful runner
who doubles and dodges until he has left all of his pur-
suers breathless. The game is played in this way. Take
almost anything—a word, a rhyme, a sentiment, a habit,
and you can think of a number of other things congruous
with it. There are many congruities, for example, to
match "moon," "fairy," "lord chancellor"; and they may
be commonplace, conventional, or at least generally acceptable; but for every possible congruity there is at least one
incongruity and to every person or thing an infinite number of incongruities may be devised. Which of these is

the most tickling to eye, mind, or fancy? Try to invent
one as startling as this of Gilbert's, or as quaint as that.
Try to equal him in his somersaults. This seems to me
the essence of the Gilbertian humour—nimbleness of wit,
an intellectual agility, a creative fancy that keeps to the
rules of the game and yet surpasses all competitors in
multiplying incongruities.

The librettos have other merits. They are most harmonious and symmetrical works of art. The results of
months of patient labour, they seem but the breath of a
moment. Their humour goes beyond mere incongruity,
it can take a tint of melancholy, or suggestions of a
deeper irony than it wishes to indicate by its mockery.
Some of the songs are as clear and sweet as the "Hesperides" of Herrick. I have given little note to the
variety of whimsy, of metrical play, of vocabulary, of
the patter songs, magnificent in their metrical pro-
ficiency—

This particular rapid unintelligible patter
Isn't generally heard, and if it is, it doesn't matter.—

of the irresistible fitness of proper names or of exotic
polysyllables, of all the manifestations of an artistry as
perfect in its way as that of Keats. Yet the mind lingers
last on the phrase or refrain that embodies a matchless
incongruity, like that which helped to win the first great
popular success—

Stick close to your desks and never go to sea
And you all may be Rulers of the Queen's Navee!

Or that more intricate suggestion of the enigma of life:

String the lyre and fill the cup,
Lest on sorrow we should sup.
Hop and skip to Fancy's fiddle
Hands across and down the middle—
Life's perhaps the only riddle
That we shrink from giving up!

Or, the simplest and best of them all—most unforeseen:

> The flowers that bloom in the spring,
>   Tra la,
> Have nothing to do with the case.

CHAPTER XXII

THE NEW BIRTH OF COMEDY, 1890-1900

THE revival of comedy which became manifest during the last decade of the nineteenth century and has continued to the present time must be credited in considerable part to Gilbert's librettos. They had made topsy-turvydom immensely popular on the stage, but manifestly had not exhausted the almost infinite possibilities of this method of humour. A *reductio ad absurdum* could by the exercise of a little ingenuity be applied to whatever was established by custom, convention or tradition; and the public was now prepared to be delighted as well as startled at the most insouciant incongruities. Gilbert, moreover, was a stylist, a master of verbal device and invention, and his example did much to evoke literary effort from subsequent writers of comedy. Though it was hopeless to compete with him in his particular manner, his success opened new vistas of gaiety and mockery which were soon being ventured upon by Oscar Wilde and Bernard Shaw. In fact, few comedies of mark since Gilbert's day have been altogether lacking in deftness and neatness of style and in surprising whimsy and paradox —qualities almost unknown in English comedy for a century before "Pinafore."

The reawakening of the comic spirit, however, was but one sign of many that a new era was beginning in European drama. The great leader was Henrik Ibsen, whose "Pillars of Society" (1877), "A Doll's House" (1879) and "Ghosts" (1881) were hailed everywhere as soon as they were known as heralds of dramatic revolution. Towards the end of 1887 André Antoine and a few others established in Paris the Théâtre Libre, an experimental playhouse supported by subscriptions of a club, devoted to naturalistic dramas, and opposed to "well made" plays and theatrical artificiality. The Freie Bühne in Berlin followed in 1889 and the Independent Theatre in London in 1891. Ibsen's plays quickly took the post of honour in these free theaters, "Ghosts" being performed in Berlin in 1887, in Paris in 1890, and in London in 1891. Within a few years Hauptmann and Sudermann had appeared in Germany, Maeterlinck and Brieux in France, Bernard Shaw and Oscar Wilde in England. The new movement in the drama was far wider in scope than could have been surmised from the theories of the Théâtre Libre or even from the revolutionary theses of "A Doll's House" and "Ghosts." It has not yet subsided, and perhaps the time is not yet ripe for the appraisal of its significance, but certain salient characteristics may be noted. It began as a protest against the commercial theaters and conventionalized practices of the time and in favour of free experimentation both in form and substance; and although it has not removed commercialism from the drama, it has been successful in increasing enormously the opportunities for innovation and variation on the stage. It began also as a protest against the artificial and theatrical methods of the well-made plays and melodramas of the time, against the Scribe-Sardou-Boucicault technic and in favour of more natural dialogue, less sentimentality and claptrap, and a sincere effort to make the stage the mirror of life; and it has succeeded in maintaining this new interest in technic, although its return to nature soon developed artifices of its own. The movement was also a protest against the romantic and sentimental absurdities and subterfuges of the older drama and in favour of naturalism in subject matter as well as in theatrical form; and it has succeeded in greatly widening the scope of drama to include a range of situations, incidents, passions and discussions that would have been impossible in any preceding theater. The efforts for naturalism in both technic and substance happily failed to result in any narrowing of the dramatic impulse. Symbolism in the plays of Maeterlinck and of Ibsen himself was soon in conflict with a Zolaesque naturalism, and the technical innovations of Ibsen were succeeded by all kinds of experiments. Though the movement began, as literary movements often do, by oppositions to the practices of the day and by proclamation of a "return to nature," it has widened its scope without losing its energy and has succeeded in bringing literature again to the theater and in making the drama a potent factor in modern life.

This European movement had another general trait, it took a serious and sincere interest in the problems of society. Protesting against the frivolity and feebleness of the older drama, it undertook to grapple with the new scientific thought and its revelations of man's nature and ways. This might result even in a single writer, in Ibsen, for example, in stark presentation of fact or in long discussion and sermon or in such fantasy as "Peer Gynt," but whatever form it took was pretty sure to be skeptical of the old moral sentiments and inhibitions. This serious inquiry is to be found in dramatists whose methods are as different as Galsworthy's and Barrie's, or as Granville Barker's and Lord Dunsany's. In the beginning it was perhaps directed by a desire for social reform, but while it might continue to tilt at special abuses or tyrannies, it was unable to unite on any constructive program of social improvement. Ibsen himself soon became confused and distrustful of himself as reformer or prophet. The movement has never rallied to any particular doctrine or morality; it has been singularly abstemious of enthusiasms or creeds, but it has kept to its original devotion to inquiry, questioning, criticism. The accepted tenets of economic, social, religious and æsthetic belief have been subjected to satire, ridicule or serious discussion. The drama has undertaken a rôle as critic of civilization.

With this dramatic activity which has been going on now for nearly a half-century, I am concerned only so

far as it has affected English comedy. At the beginning
its serious purposes naturally turned it largely to problem-
plays or domestic tragedy—to plays such as "A Doll's
House," which proposed a definite social problem of current interest, "the subjection of women," and offered a
definite answer in an appeal for woman's independence;
or such as "Ghosts," which in domestic scenes, with ordinary people, in the light of modern science, undertook to
evoke a terror and pity devastating to both our sympathy
and intelligence. But there is plenty of comedy in Ibsen,
and other dramatists were soon to find that humour was
a useful grace for both reformer and skeptic. The output
of comedy in English alone, including "Peter Pan," "The
Playboy of the Western World," "The Liars," "Man and
Superman," certainly has both variety and vitality.
Meanwhile, of course, farces, musical shows, sentimental
and domestic pieces, have filled the stage year after year
without indicating any sign of response to this movement
of ideas or to the new dignity of the drama.

My discussion is limited to comedy and still further
to comedy only at the beginning of the new dramatic revolution. I shall stop at the close of the nineteenth century because I do not think we have sufficient perspective
to form anything like an adequate judgment on the multi-
form and interesting varieties of drama produced during
the last twenty-five years mainly by men who are still
living and writing. The year 1900 is an arbitrary selection to which I shall not adhere strictly, but it serves my
purpose in marking the full initiation of the revival of
comedy. It ends a period including most notable contributions to the species by Jones and Pinero and the early
work of Shaw, the active propaganda for new ideas in the
nineties in England and the beginning of the Irish drama
in Dublin. By 1900, comedy as well as other dramatic
forms had acquired a new vitality in England, Ireland
and the United States.

At the time of the opening of the Théâtre Libre in
Paris, English drama had advanced very little since the

days of Tom Robertson twenty years earlier. Acting and
stage management had both improved under the leadership of Irving, the Bancrofts, the Kendals and others, and
through long runs, touring companies and visits to America, the possible profits for both manager and dramatist
had been greatly increased. But few signs were apparent
of any individuality or originality in dramatic composition. Most of the new plays were still adaptations from
the French and either melodramatic or sentimental.
Among those writers who had already shown technical
craftsmanship, the leaders in the eighties were Henry
Arthur Jones in melodrama and Arthur W. Pinero in
farces and sentimental comedy. They were also among
the first to respond to the new European demands for
sincerity, seriousness and ambition.

Henry Arthur Jones was born in 1851; the son of a
tenant farmer, he had little schooling and was employed
for some years as a commercial traveller. His first play
was produced in 1878, and four years later his melodrama "The Silver King" made a great hit and established him, at thirty-one, with a comfortable fortune.
Two years later his "Saints and Sinners" introduced a
little realism and sincerity into its depiction of Non-
Conformist circles in a small town, though his other plays
for a number of years were spectacular melodramas.
After "The Middleman" in 1889, however, his plays
showed increasing power in delineation of character and
in a serious criticism of society, though still yielding to
the old taste for theatrical situation and caricature. "The
Crusaders" (1891), in which social satire was prominent
and "The Masqueraders" (1894), in which satire, though
secondary, is freed from caricature, led to "The Case
of Rebellious Susan" (1894). This was the first of his
comedies to display the author's powers to full advantage,
and it shares with the nearly contemporary comedies of
Oscar Wilde and Bernard Shaw credit for leading the
revival in English comedy.

The play treats the subject of marital infidelity with

more freedom than was usual on the English stage and preaches the need of conformity on the part of the individual to social conditions which the play itself satirizes. This and other comedies of the author are sometimes criticized scornfully by radicals and doctrinaires for their compromising attitude on social questions. It must be remembered, however, that Mrs. Grundy, to whom this play was ironically dedicated, was then a very lively old lady and the censor was an official in her service. A dramatist who wished for an audience had to remember both personages. Moreover, Mr. Jones was not a revolutionary but a liberal conservative, and not a doctrinaire but a shrewd observer of social falsities and injustices for which he did not pretend to have any panacea.

In the first act various relations and friends appear to condone with Lady Susan, who has discovered her husband's infidelity, and to beg her to make up with him again. She resists their entreaties, says about all there is to say for a wife's independence and at the close of the act leaves home and husband. Before the second, ten months have passed, Lady Susan has been in Egypt, where she has an affair with Lucien Edensor, but how far it has gone is not disclosed during the play. Sir Richard Kato, worldly-wise and kindly old bachelor, is the *raisonneur* of the piece and also the manipulator of the action. He ships Edensor off to Africa and brings about a reconciliation between Lady Susan and her husband on the agreement to let bygones be bygones and to be loyal to each other henceforth. Morals as well as facts are a little enigmatical at the final curtain. Sir Richard the sagacious is to marry Inez.

Sir Richard. Do women ever tell the truth about their little love affairs?
Inez. Do men?
Sir Richard. No wise man ever tells.
Inez. No wise woman ever tells.
Sir Richard. I wonder—

Inez. Wonder at nothing that you find in the heart of a woman, or the heart of a man. God has put everything there.

Sir Richard. Let us leave these problems (*kisses her hand very tenderly*) and go in to dinner.

The play is an excellent example of the comedy of manners. The persons are sufficiently individualized and their dialogue is always in character, but they represent the manners and ideas of upper-class London society of the day. Though, compared with the comedy of Sheridan, or the contemporary pieces of Wilde and Shaw, the dialogue is singularly lacking in wit, yet as Mr. Clayton Hamilton has pointed out, the dialogue abounds in the humour that arises from the situation in which it is spoken and the person who speaks it. Lady Susan and Edensor had come in late one evening when they were supposed to be at church, and their excuse was that "the sermon was a very long one." The repetition of this phrase and of the similar one in "The Liars," "I must have taken the wrong turning," represents a very clever and superior use of the theatrical gag. The raisonneur, or personal representative of the author, adopted from Dumas fils, is of course a very old figure in the drama, conspicuous as moralist and benefactor in the sentimental comedies of the eighteenth century and as the critical surveyor of the foolish and affected in Ben Jonson. He is used very adroitly by Jones, not merely as his own spokesman but as establishing a point of view from which the persons and events of the play can be observed with humour.

Three years later (1897) appeared "The Liars," the best of his comedies and a veritable masterpiece of modern comedy. Its plot is not unlike that of "Rebellious Susan." Lady Jessica has an affair with Edward Falkner, but before it goes too far a reconciliation with her stupid husband is brought about by the raisonneur, Colonel Sir Christopher Deering; but the play has far more comic force than its predecessor, and the dramatic emphasis is placed not on any of the several love complications but on the lies everyone tells to save the lady's reputation. The play is in four acts, after the fashion then established for serious plays, with the great scene in the third act, and the final reconciliation and explanation in the last. The third act in technical excellence and cumulative effect is worthy of comparison with the screen scene in the "School for Scandal." It opens in the drawing-room at the house of Lady Rosamund, whither her sister Lady Jessica, the suspected wife, has come to take counsel how to conceal the truth from the suspicious husband. Then enter first, Rosamund's husband bound to be no longer a cipher in his own home, second, Sir Christopher; both gentlemen are induced to lie to save Lady Jessica. Enter third, Mrs. Crespin, with whom the raisonneur is in love, and spoils the lies they have been planning. Enter fourth, Dolly, who is helping them to invent new lies, when enter fifth, George Nepean, brother of Lady Jessica's husband and chief supporter of his suspicions against her. The new lie fails to work on him, when enter sixth, Dolly's husband Archibald, "fidgety and inquisitive," who is with difficulty persuaded to join in devising a new lie, when enter seventh, the suspicious husband, Mr. Gilbert Nepean and his brother. The shower of lies fails to convince him, when enter eighth, Edward Falkner, the lover with whom Lady Jessica had had the clandestine dinner about which so many lies had been told. At her request he now tells the whole truth —and the curtain falls. All these eight entrances are made through the same door to the left of center at the rear of the stage, and the entrance of the butler to announce the new arrivals stimulates the accumulating suspense.

This may not be a revolutionary attack on marriage and fashionable society but it is an excellent dramatic and humorous exposure of the pretences and falsehoods with which late Victorian society was half-heartedly guarding the sacred institution of matrimony. It owes little if any-thing directly to Ibsen and not much to French drama except its skilful technic. Of a merit comparable to that of Augier, it is a thoroughly English presentation in the discriminating and humorous portrayal of manners. Per-haps the moral is expressed in the raisonneur's con-dolences to the forsaken lover. "And all for a woman! They're not worth it. (*Aside softly*) Except one! They're not worth it." It is much more a comedy of character than "Rebellious Susan," for the difficulties arise from the temperaments of the persons and are not merely typical of a social group; yet it is more forceful than the earlier play in displaying both the difficulties and the desirability of maintaining social standards despite individual sufferings.

Pinero's first play was acted in 1877 and he soon estab-lished himself as a busy and prosperous dramatist. His "Magistrate" (1885), a farce with some real characteri-zation, made a great hit and was followed by others, "The Schoolmistress," "Dandy Dick" and "The Cabinet Minister." His "Sweet Lavender" (1888), a still greater success, was an extremely sentimental drama, manifestly under the influence of Tom Robertson. At the height of his popularity, however, he turned from farce and sentiment and made a sincere effort at a drama in the French manner, "The Profligate" (1889). Then he turned to the careful study of Ibsen and Dumas fils, aban-doned the old technic of soliloquy and asides and pro-duced in 1893 "The Second Mrs. Tanqueray," which is usually considered to have marked a new epoch in the history of the English stage.

This is a modern tragedy, sincere and serious in its dramatic revelation of human failure, and it was followed by other plays of a similar character, establishing the author's reputation as a courageous and proficient leader in the dramatic revolution. Pinero was accustomed to turn from the composition of one of these grim and realistic plays to the writing of lighter and more fanciful pieces. So in the closing years of the century along with "The Benefit of the Doubt," "The Second Mrs. Tanqueray," "The Notorious Mrs. Ebbsmith," and "Iris," he produced in lighter vein four comedies, "The Amazons," "The Princess and the Butterfly," "Trelawney of the Wells" and "The Gay Lord Quex."

"The Amazons" (1893) presents three girls trained by their mother to the costumes and sports of boys but succumbing to the first real boys who make love to them. "The Princess and the Butterfly" (1897) presents the widowed princess and the old beau, who feel poignantly the coming of middle age, caught by Cupid and happily married to their juniors. "Trelawney of the Wells" (1898) presents a picture of Sadler's Wells in the days of Tom Robertson, Pinero's first teacher in craftsmanship. These three plays have touches of the farce and sentimentality of his earlier work, and gaily avoid any approach to the sterner realities of life. "The Gay Lord Quex" (1899) in its subject matter and especially in its technic is in the author's later manner.

Pinero was a most remarkable technician. He was a master of all that Robertson, Scribe, Sardou, Dumas fils and Ibsen could teach, and in his later and greater plays was a thoroughgoing realist seeking to make everything done on the stage as natural and probable as possible. But he stuck to the ideal of the well-made play. He had none of the more recent ambitions to present slices of raw life, or medleys of fact and symbol, or eddies from the stream of consciousness without regard to unity or coherence. He began with the character of the persons and from them worked out the actions, the struggles, the mistakes which led to some definite result. Next came the technical problem of presenting on the stage a few of these actions in a certain number of scenes, which should have their appropriate climaxes of emotional interest. His technical feats are sometimes simply amazing. In "Iris," for example, he tells most powerfully on the stage a story which might easily have filled a long novel but has seemingly little fitness for the drama, the story of a disintegration of character, the downfall of a charming and much admired woman, yielding to love for comfort and luxury and descending by slow stages to the gutter. This technical skill of Pinero's, however, did not escape a certain fondness for the same patterns and devices, and the very perfection of the articulation of his structures carries the suggestion of artifice.

"The Gay Lord Quex" is not especially important for its humour or characterization or satire, but it gives a good example of Pinero's technical brilliance and indeed of the advances which were being made in the construction of comedy by Jones and Shaw as well as by himself. The story is of a middle-aged beau much in love with a young girl—a story told romantically in "The Princess and the Butterfly." The comic interest focuses on Sophy, a smart, energetic, slightly vulgar young woman, the foster sister of the heroine and now the proprietor of a manicuring establishment. She schemes to break the match between her adored Muriel and Lord Quex, aged forty-eight, and reputed a great rake, and hopes to marry Muriel to the youthful and handsome Captain Bastling. Pinero's skilful management of this not very enticing material is seen chiefly in the setting for Act I and in the complications of the chief scene in Act III. For the action it is desirable to have a place where anyone can come and may meet anyone and where one group of persons can be separated from another group. Pinero used a manicure shop, something just becoming fashionable but still novel and on the stage unknown. Across the hall from this is the office of the palmist to whom Sophy becomes betrothed, and another passage from one shop to the other is provided through a window and across the leads. It takes two pages to describe this setting, so nicely partitioned and arranged as to provide for all kinds of exits, entrances, concealments and disclosures, and yet obviously a novel, probable and amusing set.

In this four-act play, the first two acts merely prepare

the way for the crisis to be expected in the third. This
act is at Fauncey Court in the boudoir of the Duchess of
Strood, with a bedroom adjoining. Lord Quex has had
an affair with the sentimental and amorous duchess; but
now is genuinely in love with Muriel and bound in honour
to prove his sincerity by having nothing to do with any
other woman. He has, however, been persuaded by the
duchess to come to her bedroom and return her presents.
Sophy, who is very suspicious and determined to expose
the gay lord, is substituting as the duchess's maid. The
duchess dismisses Sophy. Quex enters. The duchess
makes love to him, he remains unresponsive. The clock
strikes quarter of twelve. Champagne and cigarettes.
Quex learns that the duchess has for a maid the manicure
girl, whom he has almost caught spying on him. At his
suggestion the duchess opens the door quickly and Sophy,
kneeling before the keyhole, lurches forward, then picks
herself up and runs away. The duchess is frantic. Quex
perceives that Sophy will tell Muriel and that he is done
for; so he devotes his mind to saving the duchess's reputation. He sends her off to another room and remains
alone, then rings for Sophy and as she enters locks the
door behind her. He scolds, tries to bribe, and appeals
in vain; then points out that he can tell a more probable
story than hers and one which will absolve the duchess
and condemn her. Sophy defies him but, when she
threatens to scream, he offers her the bell-rope. She finally
perceives that she is in a shocking mess and thinks of
the jealous palmist, Valma, to whom she is engaged. Now
it is her turn to plead in vain. She fingers the bell-rope,
bursts into tears and runs to the door. Quex sips his
champagne. He promises to let her go if she will sign
a letter which he dictates. She agrees with a sigh, but
then realizes that she is selling Muriel, rushes to the bell-
rope and pulls it again and again, and faces Quex in
defiance. His admiration for her courage and devotion
is now aroused. He gives her the letter, unlocks the
door. Sophy finds a pretext to dismiss the servants who

come running to answer the bell. She sobs hysterically as she turns to Quex, "you—you—you're a gentleman! I'll do what I can for you."

Both the novel setting of Act I and the suspense of Act III in a lady's bedroom, with the bell-rope an objective point—have been imitated in later plays, but they amazed theatergoers of 1899. And they contributed to a comedy of a very different sort from any of Pinero's earlier efforts. Everything is as real and plausible and up-to-date as possible; no trace is left of farce, or fancifulness or sentimentality. Here is a comedy of manners, not bothering much over ideas or reforms but presenting the surface of fashionable life with verisimilitude, frankness and great technical adroitness.

Oscar Wilde's four comedies were acted within three years, "Lady Windermere's Fan" in 1892, a year before "The Second Mrs. Tanqueray," "A Woman of No Importance," in 1893, "An Ideal Husband" and "The Importance of Being Earnest" in 1895. They are distinguished by the wit of their conversation rather than by any novelty in story, ideas or technic. The first three, in fact, tell well-worn sentimental stories, two of them presenting mothers confronted by the problems of their illegitimate children, and the third a successful man facing the discovery of the misdeed on which his success was founded. In all three, after some ingenious suspenses and surprises, sentiment and virtue triumph in the old-fashioned theatrical style. Wilde, however, was working toward a formula that has since proved very successful: provide enough virtue rising from distress to triumph to interest the sympathies of nine-tenths of your audience and then mix it with enough cynical wit to amuse the more intelligent one-tenth. In two of the plays the cynic is the villain, but in the third he is the benevolent angel who rescues all from ruin.

"A Woman of No Importance" is the most striking example of this mixture of cynicism and sentimentality. The plot is similar to that of "Lovers' Vows," an illegitimate son discovers his father and demands justice for his saintly and betrayed mother, and the last act is as tearful and oratorical and sweet as Kotzebue himself could have desired. The first act, on the contrary, is an extraordinarily brilliant conversation, mainly cynical in tone.

This act is an almost uninterrupted scintillation of repartee, epigram and paradox. It is artificial, of course, and tiring. No one could stand listening to two such acts, and perhaps no one could write them. Even Wilde ran out of epigrams and had to repeat a few before he had finished the four plays. But beyond doubt he wrote some of the most brilliant dialogue that our drama has known. Here are a few of the witticisms taken almost at random from that single act.

"American women are wonderfully clever in concealing their parents."

"What are American dry goods? American novels."

"All Americans do dress well. They get their clothes from Paris."

"The youth of America is their oldest tradition."

A fox hunt is—"the unspeakable in full pursuit of the uneatable."

"The intellect is not a serious thing, and never has been. It is an instrument on which one plays, that is all."

"The basis of every scandal is an absolutely immoral certainty."

"What do you call a bad man? The sort of man who admires innocence."

"I have so many bad qualities. Ah, don't be too conceited about them. You may lose them as you grow old."

"The book of life begins with a man and a woman in a garden. It ends with Revelations."

Most of these would not be out of place in "Pinafore" or "The Mikado." Many of them are on the pattern of

Never go to sea
And you shall be ruler of the King's Navee.

But Wilde was not making jokes and songs, only conversation. He is clever in characterization, uses both serious and silly persons as foils for his cynics and wits, and altogether makes conversation dramatic as well as amusing. The stage was witnessing in the nineties a good many things new in comedies such as it had not seen since the days of Sheridan; Wilde added another, an overflowing measure of wit.

In his last play, Wilde gave up both the strained and serious plots and the cynical pose and took his wit for a little adventure with nonsense. "The Importance of Being Earnest" is in the mood of Gilbertian extravaganza, but it maintains the mood in depicting life of today and without the aid of verse or music. We are at the same time in topsy-turvydom and in modern London, listening to preposterous nonsense and flippant epigrams, encountering only such probabilities as cucumber sandwiches and christenings, but finding them always full of fun and surprise. Wit is no longer restrained to the embellishment of conversation, it takes possession of the stage and holds revels with words, deeds, persons and plot. Though imitations have not been lacking, no one but Wilde has been able to keep such solemn fooling gay and unperturbed through a full sized comedy. If Pinero and Jones showed what could be done with plot and situation in a comedy of manners, Wilde had shown how much entertainment could be derived from mere talk, if one let his wit loose.

The most remarkable and influential innovation of the nineties in the English drama was furnished by the plays of G. Bernard Shaw. His work as a critic and his ideas as a socialist were already well known to the public when his "Widowers' Houses" was produced by the Independent Theater in 1892. His "Arms and the Man" followed in 1894 and was acted in the United States by Richard Mansfield; "Candida," written in 1895, did not get acted until two years later. Meantime Mr. Shaw had written several other pieces which for one reason or another were unacceptable for the stage, "The Philanderer," "Mrs. Warren's Profession," "The Man of Destiny" and "You Never Can Tell." In conformity with the general feeling among the reformers that plays ought to be printed and treated as literature, Mr. Shaw published these seven pieces as "Plays: Pleasant and Unpleasant," with explanatory introductions and very full descriptive and interpretative stage directions. These volumes gained him a hearing, but it was not until the next decade that his plays, old and new, won success in the theaters.

Mr. Shaw's early plays all derive from Ibsen. Some were written for the Independent Theater and all were frankly in the service of the movement to reform the drama. Although they are more like Ibsen's than like the plays of any other writer, and though in some instances they are imitative, yet they differ in many ways from the substance or the practice of the great Norwegian. They are daringly original and they all bear the marks of Mr. Shaw's personality. He had his own style of writing, incisive and audacious, he knew the theater whether he scorned or accepted its tricks, and he had plenty of ideas of his own. It is rather difficult now to recall how penetrating and novel those ideas seemed. War has taken on new realities since then, and "Arms and the Man" now seems but a mild and ladylike attack on some of war's sentimentalities, but the play was fresh and daring enough when Mansfield gave it in the nineties. In general what Shaw had to say was not altogether novel. The more intelligent part of the reading public was familiar with the novels of Meredith and Hardy, with the socialist tales and arguments of William Morris, and Samuel Butler was writing even if unheeded; but neither these nor similar voices were to be heard in the theaters. The Victorian era had already turned upon itself in fierce protest and satire, but not until Shaw had this counterattack reached the stage.

The seven early plays in themselves make up a more

notable body of satiric drama than the English stage had seen since Ben Jonson. Like Jonson, Shaw is copious and outspoken in his ridicule of follies and abuses, and like Jonson again, he sacrifices all effort for sentiment or charm in the directness of his appeal to intelligence. But his purpose and scope are larger than Jonson's and suited to another age. He is breaking his lances against the conventionality, sentimentality, romanticism and idealism, the pretenses and subterfuges which he believes conceal the grim evils of capitalistic society. In one play he exhibits the wealth derived by landlords from miserable tenants and distributed in one way or another through the capitalistic class. In another play the wealth exposed to view is that derived from the capitalization of prostitution and also widely distributed in bonds, stocks, mortgages, annuities, and even in fellowships in the universities. In another it is the glorification and idealization of war that he attacks; in another he belittles the intellect and glory of Napoleon. In others he explodes some of the most common sentimentalities and evasions that conceal the truth about love and marriage. The range of topics discussed and directly or indirectly exposed to his irony and wit is indeed much greater. In "The Philanderer" alone it includes: philandering, hysterics, medical science, vivisection, Ibsenism, mixed clubs for men and women, the female pursuing the male, neurasthenia, the new woman, her dress, her smoking, scientific discovery, jealousy. It must be admitted that this discursive satire sometimes grows a little thin or strident. Usually some sort of enfant terrible is bawling out those things which everyone knows but doesn't mention, or some rude and positive girl is opening the eyes of her elders. A play is restful or genial only for a moment, it soon returns to smart and hectic bickering. The everlasting appeal to the intelligence inevitably awakes one's distrust even in that admirable generality, and the implied reliance on a socialism which is to be a new heaven seems an even more dubious ideality than some of those which have been exploded. It is possible after the brilliant "Candida" as well as after the tedious "Philanderer" to conclude that there has been a great deal of talk without getting anywhere.

The action in each play is enveloped in talk. Or rather, the talk is the action, merely punctuated by a dance, a kiss, a shot, or what not. It is most extraordinary talk on all sorts of subjects and by all sorts of persons. Shaw has a power of realizing personalities and making them talk, and he knows all the means of bringing variety and contrast and surprise into his drama of conversation. He can point his finger like Ibsen, and the person indicated will tell the entire story of his life in a few well chosen words; or in gayer moods he will invent a pleasantry like one of Gilbert's, for example, in "You Never Can Tell," the accomplished waiter and his overpowering son, the barrister, who comes dancing on in fake nose and domino; he has Wilde's skill at paradox and repartee and he likes to mix these with matter of fact simplicities and airy persiflage. His conversations are witty, brilliant, fantastic in character, earnest, revealing, dramatic, and something more, for which I can think of no word except exhaustive. He has no mercy on his persons. When one of them in actual life would have said two sentences, under the author's direction he is good for a volume. They simply have to talk. Mr. Shaw gathers them in a room, announces a few topics, rings the bell and announces the first speaker for the negative. They are all for the negative yet each against the others, and the conversation would be perfectly dazzling if there were only occasional flashes of silence.

As we look back it is clear that already by 1900 Shaw had become the leader in the new and revolutionary movement in comedy. These plays requiring intellectual acuteness and considerable knowledge from the audience, supplying a fresh and surprising discussion of ideas, attacking the very foundations of our social structure, and relying to an unheard-of extent upon dialogue for their dramatic and humorous effects, were breaking away from most of the methods and principles that had been long accepted in English comedy. Take, for example, the use of tricks and deceptions for the plot, Shaw uses these in the old fashion in "Arms and the Man," but he abandons them in "Candida." Except for the delectable extravagance of giving Miss Proserpine champagne, the play exhibits scarcely any of the usual business of the stage. Though Shaw in this and in many other instances has a keen sense of the value of many of the old theatrical types and situations, yet he is manifestly advancing to a kind of comedy, more literary, more intellectual, more dependent on the dialogue than any yet written. His first play of the new century, "Man and Superman," was to indicate a further step onward. In his early plays he had difficulties in finding actors equal to the parts and audiences capable of following them; and as he proceeded he was inevitably to find the old stage unsuited to his novelties. Although other dramatists and other novelties were to be even more potent in straining the resources of the theater and bringing about an era, not yet passed, of experimentation and change in the stage and all its appurtenances, Shaw took the lead toward freedom from the limitations of stage mechanics and of the well made play, which still seemed fundamental to Pinero and Jones.

Shaw's plays like those of Wycherley and Congreve are comedies of satire and wit, but they reveal these in a new dramatic garb and address them to a new and wider and more fundamental list of themes. In comparison with contemporaries such as Ibsen and Brieux, Shaw has more comic vivacity and an extraordinary gift of humorous dialogue. His raisonneurs or sermonizers are rarely as tiresome as those of Cumberland or Brieux, and his observations on current topics of discussion are not less witty and much more penetrating than those of Congreve or Wilde. Yet perhaps the most noteworthy feature of Shaw's dramatic work is not its individuality and novelty but rather its service in bringing drama again into unity with the main literary tradition.

That tradition in modern England and especially the England of the nineteenth century had been the devotion of literature to reform. Whether mystic, idealistic, romantic, realistic, or utilitarian, the serious purpose to teach, to improve, to elevate, to reform had been the guiding principle which directed the imagination. As the century grew older, as modern civilization displayed itself, this purpose became more distinctly reformatory, in Carlyle, Ruskin, Tennyson, Browning, Mill, Morris, Morley, George Eliot, Meredith, Samuel Butler, and others. Social organization, religion, morality, progress, civilization itself were subjected to questioning, protest, debate, proposals of reform and revolution. Literature was concerned with little else. By the close of the century the great personalities of Ibsen and Tolstoi were stirring all Europe. But in England the drama had had little to do with literature, and nowhere had comedy been employed successfully as a main weapon in the hands of reform. Shaw bent comedy to the effective service of ideas and satire; he became another personality whose voice was heard throughout Europe and America, he restored comedy to a place in the vanguard of the cohorts of literature. Whatever posterity may think of his plays, they cannot be overlooked by the literary historian.

Though I have credited Shaw with leadership in the revival of comedy, it must not be thought that other dramatists borrowed directly from him or were lacking in initiative and originality. The awakening of the theater in the nineties was widespread and manifested in many ways. In the United States native themes were receiving able treatment by Bronson Howard, James Herne and Augustus Thomas, and in Boston an independent theater, which provided a place for Herne's more realistic efforts, gave promise of further innovation. In England new writers were being attracted to the stage, and older writers such as Sydney Grundy and R. C. Carton were writing better than ever before. Of the new men the one destined to do most for the drama was James M. Barrie.

The theater was beginning to attract the novelists by offering them larger opportunities for fame and profits and propaganda. It won Barrie after his "Little Minister," most successful as a novel in 1891, had proved even more so when dramatized in 1897. But in the earlier year he had tried his hand at drama in three plays, "Becky Sharp," "Ibsen's Ghost," a parody, and "Richard Savage." In 1892, the year of the appearance of Wilde and Shaw as dramatists, he produced "Walker, London," and two years later "The Professor's Love Story." This piece confines the author's whimsicality within the limits of domestic sentimental comedy. It was not until the opening years of the new century that his dramatic writing took on full independence. Even then his successful "Quality Street" (1902) was a reworking of two very common themes, the sweethearts separated and then united after long years (Gilbert's "Sweethearts") and the sly puss rejected, turning madcap coquette to conquer (Mrs. Cowley's "Belle's Stratagem"). But in the same year appeared "The Admirable Crichton" and in 1904 "Peter Pan." Both plays lie beyond our chronological limits, but they require a word because they connect themselves with some things in the past and also prognosticate further daring unions of comedy and fantasy.

Gilbert, Wilde and Shaw had all employed fantasy; and the general scheme of "The Admirable Crichton" might have supplied Gilbert with a libretto. The play opens in a great house in Mayfair, where no one in the family has any intelligence or energy to spare except the butler, Crichton. The imperturbable but sagacious butler had already become a stage figure, e.g., see Wilde's "The Importance of Being Earnest," but here he becomes a veritable protagonist. The family is shipwrecked on a desert island in the Pacific, where Crichton proves the

only efficient person, soon takes the leadership, becomes
the head of the social organization, acquires visions of
grandeur and habits of arrogance and is about to marry
Lady Mary, the oldest daughter, when the party is
rescued and brought back to London, where after much
falsifying they manage to forget their illuminating experience and resume their old positions.   The fantasy is thus
used in the cause of reality and reform.   Mr. Barrie
presses home the issue in his own whimsical way but
not less forcibly than does Mr. Shaw in his.   The play
ends—

Lady Mary.   Do you despise me, Crichton?   [*The
man who could never tell a lie makes no answer.*]   You
are the best man among us.
Crichton.   On an island, my lady, perhaps; but in
England, no.
Lady Mary.   Then there's something wrong with
England.
Crichton.   My lady, not even from you can I listen
to a word against England.
Lady Mary.   Tell me one thing: you have not lost
your courage?
Crichton.   No, my lady.

"Peter Pan" takes no heed of the state of England or
reform.   It is wholly fantastic and delightful.   It carries
us not to topsy-turvydom but to fairyland.   It rejoices us
not with incongruities but with inconceivabilities.   Nonsense and folly, truth and fancy take part in the gambols,
and dance as they have danced only for Puck and Ariel.
It is the comedy of playland, not without some reflections
of man's eternal youth and woman's eternal motherhood,
but as free from the smoke and dross of reality and moral
responsibility as a desert island in the Pacific or the
dreams of a child.   There had been no such extravaganza, unless "Peer Gynt," but the drama was already
turning to allegory and poetry and other-worldliness in
the later work of Ibsen, and the early work of Maeter-

linck and Yeats. Barrie has never found it easy to lean heavily on allegory, but he never afterwards was able to keep as free from moral and social implications as here. Neither has any other dramatist. "Peter Pan" has had no followers as a comedy of pure fancy. Perhaps others will come in happier days, though even then they too may be addressed to children. But Barrie did continue to bring fantasy and whimsy to aid in his analysis of human nature and social conditions; and so have other dramatists. A personality as individual as Shaw, though very unlike him, Barrie has been scarcely less potent as a comic dramatist. Writing his plays with stage directions and descriptions even more copious than Shaw's, he has been bending the stage to suit his own purpose and temperament. A little shy, though not ineffective at reform and propaganda, a bit tenuous and unsteady in his mocking and satire, always delicate and whimsical rather than robust in his humour, sometimes getting too much sentiment and nonsense for the fun to savour, he has perhaps excelled all his contemporaries in the revelation of human nature with fresh truth and humour.

By 1900 English comedy had clearly taken on new life. A great decade was before it. Shaw and Barrie were to continue; Granville Barker and Galsworthy were among the new recruits. In Dublin the Abbey Theater was to have an immediate and stirring effect on both realistic and symbolic drama and within a few years was to produce many notable plays. It is difficult to bring the pen to stop at a date when so much of interest lies before the chronicler. But happily most of the writers of that decade are still alive, and in spite of the devastation of the war, comedy is still flourishing and giving many signs of new life. It is indeed too much alive to require the service of a historian. But at one name the pen refuses to stop and begs a word for that extraordinary genius whose career, so brilliant and so full of great promise for the future, began and ended within the decade, John M. Synge.

I do not know that his plays relate themselves closely to any that preceded or have followed. The Irish theater gave him a chance, the rhythm and imagery of the Irish peasantry gave him a glimpse of beauty, the Irish people gave him a knowledge of humanity unveiled by theory, politics or social reform. "On the stage," he says simply, "one must have reality and one must have joy." What complete realism appears, for example, in the action of "The Playboy of the Western World," and what joy in its rich and startling prose; but more than these, what a new design, a new conception of comedy! Into a village on the wild coast of Mayo, where little happens and still less entertains, comes Christopher Mahon, who reports that he has killed his father at a single blow. He is a source of wonder, especially to the women. Flattered and marvelled at, he expands in conceit, gains self-confidence, and is growing rapidly from a mean snivelling fellow into a dashing hero. Pegeen Mike, best of the girls, is captivated by the romantic story-teller. Then his father, who was stunned and not killed by the blow, appears in pursuit of the rascal. Christy cowers and in a moment becomes the poltroon instead of the hero, then recovers a desperate courage and again strikes down his sire. But neither Pegeen nor the villagers relish a real murder as they have relished a narrated patricide. Christy has mastered his father, who recovers again in a humbled state of mind, but he is bundled out of the village. He goes off with his head up. "Ten thousand blessings upon all that's here, for you've turned me a likely gaffer in the end of all, the way I'll go romancing through a romping lifetime from this hour to the dawning of the judgment day." And as he disappears Pegeen cries out, "Of my grief, I've lost him surely. I've lost the only Playboy of the Western World."

Perhaps this should be called a tragicomedy, for as in other of Synge's plays the tragic motives underlie the comic action. But whatever it be named, the play presents a kind of comedy new to the stage. It has little to do with what Synge called "the intellectual modern drama." It has no propaganda, no reforming purpose, no obvious aim at its audience. Only from a remote nook like the Aran Islands could come its simplicity, its freshness of phrase, its freedom from all modernities, but only from genius, the art of its design and the lasting appeal of its humour. It has no hint of satire, and no hint of allegory. Who is this Playboy? Is he each and all of us, or is he Poetry, or Romance, or the Imagination, or Literature, or what? Synge does not say. Let us call him the Spirit of the Drama, swaying the fancies of the women, swelling in its own soul, masking reality in romancing words and passions. It is a true comic view of drama or of human nature, however we apply it. The imagination mocks and cheers, deludes and exalts, that is the humour of it for the Aran Islanders or the sophisticated Londoners. There could be no excuse for writing a history of the comedy of four centuries if we did not love our playboys.

CHAPTER XXIII

CONCLUSION

FOR four hundred years comedy has held a place among the chief of public entertainments despite an ever increasing competition. The London apprentice in Shakespeare's time who journeyed to the Bankside for amusement found the beargardens and the brothels the only rivals of the playhouses, but his successors have had a constantly widening choice of occupations and spectacles for their idle hours. In the theater itself pantomime and opera were soon rivalling comedy, and outside the drama newspapers and novels were serving the public demand for humour. Within the last century has arisen an enormous expansion in this labour of making the people laugh, by lectures, pictures, journals, and now by means of the moving pictures and radio. We spend millions of dollars daily on these new ways to persuade us to laugh or to smile, and yet comedy still draws us to the theater.

As a form of literature, also, comedy has maintained its place. In the early sixteenth century there was little writing with a comic intent and what there was turned naturally to the drama. Since then humorous writing has multiplied and has undergone a division of labour that has distributed it in every kind of reading matter and left to comedy only a small share of its total product. In the ups and downs of these changes in the business of writing, comedy has not always attracted the services of the best minds or the greatest humorists; yet from the time that the young university wits began writing for the Elizabethan theater an unceasing succession of practitioners has toiled at the difficult art of making plays that should be amusing on the stage and refreshing to

585

read. From Lyly and Greene to Shaw and Barrie, a great tradition has been created and maintained, including many masterpieces that continue to serve as spurs and examples for further artistic endeavour. In our own generation brilliant writers in both England and the United States have given new vigour to the old form, so that comedy now faces the brightest prospects.

I am using the general term comedy as applied not to a precisely defined type but to the hundreds of plays which at different times have taken that name. Our survey of these, however, has revealed similarities as often as differences and repetitions and commonplaces far more often than novelties and inventions. Indeed, anyone acquainted with the old drama will find most new plays of today built up from reminiscences of familiar scenes and persons. The startling innovation usually turns out to be only a slight variation from the normal types, for even the most inventive writer must please his actors and audience with something similar to that with which they are familiar. Shifting fashions may mean little more than the clothing of old stories in manners and sentiments to suit a different society, although changes in theatrical or social conditions bring about new opportunities for the dramatist and sometimes abrupt variations in the drama. English comedy has not kept as uninterrupted a tradition as has French comedy, nor has it held as closely to one norm, yet the many varieties that we have noticed all belong to the same family. One kind may differ entirely from another in some respect but will resemble it in others. Whatever the variants and the doubtful cases, the English stage has always been producing plays that everybody received as comedies. "The Merry Wives of Windsor," "The Wild Goose Chase," "The Way of the World," "The School for Scandal," "The Liars," and "Candida" are manifestly of the same species of drama. A modern play such as Mr. Williams's "Why Marry" or Mr. Kelly's "Show-Off" would have been accepted as comedy by Fletcher or Dryden.

In this book, however, I have been concerned in noting differences and making classifications. When we look at particular periods or men, it is easy enough to see that plays fall into definite groups under the influence of social conditions or individual leadership. In the beginning those imitative of Latin comedy differ from those based on romantic story. Shakespeare and Fletcher wrote comedies undirected by the principles to which Ben Jonson rigidly adhered. The Restoration period produced a definite fashion and criterion. A very marked difference is discernible between this comedy of manners and that of the eighteenth century sentimentalists, or between the comic melodramas and the cup-and-saucer type of the nineteenth century. Moreover, those differences in type are further accentuated by variations due to the changing fashion and the passing of time. Most persons are interested in a play, read or seen, as it relates itself to their own time, their own moment; but the historical student finds a special pleasure in tracing the reflections of different periods, of all moments. Comedy, more perhaps than any other branch of literature, must attend to the moment, to its customs, its fashions, its idiom; must not neglect the surface of things, the momentary interests, the quick mutations of society. Though it may in consequence miss the deeper currents of change, it is likely to catch the fleeting image, the passing gesture that proves a revealing record of man's infinite zest in life. How much of Renaissance valiancy and wantonness there is in Fletcher! How much of the style and hauteur of a privileged class in Etherege! How the growth of delicacy and kindness in manners is reflected in Steele and Cibber! How different the ladies, discreet and drooping now, no longer the gay belles of Congreve or the hoydens of Fletcher. What a change from the consciously superior wit of Sheridan to the cruder delights of a democratized age from Colman to Boucicault. How Victorian is Gilbert—without either a telephone or an indecency on his stage; and who but Shaw could be chosen to introduce that troubled but active century which is our own? Nevertheless, at the close of a book devoted to emphasizing these differences in time and type, it remains to be confessed that all those plays are a good deal alike.

Nearly every English comedy tells the story of a courtship resulting happily. The madcap girl sobers down, the scapegrace youth is tamed, the errant husband or wife returns, the sweet young innocents assume the responsibilities of the married state. Sexual passion scarcely receives the exaggerated fervours which it has had in modern fiction—romantic or realistic—and it may even be viewed with humour; but the incidents of minor courtships rather than the main love affair usually furnish the objects for fun or satire or ridicule. Nearly every comedy, like every novel, assumes that the love of A for B or B for A is the most important thing in the universe. Whether the passion be lawful or illicit, whether beautified by exalted sentiments or framed in vulgarities, the story is always of the love chase. The man is pursuing the woman or the woman is pursuing the man, and the interest in life is supposed to be exhausted by the capture, or the escape.

Plot, dramaturgy, characterization, sentiment, and wit must all fit into this ever repeated story of courtship. The most common way of enlarging the plot has been by multiplying the number of lovers. A and B are both in love with X. Or, A loves X while A's servant a loves X's servant x. Or, A loves X and B loves Y but Y loves A. Or, these simple algebraic formulas can be stretched into an endless chain of A—X—B—Y—C—Z—A—. I have designated the ladies by the final letters proper to unknown quantities, but there is little mystery about their intentions. She has chosen her man and usually gets him. Only rarely, as in Massinger's "Maid of Honour," and in Molière's "Misanthrope" is courtship a failure. The course of true love is delayed and hindered by the misunderstandings and perturbations of the lovers, by the machinations of rivals and parents, by poverty, separation, shipwreck, and Providence; but all these difficulties and oppositions fail to disclose a very wide range of fact or invention. From time to time the drama tends to stereotyped plots and motives. The Elizabethans, including Shakespeare, made too much use of disguise and mistaken identity. In Restoration comedy the lover and the wife deceive the husband, but he discovers them in the nick of time, but they trick him again, and so on ad infinitum and ad nauseam. The eighteenth century sentimentalists required a shipwreck or loss of fortune or some other dire calamity which interferes with the proper course of the affections until a long-lost parent, child or brother comes to life. Extraordinary cleverness has been shown in devising slight variants of those old wives' tales. Tricks, deceptions, discoveries have supplied the manipulations for the masterpieces of Shakespeare and Molière, of Sheridan and Beaumarchais, and for the "well-made plays" of Scribe and Sardou. When the theatrical manipulation of suspense and surprise has been carried to a high degree of ingenuity, then the theater may expect a reversion to characterization and conversation, but apparently it need never hope for a new plot. In general, most of the fun in comedy has been obtained by scenes rather extraneous to the main story of the love chase. The Elizabethans varied it by the antics of clowns, and Shakespeare was able to make out of them sources of perennial merriment. Low comedy or farce long continued to spice the story of courtship, and a certain amount of it was permitted even by the extreme sentimentalists. Drinking scenes, for example, have furnished much of the laughter of the theater from the time of Falstaff and Sir Toby down to the scene in "Candida" where Miss Proserpine takes champagne. On the other hand, sentiment has required song and music, and whimsy has relied on costume and scenery as supplements to the main action. But the development of the love chase requires so much time and interest on the stage that comparatively little room is left for these accessories. No dramatist except Ben

Jonson has consistently minimized the love interest for the sake of the ridicule of other aspects of life. Politics, religion, war, agriculture, commerce, manufacture, learning, art, and other of the major occupations of mankind receive but slight attention in our comedy.

The love chase has also placed a limit on the characters that can be presented within the duration of a three-hour entertainment. The lovers are of course of varied hues but of about the same attractive appearance, and both they and their parents and servants show their colours mostly in connection with the courtship. The other personages who excite merriment or ridicule are not so very numerous. Misers, fops, parvenus, cowards, braggarts, drunkards, sensualists, and religious hypocrites, repeat themselves. The frivolous wife and the thick-headed, self-complacent husband ever recur, though the latter is the more favoured at present. There have been many saucy maids since Maria in "Twelfth Night," many varieties of the clever servant besides Scrub of "The Beaux Stratagem," and several superior butlers before and since Barrie's admirable Crichton. Sillies of all sorts, male and female, of high and low estate, clownish and exquisite, have always filled up the supernumeraries. Since the spacious days of the Elizabethans, however, English comedy has not shown a great wealth of characterization. The novel has proved superior in exhibiting the humours of mankind. Literature has had no successor to Ben Jonson in the drama, but it has had Smollett and Fielding, Scott and Dickens. The novel, moreover, has succeeded in presenting the middle humour, the average persons of life, in a fashion that has proved impossible on the stage, though something of the sort was the aim of the Roman Terence, the French Augier, and the English Robertson. English comedy offers nothing like the novels of Jane Austen, still less has it anything like the quiet, humdrum but delightfully humorous characterization of Trollope. Jonson's exhaustive method of showing personality in large and in detail is probably a bad one for the stage;

certainly we are likely to wait long before any genius can equal Shakespeare's feat of creating Falstaff, Prince Hal and Hotspur in a single play; but in comparison to the Elizabethans modern characterization seems a little thin. At its best it resembles the method of the short-story rather than the novel; it shows character in relation to one situation, or one problem, or from one point of view, a method perhaps enforced by the extreme brevity of modern plays. Yet what mainly restrains the modern dramatist is not the effort for unity but the necessity of keeping to the love chase. Even Shakespeare had to dispense with that in order to get room for the full-bodied personalities of "Henry IV."

Many a comedy, however, has succeeded, though it lacked both well defined persons and an original plot, because it had wit. The excellence of English comedy by the large, its intellectual and literary humour, lies in no small measure in its style, its verbalism, under which term I would include poetry and song, dialogue and soliloquy, the expression of sentiment or satire, nonsense or wit. What felicity in the dialogues in the Forest of Arden, in the raillery of Mirabell and Millamant, in Mrs. Malaprop's blunders, in Gilbert's whimsicalities, in the paradoxes of Oscar Wilde and Bernard Shaw! Even if one could forget the stage and the story, what a revelation of humanity in a soliloquy by Falstaff or by the play boy of the western world; and what enduring charm in the songs of Fletcher or Gay! Perhaps the love chain enforces less of a limitation on style than on plot or characterization; certainly it has always been the theme for conversation, song and jest. It provokes the untiring efforts of both humorists and lyricists. And the lovers themselves are great talkers from Shakespeare to Shaw. Conversation is almost the finest art—in comedy. Talk stands forth without the elaborate apparatus of explanation and description with which it is so encumbered in the novel. We are spared an analysis of the speaker's motives or of his stream of consciousness. Rosalind and

Estefania and Kate Hardcastle can speak for themselves. The dramatist may not have much freedom in devising what his persons are to do, but, like the wits of the Mermaid tavern, he can put his whole life into a jest. One wonders if most of the humour in life does not arise in talk; at any rate it seems to do so in the drama.

Repetition, to be sure, is to be found here; everyone imitated Congreve until Sheridan displaced him, and the paradoxical, epigrammatic style that still delights us appears to have had its start in Gilbert's librettos. Moreover, much of the verbalism of comedy is mere embellishment. Every writer knows the painful task of revision when he tries to find a brighter word to replace a dull one, a fresh phrase for one often repeated, or a rhythm or a figure to deck a generalization. Possibly this revision and embellishment are more necessary in comedy than in other kinds of writing. A comedy, one suspects, is not as often written at white heat as is a tragedy or a novel. Our English examples generally lack emotional or oratorical elevation, but they often show the stylist at his prettiest. High seriousness, the quality that Matthew Arnold deemed most essential to great style is lacking, but another quality worthy of more praise than it generally receives, is sometimes present, sweet playfulness. The humorist can play with words as he plays with men and events, and he cannot lack either art or brains if he is to play the game successfully. No comedy, however amusing on the stage, is likely to tickle the humour of generations of readers unless it has extraordinary qualities of style. Those that have survived are among the most brilliant pieces of writing in our literature.

From its beginnings to the present day English comedy has tended to divide into two classes, or has shown two tendencies, the one toward satire and realism, the other toward sentiment and fancy. Though the two classes have not always been very distinct and though most plays have joined both sentiment and satire, both a delight in and a contempt of man's follies, yet the two classes represent opposing and persistent theories of both comedy and laughter. The theory of satiric comedy is the more readily stated, for it rests on a strict and narrow definition of humour as something aroused by the inferior and ugly. It is the duty of comedy to expose folly by ridicule and thus cure the social body of disease. Ben Jonson was the first to set forth this conception fully, and on the basis of classical models he attempted a realistic comedy of manners that should comprehensively diagnose and purge the society of his day. In Congreve's hands this comedy of manners sought to exemplify the difference between false and true wit, between the affectations and absurdities of fashionable society and a rational and well mannered mode of life. The moral protests of the sentimentalists made such comprehensive schemes of ridicule seem unkindly and unchristian and consequently impossible on the stage. When Murphy and Sheridan revived the comedy of manners it was well mixed with sentiment and limited in its satire, but it still excited the laughter of superiors over the unworthy follies of inferiors. The continuing sway of crude sentimentalism on the stage for nearly a century threatened to reduce wit and ridicule to trivial tasks, but since Gilbert restored a spice of satire to his fantasies, it has been abundant enough in our theater. In the plays of Mr. Shaw, this type of comedy, in fact, may be said to have received an extension in purpose, for now it aims not merely at the exposure of this or that folly but at the ridicule of the fundamentals and foundations of existing society.

The other tendency toward fancy and sentiment rests on a loose or broad definition of humour that refuses to limit it to an attitude of superiority toward the blemishes of others, but finds it capable of a sympathetic or playful response for almost everything in life. This kind of comedy has been varied in practice, because in its eagerness to minimize the satiric purpose it has supplemented ridicule by whimsy, moral, romance, sentiment, fancy, or whatever else. It has ranged from the high spirits of Fletcher and Farquhar to the tenderness of Dekker and Steele. It was inaugurated by the early Elizabethans who took little interest in probing the faults of their exuberant age but were captivated by fantastic story, by the music in words, by a union of wonder and fancy and fun. This romantic comedy Shakespeare made not of an age, but for all time. His prodigality filled the cup of mirth to overflowing with every conceivable ingredient, leaving only a pleasant tincture of the bitterness of satire. The later Elizabethans, though they were influenced by Jonson's efforts for realism, still let their fancy and fun roam freely together. After the Restoration the sentimentalists in their eagerness to displace ridicule often supplanted it by morality or sentiment rather than by a better humour. They did demonstrate that kindness and good nature and sympathy deserve a place in the theater, but they did not produce many good comedies, and the era of melodrama which followed saw comedy reduced to an idealized but commonplace love tale. In Planché, however, and later and more completely in Gilbert and Barrie, whimsy and fun again found freedom on the stage. Comedy ceased to be a schoolmistress teaching in either satiric or sentimental vein and invited its audiences to a holiday. The instincts of humour and of play again united as in Shakespeare.

Too much need not be made of the opposition between these tendencies. As I have said, most plays show a mixture of the two. Wycherley even in "The Plain Dealer" is not without sentiment; Whitehead and Kelly are not without ridicule; Shaw certainly does not lack whimsy, nor does Barrie lack satire. Nor, perhaps, are the opposing theories irreconcilable. If one laughs because, in possession of a superior gift, he perceives the inferiorities of others, and if another laughs because he likes to laugh, the result may be the same, an extensive and variegated risibility. The verdict of English comedy, however, has been clearly against a narrowing of its scope to satire and realism and in favour of a wide range for the sense of humour. Though this conception had been given exemplification before Shakespeare, undoubtedly his influence has been most potent on subsequent practice. So long as "Twelfth Night" holds the stage, it is difficult to view comedy solely as a means to reform society by ridicule, or on the other hand to accept the sentimental extreme that it should inculcate virtue by example and precept. That play asks us to take smiling delight in love's absurdities, in cakes and ale, in song and jest, and in almost everything else. But credit for the continuance in the theater of an enterprising and unfettered humour must be given to many writers, both inventive and imitative, and indeed to the general temper of English audiences.

This play world of comedy has been created only by skilful workmanship and persistent art. Immense effort, both successful and unsuccessful, has gone into building this house of mirth. Of what value is it? There are those who are fond of reminding us that the creations of art are mere illusions. Of course they are illusions, as are all our gorgeous palaces, and the great world itself, and the ions and motions into which the scientists now dissolve it. But the works of art have the lasting interest that they are man's own creations, the work of his life and mind, and the world of comedy seems peculiarly human because it is the outcome of that strange faculty of humour, of which so far as we know, man is the sole possessor. What a dreary companion he would be without it! How amazing are its powers! Intellectual as well as emotional, appealing both to intelligence and sympathy, seeking at one moment to rid existence of intolerable folly and at the next to brighten it by delightful make-believe, humour is the salt without which society would lose all its savour—is the indispensable guide to man in his search for worthy happiness. It has inspired these hundreds of plays and still summons men to create more.

Yes, we still go to the play, and we take our seats with special satisfaction if a comedy is promised, an evening of wit and fun. Perhaps it is a new piece, and one's fancy summons up other first nights and the long procession of plays that have asked for the plaudits of four centuries. A distinguished audience is gathering, and one well worth observing. Here come Sir Lucius O'Trigger and Mrs. Malaprop, swashing down the aisle, headed for the front row. Here come the belles and beaux with a great fluttering of silks—Melantha, Lady Betty Modish, Violante and Lady Gay Spanker, followed by a host of Rovers, Rangers, Dashwoods, Youngloves and Wildairs. And the fops are simpering and ogling, and the flirts and madcaps are turning up their pretty noses. Viola is in one box with her duke, but some of the other heroines in page's dress are serving as ushers; and is that not Malvolio superintending them? Portia and her party from Belmont are in another box, and Millamant reigns in a third, and Falstaff and Mrs. Quickly with Pooh Bah and Little Buttercup are crowded into a fourth. What a buzz of conversation and what laughter! What would Mrs. Grundy say!

The pit is packed. I can see Cherry and Scrub and Miss Pros and Captain Hook. Aguecheek and Slender are squeezed between Pistol and Doll Tearsheet, the Spanish curate and his sexton. Dogberry is there, and Autolycus is picking his pocket. The gallery is a riot. In the front row center, surrounded by his pals, is Tony Lumpkin, dangling something over the balustrade, fishing perhaps for his mother's tall headdress. Simon Eyre and Margery, accompanied by all their apprentices, Boucicault's Conn and Moya, Congreve's Sailor Ben, Gilbert's policemen and pirates, Jonson's motley crowd from Bartholomew Fair, are all adding to the din. In the balcony on one side are Iolanthe's fairies, on the other Titania's, with Peter and Wendy in between and the chorus of the House of Lords oscillating from one side to the other.

This is the audience which every new comedy must face.

These are the judges who determine what persons are worthy to be added to their company. These are the maintainers of our tradition, the censors of the drama, the inspirers to new effort. They are not very censorious, not insistent on rule or theory. What they chiefly ask for, is more humour.

NOTES

CHAPTER I.—Definitions

Among recent books on the subject of this chapter, are: Henri Bergson, *Le Rire, Essai sur la signification du Comique,* 1901, English trans. by Brereton and Rothwell; Sigmund Freud, *Der Witz und seine Beziehung zum Unbewussten,* 1905, English trans. by A. A. Brill; Theodore Lipps, *Komik and Humor, Beiträge zur Ästhetik,* 1898; George Meredith, *Essay on Comedy* (see ed. by Lane Cooper for bibliography); Herbert Spencer, *The Physiology of Laughter,* Essays, Vol. II; James Sully, *Essay on Laughter.* Of special importance is Max Eastman's *The Sense of Humor,* 1921; the first half sets forth the author's own theory and the second half gives a historical classification and summary of the various theories of critics, philosophers and psychologists. The notes furnish sufficient bibliographical references from Aristotle to Croce.

Page 4. Sir Philip Sidney, *Defense of Poesy.*

Page 5. Aristotle, *Poetics,* V. The full discussion of comedy is missing in the Poetics. For an elaborate attempt at reconstruction, see Lane Cooper, *An Aristotelian Theory of Comedy,* 1922.

Page 6. On tragicomedy see F. H. Ristine, *English Tragicomedy, Its origin and history,* New York, 1910.

Page 7. Dryden, *Parallel of Poetry and Painting.*

Page 9. For the problem of defining the comic and a criticism of Bergson's theory, see L. Cazamian, "Pourquoi nous ne pouvons définir l'humour," *Revue Germanique,* 1906.

Max Eastman, see introductory note to this chapter.

William Hazlitt, *On Wit and Humour.*

Page 10. Hobbes, *Leviathan,* Part I, Chap. VI. Bergson, *Le Rire,* p. 1.

Page 11. Voltaire, Preface to *L'Enfant Prodigue.* Voltaire of course was not the first to make or partially to make this discovery. For example, Sidney in the *Defense of Poesy* says "Delight hath a joy in it either permanent or present, laughter hath only a scornful tickling."

Page 12. The quotation is from Emerson's essay, *The Comic.*

Freud, see introductory note to this chapter.

"The psychologists," see Sully, Wundt, Baldwin, G. Stanley Hall, MacDougall, and E. L. Thorndike; see also discussion and references in Max Eastman, *op. cit.*

Page 13. Carlyle, *Essay on Jean Paul Richter.*

Page 14. The quotations are from Thackeray's essay, *Mr. Brown the Elder takes Mr. Brown the Younger to a Club,* I; Emerson's essay on *Scott;* and Meredith's essay on *Comedy.*

Hegel, *Philosophy of Fine Art,* trans. by F. B. B. Osmaston, Vol. IV; quoted and discussed by Eastman, *The Sense of Humor,* p. 171 ff.

CHAPTER II.—Medieval and Classical Influences

The authorities on their respective subjects are: W. Creizenach, *Geschichte des neueren Dramas,* Halle, 1893-1916. (5 vols. have appeared; vols. 4 and 5 dealing with Elizabethan drama have been translated into English); A. W. Ward, *A History of English Dramatic Literature to the Death of Queen Anne,* 1899, 3 vols.; E. K. Chambers, *The Medieval Stage,* Oxford, 2 vols. These all cover the matter of this present chapter and contain bibliographies. Creizenach's index is substantially complete for all European plays; Chambers's Appendixes contain references to editions and brief descriptions of all English plays up to Elizabeth's accession. *The Cambridge History of English Literature,* 14 vols., 1916, supplies articles on the matter of this and of subsequent chapters and gives full bibliographies. For France the authority on medieval drama is L. Petit de Julleville, *Histoire du Théâtre en France au Moyen Age,* 1800-86, 4 vols. Texts of English plays are in A. W. Pollard's *English Miracle Plays,* and J. M. Manly's *Specimens of the Pre-Shakespearean Drama.*

In general, I shall give references only to books published more recently than the bibliographies in the *Cambridge History.*

Page 18. "Mimus," see H. Reich, *Der Mimus, ein Litterarentwickelungs geschichtlicher Versuch,* Berlin, 1903.

Page 19. Text of the Wyclifite sermon is in *Reliquiæ Antiquæ,* ii, 42; Hazlitt, *Remains of Early Popular Poetry,* i, 73; see Chambers, *Medieval Stage,* I, 84, and II, 102.

"Feast of Fools," in 1207. See Chambers, I, 279.

"Interludium," text in Chambers, II, 324.

Page 20. "This religious drama seemingly had its origin," etc. For a telling criticism of this generally accepted theory, see a monograph as yet unprinted by Oscar Cargill.

Page 21. The *Towneley* collection. See article by O. Cargill,

"The Authorship of the Secunda Pastoram," *Publ. Mod. Lang. Assn.,* xli, 810.

Page 23. *Pathelin,* trans. into English by R. Holbrook, New York, 1905.

Page 25. *The Nature of the Four Elements,* Hazlitt's Dodsley, vol. i.

Page 26. *Fulgens and Lucres,* ed. by F. S. Boas and A. W. Reed, Oxford, 1926. The single copy of this play was rediscovered in 1919 in Lord Mostyn's library and purchased by Mr. H. E. Huntington, who at once made the play accessible to scholars.

Page 27. "Secular dramas . . . in Flanders." Two of these plays, *Esmoreit* and *Mary of Nimmegen,* have been translated into English by Harry M. Ayres and A. J. Barnouw, The Hague, 1924.

Page 28. See R. W. Bolwell, *Life and Works of John Heywood,* 1921, and A. W. Reed, *Early Tudor Drama,* London, 1926.

Page 30. "Neo-Latin imitations," in *University Drama in the Tudor Age,* F. S. Boas, Oxford, 1914.

Page 34. "School boys"; see Chambers, II, 196.

CHAPTER III.—THE BACKGROUND OF STORY

The matter of this chapter is touched upon in all histories of the drama. Of special interest are Samuel L. Wolff's *The Greek Romances in Elizabethan Prose Fiction,* 1912; W. P. Ker's *Epic and Romance,* 1908; and W. W. Greg's *Pastoral Poetry and Pastoral Drama,* 1906.

Page 38. "devices of later romance." In *Clitophon and Leucippe* in a single instance Dr. Wolff discovers all the sentiments of chivalric idealized love, including the regenerating effect on the hero. See *The Greek Romances,* p. 132.

Page 41. "Robin Goodfellow." I am drawing upon an as yet unpublished monograph by Miss Minor Latham of Barnard College on Folk-lore in Elizabethan Literature.

CHAPTER IV.—THE ELIZABETHAN BEGINNINGS

To the authorities cited in Chapter II, Creizenach, Ward, the *Cambridge History,* should be added F. E. Schelling, *Elizabethan Drama,* 1558-1642, 2 vols., Boston and New York, 1908, and E. K. Chambers, *The Elizabethan Stage,* 4 vols., Oxford, 1923. Professor Schelling gives a valuable bibliographical essay and a finding list or directory to modern editions of Elizabethan dramas. See also his briefer but more recent *Elizabethan Playwrights*, 1925. Sir Edmund K. Chambers supplies the latest and fullest bibliographical guides for the drama up to 1616. Other books covering special aspects of the general Elizabethan period are *Shakespeare's England*, 2 vols., 1916, for the social conditions; J. Q. Adams, *Shakespearean Playhouses*, 1917; A. H. Thorndike, *Shakespeare's Theater*, 1916; *Tragedy*, 1909.

Studies applying especially to the matter of this chapter are F. S. Boas, *Shakspere and his Predecessors*, 1896, *University Drama in the Tudor Age*, 1914; C. F. Tucker Brooke, *The Tudor Drama*, 1912; Charles W. Wallace, *The Evolution of the English Drama up to Shakespeare*, Berlin, 1912; A. W. Reed, *The Beginnings of English Secular and Romantic Drama*, 1922; *Early Tudor Drama*, 1926; R. Withington, *English Pageantry*, 2 vols., 1918, 1920. *The Revels Accounts* have been edited by A. Feuillerat, *Materialien*, 1908, 1914.

Many of the plays noted in this chapter have been reprinted in the Publications of the Malone Society. See also R. W. Bond, *Early Plays from the Italian*, 1911; A. Brandl, *Quellen des weltlichen Dramas in England vor Shakespeare*, 1898; and Hazlitt's revision of Dodsley's *Old Plays*.

Page 50. Of the plays referred to, *Like Will to Like* is in Hazlitt's Dodsley, Vol. II; *Wealth and Health, Tom Tiler and His Wife, Johan the Evangelist* and *Apius and Virginia* have been reprinted by the Malone Society.

"The Vice." For a recent discussion, see *Studies in the Development of the Fool in Elizabethan Drama*, Miss O. M. Busby, 1923.

Page 52. Of Robert Wilson's plays, *Three Ladies of London* and *Three Lords and Three Ladies* are in Hazlitt's *Dodsley*. *The Cobbler's Prophecy* and *The Pedlar's Prophecy* have been printed by the Malone Society.

Page 58. "Jack Juggler." The long epilogue suggests that the motive of mistaken identity may have reference to other matters. See Boas, *University Drama*, p. 69.

Page 59. On the authorship of *Gammer Gurton's Needle*, see Boas, *University Drama*.

Page 61. "Gascoigne." See J. W. Cunliffe's edition of Gascoigne's *Complete Works*, 2 vols., Cambridge, 1907.

Misogonus is in Brandl's *Quellen*. On its date, see Boas, *op. cit. The Bugbears* is in R. W. Bond's *Early Plays from the Italian*.

Page 64. Stephen Gosson, *The School of Abuse;* Sir Philip Sidney, *Defense of Poesy.*

Page 66. *Clyomon* and *Clamydes* is in Dyce's ed. of Greene and Peele, and also is reprinted by the Malone Society.

Page 68. "Neither of the texts." The text in Brandl's *Quellen* has 1421 lines while that in Tucker Brooke's edition (New Haven, 1915, based on Lord Mostyn's quarto) has 1904. This longer version leaves Nomides and Sabia unaccounted for, and reunites Clarisia and Lamphedon only to have them take poison, administered by the officious Common Conditions. But we are not told that they die; and, as Professor Tucker Brooke remarks, "even when the epilogue and finis are reached, the play is not properly ended."

Page 69. "The poet Churchyard." Nichols's *Progresses of Queen Elizabeth,* II, 211.

Page 70. "The . . . entertainment at Kenilworth." See Nichols' *Progresses of Queen Elizabeth.*
"pastoral personages." See "The Pastoral Element in the English Drama before 1605," *Mod. Lang. Notes,* 1899. See Feuillerat, *Revels Accounts,* for court shows, costumes, etc.

CHAPTER V.—LYLY, PEELE AND GREENE

Most of the histories and special works on the Elizabethan drama noted for Chapters II and IV deal with the dramatists of this chapter. G. M. Gayley's *Representative English Comedies,* 3 vols., 1903-14, contains both texts and scholarly articles. The standard edition of Lyly is by R. W. Bond, 3 vols., 1902; of Peele, ed. A. H. Bullen, 3 vols., 1888; of Greene, *Complete Works,* A. B. Grossart, 15 vols., 1881-6; *Plays and Poems,* by J. C. Collins, 2 vols., 1905. Among more important recent studies are: A. Feuillerat, *John Lyly,* 1910; S. L. Wolff, *Robert Greene and the Italian Renaissance, Englische Studien,* vol. 37; J. C. Jordan, *Robert Greene,* 1915.

The dates enclosed in parentheses following the titles of the plays in the text, are dates of publication. The dates for presentation in the Elizabethan period are rarely known exactly and are often much earlier than those for publication.

Page 76. The letter quoted is from Feuillerat's *Lyly,* p. 561.

Page 83. The allegory of *Endymion* has been the subject of a long debate ever since Halpin's essay "Oberon's Vision" before the Shakespeare Society in 1843. The various identifications may be traced in Fleay, G. P. Baker, Bond, Feuillerat, and Percy Long, *Modern Philology,* 1911. See Chambers, *Elizabethan Stage,* i, 327, for bibliography and summary. As I have suggested in the text, I doubt if we can arrive at any probabilities in details.

Page 85. "Thomas Nashe," *Epistle to Greene's Menaphon,* 1589.

Page 86. The quotations from Peele are from Bullen's edition.

CHAPTERS VI AND VII.—SHAKESPEARE: THE EARLIER COMEDIES—THE LATER COMEDIES

Sir Sidney Lee's *A Life of William Shakespeare,* 1922, new ed., and Joseph Quincy Adams's *A Life of William Shakespeare,* 1923, and the *Cambridge History of English Literature,* Vol. V, give general bibliographical guidance. *The Facts about Shakespeare* by W. A. Neilson and A. H. Thorndike, 1913 (a new edition in preparation), is a handbook giving bibliographical and other guidance to study. Since the suspension and subsequent curtailment of the excellent bibliographies supplied by the *Jahrbuch der deutschen Shakespeare-Gesellschaft,* Weimar, current books and articles may be best traced by the annual bibliographies in the *Publications of the Mod. Lang. Assn. of America,* the *Bulletin of the Shakespeare Association of America, Studies in Philology* (the Renaissance) and *The Year's Work in English Studies, The English Assn.*

The volumes of the *New Variorum Shakespeare,* ed. H. H. Furness, are still appearing and contain full summaries of scholarship and criticism on individual plays. Various editions supply introductory essays on the different plays; e.g., *The Tudor Shakespeare,* genl. eds., W. A. Neilson and A. H. Thorndike.

Of recent books dealing with the characteristics of Shakespeare's comedies, mention may be made of L. L. Shücking, *Character Problems in Shakespeare's Plays* (Eng. trans.), 1922; E. E. Stoll, *Shakespeare Studies,* 1927; W. W. Lawrence, *Shakespeare's Later Comedies* (in press, to include several essays already printed); *Shaksperian Studies,* Columbia Univ., 1916.

Page 96. "the latest and maturest." See George P. Baker, *Shakespeare as a Dramatist,* 1907.

"Story of Ægeon." See Brander Matthews, *Shakespeare as a Playwright,* 1913, p. 71.

For more intricate speculations on the play, see Allison Gaw, "The Evolution of The Comedy of Errors," *Publ. Mod. Lang. Assn.,* 1926.

Page 97. "a court performance in view." There has been much speculation on the occasion of the play, its contemporary allusions, and the process of its enlargement. See H. D. Gray, *The Original Version of Love's Labour's Lost,* Stanford Univ., 1916; Acheson, *Shakespeare's Last Years,* 1920; A. K. Gray,

"The Secret of Love's Labour's Lost," *Publ. Mod. Lang. Assn.,* 1924; O. J. Campbell, "Love's Labour's Lost Restudied," *Univ. of Michigan Studies,* 1925; F. E. Schelling, *Elizabethan Playwrights,* 1925, pp. 60, 61.

Page 103. I am indebted to the unpublished researches of Miss Minor Latham on Folk Lore in Elizabethan Literature.

Page 112. *The Downfall and Death of Robert Earl of Huntingdon* are in Vol. VIII of Hazlitt's revision of Dodsley's *Old Plays.* I am drawing here from my article "As You Like It and Robin Hood Plays," *Journal Eng. and Germ. Phil.,* 1902.

Page 121. On the historical plays, see F. E. Schelling, *The English Chronicle Play,* 1902. *Henry VIII* by Shakespeare and Fletcher was still later than *Coriolanus,* so Shakespeare was engaged on historical plays from the beginning to the end of his career.

Page 128. "The three plays." W. W. Lawrence's articles on these plays will be included in his volume, *Shakespeare's Later Comedies.* On "All's Well" and "Troilus and Cressida," see the introductions in *The Tudor Shakespeare,* by Professors Lowes and Tatlock respectively.

Page 131. "I have elsewhere discussed." In *The Influence of Beaumont and Fletcher on Shakspere,* 1901. See also my article on "Shakespeare as Debtor," *Shaksperian Studies,* Columbia Univ., 1916.

Page 134. "after the style of the court masques." I may refer to my paper, "Influence of Court Masques upon the Drama," *Publ. Mod. Lang. Assn.,* 1900.

CHAPTER VIII.—Elizabethan Varieties

The general authorities and bibliographies noted for Chapters II and IV continue to apply to this and the remaining chapters on the Elizabethan drama. The standard edition of Chapman is by Thomas M. Parrott, in two volumes, London, 1914, one volume being given to the comedies, with full introductions and notes. Marston's *Works* have been edited by A. H. Bullen, 3 vols., 1887, and Middleton's *Works,* 8 vols., 1885-6. *The Dramatic Works of Thomas Dekker* are to be found in Pearson's reprints, 4 vols., 1873; the *Non-Dramatic Works,* ed. A. B. Grosart, are in the Huth Library, 1884. *The Dramatic Works of Thomas Heywood,* 6 vols., are in Pearson's reprints, 1874. *The Works of John Day* were edited by A. H. Bullen, 1881. There are numerous modern editions of separate plays.

Among the more important special critical works on the material of this chapter are: R. A. Small, *The Stage Quarrel between Ben Jonson and the so-called Poetasters*, 1899; Mary L. Hunt, *Thomas Dekker*, 1911.

Page 142. The exact details of the stage and the methods of presentation have been the subjects of a vast amount of investigation and discussion. For my own views on these matters and for a bibliography, I must refer to my *Shakespeare's Theater*, 1916. This book also considers the history of the companies and the conditions of acting. E. K. Chambers, *The Elizabethan Stage*, 4 vols., 1923, covers these subjects more fully up to 1616. See also W. J. Lawrence, *The Elizabethan Playhouse*, 2 vols., 1912, 1913.

Page 144. On disguise, see V. O. Freeburg, *Disguise Plots in Elizabethan Drama*, Columbia Univ. Press, 1915.

Page 148. "Chapman." Professor Parrott in the introductions in his edition of Chapman's comedies claims for the comedies greater merits and influence than I have been able to award them. The student of the drama, however, will find these introductions thorough and informing.

Page 152. "Middleton." See W. D. Dunkel, *The Dramatic Technique of Thomas Middleton*, Chicago University Press, 1926.

Page 161. Hazlitt, *Lectures on the Literature of the Age of Elizabeth*.

CHAPTER IX.—BEN JONSON

A new edition of Ben Jonson's Works by C. H. Herford and Percy Simpson is in process of publication. Volumes I and II, 1925, contain a biography and full critical discussions of the plays. Before this, the standard edition was by Gifford, published in 1816. F. Cunningham's reprint of this with some corrections appeared in 1871 and 1875. Careful critical editions of a number of the plays have appeared in the *Yale Studies in English*. The first Folio was issued in 1616; the second Folio of 1640 was in two volumes, the first reprinting the 1616 edition.

Among the more important critical discussions are M. Castelain, *Ben Jonson, l'Homme et l'Oeuvre*, Paris, 1907; Elizabeth Woodbridge, *Studies in Jonson's Comedy*, 1898; R. A. Small, *The Stage Quarrel between Ben Jonson and the so-called Poetasters;* Gregory Smith, *Ben Jonson*, English Men of Letters Series, 1919; Mina Kerr, *The Influence of Ben Jonson on English Comedy*, Univ. of Penn., 1912. I have not seen a recent study by Esther C. Cloudman, *Ben Jonson's Art*, Northampton, Mass.

I have drawn rather heavily in this chapter upon my article

on Ben Jonson in the Cambridge History of English Literature, Vol. VI.

Page 170. In the induction, *i.e.* by the speakers of the induction, at the end of Act III, Sc. I.

Page 176. Rymer's "poetic justice." Thomas Rymer, the critic who at the close of the century attacked so fiercely the tragedies of Shakespeare and Fletcher, seems to have been the first to use this phrase, destined for a century or more to serve as a slogan in dramatic criticism.

Page 177. Mosca's boast is from Act III, Sc. 1.

Page 187. "Laws of protasis," etc., Act I at the end.

Page 189. The quotation is from my article on Jonson in the *Cambridge History of English Literature*, Vol. VI.

CHAPTER X.—BEAUMONT AND FLETCHER

The plays by Beaumont and Fletcher which had not already appeared in separate quartos were collected in the Folio of 1647. Fifty-two plays were included in the Folio of 1679. Several editions of their plays appeared before what is still the standard edition, that of Alexander Dyce in 11 vols., 1843-6. Their works were again edited by A. Glover and A. R. Waller, *Cambridge Press Classics*, 1905 ff.; this is a reprint of the folio of 1679 with collations of previously printed texts. A variorum edition under the general direction of A. H. Bullen begun in 1904, proceeded only to three volumes. There are numerous editions of individual plays.

The following critical works have appeared since the bibliography in the Cambridge History:—R. M. Alden's introduction to Beaumont, *Belles Lettres Series*, 1910; C. M. Gayley's *Beaumont the Dramatist*, 1914; H. D. Sykes, *Sidelights on Elizabethan Drama*, 1924, and E. H. Oliphant's *The Plays of Beaumont and Fletcher*, 1927. Of special interest for this chapter are Miss O. L. Hatcher's *John Fletcher*, Chicago, 1905, and F. H. Ristine's *English Tragicomedy*. I have drawn freely in this chapter from my *The Influence of Beaumont and Fletcher on Shakespeare*, 1901, and the introduction to the edition of Beaumont and Fletcher in the *Belles Lettres Series*, 1906. I may also refer to my article "Shakespeare as a Debtor," *Shaksperian Studies*, Columbia, Univ., 1916.

Page 192. "The Woman's Prize." See *The Influence of Beaumont and Fletcher on Shakespeare* and Oliphant's *The Plays of Beaumont and Fletcher* for discussion of the date. I think no one has called attention to the evidence for date in I, iii, "These are the most authentic rebels next Tyrone, I ever read of." Tyrone submitted in 1603 and was in London that summer. In II, 1, "It had been no right rebellion Had she held off," may also allude to Tyrone's submission. These references indicate a date of 1603-4 for the play, though they might possibly fit a date of 1607-8.

Page 193. "Folio of 1679." It is generally agreed that Fletcher had no part in "The Coronation," included in the Folio, and little or no share in "The Faithful Friends" added to the Beaumont and Fletcher collection in Weber's edition, 1812. "Henry VIII," by Shakespeare and Fletcher, the tragedy "Sir John van Olden Barna-veldt" and the tragicomedy "A Very Woman" by Fletcher and Massinger were not in the folio of 1679.

"collaboration with Beaumont." See Oliphant's *The Plays of Beaumont and Fletcher,* 1927, for the latest and most thorough attempt to solve these very difficult problems of authorship.

Page 197. "dramatic romances." See *The Influence of Beaumont and Fletcher on Shakespeare.*

CHAPTER XI.—THE LATER ELIZABETHANS

Of the general authorities on the Elizabethan drama, Ward, Schelling, and the *Cambridge History* continue to be available for this period. Chambers, *The Elizabethan Stage,* and Creizenach, *Die Geschichte des neueren Dramas* close with 1616. The trage-dies of the various writers are discussed in my volume, *Tragedy.* The standard edition of Massinger is that by Gifford, 1805; reprinted, with the addition of *Believe as You List,* by F. Cun-ningham, 1870. The standard edition of Shirley is that of Gifford and Dyce, 1833. Both dramatists deserve new editions. Brome's *Dramatic Works* are available in Pearson's reprint, 1873. For other editions of collected works or of separate plays, see the bibliographies in the *Cambridge History.*

Page 218. "Those performed at court." Of those mentioned from 1625 to the closing of the theaters in 1642, thirteen are by Fletcher in whole or part, five by Shakespeare, three by Shirley, two each by Jonson and D'Avenant, and nine by other dramatists. Dr. Tannenbaum, however, has shown good reasons for believing the Caroline play-lists of 1636-7 and 1638-9 to be forgeries. See Samuel A. Tannenbaum, *Shakespeare Forgeries in the Revels Accounts,* Columbia Univ. Press, 1928.

Page 223. "William Rowley, who has been credited with the romantic and moral tone which they display." This idea was first advanced by Pauline G. Wiggin, *An Enquiry into the Authorship of the Middleton-Rowley Plays,* Boston, 1897; and has been supported by C. W. Stork, *William Rowley,* etc., Univ. of Pennsylvania, Philadelphia, 1910; and by Arthur Symons in the article on Middleton and Rowley in the *Cambridge History,* Vol. VI, 1910.

Page 225. *A Very Woman,* not in the Fletcher folios, but published in 1655 as by Massinger with a prologue stating it to be a revision of a play "long since acted." The earlier play was presumably by Fletcher, for his share in the existing play is obvious. See Oliphant, *The Plays of Beaumont and Fletcher,* p. 250.

Page 234. "Edwin Booth and Davenport." It has recently been acted by Mr. Walter Hampden.

Page 235. James Shirley has been the subject of two excellent studies: *James Shirley Dramatist, a biographical and critical study,* by Arthur H. Nason, New York, 1915; and *The Relations of Shirley's Plays to the Elizabethan Drama,* by Robert S. Forsythe, Columbia Univ. Press, 1914.

Page 237. "Of the tragicomedies." *The Duke's Mistress* is on the line between tragicomedy and tragedy. I have treated it in my volume *Tragedy.*

Page 240. "scarcely a situation." See Forsythe, *op. cit.*

Page 246. Richard Brome. See Clarence E. Andrews, *Richard Brome,* Yale Univ. Press, 1913.

CHAPTER XII.—CONCLUSION TO ELIZABETHAN COMEDY

Some of the books already mentioned bear especially on this chapter: Greg's *Pastoral Poetry and Pastoral Drama;* Ristine's *Tragicomedy;* Freeburg's *Disguise Plots in Elizabethan Drama.*

Other recent dissertations more or less applicable are: John B. Moore, *The Comic and Realistic in English Drama,* Univ. of Chicago, 1926; O. E. Winslow, *Low Comedy as a Standard Element in English Comedy from the Beginnings to 1642,* Univ. of Chicago, abstracts of theses, I, 415; R. S. Forsythe, "Comic Effects in Elizabethan Drama," *Quarterly Journal,* Univ. No. Dakota, 1927; Willard Thorp, *The Triumph of Realism in Elizabethan Drama,* 1558-1612, Princeton Univ., 1928; Emile Legouis, "The Bacchic Element in Shakespeare's Plays," British Academy, 1926.

Page 254. "as I have tried to show elsewhere." "The Influence of Court Masques upon the Drama," *Publ. Mod. Lang. Assn.,* 1900.

CHAPTER XIII.—The Restoration

A. W. Ward's *History of English Dramatic Literature to the Death of Queen Anne* covers the field of this and the following chapter. Volume VIII of the *Cambridge History of English Literature* deals with the age of Dryden; its bibliography on the Restoration drama, chapter IX, is good to 1912. G. H. Nettleton, *English Drama of the Restoration and Eighteenth Century*, 1914, is useful. The standard authority on the history of the theater is J. Genest, *Some Account of the English Stage from the Restoration in 1660 to 1830*, 10 vols., Bath, 1832. This has been supplemented and in some degree superseded by a series of volumes by Allardyce Nicoll, that for this chapter being *A History of the Restoration Drama, 1660-1700*, Cambridge, 1923. George C. D. Odell's *Shakespeare from Betterton to Irving*, 2 vols., New York, 1920, is valuable in tracing the general history of the stage as well as the particulars of Shakespearian productions. Alwin Thaler's *Shakspere to Sheridan*, Cambridge, 1922, covers a portion of the same field less exhaustively. Percy Fitzgerald's *A New History of the English Stage*, London, 1882, is not now of much value. My volume, *Tragedy*, 1909, deals with the tragedies of this and subsequent periods.

Among special studies on the matter of this chapter are: L. Charlanne, *L'influence française en Angleterre au XVIIe Siècle*, 1906; D. H. Miles, *Influence of Molière on Restoration Comedy*, Columbia Univ. Press, 1910; J. E. Gillet, "Molière en Angleterre," 1660-1670, *Mémoires de l'Acad. Royale de Bruxelles*, N. S. IX, 1913; A. C. Sprague, *Beaumont and Fletcher on the Restoration Stage*, Harvard Univ. Press, 1926; Leslie Hotson, *The Commonwealth and Restoration Stage*, Harvard Univ. Press, 1928; Joseph W. Krutch, *Comedy and Conscience after the Restoration*, Columbia Univ. Press, 1924.

The standard edition of Dryden is the Scott-Saintsbury in 18 vols., Edinburgh, 1892; Etherege has been edited by A. Wilson Verity, 1888. Montagu Summers has recently published the works of Wycherley and Shadwell, sumptuously printed with extensive and detailed introductions, Nonesuch Press, London.

Criticism of Restoration comedy includes wide variations of opinion. A good anthology of contemporary general dramatic criticism with an admirable introduction is *Critical Essays of the Seventeenth Century*, ed. J. E. Spingarn, Oxford, 1908. We shall have occasion to refer to Jeremy Collier's *A Short View of the Immorality and Profaneness of the English Stage*, 1698; and to Steele's criticisms in the *Spectator*. Of nineteenth century criticism the more important discussions are: Charles Lamb, *On the Artificial Comedy of the Last Century;* Hazlitt, *Lectures on the English Comic Writers;* Leigh Hunt's prefaces to the *Dramatic Works of Wycherley, Congreve, Vanbrugh and Farquhar;* Macaulay, *Essay on the Dramatists of the Restoration.* Recent critical discussion includes: John Palmer, *The Comedy of Manners,* 1913; Bonamy Dobree, *Restoration Comedy,* 1924; Montagu Summers, introductions to *Nonesuch editions* of Shadwell, Wycherley and Congreve.

The dates affixed in parentheses to plays acted after the Restoration are the years of presentation. For the pre-Restoration plays I have given the dates of publication, often years subsequent to time of writing.

Page 272. "Shakespeare's romantic fancy did not please." *The Tempest* was given in the Dryden-D'Avenant version. See Odell, *Shakespeare from Betterton to Irving* for a full history of productions and adaptations.

Page 274. *The Parson's Wedding* has recently been reissued by Mr. Montagu Summers in his *Restoration Comedies,* 1921.

Page 276. The quotation is from the Epilogue to *The Conquest of Granada.* See also Dryden's *Defense of the Epilogue,* and his dedication of *Marriage à la Mode* to Rochester.

Page 279. "John Wilson's two Jonsonian comedies." *The Cheats,* 1664, and *The Projectors,* probably not acted.

Page 284. The quotation is from Cibber's *Apology,* p. 99.

Page 294. Hazlitt, quoted from *The English Comic Writers.*

Page 297. Dryden's criticism. See A. W. Ward, Vol. III, p. 444.

Page 298. Steele, *Spectator,* No. 65. See also No. 51 for further criticism of Etherege.

Page 302. "Dryden's praise." The quotation is from Dryden's "Apology for Heroic Poetry," prefixed to *The State of Innocence.*

CHAPTER XIV.—MANNERS AND WIT

The books cited for Chapter XIII are nearly all useful for the present chapter. The Nonesuch press, London, has recently issued handsome editions of Congreve, 4 vols., 1923, edited by Montagu Summers, and of Vanbrugh, 4 vols., 1927, edited by Bonamy Dobree and Geoffrey Webb. The best edition of Aphra Behn is by Montagu Summers. Farquhar is available, 2 vols., ed. Alex Charles Ewald, London, 1892. Of special interest for this period is R. S. Forsythe's *A Study of the Plays of Thomas D'Urfey,* 1916-17.

Page 306. "Southerne and Otway." I have omitted any notice, of their rather feeble comic efforts, and also of the plays, near the close of the century, of Mrs. Manley and Mrs. Pix.

Page 312. "does not occur again." But see Cibber's *Lady's Last Stake* for a similar tell-tale.

Page 315. The quotation is from Dryden's poem, "To My dear Friend, Mr. Congreve, on his Comedy called The Double-Dealer."

Page 326. Leslie Stephen, article in *Dict. Nat. Biog.*

Page 331. Mr. Palmer, *The Comedy of Manners,* 1913.

Page 332. Jeremy Collier's *Short View.* Vanbrugh's reply was entitled "A Short Vindication of the Relapse and the Provok'd Wife from Immorality and Profaneness." See Krutch's *Comedy and Conscience after the Restoration* for a full bibliography of the Collier controversy, also for a bibliography of Critical Works, 1660-1700.

Squire Trelooby, in collaboration with Congreve and Walsh.

Page 338. Captain Plume. The quotation is from Act IV, Scene i, near the end.

CHAPTER XV.—THE RETURN OF SENTIMENT, 1700-1730

Of the authorities mentioned for Chapter XIV, Genest, Odell, the *Cambridge History,* Nettleton, and Ward (until the death of Queen Anne) continue available. Allardyce Nicoll, *A History of Early Eighteenth Century Drama,* 1700-1750, Cambridge, 1925; Ernest Bernbaum, *The Drama of Sensibility,* 1915, are important. Krutch's *Comedy and Conscience after the Restoration* covers this period. Of earlier scholarly works, special mention must be made of Alexandre Beljame, *Le Public et Les Hommes de Lettres en Angleterre au Dix-huitième Siècle,* 1881; and G. A. Aitken, *The Life of Richard Steele,* 1889.

Page 343. "an admirer of Collier." See Steele's *Apology,* quoted by G. A. Aitken in his excellent introduction to the *Mermaid ed.* of Steele's plays.

Hazlitt. *The English Comic Writers.*

Page 343. "Campley." Hardy's advice is in II, 1, the song in IV, 2. See *Spectator,* No. 51, for the criticism of a questionable passage, which Swift afterwards amended.

Page 345. Sir A. W. Ward, *History of English Dramatic Literature,* III, 495.

Page 349. "The Guardian," June 20, 1713. Bevil's avowal of romanticism is in I, 2.

Page 351. "European renown." For translations of the two plays, see A. Nicoll, *Early Eighteenth Century Drama*, pp. 193, 199 n.

Colley Cibber. See *Studies in the Work of Colley Cibber* by D. C. Croissant, Univ. of Kansas, 1912.

Page 352. *Love's Last Shift.* For a different view of this play, over-emphasizing, I think, its importance in the rise of sentimentalism, see E. Bernbaum, *The Drama of Sensibility*.

Page 357. "improved on Burnaby." Cf. *The Ladies Visiting Day*, II, 3.

Page 370. For a full account of Fielding's dramatic career, see Wilbur L. Cross, *The History of Henry Fielding*, 3 vols., 1918.

Page 375. "Professor Cross," *The History of Henry Fielding*, III, 373-4.

CHAPTER XVI.—PANTOMIME, OPERA AND FARCE

Genest, Nicoll, Odell, Nettleton and Bernbaum, cited in preceding chapters, continue available. The bibliography to the *Cambridge History*, Vol. X, Chap. IV, is extensive. Memoirs of actors and dramatists supply much information. *The Annals of Covent Garden Theatre*, 1732-1897, by H. S. Wyndham, 2 vols., 1906, is useful. Many of the popular pieces appear in the various collections of plays such as, *Bell's British Theatre*, 24 vols., 1776; *The Minor Theatre*, 7 vols., 1794.

Page 378. "revival of Shakespeare's long unacted comedies." For full account of revivals and alterations, see Odell, *Shakespeare from Betterton to Irving*.

Page 379. *The Tempest.* Shakespeare's play was revived at Drury Lane, 1745-6, and again in 1757.

Page 387. "In France." See Gustave Lanson, *Nivelle de La Chaussée et la Comédie Larmoyante*, 1903 (2nd ed.) and E. Bernbaum, *Drama of Sensibility*, Chap. X.

Page 388. John Weaver. See Weaver's *The History of the Mimes and Pantomimes*, 1728, and an article by W. J. Lawrence, *The Theatre*, XXV.

Page 389. For the quotation, see Davies's *Life of Garrick*, Vol. I, p. 332.

Page 391. "ballad opera." For other names, see Nicoll, *op. cit.*, p. 237.

Page 393. "a present-day moralist." Frank Kidson, *The Beggar's Opera*, Cambridge, 1922.

The Dunciad, ed. 1729, Book III, line 330.

Page 399. Swift. See Cross, *op. cit.,* for a comment on this story.

Pape 405. Samuel Foote. Foote's *Dramatic Works,* 4 vols. appeared in 1787, again in 2 vols. 1799; with a life, 1809. See also William Cooke's *Memoirs of Samuel Foote,* Esq., 3 vols., 1805.

Page 407. Dr. Johnson. See Boswell's *Life;* the story of the threatened beating, under the year 1775; that of the dinner, the year 1776.

CHAPTER XVII.—THE REVIVAL OF COMEDY, 1760-1780

The works already cited by Genest, Nicoll, Nettleton, Bernbaum, and Odell apply to this chapter. The bibliography in the *Cambridge History,* Vol. XI, Chap. XII, is ample, and has a selected list of minor playwrights. Much has been written about Goldsmith and Sheridan, but not much in regard to the other writers of this period.

Page 422. "of his five-act comedies." Arthur Murphy's comedy, *All in the Wrong,* adapted from Molière's *Cocu Imaginaire,* ought also to be mentioned. It long held the stage in the United States as well as in England.

Page 423. Dr. Johnson. Boswell's *Life,* for the year 1770.

Page 425. "deserved compliment." See Cumberland's *Memoirs* for the quotations, Vol. I, pp. 351, 364, and also for the account of the first night of *She Stoops to Conquer,* I, 365.

CHAPTER XVIII.—SENTIMENTALITY TRIUMPHANT, 1760-1780

The works cited for Chapter XVII apply to this chapter. Of special interest are *Richard Cumberland* by Stanley Williams, Yale Univ. press, 1917; *A Bibliography of Thomas Holcroft* by Elbridge Colby, N. Y. Public Library, 1922. The bibliography in the Cambridge History, Vol. XI, Chap. XII, is useful.

Page 440. Professor Bernbaum, *Drama of Sensibility,* p. 212.

Page 442. "a rivalry of renunciation." Mr. Huxley omits this debate, but his farcical substitute is scarcely less conventional.

Page 444. "the audacity to write." Preface to *It's Well it's no Worse,* 1770.

Page 447. "Mrs. Hurley . . . exclaims." Professor Bernbaum quotes in his *Drama of Sensibility,* p. 226, but omits the second half of the quotation.

"increasing vogue of sentimental pieces." See Genest's comment on *False Delicacy.*

Page 451. "in his *Memoirs,*" Vol. I, p. 274.

Page 455. "distressful interim," II, i.

Page 464. The last quotation from Mrs. Inchbald is from the introduction to *The Deserted Daughter* in her collection, *The British Theatre.*

Page 467. "Acted in New York." By this time New York was beginning to export as well as to import plays. *Tell Truth and Shame the Devil,* an afterpiece by William Dunlap, was acted at Covent Garden, May 15, 1799. It appears to have been the first importation from New York where it had already been given, Jan. 9, 1797 "with distinguished applause." See Genest, and Odell, *Annals of the New York Stage,* Vol. I, p. 429.

Page 470. "a sop to popular sentiment," etc. I may refer to my volume, *Tragedy,* where the happy ending is discussed at more length, p. 320 ff.

CHAPTER XIX.—The Illegitimate, Melodrama, Romance, and Claptrap, 1800-1840

There are no full histories for the drama or the theater of this period, or for the subjects of this chapter. Genest ends at 1830, Nicoll at 1800. H. S. Wyndham's *Annals of Covent Garden Theatre* and G. C. D. Odell's *Shakespeare from Betterton to Irving* continue to be available. Memoirs and biographies are useful, notably Macready's *Reminiscences,* William Archer's *Life of Macready,* the memoirs of O'Keeffe, Reynolds, and Colman the younger. Watson Nicholson's *The Struggle for a Free Stage in London* is valuable. Hazlitt's *A View of the English Stage,* 1818, and his *Essays on the Acted Drama* in *The London Magazine,* 1820, deal with plays of this and earlier periods. The bibliographies in the *Cambridge History,* Vol. XI, Chap. XII, and Vol. XIII, Chap. VIII, cover this chapter and the next. Perhaps the most comprehensive collections of the acting drama of the period are Cumberland's *British Theatre,* 41 vols., 1829, and *Minor Theatre,* 15 vols.

Page 472. "were suited for reading." But, of course, Byron's *Sardanapalus* and *Werner* had great stage successes.

"I have elsewhere summarized." *Literature in a Changing Age,* p. 49 ff.

Page 475. "melodrama." I may refer to my volume *Tragedy,* p. 334 ff.

Page 478. Frederic Reynolds. See *The Life and Times of Frederic Reynolds,* written by himself, 1826. His comedy, *The Will* (April 19, 1797), long held the stage both in England and the United States.

Page 480. *Reminiscences,* 2 vols., 1827, by Thomas Dibdin.

Page 481. "George Colman the younger." There is no good biography and no collected edition of his plays, though a number were translated into French. His own memoir, *Random Records,* 1830, is not very informing.

Page 484. "Mrs. Inchbald praised." In her Introduction to the play in her collection, *British Theatre.*

Page 488. "Solomon Gundy." The elder James Hackett adapted the play into *Jonathan in England,* changing Gundy into an American, Jonathan Swop. This was one of Hackett's most popular rôles.

Page 495. *The Deep, Deep Sea,* like most of Planche's extravaganzas, was at once produced in New York, Nov. 15, 1834, where it was the hit of the season. See Odell, *Annals of the New York Stage,* Vol. IV.

Page 498. Hazlitt's *Spirit of the Age* devotes a concluding paragraph to Sheridan Knowles. See also his praise of *Virginius* in the essay in the *London Magazine* for July, 1820.

Page 499. Douglas Jerrold's works were collected in 8 vols., 1851-4, and his biography, 1889, was written by his son, Blanchard Jerrold.

CHAPTER XX.—THE VICTORIAN ERA, 1840-1890

Odell and Wyndham continue available, and E. B. Watson's *Sheridan to Robertson, a study of the nineteenth century stage,* Harvard Univ., 1926, and A. Filon *Le Théâtre Anglais,* Paris 1896 (Eng. trans. by F. Whyte, *The English Stage,* 1897) are useful. The bibliography in the *Cambridge History,* Vol. XIII, Chap. VIII, furnishes guidance. A number of books that are mainly concerned with the dramatic revival at the end of the century give some consideration to the earlier years: William Archer, *Dramatists of Today,* 1882; Frank W. Chandler, *Aspects of the Modern Drama,* 1914; J. W. Cunliffe, *Modern English Playwrights,* 1927. Acting versions of many English plays are to be found in Samuel French's collections. For French drama, see Brander Matthews, *French Dramatists of the Nineteenth*

Century, 1882; R. Doumic, *De Scribe à Ibsen,* 1893; P. Ginisty, *Le Mélodrame,* 1910.

Page 507. "the first box set." But see Odell, *Shakespeare from Betterton to Irving,* Vol. II, pp. 91, 226.

Page 516. *The Life of Edward Bulwer, first Lord Lytton,* by the Earl of Lytton, 2 vols., 1913. For Bulwer-Lytton's opinion of *Money,* see Vol. I, p. 559 ff.

Page 517. See *The Career of Dion Boucicault,* by Townsend Walsh, New York. Dunlap Society, 1915.

Page 527. *Charles Reade as I Knew Him,* John Coleman, London.

Page 529. *The Principal Dramatic Works of Thomas William Robertson,* with memoir by his son, 2 vols., London, 1889.

Page 535. "an eminent critic." Probably John Oxenford, see *The Dramatic Works,* introduction, p. x.

CHAPTER XXI.—Sir William Schwenk Gilbert

W. S. Gilbert, His Life and Letters, by Sidney Dark and Rowland Gray, 1923, is the most informing work on Gilbert. Other recent books are A. H. Godwin, *Gilbert and Sullivan,* London, 1925; Isaac Goldberg, *The Story of Gilbert and Sullivan,* New York, 1926; H. A. Lytton, *The Secrets of a Savoyard,* London, 1922; H. M. Walbrook, *Gilbert and Sullivan Opera,* London, 1922; F. Cellier and C. Bridgman, *Gilbert, Sullivan, and D'Oyly Carte,* 1914.

Page 547. "Mr. George Grossmith." The story is told by Dark and Gray, *op. cit.,* p. 70.

Page 549. "a letter to Sullivan." See Dark and Gray, *op. cit.,* p. 121.

Page 553. "indelicacies." Mrs. Grundy did find some things indelicate, especially Iolanthe's son, a fairy down to the waist.

Page 558. "String the lyre and fill the cup," *The Gondoliers,* Act II.

CHAPTER XXII.—The New Birth of Comedy, 1890-1900

Many books have been written concerning this dramatic revival. Some of the more important are: William Archer, *English Dramatists of Today,* 1882, *About the Theatre,* 1886, *The Old Drama and the New,* 1923; F. W. Chandler, *Aspects of Modern Drama,* 1914; J. W. Cunliffe, *Modern English Playwrights,* 1927 (with a bibliography); Barrett H. Clark, *British and American Dramatists of Today,* 1915; T. H. Dickinson, *The Contemporary Drama of England,* 1920; Ashley Dukes, *Modern Dramatists,* 1912; A. Henderson, *The Changing Drama,* 1914; James Huneker, *Iconoclasts: a Book of Dramatists,* 1905; H. A. Jones, *The Renascence of the English Drama,* 1895; Ludwig Lewisohn, *The Modern Drama,* 1915; W. L. Phelps, *The Twentieth Century Theatre,* 1918; G. Bernard Shaw, *Dramatic Opinions and Essays,* 1907.

The plays of the leading dramatists may be found in the following editions: *Representative Plays by Henry Arthur Jones,* 4 vols., ed. with introduction by Clayton Hamilton, 1925; *Representative Plays by Arthur W. Pinero,* 4 vols., ed. with introduction by Clayton Hamilton, 1925; *Representative Plays by J. M. Barrie,* 1914; *Complete Works of John M. Synge,* 4 vols., 1912; *The Plays of Oscar Wilde,* 2 vols., 1905; *Plays Pleasant and Unpleasant* by G. Bernard Shaw.

Page 582. On Synge, see M. Bourgeois, *John Millington Synge,* 1913; P. P. Howe, *J. M. Synge, a critical study,* New York, 1912; F. L. Bickley, *J. M. Synge and the Irish Dramatic Movement,* London, 1912.

INDEX

The Index contains the titles of plays, the names of authors, and the names of a few actors. The notes are not indexed, except in a few special cases. Alterations of plays are not indexed unless they have separate titles. References of importance are indicated by heavy-faced figures.

INDEX

633